CANADIAN COMPANY HISTORIES

CANADIAN COMPANY HISTORIES

VOLUME 1

Editor
Tina Grant

An ITP Information/Reference Group Company

Changing the Way the World Learns

NEW YORK • LONDON • BONN • BOSTON • DETROIT
MADRID • MELBOURNE • MEXICO CITY • PARIS
SINGAPORE • TOKYO • TORONTO • WASHINGTON
ALBANY NY • BELMONT CA • CINCINNATI OH

STAFF

Tina Grant, *Editor*

Robert Lang, John Sabljic, *Project Editors*

Miranda H. Ferrara, *Project Manager*

Nicolet V. Elert, Janice Jorgensen, Paula Kepos,
Margaret Mazurkiewicz, Michael J. Tyrkus, *Contributing Editors*

∞™ The paper used in this publication meets the minimum
requirements of American National Standard for Information Sciences—
Permanence Paper for Printed Library Materials, ANSI Z39.48-1984.

Cover photograph: Ken Straiton, *First Light*

Canadian Cataloguing in Publication Data:

Main entry under title:

Canadian company histories

Includes bibliographical references and index.
ISBN 1-896413-06-4

1. Corporations - Canada - History. 2. Business enterprises - Canada - History.

HD2809.C35 1995   338.7'4'0971   C95-932514-X

I(T)P™ Gale Research Inc., an International Thomson Publishing Company.
ITP logo is a trademark under license.

10 9 8 7 6 5 4 3 2 1

CONTENTS

Preface vii

Company Histories

PREFACE

This first edition of *Canadian Company Histories* provides detailed profiles of Canada's largest and most influential companies, ranging from ATCO Limited to Trilon Financial, in all major industries. Written by business writers, these profiles constitute a unique one-stop source that provides context for the breaking news in tomorrow's business pages. *Canadian Company Histories* brings together widely dispersed information that will satisfy the needs of students, librarians, job seekers, researchers, and other information seekers who need historical and current background on Canada's most significant companies.

Inclusion Criteria

Companies chosen for inclusion in *Canadian Company Histories* have achieved a minimum of Can$1 billion in annual revenues in their most recent reporting year. These companies are often the leaders in their industries in Canada and, in many cases, around the world.

Gale Canada does not endorse any of the companies or products mentioned in this book. Companies that appear in *Canadian Company Histories* were selected without reference to their wishes and have in no way endorsed their profiles. As much as possible, the companies were given the opportunity to participate in the compilation of the profiles by providing information or reading their profiles for factual accuracy, and we are indebted to many of them for their comments and corrections. We also acknowledge the companies as the source of the corporate logos that appear in *Canadian Company Histories*.

Arrangement and Entry Format

Profiles in *Canadian Company Histories* are arranged alphabetically according to company name. Each profile begins with important company contact information, including legal name of company, the address of its headquarters, and its telephone number and fax number. Also included here is a statement of public, private, state, or parent ownership and the company's earliest incorporation date.

Also provided here are the most recently available figures indicating the company's annual revenue and number of employees. Revenue figures are given in Canadian dollars unless otherwise noted. For some private companies, revenue figures are estimates. For public companies, the profiles list the exchanges on which the company's stock is traded. In addition, the profiles list the four-digit Standard Industrial Classification (SIC) codes for the company, indicating the industries and lines of business in which the company is active.

To facilitate further research, *Canadian Company Histories* conveniently provides, at the end of each profile, a brief bibliography of recent articles and books about the company.

Sources of Information

The profiles were compiled from a wide range of publicly accessible sources, including annual reports; newspapers and specialized business news sources; business, general, and academic periodicals; books; and material supplied by the profiled companies themselves.

Indexes

Two indexes provide convenient access to information contained within the *Canadian Company Histories* profiles:

The **Index to Companies and Persons** arranges significant companies and people mentioned in the text in alphabetical order. Profiled companies appear in boldface type. Index citations refer to page numbers.

The **Index to Industries** arranges the profiled companies alphabetically according to broad industry classifications. Index citations refer to page numbers.

Comments and Suggestions Welcome

Gale Canada welcomes your comments and suggestions regarding this and subsequent editions of *Canadian Company Histories*. Please send your correspondence to:

Editor
Canadian Company Histories
Gale Canada
444 Front Street West
Toronto, Ontario M5V 2S9

YOUR IDEAS WANTED

Do you have an idea for a new Canadian information product?

As a Canadian who works with information, you know best what new products you need to serve your patrons and students better. Gale Canada, dedicated to responding to your information needs, would like to hear your new product ideas.

To make this easier for you, we have initiated a New Product Idea Submission Program. Send us the details of your idea and, if the idea is approved and published, you will receive a $1,000 reward from Gale Canada and recognition from your peers.

Please send your ideas, comments, or requests for more information to:

New Product Development Group
Gale Canada
1120 Birchmount Road, Suite 100
Scarborough, Ontario M1K 5GA

CANADIAN
COMPANY
HISTORIES

Abitibi-Price Inc.

207 Queen's Quay West, Suite #680
Toronto, Ontario M5J 2P5
(416) 203-5000
Fax: (416) 203-5094

Public Company
Incorporated: 1912 as Abitibi Pulp & Paper Co.
   Limited
Employees: 7,470
Sales: $2.1 billion
Stock Exchanges: Montreal Toronto Vancouver New
   York
SICs: 2611 Pulp mills; 2621 Paper mills; 2678
   Stationery products; 5112 Stationery and office
   supplies

Abitibi-Price Inc. manufactures and distributes newsprint, specialty papers, and office supplies. With 10
North American mills, it ranks as one of Canada's
largest forest products companies. Abitibi's core businesses in pulp and paper have been notoriously cyclical:
the company suffered a 14-year receivership during and
after the Great Depression; became one of the most
successful of Canada's many forest products firms in the
1980s; then suffered again in the 1990s when its parent
company, Olympia & York, turned it over to a court-
appointed guardian as collateral for a huge loan. Yet
despite its immense highs and lows, Abitibi-Price has
remained one of the world's biggest newsprint and paper
suppliers and emerged from restructuring as a force to
be reckoned with in the 1990s.

Along with much of the Canadian paper industry,
Abitibi-Price owes its existence to the bitter squabbling
that developed in the latter part of the 19th century
between U.S. manufacturers and consumers of newsprint. Ever since the newspaper industry had converted
from rag-based paper to a product made from tree pulp
in the 1870s, it had been troubled by recurring overcapacity and disastrous price wars, followed by attempts
to moderate competition by mergers and combinations.
The most ambitious of these was the creation of
International Paper Company in the 1890s from the
assets of 19 U.S. paper concerns.

In the first decade of the 20th century, International
Paper controlled nearly 75 percent of the U.S. newsprint
market, a situation that elicited charges of monopoly
and price gouging from newspaper publishers. The
publishers were able to publicize their accusations
widely, sometimes coupling them with warnings about
the need to protect freedom of the press from coercive
economic forces. They eventually convinced the U.S.
Congress to remove a long-standing tariff on imported
paper products. Lifting the tariff in 1913 prompted a
rush to build plants in Canada, which by virtue of its
abundant forests and water power was a natural site for
pulp and paper manufacturers. In 1911 alone, some 81
new forestry companies were created in Canada in
anticipation of the tariff lifting. It was in the midst of
this stampede, in 1913, that Abitibi Power & Paper
Company Limited had its origins.

Abitibi's founder was an American named Frank H.
Anson, born in Niles, Michigan, in 1859. Before coming
to the paper business, Anson had worked as a railroad
ticket agent, rubber prospector, exporter, and general
superintendent of Ogilvie Flour Mills in Montreal.
While at Ogilvie, Anson became interested in the
mining wealth of Ontario's northern reaches, and in
1909 hired two young men from McGill University to
prospect for him in that remote region of Canada. The
students found no minerals but did recommend that
Anson start a paper mill along the Abitibi River, whose
swift current could easily generate the electrical and
mechanical power necessary to run such an operation.
With the abolition of the U.S. paper tariff drawing
closer every day, Anson enlisted the financial backing of
Shirley Ogilvie, son of the Ogilvie Flour Mill family, and
in 1913 erected the Abitibi Pulp & Paper Co. Limited
mill 300 miles north of Toronto at Iroquois Falls.

In 1914, Abitibi Pulp & Paper changed its name and
reincorporated as Abitibi Power & Paper Company
Limited, since the firm also sold electric power from its
hydroelectric facility. Anson's timing was very good:
World War I soon drove up the price of newsprint to an
all-time peak of US$65 per ton, and the new Canadian
paper companies enjoyed unrestricted access to the
immense U.S. markets. So successful were the paper
companies on both sides of the border that another
round of industry investigations was launched, and in
1917 the U.S. Department of Justice began antitrust
prosecution of an industrywide cooperative group called
the News Print Manufacturers Association. The association's membership pleaded no contest, paid US$11,000
in fines, and dissolved the organization, none of which
prevented the price of newsprint from nearly doubling
by 1920 to a new record of US$112.60 per ton.

The newsprint industry's history of antitrust allegations
and cyclical depressions seemed to be a result of three
factors: the enormous cost of increasing plant capacity;
the relative inelasticity of newsprint demand, sales of
which did not tend to increase when its price dropped;
and the highly influential voice of the product's consumers, the newspaper community. Since competition often
proved fatal, newsprint manufacturers often tried to
curb competition, resulting in well-publicized accusations by the newspapers of antitrust violations.

The postwar price peak encouraged a full decade of
nonstop expansion in the Canadian paper industry,
which nearly doubled its capacity by the year 1930. The
consequence of this expansion was a long decline in the

price of newsprint, which, by the end of the decade, fell to about US$62 per ton, and a growing overcapacity, which, as early as 1928, threw the industry into a premature depression of its own.

Abitibi Power & Paper had participated enthusiastically in the decade of expansion. It entered the fine-paper business with the purchase of a sulfite pulp mill at Smooth Rock Falls, Ontario; acquired substantial interests in Manitoba Paper Company and Sainte Anne Paper Company; and built its own mills to the extent that it became one of the industry's more important competitors. Faced with the problems of increased capacity and dropping product price, Abitibi and its fellow manufacturers concluded that their best chance for collective survival was to amalgamate their holdings. Accordingly, in 1928, Abitibi engineered a quintuple merger, buying up the remainder of Manitoba Paper, Sainte Anne Paper, Spanish River Pulp and Paper Mills, Fort William Power Company, and Murray Bay Paper Company. These and a number of subsequent purchases proved disastrous, but at the time Abitibi had hoped that industry consolidation could prevent price competition and increase production efficiency. The strategy might have succeeded in a thriving economy; instead Abitibi was hit by the Great Depression and was soon in desperate straits.

By 1932 sales had dropped to a fraction of their earlier levels, while the company's $50 million debt was more than four times what it had been in 1927. This combination could not be sustained and on June 1, 1932, Abitibi defaulted on interest payments and was thrown into receivership. For the next 14 years, Abitibi was directed by a court-appointed receiver, whose task was to stabilize the company's finances, pay down the outstanding debts, and return the company to its shareholders at some future date. In 1933 the price of newsprint finally stabilized, allowing Abitibi to begin the long road back to solvency. For the remainder of the 1930s, Abitibi managed to earn a fairly steady 15-20 percent operating income for use in debt reduction and maintenance of its physical assets. World War II revived the economy, and in 1940 Abitibi sales jumped immediately and remained between $25-30 million for the duration of the war, providing the company with an excellent return and setting the stage for an end to the receivership.

In 1943, the premier of Ontario appointed a committee to take Abitibi out of receivership. When the committee's recommendations were accepted by all the creditors in 1946, the company was once again formally independent. Abitibi's 14-year receivership was the longest and most important in the history of Canadian industry, a trauma that left its mark in the form of a conservative corporate philosophy and deep skepticism about future expansion. Abitibi's experience during the Depression was only an extreme example of the Canadian paper industry as a whole; and when a remarkable postwar surge in demand for newsprint raised and prompted U.S. demands for increased capacity, Canadian producers generally chose to increase production speed at existing plants rather than add new ones.

Abitibi chief executive Douglas W. Ambridge strongly concurred with the prevalent conservatism, guiding Abitibi through two postwar decades of bountiful sales and profit increases while avoiding unnecessary capital expenditures. He was helped by the extraordinary expansion the company had undertaken in 1928, which provided Abitibi with a reserve of production capacity so great that corporate assets did not surpass those of 1928 until 30 years later. Thus Abitibi merely made use of what plants it had to meet the ever-increasing demand during the 1950s, allowing Ambridge to keep debt low and earnings per share extremely high. After the years of receivership, the 1950s were a new golden age.

Dissatisfaction among U.S. publishers with Canadian reluctance to expand capacity led to another series of industry investigations of which only one—in 1939—led to a suit filed by the Justice Department for antitrust violations. It's hard to determine what degree of collusion, if any, existed among the Canadian newsprint manufacturers during the period in question, but the continual allegations encouraged the U.S. government to offer substantial tax incentives to its domestic forestry business, which began to chip away at Canada's market share. Most of the new U.S. plants were built in the South, where trees grew faster, labor rates were lower, and an unusually strong grade of indigenous kraft paper allowed the manufacture of a more durable newsprint. In 1965, Abitibi Power & Paper Company Ltd. changed its name to Abitibi Paper Company Ltd. Abitibi had been feeling the effects of a new U.S. presence as early as 1962, when, together with the rest of the Canadian industry, it entered a decade of declining net income and diminished share of the critical U.S. market. To counteract this trend, Abitibi overcame its habitual reluctance to expand with the 1968 purchases of Cox Newsprint, Inc. and Cox Woodlands Company for US$36.58 million. Cox, located in Augusta, Ga., added 150,000 tons per year of newsprint capacity to Abitibi's Canadian holdings of 1.1 million tons, and gave the company a presence in the booming southern industry.

A new generation of leaders at Abitibi, headed up by CEO Tom Bell and COO Harry Rosier, became increasingly aggressive in the search for additional capacity. When three exceptionally lean years were followed by the upsurge of 1973-74, in which Abitibi sales soared from $307 to $552 million and its capacity was strained, Rosier suggested it would be cheaper to buy existing mills than to build them from scratch.

After a brief search for likely targets, Bell and Rosier went after and won control of 54 percent of The Price Company Ltd.'s outstanding shares in late 1974. A fellow Canadian paper concern with 1974 sales of $335 million, Price, like Abitibi, was strongest in newsprint and kraft production, but recorded a significantly higher proportion of its sales outside North America and had no fine paper and building materials divisions. Both companies had modest but profitable base-metal mining operations in Canada, and together they controlled rights to about 50,000 square miles of forest land.

Price was a company much older than Abitibi, dating back to the early 19th century and the British Navy's need for a new lumber source for its masts. In 1910, William Price had been sent by a leading London lumber merchant to Canada to organize the new operation, and Price subsequently started the company bearing his name.

No sooner had Abitibi completed its 22-day $130.1 million conquest of Price than the newsprint market collapsed, cutting the combined companies' 1975 net income by two-thirds, at a time when its debt was nearly doubling. Once again, Abitibi's poor timing led indirectly to a change in ownership. Caught in a cash squeeze, Abitibi tried to placate union demands with big pay hikes and thereby avoid a disastrous strike; instead the unions pushed their advantage and forced the strike anyway. The walkout was bitter and lasted for months. By the time the economy rebounded in 1977, Abitibi was still trying to put its shaken house in order.

In October 1978, Abitibi agreed to buy about 10 percent of Price's outstanding stock from Consolidated-Bathurst, a Canadian company that had bid against Abitibi for control of Price in 1974 and had retained a portion of Price's stock. Later that month, Abitibi purchased Price's remaining shares, paying about $95 million for the 46 percent of outstanding stock. In December, Consolidated-Bathurst bought 10 percent of Abitibi's stock and set off a prolonged bidding war for control of the company. When the dust settled 15 months later Abitibi-Price, which had assumed its present name in October 1979, was part of the Reichmann brothers' extraordinary business domain, their family-owned Olympia & York paying $670 million for 92 percent of the company's stock.

In the early 1980s, Abitibi made a concerted effort to lessen its dependence on the brutally cyclical newsprint business. Yet net sales were relatively strong ($1.6 billion in 1987, $1.8 billion in 1988 and $1.7 billion in 1989) and the company had reached its pinnacle as the world's largest newsprint producer. Even its diversified operations, run by a young man named Ronald Oberlander, had grown phenomenonally to encompass the Jaffe chain of stationary stores in Florida; a share in Australia's biggest paper company, Spicers Paper Ltd.; Price Wilson, an envelope manufacturer; Hilroy, a school and office supplier; and one of the leading producers of building materials in the United States.

In the fall of 1989, Abitibi announced plans to build a $340 million recycled newsprint mill in Gartcosh, Scotland, as a means of introducing Europeans to the company before 1992 trade barriers dropped and to begin its commitment to the wave of the future—recycling. Additionally, Abitibi's joint venture with Parsons & Whittemore Inc., a $409-million newsprint mill in Claiborne, Ala., neared its 1990 start-up date while another proposed mill in Venezuela was on the drawing board. Then after four straight years of bullish profits, including 1988's remarkable profit of $188.2 million, the bottom dropped out once again. As sales fell and profits plunged 70 percent in 1989, Abitibi's management calmly admitted in its annual report that the picture would not improve for at least 18 months—a tragic miscalculation.

Faced with a 1990 loss of $44.6 million, Abitibi began a sweeping restructuring program with Ron Oberlander installed as its new president: casualties included aging paper mills in Newfenonally and Quebec, shelving its

plans for Venezuela and Scotland, and slicing dividends by half. Then the company earmarked about $300 million for environmental cleanups and unspecified funds for converting old newsprint mills to specialized paper producers. Another blow was a September 1990 Canadian Paperworkers Union (CPU) strike, affecting most of Abitibi's newsprint mills. Next came the shutdown of the Thunder Bay mill, which would later be sold to its managers for $1 and similar plans to sell another mill at Pine Falls.

Despite savings of $30 million from downsizing in the first quarter of 1991, Abitibi still suffered a loss of $5.5 million, due in part to the continued deterioration of U.S. sales. In May, the unthinkable happened: for the first time in memory U.S. newspaper publishers purchased more newsprint from domestic suppliers than their Canadian counterparts. From bad to worse, 1991 became Abitibi's weakest year since the 1930s when it fell into receivership (net sales of $1.5 billion, net losses of $75.9 million). Yet Oberlander, who was now president and CEO, remained confident about the company's turnaround and was determined to spread optimism. The company had not only recognized its problems, but had finally taken the necessary steps to correct them: no more throwing money into obsolete mills (over $1.3 billion was spent on renovations in a decade), no more expansion of non-core operations. Instead, Abitibi-Price had to close mills, let employees go and sell off several non-core assets.

With its "no more excuses" attitude, Abitibi sold Jaffe Stationers, Spicers Paper Ltd., Innova Envelope, and its U.S.-based building products division; closed its coated paper operation in Georgetown; put its hydroelectric generating stations in Quebec and its paper distribution division on the block; cut 500 salaried positions; and put its remaining employees through week-long training seminars. Management also made it clear that if an acceptable offer was made, virtually any non-core subsidiary might be sold. Yet it was not enough: rock-bottom newsprint prices contributed to operational losses in 1992 of nearly $200 million, triple those of 1991. Then the mighty Reichmann brothers hit the skids, putting the company in the hands of a court-appointed custodian after turning over their 79 percent stake in Abitibi to creditors as collateral for US$2.5-billion loan.

All was not lost, however, for in 1993 Oberlander's predictions began to come true. First came a revolutionary six-year social contract with union workers at Abitibi's Alma, Quebec, newsprint mill, then first quarter results reported a revenue jump of 23 percent while losses were slashed by half. Again, the company reorganized, scaling back its office in Quebec City, shifting executives and putting its St. Anne de Beaupre mill up for sale. Finishing the year with net sales of $1.9 billion and an operating loss of $40 million, the comeback was bleak and far from over, but at least progressing.

The next year, Abitibi announced the closure of one of two newsprint machines in its Grand Falls mill, the small community's largest employer. The company blamed the stubborn Communications, Energy and Paperworkers Union (CEPU formerly CPU), which refused a proposal to keep the machine running with several concessions.

Though first quarter sales ($471 million) were slightly above the previous year's, Abitibi reported an operating loss of $11 million. Luckily, it would be the last, as 1994 figures were firmly in what company officials deemed "the profit zone." Year-end net sales were $2.1 billion, with an operating profit of $26 million.

In 1995, several significant factors helped Abitibi continue its upward trend including the purchase of remaining shares in Quebec's Gaspesia Pulp and Paper Co.; the start-up of its Alma mill's newly-built deinking operations, expected to produce directory paper with a 40 percent recycled content; the completion of a $9.2-million modernization of its mill in Augusta, Ga., and the expectation of returning to a full year of profitability, while holding its own during the cyclical ups and downs of the industry.

Principal Subsidiaries:

Abitibi-Price Corporation; Abitibi-Price Sales Company Limited; Abitibi-Price Sales Corp.; Gaspesia Pulp & Paper Company Limited; Azerty de Mexico S.A. de C.V.; Eurozerty B.V.

Further Reading:

Bayless, Alan, "Why Newsprint is Back on Buy Lists," *Financial Times of Canada,* May 21, 1994, pp.1,4.
Daywalker, "What Price Paper? Abitibi-Price Makes a (Bad) Deal," *Canadian Dimension,* May-June 1994, pp.33-5.
Follis, Robert, "Abitibi's Future Looks Brighter," *Investor's Digest,* July 22, 1994, p.272.
Geddes, John, "Abitibi to Get British Foothold," *The Financial Post,* August 21, 1989, p.3.
Johnson, John, "Abitibi's Share Price May Hit $35 in 1996," *Investor's Digest,* October 14, 1994, p.374.
Kennedy, Peter, "Newsprint Price Fears: Newspaper Publishers Alarmed by Abitibi's Plan to Hike Newsprint Prices Again," *The Financial Post,* January 28, 1995, p.1.
Mahood, Casey, "Abitibi Faces Tough Year," *Globe and Mail,* April 19, 1993, p.B1.
————, "Abitibi More Than Triples Loss," *Globe and Mail,* February 16, 1993, p.B15.
————, "Abitibi-Price Pares Operating Losses," *Globe and Mail,* April 19, 1994, p.B11. Mathias, Philip, "Abitibi to Build North British Newsprint Mill," *Pulp & Paper,* October 1989, p.29.
————, *Takeover,* Toronto: Maclean-Hunter, 1976.
McFarlane, Janet, "Speculation Mounts Over Abitibi Trading," *The Financial Post,* February 5, 1994, p.19.
McKenna, Barrie, "Abitibi Peace Pact a Breakthrough," *Globe and Mail,* May 7, 1993, p.B1.
————, "Abitibi to Sell Power Stations to Cut Debt," *Globe and Mail,* December 5, 1991, p.B6.
McMurdy, Deirdre, "Abitibi-Price Set for Restructuring," *Globe and Mail,* February 1, 1990, p.B9.
Melnbardis, Robert, "Abitibi's Comeback Plan," *Financial Times of Canada,* February 3, 1991, p.20.
Noble, Kimberley, "Big Changes on Way at Stumbling Abitibi," *Globe and Mail,* April 24, 1990, p.B7.
————, "Northern Mills Face Bleak Future," *Globe and Mail,* August 5, 1991, p.B1.
Stackhouse, John, "Abitibi's Last Stand," *Globe and Mail,* September 20, 1991, p.P23.

—Jonathan Martin
—updated by Taryn Benbow-Pfalzgraf

AIR CANADA

Air Canada

Air Canada Centre
P.O. Box 14000
St. Laurent, Quebec H4Y 1H4
(514) 422-5000
Fax: (514) 422-5909

Public Company
Incorporated: 1988
Sales: $4.02 billion
Employees: 18,400
Stock Exchanges: Montreal Toronto Winnipeg
  Alberta Vancouver
SICs: 4512 Air Transportation, Scheduled; 4522 Air
  Transportation, Nonscheduled.

Operated as a Crown corporation from its 1937 inception until its privatization in 1989, Air Canada is Canada's biggest airline. In the mid-1990s, the company was one of only two national airlines—all others were limited to regional and local routes. Air Canada's competition with its chief rival, Canadian Airlines International Ltd. has long represented the dichotomy between government-owned and privately owned enterprises as well as regional rivalries between Western Canada and Quebec. After losing over $1 billion in the first three years of the 1990s, Air Canada earned its first annual profit of the decade in 1994.

Twenty-four North American cities are serviced by the airline's passenger route network, and, through its domestic connector partners, the airline is able to serve an additional 62 Canadian communities and six cities in the United States. In addition, Air Canada services 24 cities in Europe and the Caribbean, and the airline's cargo division provides services to 60 destinations in Canada and around the world.

Under the administration of Prime Minister Mackenzie King, the Canadian government created Trans Canada Air Lines as a Crown corporation in 1937 to provide transcontinental airline service within Canada's borders. From its founding through 1959, the government-owned company had a complete monopoly on all of Canada's domestic air routes; it also had a monopoly on all trans-border routes (routes that crossed the Canadian border with the United States) until 1967. The federal Cabinet of Canada approved all of the airline's routes and fares, and government regulators issued licenses approved by the Cabinet for the airline.

But government sponsorship did not rule out competition. Canadian Pacific Limited, one of the country's railway giants, acquired and combined nine small private carriers to form Canadian Pacific Airlines (also known as CP Air) in the 1940s. In 1959 the Canadian government allowed CP Air to provide one flight each day in each direction between Vancouver and Montreal, Quebec. From that small foothold, CP Air grew through 1965 to acquire an average of 12.7 percent—the total it was allowed by federal regulations—of the domestic intercontinental traffic formerly held by Air Canada. In 1967 the Canadian government further relaxed its regulations and allowed CP Air two flights per day and, by 1970, CP Air was permitted to gain 25 percent of the intercontinental traffic in Canada. Also in 1967 the Canadian government allowed CP Air, which was given the right to establish international air routes across the Pacific Ocean in 1948, to establish a route from Vancouver to San Francisco, California—the first trans-border route not flown by Air Canada.

Despite the encroaching competition from CP Air and that airline's dominance in international routes across the Pacific Ocean, Air Canada held, by government fiat, a monopoly on all other international routes and intercontinental domestic air travel.

Government regulations set forth in 1966 prevented regional air carriers from competing with both Air Canada and CP Air, which were directed to work with the regional carriers to establish joint fare and commission arrangements and to cooperate on technical and servicing matters, including service to specific areas that required special equipment. Later, in 1969, the Canadian government established specific regions in which each of the five regional Canadian airlines could operate; those regulations lasted through the early 1980s.

Throughout the 1970s several pressures—many of which arose or were centered in the United States—challenged the Canadian government and the Air Canada monopoly. Larger jets for airline service provided air carriers with roomier vehicles; however, high air fares, which were regulated in both the United States and Canada by federal agencies, prevented the efficient use of those vehicles. The power of consumers increased during the decade, and customers used that power to demand lower air fares from more competitive airlines. Information on how deregulated industries would perform convinced many regulators, airline executives, and consumers that a regulated airline industry did not serve anyone's best interests. In the late 1970s these forces combined to gain the support of leading politicians in the United States. The deregulation process of the United States airline industry began, with Canadian politicians watching closely—especially as Canadian passengers increasingly chose U.S. airlines for their international and transcontinental flights because they could take advantage of lower fares and improved services.

When Parliament passed the Air Canada Act of 1978, the Crown corporation was finally subjected to the same regulations and regulatory agencies that other Canadian airlines faced, bringing it more fully into competition with CP Air and the other regional airlines that were then operating. That act ended the government's unique regulatory control over Air Canada's routes, fare structures, and services—control the government wielded over the company throughout its first 41 years of business. On March 23, 1979, the minister of transport removed all capacity restraints on CP Air's share of transcontinental traffic, and it was given a license to provide domestic transcontinental flights. CP Air established transcontinental service in May of 1980 to compete directly with Air Canada. While these changes were occurring in its domestic competition, Air Canada was also facing increasing competition in international routes from American Airlines, British Airways, Swiss-Air, and Lufthansa.

By 1984 Air Canada hinted in its annual report that, in order to continue to compete with other international airlines, it would require a tremendous amount of new capital to replace its aging fleet of airliners with state-of-the-art jets. To upgrade its fleet, Air Canada was considering buying, between the years 1984 and 1993, more than 40 new airliners at a cost of more than $135 million each; the company also said in its annual report that it did not believe it could finance such purchases from retained earnings. At that time, six airline companies were operating in Canada, and Air Canada, which had more than a 50 percent share of the market, owned and operated the country's only computer reservations system. This provided them with access to all of the major travel agents in Canada and enabled them to collect a fee from other airlines when their tickets were sold on the computerized system. CP Air, which was acquired by Pacific Western Airlines (an Alberta-based regional carrier) and renamed Canadian Airlines International Ltd. in the mid-1980s, established its own computerized reservation system, but in 1987 the two airlines' systems were merged into a single network called the Gemini Group Limited Partnership.

In 1985, then Transport Minister Donald Mazankowski said that the Canadian government was planning to allow Air Canada and the Canadian National Railways the freedom to operate as private companies. The Canadian public appeared to support that move. In its annual report for fiscal 1985, Air Canada said it was determined to resolve the challenges it faced from its competition by managing its own destiny and achieving "a standard of financial credibility that will ultimately enable the shareholder to pursue a course of private and employee equity participation." This statement pointed toward the direction the company intended to move and coincided with further relaxation of regulations that encouraged its domestic and international competitors.

The complete deregulation of Canada's airline industry was first proposed in a policy paper from Mazankowski to Parliament in July of 1985. That policy was not enacted until Parliament passed the National Transportation Act of 1987, which became effective January 1, 1988. On April 12, 1988, Mazankowski, who was then the minister responsible for privatization, announced that Air Canada would be sold to the public as "market conditions permit" with an initial treasury issue of up to 45 percent of its shares. When it was announced, the sale was seen as the most ambitious act of privatization that the Canadian government had attempted thus far;

Air Canada had assets of $3.18 billion and revenues of $3.13 billion in 1987. The sale was subjected to several conditions that were placed into the enabling legislation, which Parliament approved in August of 1988.

The legislation stipulated several things: the company's headquarters would remain in Montreal, the airline, for the indefinite future, would maintain major operational and overhaul centers at Winnipeg, Manitoba, and in Montreal and Toronto; no more than 45 percent of the company's shares would be sold and the proceeds would go to the airline, not to the government; employees would be given the first chance to buy shares in the company, small shareholders the second opportunity, followed by institutional investors and, finally, foreign investors; no individual shareholder would be allowed to hold more than 10 percent of the company's shares and foreign ownership was limited to 25 percent of the initial offering; and the government's 55 percent holding in the company would be voted in accordance with the private-sector shareholders to give the company an arm's-length relationship with the government.

On September 26, 1988, Air Canada filed a prospectus on its stock, stating that its net income after taxes was $101 million for the year ended March 31, 1988. The next day the price of the stock was set at $8 per share, and the company issued 30.8 million shares—42.8 percent of the company's total—with an option offered to brokers to buy an additional 3.5 percent of the total shares of the company at $8 per share. The company netted $225.8 million on the $246.2 million sale, with underwriting fees taking $12.3 million and with the airline absorbing $8 million in discounts to its employees. By the end of March of 1989, the company's shares were trading at $11.75 per share, and the stock hit a high of $14.83 in August that same year.

Air Canada's efficacious move to becoming a private company was seen as a result of a successful public relations program directed by the company's chairman, Claude I. Taylor, and its president and chief executive officer, Pierre J. Jeanniot. The executives focused the public relations program on the company's employees, the media, communities, customers, and potential shareholders; this was done in two carefully structured parts—pre-announcement and post-announcement—that were designed to ensure the success of the move to privatization by emphasizing the company's strengths and competitive position as it worked to improve its service and operations.

In July of 1989 the company completed its move to privatization with the filing of a prospectus for its second issue of stock. The company sold 41.1 million shares—for a total of 57 percent of its equity in the filing—at $12 per share. Proceeds from that sale went to the government. As an indication of the issue's success, by the end of the first week after the shares were issued the company's stock was trading at $12.75 per share. The company's operating results, however, did not reflect the enthusiastic welcome that its stock had met in the market. Air Canada reported losses of $74 million in 1990. The company blamed its poor performance on the recessionary economy, but it was also hurt by intensifying competition—both domestic and international—in the wake of privatization and deregulation.

In July of 1990 CEO Jeanniot surprised his colleagues at Air Canada by announcing his retirement. Jeanniot, who had spent 35 years with the company, told *Traffic World* magazine that he believed the time was right for him to retire: "I have done my time. A chief executive should not hang around forever." Claude Taylor continued in his capacity as chairman and took on the additional responsibilities of CEO while the board of directors began an extended search for a replacement.

On 20 February 1992 the company announced that it had hired Hollis L. Harris, a former top executive at Delta Air Lines Inc. and Continental Airlines Corp., as vice-chairman, president, and chief executive officer. Harris brought knowledge of the U.S. airline market that many believed was necessary for Air Canada to remain competitive in the early 1990s. The new leader sat down to a full plate at Air Canada. The airline had lost $218 million in 1991, due in part to the fact that it had nearly two million fewer passengers that year than in 1990. The war in the Persian Gulf, an ongoing recession that kept business travelers in their offices, and cutthroat fare wars combined to produce continuing losses.

Harris made the tough, but necessary decision to cut costs that his predecessor had shunned. Staff reductions came first, and started at the top. Air Canada eliminated five senior management positions, including four senior vice presidents and the position of executive vice president and chief operating officer; it also cut 250 other management positions and 100 administrative and technical support positions. In 1993 Harris announced that his pay would be cut by 15 percent for the next two years; 15 other top executives took 5 percent reductions. The CEO hoped to convince unionized employees to accept similar salary reductions, but they balked, forcing across-the-board layoffs of 21.7 percent of the company's 23,000 employees from 1988 to 1994. These efforts slashed labor costs by $63 million to $979 million.

A fleet modernization program simultaneously reduced passenger capacity by 10 percent and raised fuel efficiency by 25 percent, thereby reducing costs twice with one action. Harris also divested Air Canada's "En Route" credit card operations to Diners Club of America, sold its Montreal headquarters building, and relocated its scaled-down headquarters staff from downtown Montreal to Dorval Airport. An organizational restructuring enhanced Harris's oversight of day-to-day operations and gave him direct responsibility for the six divisions that were formed in the reorganization.

Extraordinary expenses related to the restructuring contributed to Air Canada's record $454 million loss in 1992. Unhappy shareholders watched their stock decline to $5 per share, less than half of its issued price of $12. While Air Canada's ongoing cost-cutting efforts did not bring instant profitability, they did reduce losses to $326 million and contributed to a $77 million operating profit in 1993.

Faced with ever-intensifying international competition and persistent economic difficulties, Air Canada proposed a merger in early 1992 with Canadian Airlines International Ltd., its primary Canadian competitor. Air Canada called it a "made-in-Canada" solution to industry imperatives, referring to a merger of domestic players as opposed to affiliation with U.S. competitors. However, Canadian Airlines rebuffed Air Canada's proposal, which would have given the latter company 65 percent of a unified airline. Furthermore, the idea was viewed as politically unpopular in Canada where it would have likely eliminated more than 10,000 jobs. Shortly thereafter, Air Canada abandoned the concept of a "made-in-Canada" solution, forming an alliance with United Air Lines Inc. and acquiring an equity position in Continental Airlines Corp., both of which were high-ranking U.S. carriers.

In 1994 Air Canada won long-coveted entree into the Japanese market (it had been prohibited by law from competing in Asia and South America since 1987) when the Canadian government appointed it to serve Osaka's new Kansai International Airport. A long-anticipated "open skies" agreement with the United States signed into law early in 1995 permitted Canadian airlines to expand their destinations to virtually any American airport, and vice versa. As a result, Air Canada announced that it would be adding 20 new routes in the near future. These plans for international expansion—as well as its first profitable year, 1994—served to affirm Air Canada's ability to remain competitive in the years to come.

Principal Subsidiaries:

Air Canada Vacations (Touram Inc.); Northwest Territorial Airways Ltd.; Dynamex Express Inc.; Air Nova Inc.; AirBC Ltd. (85%); Air Ontario Inc. (75%); Air Alliance Inc. (75%); Wingco Leasing Inc (75%); 176497 Canada Inc.; 152160 Canada Inc.; Galileo Canada Inc.; The Gemini Group Limited Partnership.

Further Reading:

Enchin, Harvey, Geoffrey Rowan, and Stephen McHale, "An Airline Merger Fails to Fly," *Globe and Mail,* 24 August 1992, p. A1.
Foster, Cecil, "Air Canada Searching for a New CEO after Jeanniot's Surprise Retirement," *Traffic World,* August 13, 1990.
———, "Tough Guys Don't Cuss," *Canadian Business,* February 1995, p. 22.
Gibbon, Ann, "Harris, Managers Take Pay Cut," *Globe and Mail,* 23 February 1993, p. B1.
Goldenberg, Susan, *Troubled Skies: Crisis, Competition and Control in Canada's Airline Industry,* Whitby, Ontario: McGraw-Hill Ryerson, 1994.
McKenna, Edward, "Air Canada Restructures," *Aviation Week & Space Technology,* May 4, 1992.
McMurdy, Deirdre, "The Style of Dixie," *Maclean's,* 6 July 1992, p. 96.
Ouellet, Francine Vallee, "The Privatization of Air Canada," *Canadian Business Review,* winter 1989.
Oum, Tae Hoon, W. T. Stanbury, and Michael W. Tretheway, "Airline Deregulation in Canada and Its Economic Effects," *Transportation Journal,* summer 1991.
Rowan, Geoffrey, "Air Canada Loses $326 million," *Globe and Mail,* 19 February 1994, p. B20.

Smith, Philip, *It Seems Like Only Yesterday: Air Canada, the First 50 Years,* Toronto: McClelland and Stewart, 1986.

—Bruce Vernyi
—updated by April Dougal Gasbarre

Alcan Aluminum Limited

1188 Sherbrooke Street West
Montreal, Quebec H3A 3G2
(514) 848-8000
Fax: (514) 848-8115

Public Company
Incorporated: 1902 as Northern Aluminum Company
    Limited
Employees: 42,000
Sales: $11.53 billion
Stock Exchanges: New York Toronto Montreal
    Vancouver Midwest Pacific London Paris Brussels
    Amsterdam Frankfurt Basel Geneva Zürich Tokyo
SICs: 1099 Metal Ores, NEC; 3341 Secondary
    Nonferrous Metals; 3353 Aluminum Sheet, Plate,
    and Foil; 3354 Aluminum Extruded Products;
    3355 Aluminum Rolling and Drawing, NEC.

Alcan Aluminum Limited is a primary force in the aluminum industry worldwide, competing with Aluminum Company of America (Alcoa) for the number-one ranking. The company is a fully integrated aluminum producer, handling the light-weight metal at all stages of development, from bauxite mining to high-tech component fabrication. Alcan was one of Canada's highest profit-making companies during the 1980s, although profits dipped somewhat in the late 1980s and early 1990s, reflecting weak business conditions and lower prices.

Alcan is a multinational corporation, with operations vertically integrated across many operating areas worldwide. Bauxite and aluminum are mined in several countries and primary aluminum smelters are operated worldwide to help create a variety of aluminum goods that are fabricated to differing degrees. Alcan sells primary and fabricated aluminum in more than 100 countries around the world. Historically the company has followed a decentralized corporate model; overseas subsidiaries are left to manage their own affairs, even to the extent of financing expansion on their own.

Alcan's international orientation dates back to its origins. In June 1928 the Aluminum Company of America, then the world's undisputed leader in aluminum, spun off its foreign operations, forming a Canadian holding company called Aluminum Limited. Shareholders received one share of the new company for every three

shares of Alcoa stock. For more than 20 years the two companies were controlled by the same individuals. Aluminum Limited penetrated foreign markets, and participated in international cartels away from the scrutiny of the United States Justice Department. Alcoa, meanwhile, dominated the U.S. market.

Alcan's history, however, began long before the 1928 spin-off. In 1899 The Pittsburgh Reduction Company—later Alcoa—began construction of a power plant and the first Canadian reduction works at Shawinigan Falls, Quebec. Aluminum production began two years later. This first Canadian subsidiary became known in 1902 as Northern Aluminum Company Limited.

Northern Aluminum became an important player in the global aluminum markets. Aluminum was still a new metal. A commercially feasible refinement process had been discovered in 1886, but industrial applications were somewhat slow in developing. Skepticism among manufacturers forced producers toward vertical integration. Pittsburgh Reduction, and its Canadian subsidiary Northern, were tireless in trying to develop aluminum markets, but eventually turned to fabricating products such as cooking pots to promote the metal and broaden sales.

Several countries, in addition to the United States and Canada, had one or two aluminum producers. European businesses often organized distribution in industries where demand was limited, and after the turn of the century, cartels were formed to set the prices and quotas for individual aluminum companies. The first of these cartels began in 1901, and was known as the Aluminum Association. The cartel, which was made up of the leading Swiss company, the leading British company, and a pair of French companies, in addition to the Canadian concern, divided the world into reserved markets and free markets. Each company was allotted a reserved market and given a quota on a percentage basis for the free markets. The Swiss company was the distributor for all participants. This cartel operated until 1908, then broke up over disagreements on price-setting. In 1912 a new cartel was created, this time allowing any member to sell its quota directly to customers in any market without restriction. This second cartel broke up in 1915, disrupted by World War I.

While technically Alcoa was not a member of the cartels, it did effectively participate through its wholly owned Canadian subsidiary. This association would later fuel antitrust actions against Alcoa and eventually contributed to the divestiture of Northern Aluminum and Alcoa's other foreign operations in 1928.

Demand for aluminum grew in the early years of the 20th century. Applications for the metal were found in the electrical and automotive industries. By 1914 80 percent of U.S.-made cars had aluminum crank and gear cases. Aviation, at that time a new industry, called for light-weight metals. Orville and Wilbur Wright had used aluminum in their first plane at Kitty Hawk, North Carolina.

World War I provided new applications for aluminum. Massive quantities of the metal were employed in explosives, ammunition, and machine guns. The Liberty V-12 engine, which powered Allied planes, was one-third aluminum. Military usage absorbed 90 percent of the aluminum produced during the war years. The widespread use during the war translated into widespread acceptance by consumers after the war. Furthermore, the interruption of European aluminum shipments to North America served as a boon to Northern Aluminum after the war. In 1919 Northern alone exported 5,643 tons of Canadian aluminum to the United States compared to 2,360 for all European producers combined.

The 1920s saw fantastic growth for Northern Aluminum. In the early years of the decade, Arthur Vining Davis, head of Alcoa, became interested in two or three hydroelectric plants being proposed by U.S. tobacco magnate James B. Duke on Quebec's Saguenay River, because the refinement of aluminum requires vast amounts of electricity.

Davis called upon A.W. Mellon, renowned financier and major stockholder in Alcoa, to help negotiate a deal with Duke. In 1925 a deal was struck. The aluminum company acquired the hydroelectric site at the so-called Lower Development, as well as water rights to the Upper Development. Duke took $16 million in preferred stock and 15 percent of the common stock of Alcoa. When Duke died three months after the deal was signed, Alcoa was given the opportunity to purchase a controlling interest in the Upper Development. Also in 1925, Northern Aluminum Company changed its name to Aluminum Company of Canada Limited.

These events secured the Saguenay River hydroelectric facilities, the foundation for today's Alcan operations. Growth on the site was feverish. By 1927, the power plant on the Upper Development supplied a new 27,000-ton smelter, and the refinery neared completion. The company town of Arvida, named after Arthur Vining Davis, sprang up, and the development became the world's largest aluminum production site during World War II.

In 1928 when Alcoa divested its overseas operations, the Aluminum Company of Canada Limited became the chief operating subsidiary of Aluminum Limited. Aluminum Limited also took over all of Alcoa's other non-U.S. holdings including Norwegian, Italian, French, and Spanish manufacturing and power concerns. Alcoa retained ownership of the power plants on the Saguenay until 1938, when Aluminum Limited purchased them for $35 million. At the same time, the company moved its headquarters to Montreal from New York, although some senior executives continued to work in New York.

There were several reasons for the spin-off of Aluminum Limited (AL) from Alcoa. Davis felt that Alcoa's sales force neglected overseas markets in favor of the domestic market. He believed a Canadian company, with its own directors and own staff, would be in a better position to exploit international markets throughout the British Empire and elsewhere. Also, Alcoa's domination of the aluminum industry made it a frequent target of U.S. antitrust accusations. By divesting its foreign subsidiaries, Alcoa at least created the impression that it was not excluding competition from abroad. Meanwhile, the new company was free to participate in international cartels as it pleased.

Davis was nearing retirement, and would soon be faced with choosing a successor. The choice was between his brother Edward K. Davis, and his long-time close friend and colleague, Roy Hunt. Hunt was the son of Alcoa's co-founder, Captain Alfred E. Hunt. Davis solved his problem by sending Edward Davis north to head the new international corporation.

Edward Davis, as AL's first chief, faced some difficult challenges in the company's early years. Although not truly an infant company, AL had to redefine its approach. Formerly the company had been a part of a vertically integrated whole. Now it was expected to compete worldwide, but it lacked the aluminum-fabrication capability to make finished products that Alcoa and the European producers had.

The Depression struck the company hard, and it was forced to borrow heavily to survive. Technical support and operating agreements with a benevolent Alcoa helped the company stay afloat. For the most part, AL did not compete with Alcoa in the U.S. market due to a substantial U.S. tariff on imports and the influence of Alcoa's and AL's common shareholders. As a result, AL pursued Asian and European markets.

Realizing it could not survive unless it integrated its operations, AL built fabricating plants in a number of countries worldwide. The growth of the automotive and aviation industries improved the position of AL. By 1937 the company was out of debt and operated profitably. Production capacity at the Arvida plant had doubled and the number of employees worldwide since 1928 had tripled. In 1937 the U.S. Justice Department filed an antitrust suit against Alcoa, Aluminum Limited, and 61 related subsidiaries and individuals. The suit called for the break-up of Alcoa, and its divorce from AL. The suit alleged Alcoa and its confederates had conspired to restrain imports and to preserve its U.S. monopoly. In 1942 Alcoa and Aluminum Limited were cleared of the charges. The 1942 decision was appealed and was upheld on all counts except one. The appeals court opined that at the time of the original decision, Alcoa monopolized the U.S. ingot market, but that since that time new competition seemed to have evolved. The court therefore delayed further action until an assessment of the postwar industry could be made.

In 1950 the court calculated that the same nine stockholders controlled 44.65 percent of AL's stock and 46.43 percent of Alcoa's stock. While the court said that the relationship between the two companies had been lawful in the past, it ordered the investors to divest the shares of one company or the other. It was the first time in history that U.S. investors had been ordered by their government to give up control of a foreign company. All of the investors except Edward Davis, who sold his Alcoa stock, sold their shares in the Canadian company. The suit remained open until 1957, when a Justice Department request for extended court supervision was denied. In the 20 years this case was open, the aluminum industry had undergone tremendous change, and AL had grown into a giant.

The late 1930s had seen the demand for aluminum explode, fueled by war preparations. AL was the largest supplier within the British Empire, and Britain's demand for airplanes and other military hardware was great. During the war, the Canadian company received US$78 million in low-interest loans from the British government to expand its power and reduction facilities. In return, the additional output was earmarked for the British market. The U.S. government also offered assistance to AL; the Defense Plant Corporation, the branch of the Reconstruction Finance Corporation charged with fostering war-industries production, paid US$68 million in advance for 1.3 million pounds of aluminum. AL reportedly used the cash flow to construct another dam on the Saguenay, the Shipsaw Power Plant Number 2. The purchase agreement annoyed U.S. producers, who saw it as a boost to a potential competitor after the war. AL's contribution to the war effort was, however, paramount.

The Aluminum Limited subsidiary Aluminum Company of Canada (Alcan) ended the war five times larger than it was in 1937. This expansion posed the threat of idle facilities after the war. The company's researchers worked on expanding aluminum applications in the automotive and rail transport industries.

World War II boosted other companies as well. In the United States, two new integrated concerns, Reynolds Metals Company and Kaiser Aluminum & Chemical Corporation, were born from favorable sales of government-owned aluminum plants built during the war. This new competition was not immediately threatening to Alcan, whose chief production at that time was in ingot rather than fabricated or semi-fabricated products. In addition, Alcan's Shipsaw Power plant in Quebec had indeed made Alcan's electricity costs the lowest in the world.

In 1946 Alcan announced a reduction in the ingot aluminum price to C13.25¢, or US12.04¢, per pound. This was well below most international producer's prices, and kept Alcan's price on a par with the price of US$.15. The signal was that Alcan intended to be the dominant primary—ingot—aluminum supplier worldwide.

In 1947, Nathanael V. Davis took over as CEO of Aluminum Limited from his father, Edward Davis. After a brief dip in aluminum consumption right after the war, consumer goods began to use the metal in quantities as never before. By 1950 the Korean War demanded a steady flow of aluminum for the military, and a shortage developed in the United States. U.S. producers increased their output, and several new competitors joined the field.

During the 1950s the United States imported 10 to 20 percent of its primary aluminum. Alcan controlled 90 percent of that import business. In 1951 Alcan began a $350 million expansion program, which included additions to the Quebec plants and a new hydroelectric and reduction site in British Columbia, which began operations in 1954.

In 1950, when the strong ownership ties between Alcoa and Alcan were severed, the Canadian company began to make more aggressive forays into the U.S. market. Occasionally, Alcan broke with tradition and set prices at rates lower than Alcoa. Alcoa's price leadership was followed loyally by other U.S. producers. Alcan focused on aluminum in primary-ingot form, while Alcoa,

Reynolds, and Kaiser dove into the semifabricated and fabricated products. Alcan's U.S. customers were independent fabricators, as well as Alcoa, Reynolds, and Kaiser themselves. The independents were Alcan's political allies, lobbying for low tariffs on primary aluminum.

While Alcan's exports to the United States grew in the early 1950s, market shares in other areas began to shrink. Norway and France doubled their domestic aluminum capacity, while historic importers like Germany and Japan began to develop their own industries. Although overall output increased, Alcan's percentage of world production declined from 21 percent in 1954 to 19 percent by 1960. By 1969 it had slid to 13 percent.

In 1957 Alcan's first domestic competitor, Canadian British Aluminum (CBA), was started. During the summer of 1957 a strike at Alcan's Arvida plant idled 45 percent of production capacity for four months, resulting in a loss of about 1,000 tons of aluminum production per day. Later in the year, recessionary conditions caused a global oversupply of aluminum, and Aluminum Limited's profits dipped for 1958. Sales of primary aluminum to U.S. and U.K. producers declined.

Alcan decided to bolster its fabrication efforts. In 1958 Alcan expanded fabricating operations in plants in 11 countries. The global oversupply lasted into the early 1960s, however, and as it worsened, U.S. producers slashed prices to near cost to keep plants running. Alcan was slowly being squeezed out of the U.S. market. In response, Alcan decided to build semi-fabricating plants of its own in the United States to establish stable outlets for its ingot.

In 1963 AL acquired a small U.S. metal-powders firm and an aluminum wire and cable firm. Alcan and three of its biggest U.S. independent customers, Cerro Corporation, Scovill Manufacturing, and National Distillers & Chemical Corporation, began construction of a US$45 million hot mill in Oswego, New York, that would produce coils and aluminum plate. Alcan bought out its partners in 1965, and also acquired other sheet-fabricating plants owned by Cerro and National Distillers. A U.S. subsidiary, Alcan Aluminum Corporation, was founded in Cleveland, Ohio, in 1965 to manage AL's U.S. fabrication concerns. The unit lost US$10.4 million in its first year, but persevered. By 1967 Alcan operated 12 plants in 8 U.S. states. In 1966 Aluminum Limited was renamed Alcan Aluminum Limited.

In 1968 Alcan reorganized its corporate structure. Rapid expansion taxed the company's decentralized system; 33 managing directors reported directly to CEO Davis. Subsequently, management was divided into three groups: raw materials, smelting, and fabricating and sales.

In the late 1960s another fundamental shift occurred in Alcan Aluminum's business. Higher transportation and labor costs eroded the advantage of refining aluminum in Canada, as did the availability of cheaper power in the United States. Political developments around the globe made it advantageous for Alcan Aluminum to build primary smelters in Australia, Britain, India, Norway, and Japan. By 1972, Alcan Aluminum's foreign smelting capacity equaled that of its Canadian facilities.

Alcan Aluminum had begun to develop integrated units within each country of operations.

Alcan Aluminum's shift toward finished products continued. In 1971 Alcan Aluminum shipped more fabricated and semi-fabricated tonnage than ingot for the first time. In 1972 Paul H. Leman took over as president of Alcan Aluminum Limited. Davis remained CEO and took on the new post of chairman. The French-Canadian Leman was Alcan's first president outside the Davis family. He had joined Alcan in 1938. In 1975 global recession brought on by the oil crisis, caused a decline in Alcan Aluminum's aluminum shipments by 16 percent worldwide. Profits took a dive as demand fell in all markets except Latin America. Alcan Aluminum continued to build plants overseas, however, adding an alumina refinery in Ireland, and participating in the development of new bauxite mines in Brazil in the mid- to late-1970s.

Labor troubles caused the shutdown of four of the company's five Canadian smelters in 1976. Damage to one plant, caused by molten aluminum hardening in the potlines when workers cut the power, cost an estimated US$25 million. Another strike three years later had a similar effect on Alcan Aluminum's production levels. During both of these strikes other producers took advantage of the banner growth years for aluminum. In the mid-1970s, plans to expand smelting capacity in Canada were mapped out. Uncertainty about the future of energy costs encouraged Alcan Aluminum and its Alcan subsidiary to take advantage of its own Canadian hydroelectric plants. In 1977 David Culver replaced Leman as president. The executive observed that Alcan Aluminum was the only aluminum producer in the world with the ability to expand by 30 percent without increasing its power costs. By 1978 construction on a new primary smelter in Quebec was well under way.

In July 1979 Davis stepped down as Alcan Aluminum's CEO, and was replaced by Culver but continued as chairman until 1986. Culver had joined Alcan Aluminum in 1949, and had worked his way up the sales side. He set out to bolster Alcan Aluminum's marketing efforts and strengthen the emphasis on fabricated products, eventually limiting ingot sales to 25 percent of the total. Culver initiated a new research-and-development push in 1980. Alcan Aluminum lagged in high-margin aerospace, automotive, and beverage-container markets due to dated technology.

In the early 1980s Alcan Aluminum opened new smelters in Australia and Brazil, and expanded facilities in West Germany, Britain, and Spain. The company was in a very strong financial position to face the next decade. Annual revenues had doubled since 1975 and earnings had increased eightfold. Debt was low.

Alcan Aluminum's financial strength proved a blessing when the recession of 1980 to 1982 reached the aluminum industry. Demand fell sharply. In 1982 Alcan Aluminum lost US$58 million, its first loss in 50 years. Several long-term factors came to a head in the 1980s. Increased use of scrap resulted in lower aluminum prices. New Third World producers entered the market in force. In 1960, six producers—Alcan Aluminum, Alcoa, Reynolds, Kaiser, France's Pechiney, and Switzerland's Alusuisse, controlled 70 percent to 80 percent of the free world's aluminum market. By 1981 their share was 40 percent to 50 percent. More than 80 companies, double the 1960 number, produced aluminum goods worldwide, and about 30 percent of Third World producers were owned at least in part by their governments, whose interest was oriented toward full employment and acquiring hard currency rather than toward maximizing profits or maintaining supply-and-demand equilibrium. Another factor was increased price volatility after aluminum was listed on the London Metals Exchange in 1978. Private deals between producers and buyers became obsolete, and buyers gained tremendous advantage when the exchange price was publicized daily.

The industry would adjust to these developments, but not until the latter half of the 1980s. Meanwhile, Alcan Aluminum overproduced, partly to exploit its hydroelectric power advantage while high oil prices greatly affected other producers, and partly to placate labor. Profits returned in 1983 and 1984.

In 1985 Alcan Aluminum trimmed 1,100 management jobs, cutting an estimated $40 million in costs annually. Alcan Aluminum went forward with plans to modernize its plants in Quebec, and when aluminum prices rebounded in 1985, Alcan Aluminum was better prepared to take advantage of it than any of its competitors.

In 1986 Alcan Aluminum's top managers devised a new long-term strategy to improve Alcan Aluminum's return on equity. The plan focused on technological applications of aluminum and related metals, particularly in aerospace, electronics, and ceramics. Aluminum-lithium alloys were tested in Canadian and British aircraft. Composite aluminum materials also found applications in rail-car and automotive assembly. Alcan Aluminum bought a gallium-purification subsidiary of Alusuisse in 1985, and planned to manufacture gallium arsenide semiconducting wafers. The company also reaffirmed its commitment to existing aluminum operations, including ingot production.

In 1987 Alcan Aluminum underwent a reorganization. Alcan Aluminum Limited, the parent company, was merged with its chief operating unit, Aluminum Company of Canada. All of the former parent's subsidiary units worldwide were transferred to the former Canadian operating unit, and the reorganized company took the name Alcan Aluminum Limited (Alcan). The arrangement shed layers of management. Alcan's leaner structure and clear direction helped the company earn record profits in 1988. Alcan's net of US$931 million was more than any Canadian company had ever earned. In July 1989 David Culver retired. Alcan's new chairman and CEO was David Morton, who had joined the company's British subsidiary in 1954. As Morton took over as CEO of Alcan, the world was headed for another recession.

Alcan enjoyed 1990 revenues of about $10.35 billion, about $605 million of which was netted as income. Unfortunately its primary markets continued to deteriorate and Alcan began posting disappointing losses. Sales dipped to a low of $8.96 billion in 1991 as net income plunged to a deficit of $64. Losses spiraled to more than $150 million in both 1992 and 1993. In response to the decline, Alcan executives stepped up their restructuring efforts. They jettisoned poorly performing divisions, reduced their work force, and implemented other initiatives designed to boost efficiency and shore up the companies slumping financials. In 1993 the 65-year-old Morton stepped aside as chief executive after 40 years of service to Alcan. He was replaced by Jacques Bougie.

Under Bougie, Alcan intensified its cost-cutting and restructuring efforts. Bougie's goal was to make Alcan the lowest cost producer of aluminum in the world. To that end, he initiated an aggressive cost-cutting program that slashed operating costs by more than $120 million in 1994 alone, bringing total cost reduction to more than $600 million for the three-year period. He also continued selling off assets as part of an effort to focus the company's investments solely on operations that fit in with its core smelting and rolled products businesses. In 1994, for example, Alcan sold its 73 percent stake in Alcan Australia Ltd., its U.S. metals distribution business, and its Canadian building products business. In 1995, moreover, Alcan began looking for a buyer for its non-core assets in Britain and the United States, which employed 4,200 workers at 35 locations and generated annual sales of about US$630 million.

By 1995 Alcan's work force had dropped to about 42,000 from more than 57,000 in the late 1980s. Cost-cutting efforts, combined with reviving metals markets, buoyed Alcan's sales to more than $11.53 billion in 1994, and net income recovered to a positive $105 million. Despite recent lackluster performance, the long-term outlook for the company was relatively bright going into 1995. Ongoing restructuring, improving efficiency, and Alcan's dominant market presence boded well for the company's future.

Principal Subsidiaries:

Alcan Aluminum Corporation (U.S.A.); British Alcan Aluminum plc (United Kingdom); Alcan Deutschland GmbH (Germany).

Further Reading:

"Alcan's Latest Cliff-Hanger" *Forbes,* November 1, 1977.

Farin, Philip, and Gary G. Reibsamen, *Aluminum: Profile of an Industry,* New York: Metals Week, 1969.

From Monopoly to Competition; The Transformation of Alcoa, 1888-1986, Cambridge: Cambridge University Press, 1988.

Gibbens, Robert. "John Evans Named Alcan Chairman," *Financial Post*, March 15, 1995, Section 1, p. 4.

Height, Jack. "Kingdom of the Saguenay: Canada's Sprawling Aluminum Giant," *The Iron Age,* April 5, 1945.

Kennedy, Peter. "Alcan Seeking Buyer for British and U.S. Operations," *Financial Post*, march 21, 1995, Section 1, p. 3.

Levy, Yvonne, *Aluminum: Past and Future,* San Francisco: Federal Reserve Bank of San Francisco, 1971.

McIntosh, Andrew. "Alcan Rebounds From Three-year Slump," *Gazette,* January 18, 1995, Section D, p. 1.

Ross, Alexander, "The Alcan Succession," *Canadian Business,* June 1989.

Smith, George David, Campbell, Duncan C., *Global Mission: The Story of Alcan*, 3 Vols., Montreal: Alcan Aluminum Limited, 1985-1990.

Ward, Joe. "An Alcan-Do Attitude," *Courier-Journal,* March 19, 1995, Section E, p. 1.

"Why Alcan Spends So Much," *Business Week,* July 10, 1971.

—Thomas M. Tucker
—updated by Dave Mote

ATCO

ATCO Ltd.

1600, 909 - 11th Avenue Southwest
Calgary, Alberta T2R 1N6
(403) 292-7550
Fax: (403) 292-7507

Public Company
Incorporated: 1947 as Alberta Trailer Hire Co.
Employees: 5,600
Sales: $2.02 billion
Stock Exchanges: Toronto Montreal Alberta
SICs: 1381 Drilling Oil & Gas Wells; 1382 Oil &
Gas Exploration Services; 8711 Engineering
Services; 4724 Travel Agencies

A pioneer and a commanding force in the industrial housing market, ATCO Ltd. began as an inconspicuous trailer rental company during the late 1940s before switching to the sale of trailers and then to the manufacture of housing structures designed for industrial clients. The key to ATCO's initial success was the discovery of oil in the northern reaches of North America, which suddenly positioned the company as one of the few suppliers of mobile living quarters for oil drilling crews. In later years, ATCO diversified beyond its core business by entering the real estate development and oil and gas development businesses. Then, during the early 1980s, the company plunged into the utilities business, further rounding out its enterprises.

ATCO's enormous size during the mid-1990s belied the company's humble beginnings as a small, entrepreneurial venture created to achieve a modest objective. Although ATCO was established in Calgary, the inspiration for its creation took place in Vancouver, where S. Donald Southern was spending his vacation shortly after the conclusion of World War II. A member of the Calgary Fire Department, Southern was driving around Vancouver when he saw a small fleet of rental trailers on a service station lot, a sight that prompted him to start his own trailer rental business after he returned to Calgary. With the hope of generating enough money from the rental of trailers to send his teenage son, Ronald D. Southern, to university, Donald Southern used $2,000 in credits he had earned from his military service and $2,000 from his son's summer work savings to buy a fleet of ten second-hand trailers in 1947, which he then began renting at service station lots through his newly created company, Alberta Trailer Hire Company.

Father and son worked together, each dividing their time to attend to the sundry details involved in supporting a fledgling entrepreneurial venture. The younger Southern serviced the company's fleet of vehicles when not attending his high school classes, and the elder Southern separated his time between working for the Calgary Fire Department and superintending Alberta Trailer Hire's operation. Their joint effort enjoyed moderate success, generating enough money to finance Ronald Southern's enrollment at the University of Alberta, but the foundation they laid in establishing their company would lead to much more for the two entrepreneurs. Unknowingly, Ronald and Donald Southern had created an enterprise that would spawn a new industry and begin the transformation of their inconsequential rental business into a multi-billion dollar manufacturing force.

For Donald Southern, the inspiration for Alberta Trailer Hire had come from the west, but the catalyst for his company's prolific success came from the north. In 1947, the same year Alberta Trailer Hire was founded, the discovery of oil in Leduc, Alberta, touched off a frenzied rush for oil in the region. Oil exploration companies scurried north to dig wells and explore for further evidence of the natural resource. Traditionally, oil drilling crews were housed in tents, but at the Leduc site, where it was not uncommon for temperatures to drop below −20°C, canvas tents were clearly unsuitable. To exist in the harsh climate of the north, oil drilling companies began to use mobile home trailers instead of conventional tents, giving Alberta Trailer Hire an incredible boost to business. No longer renting his trailers exclusively to vacationers, Southern was swamped with orders from oil companies, educing him to take out a $20,000 loan to purchase additional trailers, which he then began selling to his new and vastly wealthier clientele.

In the space of a few short years Alberta Trailer Hire grew into one of the largest trailer dealers on the continent, but its niche in the business world had yet to be definitively carved. That moment would arrive shortly after Ronald Southern returned from the University of Alberta in 1953 with a bachelor of science degree. Roughly concurrent with his return to the family business, an executive with Shell Oil approached Alberta Trailer Hire to ask if they could design mobile kitchens and bunk houses. This request would steer the Southerns toward the manufacturing side of the industrial housing supply industry, an industry they were already pioneering. Ronald Southern championed the shift from selling house trailers to building units properly designed for the company's industrial clients, and soon the Southerns, with the father serving as chairman and the son serving as president, built the first of six assembly plants outfitted to manufacture a series of interchangeable housing modules.

Because of the type of customers the company served and the frequently remote locations where the company's custom-designed housing units were used, Alberta Trailer Hire developed into an international company early in its history. Although the company was generating $1 million in annual sales by 1956, a remarkable total given the company's modest origins, its geographic range of operations suggested a much larger enterprise.

Shortly after beginning production of industrial housing units, ATCO was filling small orders placed by North American oil companies for shelter equipment to be used in the Middle East. As time progressed, the magnitude of ATCO's international business increased, propelling the company's growth. Ronald Southern gradually assumed control of the company, which was renamed ATCO Industries Ltd. in 1962, then ATCO Ltd. in 1979.

By the 1960s, ATCO was internationally recognized as a manufacturer able to design and produce industrial housing for any type of climate, from the intensely hot to the bitterly cold. One of the few companies in the world with such expertise, ATCO maintained resolute control over the worldwide market; its work-force housing quickly dotted the globe, supporting the enormous construction and natural resource projects that proliferated during the 1960s. In 1960 the company supplied housing units for a hydroelectric dam project in Pakistan, established factories in Australia the following year, then went on to manufacture large-scale shelter equipment for a variety of clients. During the mid-1960s the company supplied housing for construction crews erecting Minuteman missile sites in remote locations in the United States and supplied mobile camps to the Algerian state hydrocarbon authority for oil exploration crews.

As the 1970s neared, the world's insatiable demand for oil and other natural resources was sending oil companies increasingly deeper into the rugged frontiers of Alaska, Australia, and other remote regions to search for new reserves. The more remote the location and the more inhospitable the climate, the greater the need for ATCO's industrial housing. By the end of the 1960s, ATCO was regarded as one of the fastest growing companies in Canada, its growth fueled by unabated demand. Between 1956 and 1963, annual sales had climbed from $1 million to $14 million, then over the course of the ensuing five years sales leaped to $42 million. In 1968 the company first sold shares to the public, then in 1970 embarked on its most prolific decade of growth.

Sales increased eightfold between 1970 and 1979, but early in the decade revenue growth was relatively slow, the calm before the sudden storm of sales in the mid-1970s. From 1968 to 1972, annual sales increased moderately, rising by $8 million to $50 million, but in 1974 alone the company nearly doubled in size when it was awarded the bulk of more than $75 million in orders to supply housing for workers on the Trans-Alaska Pipeline. Revenue volume increased an additional 50 percent over the next two years, as orders poured in from oil-rich Middle Eastern countries for temporary housing at numerous development projects. At one such project, ATCO supplied 80 percent of the industrial housing facilities for 30,000 workers involved in a massive gas gathering project in Saudi Arabia between 1975 and 1977. This project helped bring the company's annual sales up to $261 million in 1977, a substantial increase from the $50 million in annual sales recorded five years earlier. Perhaps more important than ATCO's prodigious gain in sales was its ability to remain highly profitable as it rapidly expanded. Between 1972 and 1975, sales had increased fivefold, while the company's

net profit demonstrated even greater growth, increasing 11-fold during the same five-year span.

On the heels of this robust growth, ATCO suffered a setback that dramatically altered its future course, prompting a change in corporate strategy that would result in a much more diversified company in the 1980s. By the late 1970s, ATCO no longer had the industrial housing supply market all to itself. Competition in the lucrative industry had become intense during the roughly three decades since Alberta Hire Trailer had met the first widespread demand for industrial housing. Strong foreign competition joined the fray in force by the 1970s, when large projects in remote locations were undertaken in rapid succession. The rise of these new contenders coupled with flagging industrial housing orders contributed to a disappointing 1978 for ATCO. Annual sales slipped five percent during the year, not an alarming amount but certainly discouraging after five years of substantial and consecutive gains. More alarming was the company's waning profitability. Profits were cut in half over the course of the year, prompting Southern to accelerate the company's long-range development program hatched earlier in the decade.

In anticipation of an eventual decline in the global industrial housing market, management conferences in 1974 had developed a plan for reducing ATCO's dependency on one type of business by diversifying its interests. Specifically, management had discussed the gradual augmentation of two of its smaller operations, conventional housing and oil and gas development, into larger contributors to the company's sales volume. Sufficiently enlarged, these enterprises would give ATCO three legs to stand on and would mitigate its dependency on the cyclical industrial housing market.

When discussed in 1974, the intention had been to move in these two directions with a concerted effort in the 1980s, putting off any large acquisitions until the early part of the decade. The alarms triggered by ATCO's faltering steps in 1978, however, convinced Southern that the company should begin pursuing a more active role in conventional housing and oil and gas development sooner rather than later. Accordingly, ATCO teamed up with Genstar Ltd. and two Canadian banks in 1978 to form Alberta Land Development Company, which began constructing office buildings and single-family homes on 13,000 acres in and near Calgary and Edmonton, the two fastest-growing cities in Canada. At approximately the same time ATCO's joint venture with Genstar was begun, the company strengthened its involvement in oil and gas development by acquiring Houston, Texas-based Thomson Industries Ltd., the largest contract oil driller operating in Canada. Together with its stake in Alberta Land Development, this acquisition reduced ATCO's reliance on industrial housing as the company exited the 1970s.

Although a severe cyclical downturn in ATCO's core business of servicing energy and resources industries continued into the early 1980s, the industry-wide slump did not check the company's diversification efforts. In 1980, ATCO made a pivotal move when it acquired control of Edmonton-based Canadian Utilities Ltd., which sold natural gas and electricity throughout much of the northern half of Alberta. The addition of Canadian Utilities immediately tripled ATCO's annual revenues to $1.2 billion and doubled its annual net profit to $40.6 million, positioning ATCO as one of the largest companies in Canada. Aside from making ATCO a considerably larger company, the leap into the utilities business also provided relief from the ebbing industrial housing market, buoying the company's profitability. Between 1980 and 1983 ATCO's operating profit from its manufacturing plants was cut nearly in half, but its new utility division performed admirably during the recessive early 1980s, recording an encouraging gain in its operating profit from $99 million to $245 million. ATCO's real estate development business was also proving to be a success during the otherwise lackluster early 1980s, largely because of the company's policy to not begin constructing a building until 60 percent of its space was leased. Of 1.2 million square feet of commercial space in Edmonton and Alberta, only 27,000 square feet remained vacant, an anomaly in the depressed real estate market during the early 1980s.

After ATCO bought control of Canadian Utilities and suffered a disappointing defeat in a failed takeover of Calgary Power Ltd., annual sales climbed to $1.5 billion in 1982, making ATCO the 47th largest company in Canada. However, there the company's revenue volume remained, hovering around the $1.5 billion mark for more than the next decade. Although the company continued to expand on all fronts, the absorption and organization of the assets gained through its diversification efforts took place throughout the remainder of the 1980s. In mid-1988 ATCO restructured its organization, establishing three operating groups: ATCO Enterprises Ltd., the industrial housing manufacturing and leasing arm of the company, Canadian Utilities Unlimited, and ATCOR Resources Ltd., the oil and natural gas production and development segment of the company's business.

A fourth operating group was added in 1993, when a subsidiary company named Frontec Logistics Corp. was structured as a primary component of ATCO's corporate organization. Formed in 1986, Frontec was awarded one of its first major contracts two years later when it began operating and maintaining the North Warning System radar sites and support facilities. Commencing operations with only five employees, the company employed nearly 600 workers by the time of its reorganization as one of ATCO's four major operating groups. Over the course of those seven years, Frontec had become a comprehensive provider and manager of support services for the technical systems and system

facilities for customers in the defense, transportation, and industrial sectors.

With these four operating groups shepherding the company's business interests, ATCO entered the mid-1990s buoyed by the first substantial increases in its annual revenue total in more than a decade. In 1993, revenues rose from $1.56 billion to $1.79 billion, then broke above the $2 billion plateau in 1994 when the company generated $2.02 billion. With more than $3.8 billion in assets by this point, ATCO was solidly positioned in its various industries, having evolved into considerably more than its original father-and-son team ever dreamed.

Principal Subsidiaries:

ATCO Structures Inc.; Frontec Corporation; Canadian Utilities Ltd. (67.4%); ATCOR Resources Ltd. (35.2%); ATCO Europe kft.; Frontec Logistics Corp.; Frontec Services Ltd.; Norven Holdings Inc.; Alberta Power Ltd.; CU Power International Ltd.; Canadian Western Natural Gas Company Ltd. (96.5%); Northwestern Utilities Ltd.; Northland Utilities Enterprises Ltd. (80%); Yukon Electrical Company Ltd.; Northland Utilities (NWT) Ltd.; Northland Utilities (Yellowknife) Ltd.; CU Power Canada Ltd.; CU Power Generation Ltd.; Thames Power Ltd. (50%); Thames Power Services Ltd.; Barking Power Ltd. (51%).

Further Reading:

"ATCO Ltd.: Adding Real Estate and Oil to Industrial Housing," *Business Week,* July 9, 1979, p. 80.
Motherwell, Cathryn, "Frontec Awarded $100-Million Contract," *The Globe and Mail,* May 19, 1994, p. B10.
Schreiner, John, "Diversification Keeps ATCO on Profitable Path," *The Financial Post,* March 3, 1984, p. 1.
———, "Ronald D. Southern," *Kan'at'a,* August 1978, p. 26.
Steward, Gillian, "Southern Hospitality," *Calgary Magazine,* September 1983, pp. 24-31.
———, "Ron Southern: A Western Entrepreneur with a Multi-National Mission," *Business Life,* February 1981, p. 15.
Sylvester, Don, "ATCO Zeros in on International Business," *Business Life,* November 1977, p. 66.
Zwarun, Suzanne, "You Can't Always Get What You Want," *Maclean's,* October 20, 1980, p. 37.

—Jeffrey L. Covell

Avenor Inc.

1250 René-Lévesque Blvd. West
Montreal, Quebec H3B 4Y3
(415) 846-4811
Fax: (514) 846-4850

Public Company
Incorporated: 1941 as Pacific Logging
Employees: 6,867
Sales: $1.896 billion
Stock Exchanges: Toronto Montreal
SICs: 0800 Forestry; 2620 Paper Mills; 5110 Paper
   and Paper Products; 2621 Paper Mills; 5111
   Printing and Writing Paper; 0831 Forest Products.

Avenor Inc. is. one of the world's leading forest products companies. It was formed through the 1989 merger of Canadian International Paper Inc. (CIP) and Canadian Pacific Forest Products Ltd.. The business operated under the majority ownership of Canadian Pacific Enterprises Ltd. (itself a subsidiary of Canadian Pacific Ltd.) under the name Canadian Pacific Forest Products Ltd. from 1989 to September 1993, when Canadian Pacific Enterprises sold its controlling interest in the company to the public for nearly $700 million. In accordance with a provision of the divestment agreement, the firm's name was changed to Avenor, meaning "advantage north," in March 1994.

In the mid-1990s, Avenor ranked as North America's predominant supplier of post-consumer recycled-content newsprint. The company's overall newsprint and pulp operations accounted for more than two-thirds of its sales, most of which were exports. Industry-wide overcapacity and weak pricing of newsprint and pulp combined with high debt service expenses prevented Avenor from recording a single annual profit during the early 1990s. In fact, the company lost nearly $1.2 billion from 1990 through 1994. The first quarter of 1995 was Avenor's best since 1989; it made a profit of $66 million.

Avenor's origins can be traced through its longtime parent, the Canadian Pacific Railway Company (CP, now Canadian Pacific Ltd.). CP was founded in 1881 to build a transcontinental railroad across Canada. The federal government, which hoped that the provision of transportation would bolster western settlement, ceded 25 million acres of Crown land in Manitoba, Alberta

and Saskatchewan to the railway company. That stupendous landholding would become the foundation upon which CP built an enormous natural resources empire in the last half of the twentieth century.

The railroad first became involved in the forest industry in 1905, when it acquired Vancouver Island's Esquimalt and Nanaimo Railway and its 2 million acres of timberland. The land amounted to one-fourth of the entire island. Over the years, CP sold the vast majority of the acreage. But the 300,000 acres it kept formed the core of Pacific Logging, a pulp and paper subsidiary formed in 1941.

Although a certain amount of logging was essential to the construction of the transcontinental railway—CP had to clear a right-of-way for its train tracks, for example—the parent company didn't really begin to take advantage of the vast potential of its land and mineral rights until after World War II. That's when several trends converged to compel Canadian Pacific's diversification. Faced with competition from automobiles in the passenger sector and trucking in the freight sector, railroads began to seek out alternative ways to raise the cash necessary to build, maintain, and upgrade their operations and thereby remain competitive. Under the leadership of Norris Crump, who advanced to CP's presidency in 1955, CP was in the vanguard of a wave of diversification in its industry.

In 1962, Crump created Canadian Pacific Investments to serve as the railway's diversification vehicle. He subsequently shifted all of CP's "extracurricular" interests, including Pacific Logging, to the new subsidiary, which was later renamed Canadian Pacific Enterprises Ltd. In 1967, "Enterprises" made Canada's largest public share offering to that date, a $100 million minority stake. This stock sale helped raise funds for investment but kept a controlling interest with CP.

CP Enterprises began acquiring shares in Great Lakes Forest Products Ltd. in 1964, accelerated its purchases in 1967, and had amassed a controlling interest in the company by 1974. Headquartered in Thunder Bay, Ontario, Great Lakes Forest Products had been incorporated in 1936 to subsume a business first established in 1919. This medium-sized forester specialized in pulp, newsprint, and fine paper. Great Lakes flourished under CP Enterprise's wing: from 1974 to 1981, its net income tripled.

Departing from the way it handled its other ventures, Canadian Pacific kept its forestry interests separate from one another. During the 1960s and 1970s, Canada's vast forests made it an important (and inexpensive) supplier of pulp and paper in the global market, and CP's forestry interests continued to grow. By 1980, these businesses were generating a combined total of $674.9 million in sales and over $45 million in profits annually.

In 1981, Canadian Pacific purchased Canadian International Paper Co. Ltd. from International Paper Co. of Purchase, New York for $1.1 billion. The acquisition increased CP's annual forest products sales by more than 50 percent, and Canadian International Paper became the conglomerate's second-largest subsidiary overall (in terms of assets). Renamed CIP Inc., the new business ranked among the country's largest and most diversified integrated forest companies. CIP stood second only to Abitibi-Price Inc. in Canadian newsprint production, but it also produced pulp, packaging, paperboard, tissue and lumber at 22 production facilities in every province except Prince Edward Island and Manitoba. CIP's British Columbia landholdings ranked second only to Crown-owned land; in addition, CIP boasted more than half of the country's milk carton market, owned one of the nation's largest tissue manufacturers, and ranked as one of Canada's few suppliers to the Japanese market.

But these apparently positive factors belied a number of worrisome negatives. A 1988 *Globe and Mail* article by Kimberley Noble asserted that CIP was "widely viewed as a disorganized and geographically scattered collection of mills and product lines that [continued to suffer the ill-effects of] the neglect of its U.S. parent" for years. CIP was also cursed with some of the country's oldest and most inefficient mills, declining sales, and perhaps most disturbingly, shrinking markets. On top of these inherent problems, CP added a crushing takeover-related debt totaling $850 million.

In spite of infusions totaling more than $600 million and sales increases averaging 9 percent per year, CIP lost more than $200 million from 1981 to 1987. The CIP deal was called "probably one of the biggest corporate mistakes in recent years by a Canadian company" in Susan Goldenberg's 1983 book, *Canadian Pacific: A Portrait of Power.* Goldenberg said that "CIP was largely responsible for [Canadian Pacific Enterprise's] profit falling to $150 million in 1982 from $405 million in 1981." CIP finally earned its first annual profit, $12.9 million, in 1987, when higher pulp prices and increased shipments boosted results into the black. At some point during the decade, CP's original forestry business, Canadian Pacific Forest Products, was apparently merged with CIP. By 1988, CIP's sales totaled over $2 billion, its profits had grown to $214 million, and its debt had been whittled down to less than $125 million.

CIP's sister company, Great Lakes Forest Products, also suffered some tough years early in the decade. From 1981 to 1982, its profits were slashed 75 percent, and it recorded a loss in 1983. The company also had to lay off 1,700 employees when it shut down two mills in 1982. And although Great Lakes's sales took a precipitous plunge from $1.1 billion in 1984 to $637.5 million in 1986, its profits actually doubled during that period, from $17.9 million to $30 million. This superior performance can be credited, in part, to a $430 million modernization program launched in 1982, which clearly improved efficiency.

With the forest products industry as a whole on a roll in the mid- to late-1980s, CP proposed a merger of its disparate interests in April 1988. CP's proposition was influenced by a global forest industry consolidation. But the conglomerate couldn't move unilaterally; while it owned 100 percent of CIP, it only held 54.3 percent of Great Lakes, and therefore sought the acquiescence of a majority of its minority shareholders (a group consisting primarily of individual investors) to execute its plan. The merger called for the sale of CIP to Great Lakes Forest in exchange for 80 percent of the resulting company. Although Great Lakes's shareholders would have an even smaller voice in the proposed company, each of their shares would theoretically be worth more.

Some individual shareholders balked at the deal, noting that Great Lakes had been CP's best-managed and most consistently profitable forest company. In fact, although Great Lakes had only half CIP's annual sales from 1983 to 1988, it had generated more than $50 million more in net profits. They feared not only that the "shotgun marriage" would allow CP to pawn CIP's problems off on Great Lakes, but also that Great Lakes's management would be subsumed by that of CIP.

But in spite of their sometimes loudly-voiced reservations, 97.5 percent of Great Lakes's minority shareholders voted for the union in June 1988. The combination created one of Canada's largest forest products companies, with $3.1 billion in annual sales and $2.3 billion in assets. It was renamed Canadian Pacific Forest Products Ltd. and its headquarters was established in Toronto. (Great Lakes had been headquartered in Thunder Bay and CIP was centered in Montréal.)

Paul Gagne followed Cecil Flenniken up through CIP's ranks to become president and CEO of CP Forest in 1990. The transition was part of an industry-wide turnover that bid farewell to old-line executives who had come up through the logging ranks and ushered in a new generation of managers. Gagne came up through CIP's financial administration division. According to a 1991 article in the *Globe and Mail,* the new president was "regarded as one of the smartest people in the Canadian forest business."

Forest products prices dropped 27 percent from October 1990 to February 1991, as prices in virtually every segment of the industry softened. U.S. newsprint consumption, which accounted for two-thirds of the Canadian industry's newsprint sales, declined by 9 percent in the first quarter of 1991 alone. Major customers negotiated discounts and balked at price hikes. At the same time the Canadian dollar was trading high, thereby making the country's products costlier in comparison with U.S. goods. One *Globe and Mail* reporter vividly characterized the forest industry situation as a "bloodbath."

In 1991, Barrie McKenna of the *Globe and Mail* noted that "Prices [were] only a symptom" of the industry's malaise. "The real problem [was] oversupply. With the North American recession pounding advertising linage and forcing publishers to shrink the size of their newspapers, there's a lot more newsprint than the market can bear." Recognizing the true source of their problems, industry leaders began to take less efficient operations off line. That March, CP Forest announced the temporary shut down of individual newsprint machines. Capacity reductions accelerated in a big way in January 1992, when the company announced outright closure of an entire mill in Quebec and part of its operations in New Brunswick. These shutdowns alone reduced Canadian national capacity for newsprint production by 4.7 percent and put 1,900 workers on unemployment.

While drastic and costly (CP Forest took a $375 million charge in the fourth quarter of 1991), the move was cited as an essential step toward the resumption of profitability. Allan Robinson of the *Globe and Mail* noted that "The closing of the outdated operations means about 40 percent of the company's assets will be less than 18 months old." He quoted an unidentified analyst who agreed, saying that the closure "put CP Forest in the forefront on competitiveness in the Canadian industry."

CP Forest also sought to pare its wide-ranging interests through divestment during this difficult period. In 1991, the company sold its Facelle tissue business to the Canadian branch of America's Procter & Gamble Co. for $185 million. Sell-offs accelerated the following year, when the forester sold two Quebec cardboard box plants and two factories that produced single-serving containers. In 1993, CP Forest spun off 49 percent of Pacific Forest Products Ltd., its British Columbian lumber business, to shareholders. CP Forest's management hoped that scaling back the number and variety of products would help it concentrate on bringing its remaining lines into consistent profitability.

Nevertheless, when the company floated its first American public debt issue worth US$400 million in mid-1992, Moody's Investors Service Inc. rated the offering BA-1—"junk bond." Other rating agencies, including Standard & Poor's Corp., Dominion Bond Rating Service Ltd. and Canadian Bond Rating Service Ltd., gave the offering investment grades. But Amit Wadhwaney, an analyst with New York's M.J. Whitman & Co., pointed out that CP Forest was "borrowing to finance [its] debt," which had exploded from $115 million in 1989 to $1.4 billion at the end of 1992. By mid-1993, both Standard & Poor's and Dominion Bond had joined Moody's, placing "CP Forest on rating alert with negative implications."

Analysts weren't the only ones who were alarmed by CP Forest's ongoing woes. In 1993, Canadian Pacific Ltd. Chairman William Stinson publicly labeled the subsidiary CP's "most troublesome area." That August, the parent company announced its plan to spin off CP Forest to the public through a group of underwriters. CP had already shrunk its ownership from 79.68 percent to 70.01 percent by only buying one-fifth of a 1992 CP Forest share issue. CP sat out on another share offering the following March, thereby reducing its ownership to 60.7 percent. The conglomerate made a total of $607.8 million on the 1993 spin-off, and used the proceeds to reduce its own debt.

In accordance with an agreement with its former parent, the newly independent company took a new name in 1994. CEO Gagne hoped that Avenor, which combined the Latin root of "advancing" with the English "north," would verbally represent the company's forward-looking posture.

A five-year, $1.5 billion investment program in the early 1990s boosted productivity, reduced expenses, and added recycled paper capacity. Avenor emerged as the leader of the North American recycled-content newsprint business in the early 1990s after retrofitting two existing facilities to handle post-consumer pulp. De-inking facilities complemented these activities. The company's high level of recycled-content capacity positioned it well for the "environmental decade," when many local and regional governments (especially in the United States) began to require some recycled content in newsprint.

Given the state of the global paper market, Avenor's high level of debt, and its steep (but necessary) capital budget, the company was unable to record a single annual profit from 1990 to 1994. Avenor's consecutive losses totaled nearly $1.2 billion by the end of fiscal 1994. But the company's long-term investments appeared to be paying off early in 1995, when Avenor made its best quarterly showing since 1989. With these results in hand, president Paul Gagne was predictably confident that the company would make a profit on the year.

Principal Subsidiaries:

St. Laurent Paperboard Inc.; Pacific Forest Products Ltd.

Further Reading:

Bournette, Susan, "Noranda Forest, Avenor Post Profit Jumps," *Globe and Mail,* 19 April 1995, B3.
"CP Forest Creates New Company," *Globe and Mail,* 31 January 1994, B3.
Gibbon, Ann, "CP Profit Slips in Second Quarter," *Globe and Mail,* 5 August 1992, B9.
Goldenberg, Susan, *Canadian Pacific: A Portrait of Power.* Toronto: Methuen Publications, 1983.
Mahood, Casey, "CP Cuts Forest Subsidiary Loose," *Globe and Mail,* 12 August 1993, B1.
McKenna, Barrie, "CP Forest Debt Issue Rated Junk," *Globe and Mail,* 20 May 1992, B9.
———, "Pricing a Battlefield in Newsprint Wars," *Globe and Mail,* 4 March 1991, B1.
———, "Rash of Shutdowns Feared at Aging Newsprint Plants," *Globe and Mail,* 22 June 1991, B1.
McMurdy, Deirdre, "CP Forest To Be Leader in Recycling of Newsprint," *Globe and Mail,* 21 December 1989, B1.
Noble, Kimberley, "CP Forest Investors Now Seem Content," *Globe and Mail,* 19 April 1989, B9.
———, "CP Ltd. to Give Investment Community Rare, Incomplete Look at CIP Subsidiary," *Globe and Mail,* 27 May 1987, B6.
———, "Forest Giants Lose Ground," *Globe and Mail,* 3 November 1992, B1.
———, "Great Lakes Merger Under Fire," *Globe and Mail,* 24 May 1988, B1.
———, "Great Lakes Minority Votes overwhelmingly in Favor of CIP Merger," *Globe and Mail,* 3 June 1988, B4.
———, "Guard Changes," *Globe and Mail,* 21 May 1991, B1.
Robinson, Allan, "CP Forest to Lay Off 1,900," *Globe and Mail,* 10 January 1992, B1.

—April Dougal Gasbarre

Bank of Montreal

129 St. James Street
Place d'Armes
Montreal, Quebec H2Y 3S8
(514) 877-7110
Fax: 877-7770

Public Company
Incorporated: 1822
Employees: 34,769
Total Assets: $138.18 billion
Stock Exchanges: Montreal Toronto Winnipeg
   Alberta Vancouver London New York
SICs: 6000 Depository Institutions; 6021 National
   Commercial Banks

Two singular events in the last two decades—the arrival of an aggressive new CEO in 1975 and the deregulation of the Canadian banking industry in 1985—shook up the stodgy, traditional Canadian banking industry and forced it to deal with the increasing complexity and internationalization of the financial world. Among the leaders that emerged in the new environment was Bank of Montreal, which was the sixth largest Canadian bank going into 1995. The bank offers a full range of personal and commercial financial services and supports offices in all the Canadian provinces, the United States, Japan, and Europe.

If any bank had a right to be stodgy and traditional, it was certainly the Bank of Montreal, whose roots stretch back to the early 19th century. It first opened for business in 1817 on St. Paul Street, in the heart of Montreal's business district, as the Montreal Bank. Forced to rely on American investors for nearly half of its initial capital, the bank was established without an official charter. However, within five years the new bank had proven its worth to the community and was granted a charter in 1822 as the Bank of Montreal. By then, all but 15 percent of its capital stock had been repatriated.

During its early years, the bank engaged in bullion and foreign-currency trading in addition to its lending activities. In 1827 and 1828, it was forced to omit its dividend for the first and last time after the bulk of Quebec's fur-trading activity shifted to Hudson Bay, depressing the local economy and causing a number of loan defaults. During this time, however, the Bank of Montreal also began its long financial and managerial association with the expansion of Canada's canal and railway systems. In the late 1830s, it prospered despite political upheaval. The Bank of Montreal acquired the Toronto-based Bank of the People at that time, so when Upper and Lower Canada were united into the Province of Canada in 1841, its total assets exceeded $4 million.

During the early 1860s, the Bank of Upper Canada, which was then the Canadian government's official banker, slid inexorably toward failure, and in 1864 the Bank of Montreal was appointed to take its place. It continued in this capacity until the establishment of the Bank of Canada in 1935. The bank also began to expand its branch network when Canada achieved full political unity in 1867, opening two offices in New Brunswick. It opened a branch in Winnipeg, in 1877 and followed the Canadian Pacific Railway westward as railroad construction opened up the prairie for settlement. Bank of Montreal branches appeared in Regina, in 1883, Calgary, in 1886, and Vancouver, in 1887.

The bank already had two foreign offices by this time; it had opened one in New York in 1859 and another in London in 1870. The Bank of Montreal used its foreign representation to expand into investment banking in the late 1870s. It joined a syndicate of London bankers in underwriting loans to the province of Quebec and the city of Montreal. In 1879 it underwrote a Quebec securities issue and floated it on the New York market. It further expanded its international activities in 1892 by becoming the Canadian government's official banker in London, underwriting all of the national government's bond issues on the London market.

At the turn of the century, the Bank of Montreal embarked on an acquisition spree that would make it Canada's largest bank by the outbreak of World War I. It improved its position in the Maritime Provinces and northern Quebec by acquiring the Exchange Bank of Yarmouth, the People's Bank of Halifax, and the People's Bank of New Brunswick. In 1906, it bought out the bankrupt Bank of Ontario. In 1914 the Bank of Montreal had $260 million in assets, 179 offices, and 1,650 employees.

Nearly half of the bank's mostly male work force enlisted in the military at the outbreak of World War I, but the hiring of women in large numbers made up for the loss. In fact, the war had a rather salutary effect on the bank's finances due to the sale of war bonds, which were quite popular. World War I also marked the end the London market's role as the Canadian government's main source of external financing: the London securities markets were closed to foreign issues from 1914 to 1918, and the Bank of Montreal and the government began to float their bond issues in New York.

An economic crash in 1920 followed a short postwar boom, and the crisis forced Canadian banks to consolidate. The Bank of Montreal had already acquired the British Bank of North America in 1918; it bought the Merchants Bank of Canada in 1922 and the Montreal-based Molson Bank in 1925. These acquisitions increased its branch network to 617 offices, more than three times what it had been during the war.

The depression that struck Canada in the 1920s, however, was not as serious as the Great Depression of the 1930s. In 1933 Canada's gross national product was almost half of what it had been in 1928, and the number of unemployed increased nearly 13-fold. Bank of Montreal's assets were worth nearly $1 billion in 1929, then dropped below $800,000 for five consecutive years. The Depression finally ended with the outbreak of World War II, during which the Bank of Montreal, just as it had done during the previous war, lost large numbers of employees to the armed services and also made money from the sale of war bonds.

The years after World War II brought prosperity and rapid economic development to Canada. Canadian banks also prospered, but in a regulated and noncompetitive atmosphere. "It was sort of a clubby affair," Bank of Montreal executive vice president Stanley Davison told *Fortune* in 1979. Canadian law limited the interest banks could charge on their loans to 6 percent, and power in the banking industry was concentrated in a group of five major banks, of which the Bank of Montreal was one. During this time, however, the Bank of Montreal also earned itself a reputation for stodginess and an unwillingness to adapt to change. In the mid-1960s its earning performance began to weaken. Then, in 1967, an amendment to the Canadian Bank Act eliminated the interest-rate ceiling, opening up new opportunities in the area of consumer and small-business lending. The Bank of Montreal was caught unprepared to keep pace with its competitors.

The bank's financial performance was further eroded by its costly efforts to computerize its operations. The Bank of Montreal's accounting procedures seemed not to have changed much since the age of the quill pen; when CEO Fred McNeil assumed his post in 1968, he asked a personnel department executive for a copy of the departmental budget and the executive replied: "Budget? No one has ever asked us to prepare one." However, the necessary transfer to computers swallowed up unexpected amounts of money. Its projected cost in 1969 was $80 million, and the figure was repeatedly revised upward for several years thereafter. In another costly effort to catch up to the competition, the bank started a credit card program in 1972, becoming the last of Canada's five major banks to bring out a credit card. The start-up costs of this venture added even more to the bank's financial liabilities.

In the midst of these changes, McNeil became chairman and an American, William Mulholland, stepped into his position as CEO in 1975. Formerly a partner at the prominent investment bank Morgan Stanley, in 1969 Mulholland was named president of Brinco Limited, a Canadian mining company. After taking the top job at the Bank of Montreal, he dodged the controversy over an American heading one of Canada's largest banks by promising to consider adopting Canadian citizenship.

Mulholland's aggressive and uncompromising management style was once described as "chewing through underlings with a chainsaw" by *Canadian Business* magazine, and a number of senior executives left the bank during his tenure. But the bank's condition also improved immediately after he took office. Mulholland closed down 50 unprofitable branches during his first

five years in office, revised the Bank of Montreal's internal pricing system to reflect the cost of funds more accurately, and modernized procedures for asset and liability management. He also was unafraid to bring in outside help, as he did when he recruited IBM executive Barry Hull to get the computerization program on track. The bank opened its first computerized branch office in 1975, and all 1,240 of its branches were plugged into the computer system by 1979.

The Bank of Montreal has also sought to internationalize under Mulholland, joining a trend nearly every one of the world's major financial institutions has followed since the late 1960s. In 1978 it purchased a 25.1 percent interest in Allgemeine Deutsche Creditanstalt, a medium-sized West German bank. Also in 1978, the Bank of Montreal tried to expand into the American retail banking market when it began negotiating the acquisition of 89 branch offices from Bankers Trust Company. Mulholland forged ahead with the deal despite analysts' misgivings, but negotiations broke down in 1979 and the deal was never consummated.

The Bank of Montreal suffered in the early 1980s under the strain of loans to Latin America and to oil and real estate interests in western Canada that went sour. However, in 1984 it finally obtained entry into the American retail market when it acquired Harris Bankcorp, the third-largest bank in Chicago, for US$547 million. As with the Bankers Trust bid, banking analysts expressed their doubts over the deal; the Bank of Montreal paid US$82 per share for Harris stock, or nearly twice its trading price. Within two years, the analysts had changed their opinion entirely. The Harris acquisition made the Bank of Montreal one of the leading foreign institutions involved in U.S. commercial and industrial lending and enhanced its foreign exchange capabilities. The strong performance of regional bank stocks in 1985 and 1986 also made the deal seem like a bargain in retrospect.

In 1985 the Progressive Conservative government of Prime Minister Brian Mulroney decided to deregulate Canada's financial system, a move that blurred the traditional lines between insurance, banking, and securities brokerage. Companies that had been restricted to one business were allowed to diversify into others, increasing competition among individual firms but also the power of holding companies seeking to build financial-service empires. One immediate consequence of deregulation was a surge in merger-and-acquisition activity involving Canadian securities firms. Growing foreign investment in North America helped accelerate this trend, as did an increasing demand for stocks among domestic small investors. (One brokerage executive told *Barron's,* "It wasn't too long ago that the average Canadian's idea of a balanced portfolio was a savings bond and a lottery ticket.") The Bank of Montreal responded by acquiring Nesbitt Thomson, Canada's fourth-largest brokerage firm, in 1987, a move that spawned a string of acquisitions throughout the late 1980s and early 1990s.

William Mulholland continued to guide the Bank of Montreal into the early 1990s. Although the bank continued to grow and diversify under his leadership, the banking industry in general suffered from a global economic downturn. The Bank of Montreal was not unaffected: revenues dipped from about $10.58 billion in 1990 to less than $9 billion by 1992. Despite the decline, the bank's net income rose from about $475 million in 1990 to $576 million in 1992 and then to $641 million in 1993. The gains were largely the result of an improving loan portfolio, increased efficiency, and the success of several of the bank's forays into services.

An economic upturn combined with ongoing growth and diversification boosted Bank of Montreal's revenues to $9.11 billion in 1994, while net income grew to a healthy $756 million. The bank finished the year with about $138 billion in assets, making it the sixth largest bank in Canada. Bolstering the bank's bottom line was its expanding mortgage business and ballooning income from its brokerage services; total service, or non-interest, businesses accounted for about 20 percent of the bank's revenues in 1994. Several changes in 1994 and 1995 indicated continued diversification and growth for the bank. In 1994, Bank of Montreal became the first Canadian bank to be listed on the New York Stock Exchange. In 1995, it opened its first branch in China, indicating its ongoing expansion efforts. The same year, the Canadian government began allowing banks to compete in certain insurance businesses, an opportunity the Bank of Montreal would almost certainly pursue.

Principal Subsidiaries:

Bank of Montreal Mortgage Corporation; Bank of Montreal Securities Canada Limited; Bankmont Financial Corp. (U.S.A.); Concordia Financial Corporation (Barbados).

Further Reading:

Blackwell, Richard, "Bank of Montreal Profit Comes in Below Expectations," *Financial Post,* March 1, 1995, Section 1, p. 7.
_____, "Bank of Montreal Third Canadian Bank to Open China Branch," *Financial Post,* December 22, 1994, Section 1, p. 9.
Denison, Merrill, *Canada's First Bank: A History of the Bank of Montreal.* Toronto: McClelland and Stewart, 1967.
Haliechuk, Rick, "Bank of Montreal Profits Hit Record," *Toronto Star,* November 23, 1994, p. E1.

—updated by Dave Mote

The Bank of Nova Scotia

44 King Street West
Toronto, Ontario M5H 1H1
(416) 866-6161
Fax: (416)866-3750

Public Company
Incorporated: 1832
Employees: 33,098
Total Assets: $132.93 billion
Stock Exchanges: Alberta London Montreal Toronto
   Vancouver Winnipeg
SICs: 6000 Depository Institutions; 6021 National
   Commercial Banks

In 1995 the Bank of Nova Scotia, the second oldest bank in Canada, had more than 1,200 domestic offices as well as about 200 offices in 45 other countries. Scotiabank, as it is usually called, conducts its activities through four major divisions: retail banking and operations, Canadian commercial banking, North American corporate and investment banking, and international. It grew quickly during the 1980s and early 1990s by acquiring other institutions and entering joint ventures with overseas banks.

The first public financial institution in the colonial port city of Halifax, the Bank of Nova Scotia was formed on March 30, 1832 to handle the economic activity associated with the area's lumbering, fishing, farming, and foreign trade. None of the members of the first board of directors had any practical banking experience, but this did not deter them from setting up the necessary operations and appointing James Forman, a prominent citizen of Halifax, to serve as the first cashier (as the general manager was called then).

The bank officially opened in August, 1832, a time of unfavorable economic conditions because of massive crop failures and a cholera outbreak. Early development, therefore, focused on establishing a foreign exchange business with agents in New York, London, and Boston, while local agencies and the main office in Halifax concentrated on making domestic loans.

Over the next 30 years, the bank grew slowly in the face of increased competition from existing institutions, such as the Halifax Banking Company and the Bank of British North America, as well as from new banks

opening throughout Nova Scotia. It was not until the early 1870s that the staff also determined that growth had been stunted by Mr. Forman's embezzlement of $315,000 since 1844.

The bank gradually recovered from these losses through the efforts of Forman's successor, William C. Menzies, who guided an expansion program that increased total assets to $3.5 million by 1875. Though local industry was declining, growth continued throughout the decade as the bank found opportunities in financing coal mining, iron, and steel businesses serving the railway and steamship lines. These improvements in transportation stimulated manufacturing throughout Canada, which also served to fuel the bank's development.

The Bank of Nova Scotia expanded outside the Maritime Provinces in 1882, when it opened a branch in Winnipeg to take advantage of opportunities created by a real estate boom in the area. The boom collapsed within six months, however, saddling the bank with enormous losses and forcing the branch to close three years later.

In 1883, the Bank of Nova Scotia acquired the Union Bank of Prince Edward Island. This bank had sought a larger, stronger institution to help it weather hard times that had already forced the liquidation of one local bank and were seriously affecting others in the area. By the end of that year, the Bank of Nova Scotia was operating 23 branches in Prince Edward Island, New Brunswick, and Nova Scotia.

Although a depression in Canada in the early 1880s caused heavy losses stemming from the failure of several businesses, the bank had rebounded enough by 1885 to consider further expansion, this time in the United States. Minneapolis was chosen, because of its strong grain and manufacturing industries, to be the initial site for a direct lending and foreign exchange business. This office closed seven years later when the local environment became less favorable and other cities, such as Chicago, showed more potential.

In 1888, the bank opened an office in Montreal in a second attempt to establish a domestic presence outside of the Maritime Provinces. This office was followed a year later by an office in Kingston, Jamaica, the first time a Canadian bank had expanded outside North America or the United Kingdom. The next new branch opened in St. John's, Newfoundland in 1894 to handle the business of two local institutions that had dissolved suddenly. Credit for this vigorous expansion goes to Thomas Fyshe, who became cashier in 1876 and resigned in 1897 after 21 years with the bank.

In March, 1900 the bank moved its headquarters to Toronto, to be better able to take advantage of opportunities offered by the Klondike Gold Rush and the completion of the Canadian Pacific Railway, as well as to be closer to its other branches in Canada and the United States. Its move into Western Canada was only somewhat successful, however; several unprofitable branches closed soon after they opened, while others in Edmonton, Calgary, and Vancouver were slow to make a profit. Nonetheless, the bank considered expansion a necessary part of its overall strategic plan to achieve national growth and avoid takeover by another institution. Development in the East was more successful; 19 new branches opened in Nova Scotia and New Brunswick, 16 opened in Ontario, and four opened in Quebec between 1897 and 1909.

Beginning in 1901, Henry C. McLeod, who served as general manager from 1897 to 1910, waged a campaign to require all Canadian banks to undergo external inspection by the Canadian Department of Finance. This effort, prompted by the large number of bank failures that had occurred since 1895, was intended to win the public's confidence in its financial institutions. None of the other Canadian banks supported him, so, impatient with the government's inactivity on the issue, McLeod subjected the Bank of Nova Scotia to examination by two Scottish accountants, making his the first Canadian chartered bank to be verified by an independent, external audit. McLeod did not win his battle until 1913, when the Bank Act was revised and such inspection became compulsory.

Between 1910 and 1920 the bank embarked upon a series of major acquisitions that significantly altered its size and the scope of its operations. After two years of informal discussions, the bank officially merged with the oldest Canadian chartered bank, the Bank of New Brunswick, on December 11, 1912. The Bank of New Brunswick was a relatively small institution, confined to 31 branches in a single region and lacking the resources to expand due to its traditional practice of returning capital to shareholders. In 1914, with the acquisition of the 12-year-old Toronto-based Metropolitan Bank, the Bank of Nova Scotia became the fourth largest financial institution in Canada. Five years later, the Bank of Nova Scotia acquired the Bank of Ottawa, allowing it to expand westward again without having to establish new branches.

Joining other Canadian financial institutions in the war effort during World War I, Scotiabank experienced only minor disruptions in operations and staffing and returned to normal upon the war's end.

During the early 1920s, the bank slowed the pace of external growth to focus its attention on consolidating the operations of its three prewar acquisitions and reorganizing its departments for greater efficiency. An Investment Department was formed to handle securities transactions, which represented a significant amount of the bank's business in Toronto, Montreal, and New York.

The strong postwar recovery brought healthy earnings throughout most of the decade, until the 1929 stock market crash and subsequent depression. Between 1933 and 1935, the bank closed 19 domestic branches as profits dropped by half a million dollars, to $1.8 million. Business conditions in Newfoundland deteriorated, the Social Credit Party rose to power in Alberta and enacted troublesome legislation there, and political difficulties in Cuba and Puerto Rico pressured international activities.

Economic recovery went up and down between 1936 and 1939 as the positive effects of the growing Canadian mining industry were offset by a drought in the West. The bank's asset base continued to grow, but not without some managerial concern—it consisted largely of loans to the government for relief funds, rather than higher-yielding commercial transactions.

World War II increased the demand for banking services, particularly by the government for financing the war. By the end of the war the bank's assets had surpassed $600 million, but federal government securities represented 50 percent of the total.

In 1945, the new general manager, Horace L. Enman, renewed prewar efforts to explore new business opportunities and improve shareholders' returns. Buoyed by heavy immigration to Canada and the nation's need for capital, the bank's commercial loan activity increased after the war to restore a more favorable balance between lending to business concerns and to the government. In 1949, Enman became president and C. Sydney Frost became general manager. By this time the bank's rapid growth and extensive reach demanded greater decentralization. Regional offices gradually assumed responsibility for staffing and maintaining branch activities and credit supervision. By 1950, the bank had opened 90 new branches, half in British Columbia and Alberta.

The 1950s were a period of economic prosperity throughout Canada. Resource development and improvements in transportation increased immigration levels in major Canadian cities and provided a stimulus to growth. The change from a fixed to a floating official exchange rate allowed the bank to take advantage of the open market for the Canadian dollar and enhance its exchange-trading skills. When the National Housing Act was passed in 1954, the bank established a mortgage department, and it later developed a secondary mortgage market among pension funds to offset decreased lending activity. The bank also introduced an insured savings plan that brought in a substantial amount of new business, and more importantly, gave the bank a competitive advantage in selling banking services.

A change in the Bank Act in 1954 permitted banks to make automobile and household loans, prompting the bank to introduce a consumer credit program in 1958. In order for the bank to observe the 6 percent interest rate ceiling mandated by the Bank Act yet successfully operate in the consumer lending area on a large-scale basis, these loans required customers to deposit payments every month into a bank account that would pay off the loan by the due date and return a higher rate of interest to the bank over the life of the loan. By its second year, this plan had generated $100 million in loans and become a major contributor to the bank's overall earnings. When, in 1959, a money squeeze threatened its lending activity volume, the bank introduced a one-to-six-year term note that allowed it to compete successfully with finance and trust companies.

The bank continued its international expansion during this period, particularly in Jamaica, Trinidad, and Barbados, although the nationalization of Cuban banks in 1961 forced it, to close the eight branches it had established there at the beginning of the century.

In 1958, the bank joined with British financial interests to form the Bank of Nova Scotia Trust Company to engage in offshore and trust operations which were off-limits to foreign banks. A year later, the Bank of Nova Scotia Trust Company of New York was established.

Beginning in 1960, the bank aggressively pursued a strategy to increase its volume of deposits by resuming the establishment of new branches in Canada as well as abroad. This inflow of funds was required to support the bank's consumer credit operations while also meeting the demand for mortgages and short-term commercial loans. More than 60 percent of these new branches were in convenient suburban locations to attract new customers in and around Toronto, Montreal, Edmonton, and Calgary. Coupled with new products like term notes, certificates of deposit, and six-year certificates, this campaign increased the volume of personal savings deposits by 50 percent between 1960 and 1965.

This increased activity also enabled the bank to maintain its presence in the financial services industry despite the ceiling on lending rates, which had virtually eliminated the bank from competing effectively against trust and finance companies in all areas except for personal loans. During this time, the bank also increased its mortgage involvement by joining with two other partners to form three new ventures: Markborough Properties, a real estate company; the Mortgage Insurance Company of Canada; and Central Covenants, a mortgage financing company.

In 1963, the bank underwent a major internal reorganization, and a new profit planning system was introduced which required each branch and region to submit annual loan and deposit forecasts to be incorporated into the bank's overall plan. This system allowed the bank to further decentralize operations, to encourage competition among branches, and to better identify the services its customers wanted.

Meanwhile, business in the Caribbean continued to grow, despite the loss of the Cuban branches. Much of this growth was hotel and resort financing in areas like Jamaica and Puerto Rico, where tourism was becoming big business. The bank also opened branches in London, Glasgow, Amsterdam, Munich, Beirut, and Tokyo. Its international division became a major player in the Eurodollar market at this time.

During the early 1960s, the bank also worked to establish a stronger presence in the United States, particularly in Los Angeles and Houston, by offering financing and deposit opportunities for U.S. corporations in addition to international tax services. These efforts fueled the bank's accelerated growth in the second half of the decade.

At home, the early 1970s saw strong personal and small business lending activity, leading the bank to launch a number of new services, including automobile financing and a farm program to meet credit needs in the agricultural sector. Lending activity shifted significantly toward commercial concerns, particularly retail accounts, later that decade as inflation increased daily operational costs for Canadian businesses.

Actively involved in the precious metals market since 1958, the bank expanded this business throughout the 1970s by buying two-thirds of the country's annual production and then selling actual bullion and bullion certificates. It was also during this period that the rising expenses of branch development caused the bank to refocus its emphasis from opening new offices within Canada to improving existing operations and relocating branches to more lucrative areas.

In 1972, the bank was sued by VK Mason Construction Ltd. for negligent misrepresentation related to the building of an office and shopping complex. The contractor had required assurance from the bank that the developer, Courtot Investments, had sufficient financing to finish the construction before it would agree to take on the job, and Scotiabank had informed Mason that interim financing was available to Courtot if needed. When the project was completed, Mason was paid $1 million less than had been agreed and found that, rather than helping the developer pay its creditors, the bank called in its own loan and sold the complex when Courtot defaulted.

The Supreme Court of Canada found against the bank, though it affirmed the bank's right of first claim on the developer's assets as the mortgagee. Mason was permitted to collect damages by placing a lien on the bank's assets without having to compete with other Courtot creditors.

Organizational changes at the general office were made in the second half of the 1970s which created separate departments for each of the bank's three main customer categories: individual, commercial, and large corporate. In 1980 an operations department was formed to consolidate many of the branch, regional, and head office functions into one area, a move which signaled a shift away from decentralization toward more direct headquarters control.

The bank's total assets reached $50 billion by the end of 1981, with international business growing twice as fast as domestic operations and at a higher rate than that of any other Canadian bank. This growth was attributed to many factors, including the bank's established European and American presence, its expansion into Asia and the Pacific, and the development of a worldwide foreign exchange and banking system that operated around the clock. The year also saw the historic opening of the first and only Canadian banking branch in China.

Although a downturn in the economy during 1983 forced the bank to curtail expansion temporarily, its focus on smaller companies saved it from the large-scale losses other Canadian banks suffered from loans made to failing firms like Dome Petroleum and Massey-Ferguson, and to Mexico, Brazil, and Poland.

This focus on smaller companies and individuals did create image problems in the corporate and commercial areas. To counter the perception that the bank was not fully committed to businesses, Scotiabank embarked upon an extensive, innovative advertising campaign in 1986 using customers' case histories and games of visual illusion to show the various ways that the bank had helped companies.

During the first half of the 1980s, the bank was accused of wrongdoing in a series of cases stemming from its activities both at home and abroad. In March 1983, the bank was asked by a Miami court to release records from its Cayman Islands branch concerning certain customers under investigation for narcotics and tax violations. Although the bank was protected under Cayman Island law from such releases, a Florida judge ruled that the bank stood in contempt of court and fined it US$25,000 a day, retroactive to November 1983, for each day it did not produce the records. In order to end a stalemate which could have forced the bank into bankruptcy, the Cayman Islands Governor-in-Council intervened to authorize the bank to supply the required information, but not before the fine had reached US$1.8 million. The bank lost its appeal to the U.S. Supreme Court in January 1985.

In 1984 the bank, along with four other Canadian banks, was the subject of a one-year investigation by the Royal Commission of the Bahamas into drug dealing and money laundering by Bahamian Prime Minister Pindling and his wife. Scotiabank had lent more than $1 million to Pindling between 1977 and 1983 and had also accepted deposits from the couple totalling $114,000 from an unidentified source. Although the investigation was inconclusive, it cast a cloud on a 1985 case alleging that the bank had committed fraud against the Investment Dealers Association of Canada in its involvement in the failure of Atlantic Securities Ltd. in 1981. Although this case generated much controversy, the Nova Scotia County Court acquitted the bank.

In 1987 Scotiabank further penetrated the financial services market with the formation of Scotia Securities. That subsidiary, which provided discount brokerage and security underwriting services, allowed the bank to compete more effectively with investment banking firms. In addition to acquiring other banks during the late 1980s and early 1990s, the Bank of Nova Scotia pursued a strategy of global expansion to assure profitability regardless of any fluctuations in individual markets. It also worked to improve the quality of the loans in its portfolio and to increase the efficiency of its operations.

Scotiabank's efforts during the late 1980s and early 1990s were clearly paying off by the mid-1990s. Indeed, the bank's asset base ballooned from about $79 billion in 1992 to nearly $100 billion by early 1995—the gain was largely attributable to Scotiabank's 1994 acquisition of Montreal Trustco Inc. Similarly, the bank's sales spiraled upward to about $9.4 billion in 1994. Net income slipped in 1994 as a result of charges related to restructuring, but profitability had been improving steadily since the late 1980s and was expected to continue to improve throughout the mid-1990s.

By 1995, Scotiabank had more operations in Latin America and Asia than any other Canadian bank, and Scotiabank executives were working to set up new partnerships with banks in India, Malaysia, Brazil, Peru, and Venezuela. The bank was also branching out into new markets, such as insurance, opened up by Canadian deregulation of the banking industry. Ongoing aggressive global expansion and a robust loan portfolio boded well for the bank's long-term future.

Principal Subsidiaries:

BNS Australia Pty. Ltd.; BNS International (Hong Kong) Ltd.; The Bank of Nova Scotia International (Curacao) N.V.; The Bank of Nova Scotia Asia Ltd.; The Bank of Nova Scotia Channel Islands Ltd.; The Bank of Nova Scotia International Ltd.; The Bank of Nova Scotia Jamaica Ltd.; The Bank of Nova Scotia Properties Inc.; The Bank of Nova Scotia Trinidad and Tobago Ltd.; The Bank of Nova Scotia Trust Company (Bahamas) Ltd.; The Bank of Nova Scotia Trust Company of New York; BNS International (Ireland) Ltd.; BNS International (United Kingdom) Ltd.; Scotiabank (U.K.) Ltd.; Brunswick Square Ltd.; Calgary Centre Holdings Ltd.; Chargex Ltd.; Empire Realty (Cayman) Ltd.; Export Finance Corporation of Canada, Ltd.; First Southern Bank Ltd.; Fredericton Developments Ltd.; JPM, Inc.; Maduro & Curiel's Bank N.V.; MHM Property Ltd.; The Nova Scotia Corp.; Scotia Centre Ltd.; Scotia Leasing Ltd.; Scotia Mortgage Corporation; Scotia Realty Antilles N.V.; Scotia Realty Ltd.; Scotia Securities Inc.; Scotiabank de Puerto Rico; Scotia Export Finance Corp.; Scotia Factors (1985) Ltd.; Scotia Futures Ltd.; WBM, Inc.; The West India Company of Merchant Bankers Ltd.

Further Reading:

Blackwell, Richard, "Bank of Nova Scotia Looks to Branching Out," *Financial Post*, October 5, 1994, Section 1, p. 8.
————, "Scotiabank Expects Big Fall in Loan Losses," *Financial Post*, January 18, 1995, Section 1, p. 8.
Haliechuk, Rick, "Scotiabank Profit Hits Record in 4th Quarter," *Toronto Star*, December 1, 1994, Section E, p. 2.
Schull, Joseph and J. Douglas Gibson, *The Scotiabank Story: A History of the Bank of Nova Scotia, 1832-1982,* Toronto: Macmillan of Canada, 1982.

—updated by Dave Mote

BCE Inc.

1000 Dela-Gouchetiere, Ste. 3700
Suite 3700
Montreal, Quebec H3A 3H7
(514) 397-7000
Fax: (514) 397-7157

Public Company
Incorporated: 1880 as Bell Telephone Company of
   Canada
Employees: 116,000
Sales: $21.67 billion
Stock Exchanges: Montreal Toronto Vancouver
   Brussels Paris Frankfurt Düsseldorf Tokyo Basel
   Geneva Zürich Amsterdam London New York
SICs: 3661 Telephone and Telegraph Apparatus;
   3663 Radio and TV Communications Equipment;
   4810 Telephone Communications; 6090 Functions
   Closely Related to Banking.

The history of BCE Inc. can be traced to Alexander
Graham Bell's early communications experiments,
which eventually led to the formation of Bell Telephone
Company of Canada. Chartered by the Canadian Parliament on April 29, 1880, the company, known informally
as Bell Canada, would spend the next 100-plus years
growing and diversifying into one of Canada's largest
and most successful organizations. By 1983 Bell Canada
could be described as both a telecommunications company and a holding company, with controlling interests
in more than 80 other organizations. A move to create a
new parent company, Bell Canada Enterprises Inc.
(BCE), in 1983, left Bell Canada and its other businesses
as subsidiaries of a new holding company. The move
also changed the course of history for BCE Inc.

The Canadian phone company's history began in the
late 1870s, when Canada's first telephone exchange
opened in 1878 in Hamilton. Toronto's came second, in
1879. In 1881 the company had exchanges in 40 cities.
By 1890 the firm was offering long-distance service over
3,670 miles. From early on, the firm used the slogan, "A
telephone business run by Canadians for Canadians."

Still in its infancy, the telephone industry differed
greatly from that which most countries know today.
Initially telephone service was offered only during
business hours to about 2,100 telephones. Business
owners could use the service by buying pairs of instru-

ments to communicate from home to office, from office
to factory, or between other pairs of locations. In 1890
the company began to offer evening and Sunday service.

Although United States-based American Telephone and
Telegraph Company (AT&T) owned 48 percent of Bell
Canada's stock in 1890, Canadians began buying more
of that stock as the company grew. In 1895 Bell Canada
incorporated its manufacturing arm, Northern Electric
& Manufacturing Company Limited, which was partly
owned by AT&T's Western Electric.

Early telephone operators were also different from those
known today. In *Telephony,* April 28, 1986, one of those
early employees recalled her first days as an operator in
1924. They were times characterized by hard, fast,
manual work, usually lasting six days a week. The
operators worked on Christmas, all summer long, and
without paid sick days. For this, starting pay was $11.50
per week. In 1924 Bell Canada introduced the dial
exchange, so users could dial a party directly without
waiting for an operator to come on the line.

By 1925 the company was well on its way to living up to
its motto, as Canadians owned 94.5 percent of its stock.
The late 1920s saw several advances, including a phone
service that linked Canada to Britain via the United
States, a carrier system, and, in 1931, the formation of
the TransCanada Telephone System. The following year
the system made possible the first long distance call
from Montreal to Vancouver via an all-Canadian route.
In 1933 the U.S. federal securities act ended AT&T's
right to purchase new shares.

During the Great Depression, the need for telephone
service dropped substantially. Operators worked only
three days per week—about half the hours they had put
in previously. When World War II began all operators
were summoned back to work. Following the war, in
1945, Bell Canada installed its one millionth phone. In
1954 Bell Canada merged two subsidiaries, Eastern
Townships Telephone Company and Chapleau Telephone System. In 1956 the company merged with
Kamouraska Telephone Company and expanded once
again in 1957, when it acquired Mount Albert Telephone Company Ltd. Also in 1957, Bell Canada acquired most of Western Electric's share of Northern
Electric, which Western held through a subsidiary, Weco
Corporation. In 1964 it bought the remainder.

By 1958 customers in Canada and the United States
could dial other telephone users directly, without going
through an operator.

Bell Canada acquired Madawaska Telephone Company
in 1960. It gained control in 1962 of Avalon Telephone
Company Ltd., which would later be known as Newfoundland Telephone Company Ltd. The following year,
Bell Canada bought Monk Rural Telephone Company,
changing its name to Capital Telephone Company Ltd.
in 1966. Also in 1966, Bell Canada gained a new general
counsel, A. Jean de Grandpre, who would soon become
a major leader in the company's growth and diversification. A Montreal native, de Grandpre graduated from
McGill University in 1943, with a degree in law. He
brought two decades of experience gained in his own law
practice. Under his leadership, the firm grew rapidly
through capital expansion and acquisition. In 1970, for

example, the firm acquired control of Oxford Telephone Company Ltd. and Caradoc Ekfrid Telephone Company Ltd., as well as an interest in Telesat Canada, a communications satellite operation. The following year saw the founding of Bell-Northern Research Ltd. (BNR) to consolidate the research and development efforts of Northern Electric and Bell Canada. By 1973 de Grandpre had risen to the post of president of Bell Canada. Three years later, de Grandpre became chairman and chief executive officer.

In 1973 Bell Canada sold a portion of Northern Electric to the public, and in 1976 Northern Electric changed its name to Northern Telecom Limited. Also in 1976, Bell Canada created Bell Canada International Management, Research and Consulting Ltd. (BCI). The firm, which succeeded Bell's Consulting Services Group founded in the mid-1960s, was designed to offer expertise in telecommunications management and technical planning. Based in Ottawa, BCI's clients included common carriers, private corporations, defense companies, contractors, manufacturers, other consultants, and Northern Telecom. In addition, the firm had business dealings across the globe, including Africa, the Middle East, Europe, the Caribbean, South America, Saudi Arabia, and the United States. According to *Telecommunications*, October 1980, BCI "could serve as a case study of transfer of North American technology to other nations, be they underdeveloped, developing, or fully developed." In addition Northern Telecom and Bell Canada formed B-N Software Research Inc. for the research and development of new software. Late in 1978 Bell Canada introduced a fiber-optic system developed by Northern Telecom Ltd. Designed to simultaneously transmit telephony, data, and video, the company introduced the revolutionary new system during a video telephone conference call between Toronto and London. In 1981 the software firm was merged into Bell-Northern Research.

By 1982 Bell Canada controlled nearly 80 other companies. Switching control of the organizations, including Bell Canada, to a new parent company would simplify the business, de Grandpre believed. Consequently in 1983 Bell Canada Enterprises Inc., known since 1988 as BCE Inc., was created to act as a holding company for a corporate family whose assets amounted to $15 billion and included Bell Canada itself. By designating most of the company's businesses as separate BCE subsidiaries, Bell Canada was the only company that remained under the regulatory control of the Canadian Radio-Television and Telecommunications Commission (CRTC). This benefit led many critics to believe that avoiding CRTC supervision was the sole reason for the restructure. Such criticism was well founded, as relations between the phone company and the CRTC were not always smooth. In 1978, for instance, Bell Canada signed a $1.1 billion contract to improve Saudi Arabia's telecommunications network. Although the contract did not involve any telephone service to Canadians, the CRTC ruled that profits from the venture must be considered when determining Canadian phone rates, which meant smaller rate hikes for Bell Canada. Still, de Grandpre argued that the purpose of the restructure "was to provide the flexibility necessary for Bell to take on major competitors in telecommunications and microelectronics

around the world," reported *Maclean's*, February 14, 1983.

In addition to leadership and coordination, BCE provides equity investments to further the development of its various businesses and to finance their growth via new products, markets, internal growth, or acquisitions. Also in 1983, BCE acquired a sizeable percentage of TransCanada PipeLines Ltd. (TCPL), a move described in BCE's 1983 annual report as "a significant commitment by BCE to western Canada and to the resource sector of the Canadian economy." Although Radcliffe Latimer, president of TCPL and a personal friend of de Grandpre, cautioned shareholders to ignore BCE's offer of $31.50 per share, BCE still managed to swiftly take over 42 percent of the company. Following the feud, Latimer admitted defeat and commented in *Maclean's*, January 2, 1984, "We look at Bell as a first class major shareholder."

BCE's operations then included Bell Canada and several other locally regulated telecommunications operations: Northern Telecom Limited, a telecommunications manufacturer; Bell-Northern Research Ltd., owned by Bell Canada and Northern Telecom Ltd.; Bell Canada International Inc., a consulting firm; Bell Communications Systems Inc.; TransCanada PipeLines Ltd.; Tele-Direct (Publications) Inc., owned by Bell Canada; and Tele-Direct (Canada) Inc.

BCE's growth spurt continued through the 1980s. In fact its assets jumped from $14.8 billion in 1983 to $39.3 billion in 1989. There were investments in energy, real estate, printing and packaging, mobile and cellular communications, and financial services. BCE also became the first Canadian corporation to earn a net income of more than $1 billion. Despite that success, however, other aspects of BCE's business did not fare as well. One such failure was the firm's venture into real estate in 1985, through BCE Development Corporation (BCED), a new subsidiary. The company's experiments with printing and with oil and gas investments also brought poor reviews from shareholders.

BCE managed to succeed, despite these setbacks and several conflicts with CRTC. In 1986 the CRTC held a six-week hearing to examine Bell Canada's profits from 1985 through 1987. As a result, the CRTC ordered Bell Canada to refund to consumers $206 million worth of excess payments made earlier that year as well as in 1985. In addition the commission forced the company to decrease its predicted profits for 1987 by $234 million by lowering long distance rates in Ontario and Quebec by nearly 20 percent.

In 1989 de Grandpre retired as chairman, but remained on the board of directors as founding director and chairman emeritus. J. V. Raymond Cyr, who had been chief executive officer of BCE since May 1988, took the additional post of chairman in August 1989. Bell Canada gained a new president, Jean C. Monty. Cyr faced the monumental task of restoring the faith of BCE's shareholders, who once considered buying stock in the phone company "as safe as Canada Savings Bonds," reported *Maclean's*, July 30, 1990. To do this, the company decided to take a closer look at the types of businesses best suited to its corporate strategy. It was determined that telecommunications would naturally remain as BCE's core business and the firm's involvement in real estate would be dissolved. Management also chose to concentrate on financial services and acquired Montreal Trustco Inc., an established firm in that field. It was, however, Bell Canada that brought the most revenue to the parent company. With a record year, Bell Canada contributed $2.75 per share to BCE's 1989 earnings. In addition, BCE stock continued to be the most widely held stock in Canada.

Six years after taking control of TransCanada PipeLines Ltd., which BCE viewed as a solid, long-term investment, the company decided to sell its stake in the energy business. Owning TransCanada PipeLines was simply not consistent with BCE's core businesses in telecommunications and financial services.

In the early 1990s the holding company BCE Inc. owned subsidiaries in three primary areas: telecommunications services, telecommunications equipment manufacturing, and financial services. Although these subsidiaries made crucial contributions to the success of their parent company, many of them were successful enough to warrant widely recognized reputations of their own. While Bell Canada, the country's largest telecommunications company, provided most of the firm's services in that area, for example, Northern Telecom was responsible for the manufacturing end of the business and was the second-largest company of its type in North America. BellNorthern Research, the largest private industrial research and development organization in the country, played a vital role in BCE's research and development activities, while financial services were provided by Montreal Trust.

Throughout the early 1990s BCE boosted sales and expanded several of its divisions. One division that failed to perform up to expectations was Bell Canada. Indeed, Bell Canada experienced setbacks during the period as a result of deregulation of the Canadian long-distance industry. The net result was that Bell Canada quickly lost a significant portion of that market, which it had previously controlled as a regulated monopoly. Despite lagging performance of that division, BCE's aggregate revenues jumped from about $16.29 billion in 1990, to $19.57 billion in 1992, and then to a record $21.67 billion in 1994. The company posted a large loss in 1993, largely as a result of restructuring costs related to Bell Canada. The loss was also attributable to setbacks in the directories and Canadian Telecommunications divisions. Earnings recovered in 1994, rising to nearly $1.2 billion. The recovery was partly the result of aggressive cost-cutting initiatives designed to hew more than 10,000 workers from the Bell Canada division alone during the mid-1990s.

While many of BCE's traditional markets were sagging going into the mid-1990s, the company was posting solid gains in its wireless communications and international operations. To that end, BCE was investing heavily in communications technology related to satellites, personal communications services, and other wireless offerings. It was also reaching cross border in an attempt to, for example, boost foreign sales by Bell Canada to 50 percent of that division's revenues by the turn of the century. In addition, BCE, through its subsidiaries, was entering a number of new electronic information and media markets that benefited from the company's formidable research and development arm and complemented existing products and services.

Principal Subsidiaries:

Bell Canada; Northern Telecom Limited; Bell-Northern Research Ltd.; Bell Canada International Inc.; BCE Mobile Communications Inc.

Further Reading:

Brehl, Bob, "Phone Firms' Growth Doesn't Produce Jobs," *Toronto Star*, March 28, 1995, Section C, p. 1.
Chianello, Joanne, "$500M Bell Share Selloff," *Financial Post*, March 29, 1995, Section 1, p. 1.
_____, "BCE Rings Up Profit with Big Turnaround," *Financial Post*, January 26, 1995, Section 1, p. 7.
Hardin, Helen, "Bell Canada Marks its 100th Year by Helping Others," *Telephony*, April 28, 1980.
Wickens, Barbara, "Tough times for Ma Bell," *Maclean's*, July 30, 1990.

—Kim M. Magon
—updated by Dave Mote

BCTEL

BC TELECOM Inc.

3777 Kingsway
Burnaby, British Columbia V5H 3Z7
(604) 432-2413
Fax: (604) 434-9467

Public Company
Incorporated: 1923
Employees: 14,500
Sales: $2.3 billion
Stock Exchanges: Toronto Montreal Vancouver
SICs: 4813 Telephone Communications, Except
   Radiotelephone; 4812 Radiotelephone
   Communications

BC TELECOM Inc. is one of the largest telecommunications companies in Canada, offering telecommunications services through BC TEL, Canada's second largest telephone operating company, and through a number of other nonregulated telecommunications and related businesses that make up BC TEL Services Inc. BC TEL, the company's core business, operates as a public utility and is regulated by the Canadian Radio-Television and Telecommunications Commission (CRTC) which oversees telephone rates and services, including interconnecting agreements, competition, new entrants into markets, earnings, and issuance of share capital. With the growing movement toward deregulation initiated in the 1990s, however, BC TEL no longer exists as a monopoly and faces competition from more than 1,000 North American long-distance companies.

In addition to providing basic telephone service, BC TELECOM and its subsidiaries offer advanced personal communications services, voice and data retrieval equipment and services, wireless communications, telecommunications and satellite equipment maintenance and repair, research and development, management consulting, information technology, and financial services. Through several strategic alliances with other telecommunications companies, BC TELECOM also participates in joint agreements that include advanced technology applications for the global market.

BC TELECOM traces its corporate beginnings directly to the Vernon and Nelson Telephone Company, founded in 1891 to supply telephone service to certain areas of British Columbia. By the early 1900s, the company had purchased the assets of several smaller telephone companies throughout the province and had received authorization to extend operations to all parts of British Columbia. In 1904, to reflect its newly expanded service area, the Vernon and Nelson Telephone Company changed its name to British Columbia Telephone Company, Limited. The company obtained a federal charter from the federal government in 1916, thereby securing future rights to operate anywhere in British Columbia and to extend its lines outside the province once the company incorporated under the federal organization. In 1923, the company transferred its assets to the federal organization and became the British Columbia Telephone Company.

For the next 50 years, BC TELECOM continued to expand coverage in its operating territory by merging with and acquiring other British Columbian telephone companies. BC TELECOM also assumed responsibility for part of the Government Telegraph and Telephone Service in the province. In 1926, a major portion of the company's stock was acquired by the National Telephone and Telegraph Corporation, later named Anglo-Canadian Telephone Company of Montreal. In 1962, Anglo-Canadian became the controlling shareholder of BC TELECOM, holding a 50.2 percent interest through an arrangement with its parent company, the GTE Corporation.

In addition to increasing its territorial coverage and enlarging its customer base, BC TELECOM also expanded services and adapted new technologies to its operations. In 1941, the company's charter was amended to include operation of wireless telephone and radiotelephone systems. In 1973, BC TELECOM introduced Dataroute, the world's first nationwide digital data transmission service. Some of the more common applications of Dataroute include high volume business data transfer, on-line banking, reservations services, and computer time-sharing. In 1979, BC TELECOM acquired two electric companies and formed the Microtel Limited subsidiary. Microtel manufactured and serviced Spacetel satellite communications equipment, which provided voice and data service to remote areas.

By the late 1970s, competition in the telecommunications field heightened as industry increasingly depended on information technology. Profitability and growth, which had traditionally ensued from expanding territorial coverage, now resulted more from improving technology and customer service. In response to these market changes and the corresponding increase in customer demands, BC TELECOM underwent a corporatewide reorganization beginning in 1982. The company established several divisions and subsidiaries in an effort to compete more effectively in existing markets, as well as to facilitate the introduction of new technology. Operationally, telephone services were reorganized into five areas, each of which was accountable for service quality and financial performance. In mid-1982, the Business Telecom Equipment division was created to manufacture business terminal equipment. In 1985, BC Cellular Limited was formed to introduce and operate cellular telephone service, and, in 1986, Telecom Leasing Canada was established to offer financial services to BC Tel customers, including point-of-sale financing for terminal equipment.

Within this rapidly changing industry, management felt that future successes depended upon a committed and dedicated work force. However, BC TELECOM had a reputation for poor labor relations that dated back to the 1920s and was reinforced by a bitter six-week labor strike in early 1981, the third prolonged work stoppage in less than ten years. In response to this problem, the reorganization effort included a new program to improve management quality for both executives and labor. The new system encouraged employees to identify, analyze, and solve work area problems, provided numerous training courses and workshops, and offered cash awards to employees who proposed money-saving ideas. In 1989, BC TELECOM was one of seven recipients of the Canada Award for Business Excellence.

Early in 1988, the company created the Diversified Operations Division, designed to concentrate on highly competitive enterprises within the company. Several product-specific divisions, such as BC Cellular, Business Telecom Equipment, and Telecom Leasing Canada, were dissolved as separate entities and transferred into this new business unit. The division also included two subsidiaries: Viscount Industries Limited, which designs, manufactures, markets, and distributes building information, access, and communications systems throughout North America, and Canadian Telephones and Supplies, which implements network switching and electrical contracting and designs and installs fire alarms and security systems. Later in 1988, BC TELECOM acquired the Canadian management consulting firm of SRI Strategic Resources Inc. In 1990, BC Mobile Ltd. was established as the company's wireless communications subsidiary to provide radio-paging throughout British Columbia. Both the SRI and BC Mobile Ltd. subsidiaries were added to the Diversified Operations Division.

A strategic alliance between BC TELECOM and Northern Telecom Canada Ltd. (NTCL) in 1990 established Prism Systems Inc. to design and manufacture advanced network management systems for markets worldwide. The agreement specified 49 percent ownership of Prism by BC Tel and 51 percent by NTCL. Because Prism's operations required components of the transmission and network management systems of Microtel Limited, NTCL acquired Microtel's Central Office Switching business as part of the transaction.

Hoping to increase flexibility and readiness for future opportunities and challenges, BC TELECOM again restructured its organization in 1991. The company's new president and CEO, Brian Canfield, formed three core divisions, designed to reflect a market-driven, customer-focused operation: Business, Small Business and Consumer, and Emerging Business. The Business Division manages a broad portfolio of communications products and services for BC Tel's largest business and government customers. Monthly revenue from each client exceeds $2000; collectively, this group supplies BC Tel's core revenue. The division provides such operational services as voice mail and information retrieval. The Small Business and Consumer Division provides telecommunications products and services to BC Tel's residential and small business customers who spend less than $2000 per month.

The Emerging Business Division is responsible for recognizing and developing new business opportunities in three areas: emerging technologies, enhanced telecommunications services, and related business. The emerging technologies unit brings new and evolving telecommunications products and services to the market. The business unit includes a portable communications division as well as former divisions such as BC Tel Mobility Cellular and BC Tel Mobility Paging. The enhanced telecommunications services unit is responsible for commercializing innovative services using network-based information technology. This unit's objective is to understand the information exchange requirements of customers in three areas: message services, enhanced communications, and information network services. Message services meet voice and data message needs through such products and services as electronic mail, gateway services to information databases, and Electronic Data Interchange. Enhanced communications develops high speed data applications, such as interconnecting local area networks and wide area networks. Future projects include video conferencing and interactive video services. Information network services advise customers on problems in information exchanges.

The related business unit of the Emerging Business Division provides support services to internal and external BC Tel customers. This unit includes the formerly separate divisions of Canadian Telephones and Supplies Ltd., Microtel Limited, Telecom Leasing Canada Limited, and Viscount Industries Limited. This unit also comprises BC Tel Systems Support, the former 3S Systems Support Services Ltd., which maintains, repairs, and calibrates a comprehensive portfolio of voice and data equipment, and Pachena Industries Ltd., which provides contract design and manufactures electronic products for commercial markets in Canada and the Pacific Northwest.

BC TELECOM is a long-standing member of Stentor Canadian Network Management. The major telephone companies established Stentor in 1921 (under the name Telecom Canada) to create a route for Canadian long distance service; the cooperative alliance also provided development and government assistance to its participants. Belonging to Stentor gives BC Tel ownership and operating authority in one section of the British Columbian telephone system, including a portion of a coast-to-coast microwave radio relay system that carries telephone, special service transmission, and signals for the two national television networks.

In 1992, BC Tel and the other telephone companies reorganized Stentor, which continued to manage its members' interprovincial networks and North American connections as well as to ensure efficient division of revenues from national services. However, the alliance's other responsibilities were divided between two jointly-held companies, Stentor Telecom Policy Inc. and Stentor Resource Centre Inc. Stentor Telecom Policy began operating in February 1992 as a government relations advisory and advocacy arm for the member companies. Stentor Resource Centre began operating in January 1993, developing national telecommunications products, services, and systems with Stentor's member companies. The company also consolidated some of the telephone companies' research and development and marketing activities.

In 1992, BC TELECOM adopted a new corporate logo: BC TEL. In an effort to link the subsidiaries with BC TEL Corporation's strengths and diversified offerings, the names of some wholly owned subsidiaries were changed: B.C. Cellular LTD became BC TEL Mobility Cellular, and B.C. Mobile Ltd. became BC TEL Mobility Paging. Also in 1992, to demonstrate its commitment to a corporate environmental policy, BC TEL delivered the first telephone directories printed on 100 percent recycled paper. The directories were recycled from 1991's fully recyclable directories and furthered the corporate goal of integrating environmental protection and improvements into its plans and operations. By 1993, all directories in the BC TEL operating territory were made entirely of recycled paper.

Competitive pressures in the long distance market increased in 1992 with the CRTC decision to allow Unitel Communications, a joint venture of Canadian Pacific Ltd., Rogers Communications, B.C. Rail Telecommunications, and Lightel Inc. to offer long distance voice telephone services in all but the Prairie Provinces. CRTC expected this decision to help lower long distance prices as well as increase the services available to businesses and consumers. However, it left unresolved the disparate cost contributions of new entrants versus existing companies, such as BC TEL, which was directed to pay 70 percent of the cost of connecting the new entrants to its network. To better position itself for this more competitive environment, the company created a new public organization, BC TELECOM Inc., and changed the legal name of its core operating company to BC TEL. The restructuring plan, instituted in 1993, separated the core telecommunications from the new, emerging businesses grouped under BC TEL Services Inc. Accordingly, two new chief executives were appointed to lead the two divisions: Lynn Patterson took over as president of BC TEL, and Fares Salloum was named president of BC TEL Services Inc.

The regulatory reforms begun in the early part of the decade came to fruition in September 1994 when the CRTC handed down a historic decision that promised to redefine the Canadian telecommunications industry. The decision, which gave Canada one of the most open and competitive telecommunications markets in the world, streamlined age-old regulations; gave telephone companies the authorization to compete in new transactional services, such as home shopping and banking; allowed immediate entry into the local-service market by alternative suppliers, such as cable companies; and introduced a rate rebalancing program that increased local rates and reduced long distance rates. In a 1994 letter to shareholders, Canfield welcomed the change, calling the landmark decision a victory for companies like his "that want to compete, and for a vigorous healthy telecommunications industry."

Although the regulatory reform—and the level playing field it has promised to bring to the industry—has long been encouraged by BC TELECOM, it has forced the company to streamline its own operations and make the transition from a service-oriented to a retail-oriented business culture. While placing more emphasis on attracting customers through long-distance savings plans and additional calling features, for instance, the company has also been forced to reduce its work force in order to survive in the newly competitive environment. Despite a record-breaking 1994 performance that saw revenues near $2.3 billion and consolidated earnings reach $224.5 million, the company announced plans to eliminate approximately 2,000 jobs by the end of 1996, in an attempt to reduce operating costs by $100 million and offset a decline in its core business.

The future success of BC TELECOM will depend not only on its ability to lower costs and increase efficiency, but also on how well the company can take advantage of opportunities in new information technology, such as electronic mail and the Internet. "I believe we're an active agent in a paradigm shift in communications," said BC TEL president Fares Salloum in a 1994 letter to shareholders, one "that will touch every area of our lives, including government, business, medicine, education, and the arts." Exactly what affect the evolution of the Information Age will have on the balance sheets of the century-old telecommunications giant, however, remains to be seen.

Principal Subsidiaries:

BC TEL; BC TEL Systems Support Inc.; BC TEL Mobility Cellular; Canadian Telephones and Supplies Ltd.; MPR Teltech Ltd.; Telecom Leasing Canada (TLC) Limited; ISM Information Systems Management (B.C.) Corporation (75%).

Further Reading:

"BC TEL Perspectives," *BC Tel Corporate Newsletter,* June/July 1992.
Champion, Don W., "Quality: A Way of Life at B.C. Tel," *Canadian Business Review,* Spring 1990.
Mackin, Bob, "Ads Take Cellular to the Next Century," *Marketing,* October 11, 1993, p. 2.
————, "BC TEL Calls for Feedback," *Marketing,* January 31, 1994, p. 2.
————, "They're Calling It the Phone Wars . . . BC Tel Is—Under Fire," *BC Business,* November 1994, pp. 48-50, 53-56.
Ramsey, Laura, "BC Tel Learns How to Deal With Bad Bosses," *The Financial Post,* July 23, 1994, p. S13.
Stacey, John, "How B.C. Tel Stacks Up," *Investor's Digest,* January 18, 1991, p. 23.

—Allyson S. Farquhar-Boyle
—updated by Jason Gallman

Bell Canada

1050 Cote du Beaver Hall
Montreal, Quebec H2Z 1S4
(514)870-1511
Fax: (514)876-8726

Wholly Owned Subsidiary of BCE, Inc.
Incorporated: 1880 as Bell Telephone Company of
 Canada
Employees: 45,000
Sales: $8.06 billion
SICs: 4810 Telephone Communications

The Bell Telephone Company of Canada, which came to
be called Bell Canada, was the country's largest provider
of telecommunications services in 1995, supplying
voice, data, and image communications to seven million
customers in the provinces of Quebec and Ontario and
in the Northwest Territories. Most of Bell Canada's
revenues are generated from its provision of local
telephone service and long-distance service, which includes various toll-free, message, and data transmission
services. The company also owns a one hundred percent
interest in the directories division of Tele-Direct Inc.,
which sells telephone directory advertising and publi-
ishes white pages and Yellow Pages phone books.

The history of telephone service in Canada can be traced
back to 1874, in Brantford, Ontario, where Alexander
Graham Bell discovered a way to transmit speech
electrically. Bell transferred his Canadian patent rights
to his father, Alexander Melville Bell, who established
Canada's first telephone network by leasing telephones
in pairs to be used on private lines and by contracting
with the Dominion Telegraph Company to create exchanges in concentrated areas.

Telephone service did not begin as a monopoly. The
Montreal Telegraph Company used Thomas Alva Edison's version of the telephone to establish competing
service in that city. The telegraph companies, seeing
telephone service as auxiliary to their main function,
offered it at low rates or even free of charge. Its value
was not perceived to be very high; when Melville Bell
offered his patent for sale in 1879, no Canadian would
pay his price of $100,000.

The National Bell Telephone Company of Boston
eventually took the patent off Melville Bell's hands. The
company enlisted the aid of Hugh C. Baker, head of the
Hamilton District Telegraph Company, to apply for a
charter from the Canadian Parliament. On April 29,
1880, a Special Act of Parliament incorporated the Bell
Telephone Company of Canada.

Next, National Bell Telephone Company of Boston
hired a former sea captain and insurance executive,
Charles Fleetford Sise, to negotiate with the telegraph
companies for their interest in the telephone business.
Sise's labors resulted in his appointment as vice-president and managing director of the new company, and
his successful efforts to organize the company led to his
reputation as the founder of Bell Telephone Company of
Canada.

By the end of the company's first year, telephone
exchanges had been established in 14 major cities-
including Montreal, Ottawa, and Quebec-and agencies
to obtain subscribers and develop exchanges opened in
dozens more. Over 2,000 telephones were in service,
and the company employed 150 people. Bell Canada's
early goal was to extend service throughout Canada.

The country's vastness, however, precluded one company managing all of it. Bell Canada never held a license to
provide service in British Columbia, and it sold its plant
and interests in Prince Edward Island in 1885. Within
four years, it had sold its interests in New Brunswick
and Nova Scotia. Early in the next century, many
citizens of the Prairie Provinces wished to transfer the
ownership of telephones to the government, so the
company sold its interests in Manitoba and Alberta in
1908 and in Saskatchewan in 1909. Bell Canada maintained its operations in the remaining provinces of
Ontario, Quebec, and the Eastern Arctic.

The company was most successful in establishing service
in urban areas, since voice clarity was possible only over
distances of less than 20 miles. To provide rural
residents access to the city, public telephones were
installed at the end of the lines.

Although long-distance lines were originally considered
the lines from a large city to neighboring towns, Bell
Canada was already attempting a line between Toronto
and Hamilton in 1881. It succeeded in October of that
year, but the expense forced the company to operate
with funds borrowed from Sise. A continuous but
undependable route was created from Montreal to
Detroit in 1885. In 1886 the advent of copper wire
vastly improved transmission over long distances.
Northern Advance reported in 1886, "Officials say they
could easily guarantee a satisfactory conversation from
Buffalo to Owen Sound about 290 miles if anyone ever
required to use a line of that length."

An amendment to Bell Canada's charter in 1892 read,
"The existing rates shall not be increased without the
consent of the Governor in Council." Although the
company was now subject to regulation, it still had to
contend with competitors. Bell bought out several rival
companies between 1890 and 1925, including the Federal Telephone Company, whose competition had forced
Bell to lower rates in Montreal from $50 to $25 dollars a
year. Rural territory was an open field, but Bell's more
extensive network and resources forced many competitors into bankruptcy.

The twentieth century brought several innovations that improved Bell Canada's service, including underground cables with hundreds of pairs of wires, which replaced poles in cities, and the common battery, or central energy switchboards, which eliminated the need for batteries on the subscriber's premises. Perhaps the greatest innovation of that time was the phantom circuit. Two pairs of wires with special equipment at each end could transmit a third conversation, and the phantom circuit actually had a higher transmission quality than the physical circuits. Bell's first installation of this early form of multiplexing linked Montreal and Ottawa beginning in 1908.

Bell Canada became increasingly regulated in the early 1900s. In 1902 the company's charter was amended to include a regulation requiring the company to provide service to whoever applied for it, on the condition that the instrument would not have to be placed far from a road. In 1906 the government decided that Bell Canada should be included in the Railway Act of 1903, meaning rates would be regulated by the Canadian Board of Railway Commissioners.

In 1905 a detailed examination of Bell Canada was made by a special committee appointed by Parliament. After producing approximately 2,000 pages of testimony and exhibits, the committee concluded the investigation without coming to any determination. The company issued the following statement in response, "Although the records of the Company have been searched from its organization twenty-four years ago, not a single fact has been adduced which reflects discreditably on the integrity or the justice of the management."

Also in the early 1900s many independent telephone companies provided service in Ontario and Quebec. Some, fearing they would be taken over by Bell Canada, refused to interconnect their lines with those of the huge company. Many others, however, readily exchanged business with Bell Canada, taking advantage of the company's established long-distance lines. During the next few decades, Bell Canada integrated systems throughout Quebec and Ontario.

Long-distance telephone service changed significantly when the vacuum tube repeater was introduced in 1915. The device, which theoretically could transmit a voice an infinite distance, allowed the development of a transcontinental network. In 1917 Bell Canada installed its first repeater at Kingston, Ontario, and within six years the Bell system's use of repeaters was estimated to have saved approximately $100 million in construction costs of long-distance lines.

A shortage of materials during World War I led to an extended delay in providing service to new applicants. Orders accumulated, reaching a peak of 22,000 at the beginning of 1924. Bell Canada, however, remained committed to providing service to rural residents.

Bell introduced overseas service by radio in 1927. A three-minute call from Quebec City, Ottawa, Toronto, or Montreal to London, England, cost $75. Another important innovation, the carrier system, was first installed by Bell Canada in 1928 from Montreal to Ottawa, Sherbrooke, and Trois Rivieres. The new technology simultaneously sent several conversations over the same pair of lines, avoiding interference by transmitting each call at a different frequency. Now known as a form of multiplexing, it was originally referred to as wired wireless.

The Great Depression of the 1930s affected even the phone company. Revenues from long-distance service were down five percent, and new orders for service decreased. In addition, the few new telephones Bell Canada did install could not match the surging numbers of telephones being disconnected. In 1931 the number of residential telephones leased by the company decreased by 11,321; in 1933 the net loss of telephones was 41,829. By 1934, though, recovery seemed to have begun: the company had a net gain of approximately 3,000 telephones. In an attempt to regain some of its losses, Bell Canada intensified its efforts to subscribe rural residents. Stock prices and dividends also fell during the Depression. In 1932 the stock price dropped to $75 a share, down from $125 in 1929. Bell Canada had been paying dividends of $2 a share since 1891. It was forced to reduce that in 1932 and could not return to that level until 1937.

World War II brought about restrictions that taxed Bell Canada's resources. In 1942 the Wartime Prices and Trade Board ordered telephone companies to conserve facilities for war purposes, restricting the installation of nonessential orders for service. By the end of the war, more than 100,000 orders had accumulated. The company's plans to replace most of its long-distance lines were altered by the wartime need for metals. By employing strict conservation procedures, however, the company managed to complete the project and still replace the copper it drew from the national reserves.

Postwar prosperity meant a boom in telephone installations for Bell Canada. In 1945 it installed its one millionth telephone, and in the next eight years it established another million. In 1946 the company was installing telephones at the rate of 6,800 per month.

The number of Canadian holders of the Bell's stock quickly increased after World War II. An amendment to the company's charter in 1948 increased the authorized capitalization from $150 to $500 million and required stock to be divided into shares of a par value of $25 rather than $100. Canadian investors took advantage of the inexpensive, widely available stock. Investors in the United States could not buy the new issues since they were not registered with the Securities and Exchange Commission (SEC) in the United States. In 1948 American Telephone and Telegraph Company (AT&T) held 14.6 percent of Bell Canada's stock. By 1975, when AT&T sold the remainder of its holdings, it held only two percent of the Bell Canada's stock.

The 1950s began an era of rapid technological innovation for Bell Canada. It installed the first permanent television link between two countries in 1953, bringing programs from Buffalo, New York, to the Canadian Broadcasting Corporation (CBC) in Toronto. Bell opened the first intercity microwave radio relay between Toronto and Montreal in the same year, allowing audiences in the two cities to view the same live program simultaneously. In 1958 the company completed its microwave network, making its coast-to-coast coverage the longest system in the world. Also in 1958,

Bell Canada offered Dataphone service, which enabled subscribers to transmit data or text over voice channels at speeds of up to 800 words a minute.

In the 1960s Bell Canada introduced a myriad of services: Wide Area Telephone Service (WATS), which applied flat-rate calling to long-distance service; Teletypewriter Exchange Service (TWX), a system linked to TWX in the United States in 1963 and to International Telex in 1965; PHONE-FAX, which was the first facsimile service in the world offered by a telephone company; Message Switching Data Service (MSDS), which used a computer to switch between private-line data circuits; and DATACOM and DATA-LINE, a provider of inexpensive communications between remote users and time-sharing computers.

In 1973 Bell Canada introduced Dataroute, the world's first nationwide digital data transmission system. The company began experimenting with fiber optics and in 1978 became the first in the world to test optical fiber service on home telephones.

Bell Canada's organization changed in several ways during the 1970s. First, it became independent of AT&T, which sold the remainder of its stock in Bell Canada in 1975. That same year, the companies terminated their 52-year-old service agreement. Second, Bell Canada created a number of new subsidiaries, including Bell Northern Research (BNR) and Tele-Direct Limited in 1971 and Bell Canada International Management Research & Consulting Limited (BCI) and B-N Software Research (BNSR) in 1976. In addition, Bell Canada's manufacturing arm, the Northern Electric Company, became Northern Telecom Ltd. in 1976.

The 1970s were a period of international growth for Bell Canada. Northern Telecom reported C$1 billion in sales in 1975, and sales to the United States accounted for ten percent of that. The following year, Northern Telecom began an aggressive marketing strategy in the United States to boost that percentage even higher. In addition, Bell Canada won several international contracts, not the least of which was a $1 billion consulting contract with Saudi Arabia.

In order to free its nonutility business concerns from regulation, Bell Canada planned to reorganize in 1982. A new holding company would be established, Bell Canada Enterprises (BCE), Inc., and Bell Canada would become a subsidiary, retaining only its telephone utility functions. Since its incorporation in 1880 by a special act of Parliament, Bell Canada had been regulated by various government commissions, concluding with the Canadian Radio and Telecommunications Commission (CRTC). The CRTC took all of Bell Canada's profits into consideration when rates were set, despite the fact that by 1982 half of Bell's revenues came from nontelephone business. In effect, telephone rates were being subsidized by Bell's other businesses.

Bell Canada first made–and won–an application for continuance under the Canadian Business Corporations Act. The shift allowed Bell to begin implementing its plan without regulatory approval. Opposition came from consumer groups, who feared the reorganization would greatly increase telephone rates, and the government, who claimed the change would make Bell Canada

too difficult to regulate. Government officials worried that telephone subscribers could end up subsidizing Bell's sister corporations. For example, Bell could buy overpriced equipment from Northern Telecom and pass the expense on to its subscribers. Bell Canada, however, claimed the reorganization would merely free its non-telephone subsidiaries to compete on equal footing with unregulated businesses, particularly internationally. The Quebec Superior Court eventually ruled that Bell did not need CRTC approval for the restructuring. So, barring an act of Parliament, the company was free to implement its plan.

The price of Bell's shares steadily increased-from $13.25 to $27.13 on the New York Stock Exchange as the company reorganized. Shareholders approved the restructuring and exchanged their Bell Canada shares for those of the new holding company, BCE, Inc. The gradual deregulation of the telecommunications industry in the United States during the 1970s and early 1980s encouraged Canadians to lobby for lower long-distance rates through deregulation. CNCP Telecommunications applied to the CRTC for an opportunity to break into Canada's long-distance market, promising consumers 30 percent lower rates. In 1985 the CRTC rejected CNCP's request on the grounds that Bell Canada needed the long-distance revenues to subsidize local phone rates.

In 1990, however, the CRTC ruled that companies could buy time on private telephone lines in bulk from the phone companies and resell it at a discount. Within two years, the resellers had captured two to four percent of the phone companies' long-distance business. In 1992 the CRTC was expected to institute even greater changes in the long-distance market, such as allowing companies to resell discount packages like WATS. Resellers, however, wanted the CRTC to go further and allow them to own their own lines, an idea Bell Canada was fighting. *Canadian Business* quoted Bell Chairman Jean Monty as saying that "the presence of resale means Canada already enjoys a workable balance between competition and monopoly."

Although between 1987 and 1992 Bell Canada had already lowered its long-distance rates, sometimes by as much as 51 percent, its rates remained almost double those in the United States, which was not helping the company fight competition from that country. AT&T, US Sprint Communication Co., and MCI Communications Corp. were all selling services to Canadians whose networks crossed into the United States.

While Bell Canada still maintained a monopoly in the telecommunications industry in Ontario, Quebec, and the Northwest

Territories in 1992, increased competition and the likelihood of further deregulation pointed toward major changes for the company. Although some feared competition would force Bell Canada to raise local phone rates, others saw competition as encouragement to revitalize Bell's operations and offer better service at lower prices.

Deregulation and competition did, in fact, confront Bell Canada in the mid-1990s. During the early 1990s the Canadian government began deregulating the telecommunications industry in an effort to create competition.

On July 1, 1994, for example, new legislation went into effect that gave other providers the right to compete for Bell customers in basic services. The effects of deregulation on Bell Canada were immediate. The overall result of new competition was that by the end of 1994 Bell Canada had lost 22 percent of the entire Canadian long-distance market. Part of the loss was due to the fact that Bell's prices and activities were still being regulated as part of a government effort to help newcomers to the telecommunications industry. Bell's net income dropped from more than $1 billion in 1992 to just $793 million in 1994.

Many Bell customers welcomed deregulation as a way to lower rates and improve service. Bell management, however, realized that it would face major changes in its future. To usher the company into the new era of Canadian telecommunications, Bell hired John McLennan early in 1994. The 49-year-old McLennan went to college in the United States under a hockey scholarship. He later served in management positions with Canadian telecommunications competitors Mitel Corp., Cantel Inc., BCE Mobile Communications, and Bell Ontario. Finally, he was tapped to lead Bell Canada.

Shortly after his arrival, McLennan designed a major restructuring plan designed to cut costs and pave the way to improved services. The company jettisoned hundreds of employees before announcing its intent in mid-1995 to reduce its 46,000-member work force by as many as 10,000 employees within two years. The restructuring plan also called for a $1.7 billion investment in a program to redesign the company's methods and systems for serving customers—the program identified 125 different goals related to updating technology and internal processes.

On January 1, 1995, Bell Canada was organized into operating divisions. A new corporate group was established to develop new technology and services in areas such as multimedia, personal communication services, and advanced intelligent networks. The second management team, headed by CEO McLennan, was leading Bell's efforts in the more traditional information arena. Bell Canada expected to suffer, at least in the short term, from increased competition. At the same time, surging demand for all types of telecommunications services combined with gradually diminishing government restraints on its operations suggested a bright long-term future for Bell Canada.

Principal Subsidiaries:

Tele-Direct (Publications), Inc.; Bell Sygma Inc.; Worldlinx Telecommunications Inc.

Further Reading:

Fetherstonhaugh, R.C., *Charles Fleetford Sise,* Montreal: Gazette Printing Co. Ltd., 1944.
The First Century of Service, Montreal: Bell Canada, 1980.
Fleming, James, "Divided, Bell Prospers," *Maclean's,* February 14, 1983.
Hawkins, Jeffrey, "Trade Benefits of CFTA: Telecommunications," *Business America,* April 20, 1992.
Mandelman, Avner, "The Belle of Bay Street," *Barrons,* October 8, 1984.
Misutka, Frances, "More Talk, Less Money," *Canadian Business,* April 1992.
Ravensberg, Jan. "Bell Gets a Wake-UP Call; New President Leads Fight Against the Competition, Often by Fighting Bell Empire Itself," *Gazette,* March 4, 1995, Section G, p. 1.
————. "The Gloves are Off; For Decades Bell Was Spoiled," *Gazette,* April 1, 1995, Section G, p. 1.
"Up the Down Stairs at Bell Canada," *Business Week,* April 12, 1976.
Walmsley, Ann, and Ken Pole, "Putting CNCP on Hold," *Maclean's,* September 9, 1985.
Willoughby, Jack, "Apres AT&T, le deluge," *Forbes,* October 22, 1984.

—Susan Windisch Brown
—updated by Dave Mote

Bombardier Inc.

800 Rene-Levesque Blvd. W., 29th Fl.
Montreal, Quebec H3B 1Y8
(514) 861-9481
Fax: (514) 861-7053

Public Company
Incorporated: 1942 as L'Auto-Neige Bombardier
   Limitee
Employees: 37,000
Sales: $5.94 billion
Stock Exchanges: Montreal, Toronto, Brussels,
   Antwerp
SICs: 3711 Motor Vehicles and Car Bodies; 3721
   Aircraft; 3740 Railroad Equipment

Bombardier Inc. is a diversified, global conglomerate primarily focused on industries related to transportation, aerospace and defense, and motorized consumer products. About 90 percent of its revenues in the mid-1990s came from sales outside of Canada, and the company operated production facilities throughout North America and Europe. The company boasts a rich legacy of innovation in the motorized transportation industry and is among the most successful manufacturing companies in Canada. After stumbling in the 1970s, Bombardier reemerged as a force in several of its key industries and was enjoying healthy sales and profit gains as it moved toward the new century.

Bombardier Inc. is the progeny of inventor and entrepreneur Joseph-Armand Bombardier, who was born near the eastern Quebec village of Valcourt in 1902. An inveterate tinkerer, Bombardier took it upon himself early in life to devise a solution to the difficulty of traveling during the winter when snow-covered roads in his native Quebec kept people isolated. At the age of 19, Bombardier started his own garage and worked as a mechanic, while he labored diligently in his spare time to create a vehicle that would allow easy winter travel, eventually building several prototypes that could travel on snow. Over a ten-year period, in fact, he crafted motorized test vehicles ranging from one-seat units to multi-passenger carriers.

Bombardier finally came up with what he believed was a suitable solution to winter travel. In 1936 he submitted his patent application for the B7, a seven-passenger snowmobile that sported a revolutionary rear-wheel drive and suspension system. Bombardier soon found himself besieged with 20 orders for the innovative vehicle, and he quickly assembled a work crew—comprised largely of relatives and friends—in order to begin manufacturing B7s for country doctors, veterinarians, telephone companies, foresters, and others that benefited from easy winter travel. In 1940 he built a modern factory with an annual production capacity of 200 vehicles, and in 1941 he introduced a bigger version of the B7 named the B12. The B12, used for cargo and mail transport as well as ambulance and rescue services, resembled a small blue school bus with round passenger windows, tank-like treads on the rear, and skis on the front.

Despite strong demand, wartime material and fuel restrictions reduced Bombardier's output during the early 1940s. Nevertheless, the optimistic Joseph-Armand incorporated the company in 1942 as L'Auto-Neige Bombardier Limitee, or Bombardier Snowmobile Limited. The war eventually turned out to be a boon for the company—in 1942 the government ordered 130 B1s, which were a specially tailored version of the original B12. Moreover, in 1943 Bombardier was asked to design and produce a special armored all-track snowmobile—the Kaki—which led to the development of the armored Mark I. Between 1942 and 1946 Bombardier produced more than 1,900 tracked vehicles for the armed forces. Unfortunately, the company reaped few profits from the sales, and Joseph-Armand was even forced to give up the royalties for the use of his patents in all military vehicles.

The massive production boom did help Bombardier to hone his manufacturing and design skills, experience that proved useful after the war, when civilian orders for the company's snow vehicles ballooned. Between 1945 and 1952 the company shipped 1,600 B12s. It also began producing the C18, which was a larger version of the B12 that could carry 25 school children. By 1947 the company was generating annual sales of $2.3 million and capturing profits of more than $300,000. Unfortunately, sales plummeted to less than $1 million in 1949 after the Quebec government implemented a snow-removal program for rural roads. Joseph-Armand scrambled to compensate for the setback, relying on his inventiveness to come up with new products that could utilize his patented technologies.

Among several new products the company tested during the late 1940s was the Tractor Tracking Attachment, a patented tread mechanism that could be attached to a tractor, thus improving performance in muddy terrain. Between 1949 and 1954 Bombardier sold thousands of the devices throughout North America, and cash from that successful product was dumped into research and development of a variety of all-terrain vehicles for the mining, oil, agriculture, and forest industries. Two of the most successful innovations introduced during that period were the Muskeg and the J5. The Muskeg was a breakthrough tractor-type machine that could perform multiple functions in difficult terrain. Joseph-Armand considered it one of his greatest inventions, and modern versions of the vehicle were still being produced in the early 1990s. The J5 was the first tracked vehicle designed specifically for logging.

By the end of the 1950s Bombardier's sales were approaching $4 million annually as profits soared toward the $1 million mark. It was during that time that Joseph-Armand, who was still managing the business, renewed his childhood dream of building a small snowmobile that could whisk a person over snow-covered terrain. With the advent of lighter engines, high-performance synthetic rubbers, and an improved tracking technology patented by his son Germain, Joseph-Armand believed that he could accomplish his goal. By 1959 the Bombardier team had developed a working prototype that lived up to Joseph-Armand's dream, and that year the company began mass production of the acclaimed Ski-Doo snowmobile. The first model sported five-foot wooden skis, a coil-spring suspension system, and could travel at speeds of 25 miles per hour.

The vehicles, which originally sold at a price of $900 each, launched an entirely new industry that would explode during the next two decades. Although demand for the new snowmobile was slow in the first two years after its introduction—production rose from just 225 in 1959 to about 250 in 1960—in 1961 unit sales lurched to 1,200 before rocketing to more than 2,500 in 1962. Besides capturing the interest of trappers, foresters, prospectors, and other workers, the Ski-Doo became popular as a sport vehicle.

Bombardier continued to improve the vehicle and began introducing new lines. By 1964 the company was shipping more than 8,000 Ski-Doos annually, and Joseph-Armand died knowing he had realized his original dream of providing safe, practical, and economical transportation in isolated, snow-covered regions. During his career, Bombardier secured more than 40 patents, and he left his sons in charge of a financially sound company with more than $10 million in annual sales and profits of more than $2 million annually. Germain, Joseph-Armand's eldest son, assumed the presidency, but passed the torch to his brother-in-law, Laurent Beaudoin, in 1966.

Beaudoin was only 27 years old when he assumed the presidency at Bombardier Limited, as it was named in 1967. Also, he was joined by an aggressive young group of top managers that averaged 30 years in age. That group of executives successfully guided the company through its headiest growth stage—North American snowmobile shipments vaulted from 60,000 units in 1966 to a peak of 495,000 units annually in 1972, and Bombardier produced more than one-third of that number. During that period the company's sales and profits surged from $20 million and $3 million, respectively, to $183 million and $12 million, a growth that was achieved by attacking the giant U.S. market, unveiling a broad line of new snowmobiles, and pursuing an aggressive marketing initiative.

In 1969 Beaudoin took Bombardier public, planning to use the resulting cash to vertically integrate the company and profit from related economies of scale. In fact, during the 1960s and early 1970s Bombardier acquired several new companies, the largest of which was the Austrian firm Lohnerwerke GmbH. The two companies were merged to form Bombardier-Rotax in 1970—Lohnerwerke's subsidiary, Rotax, had previously supplied engines for Bombardier's Ski-Doos. Lohnerwerke, a tramway manufacturer founded in 1823, gave Bombardier an entry into the tram and rail transit industry. A year later, Bombardier also purchased its largest competitor, Bouchard Inc., which produced the third best-selling snowmobile on the market. As it turned out, Bouchard exited the snowmobile industry at an opportune time, as demand for the vehicles began tumbling shortly after the buyout.

Indeed, the energy crises of the early 1970s left the snowmobile industry gasping. Of 100 North American manufacturers, only six survived the ugly industry shakeout of the mid-1970s. The ever-resilient Bombardier was one of those left standing. Confident that the industry would one day recover, Bombardier management remained committed to sustaining its leadership position and capturing as much market share as possible. Still, Bombardier suffered serious sales and earnings declines. Just as it had done following the creation of the Quebec snow-clearing program of 1949, Bombardier scrambled during the early and mid-1970s to develop new products to bolster sagging snowmobile sales. The Can-Am off-road motorcycle, which used parts supplied by manufacturers of Ski-Doo components was introduced in 1972, and two years later the company began manufacturing a fiberglass sailboat. Bombardier also landed a big contract to produce stadium seats for the 1976 Montreal Olympic Games. In addition, the company entered the aviation industry in 1976 when it purchased a controlling interest in Herous Limited, a manufacturer of aircraft maintenance and landing gear.

In 1974 Bombardier had won a $118 million contract with the city of Montreal to supply 423 subway cars by 1978. At the time, snowmobiles still accounted for about 90 percent of the struggling company's sales, so the subway car contract represented a major new push for Bombardier. Some analysts, however, frowned upon the move because most of North America's rail equipment manufacturers had already exited the business in the 1960s in light of foreign competition and stagnant demand. In contrast, Bombardier worked to acquire and master related technologies during the 1970s as part of an effort to position itself as a major player in the global rolling stock industry. In addition to the Montreal contract, Bombardier supplied 36 self-propelled commuter cars to Chicago in 1977, 21 locomotives and 50 rail cars to VIA Rail Canada in 1978, and 117 commuter cars to the New Jersey Transit Corporation in 1980. In 1981, moreover, Bombardier received an order for 180 subway cars to be used in Mexico City.

After slogging through the snowmobile industry downturn of the 1970s, Bombardier was beginning to reshape itself into a successful manufacturer of transit equipment by the early 1980s. Importantly, Bombardier landed a huge contract in 1982 to supply New York City with 825 subway cars. Also during the early 1980s, Bombardier diversified into military equipment, believing that it could implement the same strategy it was using to dominate the North American rail transit market. In 1977 the company had purchased the marketing rights, at a discount, to a truck developed by Am General Corporation of the United States, a deal that turned out to be a boon for the company. In 1981 the Canadian government awarded Bombardier a contract to supply 2,767 trucks. Bombardier delivered the last truck ahead of schedule in 1983, leading to a second order for 1,900 of the vehicles. The company also received a contract in 1985 to supply 2,500 trucks to the Belgian Army.

By the mid-1980s Bombardier was again generating hefty profits, despite turbulence in the North American transit market and ongoing sluggishness of snowmobile sales. Beaudoin, who was known as a savvy dealmaker, capitalized on the downturn in the transit industry to increase market share and bolster its competitive position. In 1987, for example, Bombardier acquired Pullman Technology, a division of Pullman-Peabody, followed the next year by the purchase of the Transit America division of The Budd Company. The company also acquired major interests in transit companies in Belgium and France. In the early 1990s Bombardier acquired UTDC, a major Canadian competitor, and Concarril, Mexico's top manufacturer of railway rolling stock. Those purchases cemented Bombardier's role as a leading global supplier of transit cars. That status was confirmed when Bombardier was awarded the contract to build specialized rail cars for the massive Eurotunnel, a transit system linking England and France beneath the English Channel.

At the same time Bombardier was expanding in the transit industry, the company was also launching an aggressive diversification drive into the aerospace market. That drive began with the 1986 purchase of the troubled air carrier Canadair from the Canadian government. The government had dumped US$2 billion into the development of the Challenger corporate jet, a nine-seat craft that was to be the foundation of Canadair. Bombardier paid just US$121 million for the company and was quickly able to turn the operation around through cost-cutting and aggressive marketing of the project's sophisticated technology. The acquisition effectively doubled Bombardier's size and represented its intent to become a player in the aerospace industry. To that end, in 1989 Bombardier purchased Short Brothers PLC, a Northern Ireland aircraft producer, and the following year bought Learjet Corporation, builder of the well-known business jets. In 1992, moreover, Bombardier snagged Ontario-based De Havilland, a manufacturer of turboprop aircraft.

Meanwhile, Bombardier continued to firm up its position in the sporadic snowmobile market. Although the business represented less than 10 percent of sales by the early 1990s, Beaudoin refused to exit the market, citing Bombardier's historic expertise in the industry. Throughout the mid-1980s, in fact, Bombardier continued to beef up its snowmobile division with new technology and products. By the early 1990s Bombardier was still controlling about 50 percent of the Canadian snowmobile market and more than 25 percent of the entire North American market. In addition, Bombardier introduced the Sea-Doo watercraft in 1988 to compete in the growing market for individual sit-down jet-boats—the design was actually the offspring of a 1968 effort by Bombardier's research staff, and it was chosen as the number-one watercraft of its type by *Popular Mechanics* in 1988. By the early 1990s Bombardier was serving about 40 percent of that emerging North American segment. Bombardier was also branching out globally with its motorized consumer products division, as evidenced by its 1993 buyout of the leading Finnish snowmobile maker.

Throughout the 1980s and early 1990s Bombardier grew and prospered by purchasing undervalued operations and turning them around with sound management, but not all of its efforts proved profitable. For example, several of its transit deals, including the giant Eurotunnel contract, actually lost money for the company. In general, though, Beaudoin's deals were successful and most of the company's operations thrived. As a result, Bombardier's sales mushroomed from $1.4 billion in 1987 to an impressive $4.4 billion in 1992. Profits rose at a rate of 15 percent annually during the period to $133 million in 1992. Bombardier had become one of Canada's largest and most successful manufacturing companies, and it was steadily expanding throughout Europe and North America.

Bombardier continued to expand its operations and acquire new companies going into the mid-1990s. In 1994, for example, it purchased German transportation equipment manufacturer Waggonfabrik Talbot, which employed a work force of about 1,200, and Bombardier's aerospace division was working to add a 70-seat jetliner to its product line. Importantly, the wisdom of Bombardier's decision to retain its motorized consumer craft business became evident when that market rebounded in 1994. Buoyed by new product introductions, sales by that division surged 39 percent in 1994 to account for roughly 17 percent of company revenues. More importantly, profits from Ski-Doo and Sea-Doo products represented 37 percent of total company profits, making that division central to Bombardier's gains in that year.

As a result of new acquisitions and improving markets, Bombardier's revenues sailed from $4.8 billion in 1993 to $5.9 billion in 1994, as net income climbed from $176 million to $242 million. In addition, investor confidence in Bombardier's long-term prospects was evidenced by the company's surging stock price, which doubled during 1994.

Principal Subsidiaries:

Bombardier Inc. Canadair; Learjet Inc.; De Havilland Inc.; Short Brothers PLC; Bombardier Rotax Gmbh; Bombardier-Concarril; Bombardier Eurorail.

Further Reading:

Bombardier: A Dream With an International Reach, Montreal: Bombardier Inc., 1992.
Crowe, Nancy, "Bombardier Gears Up," *Vermont Business,* December 1986, Section 1, p. 89.
Ferrabee, James, "Bombardier Stock on a Magic Carpet Ride," *Gazette,* December 19, 1994, Section C, p. 2.
————, "Confident Chunnel Man," *Gazette,* February 1995, Section D, p. 7.
Ford, Royal, "Red Line Cars are Born in Vermont," *Boston Globe,* November 7, 1993, Section 1, p. 69.
Gibbens, Robert, "Bombardier is Aiming High," *Financial Post,* April 11, 1991, Section 1, p. 21.
————, "Bombardier Buys German Railcar Firm," *Financial Post,* February 25, 1995, Section 1, p. 19.

Hadekel, Peter, "Bombardier's Ski-Doo Division is Profiting from Borrowed Techniques," *Gazette,* April 16, 1993, Section F, p. 1.

Koselka, Rita, "Let's Make a Deal," *Forbes,* April 27, 1992, p. 62.

Lang, Amanda, "Dynasties," *ROB Magazine,* June 1, 1995, p. 60.

McGovern, Sheila, "On the Move; The Snowmobiles Bombardier Built for Rural Quebec are the Still-Thriving Roots of a World Transportation Empire that Includes Planes, Trains, and Sea-Doos," *Gazette,* November 1, 1993, Section C, p. 8.

Moorman, Robert W., "The Deal Maker; From Selling Snowmobiles to Saving Aircraft Companies, Laurent Beaudoin Has Made Bombardier a World-Class Player," *Air Transport World,* July 1992, p. 44.

Shalom, Francois, "Firefighting; Canadair Says Bomber's Problems are Merely Glitches, and Promises to Fix Them for Unhappy French," *Gazette,* March 18, 1995, Section C, p. 3.

Yakabuski, Konrad, "Bombardier Sets Out On a European Odyssey; Canadian Firm Establishes New Trade Beachhead On Old Continent," *Toronto Star,* December 19, 1993, Section D, p. 1.

—Dave Mote

British Columbia Hydro and Power Authority

333 Dunsmuir Street
Vancouver, British Columbia V6B 5R3
(604) 528-3056
Fax: (604) 528-3137

Government-Owned Company
Incorporated: 1962
Employees: 6,048
Sales: $2.18 billion
SICs: 4911 Electric Services

The third-largest utility in Canada, British Columbia Hydro and Power Authority served 1.4 million customers during the mid-1990s. Through more than 70,000 kilometers of transmission and distribution lines, the utility's electricity was fed to a service area containing more than 92 percent of British Columbia's population. The bulk — more than 70 percent — of the electricity distributed by B.C. Hydro was derived from major hydroelectric generating stations on the Columbia and Peace rivers.

Although B.C. Hydro was formed in 1962 when the British Columbia Electric Company Limited and the British Columbia Power Commission were amalgamated, the roots of the company stretch back considerably further, to the late 19th century and the incipient years of electricity and electrically powered transportation in the province. Much of the groundwork for the creation of B.C. Hydro's primary predecessor, the British Columbia Electric Railway Company Limited, was established between 1885 and 1890, when a collection of electric companies and electric railway companies were organized on Vancouver Island and the mainland. In and around Vancouver and Victoria, these fledgling utilities and public transportation companies were established, then shortly thereafter, when financial difficulties threatened their survival, the electric companies and the railway companies united, creating the first major utility in British Columbia, the Consolidated Railway and Light Company, the formation of which was credited largely to one individual, Robert M. Horne-Payne. Prior to Horne-Payne's involvement in the organization of Consolidated Railway and Light, the Vancouver Street Railway Company was organized by a group of local capitalists in 1886. Approximately two years later Vancouver's first electric company, Vancou-

ver Electric Illuminating Company Limited was formed by a separate group of promoters who directed the construction of a steam plant within the city to give the community its first electricity. Less than 24 months later, however, both companies found their pioneering efforts unable to produce sufficient revenue to stay in business and both quickly began to flounder. In the first of many mergers to follow, the directors of Vancouver Electric and Vancouver Street Railway consolidated their companies, convinced that the union of their operations offered the only viable solution to their salvation. From the merger the Vancouver Electric Railway and Light Company was created, but before the company's inaugural year was through, it too was reeling from financial difficulties and its bondholders threatened foreclosure.

During the same period when Vancouver Electric and Vancouver Street Railway were formed and then united to create Vancouver Electric Railway and Light, the Westminster and Vancouver Tram Company and the Westminster Street Railway Company were formed to build a tramway to provide interurban rail passenger service between Vancouver and New Westminster. These two railway systems, however, quickly floundered, remaining bankrupt for several years before bondholders foreclosed in 1893.

Such was the state of the electric and railway industries during the early 1890s when Robert Horne-Payne first visited the province. The son of an English barrister, Horne-Payne grew up in London, securing his first job there when, through his father's influence, he began working for the London branch of the Bank of Scotland. From there, Horne-Payne joined a stock brokerage firm named Sperling & Company that concentrated on railway and industrial stocks, bonds, and government loans. At Sperling & Company, Horne-Payne quickly distinguished himself, becoming a partner of the firm at age 24 when he also was entrusted with overseeing company business in Canada. Horne-Payne left for Canada in 1894 and once there met Sir William Van Horne, president of the Canadian Pacific Railway. Van Horne invited the recently-arrived Horne-Payne on his annual inspection of Canadian Pacific Railway's lines, a trip that took the pair across the country and into British Columbia, where Horne-Payne discovered an enticing business opportunity.

During his coast-to-coast journey Horne-Payne realized that Canada offered ample opportunities for investment. The vast natural resources in Canada were indicative of a country that soon would become a major commercial center, but its burgeoning manufacturing and commercial industries were under-capitalized, as the condition of the utility and railway industries in British Columbia evinced. Horne-Payne set himself to the task of removing this stumbling block, embarking on a career as a financier that would credit him with directing $500 million of British capital into Canadian industry and helping struggling business ventures surmount formidable obstacles. Horne-Payne immediately set to work where his cross-country trek ended, offering his assistance in obtaining capital for the numerous failed or failing railway and electric companies in the Vancouver region.

Concurrent with Horne-Payne's arrival in British Columbia in 1894, the bondholders of the Vancouver and New Westminster railway systems petitioned the legislature for an act consolidating the Westminster and Vancouver Tram Company and the Vancouver Electric Railway and Light Company. The company created from their successful petition was named, aptly enough, Consolidated Railway and Light Company, a combination of the pioneer electric and railway companies in Vancouver and in Victoria, where much of the developmental progress of electric and railway companies had occurred contemporaneously with the development of Vancouver's electric and railway companies. Consolidated Railway and Light represented the latest effort to keep the numerous railway and electric operations involved financially stable, but, like the company's constituents, Consolidated Railway and Light suffered from a lack of capital, a deficiency Horne-Payne sought to ameliorate.

Horne-Payne left British Columbia promising to raise the money required for Consolidated Railway and Light's survival and arrived in London in late 1894, where he immediately began campaigning for funds to liquidate Consolidated Railway and Light's debts and to enable the company's expansion. Through his efforts the British Railway Amalgamation Syndicate was formed in London, guaranteeing sufficient capital for Consolidated Railway and Light to meet its financial obligations. The consortium of investors also promised to provide for necessary plant additions and the extension of railways, as well as to provide money for the potential development of hydro-electric facilities.

Consolidated Railway and Light's promising beginning came to an abrupt end in May 1896, however, when the Point Ellice Bridge collapsed, sending a Victoria streetcar carrying nearly 200 people plunging down with it. Fifty-four people were killed when the streetcar fell to the water below and immediately Consolidated Railway and Light was presumed the negligent party. In response to the catastrophe, the British Railway Amalgamation Syndicate withdrew its offer to finance Consolidated Railway and Light, forcing the company into receivership six months later. Horne-Payne hurried back to England in search of capital to tie together the loose threads of Consolidated Railway and Light, a quest that was made easier after the company was cleared of any blame in the streetcar accident and the City of Victoria, owner of the bridge, was ruled to be at fault. All of the assets formerly belonging to Consolidated Railway and Light were then purchased at an auction, and in 1897, with Horne-Payne elected chairman, the British Columbia Electric Railway Company Limited (B.C. Electric) was formed, establishing at last, after a more than a decade of failed attempts, a financially stable railway and electric company in the province.

One year after its formation, B.C. Electric constructed its first hydroelectric generating plant, a facility that used two water wheels connected to two 360 kilowatt generators. Located at Goldstream, near Victoria, the company's generating plant was expanded to 1,500 kilowatts between 1903 and 1904. The Goldstream plant was the first of many hydroelectric facilities to follow, as B.C. Electric's generating capacity and geographic coverage expanded with the growth of the areas

its served. In 1903 another hydroelectric plant was constructed at Lake Buntzen, a project that was known as the Coquitlam-Buntzen development, then two years later a 2.5 mile-long tunnel — the longest hydroelectric tunnel in the world at the time — was completed, connecting Lake Coquitlam and Lake Buntzen. Concurrent with the construction of this mammoth project, B.C. Electric strengthened its involvement in the distribution of gas, acquiring five Vancouver gas companies in 1904 and the Victoria Gas Company in 1905.

As time progressed, B.C. Electric continued to develop hydroelectric resources and purchase smaller electric power plants and companies, relying on both acquisitions and its own construction projects to meet the growing need for electricity. A hydroelectric plant was constructed along the Jordan River in 1912, a second plant was added on Buntzen Lake in 1914, and the Western Canada Power Company was acquired in 1921, before B.C. Electric embarked on one of the largest development projects in its history. In 1924 a group of B.C. Electric engineers began an extensive study of the power resources of the Bridge River, which the company began developing three years later, constructing over a 33-year period three dams for four generating stations.

In 1926 British Columbia Electric Power & Gas Company, Limited was formed through the amalgamation of Vancouver Gas Company, British Columbia Gas Company, and New Westminster Gas Company. For the next two years B.C. Electric Power & Gas functioned as a holding company for B.C. Electric until the British Columbia Power Corporation, Limited was formed in 1928 to serve as the holding company for B.C. Electric and B.C. Electric Power & Gas. Under B.C. Power Corporation's corporate umbrella were the company's two primary operating companies, B.C. Electric and B.C. Electric Power & Gas, plus a host of affiliated companies, including Vancouver Power Company, B.C. Rapid Transit Company, Western Canada Power Company, Bridge River Power Company, Burrard Power Company, Vancouver Island Power Company, Victoria Electric Company, and Victoria Gas Company.

Organized as such, the group of companies that had gathered around B.C. Electric since its formation in 1897 represented a prodigious force in both the transportation and electric utility industries; the result of nearly 50 years of consolidations and acquisitions springing from the early failed companies formed between 1885 and 1890. Together these companies expanded their territories of service to embrace the entire province, absorbing electric and gas properties scattered throughout the region. By the beginning of the 1940s, rumors were circulating about the possibility of the government acquiring B.C. Electric, foreshadowing the formal birth of B.C. Hydro by nearly two decades.

The first step toward government ownership was taken in 1945 when the British Columbia Power Commission was formed in 1945 to consolidate generation and distribution of electricity in particular regions of British Columbia and to superintend the extension of electrical service to regions receiving insufficient service. One year after its creation, the B.C. Power Commission initiated proceedings to seize B.C. Electric plants in Port Alberni and Kamloops with B.C. Electric's consent. At roughly the same time, B.C. Electric Power and Gas Company changed its name to B.C. Electric Company Limited, one of the two primary companies operating under the aegis of B.C. Power Corporation, which assigned all electric power and gas activities to the newly named B.C. Electric Company, while B.C. Electric Railway handled all of the holding company's transportation activities.

Over the course of the ensuing decade, B.C. Electric and B.C. Power Commission constructed several hydroelectric generating plants before the two companies became a single entity in 1962. One year prior to the merger of the two utility companies, B.C. Electric Company was purchased by the provincial government, becoming a Crown corporation under the Power Development Act. The following year, in 1962, the B.C. Hydro and Power Authority Act was passed, amalgamating B.C. Electric Company and the B.C. Power Commission to create the British Columbia Hydro and Power Authority.

The decision by the government to amalgamate the B.C. Power Commission and B.C. Electric had been prompted by the mounting need for electricity, the development of which, in the government's estimation, required the concerted effort of both utility companies. Specifically, the government realized that the time had come to harness hydroelectric power from the Peace River and the Columbia River, two major rivers that would require enormous amounts of labor and money to develop. Toward this objective, the government had purchased the Peace River Power Development Company at the same time it had acquired B.C. Electric, then once B.C. Hydro had been formed, it began hydroelectric development projects on the two rivers. B.C. Hydro's first hydroelectric project along the Peace River was completed in 1968, giving the utility an additional 2.4 million kilowatts of generating capacity. On the Columbia River three dams were constructed — Duncan Dam, completed in 1967, Keenleyside Dam, completed in 1968, and Mica Dam, completed in 1973 — as an era of large-scale hydroelectric projects, commonly referred to as "megaprojects," characterized B.C. Hydro's first two decades of existence.

During the 1960s and early 1970s, B.C. Hydro also acquired more than a dozen smaller utilities, which coupled with the additional generating capacity realized from the development of the Columbia and the Peace rivers, more than doubled B.C. Hydro's generation capability by 1972. The construction of megaprojects continued into the 1970s, when construction was begun at Seven Mile on the Pend d'Oreille River, Peace Canyon on the Peace River, and Revelstoke on the Columbia River.

B.C. Hydro entered the 1980s looking to expand further, its directors convinced that the province's electricity needs would soon eclipse the utility's generation capability. The perpetual drive to develop additional hydroelectric facilities had propelled B.C. Hydro's growth and, in fact, had predicated its formation, but in the 1980s the consistent development of hydroelectric resources would come to a stop. When B.C. Hydro announced plans to build another dam on the Peace River in 1981, the impetus for which was based on prognostications that the demand for electricity would increase substantially during the coming decade, the utility faced considerable opposition. The B.C. Utilities Commission, which had been created a year earlier, bringing B.C. Hydro's electricity and gas operations under regulatory control for the first time, questioned the reliability of the utility's estimates regarding the projected increase in demand for electricity. Additionally, environmental concerns were raised about the construction of further dams and generation facilities, and quickly B.C. Hydro found its historical pattern of building new hydroelectric facilities whenever and wherever it chose no longer an approach it could take in the 1980s.

An economic recession during the early 1980s exacerbated the utilities position, putting its plan to build a dam on Site C along the Peace River temporarily on hold. B.C. Hydro's estimates for a substantial increase in the demand for electricity had been largely based on a projected increase in the number of industrial customers the utility expected to serve, but with the onset of the recession many of the companies that had intended to establish facilities in British Columbia opted to abandon their plans. As a result, B.C. Hydro was left with a surplus of power rather than a projected lack of it, forcing the utility to re-examine its role as the province's electricity and natural gas supplier.

Later in the decade when economic conditions improved, B.C. Hydro again proposed constructing a dam on Site C along the Peace River, but again the utility met with fierce opposition. After selling its natural gas distribution division to Inland Natural Gas Company Limited in 1988 for $741 million, B.C. Hydro began to take the first steps toward becoming a different type of utility company. It launched its energy conservation program, dubbed Power Smart, in 1989, beginning B.C. Hydro's pivotal switch from a utility that previously had concentrated on generating electricity by building more and more dams to a utility that regarded energy conservation as a strategic resource.

With this new approach — using conservation measures and products as a means of increasing electrical generation capability rather than relying on the development of additional generation facilities — B.C. Hydro entered the 1990s, buoyed by the success and popularity of its Power Smart program. By 1994, the utility's strategic approach to conservation had been adopted by nearly every utility in Canada, proving to be a practicable course for Canadian utilities to take during the 1990s and beyond.

B.C. Hydro began what one company executive in an interview with *The Globe and Mail* referred to as, "the most profound change since the formation of the company," in 1994 when the utility began to streamline its operations and re-focus its efforts for the remainder of the decade and into the 21st century. The future promised the erosion of the utility's long-held monopoly over the production and distribution of electricity, as the deregulation of the North American electricity trade spawned a host of independent power companies, forcing B.C. Hydro to reduce the size of its work force dramatically. Six vice-president positions were eliminated as were hundreds of lower-level positions and more than 40 senior manager positions with the hope of improving the utility's efficiency as it positioned itself for the future.

Principal Subsidiaries:

Powertech Labs Inc.; Western Integrated Technologies Inc.; British Columbia Power Exchange Corporation; British Columbia Hydro International Limited; Power Smart Inc.; Columbia Estate Company, Limited

Further Reading:

Adams, E.H., "Scaling Our Family Tree," *The B.C. Electric Employees' Magazine,* December, 1931, p. 3-8.
"Events in the History of B.C. Hydro and its Predecessors," *British Columbia Hydro and Power Authority Annual Report,* 1971.
Glover, F.R., "Birth of the B.C.E.R. Company," *The B.C. Electric Employees' Magazine,* October 1928, pp. 5-7.
Howard, Ross, "B.C. Hydro Denies Conflict of Interest," *The Globe and Mail,* December 21, 1994, p. A6.
"Hydro-Electric Development in Canada," *The B.C. Electric Employees' Magazine,* March 1933, pp. 6-8.
McFarlane, Don, "History of Electric Power in British Columbia," *IEEE Power Engineering Review,* October 1984, pp. 11-13.
Mulgrew, Ian, "Chairman of B.C. Hydro Resigns, Cites Personal Financial Problems," *The Globe and Mail,* January 12, 1985, p. P5.
Sheppard, Robert, "B.C. Hydro Taking Aim at Markets in California," *The Globe and Mail,* May 30, 1988, p. B1.
Sigurdson, Albert, "B.C. Hydro Scrambles To Meet Rising Energy Demand," *The Globe and Mail,* May 25, 1981, p. B27.
Williamson, Robert, "B.C. Hydro Eyes Two Kinds of Green," *The Globe and Mail,* November 5, 1992, p. B1.

—Jeffrey L. Covell

Canfor Corporation

2900-1055 Dunsmuir Street
P.O. Box 49420
Bentall Postal Station
Vancouver, British Columbia V7X 1B5
(604) 661-5241
Fax: (604) 661-5235

Public Company
Founded: 1938
Employees: 4,360
Sales: $1.4 billion
Stock Exchanges: Toronto Vancouver
SICs: 2421 Sawmills & Planing Mills, General; 2611
   Pulp Mills; 5031 Lumber, Plywood, Millwork, &
   Wood Panels; 5039 Construction Materials, Nec;
   5211 Lumber & Other Building Materials Dealers;
   6719 Offices of Holding Companies, Nec

Located among the world's second-largest forests, Canfor takes full advantage of its Vancouver location to manufacture and market a variety of integrated forest products, including lumber, bleached and unbleached kraft pulp (for paper, tissue, newsprint, etc.), hardboard paneling, and several environmentally friendly fibre products. Canfor's extensive forestry operations, from the southern coast of Canada to the northern interior of British Columbia and into Alberta, boasts customers in 28 countries and offices throughout Canada, Europe, the United States, and Asia. In an era of dwindling resources and increased environmental responsibility, Canfor, which regards itself as a "forest manager," has survived in part because of its commitment to reforestation, pollution control, and other measures designed to reap the forests' benefits while replacing them for future generations.

British Columbia's third-largest company and the province's biggest employer evolved from a small family-run business in New Westminster, whose origins can be traced to the late 1930s when Adolf Hitler was flexing his muscles in Germany and its surrounding countries. Not waiting for an official vote to annex Austria, the Nazis invaded, and two families, the Bentleys and the Prentices, fled while it was still possible to do so. Narrowly escaping with little more than the clothes on their backs, John G. Prentice and L. L. G. ("Poldi") Bentley, brothers-in-law and textiles merchants, left their homeland to begin a new life elsewhere. Having

visited Canada, Poldi suggested the families settle there, and they booked passage on the *Empress of Britain.*

After arriving in British Columbia, Prentice and Bentley immediately sought employment. Collecting outstanding debt due their textiles mill from countries outside Nazi control, they pooled their resources and prepared to go into business. Introduced by associates at the Bank of Montreal to a man named John Bene, who had extensive forestry experience, Prentice and Bentley were enthused about Bene's idea for a hardwood veneer factory. Though Prentice and Bentley had neither background nor experience in the forest industry, they did possess a keen business sense and the prescience to know timber and its byproducts could be a sound business venture. On November 12, 1938, after receiving a tax break to base their company in the town of New Westminster, Pacific Veneer Company Ltd. (PV) was incorporated with Prentice and Bentley as equal partners.

Construction of a mill on the Fraser River commenced in April 1939, and the partners bought a clipper, conveyor dryer, lathe, and 16-foot slicer and contracted to have a 60-by-16-foot boiler built on their Braid Street premises. Having begun with just over two dozen employees, PV was selling single-ply veneer to local furniture manufacturers when the advent of World War II spelled rapid expansion. The British Air Force, cut off from its lumber supplies in Finland and Sweden, asked the company to supply massive quantities of plywood for aircraft production. With the exception of the prototype, every *Mosquito* bomber flown during World War II had wings crafted from PV's birch or spruce plywood. By this time, PV employed nearly 1,000 workers, almost two-thirds of them women.

Even after war production slowed, plywood was still very much in demand for postwar rebuilding throughout Europe, though PV sold fir plywood for this purpose, rather than birch or spruce plywood. Believing the company's long-term survival depended on diversification, Bentley and Prentice initiated a series of acquisitions in the 1940s and 1950s to round out their holdings and strengthen their position in the timber industry. Among these early acquisitions was Eburne Saw Mills Ltd., with a decrepit mill purchased primarily for its location, three logging operations, and a shingle manufacturer in 1943. Bill McMahan, a veteran of the area's lumber industry, joined the company at this time to rehaul the Eburne facilities. In 1944, PV arranged what Bentley later deemed the company's "wisest move": purchasing the Beaver Cove Timber Company Ltd.

As part of the Beaver Cove deal, PV acquired several densely forested land tracts along the Nimpkish River on Vancouver Island, as well as a timber holding company called Canadian Forest Products Limited (CFP). Intrigued by the appropriateness of the name, Prentice and Bentley decided to claim it as the overall title of their burgeoning operations and rolled all of PV's assets into the new corporation in 1947. When the new Canadian Forest Products Ltd. came into existence, the company reorganized into four parts: the Eburne Saw Mills Division; the Englewood Logging Division; the Harrison Mills Logging Division; and the Pacific Veneer and Plywood Division. The same year, CFP acquired two more logging operations, another shingle manufacturer, and a new board member in the name of Victor Whittall, well known in the U.S. and Canadian shingle industry. Meanwhile, John Bene parted ways with Bentley and Prentice and helped create Weldwood of Canada Limited, which later merged with CFP in 1989.

Back at Pacific Veneer in 1948, a new product called "hardboard" was made using the leftover residue from plywood operations. Hardboard not only turned waste into a viable product, but its versatile applications soon propelled CFP into manufacturing an entire line of woodgrain products.

By the 1950s, CFP had established a distribution system in British Columbia through its own fleet of railcars, warehouses, and retail centers—all of which became the Building Materials Division. Another critical step in CFP's history was the 1951 purchase of controlling interest in the Howe Sound Pulp Company Ltd. and its Port Mellon mill. Once again, a declaration of war cranked up demand; this time it was the Korean War and the product in demand was unbleached kraft pulp—just what the Howe Sound mill produced. Two years later, CFP purchased the remaining shares of Howe Sound and expanded its operations.

In 1955, the CFP crossed into Grand Prairie, Alberta, and began acquiring properties owned by the Bickell family. Forming a subsidiary called North Canadian Forest Industries Ltd. to oversee operations, its holdings eventually encompassed several sawmills, a plywood plant, and varied timber rights. CFP then shifted its focus to pulp when British Columbia began issuing Pulpwood Harvesting licenses. Granted its first license in 1962 for an 8-million acre tract in the Prince George area, CFP formed a joint venture with Britain's Reed Paper Ltd. to construct the $84-million Prince George Pulp and Paper mill in 1964. Another partnership, Takla Holdings Limited, was created in 1965 to harvest timber and construct a sawmill and veneer plant at Fort St. James (100 miles north of Prince George).

In 1966 the Prince George mill began operations; the same year, Peter Bentley, who began working summers at the family business some 15 years earlier, was named one of CFP's directors. Bentley had studied forestry at the University of British Columbia and worked for an outside forest products company in Chicago; the appointment of Poldi's son to the board heralded the arrival of the second generation. The success of the Prince George mill inspired a new venture for $60 million between CFP, Reed, and West Germany's AG Feldmuehle for a second pulp mill. Called the Intercontinental Mill, it commenced production in 1968, situated near its Prince George predecessor. Two years later, another shift in CFP's management took place when John Prentice became chairman of the board, Poldi Bentley was named president, and Peter Bentley became executive vice-president.

Flushed with increasing success as an integrated forest products manufacturer, CFP continued spending substantial sums of money to broaden its operations. Although most acquisitions were related to the timber industry—like the 1973 purchases of lumber and plywood producer Balco Industries Ltd. and Westcoast Cellufibre Industries Limited—the company also departed into noncore assets, like acquiring a 46 percent controlling interest in Yorkshire Trust Co. and 39 percent of industrial conglomerate Cornat Industries Ltd. (later renamed Versatile Corporation). When CFP's fortunes changed dramatically in the next decade, most analysts pointed to the Yorkshire and Versatile acquisitions as expensive missteps.

In January 1975, Peter Bentley succeeded his father as president, Poldi became the company's vice-chairman to John Prentice's chairman, and the three planned CFP's next slew of acquisitions. Returning their attention to the pulping industry in 1978, CFP's top three decided the company should pay $60 million to buy out Reed Paper's shares in the two Prince George pulp facilities and its nearly 44 percent stake of Takla Forest Products at Fort St. James. As the decade closed, CFP's balance sheet seemed secure: 1980's total sales reached almost $700 million, comprising $300 million or about 43 percent from pulp, $150 million from lumber, and the rest from building materials and other byproducts. The company continued expanding, extensively upgrading Howe Sound in 1980 with the addition of a huge warehouse capable of storing 20,000 tons of product awaiting shipment by deep-sea vessels. In 1981, CFP was again on the move, this time acquiring Swanson Lumber Co., with sawmills in British Columbia and Alberta.

Yet as CFP's operations hummed along at a breakneck pace, a cyclical slump was deepening into a devastating, long-reaching recession. The pulp and paper market's decline in the early 1980s was a surprise, though CFP and most integrated producers believed their other products would pick up the slack. When pulp didn't improve and higher interest rates and inflation kicked in, however, the situation turned desperate, and exporters worldwide began voluntary currency devaluations. Sweden's devaluation of 65 percent proved particularly harmful to CFP's cash reserves, and closer to home, the New Westminster plywood facility was losing millions. Hoping for a turnaround or buyout from management and employees, CFP decided against closing New Westminster's operations.

In addition, the company formed a partnership for the Heffley Reforestation Centre Ltd. at Kamloops, as a seed orchard and nursery. It then turned its attention to the United States, paying $3 million in 1982 for the Idaho-based Chandler Corp., a building materials distributor the company bought principally for its excellent rail access in the highly regulated United States. Yet this deal turned as sour as the economy when the United States deregulated, leaving CFP with an unstable asset that added to an already sizable debt burden. After years of cautious yet nonetheless free spending, CFP found itself with a whopping 72 percent debt load and skyrocketing interest payments. To augment its shallow (28 percent) equity and cash flow, the company went public, raised about $100 million, and officially changed its name to Canfor in 1983.

After continued losses, Canfor took several measures to slacken the flow of red ink: it closed the New Westminster plywood facility; sold its York Trust holdings and the majority of its stake in Versatile Corporation; sliced working capital by $20 million; and prepared to sell or close other underperforming assets. The company also made another executive change, naming Roy Bickell (whose parents sold their Alberta properties to CFP around 1960) the company's first non-family president and Peter Bentley the chairman and CEO. Despite belt-tightening across the board, Canfor did, however, buy up the remaining interest in both Takla Forest Products and the Intercontinental pulp mill in 1985 from AG Feldmuehle of West Germany, betting on the renovated Howe Sound facilities as a major draw when the pulp market recovered. Three years later, Howe Sound was the jewel Canfor had envisioned when the company formed an alliance with the Oji Paper Co. Ltd. (later renamed New Oji Paper), Japan's biggest paper producer, to create Howe Sound Pulp and Paper Limited. Canfor brought its established Howe Sound operations to the partnership, and the Japanese put up $307 million in cash towards the facility's extensive remodeling. Although Canfor had poured $122 million into Howe Sound from 1980 to 1987, this refurbishment (estimated at upwards of $1 billion) would enable it to produce 1,000 tons of high-quality kraft pulp daily (versus previous output of 665 tons per day) and an additional 585 tons of newsprint per day for Oji Paper to export and sell in Japan.

The following year, 1989, Canfor reunited in a fashion with John Bene by merging with rival Weldwood of Canada Ltd. to become Canfor-Weldwood Distribution Ltd. In 1990, Canfor sold its sawmill and logging operations in Alberta for $78 million and closed its Grande Prairie plywood mill. Although plywood represented Canfor's origins and was once its primary source of income, it had been pushed aside to make way for the wave of the future: Canada's first wood fiber composite plant, manufacturing an entire new line of forestry-related products. The same year, Arild Niellsen took over as president after Roy Bickell retired. In 1991 Canfor issued another 3 million shares of stock, netting the company $75 million, and year-end sales hit just over $822 million. However, income still evaporated into a staggering loss of $99 million.

In 1992, Canfor embarked on further compensatory actions with a $5 million reorganization of its New Westminster Panel and Fibre Division; a $6.5-million write-off to rationalize its sawmilling assets; and another public offering of 2 million shares for $51.7 million. Though the worst appeared to be over, Canfor's management knew it would be some time before their restructuring measures returned the company to full profitability. Net sales for 1992 grew to $976 million, and the company managed to reduce its losses to half 1991's figure at just under $50 million.

By the next year, Canfor was once again swimming in black ink with sales just shy of $1.2 billion and a profit of $41.3 million. Though 1993 was still a poor year for pulp, the company positioned itself for a full recovery with a $51-million upgrade of Intercontinental's boiler and the $53-million installation of oxygen delignification equipment. The new equipment, considered one-of-a-kind, significantly decreased the chlorine necessary for bleaching pulp, saving the company money and making the mill more environmentally sound. Other 1994 projects included the modernization of five sawmills for

$35 million and the installation of a new $32-million newsprint press at Howe Sound's newsprint mill.

Coupled with the costs of upgrading, strict new fiber requirements brought by the B.C. government's Forest Practices Code and the newly created "Forest Renewal Program" in 1994 threatened Canfor's recovery. However, despite an increase in stumpage fees by 115 percent from 1993 to 1994, Canfor still finished the year with an impressive of $1.4 billion in net sales and earnings of $124.5 million, representing a third consecutive year of marked improvement. Helping out in this regard was a boon of $48.2 million, part of a proposed $80-million refund of countervailing duties imposed on Canadian softwood lumber exports to the United States.

At the end of 1994, Canfor initiated a friendly takeover of a smaller B.C. rival, Slocan Forest Products Ltd., to secure a supply of wood chips for its pulping operations. Though the cash and stock swap bid was ultimately unsuccessful (due in large part to the intervention of Forests Minister Andrew Petter), the battle rocked the forest products industry. Canfor's management was left bitter when Slocan partnered with Weyerhaeuser (another rival) for $80 million and a 10-year contract for 20 percent of its wood chip production. Yet Canfor quickly recovered by signing Ainsworth Lumber Co. Ltd. as its chips supplier; initiated a $12.9-million state-of-the-art renovation of its Hines Creek mill; and formed a new partnership for a fiberboard plant and wood residue co-generation facility in Prince George.

In April 1995, Peter Bentley turned his duties as CEO over to Nielssen, but remained Canfor's chairman. First quarter results were strong, with net sales of $487.8 million and income of $14.7 million. The company moved forward with the development of several new low-impact harvesting methods, computer graphics programs, and satellite mapping systems for environmentally sensitive areas.

Principal Subsidiaries:

B.C. Chemicals (50%); Balfour Guthrie Forest Products Inc.; Balfour Timbre Limited; Canfor Europe; Canfor Japan Corporation; Canfor U.S.A. Corporation; Canfor-Weldwood Distribution Ltd. (50%); Heffley Nursery (50%); Howe Sound Pulp and Paper Limited (50%); Westcoast Cellufibre (50%).

Further Reading:

Chipello, Christopher, "Slocan to Buy Back Shares to Fight Canfor Corp.'s Bid," *Wall Street Journal,* January 24, 1995, p. A6.
———, "Canfor Increases Up-Front Cash Part of Bid for Slocan," *Wall Street Journal,* January 30, 1995, p. B4.
De Santis, Solange, "Canfor Makes Bid Put at $470 Million for Slocan Forest," *Wall Street Journal,* December 13, 1994, p. A6.
Lush, Patricia, "Canfor for Chairman Optimistic," *Globe and Mail,* April 30, 1991, p. B11.
———, "Canfor's Bentley Bets Big," *Globe and Mail,* December 16, 1994, p. B1.
Mahood, Casey, and Lush, Patricia, "Canfor Bids for Slocan,"

Globe and Mail, December 13, 1994, p. B1.

Noble, Kimberley, "Canfor, Weldwood to Merge Division," *Globe and Mail,* January 31, 1989, p. B1.

"Score One for Canfor," *BC Business,* August 1994, p. 7.

Sigurdson, Albert, "Forest Giant Canfor Plans to Go Public," *Globe and Mail,* May 31, 1988, p. B1.

Sorenson, Jean, "Coping with Crisis," *B.C. Business,* January 1986, pp. 18-21,23,25,26.

Tribute to the Founders, Canadian Forest Products Ltd., 1978.

Williamson, Robert, "Slocan Reveals Key Backer," *Globe and Mail,* February 6, 1995, p. B1.

————, "Canfor Kills Bid for Slocan," *Globe and Mail,* February 8, 1995, p. B1.

Willis, Andrew, "Chipping Away at the Future," *Maclean's,* February 27, 1995, pp. 42-43.

—Taryn Benbow-Pfalzgraf

Canadian Airlines Corporation

Suite 2800
700 2nd Street S.W.
Calgary, Alberta T2P 2W2
(403) 294-2000
Fax: (403) 994-2066

Public Company
Incorporated: 1987 as PWA Corporation
Employees: 17,000
Sales: $2.95 billion
Stock Exchanges: Toronto Alberta Vancouver
SICs: 6719 Holding Companies Not Elsewhere
  Classified

Owner of the second-largest airline in Canada, Canadian Airlines Corporation and its primary operating subsidiary, Canadian Airlines International Ltd., provided domestic and international air service to more than 140 destinations on five continents. Canadian Airlines International owned Canadian Holidays Ltd., Transpacific Tours (Canada) Limited, and Canadian Regional Airlines Ltd. The airline also provided aircraft and engine overhaul and maintenance services to other carriers, as well as ground handling and cargo services, flight simulator and equipment rentals, and employee training programs.

Months before the January 1988 National Transportation Act ushered in the era of airline deregulation, permitting Canadian carriers for the first time to set their fares and routes with almost total freedom, PWA Corporation, the predecessor to Canadian Airlines Corporation, was established. The company formally came into existence on April 26, 1987, after the merger of Pacific Western Airlines and Canadian Pacific Airlines nearly five months earlier, but if the parts are equal to the whole then the roots of the airline holding company stretch back considerably farther than 1987, reaching back to the dawn of the aviation age in Canada when the first of the numerous airlines composing Canadian Airlines Corporation was established.

From the inception of the first airline in Canadian Airlines Corporation's ancestral tree in the late 1920s to the merger of Pacific Western Airlines and Canadian Pacific Airlines on December 2, 1986, a series of mergers and acquisitions took place that brought together small, regional airlines—each the product of numer-

ous smaller aircraft companies—to create Canada's second great transcontinental airline, Canadian Airline Corporation.

The first rumblings of what later would become the second-largest airline in Canada occurred in 1928 when Inter-Provincial Airlines was formed in eastern Canada and Western Canada Airways was formed, appropriately enough, in western Canada. Two years later these two airlines merged to form Canadian Airways Limited, which then was merged in 1942 with nine small airlines owned by Canadian Pacific Railway. The resulting Canadian Pacific Airlines became one of the two major airline companies that spawned Canadian Airline Corporation.

Combined, the nine airlines owned by Canadian Pacific Railway served small portions of Alberta, the Yukon, Manitoba, Ontario, Saskatchewan, British Columbia, and Quebec. Its consolidated fleet of small aircraft, coupled with the fleet amassed by Canadian Airways Limited, gave Canadian Pacific Airlines 78 airplanes during the new company's inaugural year of business, but during the war years each of the constituents of Canadian Pacific operated under their own names. Not until the conclusion of World War II did Canadian Pacific emerge as a distinct airline entity. Once it did, the airline grew quickly, particularly after the United States Army contracted Canadian Pacific to airlift large numbers of troops during the Korean War. The airline transported more than 39,000 military personnel during the war, which spawned a lucrative service route shortly thereafter that carried immigrants between Hong Kong and Canada. This route precipitated the extension of Canadian Pacific's geographic coverage during the remainder of the 1950s and into the 1960s. Canadian Pacific air service reached South America and Mexico City in 1955, Amsterdam, Madrid, and Lisbon in 1957, then Rome in 1965 and Athens in 1968.

Although the airline was recording remarkable progress, its growth was held in check by government-owned Trans-Canada Airlines (later renamed Air Canada), the only airline in the country permitted to provide transcontinental air service. The battle between Trans-Canada Airlines and Canadian Pacific would intensify in later years, but during Canadian Pacific's formative first decades it was unable to mount a serious threat against the much larger Trans-Canada Airlines. After numerous attempts to convince federal authorities to end Trans-Canada Airlines exclusive Canadian ambit, Canadian Pacific was awarded unlimited transcontinental authority in May 1979, thereby giving the company access to air service widely regarded as crucial to an airline's success.

The decision to open up the skies over Canada let loose the first faint murmurs of airline deregulation, which would arrive during the coming decade, and it also provided an incentive for the directors of Canadian Pacific to begin a concerted push for closing the ground separating their airline and Trans-Canada, by this point known as Air Canada. Other airlines also tried to strengthen their position in the industry, merging with others, then, in turn, being swallowed by others still. This general gathering of small airlines would eventually amalgamate as a viable competitor against industry stalwart Air Canada.

Within the Canadian Pacific organization, Eastern Provincial Airways Ltd. was the first airline to join the push toward the upper echelon in the Canadian airline industry. Acquired by Canadian Pacific in 1984 for $20 million, Eastern Provincial was established in Newfoundland in 1949, the same year the province entered Confederation. Initially a bush operator, Eastern Provincial was formed to provide air ambulance services and to conduct fire patrols, geological survey work, winter air mail transportation, as well as to ferry passengers within Newfoundland. The airline spent its early years flying people and equipment to remote sites in Newfoundland and Labrador. In 1958 its operational scope was broadened when the Danish government contracted Eastern Provincial to provide ice patrols and conduct photographic surveys in Greenland. Two years later the contract was expanded to include regular passenger service in Greenland, which developed into a 13,000-passenger-a-year business until the contract expired in 1965. In 1963 Eastern Provincial acquired much larger Maritimes Central Airways, an addition that swelled the company's fleet to more than 30 aircraft. Following the acquisition, the airline established its hub in Halifax, then in 1968 Eastern Provincial gained access to the Montreal market. In 1970 the company shed the bush segment of its airline operation, selling aircraft equipped to provide such service to a group of employees who then formed Labrador Airways Limited.

During the years separating the divestiture of its bush operations and its acquisition by Canadian Pacific, Eastern Provincial attempted to merge with Nordair and then with Quebecair, but both mergers failed because of governmental opposition. Eastern Provincial retained its corporate title for several years after Canadian Pacific acquired the airline, remaining a separate corporate entity until 1986, by which time Canadian Pacific had already acquired the object of Eastern Provincial's failed acquisitive bid—Nordair.

Canadian Pacific purchased a 60 percent stake in Nordair in late 1985, the second airline added in the years following the federal government's decision to grant Canadian Pacific transcontinental access. Incorporated as Boreal Airways Limited in 1947, Nordair began as a rugged, expeditionary airline entirely focused on the northern reaches of Canada. Its first aircraft was equipped with skis in the winter and pontoons in the summer, subsisting as a carrier for mining company workers, hunters, trappers, and prospectors who worked in the region surrounding St. Felicien, Quebec. A second small aircraft equipped for serving remote destinations was added two years later in 1949, but by the early 1950s the airline had begun to take on the trappings of a legitimate airline, employing more than 20 workers and offering a regular weekly flight to Fort Chimo. In 1956, Boreal Airways adopted the name "Nordair," then in 1960 acquired the heavy transport section belonging to Wheeler Airlines. Two years later Nordair inaugurated its commercial air service to Resolute Bay, the most northerly air route in the world at the time, and then the following year entered the charter business, providing service to Africa, the Middle East, and Europe.

Nordair entered the jet age in 1968, the first regional airline to do so in Canada, and from that point forward relied on its air service to western Quebec, eastern and southern Ontario, and adjacent Arctic points to fuel its growth. This service territory proved to be too meager to support an airline, however, and Nordair struggled because of a paucity of more lucrative, more populated southern air routes. After a proposed merger with Quebecair and Great Lakes Airlines collapsed in 1977, the chairman of Nordair put the airline up for sale, and the following year, in 1978, Air Canada acquired Nordair. Nordair operated as a separate corporate entity after its acquisition until Air Canada sold it in 1984 to Innocan Inc. Canadian Pacific purchased Innocan's shares in Nordair the following year, but the airline lingered on as a distinct carrier until June 1987.

Canadian Pacific's acquisition of Eastern Provincial and Nordair significantly altered the airline's position in the industry. When a commuter airline subsidiary of Nordair, Nordair Metro, purchased Quebecair, one of Canada's original five regional airlines, in 1986, Canadian Pacific stood poised as a considerably larger airline than it had a decade earlier. With deregulation imminent, Canadian Pacific had gathered its collection of airlines for the post-deregulation era, becoming in the process a substantially more formidable opponent against Air Canada. One merger remained to bring Canadian Pacific against Air Canada as an equal: the merger with an airline that had spent the past four decades growing steadily, Pacific Western Airlines.

Founded by a bush pilot and a mining executive, Pacific Western was incorporated as British Columbia Airways in 1945. The airline's initial growth was fueled by service to the B.C. Forest Service and by airlifting heavy equipment for the construction of the Alcan hydroelectric project at Kitimat, Alberta. Success with these two contracts enabled the fledgling airline to acquire several other operators: it purchased Kamloops Air Service in 1950, Skeena Air Transport in 1951, and Associated Air Taxi in 1953. The last acquisition gave the airline a scheduled flight from Kitimat to Vancouver and raised the size of its fleet to 16 aircraft. In the wake of these three acquisitions, the company changed its name from British Columbia Airways to Pacific Western Airlines Ltd. In 1957 Pacific Western began the transformation from a bush operator solely dependent on charter business into a regional carrier after taking over Canadian Pacific's Edmonton to Regina air route.

In its bid to become a larger player in the airline industry, Pacific Western also unsuccessfully applied to become a trans-Canada airline, the first of many failed applications the government denied, giving Pacific Western and Canadian Pacific mutually discouraging experiences in attempting to elevate their stature. Moving forward after its first application for transcontinental service was denied, Pacific Western launched a charter service to the Grand Cayman Islands and to the United Kingdom in 1964, then began to divest its light aircraft fleet. In 1970, however, the airline reversed its earlier strategy of shedding smaller air routes and aircraft when it acquired B.C. Airlines and its flights into British Columbia's interior. Trans-Canada charter service was initiated during the mid-1970s, roughly concurrent with the acquisition of Pacific Western by the Alberta government for $37 million. Government officials did not retain control for long, however, and began privatizing Pacific Western in 1983, reducing its stake in the airlines from 99.9 percent to 14.9 percent. Three years after the privatization process was begun, Pacific Western made a bold move when it acquired Canadian Pacific Airlines from its parent company, Canadian Pacific Group, for $300 million. The acquisition was completed through PWA Corp., the acronymic parent company of Pacific Western, giving the predecessor to Canadian Airlines Corporation 100 percent ownership of Pacific Western, 100 percent of Canadian Pacific Airlines (which by this time owned Eastern Provincial, Nordair, and Quebec), 20 percent ownership in Air Atlantic, 35 percent of Nordair Metro, and 46 percent of Time Air.

The original agreement between Pacific Western and Canadian Pacific stipulated that the two airlines would remain separate, but less than five months later, on April 26, 1987, the two companies merged, forming Canadian Airlines International, the primary operating subsidiary of PWA Corporation and a new prodigious force in the Canadian airline industry. Leading the new airline was Pacific Western's Rhys Eyton, who *The Globe and Mail* credited with transforming "a piddling little regional carrier into Canada's second-ranked national airline," an assessment that industry observers acknowledged, given the tremendous strides achieved in closing the gap separating Air Canada and the rest of the industry. With $2.2 billion in 1986 revenues and 56 percent of the domestic market share, Air Canada was closely trailed by the $1.6 billion in revenues and 39 percent market share now supporting newly created Canadian Airlines International. In the coming year the battle between the two airline giants would become bitterly fierce, almost to the point of ruin for both, but before Rhys Eyton and Canadian Airlines launched an attack against the industry's largest airline, it shored up its second-ranking position by taking on the airline industry's third-largest competitor, Edmonton-based Wardair.

During the years immediately preceding the merger between Pacific Western and Canadian Pacific, Wardair had been struggling to make a break into the airline industry's upper reaches, relying on charter flights and international air service for the bulk of its revenue. Domestically, the airline lagged far behind Air Canada and PWA's Canadian Airlines International, controlling only three percent of the market. Proving to be a money-loser during the contentious late 1980s, Wardair was acquired for $250 million by Canadian Airlines International in 1989, making the fight for industry dominance an exclusive struggle between Air Canada and Canadian Airlines International. After Wardair was merged into Canadian Airlines International, Air Canada and Canadian Airlines International controlled 98 percent of the domestic passenger market, each maintaining roughly equal shares of the Canadian market. Increasing their grip on the domestic air travel market, the two behemoths jointly owned the computer reservation system that nine of every ten travel agents in Canada used to obtain flight information and to print tickets.

A debilitative air fare war between the two airlines ensued, severely limiting the ability of either to record encouraging profits. Between 1990 and 1992, Canadian Airlines International and Air Canada lost more than $2 billion combined, pushing both, but particularly Canadian Airlines International, toward the brink of insolvency. Canadian Airlines International was also suffering from its acquisition of Wardair, the purchase of which inflated the airline's debt and, coupled with its ongoing price war with Air Canada, forced its director's to search for immediate relief. In early 1992, Air Canada began negotiating with PWA about either merging the two companies or buying Canadian Airline's international routes, but PWA walked away from the negotiations and began talks with American Airlines with the hope that the giant U.S. carrier could provide some financial help. During the summer months of 1992 a provisional arrangement was struck in which American Airlines agreed to provide PWA with its much needed capital in exchange for an equity position in the company. In order to conclude the deal, however, PWA needed to raise some cash, but with its capital reserves dwindling and its debt swollen beyond control the company was in no position to persuade banks for a loan. Discussions with the federal government followed, touching off a rancorous public squabble in which PWA officials accused the government of refusing to help unless negotiations with American Airlines ceased and merger talks with Air Canada were renewed. The government denied the accusation that federal officials were forcing PWA into a merger with the formerly government-owned Air Canada, insisting instead that a potential merger with Air Canada was broached as a suggestion.

Against the backdrop of the acrimony created from PWA's precarious financial position, a former vice president of the company, Sidney Fattedad, developed a plan to raise the cash required to conclude the deal with American Airlines without involving Ottawa. Fattedad proposed that PWA work out an agreement with its employees to forgo a percentage of their wages for three years, then use the agreement as a guarantee for a loan. The plan failed, however, and in September 1992, while Air Canada was losing $1.8 million per day and PWA was losing $800,000 per day, a merger between the two airlines was announced, albeit with decided reluctance on the part of PWA.

The confusion and turmoil that reigned during 1992, however, had not ended. In November Air Canada announced that the terms of its pre-merger agreement with PWA were "unachievable," bringing PWA to the bargaining table once again with American Airlines. By this point PWA's financial health was grave. All debt payments were halted by the end of November and the company appeared headed for bankruptcy. Salvation finally arrived at the end of December when American Airline's parent company, AMR Corporation, signed a conditional agreement with PWA that stipulated AMR would buy one-third of Canadian Airlines International for $246 million provided that Canadian Airlines International purchase all of its information services (ranging from accounting to flight planning) for the next 20 years. For roughly the next year PWA fought to be released from its contractual obligation to the computer reservation system the company owned in partnership with Air Canada. In April 1994, after two years of halting progress, AMR and PWA concluded the deal, injecting PWA with AMR's desperately needed cash.

By the end of 1994, PWA had begun to arrest a sharp slide in its annual net income, recording a loss of $38 million in 1994 after losing $292 million in 1993 and an enormous $543 million in 1992. The airline holding company clearly needed to achieve much more before it could boast of financial stability and positive, lasting growth. In 1995, PWA Corp. was renamed Canadian Airlines Corporation, the latest name change for an organization whose existence spanned the history of airline service in Canada.

Principal Subsidiaries:

Canadian Airlines International Ltd. (71.3%); Canadian Holidays; Transpacific Tours; Canadian Regional Airlines; Time Air Inc.; Ontario Express Ltd.; Inter-Canadian Inc.; Calm Air International Ltd. (45%).

Further Reading:

Blatherwick, John, *A History of Airlines in Canada,* Toronto: Unitrade Press, 1989.

Chisolm, Patricia, "The End of Ward's Dream," *Maclean's,* January 30, 1989, p. 34.

Daly, John, "Regaining Altitude: Fewer Airlines Are Now Charging Higher Fares in the Deregulated Skies over North America," *Maclean's,* November 6, 1989, p. 46.

Enchin, Harvey, "An Airline Merger Fails To Fly," *The Globe and Mail,* August 24, 1992, p. A1.

French, Carey, "The Sky's the Limit," *The Globe and Mail,* July 17, 1987, p. P16.

Johnson, Arthur, "Up in the Air," *Canadian Business,* November 1993, p. 45.

"PWA to Conclude Services Deal with American's Parent," *Travel Weekly,* April 25, 1994, p. 8.

Rowan, Geoffrey, "Airline Deal Signals a New Era," *The Globe and Mail,* April 26, 1994, p. B1.

Smith, Philip, *It Seems Like Only Yesterday,* Toronto: McClelland and Stewart, 1986.

Wickens, Barbara, "A Possible Recovery?," *Maclean's,* March 4, 1991, p. 45.

—Jeffrey L. Covell

Canadian Imperial Bank of Commerce

Commerce Court
Toronto, Ontario M5L 1A2
(416) 980-2211
Fax: (416) 980-8185

Public Company
Incorporated: 1961
Employees: 40,897
Total Assets: $151.03 billion
Stock Exchanges: Montreal Tokyo London Jamaica
   Barbados Trinidad
SICs: 6000 Depository Institutions; 6021 National
   Commercial Banks

The Canadian Imperial Bank of Commerce (CIBC) is Canada's second largest bank. The result of a 1961 merger between the Imperial Bank of Canada and the Canadian Bank of Commerce, CIBC is headquartered in Toronto and in 1994 operated about 1,500 branches in Canada and more than 100 overseas offices. The bank has grown by innovating to meet the needs of an increasingly complex international marketplace.

The older of CIBC's two predecessors, the Canadian Bank of Commerce, was founded in 1867, the same year as Confederation. While Canadian statesmen discussed the advantages of uniting the British North American Colonies under one parliament, a prominent Toronto businessman, William McMaster, was busy acquiring a bank charter from a group of financiers who had been unable to raise the necessary capital to put it to use. McMaster opened the Canadian Bank of Commerce on May 15, 1867, and under his leadership, the bank grew at a tremendous rate. The bank's paid-up capital swelled from $400,000 to $6 million in its first seven years, and it soon had offices in New York and Montreal as well as throughout Ontario. Canada was in the midst of rapid industrial growth at this time, and the Bank of Commerce was instrumental in financing a number of large capital projects. For its first 20 years, the bank's prosperity fluctuated with economic conditions, but in general it grew and was profitable.

In May of 1893 the bank joined the Canadian push westward by establishing a branch in Winnipeg. In 1898 branches were established in Dawson City, Yukon Territory; Vancouver, British Columbia; and Skagway,

Alaska. In 1900 the bank acquired the Bank of British Columbia, strengthening its position on the Pacific Coast. During the next ten years the Canadian Bank of Commerce acquired several other financial institutions; at the start of World War I, it had 379 branches.

During the 1920s the bank nearly doubled its branch network by acquiring the Bank of Hamilton and later the Standard Bank of Canada. The general prosperity of the 1920s was reflected in the bank's growth. At the time of the stock market crash in 1929, the Canadian Bank of Commerce's assets were $801 million. The Depression that followed, however, took a heavy toll on the bank, and its assets did not return to their pre-Depression high until 1940.

World War II finally brought economic recovery to Canada. The Canadian Bank of Commerce was active in the war effort, leading victory loan drives among other things. After the war, the bank grew steadily. By 1956, assets had reached $2.5 billion, and by 1960, they had passed $3 billion. Despite this success, however, the bank felt pressured by increasing competition and in 1961 agreed to a merger with the Imperial Bank of Canada.

The Imperial Bank of Canada was established in 1875. Its first president, Henry Stark Howland, had been the vice president of the Canadian Bank of Commerce. The bank's first office actually had no vault—overnight deposits were stored at another bank—yet in its first year of operation, the Imperial Bank made a profit of $103,637. Reluctant to open too many branches too soon, the Imperial Bank's growth was somewhat slower than that of the Bank of Commerce during the same period. By 1880, however, the Imperial Bank had frontier fever. That year it opened a branch in Winnipeg, and the next year it branched out to Brandon and Calgary. By 1900, the Imperial Bank had 32 branches spread across the continent. Between the turn of the century and World War I, Canada began to tap its mineral resources with amazing speed. The Imperial Bank of Canada earned the nickname the "Mining Bank" because of its ties to that industry.

After the World War I, the bank opened about 50 branches within just a few years, but not all of them survived the volatile economic conditions that followed the war. In the 1920s, deposits reached record levels, but the stock market crash in 1929 caused severe problems for the bank. Many of its loans went bad, and a number of branches were closed. The bank struggled to recuperate during the late 1930s and by the end of the decade it was making headway once again.

During World War II costs of operation rose faster than earnings, leading to lower dividends during the war years. About one-third of the Imperial Bank's 1,800 employees enlisted in the various services, and 53 died.

After the war, Canada entered a period of widespread prosperity and the Imperial Bank grew rapidly. In 1956, it acquired Barclays Bank (Canada) and increased assets by nearly $40 million; by 1961, the Imperial Bank had assets of more than $1 billion and 343 branches.

The amalgamation of the Canadian Bank of Commerce and the Imperial Bank of Canada in 1961 created the largest bank in Canada at the time. The new Canadian Imperial Bank of Commerce had at its helm L. S. Mackersy, of the Imperial Bank, as chairman and N. J. McKinnon, of the Bank of Commerce, as president and CEO. Altogether the new bank accounted for about one quarter of the assets of all Canadian banks combined.

In 1962 McKinnon became chairman of CIBC's board of directors and steered the bank's course from that position until 1972. The 1960s were a prosperous time for Canada, and the nation's economy grew strongly. The Canadian Imperial Bank of Commerce's net earnings increased substantially each year throughout the decade. The bank also strengthened its foreign operations. At the end of the decade, Canada relaxed some of its restrictions on the banking industry. Notably, interest rates on loans were no longer limited to six percent. In this liberalized banking climate, Canadian banks did very well. In 1969 CIBC added 46 new branches while expanding its work force by only five percent. By 1970, annual profits had risen to $43 million, more than twice what they had been at the time of amalgamation.

In the early 1970s, Canada began to invest heavily in energy development and agriculture, and the Canadian Imperial Bank of Commerce helped with the financing. Throughout the decade the bank had a close relationship with Canadian oil companies. That relationship would eventually cause the bank problems, but in the early 1970s, when oil prices were skyrocketing, investment in petroleum-related industries seemed like a gold mine.

In 1973, J. P. Wadsworth replaced McKinnon as chairman of CIBC, and remained in office until 1975. Late 1973 brought worldwide recession. Although Canadian domestic demand was adequate, overseas demand was low. This spelled trouble for Canada, whose economy was heavily dependent on exports. Nonetheless, CIBC continued to improve its earnings each year.

In 1976 Russell E. Harrison succeeded Wadsworth as chairman and CEO of CIBC. Harrison tended to run the bank in an autocratic manner. Top executives were not always given real power to make key decisions. In the late 1970s and early 1980s Canadian industry grew very quickly, and CIBC made large loans to many expanding firms. In 1980, however, this policy began to falter. Massey-Ferguson, the Canadian tractor manufacturer, was in danger of collapsing, and the Canadian Imperial Bank of Commerce was Massey's biggest lender. The Canadian government worked with Massey's creditors to try to bail the company out by allowing it to raise new capital, but it didn't work. Massey lost US$240 million in 1981, and US$413 million in 1982, leaving CIBC with a substantial amount of bad debt.

The Dome Petroleum Company was another of CIBC's large corporate debtors in deep trouble in the early 1980s. When oil prices dropped sharply in 1982, Dome lost more than $100 million; CIBC had loaned Dome more than $1 billion. The failing company was eventually bought by Amoco Canada, but again CIBC was left with a pile of bad debt. Between 1979 an 1984, CIBC had the lowest average return on assets of the five largest Canadian banks.

In May 1984 R. Donald Fullerton took over as CEO and set about restructuring the bank's operations. Fullerton eliminated branches to cut costs and service overlap and injected new blood into the bank's senior management. He also attacked the bank's bad debt, slowly eliminating bad loans from the bank's portfolio.

In 1985 a record number of farm failures caused mild concern among Canadian bankers. Canadian Imperial estimated that about 10 percent of its agricultural loans were in jeopardy. The problem was not nearly as severe in Canada as it was in the United States, however, where thousands of farmers defaulted on loans.

Under Fullerton's leadership, the bank bounced back from the troubles of the early 1980s to set a new earnings record in 1985. An aggressive new advertising campaign was launched in the United States as part of the bank's thrust internationally. In 1986 Fullerton announced that CIBC would split its operations into three separate units: the Individual Bank, the Corporate Bank, and the Investment Bank.

Each unit was to deal with a specific group of customers. The Individual Bank was CIBC's largest unit, employing three-quarters of the bank's workers to serve individuals and independent business people. The Corporate Bank was intended to provide standard financial services to a variety of Canadian and foreign companies. The Investment Bank was intended to take advantage of the upcoming liberalization of capital and other investment markets in Canada. It oversaw the operations of CIBC's brokerage firms and merchant banks overseas, and then domestically after June 1987, when Canada removed the regulations barring commercial banks from conducting investment banking activities. CIBC Securities Inc. was established in 1987 to offer stockbroker services. The bank also participated in a merchant bank, the Gordon Investment Corporation, with the Gordon Capital Corporation—each was an equal partner in the new bank. In Europe, CIBC operated CIBC Securities Europe Ltd. (formerly Grenfell and Colegrave Ltd.), and a stock brokerage for its overseas customers.

In 1987 Brazil announced that it would suspend interest payments on its foreign loans indefinitely. This action shocked the international banking community, which feared that other Third World countries would follow suit. In August 1987 the Canadian government issued a guideline that required banks to set aside a large sum to protect against possible losses on loans to Third World countries. CIBC set aside $451 million, resulting in a net loss of $63 million for 1987, though assets increased by almost $8 billion.

Worldwide deregulation, liberalization of financial markets, and information technology made banking more complex during the mid- and late-1980s. CIBC responded innovatively to a changing marketplace. The bank regained the lost ground of the early 1980s and made a greater effort to expand overseas than any other Canadian bank. But CIBC still held a significant portfolio of potential problem loans that it would have to correct if the bank was to thrive in the 1990s. To that end, CIBC management worked to improve its loan portfolio and to increase efficiency throughout its system during the late 1980s and early 1990s. It also shed employees in bloated divisions, while bolstering growing business segments.

Among the new business arenas targeted by CIBC were insurance and derivatives. CIBC's foray into insurance reflected ongoing bank-industry deregulation during the early and mid-1990s that was intended to give banks the opportunity to compete more effectively in evolving financial markets. CIBC was inundated with more than 50,000 inquiries when it began selling automobile insurance early in 1995. It subsequently began offering term-life insurance. The company's efforts related to derivatives were the result of its intent to become a major player in the burgeoning derivatives market. CIBC hired a top-notch staff to compete in the risky investment niche, and was enjoying positive results in 1995.

Largely as a result of new business ventures, CIBC boosted its asset base to more than $151 billion by 1995. Although sales remained relatively steady during the early 1990s, the bank posted a disappointing $108 million loss in 1992. Net income surged to $600 million in 1993, though, and then to a healthy $749 million in 1994. Furthermore, CIBC's loan portfolio was much more secure by 1995 than it had been only a few years earlier. In addition, the organization continued to branch out globally, as evidenced by its 1994 listing on the Jamaica, Barbados, and Trinidad stock exchanges. Improved asset quality, combined with the bank's ongoing efforts diversify globally and into new markets, suggested a bright future for CIBC.

Principal Subsidiaries:

Canadian Imperial Holdings Inc. (United States); CIBC Mortgage; CIBC Holdings Inc.; CIBC Asia Limited; CIBC Holdings Limited (United Kingdom).

Further Reading:

Blackwell, Richard. "CIBC Has Record Quarter as Loan Losses Drop," *Financial Post,* March 3, 1995, Section 1, p. 4.
_____. "CIBC Widens Insurance Effort," *Financial Post,* February 24, 1995, Section 1, p. 11.
Haliechuk, Rick. "CIBC Grooms Staff for Play in Derivatives," *Toronto Star,* January 20, 1995, p. E8.

—updated by Dave Mote

Canadian National Railway System

935 Rue De La Gauchetiere
Montreal, Quebec H3B 2M9
(514) 399-5430
Fax: (514) 399-8559

State-Owned Company
Incorporated: 1917 as Canadian National Railway
  Co.
Employees: 45,000
Sales: $4.06 billion
SICs: 4011 Railroads, Line-Haul Operating

Canadian National Railway System (CN) is the largest
transcontinental railway in Canada and ranks among the
world's biggest systems. It was formed just prior to the
1920s through the integration and nationalization of
two of the country's largest railroads, Canadian Northern and Grand Trunk. Although they were not the first
railroads to come under government control, these two
systems formed the basis of Canada's largest transportation conglomerate. After 78 years as a Crown corporation, CN was scheduled to be privatized through a late
1995 initial public offering of all its equity. Touted as
the largest privatization in Canadian history, the sale
was expected to raise between $1.6 billion and $2
billion, a large part of which would go into federal
coffers.

CN was created as a result of the near-collapse of the
Canadian Northern and Grand Trunk railways not long
after the end of the First World War. When a postwar
economic depression undermined the railroads' finances, the consolidation provided a way for the companies to avoid defaults on $1.3 billion in loans. It also
gave Canada the second largest railway system in the
world, with almost 100,000 employees and over 22,000
miles of track, nearly twice as much as its nearest
competitor.

Canada's railroads had enjoyed the support of government since the colonial era, when the Grand Trunk (GT)
emerged as the dominion's first major railway. Incorporated in 1852, GT soon dominated the railway boom
concentrated in central Canada between Montreal and
Toronto. Close government cooperation came in the
form of land grants, loans, and loan guarantees. The

railway's first president, John Ross, also held a high
government position.

Railroad and government officials, however, envisioned
disparate goals for GT—profits for its British shareholders on the one hand and settlement of the vast western
territories on the other. The public and private interests
in the railway clashed before the end of the decade. In
1858 British Columbia became a Crown colony and
western settlement became government policy. A transcontinental railway would bind the colonies together
and prevent American squatters from seizing the territory before Canadians had a chance, and as the Dominion's largest railway, the GT would naturally have been
the vehicle of choice for this western movement. Expensive construction projects, however, had drained finances to the point that the company could not make
interest payments on its loans, and shareholders—who
had yet to receive the dividends promised at the
company's inception—would not agree to what they saw
as a losing venture. Under pressure from both the
government and the company's investors, Ross and
most of his board of directors resigned in 1858. GT's
English shareholders sent Edward Watkin, a British
railway executive who represented England's preemi-
nence in the industry, as Ross's replacement.

Watkin and his managing director, Charles J. Brydges,
continued the traditional mix of public and private
support for the GT, but concentrated on financial
reorganization and capital improvements. By 1865 they
had built up traffic by 50 percent, increased net earnings, and made plans to replace iron rails with steel,
upgrade from wood fuel to coal, and standardize rail
gauges.

As did his predecessor, Watkin had a vision of a coast-
to-coast railway that would promote western settlement
and bring about confederation. Two factors stood in the
way: shareholders who wanted customers to be settled in
the west before they would build a railway to serve
them, and the Hudson's Bay Company, owner of the
territory between the eastern and western colonies. In
1863 Watkin engineered the takeover of the Hudson's
Bay Company by a London-based finance company,
bringing the possibility of a coast-to-coast railway even
closer. In 1869, however, Watkin was ousted by those
shareholders, led by Captain Henry W. Tyler, who
opposed investment in the intercolonial railway. The
Canadian government bought out the Hudson's Bay
Company, and Grand Trunk began an era of eastern
consolidation under Tyler.

During the 1880s, Tyler oversaw the absorption of 16
railways and expanded freight service to the United
States. His concentration on American markets was
rewarded—25 percent of the railway's earnings came
from meat and grain traffic between Chicago and New
England. In 1882 GT took over its largest competitor,
the Great Western, and in 1888 it assumed control of
Ontario's Northern Railway.

In the midst of all this consolidation, Prime Minister
John A. MacDonald, gave up his attempts to persuade
Tyler and the GT to build to the western coast. Instead
he contracted with a new system, the Canadian Pacific
Railway, to build a transcontinental railway from the
west. This would turn out to be a momentous decision—

privately-held Canadian Pacific Railway remained CN's largest rail competitor into the mid-1990s.

Tyler's 18-year reign at Grand Trunk was brought to an end by economic recession and, as with his predecessors, 20,000 fickle stockholders who blamed him for the loss of government support that, instead, sustained the Canadian Pacific during the "lean years." Tyler's successor, Sir Charles Rivers Wilson, hired Charles Melville Hays—an American with railroad experience—to manage the nearly 5,000 miles of Grand Trunk track. Hays brought American management techniques to the still British-owned GT, made such physical improvements as better brakes and improved grades, and rebuilt the suspension bridge over the Niagara River into the United States. All these changes improved service and, by the turn of the century, operating expenses had been reduced by 10 percent. Hays also satisfied English shareholders by enabling the company to finally pay out dividends on its shares. He quickly realized, though, that without service to the west, the Grand Trunk was just a "feeder line" for the western markets served by Canadian Pacific.

Formidable competition also came from the Canadian Northern railroad, owned by William Mackenzie and Donald Mann, partners in Mackenzie Mann & Co. Limited. The men, who met when both were working for Canadian Pacific, acquired their first railway in 1896, after they had decided to branch out on their own. Concentrating on the prairies to the north, Mackenzie and Mann built up the Canadian Northern by consolidating many small "farmer's railroads" into a system that offered transportation to 130 communities, with the motto "Energy, Enterprise, Ability." They built connecting lines with the help of provincial grants and controlled 1200 miles of track, serving Canada's bread basket by 1902.

By 1896 all of Canada was booming; Prime Minister Sir Wilfred Laurier heralded the arrival of "Canada's century." That year Grand Trunk's Charles M. Hays was finally able to announce the railroad's plan to open a line to the Pacific at the port of Prince Rupert. Grand Trunk Pacific (GTP), created as a subsidiary, was Hays's strategy for breaking out of the corner into which the railroad had been backed and ensuring Grand Trunk's future. He had tried to buy out the Canadian Northern, but Mackenzie and Mann hoped to build their own transcontinental railroad. In 1902, however, it was Mackenzie's turn to suggest that the two exchange traffic instead of building duplicate track, but by then Grand Trunk was too deep into GTP. The competition between Grand Trunk and Canadian Northern would prove to be the ruin of both systems.

The Grand Trunk Pacific line was completed in 1914, but it was an empty victory. The Panama Canal opened that same year, drawing a steady stream of traffic from Vancouver and making that city into a major port, while Prince Rupert languished. In addition, British ships no longer enjoyed the strong presence in the North Atlantic that they once did, further reducing traffic for Prince Rupert and GTP. The event that might have helped to keep Grand Trunk in private hands had it been undertaken 20 years earlier was now contributing to its failure.

By 1916 both Canadian Northern and Grand Trunk were on the brink of receivership. Overextension had stressed finances: Canada had over twice as many railway miles per capita as the United States, much of it duplicating service. A royal commission recommended nationalization of the two, including Grand Trunk's subsidiary, GTP. It took four years to bring the former competitors together—in addition to the National Transcontinental and the Intercolonial, two government lines—to form one of the country's first Crown corporations, the Canadian National Railways.

The amalgamation brought together over 90 different railways to form a system divided into four geographical regions: the Atlantic, with headquarters in Moncton; the Central, headquartered in Toronto; the Grand Trunk Western, a United States system with headquarters in Detroit, Michigan; and the Western region, headquartered in Winnipeg. Each region had its own general manager and superintendents. CN's officers were all drawn from the various systems, which helped to unify the previously rival railways.

The reorganization was directed by David B. Hanna, former vice president of the Canadian Northern. Despite the $1.3 billion debt assumed by the newly formed system, Hanna began a program to rehabilitate the railroad's physical property and bring it up to par with that of the Canadian Pacific. His task was made more difficult by a postwar industrial recession, a flu epidemic, and history-making bad weather, but the program was supported by Prime Minister Mackenzie King's Liberal government and the healthy economy of the 1920s. Hanna also began to focus on new markets for CN, especially Asia and Europe. The Canadian Government Merchant Marine, a shipping arm of the CN created in 1919, helped open Asian markets and increased the level of competition with Canadian Pacific, which was already well established in the Pacific basin.

By 1923 Grand Trunk had been officially assimilated into the Canadian National system and Sir Henry Thornton became president. Thornton continued to improve lines and equipment, reduce expenses, and improve service.

CN began to compete with Canadian Pacific for the Asia-to-New York silk trade in 1925. Competition between the two was fierce—every hour saved between the two coasts meant higher profits, because insurance on raw silk, a perishable commodity, ran as high as 6 percent per hour. The CN's "silkers"—those trains carrying the precious cargo—traveled at speeds up to 90 miles per hour and took precedence over all other trains, including express passenger lines. They averaged just four days to cross the continent. The largest CN silker ran in October of 1927. The 21-car train carried 7,200 bales of silk worth $7 million. The success of CN's Asian freight service was encouraging, but the worldwide depression that began in 1929 brought an end to that optimism.

Caught in the midst of trying to increase both the quality and quantity of services, the railway was shocked by the severity of the unexpected depression. In 1930 the support of the Liberal government was lost and by 1932 Thornton was forced to resign and business had been curtailed. By that time the system's earnings had fallen 40 percent below those in its peak year of 1928, and CN was carrying only half the traffic it had two years earlier. A smaller-than-normal grain crop and a drop in the Japanese silk trade worsened the effects of the Depression.

1932 was the low point of the Depression for Canadian National, with operating revenues decreasing a further 20 percent from those of the previous year. The Depression was not the only force moving against the CN: new modes of transportation were quickly being developed to compete with the outdated railway system. Passengers preferred the convenience of buses, cars, and airplanes; shippers preferred the lower-cost, specialized services of the trucking industry.

Trade picked up after 1932, when the British Empire employed such protectionist measures as quotas and increased customs duties on non-empire trade. Although business was generally improving by 1936, the Depression and decreased Asian trade brought about the demise of the Canadian Government Merchant Marine. A brief trade war with Japan was settled in 1935, and CN enjoyed good trade relations with that country until 1941, when the United States, Britain, and Canada froze all Japanese assets during World War II.

The years of World War II provided a boom in transportation that enabled Canadian National to make interest payments on all of its publicly held debt. At the close of the 1940s, however, the company's debts began rising, freight volumes were falling, and passenger service appeared doomed. Donald Gordon, a banker and chairman of the World War II War Prices and Trade Board, was selected as president of CN. Gordon invested in the conversion from steam to diesel and modernization of the aging railway's physical properties — three-fourths of the system's locomotives were over 30 years old. In 1952 the Canadian government gave Gordon the debt relief he needed. Recapitalization cut the system's interest charges by more than $22 million per year.

In addition to the financial difficulties facing CN, there were growing problems on the labor front. Technological advances made within the rail industry cut staffing requirements: automation of train control and clerical operations decreased the need for office staff, while diesel locomotives and higher capacity freightcars allowed carriers to operate longer and heavier trains and lengthened the distance between service stops, affecting train and repair personnel. While rail management worked to maximize productivity gains, rail labor unions fought to save their members' jobs.

Tensions between management and labor came to a head several times during the 1950s. A strike by 120,000 Canadian railway workers in August 1950 brought rail transport to a halt, shutting down traffic from coast to coast. A government injunction sent the strikers back to work within two days. Other strikes were threatened during the 1950s, but arbitration kept the trains running.

Gordon accomplished many goals during the 1950s and 1960s. These achievements included decentralized management, replacing old rolling stock with new specialized containers, adding road transport to CN's roster of services, introducing computerized processes, and improving employee training. In spite of these measures, the railroad was still commonly viewed as a tool for national development, rather than a profit-making venture. As technology continued to diminish the role of railways, Canadian government and CN officials allowed the system to become mired in deficits. Changing regulations, irregular funding, and other political machinations were often caused by party changes. These issues limited CN's ability to grow and diversify in an age when the company could not afford to be confined to rail transport.

In the late 1960s deregulation and revision of government support put CN on the road to stability and increased profits. The National Transportation Act of 1967 removed nearly all the constraints on rates that had bound both the CN and Canadian Pacific. The legislation also compensated railways for unprofitable passenger services and branch lines that had been deemed necessary for the public welfare. CN was able to end its unprofitable passenger service in Newfoundland in 1969 as a result of the new law.

During the 1970s, CN's management concentrated on increasing autonomy and profitability. The organization of profit centers improved managerial accountability and highlighted areas of government-enforced losses. CN also concentrated on diversification, spreading the company's interests into telecommunications, hotels, and oil exploration. This measure took pressure off the company's slowing railway business.

Much of the railway's success in the 1980s was credited to increased independence from government constraints. The 1983 Western Grain Transportation Act brought an end to the 84-year-old Crow's Nest Pass Act, which had fixed shipping rates at 1925 levels. Only 20 percent of the actual transportation costs had been covered, costing Canada's railways $300 million per year.

The legislative changes freed capital for investment in such technical improvements as double tracks that prevent bottlenecks, sped rail traffic, and improved the system's ability to compete with United States railroads. The late 1980s also saw CN enter the stack-car market. Having a stack of two freight containers required hefty investments in new lift equipment and higher tunnel clearances, but the increased capacity increased efficiency and helped CN compete for lucrative contracts to transport Asian auto parts.

In 1987, 46-year CN veteran Ronald Lawless was appointed president and CEO of the transport company. Over the course of his 5-year tenure, the executive oversaw a series of massive cutbacks, slashing employment from 100,000 to 40,000; eliminating over 40 percent of the railway's $3.4 billion debt, and divesting (per a 1988 government order) the corporation's hotel, telecommunications, and trucking operations.

Two major strikes in the late 1980s marred a decade-long record of good labor relations. The Associated Railway Union's 50,000 members walked out over wages, pensions, and job security in August of 1987. By the sixth day of the strike, government legislation that levied fines against workers who stayed off the job ended the stoppage. The legislation came in handy less than a week later, when 2,500 members of the Brotherhood of Locomotive Engineers threatened to strike. In an effort to head off labor disputes, CN established a forum for labor and management in 1991.

The early 1990s proved to be less financially stable for Canadian National than the previous decade. A recession reduced traffic that had already been siphoned off by competitors in the trucking and U.S. rail industries. Lingering regulatory constraints and high taxes further hampered the company's fiscal performance. To improve profitability, Canadian National's gas and oil subsidiary, CN Exploration, was privatized in 1991 and the proceeds from the sale were used to reduce the federal deficit. Early in 1992 the railway combined its United States subsidiary, the Grand Trunk Corp., with its Canadian rail interests, thereby creating CN North America. The reorganization was part of an effort to exploit continental markets, provide more efficient, cost-effective service to CN's shippers, and increase cross-border business, which stood at about 25 percent of annual sales.

But in spite of Lawless's various cutbacks and reorganizations, an internal study completed in 1990 showed that CN was still one of North America's least competitive railways. Revenues declined 22 percent from 1988 to 1992, when the company suffered a $893.7 million loss. When Lawless was called away to wield his budget axe at Via Rail in 1992, CN hired Paul Tellier as president and CEO. It didn't take the new executive long to assess the situation. In 1993, he warned that the company's annual losses would continue to surge, reaching $1.5 billion by 1998, unless drastic measures were taken. Although some questioned this career civil servant's knowledge of the rail industry, Tellier was able—by 1994—to effect CN's first profit since 1990. It wasn't an easy task.

Tellier first cut employment at all levels. To show fiscal leadership and decentralize management, he slashed administrative layers by half in some cases. By 1993, he had reduced overall payroll to 32,700 employees. Although these layoffs cost CN $80 million in 1993 alone—the company was obliged to buyout unionized workers' employment security contracts at an average of $80,000 each—they promised increased productivity in the years to come.

Tellier even initiated merger negotiations with long-time rival CP Rail in 1992. When those talks broke down, the two firms tried to work out a deal to combine their beleaguered eastern operations, which together had lost over $2 billion in recent years. More than one industry analyst had noted that overcapacity, especially east of Winnipeg, was a serious and ongoing threat to both players' profitability. A 1993 review by the National Transportation Act Review Commission asserted that "oversized rail networks" had plagued the industry in general since the 1920s; at CN in particular, 90 percent of its tonnage traversed only one-third of its total trackage. Nonetheless, late in 1994, Transport Minister Douglas Young put the brakes on CP Rail's $1.4 billion offer to purchase CN's eastern assets, noting that the purchase price undervalued the property by at least 50 percent and threatened to reduce competition as well.

After years of denying that CN was being groomed for a launch on the public markets, legislation to that very effect was introduced in May 1995. The bill proposing Canadian National's privatization restricted individual shareownership to 15 percent and called for the creation of an employee stock option plan. In light of Quebec's flirtations with succession, the legislation also required the company to maintain its headquarters in Montreal and remain bilingual. Unlike previous initial public offerings of nationalized businesses, this one did not restrict shareownership to Canadians. The sheer size of the offering, at least $1.6 billion, was expected to overwhelm the Canadian stock market. The federal government anticipated an estimated $1 billion return on the sale.

Early in 1995, however, CN still required some "primping" before it was ready to go to market. Analysts estimated that it would need to shed about $1 billion of its $2.5 billion debt to raise its debt rating and make its massive stock floatation attractive to domestic and international investors. The government offered to pay market prices of $400 million to $600 million for CN's real estate holdings, which included the CN Tower in Toronto and 85,000 acres of property. The firm also planned to sell its remaining non-rail businesses before the privatization and use the proceeds to bring down debt.

Principal Subsidiaries:

AMF Technotransport Inc.; Autoport Ltd.; Canac International Inc.; Canac International Ltd. (United States); The Canada and Gulf Terminal Railway Company; Canadian National Express Company; The Canadian National Railways Securities Trust; Canadian National Steamship Company, Limited; Canadian National Telegraph Company; Canadian National Transfer Company Limited; Canadian National Transportation, Limited; The Canadian Northern Quebec Railway Company (60%); Canat Limited (United States); Central Vermont Railway, Inc. (United States); Chapman Transport Limited; CN Exploration Inc.; C.N. (France) S.A.; CNM Inc.; CN Tower Limited; CN Transactions Inc.; Domestic Three Leasing Corp. (United States); Domestic Four Leasing Corp. (United States); Duluth, Winnipeg and Pacific Railway Company (United States); EID Electronic Identification Systems Ltd.; Empire Freightways Limited; Grand Trunk Corporation (United States); Grand Trunk Technologies, Inc. (United States); Grand Trunk Western Railroad, Incorporated (United States); GT Finance Company (United States); The Great North Western Telegraph Company of Canada (95%); The Minnesota and Manitoba Railroad Company (United States); The Minnesota and Ontario Bridge Company (United States); Mount Royal Tunnel and Terminal Company, Limited; M.O.Q. Express Inc.; M.O.Q. Rail Inc.; The Northern Consolidated Holding Company Limited (73%); 173335 Canada Inc.; The Quebec and Lake St. John Railway Company (89%); Royal Transportation Limited; St. Clair Tunnel Company (United States); St. Clair Tunnel Construction Company (United States).

Further Reading:

Bonney, Joseph, "CN + Grand Trunk = CN North America," *American Shipper,* February 1992.

Freeman, Alan, "CN Shares May Fetch $1.5 billion," *Globe and Mail,* 6 May 1995, A1.

Johnson, Bruce, "How CN Competes With U.S. Stack Trains," *American Shipper,* June 1988.

————, "Trans-Canada Double Track Nears Completion," *American Shipper,* September 1988.

————, "CN Joins Double-Stack Parade," *American Shipper,* February 1989.

MacKay, Donald, *The Asian Dream: The Pacific Rim and Canada's National Railway,* Vancouver: Douglas & McIntyre, 1986.

McKenna, Barrie, "Ottawa Big Winner in CN Sale," *Globe and Mail,* 31 May 1995, B1.

Rowan, Geoffrey, "CN Productivity Right Off the Tracks," *Globe and Mail,* 9 October 1991, B1.

Weaver, Kent R., *The Politics of Industrial Change: Railway Policy in North America,* Washington, D.C.: The Brookings Institution, 1985.

—April Dougal Gasbarre

CANADIAN PACIFIC LIMITED

Canadian Pacific Limited

910 Pearl Street
Montreal, Quebec H3C 3EA
(514) 395-5151
Fax: (514) 395-7959

Public Company
Incorporated: 1881 as Canadian Pacific Railway
  Company
Employees: 39,300
Sales: $6.58 billion
Stock Exchanges: Montreal Toronto New York
SICs: 1311 Crude Petroleum and Natural Gas; 2900
  Petroleum & Coal Products; 4010 Railroads; 5170
  Petroleum & Petroleum Products; 6531 Real
  Estate Agents and Managers

Canadian Pacific Limited (CP) operates the seventh largest railway system in North America, providing rail and intermodal freight transportation services that reach more than 150 million people. Through its various subsidiaries, CP is also engaged in oil and gas production, coal mining, real estate, container shipping services, hazardous waste management, and telecommunications. CP was battered by the economic downturn of the early 1990s. The company restructured and returned to profitability in the mid-1990s.

The building of the Canadian Pacific Railway was a demanding battle, both physically and politically. After negative reports from both explorers and surveyors, a long and sometimes bitter parliamentary dispute, and threats of refusal by British Columbia to become part of the Canadian Dominion, a contract to build the rail line was finally approved by royal assent on February 15, 1881. The following day, the Canadian Pacific Railway Company was incorporated. A group of railroad professionals, known as The Syndicate, who had come to Canada from Scotland as fur traders, headed up the railroad's first management team. The Syndicate chose George Stephen, a former president of the Bank of Montreal and one of the principals involved in the organization of the St. Paul, Minneapolis and Manitoba Railway as CP's first president. Stephen was assisted by CP vice president Duncan McIntyre, who left his post as president of the Canada Central Railway to help build the country's first and only transcontinental railroad.

Under the terms of the government contract, CP received $25 million in investor-subscribed funds and 25 million acres of timberland, which eventually included the land's subsurface resources. These important assets provided the basis for the company to raise more capital. Several stock issues were floated, and large loans were made to further finance the project. In 1882 the company issued $30 million worth of CP stock to various New York investment syndicates, followed by the sale of 200,000 shares of common stock the following year. To complete the project, CP floated a $15 million bond issue through a London-based investment house. Although the company's contract allowed CP ten years to complete the railroad's construction, the project took less than half that time. Construction of the main line was completed in 1885. At the time the Canadian Pacific Railway was the longest and costliest railroad line ever built.

The completion of the line had many effects on both the company and the Canadian economy. The subsurface resources acquired in the land deal with the Canadian Parliament put the company into the coal, zinc, lead, gold, silver, and—later—gas businesses. The railway opened the prairies for settlement, and CP was involved in agricultural development, including irrigation and wheat farming. A rail connection from the more industrialized eastern regions to the Pacific Coast enabled the company to expand into the export shipping business and opened up many opportunities in the Far East. It was also believed that the railway's consolidating effect on the Canadian provinces stifled further northern expansion by the United States. The company, then known to most Canadians as the CPR, continued its steady growth well into the mid-1900s.

The company in its early years added to its already rich natural resource holdings. In 1898 it acquired British Columbia Smelting and Refining Company, and in 1906 merged this and other properties into The Consolidated Mining and Smelting Company of Canada Limited, later known as Cominco Limited. In 1905 CP purchased the Esquimalt and Namaimo Railway and 1.5 million acres of timber on Vancouver Island.

As early as 1920 CP began using all-steel railroad cars. In many instances these units weighed nearly 60 tons, which limited the number of cars that could be pulled by a steam-powered locomotive. The Great Depression and then World War II slowed the introduction of diesel-powered engines to the railroad industry. By 1954, however, CP completed the conversion of its locomotives to diesel-power. Because of the ruggedness of much of the terrain over which CP operates, the company uses some of the largest diesel-powered trains in the world. Capable of hauling 10,000 tons of cargo, these trains are powered by as many as 11 diesel engines.

Throughout its first 75 years in business, CP's explosive growth resulted in poor record-keeping, and only in 1956 did the company institute a comprehensive inventory of its assets. The inventory took seven years. It quickly became apparent that CP's vast holdings warranted further exploitation and development. CP formed a wholly owned subsidiary, Canadian Pacific Oil and Gas Limited, in 1958 to develop and explore its mineral rights on more than 11 million acres of company-held western Canada land. With the completion of the CP's forest and real estate surveys, two more subsidiaries were formed. Marathon Realty Company Limited was incorporated to manage and develop the company's vast, nationwide real estate holdings. Pacific Logging Company Limited was to be responsible for reforestation and the development of tree farming on CP's timberlands.

As the survey of company holdings reached completion, it became clear that the development of the CP's nonrailroad assets needed to be centralized under a separate holding company. CP formed Canadian Pacific Investments Limited in 1962 to administer the development of CP's natural resources and real estate holdings and to operate as an investment holding company. In 1971 the parent company adopted the name Canadian Pacific Limited.

During most of CP's first 80 years, the company was owned by foreign interests, primarily English, French, and U.S. The transition to a majority of Canadian ownership began after the end of World War II and was completed in 1965. In that year, Ian Sinclair, CP's chairman, assumed control of the company's burgeoning enterprises. Sinclair brought to bear his influence and power to finally reverse the flow of foreign investment into the company.

In November 1967 the company offered to the public $100 million in convertible preferred shares of CP stock. At the time, it was the largest single stock issue in Canadian history and provided an opportunity for Canadians to share more directly in the resource development of their country. In 1980 Canadian Pacific Investments Limited changed its name to Canadian Pacific Enterprises Limited (CP Enterprises).

Sinclair took the company into the hotel business in the United States and to locations as distant as Jerusalem. An airline catering business in Mexico City was purchased and Canadian Pacific Airlines Limited (CP Air), which for a time was Canada's second-largest airline, was formed. Sinclair's railroading focused on the transportation of goods and raw materials rather than people. At the close of Sinclair's tenure in 1981, CP's railroad inventory comprised 69,000 freight cars, 1,300 locomotives, 3,600 maintenance and equipment cars, and only 57 passenger cars.

Sinclair was succeeded by Frederic Burbidge in 1981. Burbidge acquired leadership of a company that was about to have the worst decade in its history. A worldwide recession coupled with extremely poor crop years in the early 1980s in both Canada and the midwestern United States resulted in thousands of empty Canadian Pacific and Soo Line boxcars. Many of CP's nonrailroad businesses were highly cyclical. CP's subsidiary PanCanadian Petroleum Limited, one of Canada's largest gas and oil companies, helped compensate for the rail operations' poor performance for a time, but with the collapse of oil prices in 1986, the company was faced with profound difficulties.

William Stinson replaced Burbidge as CP's chairman in 1985. Stinson, who had been with the company for 30 years, starting with CP as a management trainee in 1955, was the youngest chairman in the company's

history. He set out to streamline the company's operations.

Stinson oversaw the sale of CP's 52 percent interest in Cominco Limited, which had become one of the world's largest zinc producers. By selling off what had been a money-loser since 1981, Stinson raised $472 million and removed an expensive liability. On the heels of the Cominco sell-off, the company divested itself of CP Air in a $300 million deal with Pacific Western Airlines. CP Air had not shown any profits since 1980; the sale also eliminated nearly $600 million in long-term debt. On December 6, 1985, with the consent of both companies' stockholders, CP and CP Enterprises merged into one company. Under the terms of the merger, CP Enterprises became a wholly owned subsidiary of CP.

After the sale of Cominco and CP Air, Stinson worked to turn around three of CP's other subsidiaries: AMCA International Limited, a producer of structural steel, the Soo Line, and Algoma Steel Corporation, an Ontario-based steel manufacturer. Stinson's plan was to focus CP in four major core businesses: freight transportation, natural resources, real estate, and manufacturing. Stinson's cutbacks, sales, and restructuring had a positive effect, and the company showed a profit of a little more than $58 million in 1987. One project that Stinson did not attempt to curtail was the construction of the longest railway tunnel in North America. The Macdonald Tunnel, located in British Columbia's Selkirk Mountains and more than nine miles in length, was completed in 1988.

The years 1988 and 1989 showed little improvement for CP's financial outlook. The Canadian economy was in a weakened condition. The company's forest products division reported a net operating loss of more than $190 million in 1989 because of the depressed market for paper products. Marathon Realty showed a net operating loss that same year of more than $17 million. The company's rail division held its own in 1989, however, and CP's waste services enterprises had a record-breaking year.

As CP entered the 1990s, the company's restructuring efforts suffered a major setback in a ruling by the Supreme Court of Ontario. Under the court's decision, CP was prohibited from spinning off Marathon Realty as a separate public company. CP had planned to distribute 80 percent of the shares of Marathon Realty to its common stock holders while retaining a 20 percent interest itself. The court ruled that the transaction would penalize CP's preferred stock holders. At the same time, it appeared that CP's performance would be further hindered by the lingering weakness in the company's forest products division.

The company's rail business increased in 1990, largely because of a resurgence in grain shipments. That year CP acquired the 44 percent of Soo Line that it did not already own. CP officials expected the transaction to make possible greater integration of the rail systems. Early in 1991 CP bought another rail company, the Delaware and Hudson Railway, operating in the northeastern United States. CP also added to its hotel operations in 1990 with the purchase of an 80 percent interest in the U.S.-based Doubletree/Compri hotel management group.

CP suffered during the economic downturn of the early 1990s. After posting a net income of $744 million in 1989 and $354 million in 1990, the company began to lose money. Part of the problem was a decline in rail traffic. But that lull was augmented by weak prices for oil and gas and a major slump in real estate markets, among other problems. Furthermore, the CP organization was relatively bloated and inefficient, despite recent attempts to boost productivity. CP executives responded to mounting losses by intensifying efforts to reorganize and increase efficiency. To that end, CP jettisoned several poorly performing operations, including several lackluster rail lines. At the same time, it beefed up its investments in its more successful divisions, particularly its shipping group.

Despite gains in its shipping division and a few other segments, CP suffered losses totaling more than $1.5 million between 1991 and 1993, which was partly the result of restructuring write-offs and accounting changes. By 1994, though, restructuring initiatives were beginning to bear fruit. Indeed, CP had slashed its work force from more than 75,000 in the late 1980s to less than 40,000 by 1994, reflecting a significant liquidation of assets. Meanwhile, company sales plunged from more than $10 billion in 1990 to roughly $6.5 billion in 1993. Finally, in 1994, CP returned to profitability with a net income of nearly $400 million.

By 1995, CP had reorganized all of its operations into eight different companies. Transportation-related businesses, including rail and container-shipping operations, accounted for about 57 of total company revenues. Energy related businesses, which included oil, gas, and coal segments, made up about 29 percent. Finally, hotel and real estate businesses accounted for 14 percent of CP's sales. Despite setbacks in the early 1990s, CP's long-term prospects were considerably brighter going into the mid-1990s. Rapidly improving productivity and recovering markets boded well for the company's future as it entered its 116 year in business.

Principal Subsidiaries:

CP Rail System; CP Ships (Bermuda); PanCanadian Petroleum Limited; Fording Coal; Marathon Realty; Canadian Pacific Hotels & Resorts Inc.; Laidlaw Inc. (19 percent); Unitel Communications Holdings Inc.(48 percent).

Further Reading:

Berton, Pierre, *The Last Spike: The Great Railway, 1881-1885,* New York: Penguin Books, 1989.
Eliot, Jane, *The History of the Western Railroads,* New York: Bison Books, 1985.
Hallman, Mark. "CP Surges Back to $393M Profit from $191 M Loss," *Financial Post,* February 7, 1995, Section 1, p. 9.
Hallman, Mark. "New CP Executives Face Difficult Times as Strike Looms," *Financial Post,* February 14, 1995, Section 1, p. 3.
Hallman, Mark. "CP President Calls it Quits," *Financial Post,* December 14, 1994, Section 1, p. 3.
Ryans, Leo, "CP Undergoing Major Restructuring," *The Journal of Commerce,* February 27, 1987.

—William R. Grossman
—updated by Dave Mote

Canadian Tire Corporation, Ltd.

2180 Yonge St.
PO Box 770, Station K
Toronto, Ontario M4P 2V8
(416)480-3000
Fax: (416)484-8872

Public Company
Incorporated: 1922 as Hamilton Tire and Rubber
 Limited
Employees: 27,000 *Sales:* $3.6 billion in 1994
Stock Exchanges: Montreal Toronto
SICs: 5300 General Merchandise Stores

Canadian Tire Corp., Ltd., was the leading retailer of
hard goods in Canada in 1995. The company sold
automotive parts through its network of over 400 retail
stores, through which it also marketed various sporting
and leisure products. Canadian tire also provided finance and credit services, and sold gasoline and petroleum products through a chain of about 200 outlets. An
estimated 80 percent of the Canadian population lived
within a 15-minute drive or walk of one of the company's outlets.

Canada Tire was started in 1922 by brothers John W.
and Alfred Jackson (A. J.) Billes. The budding entrepreneurs invested their combined savings of $1,800 in
an automobile service garage and auto parts depot in
Toronto. The company—Hamilton Tire and Rubber
Limited—stocked a small inventory of repair and
replacement goods, including tires, batteries, and automobile fluids. Although the automobile industry was
still in its infancy, the Billeses believed surging automobile sales at the time indicated a bright future for their
business. Later that year, in fact, Toronto hosted its first
"Closed Car Show," in which windshield wipers, automatic starters, and other new car parts were introduced.

The Billeses experienced what could have turned out to
be a major setback shortly after they opened their shop:
A bridge that routed traffic past their garage was shut
down for repairs. To overcome the problem, the brothers converted the garage into an overnight parking
facility and took turns sleeping in the garage at night.
Then, early in 1923, they moved the entire operation to
a better location. The new shop included retail goods
and a gas pump. The success of that outlet encouraged
the Billeses to open a second retail store nearby. Early

gains were largely attributable to A. J.'s marketing
savvy. He began offering free road maps in the company's promotional flyers, for example, because maps were
rare at the time and valued by customers.

After four years of rising sales, the Billeses changed the
name of their enterprise to Canadian Tire Corporation,
Limited, in 1927. That same year, A. J., building off of
his successful road map idea, decided to test a mail-
order offer to car owners in southern Ontario and New
York state. Response to that effort, in turn, lead him to
publish a full catalog in 1928 that featured Canadian
Tire's retail offerings and allowed customers to order by
mail. Thus, the company became a pioneer in the mail-
order and catalog auto-parts retailing industry. Indeed,
Canadian Tire's mail-order sales swelled in the late
1920s and early 1930s. Even during the Great Depression the company continued to post gains as a result of
its low prices, high-quality merchandise, and an emphasis on customer service. Importantly, shrewd marketing
always played a role.

Throughout the 1930s and into the 1960s, in fact,
Canadian Tire was a leading innovator in its industry.
Among A. J.'s most brilliant marketing schemes was
Canadian Tire "money," an innovation he concocted in
the 1950s. A. J. knew a lot of money could be made from
the sale of gasoline from his store pumps. Because of
pressure from the big oil companies, however, retailers
like A. J. were unable to lower their prices to undercut
competitors. A. J. got around that hurdle by giving his
gas customers coupons that they could use for merchandise in his stores. The scheme was a major success and
continues to be used in Canadian Tire stores. Another of
A. J.'s innovations was clerks on rollerskates. When A. J.
expanded one of his stores into a vacant supermarket he
became concerned that the longer aisles would slow
down his clerks. Besides speeding up the clerks, the
rollerskates served as an entertainment gimmick that
drew customers.

Among other firsts, Canadian Tire introduced the
unconditional tire guarantee in 1931. Until that time,
tires were guaranteed only against manufacturing defects. A. J. decided to begin offering an unconditional
"Super-Lastic" tire guarantee that would cover the tire
for almost any mishap. "In those days the guarantee on
tires was only for defects and workmanship," A. J.
recalled in company annals, "but customers would come
in with a shard of glass or a stone bruise, saying well, I
didn't do that. So I introduced the first one-year
unconditional tire guarantee. People came in looking for
a fight, and there wasn't one." Canadian Tire also
helped pioneer the profit-sharing concept, whereby
giving workers a stake in the profits of the business
generated employee motivation and loyalty.

Canadian Tire expanded in the 1930s as business grew.
In 1934 the company opened an associate store in
Hamilton, Ontario. That store was the first in what
would become a huge chain of stores that spanned
Canada. Although Canadian Tire automotive lines were
already stocked in other stores, the new outlets gave the
company higher profit margins and more control over
its products. As the chain expanded, Canadian Tire's
stores and mail order catalogs began featuring a wide
range of parts and supplies—many under the Canadian

Tire brand name—including motor and chassis parts, radio equipment, and hundreds of miscellaneous accessories. In addition, Canadian Tire was beginning to branch out into sporting goods like camping equipment. Gains at the new store spawned a flurry of expansion during the mid- and late 1930s. By 1939, in fact, Canadian Tire was operating an impressive 71 stores in addition to its thriving mail-order business.

World War II caused shortages of many goods, and Canadian Tire was forced to change many of its operating procedures. Nevertheless, the company managed to adapt and even to sustain its healthy growth rate throughout the war years. By 1946, in fact, Canadian Tire had boosted its total number of outlets to 116. As a result of spiraling demand during the postwar economic boom, moreover, sales soared. Canadian Tire built a giant new warehouse that was averaging 57 tons of new inventory daily by 1952. By 1956 even that facility had become too small to serve the company's 160-plus outlets, so Canadian Tire built a large new distribution center. Before the center was opened, president John W. Billes passed away. His brother, A. J., succeeded him.

Canadian Tire continued to prosper under A. J.'s ten-year stint as president. Warehouse and distribution centers were expanded, and the company's network of retail outlets increased to a total of 225 by the mid-1960s. A. J., always open to new ideas, was among the first retailers to use new electronic equipment and computers to handle accounting, inventory, and invoicing tasks. Canadian Tire flourished under his leadership, becoming one of the most successful retailers in Canada. Later, looking back on his career and life, A. J. would give much of the credit for the company's success to his employees: "If asked what has been my life's most rewarding experience, it is good health, strength, and a destiny which afforded me the opportunity to assist our corporate people in recognizing and more fully exploiting their God-given talents, both for their own betterment and for that of others around them, and while in the process, building a business wherein the spirit of enlightened self-interest continues."

A. J. stepped aside in 1966; J. Dean Muncaster succeeded him. Muncaster had started out working in a Canadian Tire store before working his way through the executive ranks. Under Muncaster's direction Canadian Tire continued to expand. The company began its own long-distance hauling operation in 1967, which would balloon in size to include more than 700 transport units by the 1990s. A second major distribution facility was built in 1973 to feed the growing Canadian Tire retail chain. In 1979, moreover, the company completed a giant 65-million-cubic-feet, computer-controlled, high-rise warehouse and distribution center that was among the largest of its kind in the world. That facility helped to support the company's new Auto Parts Depot division. The Auto Parts Depot, on the cutting edge of just-in-time techniques that would emerge in the 1980s, provided speedy daytime and overnight delivery of auto parts to Canadian Tire outlets.

During the late 1970s Canadian Tire upgraded its existing stores and expanded into British Columbia with a new store format. Then, in 1982, Canadian Tire reached outside its national borders when it purchased the assets of White Stores, Inc., of Wichita, Texas, for $144 million. White Stores was a chain of more than 400 automotive retail stores in the United States. Most of the stores were owned and operated by dealers, but some of the outlets were company owned, and Canadian Tire also took possession of the company's warehouse operations. Canadian Tire attempted to convert the stores into a format similar to that utilized by its Canadian stores. Unfortunately, the venture flopped and Canadian Tire elected in 1985 to sell the entire division. Shortly thereafter, Muncaster resigned. He was replaced in 1986 by Dean Groussman, the former chief executive of White Stores.

By the mid-1990s Canadian Tire was generating more than $2 billion in annual sales and operating nearly 400 stores throughout Canada (not including the U.S. White Stores division). In addition, the company was operating about 115 gas stations. Besides increasing the number of stores in its portfolio during the 1970s and early 1980s, Canadian tire had introduced a variety of new merchandise. The company had started selling a large amount of sporting and leisure items, as well as hardware, lawn and garden items, inexpensive furniture and other home products, and even luggage. In essence, Canadian Tire was becoming a general-merchandise discount store with an emphasis on automotive products.

Under Groussman's leadership, Canadian Tire continued to expand its store network and distribution facilities. Between 1986 and 1990, in fact, Canadian Tire added about 75 gas stations and 17 retail stores to its group, pushing sales past the $3 billion mark for the first time in 1990. Meanwhile, net earnings gradually rose to nearly $150 million annually in both 1989 and 1990—Canadian Tire was ranked as the 42nd most profitable company in Canada in 1990—and the company's work force swelled to nearly 25,000. Encouraged by healthy gains at home, Canadian Tire management decided once again to take a crack at the massive U.S. market. In 1991 the company announced its intent to enter the Indianapolis, Indiana, market with four new stores under the name Auto Source Inc.

Canadian Tire had started its Auto Source experiment in 1990, when it opened two stores under the banner Car Care USA. Those stores, which mimicked the successful Pep Boys centers, incorporated 14 service bays and about 18,000 square feet of space for inventory. In 1991, it decided to change the names of those stores and began construction on two new stores. The design of the new outlets was influenced by the growing trend toward superstores. Thus, the new Auto Source outlets boasted a whopping 30,000 feet of retail space and 24 service bays. Auto Source planned to open between 100 and 150 addition outlets in the United States by the turn of the century that would bring in $1 billion in sales.

During the early 1990s Canadian Tire opened six more Auto Source outlets, for a total of ten, that were soon generating more than $60 million in annual revenues. Like the company's first attempt in the U.S. market, however, Auto Source proved unprofitable. The venture lost $15.3 million in 1992 alone. Company officials explained that the loss was not unexpected considering that it was a new enterprise. In 1993, however, the division's losses increased. Part of the problem was that Auto Source was attempting a start-up in the midst of a U.S. economic downturn. But losses, according to critics, also stemmed from the fact that the company's U.S. support infrastructure was too great for the 10-store chain. Furthermore, the auto parts industry was facing increasing competition from discount stores like Wal-Mart, as well as new entrants into the burgeoning automotive discount superstore industry.

In fact, Canadian Tire's domestic operations were also suffering from increased competition, particularly from invading mega-discounters like Wal-Mart and Kmart. Indeed, by the early 1990s Canadian Tire was generating only about one-third of its revenues from automotive-related sales. The other revenue was generated from general merchandise. Canadian Tire was Canada's largest hardware retailer, for example, and a leading supplier of sporting goods. Profits from those items were increasingly being pinched by competition from discount warehouse rivals. Partly as a result of that dynamic, Canadian Tire's financial performance deteriorated in the early 1990s. Although the company's revenues grew to $3.2 billion in 1992 and then to $3.6 billion by 1994, its net income plunged to less than $100 million annually in 1992 and 1993.

Groussman left Canadian Tire in 1992 and was replaced by Stephen E. Bachand. Under Bachand's leadership, the company began implementing a strategy to help it compete in the new retail environment. That meant eliminating certain inventory items like furniture and luggage from some stores and focusing on the company's traditional core products: automotive accessories, hardware, and sporting goods. The big superstores that were popping up across Canada carried all of those items and often had larger selections. But Canadian Tire benefited from intense market penetration—and was also known for its high-quality products. Importantly, Canadian Tire launched an aggressive renewal program that called for the enlargement of 240 of its 243 stores by 1998.

Canadian Tire's net earnings plummeted to just $5.5 million in 1994, partly as a result of weak gasoline markets that were slowing down the company's gas station division. Early in 1995, moreover, the company

decided to shutter its Auto Source chain in the United States and completely bail out of that market. However, early results from the company's store expansion program were positive and management expected to realize substantial gains as it enlarged existing stores. Going into 1995, Canadian Tire was operating 423 Canadian Tire Store retail outlets and about 200 gasoline stations.

On April 3, 1995, company founder Alfred Jackson Billes passed away at the age of 93. His professional accomplishments included being invested in 1976 as a Member of the Order of Canada, the highest recognition a civilian Canadian could achieve. He was also inducted into the Canadian Hardware/Houseware Hall of Fame in 1986.

Principal Subsidiaries:

Canadian Tire Retail; Canadian Tire Acceptance; Canadian Tire Petroleum.

Further Reading:

"Auto Source Loses Money But Gains Experience," *Automotive Marketing,* May 1994, p. 20.
Brown, Ian, "Trouble in Tireland," *Canadian Business,* November 1989, pp. 95-109.
Deverell, John, "Canadian Tire Remake 'Encouraging' Sales Up 60 Percent in Revamped Stores, Shareholders Told," *Toronto Star,* May 6, 1995, p. E7.
Parent, Tawn, "A New Kind of Auto Store: Canadian Retailer to Open First U.S. Locations Here This Summer," *Indianapolis Business Journal,* p. 9A.
————, "Not Just an Automotive Chain: Canada's Largest Specialty Wholesaler Opens U.S. Headquarters Near Castleton," *Indianapolis Business Journal,* May 28, 1990, p. 1A.
Shalom, Francois, "Is 'the Tire' Going Flat? Tough Competition Is Forcing Canadian Tire Back to Its Strengths," *Gazette,* September 19, 1994, p. C8.
Total Customer Value: A Special Edition in Memory of A. J. Billes 1902-1995, Toronto: Canadian Tire Corporation, Limited, 1995.
Wirebach, John, "Canadian Tire Closes U.S. Subsidiary," *Automotive Marketing,* February 1995, p. 6.

—Dave Mote

Canadian Utilities Limited

10035-105 Street
Edmonton, Alberta T5J 2V6
(403) 420-7400
Fax: (403) 420-7400

Public Company
Incorporated: 1911 as the Canadian Western Natural
  Gas, Light, Heat, and Power Company Limited
Employees: 4,795
Sales: $3 billion
Stock Exchanges: Montreal Toronto
SICs: 4900 Electric, Gas & Sanitary Services; 1300
  Oil & Gas Extraction; 3600 Electronic & Other
  Electrical Equipment

Canadian Utilities Limited supplies gas and electricity
to a broad base of customers in the province of Alberta,
through its subsidiaries Northwestern Utilities Limited,
Canadian Western Natural Gas Company Limited, and
Alberta Power Limited. In addition, the company
provides electricity to some of the country's far northern
lands and also conducts other activities related to its
core utilities operations. The company was founded in
the early days of Canada's natural gas industry and has
continued to grow in tandem with the area that it serves.

The earliest enterprise of the Canadian Utilities group
was Canadian Western Natural Gas Company, Ltd.,
which was founded in the early 1900s by geological
engineer Eugene Coste. According to company historian
Len Stahl, Coste had become known as "the father of
the natural gas industry in Canada, having ... brought
in the first commercial discovery of natural gas in
Ontario in 1889." While employed by the Canadian
Pacific Railway (CPR) in 1909, Coste discovered a large
natural gas reserve on a bank of the South Saskatchewan
River in southern Alberta. He acquired rights to this
field, dubbed Bow Island field, from the CPR and then
went to England to raise capital, selling $4.5 million
worth of stock slated for building a pipeline from the
Bow Island site to the cities of Calgary and Lethbridge.

On July 19, 1911, Coste incorporated his company
under the name Canadian Western Natural Gas, Light,
Heat, and Power Company. In addition to planning the
construction of the Bow Island pipeline, the company
acquired two established Calgary franchises: a coal gas
plant consisting of 30 miles of pipe serving 2,200

customers and a pipeline serving about 50 customers,
including the Calgary Brewing & Malting Company. On
April 12, 1912, the company began construction of its
170 mile Bow Island pipeline. Eighty-six days later, the
completed pipeline was the third-largest gas pipeline in
North America and the most northerly gas transmission
line in the world.

Although the public initially greeted the transition from
coal to gas fuel with some skepticism, residents of
Lethbridge began using Canadian Western gas for
lighting purposes by the fall of 1912, and thereafter the
demand for gas increased dramatically. Soon the nearby
towns of Nanton, Okotoks, and Brooks were linked to
the system, and in 1913 Fort Macleod, Granum, and
Claresholm also gained the option of gas lighting. Over
the year, Canadian Western gained a client base of
3,400, whom it served from 20 wells yielding gas in the
Bow Island field. By 1914 Canadian Western's revenues
topped $1 million.

Although the years immediately following its establishment presented some challenges for the company,
Canadian Western continued to gain customers. The
company suffered a temporary setback in 1915, when
torrential rainfall wiped out its main pipeline to Calgary. The city was without gas service for two days while
the company's repair crew worked to get supplies and
repair the break in the face of severe weather conditions
that had washed out railroad tracks and bridges. This
time also marked the beginning of a legal dispute
between the company and the city of Calgary, whose
officials maintained that the company's franchise did
not cover the entire city of Calgary. Canadian Western
prevailed in 1917, when the Supreme Court of Alberta
ruled that it did have the right to provide gas to all parts
of the city.

By 1920, supplies of gas in Canadian Western's Bow
Island field had begun to wane. Because of the shortage
of gas, the company was forced to limit its service to
some industrial customers, in order to supply residential
sites. Operators at regulator stations in the city commu-
nicated by phone in order to move supplies of gas
around quickly and maintain high pressure in the lines.
As a result of these measures, Canadian Western's
revenues dropped by 10 percent.

To alleviate this shortage, Canadian Western began an
effort to develop new supplies of gas. The company
expanded its gas supply beyond Bow Island in 1921,
when it opened the Chin Coulee well 40 miles east of
Lethbridge. To cover the costs of this expansion, the
company requested its first rate increase from its
customers. This increase was grudgingly granted by the
city, on the conditions that the company also construct a
second ten-inch gas line from a site in the Turner Valley,
as well as begin a drilling program at two other sites.

Two years later, in 1923, another gas company, called
Northwestern Utilities Limited, was established in Edmonton. This company was a successor to a corporation
formed in 1914 to develop the resources of the Viking
Field, a deposit of natural gas in northern Alberta.
During the summer and fall of 1923, a pipeline was
constructed from the Viking Field to Edmonton under
tense conditions, as the company raced to beat the
winter freeze.

During this time, a controlling interest in Northwestern Utilities was held by the International Utilities Corporation, a company based in the United States, which financed, engineered, and managed a variety of public utilities. In 1925, this company also began to buy up shares in Alberta's Canadian Western, and the two utilities became sister companies, linked by ownership and shared expertise in management.

In the late 1920s, other non-gas utilities companies were established in Canada, which would later become linked to Northwestern and Canadian Western: the electric company known as Northern Power and Light, Ltd., was established in Indian Head, Saskatchewan; Mid-West Utilities, Limited, which, in turn, owned the Vegreville Utilities, Ltd., operator of a coal-fired, hand-fed steam engine and two generating units that supplied power to 380 customers; and plants in Hanna, Stettler, Lloydminster, Grande Prairie, and Raymond. During this time, Mid-West Utilities changed its name to Canadian Utilities, Limited, hoping to avoid confusion with another American utility company of the same name.

Northwestern suffered a major setback in January 1928, when shifting ice in a farmer's ditch broke the Viking pipeline, cutting off gas to Edmonton in -20 degree weather. Although gas was restored as quickly as possible, this event, and other concerns, prompted the company to begin an effort to duplicate this pipeline, increasing its capacity. Other safety measures were installed as well.

At the same time, Canadian Utilities was working to set up an electrical grid system in the areas where it served customers. The company purchased additional power plants in key locations, and then ran transmission lines between them. In this way, new communities were brought into the system, and antiquated equipment was gradually retired. In 1930, the network of Canadian Utilities companies was purchased by the Dominion Gas and Electric Company, a subsidiary of the American Commonwealths Power Corporation.

With the advent of the Great Depression in 1929, Northwestern found that demand for its products dropped significantly, as many industrial customers went out of business and residential customers were forced to resume use of coal. Northwestern Utilities also faced a spectacular misfortune in 1932, when the leak of a Northwestern gas main in downtown Edmonton caused the destruction of a leading hotel in the city and several surrounding structures. The fire broke out in the basement of the Corona Hotel on a February evening, and firemen fought it throughout the night before they were able to bring it under control. The resulting lawsuits from this event threatened to put Northwestern into bankruptcy. In an effort to ensure that no such conflagration ever took place again, the company instituted a program of odorization of its gas for safety purposes. In 1934, Northwestern was handed a legal defeat in cases resulting from the hotel fire. This blow came on top of the generally bleak economic picture in Alberta at that time.

Northwestern's sister company, Canadian Western, fared better during the 1930s, adding customers in new communities and new features to its gas distribution system. One innovation involved the storing of excess gas resulting from oil extraction at Turner Valley, gas that had previously been burned off as a waste product. P.D. Mellon, Canadian Western's vice-president, worked with geologists on his idea for storing the gas via pipes at the Bow Island site. The resulting piping system was reversible and could therefore accept gas for storage in the summer and make it available again during peak winter months.

In the mid-1930s, the electric utility company, Canadian Utilities, was merged with the Union Power company in an effort to stem the tide of losses that Canadian Utilities had suffered every year since 1928. Canadian Utilities was thereafter able to benefit from the proceeds of Union Power's coal holdings.

With Canada becoming embroiled in World World II, many employees of the gas and electric utilities of Alberta left their jobs to join the armed forces, and materials and supplies were also diverted to the war effort. In 1940, Northwestern installed heating, cooking, and water heating equipment at two air training schools being constructed in the area. Canadian Western also began serving air force training centers.

The war time economy provided opportunities for some utilities and challenges for others. For example, Canadian Utilities was able to expand into the far northern territories of Canada, via the newly constructed Alaska Highway, and began supplying electric power to the booming town of Fort St. John, British Columbia. And while Canadian Western was reporting record sales, Northwestern's efforts to meet increasing demand for gas were thwarted by the rationing of steel, which was needed to lay additional pipe.

In 1944, the Dominion Gas and Electric Company merged with the International Utilities Company, the old American partner of the Alberta companies. In doing so, International Utilities provided additional capital to the Canadian operations. The company used a portion of these funds to push forward with efforts at rural electrification. Test lines were run out to Vegreville in February 1945 and to Melfort, Saskatchewan. Moreover, International began investing in Northwestern and Canadian Utilities.

After the war's end in 1945, the utility companies resumed their normal operations and rate of growth. Alberta saw the formation of another new gas and electric company, Northland Utilities, Limited, which served customers in the Peace River area. Moreover, Canadian Utilities' operations were soon focused solely in Alberta, when the Saskatchewan Power Commission began buying up all the smaller utilities with a vision of nationalizing the industry in that province. A similar trend soon took Canadian Utilities out of British Columbia as well.

In 1947, Alberta's demand for gas began increasing rapidly due to a population boom and an accident at an oil well. Canada's oil boom began in February of that year with the discovery of oil near the town of Leduc, Alberta, and increasing numbers of people began moving to the area to share in the wealth. One year later, another well at this site, the Atlantic No. 3, went out of control, spilling oil onto the countryside for six months before igniting in September, and finally being subdued.

Northwestern was soon struggling to meet the demand for gas.

In 1954 the first step to uniting Alberta's gas and electric companies was taken, when one man, F. Austin Brownie, president of Northwestern and Canadian Western, was also appointed head of Canadian Utilities. Under Brownie, Canadian Utilities began expanding its Alberta holdings, purchasing the McMurray Light and Power Company, Limited, and Slave Lake Utilities.

In 1961, International Utilities, the corporate owner of the three linked Alberta companies, also purchased Northland Utilities, Limited, and merged this company into the group. At that time, due to changes in the Canadian tax structure, International Utilities also established itself as a United States corporation resident in Canada, hoping to blunt criticism of foreign ownership of the Alberta properties.

Later in the 1960s, International Utilities nearly doubled in size through the purchase of the General Waterworks Corporation. This move helped to pave the way for a major restructuring of the companies in the early 1970s, when Canadian Utilities became the corporate parent of Canadian Western, Northwestern, Northland, and Alberta Power, Limited, which was formed to take over the electrical operations previously run by Canadian Utilities. Northland was then merged into Northwestern. The resulting company, known as CU, became one of the largest investor-owned utilities in Canada. At this time, International Utilities also returned to residence in the United States.

In the early 1970s, a unified CU began to devote more of its attention to conservation and environmental awareness. In addition, the company began to branch out to other areas related to the utilities industry. In 1973, CU Engineering Limited was formed to provide consulting services; in 1975, CU Ethane Limited was formed to build and operate an ethane extraction plant in Edmonton as a joint venture; and, in 1976, CU Resources Limited was created to develop non-utility resource properties. One of CU's missions during the 1970s was to respond to environmental issues. Canadians were becoming increasingly aware of the need to conserve energy, and also sought to enact laws for keeping their air and waters clean and protecting wildlife. Toward that end, the company formed an environmental planning commission, headed by Gordon R. Cameron, which worked to ensure that CU was respecting the environment by modernizing facilities to emit fewer pollutants. Moreover, the company investigated such novel ideas as using natural gas to power automobiles.

At the start of the 1980s, majority ownership of CU was transferred from International Utilities to ATCO, Limited, a Canadian-based conglomerate that had started as a vendor of trailer homes in 1946. In the spring of 1980, ATCO paid $325 million for International's 58 percent share in the company, and installed its chairman as the chief executive officer of CU. In the wake of this purchase, the Calgary Power company (which then changed its name to the TransAlta Utilities Corporation) offered to buy up the 42 percent of CU's shares that ATCO did not own. This offer led to a standoff between CU and TransAlta, with legal entanglements that reached all the way to the Canadian Supreme Court. In 1982, the two companies agreed to withdraw from the dispute and gradually dispose of each other's shares.

In the early 1980s, CU also suffered from the effects of a recession that hit Alberta. The company attempted to reduce operating costs and also applied for a rate increase to offset the financial downturn. In the spring of 1982, CU also restructured its subsidiaries, creating ATCOR Resources, Limited. This group was formed from the ATCO Gas & Oil operations and the non-utility branches of CU. Shortly after this merger, CU discontinued the engineering consulting branch, after demand for these services dropped.

In the mid-1980s, ATCOR became increasingly involved in frontier exploration. In 1986, the division was reorganized again, taking the name CU Enterprises, Inc.. This entity specialized in oil and gas exploration and production, and the processing and marketing of natural gas. By 1987, it had become the largest direct marketer of natural gas to final users in Canada.

By the late 1980s, CU served more than 600,000 natural gas customers and 150,000 electric customers. The company continued to turn a profit, despite a sharp drop in growth for its main area of operation, Alberta. These earnings continued throughout the early 1990s. By the end of 1994, CU was servicing nearly 900,000 utility customers. Under the leadership of R. D. Southern, chairman and CEO, and J.D. Wood, president and CEO, the company also became involved in some new complementary operations, including the acquisition from ATCO of Frontec, a leading Canadian contractor of technical services with over $3 billion in assets and facilities. CU was also pursuing acquisitions of independent power plants in western Europe, Australia, and the United States.

Principal Subsidiaries:

Alberta Power Ltd.; Canadian Western Natural Gas Company Ltd.; Northwestern Utilities Ltd.; ATCOR Resources Ltd.; Northland Utilities Enterprises Ltd.; CU Power International Ltd.; CU Water Limited; CU Gas Limited.

Further Reading:

Atkinson, Pat, "Ten Top Shops: Canadian Utilities Automates Computer Operations," *Canadian Datasystems,* Spetember 1990, pp. 40, 42.
Sherman, Kevin, "Local-Area Networks: The Canadian Utilities Experience," *Computing Canada,* March 16, 1989, p. 40.
Stahl, Len, *A Record of Service: The History of Western Canada's Pioneer Gas and Electric Utilities,* Edmonton: Canadian Utilities Limited, 1987.

—Elizabeth Rourke

Cascades Inc.

404 Marie-Victorin
Kingsey Falls, Quebec J0A 1B0
(819) 363-5100
Fax: (819) 363-5155

Public Company
Incorporated: 1964
Employees: 7,244
Sales: $1.72 billion
Stock Exchanges: Toronto Montreal
SICs: 0800 Forestry; 2611 Pulp Mills; 2621 Paper
  Mills; 2657 Folding Paperboard Boxes

A leading manufacturer of specialty papers with diversified interests, Cascades Inc. is based in Kingsey-Falls, Quebec, a one-company town where Cascades employs nearly all of the community's residents. The company's various subsidiaries, joint ventures, and divisions are divided into six industrial groups: Boxboard, Fine Papers, Containerboard, Hygiene Products, Packaging Products, and Other Sectors & Services. With manufacturing plants in Canada, the United States, and Europe, Cascades emerged as a world leader in the pulp and paper industry during the 1980s, ranking in 1995 as the leading recycler of paper in Canada, the largest Canadian producer of de-inked pulp, both the largest Canadian manufacturer of boxboard and the world's tenth largest, and the third largest supplier of molded pulp products in North America.

Cascades grew from a fledgling upstart into one of the giant Canadian pulp and paper companies over the course of three decades; it rose through the industry's ranks through a series of joint ventures, the benefit of government grants, and an acquisitive aggressiveness that quickly enlarged the company. The three Lemaire brothers, Laurent, Alain, and Bernard, guided the company in its race to a stalwart market position, but much of the credit for Cascades' formative years was given to the eldest brother, Bernard, the driving force behind the company's formation in the small town of Kingsey-Falls.

At age 26, Bernard Lemaire was an engineering school dropout entertaining the prospect of launching his own business when he approached his father, who operated a waste paper collection business in Drummondville, Quebec, to help him fulfill his entrepreneurial desire.

The year was 1964 and Lemaire was eyeing an old kraft paper mill in Kingsey-Falls that had been closed for the past seven years. His father agreed to help, co-signing a $500,000 loan for the purchase price of the plant, and Bernard Lemaire began superintending the manufacture of paper, jumping headfirst into a business he knew little about.

Despite his inexperience, Lemaire hoped two important factors would make his fledgling enterprise a success. First, Lemaire hired many of the same employees who previously had worked at the kraft paper plant, enlisting a production staff that claimed upwards of 40 years experience in producing kraft paper, which was used in brown shopping bags. Second, he intended to take advantage of the complementary role his father's business could play by turning his collected waste paper into recycled fibre and using it as the main component to manufacture paper. However, these two factors did not remotely assure success.

From the outset customers complained about the quality of Cascades' paper, reportedly informing Lemaire that even if it was free they could not use it. In the first instance of Lemaire's participatory approach to management that later would earn the esteem of industry pundits, Lemaire talked with his workers, searching for a solution to his company's quality problems. Lemaire's employees informed him that they had always manufactured paper that way, prompting Lemaire to later confide in an interview with *The Globe and Mail*, "I began to understand why the plant was closed."

Finding no answers from his seasoned crew of production employees, Lemaire took it upon himself to discover a solution. He bought three books on paper-making and studied them assiduously, teaching himself the various techniques involved in paper-making and reportedly spending some nights sleeping beside Cascades' paper machines. When he emerged from his pulp and paper brown study, Lemaire made a switch to the manufacture of corrugated medium, a lower-quality paper used in boxes, and started anew.

Three years later Cascades recorded its first profit, generating slightly less than $100,000, and Lemaire could end his day and night vigil beside his company's manufacturing equipment. With the profit gleaned from his success, Lemaire purchased a new pulp molding machine, thereby making his first diversification from paper-making into packaging and building materials, and began his resolute rise within the pulp and paper industry.

Once pointed in the right direction, Cascades demonstrated encouraging growth, flourishing by virtue of a series of joint ventures that bolstered the company's foundation and carried it into new business arenas. In 1972 Cascades entered into a joint venture with the comparatively enormous Johns-Manville Corporation to manufacturer asbestos-based paper at Kingsey-Falls, 20 miles away from an asbestos mine. Two years later, Cascades joined with Rexfor, a provincially owned forest agency, and La Societe de Developpement du Quebec, a provincial government agency established to encourage enterprise, to open a corrugated paper mill. Alliances with much larger organizations such as these propelled Cascades' growth, lifting the company from anonymity to recognition as an up-and-comer.

Later in the decade, Cascades formed a plastics division to manufacture egg foam trays and began producing construction and insulating papers. Broadening its manufacturing scope further still, the company acquired a Victoriaville-based box manufacturer, giving it a diversified business base with which to enter the 1980s. By the end of the decade, Cascades' financial statistics told the tale of the company's vigorous growth. Sales, which were below $1 million in 1970, had risen to $9.4 million by 1977, then leaped to $20.6 million by 1980. Profits recorded a similar exponential increase, climbing to more than $500,000 by 1977, then nearly tripled in a two-year span, swelling to $1.4 million in 1979. Although Cascades' record of achievement during the 1970s was remarkable considering the inexperience of the Lemaire brothers and their troubled start during the company's early years, the 1970s would be overshadowed by the enormous growth achieved in the next decade. For Cascades, the 1970s represented merely a prelude to prodigious growth during the 1980s.

During the 1980s, Cascades would continue to expand through joint ventures and by rescuing failing properties, but the Lemaire brothers also greatly accelerated the company's growth by assuming an aggressive acquisitive posture, purchasing healthy, profit-generating companies. Diversification was also an integral contributor to the company's progress during the 1980s. The company got an early start in the decade, forming a packaging materials subsidiary in 1980 and establishing a company to make polyethylene sheeting in a joint venture with Induspac in 1981. Shortly thereafter Cascades took over a de-inking plant in Breakeyville and a manufacturer of insulation panels and roofing board in Louiseville. Then, in the space of a six months, Cascades doubled its size, acquiring the East Angus mill from Domtar Inc. in September 1983 and in March 1984 a paper mill in Jonquiere from Abitibi-Price Inc., the world's largest newsprint exporter. In 1983, Cascades became involved in its first venture outside of Quebec when the company built a towel and tissue mill in Rockingham, North Carolina, through a joint venture with Wyatt & Co. Ltd., a U.S. sanitary supplies giant.

After this burst of growth through acquisitions and alliances with much larger companies, Cascades made its biggest acquisition to date in 1985 when the company purchased the largest boxboard mill in France. By this point, in the mid-1980s, Cascades had become more than strictly a pulp and paper company. Its two other divisions, packaging and building materials, were also significant contributors to the company's sales volume, which was recording substantial gains. In 1983 the company generated $62 million in sales, a total that nearly tripled the following year to $180 million, then surged to $266 million by 1985.

Despite this remarkable sales growth, Cascades was dwarfed by the pulp and paper industry's five dominant companies, MacMillan Bloedel Ltd., Domtar Inc., Abitibi-Price Inc., Consolidated Bathurst Inc., and CIP Inc., each of which generated more than $1 billion in annual sales. Accordingly, Cascades continued to be regarded as an upstart company, a company that was making great

strides to be sure, but nevertheless ranked as a minor player in the pulp and paper industry. Lucien Rolland, chairman and controlling shareholder of century-old Rolland Inc., a Montreal-based fine-paper producer, held this view when Bernard Lemaire approached him in early 1986 about acquiring Rolland's company. Rolland refused, offering instead some of the company's assets, but Lemaire, dissuaded by an unprofitable coating operation that was included in the deal, balked at the proposal.

Undaunted, Lemaire proposed again in the fall of 1986 to buy all of Rolland's shares, which Rolland again declined to do. Lemaire then offered variations on the offer, all of which met with Rolland's now familiar refrain of refusal. In December, having achieved nothing through diplomacy, Lemaire telephoned Rolland to say he felt obliged to make a public takeover bid, controlling by this point 30 percent of Rolland Inc.'s shares. The Lemaires made a tender offer in 1987, but Rolland refused to sell his block of shares and orchestrated an active opposition to any offers by the Lemaire brothers, vowing never to sell the company to the rising triumvirate from Kingsey-Falls.

After the failure of their tender offer in 1987, the Lemaire brothers rallied forward, continuing to acquire assets, such as the carton-making operations of Djupafors AB, a unit of Munkedals AB of Sweden. By the late 1980s, however, the size of Cascades was becoming the company's biggest potential problem. No longer a minor upstart, Cascades had earned the label "mini-multinational" from the business press and had begun to inherit some of the problems that riddled large corporations. The company's failure to acquire Rolland tarnished its image, as did the unsuccessful conclusion to a joint venture with Groupe Pinault SA of France. Cascades had entered into a deal with Groupe Pinault first to manage, then acquire, Chapelle Darblay SA, France's leading newsprint producer, but Cascades was forced out of the deal in 1988 after investing considerable time managing the joint venture and gaining no assets in return. Exacerbating matters, a leakage problem at the company's carton plant in Jonquiere and labor difficulties at its kraft paper plant in East Angus seemed to signal the growing pains of a formerly entrepreneurial enterprise confronted with its own success.

Despite pessimistic prognostications by industry observers, Cascades' robust revenue growth continued through the late 1980s, reaching $818 million by 1990. A nationwide economic recession rang in the new decade, severely affecting the Canadian pulp and paper industry and dealing a repercussive blow to Cascades. Sales slipped in 1991, falling slightly to $806 million. However, the year's loss would be followed by Cascades' most daring acquisitions to that point, engendering a considerably stronger company for the 1990s and beyond. Although the pulp and paper industry was still mired in an economic slump in 1992, Cascades acquired Paperboard Industries Inc., owner and operator of 17 plants in Canada and in the United States. The addition of Paperboard Industries' plants to Cascades' 44 plants made the Lemaire-controlled company the largest boxboard maker in Canada and one of the largest in the world. The addition of the Paperboard Industries' $530 million in sales vaulted Cascades' annual revenue past the $1 billion plateau, helping the company jump from $950 million in sales in 1992 to $1.67 billion in 1993.

Perhaps the most satisfying acquisition for the Lemaire brothers, however, was the purchase, after six years of trying, of Rolland Inc. Forced into selling his shares because of the harsh economic conditions of the early 1990s, Lucien Rolland finally submitted to pressures put forth by the Lemaire brothers. Despite a last-minute attempt by minority shareholders to halt the takeover, Cascades acquired the Montreal-based fine paper producer, ending the long, sometimes rancorous, relationship between the two companies.

Cascades also acquired two corrugated container plants in 1992 from Canadian Forest Products Ltd., which, along with the acquisition of Paperboard Industries and Rolland Inc., saddled Cascades with substantial debt. Long-term debt more than doubled during 1992, rising to $660 million. After nearly 30 years in business, the rapid rise in debt was cause for concern, but the benefits were, perhaps, worth the expense, giving Cascades its two greatest contributors to annual revenue as the company entered the mid-1990s.

In 1994, with sales reaching $1.72 billion, Cascades' boxboard segment, Cascades Paperboard International Inc., contributed more than $700 million in sales, while its fine papers segment, headed by Rolland Inc., contributed roughly $400 million in sales. Long-term debt, meanwhile, had been whittled down to $476 million, alleviating some of the concern that the company would be hamstrung as it entered the late 1990s.

Principal Subsidiaries:

Cascades Cartech Inc.; Paperboard Industries Corporation; Cascades S.A.; Rolland Inc.; Papier Cascades Cabano Inc.; Cascades Niagara Falls, Inc.; Emballages Cascades VCT Inc.; Emballages Cascades Drummondville Inc.; Emballages Cascades P.A.T. Inc.; Emballages Cascades Vaudreull Inc.; Newfoundland Containers Ltd.; Industries Cascades Inc.; Cascades Industries, Inc.; Cascades P.S.H. Inc.; Cascades H.B.A., Inc.; Cascades Dismed Inc.; Cascades Dismed Ontario Inc.; Cascades Forma-Pak Inc.; Cascades

Dominion Inc.; Cascades Agri-Pak, Inc.; Cascades Diamond, Inc.; Cascades Moulded Pulp, Inc.; Plastiques Cascades Inc.; Plastichanges International Inc.; Cascades Sealed Air Inc. (50%); Cascades Re-Plast Inc.; Techno-Caoutchouc Inc. (50%); Wheel Care Retreading Inc. (50%); Cascades Conversion Inc. (50%); Cascades Multi-Pro Inc.; Cascades Sonoco, Inc. (50%); Converdis Inc. (50%); Nu-Tec, Inc. (50%); Cascades Enviropac Inc.; Cascades East Angus Inc.; Materuaux Cascades Inc.; Cascades Lupel Inc.; Bedard Lupel Inc.; Bedard Cascades Inc. (50%); Cogeneration Kingsey Regd., General Partnership (50%); Forces Motrices St.-Francois Inc. (50%); Forces Motrices Montmorency Inc. (50%); Forces Motrices Buckingham Inc. (50%); Hydrea Inc. (50%); Recuperation Cascades Inc.; Recyclage Cascades Quebec Inc.; Desencrage C.M.D. Inc. (50%); Cascades Etcan Inc. (50%)

Further Reading:

Clifford, Edward, "Cascades, a Different Kind of Forest Company," *The Globe and Mail,* September 12, 1991, p. B9.
Enchin, Harvey, "Cascades' Meteoric Rise Forces Changes," *The Globe and Mail,* December 26, 1988, p. B1.
————, "Cascades President Undaunted in Quest for Rolland," *The Globe and Mail,* January 14, 1987, p. B14.
————, "Can the Lemaires Stay Lucky?," *The Globe and Mail,* September 27, 1985, p. P80.
Gibbon, Ann, "Cascades Gets Bigger Loblaw Contract," *The Globe and Mail,* May 12, 1994, p. B6.
McKenna, Barrie, "Cascades Wins Bid to Take Over Rolland," *The Globe and Mail,* October 22, 1992, p. B1.
————, "Cascades Buys Half Share in U.S. Firm," *The Globe and Mail,* May 9, 1992, p. B1.
Neil, Boyd, "Paper Princes," *Canadian Business,* August 1984, p. 62.
Noble, Kimberley, "Cascades Squeezed Out of French Newsprint Firm," *The Globe and Mail,* July 6, 1988, p. B6.

—Jeffrey L. Covell

Cineplex Odeon Corporation

1303 Yonge Street
Toronto, Ontario M4T 2Y9
(416) 323-6600
Fax: (416) 323-6677

Public Company
Incorporated: 1977 as Cineplex Corporation
Employees: 9,000
Sales: US$539.37 million
Stock Exchanges: Toronto New York
SICs: 7822 Motion Picture and Video Tape
  Distribution

Cineplex Odeon Corporation, with headquarters in Toronto, is one of the largest motion picture theater circuits in North America. The company operates high-quality theaters in most metropolitan areas in the United States and all of the primary urban markets in Canada. In 1995, Cineplex had 1,631 screens in 357 locations in North America. In addition, Cineplex Odeon Films is the largest independent film distributor in Canada.

Cineplex Odeon commenced operations in 1979 when Garth Drabinsky, an energetic young Toronto entertainment lawyer, persuaded Nathan A. Taylor, a veteran of the motion picture exhibition business, to provide $1 million to purchase space in the basement of Toronto's Eaton Centre shopping complex. Drabinsky had first impressed Taylor several years earlier when, as a law student, he had asked the theater circuit manager to invest in a free film magazine he was distributing. Taylor refused, but he offered Drabinsky a position as editor of his own film industry paper *Canadian Film Digest,* a job Drabinsky accepted. Although Taylor had pioneered the idea of multitheater locations as early as 1948, the new site, with 18 screening rooms, was much more ambitious than anything he had previously built. In order to distinguish the Eaton Centre location, Taylor coined the name Cineplex, an abbreviation of "cinema complex," and the company was born.

From the beginning, Drabinsky was the driving force behind Cineplex's development into the second-largest theater chain in North America. He adopted a two-pronged approach that involved both the restoration of dignified old theaters and the introduction of small theaters in such locations as shopping malls. This combination of luxury and variety changed the movie-going experience and halted the decline in movie attendance that had become pronounced in the 1970s.

Nevertheless, the operation had modest beginnings. When the Eaton Centre multiplex first opened its doors, major distribution circuits controlled access to most of the expensive first-run films. Small, independent distributors, such as Cineplex, were left with less popular first-runs and second-run films that had already been playing for some time. Cineplex was also committed to showing foreign-language and independent art films with a small but loyal audience. For this reason, competitors failed to take the operation seriously at first; the consensus in the industry was that Drabinsky and Taylor would be lucky to last six months.

Cineplex confounded the experts by earning $50,000 a week during its first three years of operation. During this period, the multiplex gradually began to attract the attention of outside investors who wanted to duplicate the formula in other locations. However, in spite of its impressive performance, Cineplex was encumbered with substantial loans from the Toronto Dominion Bank and the Claridge Corporation, a Montreal development company headed by Charles Bronfman. In 1982, attendance at the Cineplex theaters dropped dramatically, and creditors threatened to call in their high-interest loans. In a bold move to avoid bankruptcy, Drabinsky flew to Montreal and persuaded The Bronfman Group to buy a large stake in the company. Cineplex went public on the Toronto Stock Exchange in October 1982 and began trading on the New York Stock Exchange in 1987.

Meanwhile, Drabinsky was tackling the problem of first-run distribution malpractice in a typically forthright way. He went to the Combines Investigation Branch, a Canadian federal investigative body, with documents proving that such competitors as Canadian Odeon Theatres and Famous Players had enjoyed preferential distribution agreements with the major United States film companies for several decades. The Canadian government threatened to take the exhibitors and the film companies to court, but a settlement was reached allowing Cineplex and other small chains to bid for first-run films on an individual basis. The settlement was widely viewed as a victory for Cineplex. Shortly afterward, using capital generated by The Bronfman Group collaboration, Taylor and Drabinsky bought the 297 screens of Canadian Odeon Theatres for a modest $16 million and in June 1985 changed the company name to the Cineplex Odeon Corporation.

From the beginning, Cineplex pursued a strategy of expansion into key markets, notably the United States, where the Los Angeles Beverly Center 14-screen multiplex opened on July 15, 1982. The Beverly 14, a collection of small theaters in the middle of a shopping complex that offered free parking, generated revenues of US$4 million in the first year, almost twice the initial projections. This set the stage for a systematic penetration of the United States market, as Cineplex began to buy up both individual movie houses and theater chains. Los Angeles remained an important focus, and the company made a number of acquisitions throughout the city in the 1980s, culminating in the June 1987 opening of the 18-screen Cineplex Odeon Cinemas at Universal City.

In November 1985 Drabinsky purchased the debt-ridden Plitt Theatres, which increased his holdings by 574 screens in 21 states in the United States. The acquisition left Cineplex in a vulnerable financial position, forcing Drabinsky and vice-chairman Myron Gottlieb to look for a major financial backer. In December 1985, Drabinsky met with Lew Wasserman and Sidney Sheinberg, chairman and president respectively of MCA, Inc.. In January 1986, MCA announced that it had agreed to buy 49.7 percent of Cineplex for US$239 million.

This injection of much-needed cash heralded a series of acquisitions of American theaters negotiated through the company's United States subsidiary, Plitt Theatres. Between April and December 1986 Cineplex purchased five movie theater chains, adding a total of 372 screens in 128 locations. In addition to these acquisitions, the company constructed 31 theaters with 163 screens in the United States and Canada during 1987. An additional 229 screens were opened in 1988. By 1989, Cineplex Odeon controlled 1,825 screens in 499 locations in North America. In order to offset the costs of the rapid expansion program, Drabinsky encouraged landlords of the new premises to invest in the company. He also adopted a practice of selling off individual properties if their real estate value increased dramatically. By constantly juggling his assets, and by the force of his confident and persuasive personality, Drabinsky managed to keep enough credit on hand to continue his policy of rapid growth, even as share prices fell in the wake of the October 1987 stock market crash. In 1988, the company moved into the United Kingdom, with the stated intention of "developing and operating" over 100 screens in the British Isles by the end of 1991. To do so, he increased the company's debt-load to over US$500 million, a level considered unacceptably high by many shareholders.

Drabinsky's ambitions went beyond operating a large number of screens. Determined to make theater-going a clean, civilized, and exciting experience, he established quality service and attractive locations as priorities in any operation that he took over. To this end, he spent millions of dollars refurbishing run-down theater complexes and in some cases painstakingly restoring historical landmarks to their former glory. Throughout the 1980s, every new acquisition was evaluated and refurbished by a 100-person design and construction team under the direction of Cineplex head architect David Mesbur. Cineplex undertook the restoration of cinemas on Vancouver's Granville Street, and the new complex quickly became one of the most profitable venues in Canada. According to company reports, the Gordon Theater in Los Angeles brought in a weekly revenue of US$6,000 before a US$650,000 facelift by the Cineplex design team. Renamed the Showcase, the refurbished cinema averaged US$30,000 a week. Art Deco motifs, plush seating, state-of-the-art sound equipment, and cappuccino bars revolutionized the way Americans thought of the cinema experience. Even Drabinsky's rivals admit that he forced the standard of service and appearance in the industry to rise. The luxurious surroundings, however, came at a high price: in May 1989 *Forbes* estimated that Cineplex spent approximately US$1,400 per leased seat compared to an industry average of US$500 a seat.

The cost of entertainment in a Cineplex theater was also high. In 1988, the average ticket price in the industry was US$4, compared with US$7 at Cineplex. The elevated prices occurred at a time when the number of movies going into production each year was dropping, and multiplexes were being forced to show first-releases on more than one screen in order to fill their playbills. Nevertheless, Drabinsky remained convinced that patrons would pay more for the opportunity to view in comfort.

They were also paying for the opportunity to snack in comfort. Concession stands in Cineplex theaters were among the most innovative in the industry, and included upscale cafes in selected locations that served cappuccino, herbal tea, and croissants. Even the more mundane establishments offered real butter on their popcorn, an executive decision that cost Cineplex a great deal of money over the years. Because concession revenues accounted for approximately one-third of overall box office revenue at Cineplex locations in 1989, the effort was judged worthwhile. Cineplex also invested considerable sums in its supervisors, most of whom participated in a six-week in-house management training program.

In view of Drabinsky's celebrated attempts to restore glamour to the movie-going experience, competitors were surprised when he introduced on-screen advertising to his Canadian venues in 1985. At a time when theaters were losing audiences to video and cable television, commercial-free screening seemed one of the movie industry's most important attractions. Drabinsky defended his decision in pragmatic terms, pointing out that the timeliness of a movie's release surpassed in importance the presence of advertising. Disgruntled patrons publicly took issue with this viewpoint, in some cases throwing objects at the screen when a commercial aired. Drabinsky refused to withdraw advertising from all but 26 art-house venues in Canada, but the experience may have influenced his decision to introduce advertising to his United States screens on a more limited basis.

Not content with celluloid success, Drabinsky soon turned his attention to live theater. In 1986, Cineplex acquired the lease to half of the Imperial Theatre in downtown Toronto. The building had an illustrious history dating back to 1920 when it opened with a combination of vaudeville and silent movies. For many years, the other half of the building had been leased by Famous Players, one of Cineplex's biggest rivals on the Canadian circuit. Cineplex acquired the lease to the second half of the building in 1986 but, due to legal wrangles, was not able to begin restoration of the theater until 1989 when it purchased half of the building outright. Renamed the Pantages, Cineplex gutted the property and spent US$18 million to restore the theater to the original design of architect Thomas Lamb. Drabinsky then bought exclusive Canadian rights to Andrew Lloyd Webber's musical *Phantom of the Opera,* which premiered to record box office advance sales in late 1989; the production was the most expensive ever staged in Canada. The company became involved in other theatrical projects during this period, including a

North American tour of songs and music by Lloyd Webber. Cineplex completed its program of diversification with the purchase of the Film House group, a postproduction facility, in 1986 and the financing of films by Oliver Stone and John Schlesinger in the United States.

Meanwhile, MCA and The Bronfman Group, Cineplex's major shareholders, were becoming increasingly concerned about the level of debt that the company had accumulated. By 1988, properties were being sold to raise money. In 1989, Cineplex's 50 percent interest in Universal Studios Florida was sold to the Rank Organisation in the United Kingdom. In early 1989, the Bronfmans indicated that they wanted to sell their 30 percent voting interest in Cineplex. Drabinsky and chief administrative officer Gottlieb recognized an opportunity to gain control of the company by acquiring The Bronfman Group's 30 percent interest. Although MCA owned 49.7 percent of the company, Canadian law allowed it only 33 percent of the voting rights. MCA president Sidney Sheinberg responded by asking that an investigation be made into Cineplex's irregular accounting practices, long a source of concern to investors. Financial improprieties were uncovered, and by the end of 1989 Cineplex's apparently healthy profit had been recalculated as a US$78.6 million loss. Drabinsky and Gottlieb were unable to secure sufficient financing to close their deal, and in December 1989 the era of Cineplex's wild leveraged expansion came to an end when both men were forced out of the company. They later purchased the Pantages theater and rights to *The Phantom of the Opera*. Cineplex, meanwhile, was left with a US$600 million debt.

In a letter to shareholders dated April 1991, Leo Kolber and Allen Karp, Cineplex's new chairman and chief executive officer respectively, stated that whereas before 1989 the company had attempted to create "an entertainment conglomerate with a presence in many aspects of the industry," the focus in the 1990s would be "the business we know best: motion picture exhibition." In keeping with this philosophy, the company entered the 1990s by selling most of its peripheral assets, including the live entertainment division, a residual interest in Universal Studio Florida, the Film House postproduction facility, the theaters in the United Kingdom, and a number of unprofitable United States screens. Plans to buy new theaters proceeded at a modest pace, and the full-time design team was reduced from 100 people to fewer than 10. The new management recognized that it would be several years before their cost-cutting efforts would be rewarded, but already in 1991 they could claim that their "fire-fighting" phase was over.

The following year, for the first time since restructuring began in 1989, Cineplex had a positive cash flow, the result of several cost-reduction and market-oriented improvement programs that led to a 46.5 percent reduction in net loss. Through its Theatre Cost Reduction Program, for instance, the company was able to significantly reduce its general and administrative expenses and, with the help of lower interest rates, cut its interest expenses by more than a third. Also continuing to further its reputation as an industry leader in customer service, Cineplex began offering patrons the option of purchasing advance tickets by phone through its CINECHARGE program. In addition to launching a new program designed to minimize disruptions, such as talking, during film performances, the company began introducing cupholders in various theaters.

Having strengthened its financial base, the company was now ready to direct its attention to a strategic vision for the future, one that would focus not only on film exhibition but on its other, often underemphasized, principal area of revenue: food concession sales. In an attempt to redefine itself as more than simply a film exhibitor that sells concessions on the side, the company developed an aggressive plan to boost concession revenue. Known as Project Popcorn, the strategy involved the introduction of modern merchandising, consisting of new graphic designs on beverage cups and new menu boards; expanded product selection, including items ranging from fresh fruit juices to cappuccinos; and innovative service methods, such as self-serve bulk candy stations and mobile auditorium carts. Although Project Popcorn resulted in a 10 percent gain in concession revenues in 1993, a well-publicized report suggesting that theater-popped popcorn was unusually high in saturated fat brought about a decline in concession revenue. Consequently, Cineplex, after conducting extensive nutrition and consumer preference tests, switched from coconut to vegetable oil, which contained 86 percent less saturated fat.

While continuing to improve upon the quality of the total moviegoing experience, introducing digital theater sound systems to many of its auditoriums, Cineplex looked to expand its operations through acquisition and merger opportunities. In March 1995 the company signed an agreement to merge with Cinemark, the fifth largest circuit in the United States, making it the world's largest theatrical exhibition company. The deal, however, failed to materialize; nevertheless, the two companies parted amiably and agreed to explore possible joint opportunities in the future.

In 1995, Cineplex outlined its strategy for the future, emphasizing its focus on new contemporary theater developments in both U.S. and Canadian major markets. To provide more resources for its theater building and refurbishment program, the company sold 28 theaters in highly competitive Florida and Georgia markets to Carmke Cinemas in May. At the same time, the company identified the primary locations targeted for expansion, announcing that it would build 5 new theaters and refurbish 11 before the end of the year. Its plans for 1996 included building an additional 26 new theaters and refurbishing 14. The program was scheduled to add more than 300 new screens to the Cinemark theater portfolio. Some of the areas slated for expansion included Illinois, New York, Maryland, Texas, Quebec, Ontario, and British Columbia.

Under the leadership of the dynamic and energetic Garth Drabinsky, Cineplex grew in less than a decade from a small independent film exhibitor in Toronto to a giant in the motion picture industry with screens in most of the major metropolitan areas of the United States and Canada. Capitalizing on the junk bond trend of the 1980s, Drabinsky financed much of his company's expansion and diversification program with expensive debt, and his unwillingness to reconsider his approach eventually unseated him. Under the direction of a new executive management team and a much more focused philosophy, the company engineered a successful turnaround, securing its financial stability and then laying the groundwork for future growth. Its future success will depend on management's continued ability to lower costs dramatically while providing the quality of entertainment that is a hallmark of the Cineplex experience.

Principal Subsidiaries:

Plitt Theatres; RKO Century Warner Theatres; Walter Reade Theatres; Neighborhood Theatres; Washington Circle Theatres.

Further Reading:

Best, Patricia, "The World According to Garth," *Globe and Mail,* March 25, 1995, p. C26.
"Cineplex Odeon Tenth Anniversary Salute," *Variety,* April 26-May 2, 1992.
Drabinsky, Garth with Marq de Villiers, *An Autobiography,* Toronto: McClelland and Stewart, 1995.
Enchin, Harvey, "Cineplex Creates Theatre Giant," *Globe and Mail,* March 3, 1995, p. B1.
Lathan, K. J. and Suzane Ayscough, "The Last Emperor," *Film Comment,* January-February 1990.
MacDonald, Gayle, "Cineplex Is No Blockbuster But It Finds Fans," *The Financial Post,* November 19, 1994, p. 25.
Siklos, Richard, "Squabbles Bring Curtain Down on Cineplex-Cinemark," *The Financial Post,* May 13, 1995, pp. 1-2.
Simon, Cecilia Capuzzi, "The Fall of Garth Drabinsky," *Premiere,* March 1991.
Wechsler, Dana, "Every Trick in the Books," *Forbes,* May 29, 1989.

—Moya Verzhbinsky
—updated by Jason Gallman

The Consumers' Gas Company Ltd.

2225 Sheppard Ave. East
North York, Ontario M2J 5C2
(416) 492-6611

Public Company
Incorporated: 1848 as The Consumers' Gas
   Company of Toronto
Employees: 3,800
Sales: $1.95 billion
Stock Exchanges: Toronto Montreal
SICs: 4924 Natural gas distribution

The Consumers' Gas Company Ltd. distributes natural gas to over 1.2 million residential, commercial, and industrial customers in south central and eastern Ontario, western Quebec, and northern New York State. Consumers' Gas also explores for and produces oil and gas, maintains underground storage facilities, and contracts well drilling for oil and gas.

The roots of Consumers' Gas date back to 1841, when predecessor gas company the Toronto Gas Light and Water Company Ltd. erected a gas works in Toronto and began distributing 50,000 feet of gas daily. That was enough to light 12 street lamps and gradually, the facilities of a number of manufacturers and merchants.

The company sold gas at $5 per thousand feet, a price eventually judged too high by consumers. A public hearing was held on September 17, 1847, for disgruntled customers. As those in attendance filed out of the hearing, they were urged to purchase stock in a new gas company at £12 10s. a share. Many did, and so was born The Consumers' Gas Company of Toronto.

On October 29, 1847, the company, led by city postmaster Charles Berczy, earned a charter from the City Hall of Toronto to supply the city with light. The charter, which incorporated the company on March 23, 1848, stated that "the great demand for a cheap and effective mode of lighting the streets and places of the said city, as well as the houses and shops, that more than one company should be established."

The nascent Consumers' Gas hired a gas engineer, purchased the lighting interests of the Toronto Gas Light and Water Company for £22,000, and contracted a host of machinery from the west coast of Scotland. In 1848, its first year of business, the company served 200 customers and charged $4 per thousand feet for its gas product, 20 percent less than the price charged by the Toronto Gas Light and Water Company. In 1850 a further 16.5 percent cut in price was effected. A year later, an additional 10 percent reduction occurred. In 1854 Consumers' Gas had 700 consumers, a 40 percent increase over the previous year.

In 1873 the company doubled its plant capacity, building new purifiers, condensers, and coal sheds. Three years later, Consumers' erected new headquarters at 17-19 Toronto Street. The five-story structure, designed by architects Grant and Dick, was built by Brown and Love Builders Ltd.

In 1887, by which time the company had 9,000 customers, the capital worth of Consumers' Gas stood at just under $1 million. By 1904 that figure had doubled, and it climbed still further to $8 million by 1924. Expansion of Toronto's population during the 1930s brought the company's capital worth to $14 million by 1936.

Consumers' Gas first encountered competition from electricity in 1880. That year the city of Toronto was granted a franchise for electric lighting. This led to the uprooting of 2,000 gas lamps, which were replaced by electric lights. In response, Consumers' Gas began in 1879 to market gas as a fuel rather than as an illuminant.

Consumers' Gas's first salvo against electricity came in 1902, when it introduced gas water heaters for homes. Six years later, the company opened a branch salesroom at 12 Adelaide Street in Toronto. To meet residential demand, the manufactured gas plant "Station B," as the branch salesroom was dubbed, was opened to produce four million cubic feet of gas a day. In 1914, though the Canadian economy had softened directly preceding World War I, demand for gas to fuel war factories climbed. By 1918 Consumers' Gas's output stood at just over 4.72 billion cubic feet of gas for the year. When the electric range became popular among consumers in the 1920s, the company responded with an improved gas model, including an insulated oven and automatic controls. The gas refrigerator was introduced in 1928.

By 1931 Consumers' Gas recognized that, while low-pressure transmission of gas was fine for the city of Toronto, a more dependable system was needed to serve outlying settlements. In April of that year the company received permission from the Ontario provincial legislature to extend its services to other municipalities. A new, medium-high-pressure system of distribution required that 305 miles of new mains be laid that year.

Expanding outside Toronto by 1938, the company's gas system stretched a distance of 17 miles east and west of the city's harbor and eight miles north. More than 9,000 new customers were added during World War II, bringing the 1947 total to 177,839. Though gas appliances were scarce in postwar Toronto, the city's population continued to grow along with its economic core; the company's future looked bright.

In 1949, to serve increased demand, the company sought to buy gas from elsewhere rather than refine it at company plants. The 1952 annual report hinted that this supply could come from the United States. What's more, that supply would be natural gas, not manufactured gas (or coal gas). In 1954 Consumers' Gas announced that natural gas would, in fact, be transported from Texas and Louisiana to its Ontario market. This would require the conversion of customers' gas-burning appliances to the use of natural gas, a task also begun that year.

The switch to natural gas brought real changes to Consumers' Gas; a new general manager, Oakah Jones, a veteran of the Oklahoma natural gas fields, was hired. In 1958, the company was reincorporated under the name The Consumer's Gas Company (it wasn't until 1990 that the firm became The Consumers' Gas Company Ltd.). Fuel started flowing from the United States in November of 1954 after a natural gas pipeline was constructed from Niagara to Sheridan, Ontario, just west of Toronto. That same year, Consumers' Gas acquired Niagara Gas Transmission Ltd., which had formerly been jointly owned by Consumers' Gas and the Tennessee Gas Transmission Company.

At that time Consumers' Gas faced public criticism for its continued purchase of United States natural gas, which it undertook despite a domestic supply available in Alberta. So when Calgary-based TransCanada PipeLines Ltd. announced in 1955 that it would build a pipeline to carry natural gas from western Canada to Ontario, Consumers' Gas began talks with the new company.

With Oakah Jones at the helm, Consumers' Gas decided at this time to expand the company through acquisition of rival gas concerns. In 1956 the company acquired Provincial Gas Co. Ltd. and thus its roughly 21,000 customers in the Niagara Peninsula. A year later, Consumers' bought Inter-Provincial Utilities Ltd., which served the Ottawa, Eastview, and Rockcliffe Park markets.

In October of 1958 the first natural gas from western Canada reached Toronto via the TransCanada Pipe Line facility. Consumers' Gas quickly closed off its United States supply line. In September of 1962 Consumers' Gas piped natural gas across the American-Canadian border near Cornwall to its subsidiary St. Lawrence Gas Co. Inc., which served the Massena-Ogdensburg area of New York State. The pipeline was attached to the bridge span over the Cornwall Canal and the St. Lawrence River.

By 1966 Consumers' Gas served 340,000 customers in 167 communities throughout Ontario, Quebec, and New York State. The annual report of 1967 offered the first glimpse of the company's new marketing message: natural gas was nonpolluting and an efficient and convenient fuel. Oakah Jones was quoted as saying: "Your company is aware of the present public concern about air pollution in large cities. For this reason in part, we have contracted for availability of much increased quantities of natural gas since it is clean burning and a pollutant-free fuel of the highest order."

In 1968 Jones, who was already president, also became chairman of the board of Consumers' Gas after the sudden death of Arthur Bishop, the previous chairman.

Two years later, after western Quebec had become yet another market that Consumers' Gas was able to serve with its Niagara pipeline, the company's shares were listed on the Montreal Stock Exchange. Expansion for Consumers' Gas continued on April 22, 1971, when it purchased 52.5 percent of Cygnus Corp Ltd., which in turn owned 43.5 percent of Home Oil Company Ltd. The hope was that by taking a stake in Home Oil, a prominent player in the Alberta oil market, Consumers' Gas could attract capital for more expansion.

Then, in November of 1971, the company purchased a further 275,506 Class B voting shares of Home Oil, keeping the oil and gas concern firmly within its sights for ultimate ownership. Home Oil had been headed since the 1950s by Bobby Brown, a well-known oil man from Calgary. A series of poor investments by Brown in the 1960s, including expensive land purchases made in Prudhoe Bay, in Canada's Arctic north, led to a steep fall in Home Oil's share price by 1970. This enabled stock purchases by Consumers' Gas. In 1972 Consumers' offered to purchase the remaining shares in Home Oil; it managed to acquire 96 percent of the outstanding shares, giving the company 46.6 percent control of Home Oil.

A year later, Oakah Jones died and Douglas Gibson was appointed chairman of the board and Joseph McCarthy, president. Their main task in 1974 was to deal with the OPEC (Organization of Petroleum Exporting Countries) "oil shock," the result of rising oil costs worldwide and an energy shortage in the United States. The company's fear was that the Alberta government might realize the worth of its gas reserves and raise the wellhead price of its fuel. Consumers' Gas responded to this concern by becoming a partner in the Canadian Arctic Gas Study Group. This consortium began looking at building a new pipeline from the Mackenzie Delta and Alaska to Alberta, where the fuel would connect to TransCanada's existing line to eastern Canada.

Nonetheless, the dreaded price hike was eventually effected, in November of 1975, when natural gas purchased from TransCanada went up from $.82 per Mcf to $1.25 per Mcf. Consumers' Gas immediately complained that too large a slice of the price increase would go toward royalties and taxes paid to the Alberta government and the federal government in Ottawa. Then, on July 4, 1977, the National Energy Board, Ottawa's fuel regulatory agency, denied the Canadian Arctic Gas Study Group permission to build their proposed pipeline.

On December 29, 1979, during the decade's second "oil shock," Consumers' Gas took full control of Home Oil, making it a wholly owned subsidiary. The company reasoned that Canada had rich natural gas resources but was still a net importer of crude oil. It was believed that Ottawa, valuing Alberta's rich oil reserves, would make it easier for energy exploration and development in western Canada. Home Oil would be an effective vehicle by which Consumers' Gas could obtain a larger slice of the Alberta oil market. The subsidiary owned rich oil and gas reserves and was engaged in potentially lucrative projects like the Elk River coal project and the Athabasca oil sands project.

In 1980 Consumers' Gas completed another large acquisition: On April 9 the company purchased Hiram Walker-Gooderham & Worts Ltd., a liquor company. This necessitated a name change from Consumers' Gas Company to Hiram Walker-Consumers' Home Ltd., which reflected the combination of the companies. Hiram Walker had earlier been a takeover target, so it turned to Consumers' Gas as a defensive partner. Linking the companies' liquor, gas, and petroleum businesses to create a company with worldwide assets of $3.6 billion and revenues of $2.6 billion produced the fifth-largest profits of any Canadian corporation.

But, early on, the marriage was not a merry one. In 1981 Home Oil paid far too much for the Davis Oil Company, purchased for US$759 million from Texas oil man Marvin Davis. It became clear in 1983 that the fallout from the Davis Oil acquisition had contributed to the poorer-than-expected profit line posted by the company that year. In 1982 Consumers' created a separate company, Congas Engineering Canada Ltd., to administer consulting worldwide. In 1988, for example, a national feasibility study was undertaken in Malaysia to develop a gas distribution system among 17 large cities in that country.

Meanwhile, Paul Reichmann, head of the Toronto-based real estate empire Olympia & York Developments Ltd. had been eyeing Hiram Walker-Gooderham & Worts for some time. In 1983 O&Y took a small stake in Hiram Walker-Consumers' Home Ltd. Reichmann waited until March 14, 1986, however, to make a $1.2 billion bid for the company's outstanding shares, through O&Y's newly purchased Gulf Canada subsidiary.

Reichmann reasoned that Hiram Walker's association with Consumers' Gas and Home Oil had been the root of its ill-conceived purchase of Davis Oil, which had weakened the company and made it ripe for takeover. The Gulf Canada bid, nonetheless, met with stiff and ultimately hostile resistance. By March 26, 1986, Hiram Walker-Consumers' Home Ltd. had lined up a white knight in Allied Lyons PLC; the British liquor and food giant agreed to buy the Hiram Walker liquor business, the heart of the company, for $2.3 billion. Hiram Walker-Consumers' Home Ltd. would essentially be split up.

On April 18 Paul Reichmann ostensibly emerged the victor after much boardroom negotiation and considerable posturing amid the media glare surrounding the takeover bid. O&Y, however, found itself saddled with a $3.3 billion price tag for 69 percent of Hiram Walker, minus the liquor business Reichmann insisted had been the main prize all along. Long-term planning for Consumers' Gas had now moved well beyond considerations of the world energy picture and technological progress at the wellhead. Now the fortunes of Paul Reichmann's O&Y empire were inextricably added to the pot.

In May of 1986 Interprovincial Pipeline paid $1.1 billion for Home Oil, leaving Consumers' Gas effectively under the control of Gulf Canada. A year later, Toronto-based GW Utilities Ltd., the Reichmann family's oil and gas subsidiary and holding company, purchased 87 percent of Consumers' Gas shares from Gulf Canada to take ultimate control.

Government regulatory policy had long proven a thorn in the side of the Consumers' Gas board. In June of 1988 the company asked the Ontario government for a 14.37 percent return on common equity from its provincial business. This compared with an allowable rate of return at that time of 14 percent. In December the Ontario Energy Board responded by approving a 13.5 percent rate of return.

In 1987 the company had founded Arbor Living Centers Inc. to own and operate nursing and retirement homes. Two years later, Consumers' established Telesis Oil and Gas to carry out all energy exploration and development work.

In 1990 British Gas plc., Britain's gas distributor, announced a $34-a-share bid for Consumers' Gas, valuing the company at $1.1 billion. British Gas sought to diversify its business beyond its home market. Its interest in Consumers raised concern that the company would end up in foreign hands. In November of 1990 a formal bid was made. With GW Utilities pledging its 82 percent stake in Consumers' to British Gas, the bid seemed assured of success.

Investment Canada, a federal agency in Ottawa reviewing all foreign takeovers of Canadian companies, ruled that the British Gas bid could proceed only if 15 percent of Consumers' shares were sold to Canadians by September 30, 1992, with the additional requirement that over the next ten years 50 percent of all additional equity financing be made available to the public. In addition, Consumers' was required to sell the assets of Telesis, its upstream oil and gas subsidiary, within three years. British Gas agreed to these terms, and the deal was completed on December 28, 1990. Soon after, Robert Martin, chief executive of Consumers', was made director, president, and chief executive of British Gas Holdings (Canada) Ltd., the British Gas subsidiary that bought Consumers'.

In 1991 British Gas announced it would spend $30 million over the next ten years on research and development of non-polluting natural gas use. Then, in February of 1992, British Gas disclosed that it was selling roughly 15.2 percent of the company to the public for approximately $170 million. The deal called for an offering of around 10 million shares.

After just three years of ownership, British Gas concluded that its goal to become a major international distributor of natural gas, much like the world's oil majors, could not be realized in Canada. Seeing greater opportunities in Asia and Latin America, in various types of power generation projects, British Gas put Consumers' Gas up for sale. And in November 1993, Interprovincial Pipe Line Systems Inc., an Edmonton-based company best known for operating Canada's longest crude oil pipeline, purchased an 85 percent stake in the natural gas giant for $1.2 billion.

The strategy behind the acquisition, according to Interprovincial Pipe Line president Brian MacNeil, was to ensure that his company has a long-term future when conventional crude oil production from Western Canada dries up. In the short term, though, the acquisition was an investment in gas technology expertise, combining Consumers' understanding of more conventional gas transportation and distribution with Interprovincial's expertise in the emerging field of batch liquids transportation—a sophisticated method of sending various types of crude oil to refineries according to their specific needs, rather than shipping a homogeneous blend of oil down the pipeline in a continuous stream.

In November 1994, after the acquisition was completed, Consumers' looked to expand its transportation capabilities by entering into an agreement with ANR Pipeline Company of Michigan, to pursue a new pipeline project called the Link Pipeline. Construction of the new pipeline—located in the region extending from the international border on the St. Clair River south of Sarnia, Ontario, to the company's storage complex in southwestern Ontario—was projected to cost approximately $10-million. In addition to providing additional transportation capacity to Consumers' Gas, the 9.4-kilometer, 24-inch diameter "Consumers' Link" was also expected to furnish transportation for third parties. In April 1995, the company attempted to further expand its market by purchasing the petroleum and natural gas rights in the Coveny gas field from Lagasco Corporation for $1.12 million.

In a market largely dependent on factors as uncertain as the weather, Consumers' Gas has experienced steady growth during the 1990s. In 1994, while approaching the $2-billion mark in revenue, the company recorded net earnings of $126-million, an increase of more than 50 percent compared to 1991. That same year the company attempted to secure its customer base by focusing its marketing strategy on customer service, implementing several new programs designed to reduce the time required to install a gas service. And in keeping with its commitment to energy-efficient products, the company initiated ten new programs as part of its "Demand-Side Management" strategy. The programs ranged from installing high-efficiency residential furnaces and water heaters to offering custom energy analyses of building designs for commercial and apartment building customers. In addition to these efficiency programs, the company planned to boost revenues in 1995 by negotiating new service contracts in Northern Ontario, while entering markets for rental products such as space heaters and water heaters.

Looking toward the more distant future, the hold that Consumers' Gas has on the Canadian natural gas market—the world's largest—is expected to grow. According to the Geological Survey of Canada, about 80 tcf, or around 40 percent of potential natural gas reserves in western Canada, are still undiscovered. Even if OPEC never again holds the world oil market for ransom, Consumers' Gas should experience healthy growth, especially since natural gas exports to the United States are expected to increase; in 1990 the Department of Energy in Ottawa forecast that Canadian exports headed south would grow by 4.9 percent during the decade.

Principal Subsidiaries:

Consumers' Corporation; Consumers' Home Services Ltd.; Consumers' LNG Ltd.; Consumers' Management Services; Consumers' Marketing Company Limited; Consumers' Realty Limited; 912176 Ontario Ltd.; 923726 Ontario Limited; The Ottawa Gas Company; St. Lawrence Gas Company Inc.

Further Reading:

Bourette, Susan, "Mild Winter Cools Consumers' Profit," *Globe and Mail,* February 3, 1995, p. B10.
"British Gas to Buy Into Consumers' Gas," *Petroleum Economist,* April 1990.
Carlisle, Tamsin, "Interprovincial Looks Abroad," *Globe and Mail,* March 3, 1994, p. B20.
Clarkson, Geoffrey, *A Gas Grievance and a Remedy,* Toronto: Claremont Press, 1860.
"Consumers' Gas Taps Former Shareholders," *Globe and Mail,* March 29, 1991.
Cook, Peter, "Canada Is Not Such a Natural Gas," *Globe and Mail,* May 20, 1994, p. B2.
"First Century of Consumers' Gas: 1848-1948," *Consumers' Gas 1948 Annual Report,* Toronto: Consumers' Gas Company Ltd.
Foster, Peter, *The Master Builders,* Key Porter Books, 1986.
Saunders, John, "Interprovincial Buys Consumers," *Globe and Mail,* November 20, 1993, p. B1.

—Etan Vlessing
—updated by Jason Gallman

Canada Trust

CT Financial Services Inc.

Canada Trust Tower
275 Dundas Street
London, Ontario N6A 4S4
(519) 663-1938
Fax: (519) 663-5114

Public Company
Incorporated: 1987 as CT Financial Services Inc.
Employees: 11,822
Deposits: $42.49 billion
Stock Exchanges: Toronto Montreal
SICs: 6282 Investment Advice

A holding company for numerous subsidiaries involved in personal banking services and trust and investment management services, CT Financial Inc. ranked as one of the largest and oldest financial services companies in Canada. Owner of The Canada Trust Company, Canada Trustco Mortgage Company, and First Federal Savings and Loan Association of Rochester, as well as other, smaller subsidiaries, CT Financial maintained approximately 500 branch offices and nearly $50 billion in assets during the mid-1990s.

Formed in 1987 as an unregulated holding company, CT Financial represented a truly modern organization created to allow the numerous financial institutions under its corporate umbrella to expand into new business arenas in a less restricted manner. The holding company's roots, however, stretch back considerably further than 1987, sprouting more than a century earlier when 25 prominent and successful merchants and businessmen gathered around a stove in the room above Daniel Macfie's dry-goods store.

The date was March 15, 1864 and the place was London, Canada West, where each of those in attendance had gained notoriety for their esteemed business acumen, helping their city become a burgeoning financial center. In the 38 years since London's first building was erected, the city had become a thriving commercial hub, supported by stores like Macfie's dry-goods store, several manufacturing factories, a fledgling oil industry, and numerous commercial enterprises. Mostly the region was dependent, as it would be for decades to come, on a flourishing agricultural industry. The region, as it existed in 1864, was predominately rural, populated by farmers and fed by their crops. Farm land, and those who cultivated it, represented the vertebrae of London's economy, underpinning and fueling its prosperity. It was this crucial, sustaining factor to London's survival that those huddled around Macfie's stove sought to preserve.

That March night, the leaders of London's business community formed the Huron & Erie Savings and Loan Society, an organization modeled after English building societies that first had appeared during the late 18th century. By the time Huron & Erie was formed, building societies, which in their early years functioned as savings pools that, in essence, aggrandized the capital of primarily middle-class investors, had evolved into rudimentary mortgage lending companies, a type of financial institution from which the founders of Huron & Erie reckoned their community could greatly benefit. Capital was scarce throughout the region, so by creating a mortgage lending company that offered established farmers or newly arrived settlers the opportunity to borrow money for the purchase or development of farm land, the founders of Huron & Erie hoped to bolster the stability and assure the prosperity of the surrounding London area, which was vital to the continued success of their other business interests. On March 15, the founders signed a declaration of their intent to form a permanent building society. Other constitutive matters were agreed upon as well: investment in the society would cost $50 per share, deposits from the public would be accepted in amounts ranging from $4 to $500. Three days later they filed their declaration and brought to life the newest addition to London's blossoming business community, an enterprise that more than century later would rank as one of the city's oldest.

Slightly more than a month later, on April 29, Huron & Erie approved its first mortgage loan: $400 to a farmer named Edward Talbott who offered land valued at $1,250 as security against the loan. Huron & Erie's first mortgage loan set the tone for the many to follow. The company would grow steadily during its first formative decades by loaning money primarily to rural applicants who were able to offer sizeable security in relation to the amount of money they borrowed, as Talbott's case exemplified. Huron & Erie's management, led by Adam Hope, the organization's first president, would become known for their prudence and caution, fastidiously examining each application for a mortgage loan (the board of directors, in fact, reviewed each application individually until the 1930s) and engaging in all business ventures with decided discretion.

Operating thusly, Huron & Erie recorded promising growth throughout the remainder of the 19th century. Two acquisitions were completed early in the company's history, the first occurring in 1865, the year Huron & Erie Savings and Loan Society was renamed Huron & Erie Loan and Savings Company, when the fledgling enterprise purchased the London Permanent Building Society, assuming its assets, liabilities, and shareholders. The next occurred the following year when a similar arrangement was concluded with the Western Counties Permanent Building and Savings Society, bringing Huron & Erie's assets up to $318,849 by 1867. Five years later the company's asset total eclipsed the million dollar plateau, then climbed vigorously, reaching $2.5 million by the early 1880s and, despite a suppressive economic depression, swelled to more than $5 million by the beginning of the 1890s.

As Huron & Erie progressed through the 1890s spurred by its encouraging growth, its management began to look toward creating other business opportunities for the concern, specifically a diversification into fiduciary business, which at that time primarily involved the management of estates. To make this strategic move, Huron & Erie needed to acquire a trust company charter, which it did in 1898 when it purchased the General Trust Corporation of Canada, a Calgary-based trust company. Shortly after the acquisition, General Trust moved its head office to London, then changed its name to The Canada Trust Company and began operating as a subsidiary of Huron & Erie when it commenced operations in 1901. From this point forward, The Canada Trust Company and Huron & Erie would forge their way through the 20th century together, with Canada Trust at Huron & Erie's side. At first Canada Trust occupied an inferior position to Huron & Erie, then later, when Canada Trust emerged as a powerful financial force, the organizations were nearly indistinguishable, forming an integral component of the financial empire CT Financial became a century later.

Three short years after Canada Trust began managing estates and conducting other fiduciary duties, its assets swelled to more than $1 million. By 1906, the trust company had paid its first dividend to Huron & Erie, marking the formal beginning of Canada Trust's long record as a contributor to its parent company's financial growth.

Increasing success soon led the management of Huron & Erie to expand further, this time geographically, after spending nearly four decades investing solely within the confines of southwestern Ontario. In 1909, the company began lending funds on farm mortgages in Manitoba and Saskatchewan, where wheat production was accelerating at a rapid pace. Two years later, the company had invested more than $2 million in the two provinces, prompting it to open a branch office in Regina, the first outside London. In 1913, an office was opened in Winnipeg to accommodate the company's expanding business in Manitoba, which combined with the Huron & Erie's other investments lifted its asset total to more than $15 million, exclusive of Canada Trust's nearly $5 million in assets.

Noting this success at Huron & Erie's 50th annual meeting the following year, then-president Thomas G. Meredith expressed the bridled restraint that still prevailed among Huron & Erie's management, commenting to shareholders, "Although it may be monotonous to hear that the past year was the most prosperous in the company's history, unless we disregard the figures in the statement just presented, no other conclusion can be reached." The company's linear path of success, however guardedly received, would record its first appreciable blip shortly after Meredith spoke those words. With the outbreak of the First World War, many Canadians joined the service, engendering a sharp decline in the demand for mortgages. Despite this decrease in business, Huron & Erie opened a branch office in Edmonton in 1916 to handle its increasing business in Alberta,

while Canada Trust's assets nearly doubled during the war years, edging toward $10 million.

Once the hostilities were concluded and the company struggled through a brief postwar slump, both Huron & Erie, which had changed its name once again during the war to Huron & Erie Mortgage Corporation and Canada Trust grew steadily, largely through a series of acquisitions. The Dominion Savings & Investment Society was acquired in 1922, the Hamilton Provident & Loan Corporation in 1926, the Southern Loan Company the following year, and The London Loan & Savings Company in 1929, bringing the company's total assets to more than $40 million by the end of the decade and its annual net profit to a robust $593,495. Both were figures Huron & Erie would not eclipse for more than two decades.

If the downturn in business experienced by the company during the First World War represented a mere blip, then the devastation wrought by the worldwide economic depression of the 1930s struck a shattering blow, bringing Huron & Erie's glowing growth to an abrupt halt. Although the stock market collapse in October 1929 was slow to affect the company — Huron & Erie opened a branch office in Vancouver in 1929 and another in Montreal in 1931 — when it did send its deleterious shock waves throughout the company in 1932, the effect lingered for a substantial duration, hobbling the company until the conclusion of the Second World War. Much of Huron & Erie's losses during the traumatic 1930s and early 1940s stemmed from its investments in Saskatchewan, whose residents were hit doubly hard by both the depression and a nearly decade-long series of natural calamities, including invading swarms of locusts, the counterpunches of drought then hail, and prodigious dust storms. Heavily dependent on wheat production, the province's economy was rocked by mounting crop failures, and Huron & Erie, with at least $18 million invested in the region at the start of the depression, bore its fair share of the losses.

Once the company was able to wrest free from the debilitative grip of the depression and its aftermath, Huron & Erie acquired two companies, London & Western Trusts Limited in 1946 and Guelph and Ontario Investment and Savings Society in 1949, signalling a return to more prosperous days. From 1947 to 1957 deposits at Huron & Erie and Canada Trust swelled from $56 million to $135 million, while combined assets of the two companies increased to more than $157 million.

Geographic expansion and diversification stood as the two main objectives Huron & Erie pursued as it headed toward the 1960s and its second century of business. By 1958, after a decade of vigorous growth during which the deposits held at Huron & Erie and Canada Trust had more than doubled, one branch had been added, giving it a total of 17. Management wanted considerably more and began concentrating on augmenting its collection of branches. During the ensuing four years, the company made significant strides toward achieving its objective, doubling the number of branches it operated to bring the total to 34, the greatest number of branches operated by any company in the trust industry.

Geographically, the company's presence throughout Canada was strengthened when it established a branch in Halifax in 1961, thereby extending the company's coverage from coast to coast. Perhaps more significant than an increase in branch offices was the increasing similarities between Huron & Erie and Canada Trust. By the late 1950s, Huron & Erie and Canada Trust were virtually indistinguishable entities, performing many of the same services. Although a merger between the two would result in costly charges and formidable legal difficulties, the directors of Huron & Erie and Canada Trust regarded the two companies essentially as one, a perspective borne out in the organization's annual report. For some time the annual reports for both companies were presented in one document, a publication entitled "The Huron & Erie Mortgage Corporation and The Canada Trust Company." Beginning in 1957, however, the annual report bore the shortened, more assimilative "Huron & Erie—Canada Trust." Five years later the names were transposed, reading "Canada Trust—Huron & Erie," beginning the gradual process of shedding the Huron & Erie name, which the wife of a Canada Trust director once remarked, "sounds like a railroad."

Moving the Canada Trust name to the forefront removed any confusion regarding the organization's business activities. It also was more reflective of the company's national scope, considering that the year discussed in the first Canada Trust—Huron & Erie annual report coincided with the establishment of the branch in Halifax. During the year of its 100th anniversary, Canada Trust—Huron & Erie, although still legally separate organizations, became a billion dollar company, serving half a million customers across the country. Growth during the company's first century had been fueled primarily by revenue generated from mortgage lending, but as the company entered into its second century of business, its dependency on mortgage lending would begin to wane, counterpoised by a more diversified portfolio.

After the acquisition of Waterloo Trust & Savings Company and Halton & Peel Trust & Savings Company in 1968, two transactions that increased Canada Trust—Huron & Erie's asset total by $400 million and gave it 165,000 additional customers, the company possessed 77 branches, more than any other trust company in the country, and $2.2 billion in assets. An intensive marketing and promotion program was effected during the early 1970s, which, by 1973, brought the company's asset total to $4.2 billion.

In the midst of this unprecedented growth, the Huron & Erie name finally was shed from the organization's corporate title in April 1976 when the company formally changed its name to Canada Trustco Mortgage Company. Two acquisitions were completed that year as well, first the Lincoln Trust and Savings Company and then the Ontario Trust Company, the addition of which solidified the newly named Canada Trustco's presence in key regions and raised the number of branches operated by the company to 123.

The next pivotal event in Canada Trustco's storied history occurred during the mid-1980s, when the company and its rapidly growing collection of diverse subsidiaries became the object of a hostile takeover. The unsolicited suitor was Genstar Corporation, a multi-billion dollar industrial and financial conglomerate that ranked as the leading manufacturer of cement in western Canada and a major producer of lime products and building materials, among numerous other business activities. Stewarded by Angus A. MacNaughton and Ross J. Turner, Genstar first entered the financial services field in 1981, when it acquired Canada Permanent Mortgage Corporation, founded in 1885, nine years before Huron & Erie. Reportedly, MacNaughton had wanted to enter the financial services industry for decades and the acquisition of Canada Permanent satisfied that ambition, but only for a few short months. Genstar's acquisition of Canada Permanent led to discouragingly lackluster results and left MacNaughton dissatisfied. Hoping to ameliorate Canada Permanent's torpid profit growth, MacNaughton decided Genstar needed to carve a greater presence in the banking industry and, consequently, he began pursuing Canada Trustco with the eventual aim being the merger of Canada Permanent and Canada Trust.

On April 29, 1985, Genstar Acquisition Corporation, a subsidiary of Genstar Corporation purchased 650,000 shares of Canada Trustco. The next day an additional 15,900 shares were purchased, then over the next several days a further 1.15 million shares were purchased, tripping alarms at Canada Trustco. Although Canada Trustco's management resisted Genstar's attempt to take over their company, Genstar eventually purchased the remaining shares and the deal was completed on August 27, 1985.

Less than a year later another nonbanking company wishing to enter the financial services industry made a bid for Genstar. The company was Imasco Limited, a giant holding company that originated as the Canadian subsidiary of the British-American Tobacco Company Limited. Later in its corporate life, Imasco diversified into fast-food and drug-store chains, and now, on the heels of Genstar's acquisition of Canada Trustco, the company looked to diversify further. Imasco acquired Genstar in 1986, giving Canada Trustco new owners once again, less than a year before CT Financial Services became the newest addition to the Canada Trustco corporate family.

Facing what they regarded as an uncertain legislative environment, the directors of Canada Trustco restructured their company and, in the fall of 1987, formed CT Financial Services Inc. to sidestep existing and future legislative barriers precluding Canada Trustco and its numerous subsidiaries from engaging in particular business activities. Soon after its formation, CT Financial, which was immune from both provincial and federal loan and trust company legislation, became the 100 percent owner of Canada Trustco, while, in turn, Imasco Financial Corporation, a subsidiary of Imasco Limited, assumed 98 percent ownership of CT Financial.

The following year, in 1988, CT Financial began looking to enter the savings and loan business in the United States, spending roughly two years studying the market in the northeastern United States before it acquired a majority stake in First Federal Savings and Loan Association of Rochester in 1991. The acquisition of

First Federal added $5.6 billion in assets (compared to Canada Trust's $33 billion in assets) and 65 branches in New York State to CT Financial's financial services empire. Two years later, assets had climbed an additional $10 billion, despite an economic recession during the early 1990s. The bulk of the company's more than $40 billion in assets at this point consisted of residential mortgage loans, which presented the lowest risk in the market, enabling the company to withstand the pernicious downturn.

As CT Financial headed toward the mid-1990s, its conservative management and aggressive marketing continued to predicate the company's enviable record of growth. Between 1992 and 1994 assets climbed from $44 billion to $49 billion, deposits from $39 billion to $42 billion, and the number of branch offices from 441 to 491, representing a financial services powerhouse that would stagger the minds of those gathered around Daniel Macfie's stove on March 15, 1864.

Principal Subsidiaries:

Canada Trustco Mortgage Company; The Canada Trust Company; CT Fund Services Inc.; CT Investment Counsel Inc.; CT Private Portfolio Management Inc.; CT Corporate Services Inc.; Canada Trust Bank N.V. (Netherlands); Canada Trustco International Limited (Barbados); Truscan Realty Limited; First Federal Savings and Loan Association of Rochester (United States) (99 percent); First Diversified Financial Services Inc. (United States); First Performance Mortgage Corporation (United States); CT Insurance Company Limited (Barbados); CT Realty Franchising Inc.; Canadian Trinity Life Insurance Company (40 percent); CB Commercial Real Estate Group Canada Inc. (25 percent); Meridian Securities International Limited (75 percent)

Further Reading:

"Canada Trust Co.," *The Financial Post,* June 3, 1961, p. 40.
"Canada Trust Co.," *The Financial Post,* February 9, 1963, p. 22.
"Canada Trust Co.," *The Financial Post,* June 1, 1963, p. 52.
"Canada Trust Co.," *The Financial Post,* January 29, 1966, p. 3.
"Canadian Trust Companies: All Pull Apart," *The Economist,* August 31, 1985, p. 72.
Enchin, Harvey, "Trust Baffled Why It Can't Be a Bank," *The Globe and Mail,* March 16, 1991, p. B12.
Freeman, Alan, "Central Guaranty Concerns Expressed," *The Globe and Mail,* June 9, 1992, p. B7.
Galt, Virginia, "Imasco Waiting for Ottawa Before Deciding on CT Financial Stake," *The Globe and Mail,* March 23, 1989, p. B14.
Hartley, Tom, "Canadian Bank Eyes Operation in Buffalo," *Business First of Buffalo,* May 20, 1991, p. 2.
Howlett, Karen, "Real Estate Powerhouse Formed," *The Globe and Mail,* October 13, 1993, p. B1.
Milner, Brian, "CT Financial's Quarterly Profit Slips," *The Globe and Mail,* October 25, 1990, p. B11.
Partridge, John, "Trust Firms Bemoan NDP Inaction," *The Globe and Mail,* April 22, 1995, p. B5.
Smith, Philip, *The Trust-Builders: The Remarkable Rise of Canada Trust.* Toronto: Macmillan of Canada, 1989, 275 p.
Westell, Dan, "Montreal Trust Joins Bidding for Central Guaranty," *The Globe and Mail,* June 11, 1992, p. B21.

—Jeffrey L. Covell

DOFASCO

Dofasco Inc.

P.O. Box 2460
Hamilton, Ontario L8N 3J5
(905) 544-3761
Fax: (905) 545-3226

Public Company
Incorporated: 1912 as Dominion Steel Castings
    Company, Ltd.
Employees: 7,000
Sales: $2.26 billion
Stock Exchanges: Toronto, Montreal
SICs: 5050 Metals and Minerals Except Petroleum

Dofasco Inc., one of the world's largest integrated steelmakers, ships over three million tons of flat rolled steel products annually. Once Canada's largest steelmaker with over 40 percent of the country's total raw steel production, Dofasco and its subsidiaries have provided North America with a myriad of products including hot and cold rolled, galvanized, Galvalume and prepainted steel; tinplate and chromium coated steel in coils, cut lengths, and strip; as well as welded pipe and tubular steels. In over eight decades of service, Dofasco's motto has remained the same: "Our product is steel, our strength is people."

Clifton W. Sherman built a foundry that served as the cornerstone for Dofasco in Hamilton, Ontario, in 1912. Then known as the Dominion Steel Castings Company, the foundry initially made steel castings for Canada's expanding railway system. The original plant covered five acres. In 1913 Dominion merged with Hamilton Malleable Iron Company and took the new name of Dominion Steel Foundry Company.

In 1914, Clifton's brother, Frank A. Sherman, joined the firm as production for war goods began to roll. As World War I progressed, orders for stirrups, bridles, and clevises were replaced with orders for munitions, marine forgings, and steel plate, reflecting changes in the nature of warfare. The company purchased a plate mill in 1917, and a new forging plant began churning out shell forgings. The company's name changed again that year to Dominion Foundries and Steel, Limited, even then known as Dofasco. When the war drew to a close in 1918, Dofasco had 11 open-hearth furnaces producing about 750 tons of steel per day. The plant had sprawled

to 26 acres with about 2,280 workers on the payroll, nearly 10 times the number just four years earlier.

The 1920s were a difficult decade for the Canadian steelmaker. Following the end of World War I, demand for steel dropped off drastically. To make matters worse, low tariffs allowed U.S. steel producers to control a sizable chunk of the Canadian steel market. Dofasco operated Canada's only heavy plate mill capable of producing 6- to 42-inch universal steel plate. It was completed in 1921, but tough foreign competition kept the mill working below capacity for most of the decade. The foundry, however, picked up the slack for the mill during the 1920s, and the company's expertise in steel castings improved accordingly. By 1928, the market for Canadian steel plate improved, and in 1929 a second shift was operating at the universal plate mill.

In 1930, Dofasco's foundry poured a 95,000-pound casting for a hydroelectric development in Quebec. It was the largest such casting ever produced in Canada. During the Great Depression, demand for steel fluctuated: sometimes the foundry was overbooked, at others it was virtually idle. Canada's rail system continued to expand, yet provided orders sporadically. The second half of the decade saw many improvements at Dofasco, including a 20-inch cold reducing mill brought on line in 1935 and the production of Canada's first tin plate.

Dofascolite, the name under which the company's tin plate was marketed, was a tremendously successful product. In 1937, the company built a 42-inch cold mill, which produced 100 tons of cold-rolled steel per day. By the late 1930s war again loomed on the horizon, and Dominion Foundries and Steel geared up to meet Canada's war demands. Between 1935 and 1940, the company spent $5.8 million on new facilities. At the time three-quarters of all steel and one-third of all tin produced in Canada came from Dofasco. The company became Canada's only domestic producer of armor plate in 1941, supplying the Canadian armed forces until the end of the second World War.

After World War II, the company continued to produce at record levels. In August 1951, Dofasco ignited its first blast furnace. Three years later, it became the first North American company to produce basic oxygen steel. This new process resulted in higher quality steel at reduced costs. Also, in 1954, Dominion Foundries and Steel acquired the galvanized sheet division of Lysaght's Canada, Limited. A year later, the company began operating a 56-inch cold mill with a continuous galvanizing line. It was in this year, 1955, that founder Clifton Sherman died and was succeeded as president by his brother, Frank.

The next year, 1956, a second blast furnace began operations. Substantial facility renovations were made during the next five years; between 1950 and 1959, Dofasco invested $120 million in new plant facilities. Dofasco's postwar growth continued into the next decade. In 1960, the company installed a second galvanizing line, raising steel production potential to one million tons per year. Dofasco's next growth came through acquisitions: in 1961, a joint venture to run the Wabush Iron Company was initiated; in 1962, National Steel Car Corporation, a leading manufacturer of railroad cars, was purchased; then the Temagami property, destined to become the Sherman mine, was purchased.

In 1964, four years before the Sherman mine delivered its first iron ore pellets, there was a second changing of the guard at Dominion, when Frank A. Sherman stepped down from the presidency in favor of his son, Frank H. Sherman. Two years later, the company expanded its iron ore capacity by purchasing the Adams mine in northern Ontario.

Capital investments had continued throughout the 1960s. When industrial impact on the environment became a growing concern in the late 1960s, Dominion Foundries and Steel reacted, installing pollution-control equipment to improve the quality of water returned to Lake Ontario from the plant. By 1994, the company had invested about $450 million to install, retrofit, and operate a myriad of pollution abatement equipment at its facilities.

Steady demand for steel kept the facilities at Dofasco humming into the early 1970s and inspired more acquisitions. In March 1973, Dofasco bought the Beach-viLime Ltd. quarry, insuring a steady supply of lime. A month later, it acquired a pipe manufacturer, Prudential Steel. In the mid-1970s massive construction was underway to double steel output within 20 years and a second five-stand cold mill was built in 1974. By 1976, sales rebounded from the recessionary trough, reaching record levels in some areas. Two years later, the company launched what was at that time its largest construction project, a second melt shop that would be a technological wonder run with computers and video cameras. It also purchased Guelph Dolime that year, a lime quarry to be operated as a part of the BeachviLime unit. As the 1970s drew to a close, Dofasco announced its plans to build a fourth galvanizing line and a second hot strip mill.

In October 1980, Dominion Foundries and Steel, Limited, officially changed its name to Dofasco Inc. A severe recession struck Canada in the second half of 1980, causing the company to shut down a plant for part of July. The steel industry was hard hit, but Dofasco continued with the new plant's construction on schedule. As the recession deepened, however, Dofasco was finally forced to take cost-cutting measures; demand for steel was critically low. In November 1982, the company laid off 2,100 employees; net income for the year had dropped to $63.8 million from $169.3 million the previous year.

In 1983 Paul Phoenix, a Dofasco employee since 1951, became president and CEO, only the second nonfamily member to hold the titles. That year, production levels improved, with all laid off employees returning to their jobs. Also, rival steelmaker Ivaco Ltd. made the first of several purchases of Dofasco stock in 1983. Demand for premium-quality steel prompted Dofasco's conversion in 1984 of its number-one galvanizing line to production of a new corrosion-resistant steel, Galvalume. By 1985, Ivaco Ltd. had acquired nearly 12 percent of Dofasco's shares, making it the single biggest shareholder and alarming Dofasco's management. Rather than gamble with the company's future, Dofasco issued $325 million in new voting convertible shares, lessening Ivaco's stake to 9.7 percent, and denied the latter's request for a seat on the board. Once this crisis had ended, Dofasco directed its attention to a $750 million cast slab expansion, the company's most expensive project ever.

The new facilities enabled Dofasco to produce new and higher- quality steel products. Several major acquisitions helped Dofasco's sales jump from $1.9 billion in 1985 to $3.9 billion in 1989. In December 1986, Dofasco acquired the Whittar Steel Strip Company of Detroit, which specialized in strip products used in the automotive industry. As revenues continued to climb, Dofasco posed a $154-million profit on $2.2 billion in sales in 1987 and was widely regarded as Canada's most profitable steel company.

Yet Dofasco's fortunes were to change dramatically after the 1988 acquisition of the Ontario-based Algoma Steel Corp. Ltd. for $560 million. Though the purchase was considered a boon for the steel industry, Algoma's troubled history included substantial losses, a heavy debt load, and wildly fluctuating production costs. Yet Dofasco's management believed Algoma's core business was sound and found the benefits of an enhanced product line and combined manufacturing capabilities worth the risk. Buying Algoma saved Dofasco the immense costs of building several new facilities to keep up with ever-growing demand; together, the two would yield over six million tons per year, making Dofasco Canada's largest steel producer. Continuing its acquisitive trend, Dofasco bought first 25 percent and then the remaining shares of Quebec Cartier Mining Co. in 1989, one the largest iron ore mines in the country. The company then announced $1 billion in renovations and new construction to its Hamilton operations, including a $465-million cold roll mill. Then came many unexpected factors: Algoma's 112-day strike resulting in $75 million in lost revenues (a new experience for the nonunion Dofasco), continued high interest rates, an inflated Canadian dollar and falling steel prices, all of which brought Algoma to the brink of bankruptcy. When Algoma was unable to pay a $32.5-million loan payment, Dofasco paid it; when another installment came due and Algoma had no funds, Dofasco declined to pony up. Disavowing further financial support, Dofasco wrote off the entire Algoma operation in 1991 for $713 million.

Demand for durable consumer goods continued to be weak during the early 1990s, and as a result Dofasco's major customers—the automotive, appliance, and construction industries—cut orders. For the first time in a decade, Dofasco posted a second-quarter loss of $27 million on revenue of $535 million (previous year results were $6 million profit on $713 million in revenue). Staying true to its motto of "Our product is steel, our strength is people," Dofasco began the first of several early retirement offers to the company's 11,000-plus employees, rather than massive permanent layoffs. In 1992, Dofasco reported a second-quarter loss of $65.9 million attributed to the closing of its original foundry and costs of its second early retirement package, then announced its plans to sell National Steel Car Ltd., Prudential Steel, and BeachviLime Quarry.

On the positive side, Dofasco had combated overcapacity problems by building a hot-dip coated steel plant with Japan's NKK Corp. and the United States's National

Steel Corporation. The alliance was the first steel industry joint venture involving companies from three countries. In another venture, with Co-Steel Inc. of Toronto, the two formed Gallatin Steel and commenced building a US$400-million flat-rolled steel minimill on the Ohio River in Kentucky. The revolutionary minimill (based on Nucor's phenomenally successful prototype in Crawfordsville, Indiana), would produce hot rolled steel from scrap, replacing the traditional blast furnace method using iron ore and lime.

Additionally, Dofasco, the National Research Council, and five other steel companies (including rival Stelco, Canada's top steelmaker), had begun "Project Bessemer," a study researching the feasibility of direct strip coating. Then in late 1993, Dofasco was forced to initiate its first involuntary layoff after only 400 of 1,400 employees accepted its latest voluntary retirement package. By April 1994, Dofasco completed its restructuring and layoffs and could finally concentrate on regaining its edge. Income from operations in 1993 reached a solid $65.9 million and grew substantially to $179.7 million in 1994, heralding optimism for the steelmaker's future.

To capitalize on its growing stability and stay ahead of the competition, Dofasco reported a $200-million expansion to combine its latest minimill technology with the company's Hamilton blast furnace operations. If successful, the partnership of the two facilities would raise annual capacity, slash imports of cast steel slab and reduce the minimill's dependence on scrap by substituting liquid iron from Hamilton's furnaces and coke ovens. As 1995 neared an end, a trimmer and wiser Dofasco prepared for the remainder of the decade: it not only hoped to have a more open trade relationship with Mexico after NAFTA, but was poised to take full advantage of the steel industry's latest technological leaps.

Principal Subsidiaries:

Dofasco U.S.A. Inc.; Iron Ore Company of Canada (6.4%); Quebec Cartier Mining Co. (50%); Wabush Mines (22.1%); Baycoat (50%); DNN Galvanizing Limited Partnership (50%); Ferrum Inc. (50%); Gallatin Steel Company (50%); Sorevco and Company Ltd. (50%).

Further Reading:

Dofasco 75: 1912-1987, Hamilton, Ontario: Dofasco Inc., 1987.
Dofasco to Cut 10% of Work Force, Close Steel Castings Division, *Wall Street Journal,* April 23, 1992 p. B9.
Dofasco's Wallace Resigns in Dispute Over Strategic Plan, *Wall Street Journal,* July 21, 1992 p. B10.

Estok, David, "Algoma Fuels Dofasco's Corporate World Strategy," *The Financial Post,* April 24, 1989, pp. 1, 8.
Fleming, James, and Olive, David, "Dofasco's Big Misadventure," *Globe and Mail,* May 17, 1991, p. P32.
Hallman, Mark, "Dofasco Mulls Selling, Shutting Businesses," *The Financial Post,* April 30, 1990, p. 1.
————, "Big Steelmakers Get Rolling," *The Financial Post,* January 29, 1994, p. 15.
"Industry Makes Marketing Changes: A Steely Will to Get Ahead—Again," *Marketing,* June 29, 1987, pp. B1, B18.
Keenan, Greg, "Dofasco Unveils $200-Million Project," *Globe and Mail,* April 11, 1995, p. B7.
Kilpatrick, Lynne, "Dofasco Inc.: Due for a Comeback," *Financial Times of Canada,* January 23, 1993, pp. 11-12.
Languedoc, Colin, "Dofasco President Sees Salad Days Ahead for the Steelmaker," *The Financial Post,* May 2, 1988, p. 10.
Lem, Gail, "Trade Tribunal's Steel Ruling 'Scary'," *Globe and Mail,* May 8, 1993, p. B3.
————, "From Scrap Heap to Treasure," *Globe and Mail,* July 13, 1993, p. B1.
Luke, Anick M., "Dofasco's Credit Outlook Positive, Rating Reaffirmed," *Investor's Digest,* July 22, 1994, p. 272.
Mayberry, John T., "Total Quality Management at Dofasco," *The Business Quarterly,* Summer 1992, pp. 120-22.
Parkinson, David E., "Dofasco to Close Ingot Plant, Take 4th-Period Charge," *Wall Street Journal,* November 27, 1992, p. C13.
Partridge, John, "Dofasco Bid for Algoma Stuns USW, Pleases Rival," *Globe and Mail,* July 19, 1988, p. B1.
Ritts, Morton, "Industrial Evolution," *Canadian Business,* February 1987, pp. 46-49, 51.
Romain, Ken, "Dofasco Hits Big Time with Algoma Takeover," *Globe and Mail,* August 22, 1988, p. B1.
————, "Dofasco New Owner of Big Ore Mine," *Globe and Mail,* July 1, 1989, p. B1.
————, "New Building Is Dofasco's Latest Leap Forward," *Globe and Mail,* July 8, 1989, p. B3.
Siklos, Richard, "Dofasco, the Heir Apparent to the Throne in Steel Town," *Financial Times of Canada,* July 25, 1988, p. 8.
Steacy, Anne, "Union-Free Workplace," *Maclean's,* July 13, 1987, p.35.
Stinson, Marian, "Dofasco Discards Algoma," *Globe and Mail,* January 24, 1991, p. B1.
————, "Dofasco Posts $24.6-Million Loss," *Globe and Mail,* July 31, 1991, p. B7.

—Thomas M. Tucker
—updated by Taryn Benbow-Pfalzgraf

Dominion Textile Inc.

1950 Sherbrooke St. West
Montreal, Quebec, H3H 1E7
(514) 989-6000
Fax: (514) 989-6214

Public Company
Incorporated: 1905 as the Dominion Textile
  Company Limited
Employees: 8,700
Sales: $1.33 billion
Stock Exchanges: Montreal Toronto
SICs: 2200 Textile Mill Products

Dominion Textile Inc. is one of Canada's largest textile companies and the world's largest manufacturer of denim. Dominion grew slowly throughout the twentieth century, first strengthening its role as a Canadian manufacturer before acquiring a number of companies in the United States, mostly in the 1970s and 1980s. By 1994 Dominion posted sales of $1.33 billion and held strong market positions in denim, yarn, technical fabrics, apparel fabrics, and nonwovens.

The roots of Dominion Textile reach back to 1890 with the formation of the Dominion Cotton Mills Company. Eight small, struggling textile firms had banded together to pool their resources; each had suffered from the high costs and inefficiencies associated with producing a small number of many items. Dominion, like many other Canadian textile firms, grew to depend on the profitable trade to the Far East, which had become possible with the completion of the Canadian Pacific Railway in 1885. However, the Boxer Rebellion in China in 1900 disrupted trade to that lucrative market.

In 1905, in a further effort to stave off financial ruin, a handful of companies again banded together. They were the Dominion Cotton Mills, Ltd. (which by that time had plants in Halifax and Windsor, Nova Scotia; Moncton, New Brunswick; Montreal, Magog, and Caoticook, Quebec; and Kingston and Branford, Ontario), the Montmorency Cotton Mills Company, the Montreal-based Merchants Cotton Company, and the Colonial Bleaching and Printing Company, also of Montreal, for a total of eleven plants. The new entity was called the Dominion Textile Company Limited.

Montreal financier David Yuile was the company's first president, but it was Charles B. Gordon, who became president in 1909, who dominated the early history of the company. One of the first battles the company weathered was brought on by security holders of the former Dominion Cotton Mills Company and Merchants Cotton Company who had refused to sell their stock in 1905. The case was heard by the Privy Council, which ruled in favor of Dominion.

With the advent of World War I, Gordon was put in charge of war-purchase missions in the United States by the British and Canadian governments; he was later knighted for his duties. Dominion's plants ran continuously to supply goods for the war. The plants' overuse during the war meant that in the years immediately following, much of the company's resources were put into repairing and refurbishing its manufacturing facilities, which included the facility that it acquired in 1919 when it bought the Mount Royal Spinning Company of Montreal.

A stock offering in 1922 brought Dominion $2,500,000 in new capital. A new entity, the Dominion Textile Co. Limited, sometimes called Domtex, took over the assets of the Dominion Textile Company. A series of technological upgrades (after the introduction of long-draft spinning and multiple loom sets) and acquisitions swiftly followed. In 1928 Dominion bought two American companies that made tire fabric: the Jenckes-Canadian Company became a subsidiary known as Drummondville Cotton Company Limited, and the Canadian Connecticut Cotton Mills became Sherbrooke Cotton Company Limited. (In 1934 Sherbrooke was converted into a sheeting-fabric manufacturing plant, and tire manufacture was concentrated in Drummondville.) In 1930 Dominion took over the management of Montreal Cotton Limited, a company in which it had an interest since 1908. In 1948 Dominion bought the last of Montreal Cotton's shares, and by 1953 it was completely folded back into Dominion.

As with many other industries, the onset of World War II put a spur to textile production, which had suffered during the Depression. A plant that had lain dormant from 1934 was reactivated in 1940, and Dominion made a range of products for military purposes, from camouflage nets to bootlaces. With an eye on the postwar economy, Dominion entered a joint venture in 1945 to make rayon with the Burlington Mills Corporation of North Carolina, called Dominion Burlington Mills Limited. In March 1952 Dominion bought Burlington's 50 percent share and the company's name was changed to Domil Limited (those plants became fully integrated with the company in 1966).

During the 1960s, Dominion built four new plants in Quebec and Ontario, where a popular new fabric, the polyester/cotton blend, was spun, woven, and finished. One print ad created during this time featured "the unwrinkable Molly Brown," a little girl whose clothing, made of Dominion's Truprest fabric, stayed smooth and wrinkle-free. Also during this time, Dominion acquired Penmans in Ontario, a company engaged in the manufacture of knitted leisurewear. This represented Dominion's first move outside the primary textile industry.

In November 1969, the company's name was changed to Dominion Textile Limited. A string of acquisitions and divestitures followed as the North American textile industry tried to come to terms with the flood of cheap imports from the Far East. In 1969 Dominion bought Fiberworld Limited and Jaro Manufacturing Co. Ltd. In 1972 it formed a joint venture—DHJ Canadian, Ltd.—with New York-based DHJ Industries, Inc. Three years later, Dominion bought DHJ Industries Inc., which consisted of eight plants in the United States as well as affiliates and distributors throughout the world. That purchase strengthened Dominion's hand in the international marketplace as the textile industry continued to rapidly shift out of North America.

The DHJ takeover was an unfriendly one. The financially troubled company (with US$64 million in debt, US$20 million from the first nine months of 1975 alone) was dominated by chairman and founder Herbert Haskell. Much of his family's holdings in the company were held as collateral for personal loans made by Chemical Bank of New York. When Haskell refused to sell to Dominion, Dominion went to his banker and negotiated a deal without him, purchasing DHJ for US$9.2 million. Haskell sued and vowed to go into direct competition with Dominion, but he eventually settled. Dominion got a lot out of the deal, for DHJ owned one of the largest denim manufacturing facilities in the United States through its Swift Textiles, Inc. subsidiary and had sales of US$191 million for the fiscal year ending June 1974.

In 1979 Dominion, which had been renamed Dominion Textile Inc., continued to try to move away from "commodity" fabrics, which were dominated by imports. In October 1979, DHJ and Facemate Corporation of Chicopee, Massachusetts, formed a joint venture—DHJ-Facemate Corporation—and merged their interlining operations. In 1980 Dominion bought Linn-Corriher Corporation of Landis, North Carolina, which made cotton and synthetic yarns, for $25 million. In 1981 it acquired Mirafi, Inc., the civil-engineering fabrics division of the Hoescht Celanese Corp. of Somerville, New Jersey. Mirafi made plastic-based materials used in roadbeds and drainage systems. In 1988, Dominion acquired Wayn-Tex, a manufacturer of carpet backing, based in Virginia. Also that year, the company acquired the London-based Klopman International, Europe's largest producer and distributor of workwear fabrics.

Recession exacerbated the difficulties brought by the inexorable growth of cheap imports, and from 1982 to 1985 Dominion lost money. Dominion responded by paring down operations. In 1981 it sold its 50 percent interest in DHJ-Facemate. Between 1983 and 1986 Dominion closed 13 of its 26 plants. Most of these facilities were in Quebec, where the company had repeatedly locked horns with the aggressive union Centrale des Syndicats Democratiques. As opposed to the United States, where most textile workers were not unionized, most of the workers in Canada at that time were, and wages ran approximately 7 to 10 percent higher than in the United States. Canadian textile executives also complained of the difficulty in competing against U.S. makers when U.S. plants were flexible

enough to run seven days a week if necessary; strict union rules prohibited such flexibility, they said.

In 1986 Dominion again tried to make an incursion across the border when it tried to purchase Avondale Mills, a denim and yarn maker in Sylacauga, Alabama. Dominion lost out to AM Acquisition, which had countered its US$26-a-share bid with an offer of US$28. Dominion was not daunted by the effort and simply went after a bigger prize. That prize was none other than its former joint-venture partner Burlington Mills Corporation of Greensboro, North Carolina. By 1987 Burlington Mills was the largest textile company in the United States, with fiscal year 1986 sales of US$2.8 billion. Dominion's sales in fiscal 1986 were US$671 million.

Burlington was vulnerable, having become dependent on selling commodity fabrics in a market that was dominated by overseas makers. Dominion teamed up with renowned New York raider Asher Edelman to try and win Burlington. Edelman first quietly gained control of 7.6 percent of Burlington stock. Edelman and Dominion then bid US$1.51 billion for the company on April 24. Some suspected that Dominion was interested in only a handful of Burlington's plants and planned, if it won control of the venerable manufacturer, to sell off the rest. Burlington's denim plants contributed 25 percent of its revenues and were considered Dominion's real goal. Dominion was also eager to put down roots in the United States in an effort to get around the expected results of lower tariffs in negotiations that were then taking place between the United States and Canada. Dominion was fearful of being undercut by larger volume, lower cost facilities in the United States, where Dominion earned more than a quarter of its sales.

The struggle for control of Burlington raged for over seven weeks, with a series of offers and counteroffers made until Dominion made a final offer of US$2.1 billion. Lawsuits were filed on both sides. In the end Dominion lost the battle—Burlington took itself private in a leveraged buyout—but won the war. Edelman and Dominion agreed to drop their hostile takeover attempt in exchange for US$25 million and certain Burlington properties. Edelman and Dominion sold their 12 percent stake for a post-tax gain of US$15.2 million. Further, Dominion snapped up several of Burlington's most desirable facilities: a denim plant in Erwin, North Carolina, which it bought for US$205 million (the purchase contract included an agreement to drop all litigation from the takeover attempt); Klopman International, the largest producer in Europe of polyester- and cotton-blended fabrics for workwear, purchased for US$90 million; as well as Klopman International SpA (Italy), Burlington Industries Limited (Ireland), Burlington Deutschland GmbH, and Burlington AC. These moves seemed to say that Dominion would place the bulk of its future investments outside of Canada. After the purchase of Burlington's denim factories, Dominion became one of the world's largest denim manufacturers.

The acquisitions of the 1980s left the company in debt, and the recession that hit the apparel industry in 1989 meant that Dominion lost money in 1990 and 1991. Dominion restructured to bring focus to the company's sprawling assemblage of plants and subsidiaries, which made everything from electrical insulation to book bindings to bedding to upholstery. Plants were closed and divisions sold. Mirafi was sold off during this time, and Dominion merged its Caldwell towel division with the operations of New York-based C.S. Brooks Corporation. In 1992 it sold off its Wayn-Tex and Dominion Fabrics Co. divisions. Poly-Bond Inc., a wholly owned subsidiary, became the focus of its nonwovens efforts in North America, and heavy investments were made at its Waynesboro, Virginia, facilities.

Thus Dominion's emphasis was on denims, nonwoven fabrics, and commodity yarns. In 1990, Dominion had acquired Quebec-based Textiles Dionne, which specialized in cotton and synthetic yarns. The company acquired Nordlys S.A., a nonwovens manufacturer in Bailleul, France, and in 1991 completed construction on a modern new facility to house all of the operations. In 1992, another nonwovens plant was built in Malaysia.

In further efforts to strengthen its core businesses, Dominion agreed in 1995 to sell DHJ Industries to Chargeurs Textiles of France. The company restructured Dominion Specialty Yarns in Canada to focus on its most profitable product lines, and the Poly-Bond subsidiary entered into a joint venture with Corovin GmbH to produce new high-technology nonwovens.

The popularity of denim in the early 1990s (denim demand grew by 30 percent from 1990 through 1993) and a 20 percent drop in cotton prices helped Dominion's financial position. In 1994 sales were $1.33 billion, with a net income of $33.5 million, a turnaround from two years before when it had lost $74.8 million. In 1994, the bulk of its business was derived from denim, which accounted for 39 percent of sales ($518.3 million), yarns, which made up 21 percent ($281.4 million), and technical fabrics, 17 percent ($228.4 million). Apparel brought in 13 percent of sales ($178.1 million).

Principal Subsidiaries:

Swift Textiles, Inc.; Swift Textiles Canada; Swift Textiles (Far East) Ltd.; Dominion Yarn Corporation; Dominion Yarn Company; Dominion Specialty Yarns; Dominion Textile (USA) Inc.; Dominion Cotton Services; Intech-PEM Inc.; Vivatex; Dominion Textile International B.V.; Dominion Textile International (Asia) Pte. Ltd.; Nordly's S.A.; Klopman International S.r.l.; Klopman International Ltd.; Poly-Bond Inc.; Dominion Industrial Fabrics Company.

Further Reading:

"Dominion Textile Inc. Ends Bid for Avondale," *Wall Street Journal,* April 4, 1986, p. 4.
Foust, Dean, "Burlington Almost Invited Edelman to Attack," *Business Week,* May 1, 1987, p. 50.
——, "Dominion's Unraveling Bid," *Business Week,* June 1, 1987, p. 49.
"How Domtex Staged Its Coup at DHJ," *Business Week,* June 9, 1975, p. 26.
O'Connor, D'Arcy, "To Fade or Not to Fade," *Canadian Business,* June 1988, p. 45.
"Who's the Real Winner in Burlington Match," *Textile World,* June 1987, p. 23.

—C. L. Collins

Domtar Inc.

395 de Maisonneuve Blvd. West
Montreal, Quebec H3A 1L6
(514) 848-5400
Fax: (514) 848-6878

Public Company
Incorporated: 1929 as Dominion Tar & Chemical
    Company Ltd.
Employees: 9,000
Sales: $2.41 billion
Stock Exchanges: Montreal Toronto Vancouver New
    York
SICs: 1479 Chemical & Fertilizer Mineral Mining,
    Nec; 2611 Pulp Mills; 2621 Paper Mills; 2819
    Industrial Inorganic Chemicals, Nec; 2869
    Industrial Organic Chemicals, Nec; 6719 Offices
    of Holding Companies, Nec

Domtar is one of Canada's leading suppliers of pulp and paper products with a network of facilities across the country involved in every aspect of the pulp and paper business, from logging to pulp production and from manufacturing to selling fine papers and newsprint. Domtar also became a major manufacturer of construction materials, such as gypsum wallboard, and offered a diversified line of packaging materials. In 1989, the company completed the sale of its original chemical and energy businesses, eliminating the last vestiges of what had once been known as the Dominion Tar & Chemical Company Limited.

Dominion started in 1903 with the construction of a coal tar distillation plant in Sydney, Nova Scotia. Coal tar distillation was the process of removing a range of valuable chemicals from tar, which itself was obtained by a preliminary heating and distillation of coal. The resulting commercial by-products were divided into three categories: hydrocarbons, such as benzene and napthalene; acids, such as phenol and creosols; and bases, such as aniline, which provide a variety of dyes. In addition, the pitch residue of coal tar distillation was useful in the construction of roads, an application first made only a few years before the founding of Domtar in 1903. At that time, the commercially valuable properties of coal tar were just beginning to be explored, but as Canada's economy rapidly industrialized the Dominion plant turned out an increasing number of products, and the company grew quickly.

World War I culminated in a period of great prosperity for Canada and Dominion Tar. The ensuing slump was fortunately brief, and by the mid-1920s industrial activity was again strong. Dominion's sales increased accordingly. The widespread growth of automobile traffic required the construction of secure, all-weather roadways, boosting Dominion revenue from the sale of pitch; while the coal tar distillates continued to find an increasing number of applications in the chemical, textile, and steel industries. The relatively new field of pharmaceuticals also derived a variety of compounds from coal tar, as did the even-more-recent science of plastics. As a sign of its vigorous growth in these many areas, and in order to raise capital for further expansion, Dominion Tar was incorporated in 1929 and shortly thereafter offered its shares for public sale.

Though perhaps not the most ideal time to incorporate, the company nonetheless did so and the October crash of the Montreal and Toronto stock markets, along with virtually every other in the world, precipitated 10 years of economic depression in Canada. Dominion, which had by this time relocated to Quebec, weathered the storm with considerable success, although failing to pay a stock dividend as regularly as its leaders might have wished. Due to the wide variety of industries for which it manufactured goods, Dominion was able to maintain a minimum amount of business during even the leanest years and, after enduring a series of enforced layoffs and cuts in capital spending, emerged as a stronger, more efficient company by the end of the decade. By that time Canada had joined the Allies in World War II and the Canadian economy tooled up for what would become a 30-year boom.

The 1950s were not only a period of sustained growth at Dominion, but also marked the beginning of the company's expansion into the paper and construction businesses. With its enormous forests, Canada had become the world's leading manufacturer of paper products, in particular supplying the United States with a good portion of its paper needs. By the mid-1950s, Dominion had closely studied the growing worldwide paper market and, flush with cash after a series of excellent years, acquired 33 percent of Howard Smith Paper Mills Limited in 1957, with major mills in both Cornwall, Ontario, and Windsor, Quebec. Howard Smith was a maker of fine paper for printing and writing purposes and of kraft paper for applications requiring strength.

Dominion's entry into the paper business, though limited, was viewed by most observers as somewhat unorthodox, and many doubted such a combination would prove manageable. The Dominion picture was complicated further the following year when it purchased an interest in Gypsum, Lime, & Alabastine Canada Limited, producers of gypsum wallboard for the construction industry. The company was now stretched across the three distinctly different enterprises of chemicals, paper, and construction materials, but the financial results were excellent, encouraging the even bolder moves that soon followed.

At the close of the 1950s, Dominion was faced with a fundamental and recurring question about the direction of its future growth, a question it answered differently during the next several decades. As President Wilfred

Hall expressed in 1964, in Canada as elsewhere businesses could not afford to remain small, yet Canada was unusual in the limited size of its internal markets. Dominion would therefore either have to concentrate exclusively on one of its businesses and expand internationally, or remain a fundamentally Canadian concern and diversify its interests across a number of industrial boundaries. In 1960, Hall and his advisors at Dominion chose the latter alternative; 30 years later, in an age of global competition, Domtar would reverse itself and begin paring down its holdings. Accordingly, in 1961, Hall announced a complex multiple-merger combining Dominion; the remaining shares of Howard Smith Paper; a maker of newsprint, St. Lawrence Corporation Limited; and Hinde & Dauch Limited, a manufacturer of corrugated containers and merchandising displays. The result was an early example of the conglomerate, one of Canada's ten largest companies with sales approaching C$400 million and some 18,000 employees at over 270 facilities across the length of Canada. By any measure it was a complex and somewhat ungainly mixture of diverse businesses, and its sorting out and eventual coordination would take the better part of the decade to finish. Many industry analysts doubted it would ever happen.

The newly reformed Dominion Tar & Chemical Company consisted of six operating groups, each of these in turn broken down into many divisions. Domtar Chemical represented the company's original interests in coal tar by-products such as creosols, dyes, and pitch, as well as recent acquisitions in salt mining and lime; Domtar Construction Materials handled wallboard products and a growing business in wood laminates for use in home furnishings; the pulp and paper products were split among three groups; and Domtar even entered the consumer products market via the Javex Company, maker of various cleaning agents.

Within a few years, the company had added the beginnings of an overseas presence—paper and plastics in the United Kingdom, bleach in the West Indies, and lime in Washington state. More substantial yet was the 1963 purchase of a 49 percent interest in Cellulosa d'Italia, an Italian paper company. Dominion's focus, however, remained firmly on Canada and the United States, and from the beginning it proved remarkably adept at melding its diverse interests into a coherent whole. The various divisions did quite a bit of business with each other, allowing the company to keep product runs at their maximum and most efficient lengths while saving money on marketing expenses. Perhaps most impressive was Domtar Inc.'s (the name was officially changed in 1965) smooth absorption of its new paper businesses, which soon provided more than 50 percent of corporate sales. In the space of a few years, Domtar had transformed itself from a medium-sized company into a huge conglomerate, best described as a pulp and paper manufacturer.

By the time T. N. Beaupre had replaced Hall as president in 1967, the new Domtar had taken shape. Beaupre simplified the company's structure by grouping its divisions into chemicals, construction, and pulp and paper units; then he sold off the consumer products division to Bristol-Myers for $37 million, recognizing the company could not compete with larger marketers of consumer goods. Domtar was now Canada's leading producer of fine papers, with more than 500 different grades in production; but its success in paper brought with it a long series of bitter disputes with organized labor, traditionally strong in the paper industries and hungry for a larger share of the profits generated by the robust economy of the late 1960s. Domtar rarely enjoyed a year without either a strike, the threat of a strike, or the need to negotiate important and hard-fought contracts with labor, all of which tended to complicate every aspect of its business planning.

After a number of excellent years at Domtar and Canada in general, the bottom dropped out of the world economy in 1973 when the Organization of Petroleum Exporting Countries (OPEC) quadrupled the price of oil. In the ensuing recession of 1974-76, the downturn in Domtar's pulp and paper business was so severe the company thought seriously of getting out of the industry altogether. Canada's share of the world market had shrunk from 25 to 19 percent in 1961, yet the prosperous 1960s had saddled Domtar with high labor costs at a time of shrinking sales and margins. New president Alex D. Hamilton adopted a conservative policy of closing marginally profitable mills while looking for further investments in construction, preferably in the United States. In 1978, Domtar satisfied both of these goals with its C$35 million purchase of Kaiser Cement's California wallboard facilities, which also helped balance the flow of Canadian and U.S. dollars at Domtar, a company increasingly dependent on exports to the United States. Industry analysts described the move as typical of Domtar's recent tendency toward a conservative policy—and though the purchase was made a little late and at rather too high a price, but it was basically sound.

It was at about this time that Domtar became involved in a lengthy series of takeover bids. When the Argus Corporation (owner of about 20 percent of Domtar's stock) decided to sell its Domtar holdings, they were quickly snapped up by MacMillan Bloedel, a West Coast paper competitor. MacMillan then made an offer for Domtar's remaining shares, which elicited a counteroffer by Domtar for all of MacMillan's stock. At that point Canadian Pacific, a third paper company, also made a bid for MacMillan, prompting the premier of British Columbia to decree that MacMillan couldn't be purchased by any company outside the province.

Chastened, MacMillan sold its 20 percent of Domtar to an agency of Quebec provincial government, the Caisse de Depot et Placement du Quebec, entrusted with the investment of pension funds. A short time afterward, a second Quebec agency, the Societe Generale de Financement du Quebec, also acquired a piece of Domtar, and by August 1981 the Quebec government thus controlled more than 40 percent of the company's stock.

Under new president and CEO James H. Smith the company quickly underwent a thorough restructuring of its board of directors, which, together with the Quebec government's stock control, led to concern that Domtar would become an appendage of the Quebec government. The issue came to a head when Domtar asked the Canadian government for help in funding the $1 billion rehabilitation of its massive paper mill in Windsor,

Ontario. The request was denied, fueling the conviction of Quebecois separatists that their province would never receive fair treatment at the hands of the federal government. As it turned out, Domtar went ahead with the work at the Windsor mill, creating a world-class fine-paper facility, while the Quebec government tried unsuccessfully to sell off the Domtar stock it still held.

In the meantime, Domtar sales had passed the $1 billion mark in 1977 and leapt to $1.7 billion in 1981. Yet the severe recession of the early 1980s had forced the company into a belt-tightening strategy, which in turn led to its request for federal aid on the Windsor mill project. However, in general, the decade was good to Domtar. The company was again faced with the question of how best to expand beyond its already considerable size, and this time Smith and his board of directors decided to concentrate on a fewer number of global products. In essence, this decision meant the end of Domtar's chemical businesses, which had long been dwarfed by the company's paper and construction interests, and by 1990 the chemical assets had been sold for about $100 million. On the other hand, in 1987 Domtar paid US$241 million for the Genstar Gypsum Products Company's family of wallboard plants in the United States, a move the company would later regard as a costly mistake.

In the early 1990s, Domtar was again forced to focus its energy on a limited number of products, drastically paring down other divisions. In January 1991, after poor sales in both the Canadian and U.S. markets, Domtar announced a restructuring plan that, among other factors, required the elimination of its annual dividend and some 1,300 jobs (about 30 percent of its white-collar work force). With operating losses for 1990 at $379 million and a $1.1 billion debt load, Domtar hoped a changing of the guard would help and appointed Pierre Desjardins, formerly of Labatt Breweries of Canada and an ex-lineman of the Canadian Football League, as its new president and CEO and Quebec nationalist Jean Campeau as its chairman.

Despite a reduction of its debt load and year-end operating losses falling to $125 million in 1991, Domtar suffered another setback in February 1992 when Standard & Poors downgraded its rating to junk bond status or double-B (minus). Yet a year later the company rallied after securing patents and licensing rights for a new recycling process capable of using both recycled (old corrugated containers) and virgin fiber to make fine-paper products. The process also cut sludge by over 20 percent while producing a cleaner, brighter bleached product company reps said was "virtually indistinguishable from virgin paper."

By 1993, Domtar had lost more than $600 million in the preceding three years and had laid off more than 4,000 of its 14,000-plus workforce since 1989. However, the company was slowly regaining its strength, beginning with a new union agreement in March, then a $3-million operating profit in the third quarter (its first since 1990). Helped by the building boom in the United States after Hurricane Andrew and midwestern-state flooding, Domtar was poised for a recovery. Once again, an unexpected setback came with a $320-million cleanup bill to bring nine of its mills in Quebec and Ontario up to code with new national and provincial environmental standards over the next three years.

To shoulder the immense cost, Domtar announced the formation of Alliance Forest Products Inc. from its groundwood printing division (comprised of two saw-mills, two paper mills, and cutting rights in the Lac St. Jean area), which eventually generated $289 million in gross proceeds. Domtar then renamed its gypsum and decorative panel enterprises America North Industries (ANI), selling shares to the public and retaining 40 percent ownership. Lastly, Domtar considered putting its Construction Materials Group and roofing and insulation division, Techni-Therm, on the block.

The fall of 1994 brought another change in executive management, with the contract termination of Desjardins and Paul Gobeil (Campeau's 1993 replacement). Stephen Larson, who left the company in July after clashing with Desjardins, was named president and chief operating officer. By year's end, Domtar's operating profits reached $188 million from revenues of $2.14 billion, a sales increase of 25 percent (as opposed to an operating loss of $52 million and revenues of $1.7 billion in 1993). The company then began extensive renovations of its mills, including a $245 million investment in its Lebel-sur-Quevillon mill in Quebec to increase output, improve quality, and meet higher environmental standards.

In 1995, Domtar had completely reversed its financial status from 1990's near bankruptcy to record sales of just under $1.4 billion (up 40 percent in the second quarter alone) and net earnings of $166 million, more than 1987's earnings for the entire year. Moreover, the company increased liquidity by decreasing its debt load from 55 percent to 43 percent, and hoped to further reduce this figure to between 30 percent and 35 percent by the next fiscal year. On a roll, Domtar negotiated the purchase of Quebec's La Compagnie J.B. Rolland et Fils (a fine papers distributor) and Produits Forestiers Gatineau Inc. (a sawmill) in the fall of 1995. The former acquisition allowed Domtar to diversify its product line and distribution, whereas the latter increased capacity by over 20 percent and helped Domtar retain its competitive edge in the lumber industry.

Principal Subsidiaries:

America North Industries Ltd.; Bisson & Bisson Inc.; Brompton Lands Ltd.; Domtar Enterprises Inc.; Domtar Holdings Inc.; Domtar Industries Inc.; Domtar International Ltd.; Domtar Realties Ltd.; Jellco Packaging Corp.; La Compagnie J.B. Rolland et Fils; Laberge & Laberge Ltd.; Lithotech Inc.; Maine Timber Holdings Limited; Pacos Carrier Inc.; Produits Forestiers Gatineau Inc.; St. Georges Gypsum Mines Inc.; San Marcos Carrier Inc.; Techni-Therm Inc.; 804736 Ontario Limited.

Further Reading:

Boardman, Anthony, Ruth Freedman, and Catherine Eckel, "The Price of Government Ownership: A Study of the Domtar Takeover," *Journal of Public Economics,* 1986.

96   Domtar Inc.

Chipello, Christopher, "Domtar Board Ousts Chairman, Chief, Citing Differences," *Wall Street Journal,* October 25, 1994, p. B4.

"Domtar Breaks Ground with Unions," *Pulp & Paper,* May 1993, p. 23.

"Domtar Continues Sales of Non-Core Operations," *Wood Technology,* July/August 1994, pp. 12-13.

"Domtar Joins Spinoff Movement," *Pulp & Paper,* May 1994, p. 23.

"Domtar Outlines Financing Plan, Reports a Loss," *Wall Street Journal,* February 14, 1992, p. A8.

"Domtar Restructures Fine Paper Business," *Pulp & Paper,* June 1991, p. 31.

"Domtar Slates $320-Million Program," *Pulp & Paper,* March 1994, p. 23.

"Domtar to Form New Firm Through Public Offering," *Wall Street Journal,* March 24, 1994, p. C17.

"Domtar to Give Mill a Facelift," *Globe and Mail,* March 18, 1995, p. B6.

"Domtar to Turn OCC into Fine Papers," *Pulp & Paper,* April 1993, p. 25.

"Domtar Wants Help in Cleanups at Mills," *Pulp & Paper,* April 1994, p. 21.

Gibbon, Ann, "Domtar Faces $320-Million Cleanup," *Globe and Mail,* January 22, 1994, p. B7.

———, "Domtar Ousts Its Chiefs," *Globe and Mail,* October 24, 1994, p. B1.

———, "Domtar Posts Record Profit," *Globe and Mail,* April 21, 1995, p. B3.

Mackie, Richard, "Domtar Spins Off Units in Bid to Return to Black," *Globe and Mail,* April 29, 1994, p. B15.

McKenna, Barrie, "Cuts at Domtar Continue," *Globe and Mail,* February 6, 1991, p. B9.

———, "Domtar Falls to Junk Bond Status," *Globe and Mail,* February 25, 1992, p. B9.

———, "Domtar Invests $200-Million in Recycling Breakthrough," *Globe and Mail,* February 12, 1993, p. B1.

———, "Domtar Loses $294-Million," *Globe and Mail,* February 1, 1991, p. B1.

———, "Domtar Repair Plan Hopes to Raise Millions," *Globe and Mail,* February 14, 1992, p. B1.

———, "Domtar Turning Corner on Profit," *Globe and Mail,* January 14, 1994, p. B4.

———, "Giant-Fighter Desjardins Tackles Troubled Domtar," *Globe and Mail,* April 27, 1991, p. B1.

———, "Jean Campeau Not Coming Back to Domtar," *Globe and Mail,* March 18, 1993, p. B4.

Nichols, Mark, "One City's Water Problem," *Maclean's,* January 15, 1990, p. 41.

Noble, Kimberley, "Quebec Denial Fails to Scotch Speculation on Domtar Sale," *Globe and Mail,* February 22, 1988, p. B3.

Ross, Val, "Paper Tigers," *Canadian Business,* September 1978.

Sinclair, Sonja, "Domtar: Case History of a Corporate Trend," *Canadian Business,* September 1964.

———, "Domtar: Case History of a Corporate Trend—II," *Canadian Business,* October 1964.

—Jonathan Martin
—updated by Taryn Benbow-Pfalzgraf

Dylex Ltd.

637 Lakeshore Boulevard West
Toronto, Ontario M5V 1AB
(416) 586-7000
Fax: (416) 586-7277

Public Company
Founded: 1967
Employees: 14,000
Sales: $1.75 billion
Stock Exchanges: Toronto
SICs: 5650 Family Clothing Stores

One of the leading apparel retailers in Canada, Dylex Ltd. operated more than 700 stores across the country in 1995. Its store chains included BiWay, Braemar, Club Monaco, Fairweather, Harry Rosen, Thrifty's, and Tip Top Tailors. Dylex also operated five stores in the United States under the Harry Rosen and Club Monaco names, and owned an apparel manufacturing unit. Dylex expanded rapidly during the 1970s and 1980s before experiencing financial problems in the early 1990s.

Dylex was founded in 1967 by Wilfred Posluns and James Kay, who purchased the 52 stores of Tip Top Tailors, a men's clothier, and Fairweather, a women's clothier. Although the chains were well established, Posluns and Kay felt that they were performing below their potential. In what would become a common pattern at Dylex, both chains improved financially under new ownership and expanded rapidly. During the 1970s Kay and Posluns expanded their business by purchasing other retailers that they believed had growth potential.

Their purchases included BiWay Stores Ltd., a discount retailer of food and general merchandise, Town and Country, and controlling interests in chains like Monaco Group Inc., a seller of men's and women's apparel, and Harry Rosen, a retailer of fine men's wear. By the end of the 1970s Dylex was operating a diversified group of growing retail chains with outlets across Canada. It controlled a full seven percent of the combined men's and women's wear markets in Canada and was generating revenues of more than US$500 million annually. Few people had ever heard of Dylex—the company's stock was still owned largely by Kay and Posluns—but

many of them were regular shoppers at the holding company's stores.

During the late 1970s and early 1980s Dylex expanded rapidly to include more than 1,000 stores in 17 different retail chains, many of which were leaders in their market segments. For example, Dylex holdings Harry Rosen, Braemar Apparel, and Fairweather were located in nearly every shopping mall in Canada. Also well known were Suzy Shier, BH Emporium, L.A. Express, and Big Steel Man; the latter three originated as in-store departments of Fairweather stores. 1983 revenues approached US$1 billion, about US$31 million of which was netted as earnings, as Dylex's share of the Canadian men's and women's apparel market jumped to a 11 percent. Importantly, the company also improved its profit margins and overall financial condition, reflecting an apparently sound operating strategy that complemented its expansion tactics.

By 1984 Dylex had become the largest clothing retailer in the country and one of the 100 largest companies in Canada. Its hefty gains throughout the 1970s and into the 1980s were largely the result of a savvy management incentive plan. Indeed, Kay and Posluns were generally disengaged from the operations of their subsidiaries. While they worked on buying new chains and managing the company's finances, the managers of their chains operated independently, with little direction from corporate headquarters. Thus, Dylex was effectively a loose conglomeration of companies linked by mutual ownership. If the company managers were successful, they were rewarded. If they failed, they were fired. "If you made it work, I didn't care what you did," Posluns recalled in the November 1990 *Canadian Business*.

During the 1970s and early 1980s the Dylex management system was undeniably effective. Dylex would purchase or invest in a subsidiary and allow existing or appointed managers to run the chain as they saw fit. Subsidiary managers did their own financial planning, merchandise selection, store design, and hiring and firing, and they reported to headquarters only during weekly meetings with Posluns. To ensure their best efforts, Dylex based managers' compensation on the performance of their division with no limit on pay. As a result, several of Dylex's managers were earning more than US$1 million annually by the early 1980s. "It's absolutely a dream," said Gord Edelstone, vice-president of the Tip Top men's wear chain, in the September 1986 *Dun's Business Month*. "Your really feel like you're running your own business. If he [Posluns] has an insight we might have missed and we get our backs up, he'll try it our way first and see what happens."

Although Dylex maintained an arms-length relationship with its subsidiaries, the company did provide financial and operations support that the chains would have missed without a corporate parent. For example, Dylex furnished real estate services to help subsidiaries find space and negotiate rent for new stores. It also maintained a computerized point-of-sale inventory system that was considered among the best in the industry. Dylex's greatest requirement was that each chain maintain a sharp focus on a carefully selected market niche. In addition, the home office set sales goals against which manager's performance would be measured. Dylex's stores were generally successful; indeed, Dylex was credited with turning around a number of the chains that it had purchased. As evidence of that success, Dylex's outlets averaged US$260 per-square-foot in sales annually in the early 1980s, compared to the industry average of just US$176.

Encouraged by solid gains in Canada, Dylex decided to try to implement its strategy in the massive U.S. retail market. The company had already wetted its feet in the United States in 1980 when it purchased clothing manufacturer Tobias Kotzin. Posluns believed that applying his retailing strategy in the United States could boost Dylex's sales more than five-fold by the end of the 1980s. To that end, the company launched an aggressive acquisition drive in 1984 when Dylex and an investment partner paid about US$350 million for Brooks Fashion Stores, a 700-plus chain of shops that sold medium-range clothing to young women. In 1985 Brooks executives convinced Dylex to fund the acquisition of a competitor, Foxmoor. Foxmoor brought about 600 more stores to the Dylex portfolio. As it did with its Canadian operations, Dylex allowed Brooks and Foxmoor managers to run the companies as they wished.

The Brooks and Foxmoor deals seemed encouraging at first. Sales at Foxmoor, for example, jumped 30 percent in 1985 following a change in the chain's inventory. In addition to the huge Foxmoor and Brooks deals, Dylex launched a number of new U.S. retail efforts during the mid-1980s. For example, in 1984 it purchased a controlling interest in Wet Seal, a California-based junior fashion chain with 18 outlets, and in 1985 it started a division of its Tip Top chain in Chicago. Also in 1984, Dylex purchased a controlling interest in National Brands Outlet (NBO), a 14-unit men's off-price clothing retailer in New York. By 1986 Dylex had amassed a total of 1,700 stores in the United States that were capturing nearly $800 million in annual sales. Including its Canadian divisions, Dylex owned or had significant interests in chains with 2,700 stores.

Dylex's achievements during the 1970s and even going into the mid-1980s were the result of efforts by both Posluns and Kay. During the early 1980s, however, their relationship became increasingly strained. In 1982 Kay used his 40 percent voting stake in the company to secure a large loan. The move angered Posluns, who owned a 50.1 percent voting stake in Dylex. Posluns succeeded in ousting Kay as chairman of Dylex in 1983, claiming that Kay had breached their agreement to share control of the company. The outraged Kay argued that the agreement was still intact. Although Kay continued to be active in the company following his effective ouster, the whole episode sparked a decade-long battle over control of the company that was punctuated by threats of retaliation and lawsuits. Posluns had assumed day-to-day control of the company by the mid-1980s, though the disagreement with Kay continued throughout the 1980s and into the 1990s.

Unfortunately, the tiff between Kay and Posluns signaled the start of a succession of problems that would plague the company during the late 1980s and early 1990s. Importantly, Dylex's overall U.S. effort soured shortly after it had begun. The U.S. apparel industry turned out to be vastly different from the one in Canada,

and Posluns's strategy rapidly ceased to be ineffective. The Brooks chain racked up record sales and earnings for two years, but began to nosedive in 1986. Among other problems, the family that was managing the operation was unmotivated to run the division aggressively. Posluns eventually took control of the operation, but it didn't help. The company was loaded with debt, and Posluns had failed to recognize the competitiveness of the U.S. market. Brooks filed for bankruptcy in 1987 and Dylex was forced to write off a painful loss.

Foxmoor followed a similar pattern. After initial gains the chain's performance waned, and Foxmoor began posting big losses. Like Brooks, Foxmoor was burdened with heavy debt as the result of a leveraged buyout. When cashflow slowed, the company was pushed to the edge of financial disaster. Dylex sent its own managers south to whip the faltering organization into shape, but were unsuccessful. Foxmoor eventually filed for bankruptcy in January 1990, following Dylex's 1989 write-off of $77.8 million related to the chain. By 1990 Dylex had sold more than 1,500 U.S. stores and suffered losses of more than $200 million. "It was a fiasco," Posluns said in the November 1990 *Canadian Business.* "We had to move out of it before it really cooked us." As Dylex's chief U.S. operations crumbled, it put its acquisition program on hold and labored to improve existing operations. It continued to operate some of its smaller, successful U.S. chains, including the profitable Wet Seal and NBO divisions, which had grown to include about 170 stores by the early 1990s.

Dylex's setbacks in the U.S. market were not completely attributable to differences in the U.S. and Canadian markets. In fact, the problems were also the result of evolving apparel and retail industries throughout North America. The laissez-faire management approach utilized by Posluns was becoming outdated in light of consumer and technological changes. Consumers were becoming more sophisticated, spending less on apparel, and demanding more than they had during the 1970s and early 1980s, and Dylex's competitors were becoming increasingly efficient. The chains that were most effective were those that could run a tightly integrated, geographically diverse organization that was on the cutting edge of consumer preferences and information technology.

The new environment required changes at Dylex. For example, Dylex's chains tended to cannibalize each others' sales because there was no central command managing a comprehensive product mix. To bring change to Dylex, Posluns transferred many of his responsibilities to Lionel Robbins, who was serving as president of the company in the mid-1990s. Under Robbins's direction, the company became more centralized, although it still maintained much of its entrepreneurial flavor. Robbins also stepped up the company's emphasis on technology, as evidenced in 1990 by a newly renovated, $12 million computerized warehouse in Ontario. The efforts succeeded in cutting operating costs. However, an industry downturn in the late 1980s and early 1990s effectively absorbed those gains and left Dylex scrambling for profits. Sales rose from $1.4 billion in 1988 to $1.7 billion in 1990, but net earnings plummeted from $30 million to a depressing loss of $60 million in 1989 and $3.2 million in 1990.

By 1991 Dylex had slashed the number of stores in its chains to about 1,500, but its balance sheet continued to bleed. While sales hovered below the $2 billion mark through 1993, Dylex suffered a combined loss of nearly $75 million during those three years. By 1993 Dylex had reduced the number of stores under its control to just 1,047, about 170 which were located in the United States. Still, the company's financial performance languished. Under pressure from stockholders, Dylex continued to shed employees, jettison poorly performing stores, and cut costs. Unfortunately, these efforts were insufficient to salvage the situation.

The company's stock price plunged from about US$15 in the late 1980s to a pitiful 34 cents by early 1995. That price reflected the market's disappointment over Dylex's crushing $250 million loss in 1994, which included write-offs related to restructuring. The beleaguered Dylex sought court protection from its creditors in January 1995 under Canada's Companies' Creditors Arrangement Act. In mid-1995, Dylex was operating only about 700 stores in Canada, and with the exception of five outlets, it had squelched its entire U.S. operation. Its remaining chains included Braemar, Club Monaco, Fairweather, Harry Rosen, Thrifty's, and Tip Top Tailors.

Principal Subsidiaries:

Braemer; Club Monaco; Fairweather; Harry Rose; Thrifty's; Tip Top Tailors.

Further Reading:

Brauer, Molly, "What Is Dylex and Why Is It Looking at U.S.," *Chain Store Age Executive,* October 1984, p. 31.

Brent, Paul, "BiWay Loss Clouds Dylex 1993 Outlook," *Toronto Star,* July 1, 1993, Section 1, p. 11.

_____, "Dylex Founder Gets Day in Court," *Financial Post,* May 28, 1994, Section 1, p. 3.

Furman, Phyllis, "Finally, Shoes: New NBO Chief Suits Himself," *Crains New York Business,* July 4, 1988, Section 1, p. 3.

Girard, Daniel, "Dylex Axes Money-Losing Men's Wear Chain," *Toronto Star,* October 21, 1993, Section D, p. 1.

_____, "Retailer Dylex Takes $236 Million Loss—Restructuring Has Already Cost $84 Million," *Toronto Star,* February 28, 1995, Section C, p. 10.

Matthews, Jan, and Greg Boyd, "Can Lionel Robins Rescue Dylex?" *Canadian Business,* November 1990.

Mayers, Adam, "Dylex Isn't Admitting Lousy Excuses for Woes," *Toronto Star,* January 14, 1995, Section C, p. 2.

"Rough Crossings: Canadian Retailers Have Paid a Heavy Price for Not Doing Their Homework," *Toronto Star,* February 28, 1993, Section H, p. 1.

Stern, Aimee, "The Intrapreneurs of Retailing," *Dun's Business Month,* September 1986, pp. 54-55.

"White, Lucy, Dylex Feeling the Effects of Still-Soft Retail Market," *Financial Post,* June 8, 1991, Section 1, p. 23.

—Dave Mote

Empire Company Limited

115 King Street
Stellarton, Nova Scotia B0K 1S0
(902) 755-4440
Fax: (902) 755-6477

Public Company
Incorporated: 1963
Employees: 15,300
Sales: $2.58 billion
Stock Exchanges: Toronto Montreal
SICs: 5149 Groceries & Related Products Not
    Elsewhere Classified; 6530 Real Estate Agents &
    Managers; 8900 Services Not Elsewhere Classified.

A diversified food and drug distributor with related real estate investments, Empire Company Limited originated as a small Nova Scotian grocery store, then evolved into a diverse collection of businesses shepherded by the Sobey family. A genuine corporate dynasty, Empire served as the holding company for the 119-store Sobey supermarket chain, the 80-store Lawtons Drugs pharmaceutical chain, and 27 shopping centers owned by Atlantic Shopping Centres Limited. In addition to these primary operating companies, Empire maintained investments in various other business ventures that extended the company's presence throughout North America.

Shortly after the turn of the century, John William Sobey decided to test his entrepreneurial talents and start a new business. A farmer and carpenter by profession, Sobey was surrounded in his hometown of Stellarton, Nova Scotia, by enticing signs of prosperity. Coal-mining and the close proximity of the railroad had proved to be a boon to the small but burgeoning town of Stellarton, creating a robust economic climate that offered enterprising individuals like Sobey an opportunity to share in the spoils created by the town's two most important industries. Though his first step was a modest one, Sobey's decision to start his new business would enrich generations of Sobeys to come and mark the birth of what would become a multibillion dollar company, the Sobey family's aptly named Empire Company Limited. Sobey bought his way into his new line of work when he purchased a meat-peddling business in 1907 and began selling cuts of beef, pork, and lamb from a horse-drawn covered wagon. Five years later Sobey assumed a more sedentary lifestyle after his delivery

runs in and around Stellarton had demonstrated enough success to warrant the construction of a wooden store, which he and his brother Charles Sobey built. The wooden structure in Stellarton was the first of many Sobey stores to come, the incipient step that would lead to the Sobey family's giant strides across Atlantic Canada. As if to foretell this expansion, the first store was known as "No. 1," a precursor to the grocery store empire to come.

From No. 1, Sobey sold meat and vegetables until his son suggested that the store offer a greater variety of foods and goods. Sobey's son, Frank Hoyse Sobey, would be chiefly responsible later in life for transforming his family's stores into a highly coveted chain of supermarkets, but early in life he demonstrated himself to be an underachiever, dropping out of the eighth grade at age 16 in 1918 to work for the family business and, ironically, to take a business course.

Not long after Frank Sobey began working for his father as a butcher, he convinced him that No. 1 should also sell tea, coffee, spices, butter, cheese, and tinned goods, adding a host of food products to complement the store's limited selection of meat and vegetables. Once these additional products were added to the shelves of No.1 during the years immediately following the conclusion of World War I, the Sobey store became a genuine grocery store, a transformation that spawned the establishment of additional stores.

Shortly after the end of another global war, the Sobey family business would make another definitive transformation, once again initiated by Frank Sobey, who by the end of World War II was firmly in control of the burgeoning Sobey dynasty. By 1947, the year Frank Sobey steered the family business toward a new and prosperous direction, the Sobeys owned two dozen small stores, each operated by sales clerks who fetched, weighed, and bagged goods for customers. Frank Sobey, however, envisioned a different type of Sobey food store for the future, one that borrowed from a relatively new entry in the retail food industry: the modern supermarket.

For nearly a decade before he made the signal leap into the supermarket business, Frank Sobey had studied the success of what was promising to be a revolutionary concept, perusing Canadian and American magazines for coverage of successful supermarkets throughout North America. In 1940 Frank Sobey and his wife drove to California, ostensibly to take a vacation, but the aspiring supermarket operator spent the duration of the trip frequenting supermarket stores stretched between Nova Scotia and California. Sobey canvassed the operators of these new, much larger grocery stores that stocked a comprehensive collection of products, carefully noting what characteristics made each a success and assembling his plans to build a Sobey supermarket. Five years after this junket across North America, the opportunity to build a supermarket arrived when the Empire Theatre burned to the ground in New Glasgow, a town near Stellarton.

The largest town in Pictou County, New Glasgow could support a large-scale grocery store more readily than Stellarton, educing Sobey to purchase the lot the charred theater previously occupied by acquiring its owner, the

Empire Company Limited. On this lot Sobey planned to build his first genuine supermarket and put to use all the research he had conducted over the previous years. His critics were many, including his father John, but Sobey was confident his concept would prove successful and make the family business substantially more profitable. In 1947, two years after acquiring the Empire Theatre lot, Sobey's store, known as No. 25, opened for business, the first building with electronic-beam doors in Pictou County and the largest food store many had ever seen. Although the store was nearly seven times smaller than the Sobey supermarkets that would be built decades later, the 6,150 square feet it occupied was seven times larger than any other Sobey store: enormous when compared to competing food retail stores in the region.

From the start, Sobey's cash-and-carry, self-serve groceteria was an extraordinary success. Frequently its inventory was sold before it was paid for, quickly enriching the Sobeys and giving them the financial means to convert existing smaller stores into large-scale supermarkets. Those who mocked the idea that a large food store could survive in New Glasgow were quickly silenced, many of whom now found themselves competing against the formidable Sobey supermarket. By the early 1950s, the supermarket had caused six meat merchant businesses in New Glasgow to collapse from the pressure, and as time progressed Sobey supermarkets evolved into a chain of stores spreading across Atlantic Canada.

Over the next 30 years, Frank Sobey built upon the foundation laid by the establishment of No. 25, creating a supermarket chain that positioned his family as stalwart regional competitors in the retail food industry. Empire Company Limited, the company he acquired to obtain the lot for No. 25, was kept alive as a conduit for stock market investments, becoming, as the Sobey empire spread across the Maritimes, the holding company and investment arm of the Sobey family. In these investments, Frank Sobey displayed a penchant for targeting companies with particularly strong management, acquiring enough of the company to gain a seat on its board of directors, then exerting his influence over the company and protecting it from any potential hostile takeovers. Additionally, instead of purchasing a mall location for one of his supermarkets and then selling it back to a developer who would then rent the supermarket site to Sobey, Sobey retained possession of the entire mall.

By expanding in this manner, Sobey remained in control of everything: the rent his supermarket paid, the rent paid by other businesses, and ownership of the land and buildings surrounding a Sobey supermarket. The result was a highly successful supermarket chain supported by a host of subsidiary companies involved in an increasingly diverse collection of business interests. To the real estate investments held by Empire were added a chain of pharmaceutical stores named Lawtons Drugs, automotive and insurance agency businesses, and movie theaters, plus additional investments in major Canadian companies. An enormous leap from John William Sobey's inconsequential meat-peddling business, Empire nonetheless ranked as only a minor player in the Canadian retail food industry; a strong regional competitor dwarfed by substantially larger national chains. In

the mid-1970s, however, the Sobeys set their sights on elevating Empire's stature and embarked on a new era in the history of their family business.

This new era began in 1976 when Empire, led by David Sobey, William Sobey, and Donald Sobey—the third generation of Sobeys to superintend the family business—acquired control of Atlantic Shopping Centres Ltd., a Halifax-based real estate developer with properties appraised at $80 million. Empire's stake in Atlantic Shopping Centres ushered in a period of rapid growth, marking the beginning of the company's aggressive strategy to grow by acquisitions and amplify its presence in the national retail food industry. One year after acquiring Atlantic Shopping Centres, Empire attempted the takeover of Ottawa-based food-wholesaling giant M. Loeb Ltd., a much larger company whose addition would elevate Empire from its stature as a strong regional company to a genuine national competitor. In response to Empire's aggressive bid, Caisse de depot et placement du Quebec, M. Loeb's largest shareholder, sold its shares to Provigo Inc., a Montreal-based wholesaler and retailer of food, prompting Frank Sobey's three sons to reposition Empire's turret toward Provigo. Empire quickly began acquiring stock in Provigo, touching off rumors in the financial community that Empire was attempting a takeover of Provigo. By autumn 1977 Empire had acquired 18 percent of Provigo, giving it, in turn, majority control of M. Loeb, the primary reason the Sobeys had begun their raid on Provigo.

By 1982, Donald Sobey and David Sobey each had gained a seat on Provigo's board of directors—in typical Sobey fashion. Meanwhile, Empire continued its expansion program by investing in other companies, including a 25 percent stake in a New England supermarket chain named Hannaford Brothers Company and a 10 percent stake in Nash Finch Company, a major retailer and wholesaler of food in the midwestern United States. In 1988 Empire once again sought to increase its stake in Provigo by joining forces with Unigesco Inc., a Montreal-based food distributor and processor, to together control 51 percent of Provigo's shares. Provigo by this time represented an enviable property to control, generating $6.2 billion in annual sales and ranking as the largest food distributor in Quebec and the second-largest in Canada. With the successful completion of its joint bid for 51 percent of Provigo, Empire represented a powerful force as well, collecting $1.6 billion in sales in 1988 and ranking as the largest food retailing conglomerate in the Maritimes. Despite Empire's multifarious investments, Sobey Stores Co. Ltd., the supermarket subsidiary, still stood as the main engine driving Empire's growth, contributing $1.4 billion in sales of the holding company's 1988 $1.6 billion sales total.

By the end of the 1980s, Empire had achieved a remarkable record of financial growth. Between 1980 and 1990, the company's annual sales total had made a meteoric leap from $38 million to $1.8 billion, a prodigious increase engendered largely by the third generation of Sobeys. The $2 billion plateau was reached the following year, in 1991, when annual sales crept to $2.09 billion, then Empire began strengthening its control over its various operating companies. By 1993, with $2.36 billion in sales, Empire ranked as one of the premier food retailing conglomerates in Canada, its sales total still derived chiefly from Sobeys Inc.'s 123 supermarkets. The company's other primary operating companies were important contributors as well, particularly Lawton's Drug Stores Limited, which operated a chain of 72 stores during the early 1990s. Atlantic Shopping Centres Limited, whose acquisition had sparked Empire's rapid growth during the 1980s, owned and managed 5.6 million square feet of space by 1993, and Halifax Developments Limited, another real estate concern partly owned by Empire, controlled nearly all of downtown Halifax.

In 1994, Empire's 35 percent stake in Halifax Developments Limited was increased to 100 percent, as the holding company continued to exert more resolute control over its properties. Sales for the year rose to $2.58 billion, and with a fourth generation of Sobeys waiting to take the place of Frank Sobey's children, expectations of future financial growth were optimistic. With 94 percent of the company's annual revenue derived from food and drug distribution, another four percent from real estate, and two percent from other operations and investments, this expected growth was most likely to come from the further augmentation of the company's original and mainstay business, the retailing of food.

Principal Subsidiaries:

Sobeys Capital Inc.; Sobeys Inc.; Lumsden Brothers Limited; Burgess Wholesale Limited; Sobeys Land Holdings Limited; Sobey Leased Properties Limited; Atlantic Shopping Centers Limited; Canadian Shopping Centres Limited; Halifax Developments Limited; Lawton's Inc.; Lawtons Drug Stores Limited; Empire Theatres Limited; Amteco Leasing Limited; Empire Automotive Limited; E.C.L. Investments Limited; Kepec Resources Limited; Empro Holdings Limited; Empjan Holdings Limited.

Further Reading:

Bruce, Alexander, "Empire Wants Bigger Piece of Ontario Market," *The Globe and Mail,* September 12, 1989, p. B13.
Bruce, Harry, "The Sobey Boys Meet the Man from Provigo," *Canadian Business,* November 1985, p. 87.
Clifford, Edward, "Look for Empire to Shed Assets," *The Globe and Mail,* October 21, 1993, p. B11.
Farnsworth, Clyde H., "Canadian's Family Feud," *The New York Times,* October 30, 1994, p. F3.
Flinn, Brian, "All in the Family," *CA Magazine,* May 1995, p. 14.
Hunter, Nicholas, "Empire Co. Eyes Acquisitions," *The Globe and Mail,* August 12, 1983, p. B1.

—Jeffrey L. Covell

Federated Co-operatives Limited

401 22nd Street East
P.O. Box 1050
Saskatoon, Saskatchewan S7K 3M9
(306) 244-3311
Fax: (306) 244-3403

Private Company
Incorporated: 1955 as Federated Co-operatives
  Limited
Employees: 2,401
Sales: $1.98 billion
SICs: 2431 Millwork; 2048 Prepared Foods Not
  Elsewhere Classified; 2911 Petroleum Refining;
  2047 Dog & Cat Food; 5141 Groceries—General
  Line; 5072 Hardware

Federated Co-operatives Limited, the second largest co-operative in Canada, functions as the manufacturing, wholesaling, and administrative organization for more than 300 autonomous retail co-operatives spread across western Canada. During the mid-1990s an estimated 750,000 members owned these co-operatives, which, in turn owned Federated Co-operatives. For its members—the independent retail co-operatives—Federated Co-operatives supplied food, petroleum, hardware, building products, crop supplies, livestock feed, and family fashions, as well as advertising, accounting, training, and member relations services. Through Federated Co-operatives, the retail co-operatives realized the added buying-power and cost-efficiencies normally accorded to large retail conglomerates, yet retained their autonomy, making the West an economically hospitable region for smaller independent retail concerns. In accordance with the desire to protect autonomy, retail co-operatives were not obligated to use the products or services provided by Federated Co-operatives; it was the general and overriding task of Federated Co-operatives to attract member retail co-operatives. Those retail co-operatives that were members during the mid-1990s shared ownership in a Saskatoon-based home office, regional offices in Regina, Saskatoon, Winnipeg, Calgary, and Edmonton, feed plants in seven locations across western Canada, a sawmill and plywood plant in Canoe, British Columbia, control of Consumers' Co-operative Refineries Limited, and control of Grocery People Limited.

Together, the independent retail co-operatives and Federated Co-operatives composed the Co-operative Retailing System, whose roots stretched back to the early 20th century when locally-owned retail co-operatives banded together to form provincial wholesale organizations, the predecessors to Federated Co-operatives. The earliest genuine retail co-operatives were organized in the wake of popular support for co-operative farming organizations, which spawned the Saskatchewan Wheat Pool, the Manitoba Pool Elevators, and the Alberta Wheat Pool. Encouraged and aided by the efforts that created these wheat co-operatives, retail co-operatives first began to appear in western Canada in 1913, with the earliest connection to Federated Co-operatives emerging in 1914, when the Saskatchewan Grain Growers' Association opened a trading department to sell bulk supplies to Grain Growers' members.

Both the wheat co-operatives and the retail co-operatives shared the common goal of assisting largely powerless independent farmers and businesses to ameliorate their precarious positions by forming more powerful co-operative organizations. However, the agricultural co-operative movement enjoyed more success initially, emerging resolutely between 1923 and 1924 when the three provincial wheat pools were formed. A debilitative postwar economic recession struck a serious blow to the retail co-operatives that had formed during the 1910s, forcing numerous associations to collapse during the 1920s and thereby arresting the groundswell of support for retail co-operatives. By the late 1920s, however, retail co-operatives were enjoying a rebirth and once again small associations of retail concerns began appearing across western Canada. It was during this second surge of growth that the predecessor organizations to Federated Co-operatives were formed, bringing to life the provincial wholesale organizations that would later amalgamate and form one of Canada's largest co-operatives.

The oldest provincial retail co-operative of Federated Co-operatives lineage was incorporated in 1927 as Manitoba Co-operative Wholesale (MCW) after 13 retail co-operatives in the province agreed to join together. The following year, MCW opened its first office—located in Winnipeg—concurrent with the establishment of another major constituent of Federated Co-operatives in Saskatchewan. Saskatchewan Wholesale Society Ltd. was incorporated in 1927 as a preliminary organization to a co-operative incorporated the following year as Saskatchewan Co-operative Wholesale Society Ltd. (SCWS). Created by an act of the provincial legislature, SCWS assumed the assets and liabilities of the trading department formed by Saskatchewan Grain Growers' Association in 1914 and immediately attracted 29 retail co-operative applicants, the most by any of the four original provincial retail co-operative organizations.

The organization of provincial retail co-operative associations continued to spread westward after the incorporation of SCWS, moving across the country in chronological order, but the wholesale co-operatives formed in Alberta and British Columbia would join Federated Co-operatives after its formation instead of amalgamating to create it, as did MCW and SCWS. In the interim, before all four co-operatives were joined together under

Federated Co-operatives' corporate umbrella, MCW and SCWS struggled to establish themselves as stable co-operative entities, a challenge that MCW found more difficult. The fledgling co-operative recorded a financial loss during its first two years of existence, while the Saskatchewan co-operative registered in the black from the outset. By 1930, MCW had reversed its fortunes and began recording what retail co-operatives preferred to call net savings rather than profits. The Manitoba co-operative generated $334,000 in sales during the first year of a nearly decade-long economic depression and recorded $7,000 in net savings, but the organization only employed three people and, as further evidence of its shaky financial status, the directors of the co-operative offered their personal property in order to guarantee MCW bank loans.

Caught in the grip of the Depression, MCW, SCWS, and the Alberta Co-operative Wholesale Association agreed in 1930 to work together in the purchase of twine, oil, and other products, foreshadowing their union three decades later and setting the foundation for the formation of an interprovincial bulk commodity purchasing committee eight years later. When this committee was organized in 1938, the ties linking the three co-operatives together were formally established, ushering in an era of consistent sales growth and increasing the importance of the role played by the three organizations for retail co-operatives.

Once this concerted effort began, its effects were readily discernible, enabling both SCWS and MCW to enter into business lines that were indicative of Federated Co-operatives' core business during the mid-1990s. SCWS implemented a life insurance plan for employees in 1938, then the following year acquired a flour mill and imported the first tractor from the United States, marking the beginning of co-operative involvement in the farm machinery business. MCW, meanwhile, inaugurated grocery service in 1941, started feed manufacture in Saskatchewan in 1942, and opened a feed plant in Regina in 1943, further broadening the scope of its business.

Groceries, livestock feed, farm machinery, and flour production had been added to the two co-operatives' range of businesses during the years immediately following the establishment of the interprovincial committee; oil was added to the list when the Consumers' Co-operative Refineries Limited amalgamated with SCWS and created a more well-rounded predecessor to Federated Co-operatives. The Consumers' Co-operative Refineries Limited (CCRL) had been organized in 1934 when 10 petroleum co-operatives in south-central Saskatchewan joined together and invested $32,000 in a small plant that began processing 500 barrels of crude per day, enabling the small petroleum co-operatives to remain independent. SCWS and CCRL began working together in 1937 when the two organizations entered into a joint agreement to market tires, then united in 1944, creating a new provincial co-operative named Saskatchewan Federated Co-operatives Limited (SFCL).

Once oil processing had come under SFCL's purview, the co-operative moved into other business areas, establishing a dry goods department shortly after CCRL was absorbed and a hardware department the following year,

in 1945. The conclusion of World War II also marked the beginning of the co-operative's wholesale grocery service, its acquisition of a coal mine, the purchase of Shuswap Lumber Company in Canoe, British Columbia, and the opening of grocery departments in Saskatchewan, broadening SFCL's scope as the date approached when it would become one of the two provincial co-operatives forming the foundation of Federated Co-operatives.

Discussions between the directors of SFCL and MCW about a possible merger of the two organizations began in 1954, leading to their amalgamation in 1955 and the birth of Federated Co-operatives Limited. Together, the two co-operative wholesales and CCRL, which by this point was processing 12,000 barrels of crude per day after its production capacity was increased in 1951 and 1954, represented an interprovincial co-operative force involved in an array of businesses that would compose the core of Federated Co-operatives activities for the next three decades and into the mid-1990s. Two more provincial wholesale co-operatives would be merged into Federated Co-operatives in the first decade-and-a-half after its emergence as a combination of MCW and SFCL. The first, Alberta Co-operative Wholesale Association, which had joined forces with both MCW and SCWS to purchase twine, oil, and other products in 1930, was merged into Federated Co-operatives in 1961. The second co-operative to join Federated Co-operatives was the British Columbia Co-operative Wholesale Society, which was almagamated into Federated Co-operatives in 1970.

The Alberta Co-operative Wholesale Association (ACWA) had been organized in 1928, the same year the Saskatchewan Co-operative Wholesale Society had been incorporated. Formed by nine retail co-operatives located in and near Killam, Alberta, ACWA signed a large contract to handle lumber early in its history, entering the lumber business 16 years before SFCL. Its lumber contract, however, quickly sent the co-operative into a financial tailspin and for much of the Depression era ACWA remained hobbled by its disastrous foray into lumber. In 1938, ACWA re-emerged completely reorganized with new management and a new head office in Edmonton. In the years leading up to its merger into Federated Co-operatives, ACWA moved into the distribution of feed and petroleum, expanding at a rapid pace until the mid-1940s when financial problems once again affected the co-operative's stability. At the co-operative's annual meeting in 1954, its directors discussed a potential merger with SFCL at roughly the same time similar discussions between SFCL and MCW were conducted, but ACWA remained a separate co-operative entity for seven more years before it united with Federated Co-operatives.

During this period from 1954 to 1961, ACWA diversified its interests, becoming involved in several business areas that were identical to those occupying the efforts of Federated Co-operatives. A lumber department was opened in 1956, followed by the establishment of a farm supplies department in 1956. In 1959 the annual meetings of Federated Co-operatives and ACWA approved their merger, to be effected in 1962, of the two organizations, but during the following year the timetable for the proposed merger was shortened, leading to the merger of ACWA into Federated Co-operatives in 1961, giving Federated Co-operatives a much larger territory of service and adding the ACWA's interests in lumber, petroleum, feed plants, and warehouses.

During the 1960s, Federated Co-operatives' business interests became increasingly diverse, embracing a wide range of retail fields that positioned the co-operative as a comprehensive support and services institution for retail co-operatives in Manitoba, Saskatchewan, and Alberta. A fresh meats program was instituted in 1961, followed by the establishment of an agricultural department in 1964 to oversee the co-operative's activities in chemicals, fertilizers, and twine. Federated Co-operatives' lumber activities in Canoe were expanded, including the establishment of a plywood plant in 1966, and CCRL's processing capacity was increased to handle 22,500 barrels of crude per day.

By the end of the 1960s, Federated Co-operatives' was firmly established in a collection of businesses integral to retail co-operatives operating in its service territory. The amalgamation of western Canada's fourth provincial wholesales co-operative, the British Columbia Co-operative Wholesale Society (BCCWS), in 1970, added to Federated Co-operatives' stature, both in terms of its geographic range and its assets. BCCWS had been incorporated in 1939 when representatives of 23 retail co-operatives gathered in a Vancouver hotel and agreed to join together for many of the same reasons that had precipitated the formation of the three other provincial wholesale co-operatives.

During the years bridging its incorporation and its amalgamation with Federated Co-operatives, BCCWS established a farm supplies department in 1945 and created a merchandising department in 1946, the same year it leased its first warehouse. By the end of the 1940s, BCCWS had nearly 70 member associations, a total that would approach 100 by the mid-1950s. Expansion accelerated during the late 1950s when co-operative operated warehouses were expanded and additional warehouses were acquired, enabling BCCWS in 1959 to double the number of merchandise lines it handled. With 125 member associations by the beginning of the 1960s, the co-operative began to consolidate its assets, arresting its program of expansion to take stock of its position in British Columbia's retail co-operative community. Negotiations were initiated with Federated Co-operatives in 1960 regarding the merger of BCCWS into Federated Co-operatives, then the following year, like ACWA in the early 1950s, BCCWS began to suffer from financial shortages. Less than a decade later, BCCWS was amalgamated into Federated Co-operatives, the fourth provincial wholesale organization to join the interprovincial wholesaling force that now provided support and service to member retail co-operatives across all of western Canada.

During the late 1980s the co-operative's annual sales would approach $1.5 billion, dwarfing its sales volume of the late 1970s, but early in this decade of exponential growth an economic recession severely affected retail co-operatives operating in western Canada, getting the decade's robust growth off to a discouragingly slow start. Retail co-operatives suffered their most serious financial losses in 1982, when as a group they recorded a deficit,

but were bailed out by financial help from Federated Co-operatives. Although the situation was grave, the pernicious economic climate accentuated the role Federated Co-operatives played in supporting independent retail co-operatives, clearly demonstrating to the owners of struggling retail concerns the benefits of operating under the supportive tutelage of Federated Co-operatives.

Federated Co-operatives responded to the onset of the recession by closing its regional office in Vancouver, closing a sawmill, discontinuing a newspaper, cutting staff by 10 percent, and closing retail co-operatives that were mired in financial difficulties. More fundamental changes in the way the Co-operative Retailing System operated followed, particularly in terms of increasing the focus on service to members, rather than concentrating on growth and expansion. Dilapidated retail establishments were refurbished and a greater emphasis was placed on advertising, making the retail facilities more attractive to the consumers they desperately needed.

By 1986, recovery was in full swing, with all of Federated Co-operatives' departments contributing positively to net savings growth for the first time since 1973. Efforts toward improving the image of retail establishments continued throughout the late 1980s, helping to spur growth as Federated Co-operatives moved past its 60th anniversary year. Annual sales eclipsed the $1.5 billion mark in 1990, while net savings amounted to $91 million, nearly three times the total recorded five years earlier. The following year, in 1991, retail co-operatives registered the largest combined local savings in Federated Co-operatives' history, instilling confidence in the value of the wholesale organization's services. In 1992, Federated Co-operatives completed the $12.3 million takeover of Edmonton-based Grocery People Ltd, which was then organized as a subsidiary of the wholesale organization, increasing its ability to wholesale groceries to independent retail outlets in northern Alberta, northern British Columbia, the Yukon, and in the Northwest Territories.

By 1994 Federated Co-operatives' annual sales were flirting with the $2 billion mark, reaching $1.98 billion as the wholesaling giant plotted its course for the future. Food and petroleum ranked as the company's two largest contributors to annual sales, generating $973 million and $601 million respectively, but its other primary businesses—crop supplies, family fashions, feed, forest products, and hardware and building products — were also integral components of the company's business, giving Federated Co-operatives a diversity reflective of its constituent locally-owned retail co-operatives. As Federated Co-operatives prepared to move toward the 21st century, its stability, growth, and prosperity were inextricably tied to the success of the retail co-operatives the company represented. This was true in the mid-1990s just as it had been true in the late-1920s when small provincial wholesale co-operatives first emerged and laid the foundation for Federated Co-operatives' birth in 1955.

Principal Subsidiaries:

Consumers' Co-operative Refineries Limited; The Grocery People Ltd.

Further Reading:

Building a Dream: The Cooperative Retailing System, 1928-1988, Saskatoon, Western Producer Prairie Books, 1989.

Fairbairn, Brett, "Co-op Savvy," *Saskatchewan Business,* January/February 1991, pp. 7-12.

"Federated Co-operatives Chief Warns Movement Threatened," *The Globe and Mail,* October 14, 1982, p. B6.

Motherwell, Cathryn, "New Offer in Oil Upgrader Dispute," *The Globe and Mail,* June 14, 1993, p. B5.

"'Value, Service . . . Guaranteed' Key to Marketing Success," *Trade and Commerce,* July/August 1990, pp. 43-86.

Wattie, Chris, "Province Seeks Control of Heavy-oil Upgrader," *The Globe and Mail,* May 29, 1993, p. B5.

York, Geoffrey, "Co-op Giant Comes Out Swinging as Prairies Fight Economic Slump," *The Globe and Mail,* December 21, 1989, p. B5.

—Jeffrey L. Covell

Finning Ltd.

555 Great Northern Way Vancouver, British
  Columbia V5T 1E2
(604) 872-4444
Fax: (604) 872-2994

Public Company
Founded: 1933 as Finning Tractor and Equipment
  Co.
Employees: 3,900
Sales: $1.46 billion
Stock Exchanges: Montreal Toronto
SICs: 3500 Industrial Machinery & Equipment;
  7353 Heavy Construction Equipment Rental

Finning Ltd. is a leading global heavy equipment dealer, and is distinguished as the largest dealer of Caterpillar equipment in the world. The Vancouver-based company sold, leased, financed, and serviced heavy equipment going into the mid-1990s on three continents for use in forestry, agriculture, mining, oil, pipeline, and construction industries. Savvy management has allowed Finning to post consistent profits for nearly all of its 60-plus years in business, despite cyclical industry downturns.

Finning was founded in 1933 during the dawn of the heavy equipment industry by "British Columbia's Tractor King" Earl Finning. Steam-powered and later gas-powered agricultural tractors had been in wide use since the early 1900s, but they were relatively clumsy, problematic machines that rested on spiked or cleated metal wheels. It wasn't until 1920 that the early agricultural tractor was replaced by the general purpose tractor, which became useful in other applications such as construction. In the early 1930s, moreover, pneumatic rubber tires were introduced. Another major breakthrough during the period was the continuous tread, which was wrapped around geared wheels. Treaded machines, which became known as crawlers or caterpillars, were useful for applications involving rough terrain. The result of improvements to the original farm tractor was that heavy equipment was developed for uses ranging from mining and forestry to construction and warfare.

Earl Finning's burgeoning venture, Finning Tractor and Equipment Co., benefitted throughout the 1930s and 1940s from steady growth in heavy equipment sales as its Canadian customers purchased tractors, crawlers,

and adaptations of those machines for a growing number of uses. By 1943, Finning was employing a work force of about 50 people. Among the new employees hired in that year was 16-year-old Jerry Holmes, who would watch Finning's work force balloon to more than 2,500 before he retired in the late 1980s. Sales were particularly brisk during the postwar North American economic boom that began in the late 1940s and lasted into the 1960s. Indeed, during that period Finning shipped thousands of pieces of gear to build Canada's highway system, erect new cities and skyscrapers, mine construction materials and minerals, and supply the country's increasingly automated agricultural and forestry industries.

Finning grew explosively during the 1960s and cemented its position as a leading supplier of heavy equipment in Canada. Besides its core British Columbian territory, the company by the 1960s was branching out into parts of Yukon and the Northwest Territories, where logging and mining were big business. Throughout the period, new product introductions continued to expand Finning's market scope and to boost sales. Importantly, Finning benefitted from agreements with heavy equipment manufacturer Caterpillar to distribute its equipment. The U.S.-based Caterpillar became the dominant global supplier of heavy equipment following World War II and was recognized by many consumers as the leader in quality and innovation. Thus, dealers like Finning that could win Caterpillar's favor benefitted greatly. By the late 1960s, in fact, Finning was generating $50 million in annual revenues and had recorded profits for several consecutive years.

Finning's rapid expansion during the 1960s was the result of keen management and a hard-driving sales force. After Earl Finning had gotten the company started, a number of shrewd managers had contributed to the company's gains. For example, W. M. (Maurice) Young, Earl Finning's son-in-law, lead the company during its expansion in the 1960s and into the 1970s. Working with him were other talented executives, including John Frazee, R. E. Lane, Vinod Kumar Sood, and others. Interestingly, several of Finning's top executives had attended the Massachusetts Institute of Technology's Sloan School of Management, where they had received advanced degrees. Young and Frazee had attended the school together, in fact, and attracted fellow students to Finning's executive ranks.

Young and Frazee's most notable contact through the Sloan School was Vinod Kumar Sood. Sood, working part of the time with both Young and Frazee, was credited with maneuvering Finning through troubled waters. He then lead it through a period of unprecedented growth that effectively doubled the company's size during a cycle of industry malaise. Sood was born in India, where he graduated from college at the age of 19. He went to work for Bajaj Electricals in India for a few years before deciding that he wanted to lead a major corporation. With that goal in mind, Sood applied to MIT's respected Sloan School. Because most entrants to the program were ten years older than Sood and had years of management experience, Sood's application was rejected out of hand, two years in a row.

Evidencing his tenacious nature and salesmanship ability, Sood cornered Sloan's dean of admissions while he was touring in Bombay. Sood, in an impassioned plea, convinced the dean to accept him into the school the following year. At the age of 28, Sood was the youngest person to ever enter the program. Sood's employer flew Sood and his wife to the United States, where the cash-strapped student convinced MIT to wave his tuition and even provide a $2,000 living stipend. At Sloan, Sood made the contacts that would lead him to Vancouver and later to the head of Finning. He returned to India, but eventually became convinced that his dream of running a corporation was most likely to be realized in North America. Sood flew back to the United States in 1968 to interview with several companies, including General Motors.

Among the companies that interested Sood most was Finning, where he believed he could have a real impact because of its relatively small size. Young and Frazee wanted to extended an offer to Sood, even though they were not sure what he would do at the company or how much he would be paid. Sood asked his new employers to give him 90 days to look around and see what he could do for the company, at whatever salary they desired. Sood initially took on the title of operations manager. His superiors were so impressed by his performance that they promoted him within a few months. Sood was still only 32 years old when he was given his first major project—to take Finning public. Sood had pushed for the move because he believed that Finning could use the proceeds from a public offering to fund a program whereby Finning would finance its customers' equipment purchases. The offering was a success and Sood found himself promoted to vice-president of finance at the age of 33.

Sood came to Finning at a good time. Indeed, Finning thrived during the 1970s because of booming forestry and mining industries. Sales and financing of heavy equipment surged while Finning's revenues and profits spiraled upward. Frazee took over as president of the company in 1976. Earnings in that year hit $8.6 million. Markets heated up during the late 1970s, moreover, partly as a result of heavy equipment demand from the oil industry. By 1979, in fact, Finning was churning out $19.4 million in earnings from about a half million dollars in revenue. And demand from Finning's core forestry, mining, and construction markets continued to swell. Unfortunately, the party started to die down in 1980. Earnings in that year slipped to $18.2 million and orders late in the year dropped drastically.

It quickly became apparent to even the casual observer that North America was heading into a recession. Frazee took early retirement in the fall of 1981 after 31 years of service to Finning. He was replaced by Sood, who had finally achieved his goal of becoming a corporate president. Sood's victory was bittersweet, though. In an unusual turn of events Finning's three major market segments simultaneously crumbled. Importantly, the forestry industry, which supplied more than 50 percent of the company's revenues, plunged into a severe depression. Finning's earnings dropped 44 percent in 1981, to about $5.2 million, and orders continued to slow going into 1982. Sood, realizing the urgency of the situation, called all of his managers together. In that

meeting they decided to reduce their 1982 sales goal from $500 million to $300 million, and to figure out a way to break even for the year.

In their effort to break even, Sood executives laid off nearly half of the entire 2,400-member work force. They also adopted Sood's proposed salary deferment plan. Under that program, employees agreed to have 15 percent of their salary withheld (20 percent for management), which would be payable from earnings in 1983. Sood also sought out new markets to boost sales. Importantly, he purchased two Caterpillar dealerships in the United Kingdom that were immune to the changes in the Canadian market. The move was controversial at the time, but turned out to be a major coup. Sood combined the dealerships into a subsidiary called Finning Limited. In 1984 Finning automated the division and added financing operations. By 1985, Finning Limited was contributing one-third of the organization's total revenues and a significant portion of its profits.

Finning finished 1982 with sales of $315 million and a positive net income of $285,000, allowing it to continue its legacy of profitability despite the worst downturn in its history. Sood's efforts during 1981 and 1982 were praised by his peers that were still working for the company. Indeed, fellow managers at the time attributed Finning's success to Sood's respected sales abilities as well as his uncanny knack for handling money, numbers, and detailed information. He was also commended for his unique management style. Sood operated Finning during the 1980s as a very loose, decentralized company. Employees were generally empowered to make important decisions, and Sood held things together by getting out and speaking directly with workers on the floor and in the field. In 1986, in fact, Finning was recognized by the *Financial Post* as one of the best 100 companies to work for in Canada.

Although Finning laid off about 1,100 workers in the early 1980s, huge sales gains during the middle 1980s allowed it to hire back many of those employees. Indeed, Finning benefitted during the mid-1980s from healthy gains both at home and in the United Kingdom. Sales bolted back past $500 million by 1986, to about $550 million, and then to a big $660 million in 1987. Also in 1987, net income rocketed 28 percent to $26.6 million—the company changed its name in that year from Finning Tractor and Equipment Co. to Finning Ltd. By 1988 Finning was employing 2,600 workers—about 200 more than were working at the company before the 1981 layoffs began. It was selling its equipment in 55 Canadian communities and about a dozen cities in the United Kingdom. In addition to its Caterpillar distribution business, the company was also selling other manufacturers' drilling equipment and cranes in the United States and the United Kingdom.

Finning continued to prosper into the early 1990s. Importantly, Sood engineered the 1989 buyout of Alberta Caterpillar dealer R. Angus Alberta Ltd., which broadened Finning's presence in the oil drilling market and reduced its dependence on the forestry industry to just 18 percent of revenues. The purchase also helped push Finning's sales to a record $1.1 billion in 1990. By that time, Finning's work force was approaching 4,000. Unfortunately, another recession came and Finning was again forced to start cutting costs. To that end, Finning began reducing its number of employees through early retirement and by implementing a hiring freeze. It also started reevaluating and reorganizing existing operations and adapting them to an environment of declining demand.

Sood handed his chief executive duties off in 1991 to 52-year-old James Shepard. Shepard joined Finning along with Sood in 1968. He trailed Sood's advance, rising from a branch manager to president of the company's Canadian operations, and finally to chief executive of the company in June of 1991. Shortly before he took the helm, Finning expanded in Europe when it became the designated dealer for Poland. That gave Finning three European divisions—the third division was a lift-truck dealership in Holland that Shepard sold in 1993. In 1993, Finning also branched out into Chile with the purchase of a Caterpillar dealer in that emerging nation. That move reflected Shepard's drive to divest Finning of the operations that were dragging down the bottom line and invest in areas of opportunity. Importantly, the purchase of Gildemeister S.A.C. in Chile increased Finning's total revenue pool by about 25 percent.

Despite Finning's efforts to cut costs and improve margins, a general economic recession in North America and Europe hurt sales and earnings. Sales dipped to $832 million in 1992 while net income plunged to a low $2.8 million. Markets began to recover in 1993 and Finning began to enjoy sales contributions from its new

Chilean division. Revenue surged to $1.04 billion in that year and earnings rocketed back to a healthy $22.2 million. Better yet, Finning's Chile acquisition helped to push sales to a record $1.46 billion in 1994, a whopping $61.42 million of which was netted as income. Going into 1995, Finning was employing 3,900 people in western Canada, the United Kingdom, Poland, and Chile. It remained the largest Caterpillar dealer in the world, but also sold and leased trucks, cranes, compressors, and other equipment for a wide variety of markets. A diverse market mix and increasing efficiency complemented the company's legacy of profitability.

Principal Subsidiaries:

Finning Equipment Hire Limited; Finning Finance Limited; Finning Poland Sp. z o.o.; Gildemeister S.A.C.

Further Reading:

Nutt, Rod, "Finning Digs Up $12 Million in Profits in the First Quarter," *Vancouver Sun,* April 23, 1994, Section H, p. 3.
Schreiner, John, "Analysts Just Can't Resist Finning," *Financial Post,* July 20, 1991, Section 1, p. 19.
Van Halm, Rochelle, "Finning's Guru," *BC Business,* May 1988, Section 1, p. 112.

—Dave Mote

Weston.

George Weston Limited

22 St. Clair Avenue East, Suite 1901
Toronto, Ontario M4T 2S7
(416) 922-2500
Fax: (416) 922-4395

Public Company
Incorporated: 1928
Employees: 63,700
Sales: $13 billion
Stock Exchanges: Toronto Montreal Vancouver
SICs: 2026 Fluid Milk; 2051 Bread, Cake & Related
  Products; 2064 Candy & Other Confectionery
  Products; 2091 Canned & Cured Fish & Seafoods;
  2611 Pulp Mills; 5149 Groceries & Related
  Products Nec; 5411 Grocery Stores

George Weston Limited, a diversified food processor and distributor, carries the name of the baker's apprentice who started this family-run business in 1882 with two bread routes. It has since grown, mainly by acquisition, to become one of the largest companies in Canada.

George Weston's early success at selling bread led to a rapid increase in the number of routes he managed, and soon encouraged him to establish a bread and cake bakery in Toronto, in 1897. At George Weston's death in 1924 his son Garfield Weston took over a growing business. In 1928 he incorporated George Weston Ltd.

Under Garfield's leadership, the firm built its bread and biscuit businesses in Canada and the United States. Weathering the Depression, the company was able to take advantage of its position as a low-cost producer to take over other competitors in the baking industry. Its 1938 acquisitions of the Inter-City Western Bakeries and the Associated Biscuit Company, for example, provided Weston with the facilities and resources to produce 370 varieties of candy and 100 types of biscuits, in addition to its breads and cakes.

Despite World War II, expansion continued smoothly throughout the 1940s. In 1944 the company bought the Southern Biscuit Company, and the acquisition of Western Grocers marked the firm's initial entry into food distribution. This growth was strengthened by purchases of the Edmonton City Bakery in 1945 and Dietrich's Bakeries in 1946. After the war, the company acquired William Neilson, a major Canadian producer

of chocolate, cocoa, milk, and dairy specialty products. In the 1980s Neilson acquired licenses to produce Haagen-Dazs ice cream and Danone yogurt in Canada. This subsidiary's 1987 acquisition of the confectionery operations of Cadbury Schweppes Canada Inc. gave Weston a commanding one-third share of the Canadian chocolate bar market and made it Canada's largest chocolate manufacturer.

During the 1940s and early 1950s, Weston began buying shares of Loblaw Groceterias, a food distributor, as part of a strategy designed to reach consumers directly with its products. By 1953 the firm had acquired a majority interest in Loblaw, a position that made possible Loblaw's subsequent acquisitions of other food distributors across Canada and the midwestern United States, including National Grocers of Ontario in 1955; National Tea, a U.S.-based retailer, in 1956; Kelly, Douglas and Company, a British Columbia wholesaler, in 1958; the Maritime-based Atlantic Wholesalers in 1960; and the Zehrmart supermarket chain in 1963.

During the 1960s the company pursued further diversification in an attempt to improve its value to shareholders by expanding into natural resources. Weston bought Eddy Paper Company in 1962, and five years later, British Columbia Packers, a salmon processor, and Connors Brothers, the largest herring and sardine processor in Canada.

Growth was temporarily curtailed in the 1970s as management focused on reorganizing the company's activities and operations to achieve greater control and efficiency. W. Galen Weston, one of Garfield's sons, had become president in 1970, and the firm began to refocus on food as its primary area of emphasis. By the next decade, Weston had successfully consolidated its many businesses into three major groups which managed daily operations autonomously within the framework of defined corporate goals and objectives.

Weston Foods Ltd., the food processing group, was formed in 1986. Its operations include baking and milling, biscuits, chocolate, dairy, and specialty products, providing food and ingredients both to intermediate processors and directly to consumers all over North America. This group employs more than 12,000 workers and accounts for 11 percent of the company's total sales.

The food processing group includes Weston Bakeries, Canada's largest baker of fresh bread, buns, and cake products (distributed under a variety of brands and private labels), Neilson/Cadbury, and the Stroehmann Bakeries. Stroehmann was acquired in 1980 and today is one of the largest wholesale baked goods producers in the northeastern United States. Another member of the food processing group is the Interbake Foods specialty biscuit division, which consists of the cookie and cracker businesses acquired between 1928 and 1960, including the Southern Biscuit Company, the focus of operations in the United States. This group also includes the Soo Line Mills and McCarthy Milling, which manufacture and distribute various types of flour inside Canada and abroad, and Bowes Company, a food specialties supplier.

Weston Resources, divided into two areas, accounts for 11 percent of Weston's total sales. Operations of the

Forest Products division are handled primarily by the Ontario-based E. B. Eddy Forest Products, established in the mid-1800s. Today this company mills and processes pulp, lumber, and paper products for North American distribution. The Fisheries division, comprising British Columbia Packers and Connors Brothers, markets canned, fresh, frozen, and processed fish and herring products throughout the world.

Loblaw Companies, Weston's food distribution group, is the largest wholesale and retail food distributor in Canada, and has a sizeable retail business in the United States as well. Staffed by more than 46,000 employees and representing 78 percent of total company sales, the group's aim is to customize its stores to meet the needs of specific markets and to develop a large number of products under the private labels of "No Name" and "President's Choice." In 1986 Weston's National Tea subsidiary acquired 26 stores in St. Louis owned by the Kroger Company. Ten years earlier, however, National Tea had encountered serious financial problems in its food distribution area, forcing it to sell 75 percent of its supermarkets. This set the stage for a period of consolidation which lasted into the 1980s.

The firm also faced major labor problems in the early 1980s involving the unionized employees of its Super Valu stores in Manitoba. These difficulties resulted from Weston's aggressive penetration of the Winnipeg retail food market. In order to convert its existing Loblaw stores in the area to larger-scale supermarkets and hire away experienced employees from other retailers, Weston offered to recognize the Manitoba Food and Commercial Workers Union and to match its current contract with Safeway Foods in return for a six-year, no-strike, no lockout agreement which effectively eliminated the union's contract negotiation rights. Shortly after concluding this arrangement, Super Valu was accused by its employees of violating a number of contract provisions related to seniority, scheduling, and full-time employment; however, a compromise was eventually reached.

During the late 1980s and early 1990s the company slowed its growth and focused on improving the profitability of its existing activities. Guided by a corporate philosophy that positioned the company as a low-cost supplier of superior products, the firm continued to be managed by Galen Weston, who assumed the additional position of chairman in the mid-1970s. Weston has earned a reputation as a turnaround specialist and expert retailer. He has maintained a very private lifestyle, partly because of a foiled kidnap attempt by the Irish Republican Army in 1983.

Going into the 1990s, George Weston was a dominant force in its three primary business segments. Unfortunately, economic recession and sluggish key markets hindered the company's success. Weston responded to the tight economy by stepping up its restructuring efforts and consolidating its businesses. It eliminated several hundred employees, in fact, and flattened its management structure. In 1994 Weston even eliminated its chief financial officer and transferred responsibilities from that position to another executive, effectively combining two positions.

Besides the economic downturn, Weston also suffered during the early 1990s from labor conflicts and price wars with major competitors. The company still posted a healthy $57 million profit in 1993. In 1994, moreover, sales jumped to the $13 billion mark as net income more than doubled to $117 million. With a renewed emphasis on product superiority and low-cost production, Weston was positioned to remain a leader in its industry.

Principal Subsidiaries:

Weston Foods; Loblaw Companies; Weston Resources.

Further Reading:

Davies, Charles, *Bread Men: How the Westons Built an International Empire.* Toronto: Key Porter Books, 1987.

MacDonald, Gayle, "Hoop Dreams Hit Corporate Canada," *Financial Post,* February 25, 1995, Section 1, p. 3.

Paul, Brent, "Weston CFO Resigns in Shuffle," *Financial Post,* March 11, 1995, Section 1, p. 5.

———, "Weston Jumps 29 Percent in Quarter," *Financial Post,* May 7, 1994, Section 1, p. 10.

"Weston Foods President Announces Resignation," *Financial Post,* July 9, 1994, Section 1, p. 48.

"Weston Profit Soars," *Globe and Mail,* February 17, 1995, p. B2.

—updated by Dave Mote

Great-West Lifeco Inc.

100 Osborne Street North
Winnipeg, Manitoba R3C 3A5
(204) 946-7705
Fax: (204) 946-7838

Public Company
Incorporated: 1891 as The Great-West Life
   Assurance Company
Employees: 6,672
Total Assets: $34.30 billion
Stock Exchanges: Winnipeg Toronto Montreal
SICs: 6311 Life Insurance; 6719 Holding Companies
   Nec

Great-West Lifeco is the holding company for The Great-West Life Assurance Company, a company begun during a major recession in a small Canadian western prairie town almost a century ago. Great-West Lifeco is, in turn, primarily owned by Power Financial Corporation. The Great-West Life Assurance Company was meeting the insurance, retirement, and investment needs of more than four million people across North America going into the mid-1990s. A combination of conservative investment strategies, adaptation to the changing business environment, and innovation in both products and policy have brought Great-West into its second century of business.

In the early 1890s, Winnipeg was a frontier town of lumbermen and plains traders. As a stop on the slowly growing Canadian Pacific Railway, it was a promising growth point in Manitoba. The difficulty of transportation combined with drought created hard economic times for the region during the decade, however. An optimistic local businessman, Jeffry Hall Brock, recognized that capital was needed to invest in local farm and retail development. He envisioned collecting western Canadians' savings via insurance sales, thereby offering them security and protection while financing development. At the time, only 9 of the 40 insurance companies in Canada were Canadian. Not one of these companies was based in western Canada.

The Great-West Life Assurance Company was incorporated in 1891 with a name that reflected the company's regional pride; the hyphen was a typesetter's error. In the first year, 834 policies were sold, representing more than $2 million worth of protection, by a sales force of

three that included Brock. The bold enterprise attracted the involvement of the area's outstanding businessmen, and early shareholders included bakers, farmers, a harnessmaker, and the sheriff. Support came from bustling Toronto as from well as many local rural communities. The mayor of Winnipeg, Alexander Macdonald, became Great-West's first president in 1892. Brock was made managing director.

The company issued its premier manual in 1892, offering six insurance plans. The first claim was received that same year. By the end of 1893, Great-West—competing with 5- to 50-year-old companies across Canada—had the eighth highest returns. At this point, the self-confident young company made the remarkable decision to enter the eastern Canadian markets. Its well-established competitors were situated in the East, as were the country's banking, financial, and manufacturing institutions. The West had essentially one industry: agriculture. In Great-West's first three years, it had achieved the financial backing and business volume that had taken other companies up to 15 years to reach.

Great-West's prosperity continued during the next two decades. By the turn of the century, the company was represented in every province and was the country's fastest-growing life insurer. As the economy improved when the region's depression lifted, the service industry benefited. In 1896 Great-West gained the largest percentage of new business written out of 21 Canadian life insurance companies, placing it only $80,000 behind the industry leader. The first shareholder dividends were paid in 1901, and dividends have been paid every year since.

In 1906 the company crossed the border and established U.S. operations in North Dakota. The next year, Great-West topped all Canadian companies in paid-for business. From 50 applications a month in 1893, the company received an average of 375 applications a month by 1909. However the growth proved a strain on the founder's health. Brock essentially left the company in 1912 for health reasons, and he died in 1915. C. C. Ferguson succeeded Brock as CEO in 1915, one year after the onset of World War I. With the war came a boost to the area's economy, which had declined as the wheat boom receded and freight rates climbed, but the war presented the life insurance industry with the problem of wartime policies. Most firms charged extra premiums for those in the service, but Great-West kept its extra charges at a minimum as part of its war effort. Throughout the war, the company managed to keep up its record, maintained since 1906, for writing more ordinary business in Canada annually than any other company. Nevertheless, the war's impact was felt: claims for wartime deaths totaled $1.5 million. Almost as catastrophic was the flu epidemic that flared up at the war's end from 1918 to 1919, which cost Great-West more than $1 million in death claims.

Canada, like other countries, then contended with conditions following the war: high rates of inflation and unemployment, labor unrest, and slowed agricultural output. Though economic conditions worsened through the 1920s, Great-West showed a steady increase in business. In 1920 U.S. operations were extended into Michigan and Minnesota. That same year, Great-West became one of the first companies to offer group insurance. The concept took many years to catch on. In 1940 group insurance was still only nine percent of the company's total business. In later years it comprised more than half. In 1926 Macdonald retired as president, succeeded by G. W. Allan, who had been company director for 22 years.

Great-West, which had initially concentrated its investments in farm mortgages, had diversified since the war into government bonds and city mortgages. Because of its diversified investments and the fact that stock holdings were a very small part of the company's portfolio, Great-West was well insulated when the market crash of 1929 occurred. In fact, that year was the best to date in the company's history.

The Great Depression years of the next decade provided a new challenge. Business declined between 1932 and 1937, but Great-West managed a gradual increase in assets during the period. By the company's 45th anniversary in 1936, it provided coverage for nearly one million people in North America, issuing an average of 60 policies per business day. New insurance plans were introduced during the Depression, including a policy for the professional woman and a family protection policy. By summer of 1939, Great-West was again enjoying record-breaking figures in applied business.

The decade of depression was ended by the outbreak of World War II, which stimulated employment and industrial activity. The life insurance industry was dramatically revived, and between 1939 and 1945 Great-West enjoyed a tremendous growth in the business, as well as expansion into Indiana, Missouri, Ohio, Kansas, California, and Pennsylvania. Group insurance and group pension plans steadily increased. Also during the war years, Great-West entered into the individual accident and health insurance fields. The company changed presidents in 1940, when M. F. Christie took the job, and again in 1943, when W. P. Riley assumed the position.

During the postwar boom, the company's business boomed too. In 1946 Great-West's business-in-force reached the $1 billion mark. It would reach its second billion only six years later and its third three years after that. The company continued its expansion in the United States entering seven more states between 1946 and 1952. In 1958 it started doing business in five more states and the District of Columbia. Also in 1958 Great-West began technological expansion; it purchased the first computer in western Canada.

Growth continued throughout the prosperous 1960s. In 1968 Great-West became the first Canadian company authorized to sell a variable annuity in the United States. More than $1 billion of new business was placed in that year.

Business in the United States grew rapidly. By 1973 Great-West was licensed in 28 states and the District of Columbia, and opened a marketing office in Denver, Colorado, in 1973. The company separated its Canadian and U.S. operations, except for investment and corporate operations, in 1979. It also opened the company's U.S. headquarters in Denver that year. By then Great-West Life was operating in 45 states. From 1979 to 1983 U.S. business nearly doubled.

During the next decade, Great-West concentrated on product development, asset management, and developing the two regional operations. The Canadian and U.S. markets developed different needs during the 1980s. One of the company's new products was a universal life policy, first introduced in 1982—the first of its kind designed for the Canadian market. A similar policy was introduced in the United States the following year.

Another Great-West innovation was a system it introduced in Canada that paid agents levelized commissions and offered loan arrangements for agents needing additional income. It was the first insurance company in North America to adopt such a system. This arrangement allowed the sales force to experiment with the sale of new products with less fear of financial repercussion. As a result, universal life business increased from 30 percent in 1983 to almost 60 percent in 1985. Over those three years, career agents enjoyed a 65 percent compound growth in average earnings.

In the mid-1980s, the company's structure changed. Great-West had been a joint shareholder-policyholder-owned company from its inception 1891 to 1969 when the Investors Group acquired controlling interest in the company's common shares. Investors Group was subsequently acquired in 1969 by Power Corporation, a Montreal-based holding company with interests in publishing, pulp and paper, and financial services. Then in 1984 Power Corporation formed a subsidiary to hold Great-West and its other financial-service companies. This corporation, called Power Financial, created a holding company in 1986: Great-West Lifeco now holds nearly 100 percent of Great-West Life Assurance Company's stock.

In 1988 Great-West entered into a joint venture with New England Life Insurance Company of Boston. The arrangement allowed Great-West to provide New England Life with a range of services including group life and health products, with both companies sharing in the risks and profits. This innovation allowed New England Life to benefit from Great-West's product line while Great-West gained from New England Life's sales force and established markets. In 1989 Great-West Life also acquired Crown Life's group life and health business in the United States. Several other acquisitions during the early 1990s bolstered Great-West's portfolio, bringing the company's total asset base to about $25 billion going into 1994. Those acquisitions, combined with efforts aimed at cutting costs and consolidating operations, boosted the organization's assets to about $30.41 billion in 1993, from which a net income of about $196 million was generated.

Great-West's rapid growth during the early 1990s reflected its attempt to reposition itself for future gains. In fact, the life insurance market had been relatively stagnant for several years, meaning that growth in the company's traditional line of business—life insurance—was waning. People were shifting their assets out of traditional life insurance products into annuities, health plans, and various retirement accounts. Recognizing the limited future of their bread-and-butter business, Great-West executives began emphasizing the sale of financial services ranging from health plans and retirement savings plans to benefit plans and asset management services. To that end, Great-West reduced its life insurance work force, shifting many of those workers to newer divisions. It also stepped up investments in non-life financial businesses. "The worst thing you can do is stay in a bad business," said Bill McCallum, chief executive, in the April 22, 1994, *Denver Business Journal.*

Great-West's asset base careened to $34.30 billion in 1994 as net income rose to $242 million. It entered 1995 as the largest Canadian provider of group insurance, and it sported the most comprehensive and diversified disability income insurance lines in the country. It also supported a distribution network of about 10,000 agents, brokers, and representatives of financial institutions. Among other forays, the company initiated its first health maintenance organization in the United States in 1995.

Principal Subsidiaries:

Great-West Life & Annuity Insurance Co. (United States); The Great-West Life Assurance Company.

Further Reading:

Fleming, James, *Merchants of Fear,* New York: Viking Press, 1986.

Hicks, L. Wayne, "Great-West Reinventing Itself," *Denver Business Journal,* April 22, 1994, Section 1, p. 3.

McFarland, Janet, "Great West Takes Control of Confed," *Financial Post,* April 30, 1994, Section 1, p. 1.

McQueen, Rod, "The Story Behind the Death of a Giant: Getting Through the Smoke and Mirrors Swirling Around the Demise of Confederation Life," *Financial Post,* September 24, 1994, Section 1, p. 10.

"United States Operations Span 75 Years," *Key News,* January 1981.

—Carol I. Keeley
—updated by Dave Mote

The Horsham Corporation

BCE Place
181 Bay Street, Suite 3900
P.O. Box 768
Toronto, Ontario M5J 2T3
(416) 682-8600
Fax: (416) 364-1560

Public Company
Incorporated: 1987
Employees: 1,800
Sales: $2.49 billion
Stock Exchanges: New York Toronto Montreal
  Frankfurt Berlin
SICs: 2911 Petroleum Refining; 1041 Gold Ores;
  6512 Nonresidential Building Operators

The holding company for operating companies involved in oil, gold, and real estate, The Horsham Corporation ranked as one of Canada's largest conglomerates, a position it earned after recording prodigious growth during the late 1980s and early 1990s. Supported by controlling interests in four main operating companies, Horsham generated nearly $2.5 billion in revenue in 1994, seven years after commencing operations as a $200-million company. During the mid-1990s, Horsham controlled Clark USA, Inc., the fourth-largest independent petroleum refining operation in the United States, Trizec Corporation Ltd., the largest public real estate company in North America, and Barrick Gold Corporation, the third-biggest gold producer in the world. The threads that connected Horsham to these disparate, industry-leading companies were spun by one individual: Peter Munk, the eminently successful entrepreneur who faltered on two notable occasions before founding Horsham to plough the profits gleaned from his gold production business into other business ventures, such as Trizec and Clark USA. Although others contributed to Horsham's prolific rise during the late 1980s and 1990s, it was Munk who orchestrated it all, transforming his shrewd and favorably timed investments into one of the largest conglomerates in Canada.

Born into a wealthy Hungarian banking family, Munk escaped probable internment in a Nazi concentration camp when he fled Budapest at age 16 after his grandfather arranged for the Jewish Munk family to emigrate to Switzerland in 1944. After a brief stay in Switzerland, Munk relocated to Liverpool, England,

then left Liverpool in 1948 with plans to attend the University of Toronto. Munk boarded the *S.S. Arcadia* with enough money to pay one year's tuition, then spent it on the passage across the Atlantic entertaining a female passenger who reportedly had an expensive penchant for champagne. His tuition money gone, Munk worked on a tobacco farm near Dehli, Ontario, to recoup his tuition money, then attended the University of Toronto where he studied electrical engineering.

After leaving the University of Toronto, Munk put his knowledge of electrical engineering to use by forming a consumer electronics manufacturing company named Clairtone Sound Corporation in 1958. Success came quickly to Clairtone, propelled by the popularity of the stereos Munk and his partner, David Gilmour, produced, particularly after singer Frank Sinatra began endorsing the company's products. Only 30 years old when he formed Clairtone, Munk was fast becoming one of Canada's most celebrated business leaders and one of its youngest, stewarding what eventually became the fastest growing industrial company in Canada. In the mid-1960s, when Clairtone was generating more than $15 million in annual sales and had diversified into the manufacture of color television sets and automobiles, Munk learned from a government representative that Nova Scotia was offering cheap financing to businesses able to bring jobs to the economically depressed province. Munk made the move and set to work superintending the construction of a $9 million factory, but part of the deal stipulated that Munk relinquish partial control of Clairtone to the provincial government. Union labor difficulties ensued, exacerbated by production problems with Clairtone's color television sets, and soon, in 1968, the Nova Scotia government converted its bond holdings into a majority stock position and forced Munk and Gilmour out.

Later in his career, Munk summed up his meteoric rise and equally sudden fall before an audience gathered at Upsala College in New Jersey by explaining, "The man who was held out to be a national symbol of creative genius," was transmogrified into, "an incompetent idiot." On the heels of this discouraging experience, however, Munk quickly responded by delving into another business venture with Gilmour. The two publicly castigated entrepreneurs retreated to Fiji and built a resort, Pacific Harbour, that subsequently flourished as one of the South Pacific's most popular resorts. Encouraged by his success, Munk bought control of the region's largest hotel chain, Travelodge Australia Ltd., in 1972 through his new company, Southern Pacific Properties. For Munk, success begat success in the South Pacific, and soon, in 1974, he was attempting to build a $400 million resort at the base of the Egyptian pyramids. Supported by the financial backing of arms dealer Adnan Khashoggi, the resort project appeared ready to go, having received the full acceptance by Egyptian president Anwar Sadat, but the project eventually was derailed by mounting opposition from Sadat's political foes.

Even with the failure of Munk's plan to erect a resort near the pyramids, his foray into the resort management field proved to be highly successful; his first business venture that began and ended successfully. Munk sold his hotel chain in 1981, which had since been renamed

Southern Pacific Hotel Corporation, for $130 million, giving Munk a sevenfold profit on his initial investment. With the profits gleaned from his South Pacific venture, Munk began buying oil and gas properties during the early 1980s, an ill-timed decision that once again deflated the swelling public recognition he had garnered from his stint as a hotelier. Through his newly formed petroleum company, American Barrick Resources Corporation, Munk had made his investments just as the oil and gas market had crested, resulting in what Munk later confided to *Business Week* as "a classically stupid error."

In 1983, as oil prices were plummeting, Munk made an about-face and began investing in gold properties, using American Barrick, his floundering petroleum company, as the financial conduit for his new business interests. Although the shift from oil to gold was sudden, Munk's decision to forego oil exploration and bank his future on gold was not rash, despite the fact that Munk reportedly had made the decision in the middle of the night while pacing the hallways of his home in Switzerland. Munk's decision was predicated on the belief that the price of gold was reaching its nadir and that the political and social upheaval occurring in South Africa at the time would engender a greater demand for other sources of gold. As such, Munk was taking a calculated risk, but no matter the soundness of his theory, the decision to enter the gold business represented a gamble, a gamble Munk would win.

Beginning in 1983, Munk started purchasing gold mines. The first was called Renabie; soon others followed: Valdez Creek, Camflo, and Mercur. Munk waited for each to turn into a producer before purchasing the next, establishing a short pattern of success that continued until 1986, the year Munk made his biggest gamble and most fateful decision to date. In early 1987, Munk paid $62 million for the Goldstrike Mine in Nevada, a price industry pundits thought exorbitant, but the mine proved to be aptly named, representing a mother lode of gold in the Western Hemisphere. Projected to contain 19 tonnes of gold, Goldstrike actually contained more than 900 tonnes of gold reserves, which in the years to come would make American Barrick the largest and most profitable gold producer in the Western Hemisphere.

Shortly after the Goldstrike Mine was purchased, Munk took command of Horsham Corporation (formerly called United Siscoe Mines Inc.). Transformed into an investment company to acquire properties with significant growth prospects, Horsham gave Munk the corporate and financial means to diversify his business interests beyond gold. Roughly a year after forming Horsham, which owned 22 percent of American Barrick, Munk began to explore the possibility of acquiring St. Louis-based Apex Oil Company, the fifth-largest private company in the United States. Several months earlier, in December 1987, Apex had filed for Chapter 11 bankruptcy protection, paving the way for Munk's bid and the acquisition of Apex' main asset, Clark Oil & Refining Corporation, operator of 1,017 service stations in the U.S. Midwest and owner of two oil refineries in Illinois. Through AOC Acquisition Corporation, a wholly owned subsidiary of Horsham, Munk acquired 60 percent of Clark in late 1988, giving Horsham control of the fourth-largest independent oil refining and marketing company in the United States.

Having secured a solid presence in the oil and gold markets, Munk next set his sights on carving a niche in the real estate market. Revenues at Horsham recorded an exponential leap in the years following the acquisition of Clark, jumping from roughly $200 million in 1988 to more than $2.5 billion by the beginning of the 1990s. Munk, however, was not satisfied and began looking to take Horsham in a new direction. The inspiration for his next move came from well outside the boundaries of Horsham's activities, taking Munk back near his native Hungary. Shortly after the collapse of the Berlin Wall in late 1989, Munk hurried to East Berlin for a private meeting with the city's mayor, during which he laid out a proposal to rebuild vast sections of the city with Western-style offices, residences, and shopping centers. Although the project never materialized, Munk was not finished in Germany. In September 1991, less than two years after his meeting with East Berlin's mayor, Munk purchased 500 acres of farmland outside the city from Treuhandanstalt, the state agency responsible for privatizing East German assets. "Brandenburg Park," a large-scale business subdivision, was opened on the site two years later, in June 1993, giving Horsham a new source of revenue and a third operating company, wholly owned Horsham Properties GmbH.

Next, Munk led Horsham toward a considerably more ambitious real estate venture when he acquired control of Trizec Corporation Ltd., North America's largest publicly traded real estate company. Based in Calgary, Trizec at the time held interests in 85 office buildings and shopping centers spread across Canada and the United States, but, like Clark Oil & Refining, was struggling mightily to survive when Munk cast his acquisitive glance in its direction. Despite its precarious financial health, Trizec represented a significant addition to Horsham's disparate collection of operating companies when Munk's holding company acquired a 48 percent stake in July 1994 for $700 million. This purchase brought Horsham's real estate assets to more than $5 billion.

Before the dust had settled from the Trizec deal—in fact, the same day the Trizec transaction was concluded—American Barrick announced the acquisition of gold miner Lac Minerals Ltd. for $1.3 billion. The addition of Lac Minerals increased American Barrick's gold reserves by more than 40 percent, gave it substantially more exploration and development potential, and made the Horsham subsidiary the largest gold producer in North America, as well as the largest in the world outside of South Africa.

As 1994 ended, Horsham's most pressing need was the efficient consolidation of its acquisitions into the fold. Trizec, in particular, required the most attention, receiving a major financial overhaul and the infusion of more than $1 billion in equity during the months following its acquisition by Horsham. With interests in Barrick Gold Corporation (formerly American Barrick Resources Corporation), Trizec Corporation Ltd., Clark USA, Inc., and Horsham Properties GmbH fueling Horsham's growth, the company's management plotted their course for the mid-1990s and beyond.

Principal Subsidiaries:

Barrick Gold Corporation (16.5%); Trizec Corporation Ltd. (48%); Clark USA, Inc. (60%); Horsham Properties GmbH (Germany).

Further Reading:

"Canada's Goldfinger," *The Economist,* April 1, 1995, p. 58.

Kovski, Alan, "Horsham to Put One-Third of Clark Shares on Market to Help Fund Refinery Purchase," *The Oil Daily,* September 22, 1994, p. 1.

McKenna, Barrie, "Munk Defends Berlin Project," *The Globe and Mail,* May 1, 1992, p. B15.

Noble, Kimberley, "Can Munk Make It Last," *The Globe and Mail,* September 19, 1994, p. B1.

Reingold, Jennifer, "Horsham Corp.: Black and Yellow Gold Cheap," *Financial World,* March 16, 1993, p. 14.

Robinson, Alan, "Bid for Apex Oil Launched by Munk," *The Globe and Mail,* June 30, 1988, p. B1.

Rudnitsky, Howard, "If at First You Don't Succeed...," *Forbes,* April 2, 1990, p. 146.

Symonds, William C., "A New Empire Rises North of the Border," *Business Week,* July 11, 1994, p. 106.

———, "After Stereos, Hotels, Oil, and Gold, What's Next?," *Business Week,* October 14, 1991, p. 82.

—Jeffrey L. Covell

Hudson's Bay Company

401 Bay Street
Toronto, Ontario M5H 2Y4
(416) 861-6112
Fax: (416) 861-4720

Public Company Incorporated: 1670
Employees: 62,000
Sales: $5.83 billion
Stock Exchanges: Montreal Toronto
SICs: 5311 Department Stores; 5300 General
   Merchandise Stores

Hudson's Bay Company is Canada's oldest corporation. On May 2, 1670, King Charles II granted 18 investors a charter incorporating them as the Governor and Company of Adventurers of England. In its first century, the company traded with the North American Indians, established forts on Hudson Bay, and successfully fought with French competitors to build its fur trade. By the mid-1990s, it constituted a coast-to-coast operation accounting for about eight percent of Canadian retail sales, excluding food and automobiles, and roughly 40 percent of total Canadian department store sales. The company owned and managed about 400 stores in 1995 in two retail divisions, the Bay and Zellers.

The development of the company is tied to the growth of Canada and settlement of its western region. Those who were important to the development of the company were also important politically and historically to the economic and political growth of the New World. The list of well-known people associated with the company is long and includes Peter Skene Ogden, Solomon Juneau, Henry Kelsey, James Knight, Samuel Hearne, Peter Pond, Alexander Mackenzie, Sir George Simpson, Sir James Douglas, John McLoughlin, and many others. The chartering of the company on May 2, 1670, with Prince Rupert—a cousin of Charles II—as the company's first governor, followed the successful fur trading voyage of the ketch *Nonsuch* that brought back beaver pelts for the English market, used by felters and hatters to make the beaver hats that were fashionable at the time.

The Adventurers' charter of 1670 gave it 1.49 million square miles of virgin territory, or nearly 40 percent of today's Canadian provinces, including what would become Ontario, Quebec north of the Laurentian water-shed and west of the Labrador boundary, Manitoba, the better part of Saskatchewan, southern Alberta, and much of the Northwest Territories. The group's rights to the lucrative fur trade did not go uncontested, and it was not until 20 years later that the company made its first inland expedition. Henry Kelsey, an apprentice who joined the company in 1677 and who later became a company governor, made the first journey into the prairie in 1690, learning the Cree language and adapting to Indian life. He wished to encourage peace among the Indian tribes so that they could bring beaver pelts to the forts without being attacked. Three forts on James Bay—Rupert's House, Moose, and Albany in the east—and a fourth, York Factory, on the west coast of Hudson Bay, were the sites of battles for nearly 30 years between the French and English contesting the territory and the right to conduct trade. The Treaty of Ryswick in 1697 brought peace, but by then the company was near ruin. Most of the company's first century of business was devoted to establishing forts and territorial rights and making peace with the Indians and the French merchants who wanted to be a part of the fur trade in the New World.

One of the Hudson's Bay Company's fiercest early competitors was North West Company, established in 1779 by a Scottish-Canadian group of nine traders that moved into the Canadian interior around 1780 and claimed to be the rightful successor to the early French traders who had opened up the land. North West Company had two types of shareholders: the eastern partners, merchants in Montreal and Quebec who supplied the venture capital, and the "wintering" partners, who became responsible for exploratory and sales operations. By 1800 North West became a serious competitor, forcing Hudson's Bay Company to become increasingly more adventurous, pushing the trade boundaries westward from the Hudson Bay, in fear of losing trade with the western Indians. Each company drove the other toward new expeditions, so that by the turn of the century, they each had men trading on the upper Missouri River. North West's Alexander Mackenzie, who later was knighted, was the most famous fur trader of his day. Mackenzie pushed the trade boundaries farther westward. Several of his trade expeditions were historical achievements: in 1789 he covered 1,600 miles and back in 102 days, and in 1793 he crossed the Rocky Mountains to reach the Pacific Ocean.

Other companies also envied the apparent monopoly of Hudson's Bay Company. U.S. traders wanted a share in the fur trade following the Lewis and Clark expedition of 1804-06. In 1808 Pierre Chouteau, William Clark, and five others established the Missouri Fur Company, and in New York John Jacob Astor, the leading fur dealer in the United States, started the American Fur Company, capitalized at US$300,000, of which he owned all but a few shares.

Peter Skene Ogden, who worked for a time for the American Fur Company, moved to Quebec after being appointed judge of the Admiralty Court in 1788. Ogden wanted to be among the first white men to see the great wilderness. After living in Quebec for six years with his wife and children, he was sent by North West into the interior of North America to clerk at the company's post in what is today Saskatchewan. Ogden wintered on the prairies for the first time in September 1810, where he met Samuel Black, a Scots clerk, who would become a lifelong friend. The two men made a sport of harassing Hudson's Bay men. Among the tales cited by Gloria Cline, author of *Peter Skene Odgen and the Hudson's Bay Company,* was that of the harassment of Peter Fidler of Hudson's Bay Company. Fidler departed in three boats with 16 men for Churchill on Hudson Bay, an important post, and Ogden, with two canoes-full of Canadians, taunted the British traders for six days by keeping just ahead of them in order "to get everything from Indians that may be on the road, as they can go much faster than us," according to Fidler. Ogden was a much-valued employee of North West and was promoted as a result of his antics with Black.

The North West Company also entrusted its goal of westward expansion to David Thompson. In 1807 Thompson had crossed the Rockies and reached the headwaters of the Columbia. In 1809 he again crossed the Rockies and established an outpost in what is now northern Idaho; from there he proceeded into Montana. Directly ahead of Thompson's trading party was the first far-western expedition of John Jacob Astor's Pacific Fur Company, the West Coast subsidiary of American Fur Company. Although a U.S. company, it was managed by three Canadians, former Nor'westers—employees of North West. The War of 1812 altered hopes for Astor's company, and the following year Pacific Fur Company sold all of its interests in the region to North West Company.

During the fall of 1818, Ogden took charge of David Thompson's old post, near what is now Spokane, Washington. The following year, Ogden returned east. In 1821 the two companies merged under the name of the Hudson's Bay Company after the Nor'westers learned that their company was in poor financial condition. Ogden was excluded from the merger by the company because he had fought so fiercely, although he continued working for the new firm as an explorer and trapper.

The next phase of the company's growth was shaped by the 1849 gold fever that caused a great rush westward: almost 40,000 '49ers came west that year. The Bay Company suffered as a result. Demand made the cost of basic goods skyrocket. Lumber rose from $16 to $65 per thousand feet; unskilled labor received $5 to $10 a day; sailors were paid $150 a month. The steady flow of gold, however, created a favorable balance of trade. With settlement, though, came new tax laws. In 1850 the Treasury Department prohibited trade between Fort Victoria and the English Vancouver Island and Fort Nisqually on the U.S. Puget Sound. This hurt Hudson's Bay Company considerably because it legally tied up all vessels for custom inspection, which took them 350 miles off course, subjected them to twice crossing the hazardous Columbia sandbar, and made them pay heavy piloting fees at the custom house port. To add to Ogden's troubles in the western outposts of the company, the gold fever created labor difficulties, with many crewmen deserting to seek gold. After several years of health problems, Ogden returned east for 18 months. Upon returning to his post in the North West, the strenuous trip and his advancing age took their toll: Ogden died in 1854.

Equal in importance to the growth of the company was Sir George Simpson, who served as administrator of the company for 40 years following the merger with North West. John McLoughlin, called the Father of Oregon, governed the district under Simpson with wide powers. Sir James Douglas assisted McLoughlin; he later became Governor of the Crown Colonies of Vancouver and British Columbia.

When the westward settlement reached St. Paul, the British government tried to break the Bay Company monopoly by charging it with poor administration. A select committee of the House of the Commons investigated the charges, and with Sir George Simpson as one of the principal witnesses, the charges were dismissed. Most of the company's territory and the North West territories became part of the Confederation through the British North America Act of 1867. Canada bought Rupertsland in 1870.

Demand for general merchandise increased, and shops were established on the outskirts of the forts. In 1912 a major remodeling and reconstruction of retail trade shops was interrupted by World War I. Following the war, the company diversified, incorporating elements of oil exploration in Alberta, revitalizing its Fur Trade Department, and venturing into the oil business as a favored partner of Hudson's Bay Oil and Gas. After the 1929 stock market crash and the subsequent Great Depression, the fur department revitalized itself, improving working conditions, and in some areas acted as an agent for Inuit carvings.

Early in the 20th century, the company made retail stores its first priority, building downtown department stores in each of the major cities of western Canada, moving east through acquisitions, and expanding into the suburbs of major Canadian cities beginning in the 1960s. Hudson's Bay Company acquired Markborough Properties, a real estate company, in 1973; Zellers, a chain of discount stores, in 1978; and Simpsons, a group of Toronto-area department stores, the following year. Kenneth Thomson, representing the family of the late Lord Thomson of Fleet, acquired a 75 percent controlling interest in the company in 1979.

In the 1970s, the company's governor was Donald McGiverin, and George Kosich was chief operating officer. In that decade and into the 1980s, sales and oil prices slipped, while debt from acquisitions piled up. By 1985 the company owed $2.5 billion and with feeble operating profits wiped out by $250 million in interest payments, the company suffered its fourth consecutive yearly loss. In response, management shed assets, including the Bay's 179 northernmost stores, some of which could be traced back to the fur-trading days of Ogden. In a strong attempt to survive, Thomson shook up top management, eventually appointing George Kosich, a career merchandiser, president. Thomson revamped retail operations, and the combined market share of the three department store chains rose to 33 percent from 29 percent in two years.

Kosich refocused Simpsons to the upscale market and the Bay toward the middle-to-lower-priced market. In repositioning the Bay, Kosich put the 300-year-old Canadian giant up against its closest U.S. counterpart, Sears. In 1985 the Bay had 10 percent of the market,

Sears 27 percent. Employing an intensive advertising campaign—$75 million—the Bay produced a bold and aggressive image before Canadians. In the first half of 1986, sales rose 13.2 percent over that of 1985. Operating profit rose to $31 million in 1985, and to $83 million on $1.8 billion in total sales in 1986. Sears was feeling the results, reporting barely a three percent rise in 1986 and a continuous downturn ever since.

Zellers was positioned to appeal to the budget shopper as a "junior" department store. Club Z, a frequent-buyer program that allowed customers to accumulate points for prizes, boasted three million members. Hudson's Bay Company reversed a formidable debt picture in 1987 by shedding non-strategic assets such as its wholesale division and getting out of the oil and gas business. In 1990 it spun off its real estate subsidiary, Markborough Properties, as a separate, public company. Shareholders received one share of Markborough for each share they held of Hudson's Bay, with the Thomson family retaining a majority interest in Markborough. Also in 1990, the company bought 51 Towers Department Stores and merged them with Zellers. In January 1991 Hudson's Bay Company permanently left the Canadian fur trade, an estimated $350 million market, because its own share of that market had degenerated to a paltry $7 million in 1990. Furthermore, the company had been targeted by increasingly vocal antifur groups. Early in 1991, the company sold three million new common shares, with net proceeds of $72.5 million. It also repurchased slightly more than two million Series A preferred shares for $42.5 million. Company officials said these transactions would result in a stronger financial position. Because of declines in interest rates in the early 1990s, the Series A shares, with an eight percent dividend, had become more expensive to service than debt. Later in 1991 the company broke up its Simpsons division when it sold eight Simpsons stores to Sears Canada Inc. and moved the remaining six stores into the Bay division.

The company entered the 1990s expecting a recession to adversely affect both retail sales and earnings. To brace for the downturn, Hudson's executives developed a restructuring plan designed to shed underperforming stores and divisions, increase retail activity in more promising locations, and boost productivity. The retail industry did indeed slump during the early 1990s. Hudson's responded with beefed up capital investments in technology, marketing, and new Bay and Zeller stores. The net result was that company revenues rose steadily from $4.98 billion in 1990 to a record $5.44 billion in 1993. More importantly, earnings grew from $98 million to a all-time high of $148 million. Much of the growth was attributable to the Zeller chain, which grew to 285 stores by 1985.

Although Hudson's early 1990s gains were impressive when compared to the performance of many other retailers, its success was being shadowed by changes looming on the retail industry horizon. Wal-Mart began to invade the Zeller's turf in the Canadian discount market in 1994. By the end of that year, in fact, the formidable U.S. discounter was having a marked impact on Hudson's business in the areas that it had entered. Specifically, Wal-Mart was boosting competition and exerting pressure on some Zeller store's profit margins. The Wal-Mart threat was evidenced by a decline in Hudson's stock price during 1994 and early in 1995. Still, Hudson's revenues and earnings soared to $5.83 billion and $151 million, respectively, in 1994.

To combat Wal-Mart, Hudson's was scrambling to expand its chains and increase efficiency. Hudson's earmarked $200 million early in 1995, in fact, to add, expand, and renovate its stores. "We will probably open more stores this year naturally [not through acquisitions] than we have ever done in the history of the company," said Don Rogers, vice-president of real estate, in the February 9, 1995, *Financial Post*. In early 1995 Hudson's was operating 101 Bay stores and 292 Zeller discount stores throughout Canada. 1995 marked the company's 325th anniversary, making it the oldest company in Canada and one of the oldest in the world.

Principal Subsidiaries:
The Bay; Zellers.

Further Reading:

Brent, Paul "HBC Profit Less Than Expected," *Financial Post*, August 26, 1994, Section 1, p. 6.
———, "Hudson's Bay to Buy Three Comark Stores," *Financial Post*, February 9, 1995, Section 1, p. 15.
Cline, Gloria G., *Peter Skene Odgen and the Hudson's Bay Company*, Norman: Oklahoma, University of Oklahoma Press, 1974.
Deverell, John, "Jubilant Bay Chief Celebrates Record Year," *Toronto Star*, April 7, 1995, Section C, p. 1.
Innis, Harold, *The Fur Trade in Canada*, Toronto: University of Toronto Press, 1967.
Newman, Peter C., "The Hudson's Bay Company: Canada's Fur-Trading Empire," *National Geographic*, August 1987.
Ray, Auther J., and Donald B. Freeman, *Give Us Good Measure: An Economic Analysis of Relations between the Indians and the Hudson's Bay Company before 1763*, Toronto: University of Toronto Press, 1978.
Rich, Edwin Ernest, ed., *Minutes of the Hudson's Bay Company, 1671-1674*, London, Ontario: Hudson's Bay Record Society Publications, 1942.

—Claire Badaracco
—updated by Dave Mote

Hydro-Quebec

75 Ouest Boulevard Rene Levesque
Montreal, Quebec PQ H2Z 1A4
(514) 289-2211
Fax: (514) 289-3658

*Wholly Owned Subsidiary of the Government of the
   Province of Quebec*
Incorporated: 1944
Employees: 20,528
Sales: $7.30 billion
SICs: 4911 Electrical Services

Hydro-Quebec and its subsidiaries constitute the third
largest electric utility in North America, serving over 3.3
million customers in the Canadian province of Quebec
through over 54 hydroelectric plants and 26 thermal
plants. Hydro-Quebec is also involved in energy-related
research and testing through its high-voltage, high-pow-
er research center, IREQ, located southeast of Montreal.
Hydro-Quebec is one of the province's largest employers, with over 25,000 temporary and permanent workers
in 1994. The company was created in 1944 by an act of
the provincial legislature.

The province of Quebec emerged as one of the world's
major producers of hydroelectricity in the late 19th
century. Construction of the province's first large dam
began in 1898, just three years after completion of the
world's first hydroelectric plant at Niagara. Hydroelectricity was a powerful force behind the development of
Quebec's economy, since many other industries, including aluminum and carbide production, relied on the
cheap, abundant power produced on Quebec's raging
rivers.

Montreal Light, Heat & Power Company (MLH&P) was
formed in 1901 under the leadership of two powerful
Montreal financiers, Louis-Joseph Forget and Herbert S.
Holt. Holt was an Irish Protestant immigrant who began
his engineering career as a contractor for the Canadian
Pacific Railway. He made his fortune in Montreal as
president of the Royal Bank and held directorships in 26
companies by 1912, including MLH&P. Forget and his
nephew and partner Rodolphe Forget were securities
brokers who made substantial fortunes and became
shareholders in many companies by engineering corporate reorganizations and mergers.

Holt served as director of the Royal Electric Company
and was elected president of the Montreal Gas Company
in 1894. He began building the conglomerate that would
become MLH&P with the acquisition of Consumers'
Gas Company, a competitor for the city's gas streetlight-
ing contract. While Royal Electric concentrated on
commercial and industrial service, its rivals vied for the
domestic suburban market.

The most threatening new force was the Lachine Rapids
Hydraulic and Land Company. Lachine was able to
produce power at much lower rates than Royal Electric,
and in 1899 Royal was forced to cut its rates by 33
percent to remain competitive. Holt and other investors
tried to build their own hydroplant on the Richelieu
River, but their Chambly plant suffered from low water
and defective construction. As Lachine continued to
undercut Royal, a group of Royal Electric shareholders
led by the Forgets took over the company in 1898.

They began to build their hydroelectric empire by
consolidating interests in the Chambly plant, the Montreal Street Railway, and the Royal Electric Company
during the late 1890s. As financiers, the Forgets knew
that centralizing ownership of the various electric concerns would enable them to generate more capital
through the combined collateral of the subsidiaries.

Forget and Holt created the MLH&P system in 1901
from three electric companies (Royal Electric Company,
Montreal & St. Lawrence Light & Power Company, and
Imperial Electric Light Company) and one gas company
(Montreal Gas Company) that soon monopolized power
distribution in and around the city of Montreal. The
industries complemented each other. After Chambly
was upgraded, it provided cheap power to Royal, which
distributed that power to the Montreal Street Railway
and other industrial and commercial customers. The gas
company brought profits in its own markets.

Competition among the many utilities around Montreal
remained fierce, and the appearance of the Shawinigan
Water and Power Company threatened to put MLH&P
out of business. The Shawinigan plant on the Saint-
Maurice River Valley was the largest system in the area.
The company offered to sell power to MLH&P, but Holt
and Forget, seeing that the asking price was too high,
built another small plant at St. Therese. In 1902 a flood
wiped out the St. Therese station and shut down the
Chambly plant. Holt and Forget were forced to buy
power from the rival Lachine plant and soon realized
that the only way to put an end to the competition and
come out ahead was to buy out their competitors.

In 1903 they raised $4.5 million and purchased the
Lachine Rapids Hydraulic and Land Company, including its generating station, distribution system, and the
contract for virtually all the power that Shawinigan
Water and Power could sell. After winning a monopoly
over the Montreal power market, Holt and Forget did
their best to buy out competition and control waterpow-
er in the region.

In 1916, the Civic Investment & Industrial Company, a
holding company, was created to acquire the capital
stock of MLH&P and the Cedars Rapids Manufacturing
& Power Company. The company name was changed to
Montreal Light, Heat & Power Consolidated in 1918 to

reflect the incorporation of practically all the gas, electric light, and power business in Montreal as one enterprise.

Consolidation was the key word for the 1920s. By 1930, MLH&P owned or controlled six of its former competitors, an electric railway, and a coal and coke plant. The monopoly allowed MLH&P to set prices and reap big profits. From 1910 to 1930, domestic electric rates dropped from 9¢ to 3¢ per kilowatt hour, and costs fell even faster. Holt held Quebecers' domestic rates at twice those offered in Ontario.

Opposition to the "electricity trust" focused on these big profits and came primarily from local businessmen. Others were outraged at the perpetual land leases granted to the MLH&P along with rights to use the streets in suburbs within 100 miles of Montreal.

The Great Depression undermined the finances of many hydroelectric companies around Montreal during the 1930s. MLH&P gained control of Beauharnois Power Company, a large producer of energy on the St. Lawrence River, in 1933. It also took advantage of the economic downturn by acquiring municipal utility companies in Pointe Claire, Baie d'Urfe, and St. Anne de Bellevue. By 1941, MLH&P owned three hydroelectric plants and operated a fourth in cooperation with Shawinigan Water and Power.

The Lapointe Commission, formed in 1934, recommended the creation of an Electrical Commission in 1935. The Electrical Commission (later named the Provincial Electricity Board), regulated electric distribution, focusing on rates and services. In 1937, the provincial government adopted a bill that favored municipal control of electrical service.

The Quebec Hydro-Electric Commission, better known as Hydro-Quebec, was created on April 14, 1944, and took over the assets of Montreal Light, Heat & Power Consolidated the next day. The new commission compensated MLH&P shareholders in 1947, but did not settle contracts with minority shareholders in MLH&P subsidiaries Beauharnois Light, Heat & Power and Montreal Island Power until 1953. By 1948, the government had gone a long way toward achieving its goals of reducing rates and standardizing service: residential rates were cut by 20 percent and commercial power prices went down 26 percent.

In 1948, Hydro-Quebec gave new impetus to its exports to the United States when it contracted with the Cedar Rapids Company, a subsidiary of Aluminum Company of America in Massena, New York. In the 1940s and 1950s, Hydro-Quebec concentrated on developing the hydroelectric potential in the province. In 1957, the company sold its gas system to concentrate on hydro power. After that year, virtually all of Hydro-Quebec's generating capacity came from hydroelectric generators.

Demand for cheap power was driven by the defense industry. Aluminum, copper, and nickel refining were in high demand during World War II and on into the military build-up during the Cold War. As a result, many major hydro projects were undertaken in the 1950s. By the end of the decade, the province of Quebec produced 48.9 percent of Canada's hydroelectricity and was the greatest producer of power per capita in the country. Hydro kept costs low, too: the price per kilowatt hour in Quebec was 33 percent less than that of the United States.

Hydro-Quebec's first bond offering to American markets was used to finance the Bersimis River project. Twenty-five year bonds were sold for a total of US$50 million to finance the generating station, which was completed in 1958. In 1953, Hydro-Quebec undertook a project to widen the Beauharnois canal, which diverted water from the St. Lawrence River to drive hydroelectric plants. The project kept Quebec in the forefront of hydroelectric development in Canada. The next year, the company installed the world's largest submarine power cable, connecting the Bersimis generating facility with the Gaspe Peninsula. The discovery of rich copper mines in this previously undeveloped region raised demand for inexpensive power. The area had been electrified by diesel generators, which cost two to three times as much as hydropower. The cables provided for the complete electrification of the area, 20 percent of which had been without power up to that time.

The 1960s were characterized by the purchase by Hydro-Quebec of the private electrical distribution companies. The Shawinigan Water & Power Company, Quebec's largest nongovernment hydroelectric company, was bought out in 1963 in an effort to standardize rates and services throughout the province. Between 1963 and 1965, 45 rural electrical cooperatives and 19 municipal systems came under government control. They had constituted about one-third of Quebec's power sources. The 1960s also brought technological strides for Hydro-Quebec. In 1963, the company cosponsored extra-high voltage experiments with Pittsfield Massachusetts's General Electric Company. The 700-kilovolt tests surpassed U.S. voltage limits by 200 kilovolts.

During the 1950s an unfavorable balance of trade with the United States led the Canadian Exporters Association to discourage electric exports because of U.S. quotas and tariffs on many Canadian products. But in 1963, the federal government began to encourage the export of hydroelectricity to U.S. markets. In 1966, after two years of talks, Hydro-Quebec entered into agreements with British Newfoundland Corporation (Brinco) to begin a massive project at Churchill Falls, Newfoundland. The falls at Churchill were a tremendous untapped resource: at 245 feet (50 percent higher than Niagara Falls), Churchill was considered the western world's largest single source of power. Work began at the site in 1967 and was completed in 1970. Hydro-Quebec cosponsored the project, which diverted the river above the falls into a tunnel to an underground powerhouse. When finished, the project produced more power than all the American and Canadian plants at Niagara Falls.

In 1971, the James Bay Development Corporation was created by an act of the Quebec National Assembly to develop natural resources. Increased demand for electricity inspired a plan known as the James Bay project to develop generating stations on La Grande River. The venture has been controversial since its inception and throughout its development, with plans calling for the construction of over 200 structures that would alter the courses of 19 waterways in northwest Quebec.

The James Bay project consisted of three different complexes hundreds of miles apart. The La Grande Complex, commonly referred to as James Bay 1, consisted of a series of dams and dikes stretching a total of 41 miles, guiding regional rivers through three generating stations. Despite efforts to stop the project, the undertaking was completed in 1985. James Bay 2, commonly known as the "Great Whale" project, began in 1987. The $13.5 billion plan called for the construction of a hydroelectric plant on the Great Whale River and the construction of facilities on the Nottaway, Broadback, and Rupert Rivers.

The project drew opposition from Cree and Inuit Indians, and from international environmentalists, who cited the possibility of higher mercury levels in fish, destruction of caribou habitat, and the unpredictable geological impact of massive man-made reservoirs on the earth's crust as reasons to stop the project.

Utility and government officials, on the other hand, pointed out that hydro power does not produce air pollution or wastes, and that if the equivalent of the annual production of the Great Whale complex was produced by thermal power stations, it would be necessary to burn at least 26 million barrels of oil per year. Furthermore, the James Bay Project has created thousands of jobs and opened up more than 1,000 miles of roads in previously inaccessible areas. Utility officials also dispute the impact of the project on the environment. Hydro-Quebec's increased generating capabilities have also enabled the company to sell surplus electricity to neighboring provinces and to export power to utilities in Connecticut, Maine, New Hampshire, Massachusetts, Rhode Island, Vermont, and New York.

Hydro-Quebec took a variety of steps to resolve the problems that impeded the conclusion of the James Bay projects. In cooperation with the provincial government and native groups, the company participated in environmental impact studies and drafted agreements to hire Native people and to award contracts to their firms. Negotiations continued during the early 1990s, with the target start up date for the Great Whale plant scheduled for 2001.

Although Hydro-Quebec's own $400-million study suggested that the demand for electricity would justify the $13-billion project, a number of forces caused Premier Jacques Parizeau to cancel the project in November 1994. The most vocal opposition to Great Whale came from the Quebec Crees, who argued that the 3,000-megawatt project and the 3,400 acres of their land that would be flooded, would serve to "extinguish aboriginals' rights" and cause irrevocable environmental damage. While the well publicized speeches by Cree leaders, such as Grand Chief Matthew Coon Come, and the various environmentalists who championed their cause, no doubt, contributed to the decision, a significant decrease in energy demand may have proved to be just as important. In 1992, for example, New York canceled a $17-billion contract to buy 1,000 megawatts of electricity; other cancellations from border states soon followed. "The [Premier] had sound economic, political and environmental reasons to act," wrote one *Globe and Mail* editorialist. "Any one of them might have made

the case effectively; together, the reasons were overwhelming."

Despite the negative publicity it received from Great Whale, Hydro-Quebec has instituted several successful programs during the 1990s that have improved both customer and employee relations. In 1993, the company reorganized the administrative structure of its major activities, in hopes of improving efficiency and lowering operating expenses—two of the primary goals behind its growing *Defi performance* or "performance challenge" program. This long range project, with its 400 improvement teams involving more than 3,000 employees, played a large part in boosting customer approval ratings to 95 percent in 1994. A broad range of Energy Efficiency Projects, such as Econo-Confort, in which company representatives visit customers and install more efficient equipment and offer tips on energy conservation, helped to save customers money without a reduction in comfort.

Hydro-Quebec has also earned high marks during the 1990s for its commitment to research and technology. Devoting almost two percent of its revenues and more than 800 employees to developing new computer software, electronics equipment, and various other high-tech projects, the company is generally acknowledged to be one of the Canadian leaders in R & D. And in May of 1995, the company was named a finalist for the Edison Award, in recognition for its many technological breakthroughs during the previous year, which ranged from the Language Expert System, a sophisticated diagnostic software program, to the Organic Electrosynthesis Program, a more efficient method of producing a wide array of chemicals and pharmaceuticals. Once new technologies such as these are developed at its two research sites in Quebec, they are marketed by one of the company's subsidiaries, Nouveler, which negotiated licensing agreements that brought about sales of around $14 million during 1994, while also launching several new companies, such as Scompitech, a firm engaged in the manufacture of a Hydro-Quebec's own newly developed robotic solder system.

Hydro-Quebec has maintained an impressive record of performance since its inception. Between 1944 and 1979, the company doubled its electric production capacity every ten years. As the company has looked forward to the year 2000, however, competition in the North American electrical industry has been intensifying and the rate of demand growth has been declining. As a result, nearly all major producers have had a surplus of energy at their disposal, leading to price rivalries among gas, oil, and electricity—and lower profit margins for the industry as a whole. The deregulation of U.S. energy markets, combined with the entrance of several private and independent producers, suggests that the future of Hydro-Quebec will depend largely on its ability to maintain its excellent record of customer service and continue to improve the efficiency of its operations, while avoiding the environmental and political battles that have at times overshadowed the company's strengths.

Principal Subsidiaries:

Hydro-Quebec International; Nouveler; Societe d'energie de la Baie James; ACEP (50 percent); CITEQ (50 percent); Churchill Falls Corporation (34.2 percent).

Further Reading:

Armstrong, Christopher, and H.V. Nelles, *Monopoly's Moment: The Organization and Regulation of Canadian Utilities, 1830-1930,* Philadelphia, Temple University Press, 1986.

Bolduc, Andre, Clarence Hogue, and Daniel Larouche, *Hydro-Quebec After 100 Years of Electricity,* translated by Sheila Fischman, Libre Expression, 1989.

Coffee, Hoyt E., "James Bay Power Project Hits a Dam," *Site Selection,* February 1992.

Gagnon, Lysiane, "Great Whale Was Headed for the Beach Long before Coon Come's Speech," *Globe and Mail,* November 26, 1994, p. D3.

Gibbon, Ann, "Druin Quitting Hydro-Quebec Early," *Globe and Mail,* May 4, 1995, p. B10.

————, "Hydro-Quebec Loses Court Fight," *Globe and Mail,* February 25, 1994, p. A1.

Linteau, Paul-Andre, et al, *Quebec: A History, 1867-1929,* Toronto, James Lorimer & Co., 1983.

McKenna, Barrie, "Study Backs Great Whale Plan," *Globe and Mail,* September 1, 1993, p. B1.

McNish, Jacquie, "Hydro-Quebec Facing Loss of Second Contract," *Globe and Mail,* March 30, 1994, p. A1.

"People," *Electrical World,* February 1992.

Picard, Andre, "Is Hydro-Quebec the Wal-Mart of Energy?," *Globe and Mail,* May 19, 1994, p. A29.

Selby, Beth, "Hydro-Quebec's Big Power Play," *Institutional Investor,* February 1992.

—April S. Dougal
—updated by Jason Gallman

Imasco

Imasco Limited

600 de Maisonneuve Boulevard West
Montreal, Quebec H3A 3K7
(514) 982-9111
Fax: (514) 982-9369

Public Company
Incorporated: 1912 as Imperial Tobacco Company of
   Canada Limited
Employees: 200,000
Sales: $16.43 billion
Stock Exchanges: Montreal Toronto Vancouver
SICs: 2111 Cigarettes; 5331 Variety Stores; 5812
   Eating Places; 5912 Drug Stores & Proprietary
   Stores; 6162 Mortgage Bankers & Correspondents

Imasco Limited dominates the Canadian cigarette market; its Imperial Tobacco Limited subsidiary had a 60 percent market share in the early 1990s and produced Canada's two most popular brands of cigarettes—Player's and du Maurier. Imasco also has interests in a broad range of other businesses. Subsidiary CT Financial Services Inc., popularly known as Canada Trust, is a leader in retail financial services. Imasco also operates fast-food restaurants, through Hardee's Food Systems; drugstores, through Shoppers Drug Mart/Pharmaprix; and specialty retailing, through The UCS Group.

The British-American Tobacco Co., Ltd., owned a controlling share in Imperial Tobacco at its founding, and as of 1995 its successor, BAT Industries, still owned 40 percent of Imasco. One month after Imperial Tobacco's establishment in 1908, it assumed the businesses of two other companies controlled by British-American Tobacco, American Tobacco Co. of Canada Ltd. and the Empire Tobacco Co., Ltd., founded in 1895 and 1898, respectively. American Tobacco of Canada was the largest tobacco manufacturer in Canada. Its holdings included D. Ritchie & Co. and the American Cigarette Co. Empire Tobacco had been 80 percent-owned by American Tobacco of Canada, and produced plug tobacco from Canadian-grown leaf in its Quebec factory. Imperial also obtained about 80 percent of cigarette-maker B. Houde Co. and 50 percent of the National Snuff Company, both of which had been controlled by American Tobacco of Canada. Imperial grew through acquisition as well as by increasing brand recognition. In 1930 Imperial acquired Tuckett Tobacco Co., followed in 1949 by Imperial Tobacco Company Limited, of Newfoundland, and in 1950 by Brown & Williamson Tobacco Corporation (Export) Ltd. By the late 1950s Imperial controlled slightly more than 50 percent of the Canadian cigarette market. Imperial's only venture outside the manufacture of tobacco products was its United Cigar Stores, a wholly owned subsidiary operating 200 tobacco stores.

The impetus for Imperial's diversification, begun in 1964 under President John Keith, was the increasing evidence that smoking caused disease, which was expected to affect the industry's future growth. Health concerns about the habit had increased during the 1950s, but the real end of care-free smoking was the U.S. surgeon general's 1964 report linking cigarettes with lung cancer. The report sparked an initially sharp decline in cigarette sales, which leveled off after several months. Imperial slated layoffs in anticipation of a drop in smoking, converted some factories to cigar production, and, most significantly, acquired non-tobacco interests—a foil packaging company and two winemakers—within a year of the report's publication. By 1967 the diversification plan was stepped up, and two vice-presidents left, reportedly because of disagreements over company strategy.

In the late 1960s Imperial introduced an array of new cigarettes—some smaller, others equipped with the new filters. None of these was especially successful, and the company's market share shrank. In another effort to increase sales, Imperial included a gambling game in its 1969 Casino brand. Sales rose, but only because the game was so easy to crack that buyers won more than US$250,000 before the company took the brand off retail shelves. Among other tactics, Imperial introduced an unsuccessful cellulose-based tobacco substitute in the early 1970s. In a more successful venture, Imperial was the first company to introduce low-tar cigarettes; its four new brands, brought out in 1976, were a hit with the public and helped the company's market share rebound from 35 percent in 1980 to 47 percent in 1981.

Under Paul Paré, who became Imperial's president and chief executive officer in 1969, expansion accelerated. Paré formed Imasco Limited in 1970 as a holding company for potential diversifications as government sanctions began to curtail the tobacco industry. Canadian regulators in 1972 persuaded the industry to put warnings on cigarette packages and restricted advertising spending.

Imasco was also busy developing its other ventures. By 1976 Imasco had completely disposed of its wine businesses. A ten-year stint in sporting goods retailing began with the purchase of the Collegiate Sports Ltd. chain in 1973 and ended with its sale in 1983. In the late 1960s and early 1970s, Imasco made a concerted effort to establish a presence in the prepared-foods industry. Forming the triangular hub of this enterprise were Piñata Foods, Progresso Quality Foods, and S&W Fine Foods. Although the companies were regional successes when acquired, none had the strength to go national as Imasco intended.

Progresso, for example, when it joined Imasco in 1969, was the top Italian-food producer in the United States. Progresso's success, however, came substantially from the entrepreneurial spirit of its founder and president,

Frank Paormina, who retired a year after the acquisition. Ragu soon overtook Progresso in sales. Similarly disappointing experiences with Piñata and S&W resulted in the sale of all three by 1979.

Imasco's difficulties were typical of Canadian companies attempting to break into the tough U.S. market. Although it may have preferred to expand in Canada, Imasco's Canadian activities were curtailed by the Canadian government's limits on foreign investment, which applied to Imasco since it is substantially owned by BAT. These restrictions were lifted in 1985 when Imasco was granted "deemed Canadian status" by the government.

Imasco began to land better investments in the mid-1970s and early 1980s. The company set criteria for new ventures by the late 1970s: acquisitions had to be consumer-oriented businesses with good management teams and excellent growth potential, and of sufficient size and profitability to immediately increase corporate earnings. Acquisitions also had to be in North America, Canada preferred. Among the industries that fit this profile were fast food, drugstores, and financial services.

Expansion into fast food came with Hardee's restaurants. Wilbur Hardee opened his first drive-in hamburger restaurant in 1960 in Greenville, North Carolina. It eventually grew into a chain. By 1976, however, Hardee's had gotten into financial trouble while expanding to about 1,000 restaurants. That year Hardee's sold Imasco a 28 percent interest in the chain for US$15 million. In 1980 Imasco increased its holding to 44 percent and placed a member on the Hardee's board. In 1981, by which time Hardee's had 1,300 restaurants, Imasco bought out the remaining shareholders for US$85 million. With new financial resources, Hardee's remodeled, expanded its menu, and increased sales per store 47 percent from 1977 to 1981. In 1982 Hardee's purchased and converted 650 Burger Chefs, intensifying Hardee's already strong presence in the midwestern United States. Expanding via regional strength there and in the Southeast, Hardee's was the third-largest fast-food sandwich restaurant group in the United States in 1990, with 4,022 outlets—1,352 company-operated and 2,670 licensed to other operators. Over the years, Imasco acquired two other restaurant chains, Grisanti's Italian restaurants and Casa Lupita Mexican restaurants, but these were both disposed of by 1989 in order to concentrate resources on Hardee's.

Imasco acquired its first Canadian drugstores in 1973. Pharmaprix Stores and others were added in 1974, and Shoppers Drug Mart in 1978. The Shoppers Drug Mart/Pharmaprix group has become Canada's largest retail drug chain, claiming 30 percent of the market with 645 stores as of 1990. Encouraged by Canadian success, Imasco moved Shoppers into Florida in the early 1980s. Due to the troubled U.S. economy and glutted Florida market, by 1983 the company had lost $3 million on this operation. Imasco was prepared to try again and in April 1984 bought Peoples Drug Stores, Inc. Peoples, however, did not generate the returns Imasco desired, and was sold to Melville Corporation for US$325 million in 1990.

Imasco's 1986 $2 billion takeover of Genstar Corporation brought Canada Trustco Mortgage Company, the country's trust company, into the Imasco family. The mortgage company and the Canada Trust Company are the principal operating companies of CT Financial Services Inc. CT derives most of its earnings from intermediary services. Its funds are provided mostly by depositors in personal savings accounts, term deposits, or specialized accounts like retirement savings plans. For the most part, the funds are invested in residential mortgages.

Because Imasco made its bid during a lengthy controversy over Canadian laws governing the ownership of trust companies, the deal was of concern to the federal government. These concerns were resolved when Imasco made a series of assurances to the government. Principal among these was Imasco's agreement that the government could require whole or partial divestment of CT pending a legislative review. Legislation was subsequently introduced that would require Imasco to reduce its voting stake in CT to 65 percent over a five-year period. The law was expected to be enacted in 1992.

The UCS Group is the progeny of United Cigar Stores. This division operates sundry retail stores in five divisions: Woolco/Woolworth Specialty Stores, Hotel Airport Shops, Den for Men/Au Masculin, and Tax and Duty Free Shops. Because of product mix—confections, reading materials, tobacco, and gifts and souvenirs—these stores face stiff competition from supermarkets, drugstores, and other vendors. UCS relies on prime airport and resort location for its advantage, and gains 56 percent of its sales from tobacco products and accessories. While UCS outlets placed in Woolco and Woolworth stores led UCS's record sales increases during the late 1980s, the group entered the 1990s with the highest growth prospects in the tax and duty free shops in airports.

Imasco encountered further difficulties in its tobacco business in the late 1980s. In 1988 the Canadian government enacted the Tobacco Products Control Act, which required further health warnings on cigarette packages and severely limited the tobacco industry's advertising and promotional options. Imperial and other Canadian tobacco makers challenged the constitutionality of the act in court. In 1991 the Quebec Superior Court upheld the companies' challenge, but the government appealed the case to Canada's Supreme Court, where it was pending in the early 1990s. Also in the early 1990s, Imasco made further investments in the restaurant business, as Hardee's acquired the Roy Rogers restaurant chain. Plans called for converting many of the Roy Rogers restaurants, located primarily in the eastern United States, to Hardee's.

Despite difficulties, Imasco's diversification during the 1970s and 1980s was successful, and was duly noted by the financial community in the early 1990s. BAT, Imasco's substantial stockholder, deflected a takeover attempt during the early 1990s. Although the bid lapsed, it generated increased attention for Imasco from international investors. With its particularly strong positions in the financial and fast-food markets, Imasco headed into the 1990s with potential to expand lucratively under the stewardship of Purdy Crawford, who assumed the presidency in 1986 and the chairmanship in 1987.

Despite ongoing difficulties in the tobacco industry, Imasco thrived under Crawford's direction. The company increased its emphasis on food service and drugstores, and sales grew steadily, although profits from those divisions were lackluster. Conversely, Imasco continued to post healthy profits from its tobacco and financial services divisions despite revenue decreases in those two segments. Overall, Imasco's sales surged to about $15 billion by 1990 before rising steadily to more than $16 billion in 1992 and 1993. Similarly, aggregate earnings climbed from $295 million in 1990 to $409 million in 1993.

In February 1995 Crawford handed over Imasco's presidency to Bran Levitt, the company's former chief operating officer, with Crawford retaining his position as chairman. Crawford had led the company to an undeniably strong financial and competitive position. During his ten-year presidency, Imasco's annual earnings had nearly doubled and sales nearly tripled—1994 sales and earnings were $16.43 billion and $506 million, respectively.

Principal Subsidiaries:

Imperial Tobacco Limited; CT Financial Services Inc.; The UCS Group; Hardee's Food Systems, Inc.; Shoppers Drug Mart/Pharmaprix; Genstar Development Company.

Further Reading:

Bott, Robert, "Anatomy of a Bloodless Coup," *Canadian Business,* June 1986.
Gibbens, Robert, "Imasco Profit Higher than Expected," *Financial Post,* October 28, 1994, Section 1, p. 11.
Heinrich, Jeff, "Imasco Posts Record 1st Quarter Profit of $75 Million," *Gazette,* April 29, 1994, Section D, p. 1.
Thompson, Tony, "Imasco Gaining Experience in U.S. Retailing," *Advertising Age,* November 30, 1981.
Weber, Terry, "Imasco Chief Gets 21 Percent Pay Hike," *Financial Post,* March 31, 1995, Section 1, p. 5.
———, "Levitt to Replace Crawford as Imasco's CEO," *Financial Post,* February 3, 1995, Section 1, p. 3.

—Elaine Belsito
—updated by Dave Mote

Imperial Oil Limited

No. 2000-4720 Kingsway
Burnaby, British Columbia V5H 4N2
(604) 451-5900
Fax: (604) 451-5005

Public Company
Incorporated: 1880 as The Imperial Oil Company,
    Limited
Employees: 8,252
Sales: $8.9 billion
Stock Exchanges: Montreal Toronto American
SICs: 1311 Crude Petroleum & Natural Gas; 2821
    Plastics Materials & Resins; 2870 Agricultural
    Chemicals; 2911 Petroleum Refining

Imperial Oil Limited is Canada's largest producer of
crude oil and one of the country's largest suppliers of
natural gas. Imperial, which is 69.9 percent owned by
the U.S. corporation Exxon, is Canada's largest refiner
of petroleum products. It provides a wide variety of
products and services that appear with the Esso brand
name, and produces and markets coal, fertilizer, and
petrochemicals, among other products. Imperial has also
made itself known for its support of Canadian culture,
health, education, and community services.

When Imperial Oil Company was founded in London,
Ontario, in 1880, oil did not appear to be a fast route to
riches. The Canadian oil boom, triggered in 1857 with
the sinking of the first oil well, had gone bust in 1876.
Domestic overproduction and liberal trade policies had
resulted in the saturation of the Canadian market. The
industrial boom and rampant land speculation, begun in
the 1850s, were coming to a halt. During the boom
many Canadians had jumped to join the oil rush, and
contributed to the flooding of the local market. This,
coupled with worldwide depression, resulted in deflated
oil prices that were one-third of their former value.
Thus, in 1876, Canadian refiners who had glutted their
own market began to desert their businesses at bailout
prices.

It was at this crisis point that 16 well-established
London and Petrolia, Ontario, businessmen banded
together and decided to buy into the petroleum business.
On September 8, 1880, with $25,000, The Imperial Oil
Company, Limited was formed. Its charter was "to find,
produce, refine and distribute petroleum and its prod-

ucts throughout Canada." With two refineries, one in
London and the other in Petrolia, the total capitalization was an impressive $500,000.

Frederick Fitzgerald, a builder of the London Water
Works who dabbled in furniture, liquor, groceries, and
oil, became Imperial's first president. The mastermind
of the group's success was its vice president, Jacob
Englehart, who by age 33 had 14 years experience in oil,
having started his first refinery at age 19. William
Spencer and Herman and Isaac Waterman brought their
knowledge of refineries to the association. Isaac Waterman's involvement in municipal politics and the railway
later proved a valuable asset to the group. John Geary, a
lawyer-turned-refiner, and John Minhinnik a plumber-
turned-refiner, were more than ready to deal with the
business' logistical and physical problems. Thomas
Smallman and John Walker brought the experience they
had gained when producing sulfuric acid with the first
Canadian chemical company. No less valuable was
Walker's involvement in federal politics. It was no
accident that Thomas Hodgens, a former wagon maker,
and his brother Edward, a barrel-maker, were brought
into the deal. Edward Hodgens, in 1879 had also
patented a process that sweetened the odor of the
rancid-smelling Canadian crude, making it more competitive with relatively odorless U.S. crude.

The group immediately began trying to set its products
apart by improving their quality, as well as trying to find
new uses for the products and to increase distribution.
Imperial acquired rights to Hodgens's patent and started
deodorizing its oil. It began importing a new kerosene
lamp from Germany that burned with a brighter, whiter
light. It sent dealers out into the previously unpenetrat-
ed west to hustle up sales. In the space of one year,
Imperial was selling to Winnipeg, a frontier town of
8,000, as well as opening up an office in Montreal.

Imperial oil, carried in Imperial's hand-made barrels,
rode on Imperial-built wagons across the prairies of the
Northwest Territories to Hudson's Bay Company posts.
Imperial became so well known for its sturdy oak
barrels, that, although the company offered a generous
$1.25 refund for each, most homesteaders chose to keep
them and convert them to washtubs, rain barrels, and
armchairs. By 1883, Walker's position as vice president
of Canadian Pacific Railway had helped Imperial to
become the basic supplier to railroad construction crews
as well as to the settlers who followed in the wake of the
railway.

After three years of growth, Imperial Oil suffered a
major setback. During a thunderstorm in July, lightning
hit an Imperial refinery, sparking a fire that burned its
London processing operation to the ground. In 1884,
when Imperial requested of the city of London a
$20,000 grant to build a new line to pipe crude from
Imperial's Lambton Wells into the city, its political
connections were not enough. Londoners had had
enough of the flash fires and the stench rising from
streams of gasoline that ran from where it was dumped
on the streets down to the river. Gasoline, a useless by-
product of kerosene, created problems elsewhere as well.
Some refiners, trying to get the most dollars per barrel,
illegally cut kerosene with gasoline, frequently causing
lamps to explode when ignited.

Rather than rebuilding in what it felt to be a now-hostile London, Imperial moved its head offices first to Petrolia then to Sarnia, Ontario. Within a short time almost all related industries followed Imperial from London to Sarnia, which was becoming the new oil center.

By 1893 Imperial had 23 branch offices spread from Halifax to Victoria. Imperial had developed new markets so well that it could no longer keep up with demand. Imperial lacked the money necessary to expand to meet its consumers' needs, and feared losing market share to larger U.S. companies.

Unable to convince Canadian or British banks or private investors to gamble with large amounts of capital, in 1898 Imperial turned to the U.S. Standard Oil Company of New Jersey, who had offered to purchase Imperial years earlier. On Dominion Day in 1898, Standard Oil (now called Exxon) assumed a majority interest in Imperial. Imperial took over Standard Oil's Canadian assets on February 23, 1899, including its refinery in Sarnia. Standard worked to keep its ownership of Imperial secret, giving Canadian government officials Imperial Oil stock as hush money.

After laying a pipeline to bring in its crude from Petrolia, Imperial was ready to start servicing all of Canada, producing 143 cubic meters per day at its Sarnia plant alone. Imperial's business got another boost with the growing popularity of the automobile. By 1910 there were about 6,000 of these gasoline-consuming machines chugging down Canadian streets. Gasoline, a by-product of kerosene that previously had been thrown away, came to be in such demand that oil companies were not prepared to dispense it at a rate sufficient to satisfy need. People bought gas in open buckets from grocery stores or even went to the oil companies' warehouses. The first service station got its start when a car pulled up to Imperial's Vancouver warehouse in between the horse-drawn oil wagons, and backfired. By the time the workers had gotten their horses settled, the foreman had banished automobiles forever. C.M. Rolston, Imperial's Vancouver manager, solved the problem the next day when he opened up Canada's first service station, a one-room metal shack with a garden hose and a water tank full of gasoline.

Building a service station did not, however, meet all the demands awakened by automobiles. The use of automobiles increased so rapidly, that Imperial almost immediately was forced to begin looking for ways to increase its supply of crude, to produce more gasoline. In 1914 Standard licensed Imperial to use its cracking technique, a process that yielded much more gasoline per barrel of crude, and installed the first units in its Sarnia refineries. Cracking involved the use of heat and pressure coils to chemically decompose the crude. In that same year, it formed the International Petroleum Company, Limited, to search for oil in South America; ordered an exploratory geological party to Turner Valley to confirm the discovery of crude near Calgary; laid a pipeline from Sarnia to Cygnet, Ohio, connecting Imperial refineries to some of the most productive oil fields in the United States; and built the first refinery in British Columbia, on Burrard Inlet. Before long World War I broke out, creating a whole new market hungry for gasoline.

In 1919 the Imperial Oil Company, Limited changed its name to Imperial Oil Limited. To meet the new demands of war, Imperial grew rapidly. Within five years it quintupled the number of its refineries and doubled its refining capacity. By 1920 there were four times as many cars in Canada as five years prior, and once again Imperial began to search for more efficient ways to refine gasoline. In 1923 Imperial obtained Canadian rights to use pressure stills, which enhanced the cracking process, yielding a greater quantity and quality of gasoline.

In 1924 Imperial hired R.K. Stratford, its first research worker. He discovered that sulfur corrosion of the cracking coils could be prevented by adding lime to the crude. He also came up with a way to keep gasoline from gumming up engines by running the cracked product through a slurry of clay.

For Imperial, the 1930s, were full of changes. Previously, geologists searching for oil depended on a hammer, a chisel, maybe a pair of field glasses, and a lot of luck. In the 1920s, the rotary drill rig came along, and it became possible to drill deeper beneath the surface. The biggest change did not come until the 1930s, when Imperial started investigating the possibilities of seismology. Its geologist bounced shock waves off of underground rocks, and judging from the waves' reflection, the shape and size of possible oil formations could be determined. Imperial had started implementing these procedures, before the outbreak of World War II, when the Allies needed all the fuel they could get.

Imperial was able to produce a large amount of the 87-octane aviation fuel that the Commonwealth Air Training Plan needed for its training aircraft by selecting crude oils containing the most useful fractions and by modifying its distillation equipment. Imperial also helped to produce 100-octane aviation fuel for combat aircraft. The company aided in the development of portable runways, which could be rolled up, taken to a flat field almost anywhere, and laid in place. Imperial was a key player in Operation Shuttle, which kept oil flowing to Great Britain for a full two years before the United States entered the war.

Alaska's importance grew when Japan entered the war, and airports popped up there for U.S. defense. In 1942 the U.S. Army requested that Imperial build a refinery in the Yukon at Whitehorse, to supply the Alaskan airfields. By 1944 a ten-centimeter pipeline snaked out from the Whitehorse refinery to supply the much-needed fuel for a full year before the war ended.

When the war ended, Imperial welcomed back its employees who had served. Throughout the war, Imperial had made up the difference between military pay and salaries at Imperial when military pay was lower. On enlistment, Imperial had given its employees one month's salary as a bonus.

In 1946 Imperial sold 6.275 million cubic meters of crude, more than any previous year. The company's officers, realizing that there had been no meaningful field discoveries since 1920, launched a full-scale exploration to assure supplies for the future.

At the end of the 1940s, 90 percent of all crude oil refined in Canada was imported. Imperial drilled 133 consecutive dry holes. The future looked so bad that Imperial was debating the expensive conversion of natural gas to gasoline. If things did not change, it decided, it would have to close its Sarnia refinery and rely on off-shore crude shipped in to Montreal. Before Imperial shut down Sarnia and began building in Montreal, however, the company's leadership decided to drill once more in the Hinge Belt, south of Edmonton. Seismograph crews picked a sight in Leduc. On February 13, 1947, the Leduc well gushed oil in huge quantities. The extent of Leduc's success is best measured by the fact that the wells that quickly sprouted up in that area provided 90 percent of all oil produced in Canada. With Leduc's success came the call for a neighboring refinery. Imperial dismantled the idled Whitehorse refinery and reassembled it in nearby Edmonton.

With the Leduc strike, domestic oil production was so greatly increased that Imperial began searching for ways to export it. To aid in exportation, Imperial and others joined to form Interprovincial Pipe Line Limited in 1949. Imperial owned 49.9 percent of Interprovincial's stock. By autumn of 1950, a pipeline had been laid from Edmonton, Ontario, to Superior, Wisconsin. Imperial still holds the most shares of any owner. In 1957 the line was extended to Toronto, then in 1976 it stretched to Montreal.

The surplus of oil in the 1950s and price wars that ensued lead Imperial to analyze gasoline markets, eliminate unprofitable stations, and set up stations in the right places—some were simple gas stations, others were full-service auto "clinics." Imperial was responsible for introducing Canada's first car clinic complete with electronic diagnosis. It was not long before highway service stations became a familiar sight, offering everything from gas to snacks. In 1970 self-service stations began popping up under the Esso name, Imperial's brand name.

Canadian gas and oil reserves once again had begun to dwindle as demand continued to grow. Imperial went so far as to explore the far northern waters off Canada's eastern coast. In January 1970 that extremely expensive search paid off when Imperial hit medium-gravity, low-sulfur crude at Atkinson Point on the Beaufort Sea in the western Arctic, 1,700 meters deep. As a result of this and other offshore searches Imperial, pioneered the artificial island. The first artificial island, Immerl, was built by Imperial at the cost of $5 million, not including the cost of the well, which turned out to be dry. The offshore oil search continues both in the farther north Queen Elizabeth Islands as well as in the Atlantic seabed.

One of Imperial's most important steps toward growth was taken in the late 1980s. In 1988 Imperial began talking to Texaco Canada about a possible merger. In February 1989 Imperial bought Texaco Canada, now McColl-Frontenac Inc., for C$4.96 billion, making it the largest acquisition in Imperial's history and the second-largest in Canada's. The actual merger did not take place until February 1990; it was held up awaiting approval from the Canadian competition authorities. One of the most remarkable features of the merger was the speed with which Imperial was able to reduce the initial debt incurred by the merger, taking it from C$4.96 billion to C$3.1 in 1989.

During the early 1990s, Imperial remained the largest and one of the most profitable oil companies in Canada. In fact, many analysts feared that Imperial had grown about as large as it could get. After years of tapping into its giant base of oil reserves—particularly Leduc—Imperial was finding it increasingly difficult to increase its oil business. The company had become a cash cow, stashing more than $1.2 billion in its war chest by 1994. But it was hesitant to spend that money exploring for new crude reserves because—while smaller companies could strike a small well and double production, it was assumed that there were few if any reserves in Imperial's region of activity that could have a significant impact on the company's bottom line. That attitude was evidenced by a reduction in drilling activity from more than fifty new wells in 1990 to just five in 1995. "While we believe there is some undiscovered crude oil potential in Western Canada," said Doug Baldwin, senior vice president, in the April 1, 1995, *Calgary Herald*, "we don't think it's strategically significant for us to pursue it."

So, rather than concentrating on developing new reserves during the early 1990s, Imperial focused on cutting costs, eliminating poorly performing divisions, and improving its efficiency. As a result, the companies asset base shriveled to $10.4 billion in 1992 and then to just $8.5 billion in 1993. Sales remained relatively steady as a result of strong performance from key divisions, and hovered between about $200 million and C$400 million annually. By 1994 Imperial's work force had dwindled to about 8,300, about 250 of which were expected to be released during 1995. The cutbacks and reorganization reflected, in part, parent company Exxon's desire to shift resources away from Imperial to its U.S. and international operations.

Imperial's long-term future will depend partly on its forays into businesses other than petroleum—its Leduc oil fields, for example, were expected to start producing significantly less oil in 1997. From its beginning, Imperial's interests have branched through all aspects of the business, including the manufacture of wagons, barrels and lamps, as well as chemicals for its treatment plants. Going into the mid-1990s, the company continued to be a leading Canadian manufacturer of aviation fuel, marine fuel, railway lubricants, and domestic heating fuels in Canada. It also had petrochemical interests and marketed, through its subsidiaries, such things as vinyl siding, plastics, and ropes. The company still generated more than 80 percent of its revenues from petroleum-related products in 1995, though, and maintained 11,000 natural gas wells, 7,600 kilometers of pipeline, and about 3,000 service stations.

Principal Subsidiaries:

Esso Resources Canada Limited; Esso Resources N.W.T. Limited; Esso Resources (1989) Limited; McColl Frontenac Inc.

Further Reading:

Boras, Alan, "Imperial's Loss Linked to Buyout," *Calgary Herald,* July 22, 1994, Section D, p. 3.

————, "Imperial Swings Its Axe," *Calgary Herald,* April 27, 1994, Section E, p. 1.

Campbell, Donald, "No More Leducs: Oilpatch Giant Imperial Raises Eyebrows with Declining Exploration," *Calgary Herald,* April 1, 1995, Section A, p. 12.

Haliechuk, Rick, "Imperial Oil Posts 29% Jump in 1994 Profits," *Toronto Star,* January 24, 1995, Section D, p. 9.

Malone, Mary, "Imperial Beginnings," *London Magazine,* December 1986.

—Maya Sahafi
—updated by Dave Mote

INCO

Inco Limited

Royal Trust Tower
Toronto-Dominion Centre
Toronto, Ontario M5K 1N4
(416) 361-7511
Fax: (416) 361-7781

Public Company
Incorporated: 1916 as International Nickel Co. of
    Canada, Ltd.
Employees: 15,709
Sales: US$2.48 billion
Stock Exchanges: Toronto Montreal New York
    London Paris Amsterdam Brussels Zurich Berne
    Basel Geneva Lausanne
SICs: 1021 Copper Ores; 1041 Gold Ores; 1061
    Ferroalloy Ores, Except Vanadium; 2819 Industrial
    Inorganic Chemicals, Not Elsewhere Classified;
    3339 Primary Smelting and Refining of
    Nonferrous Metals, Except Copper and Aluminum;
    3356 Rolling, Drawing, and Extruding of
    Nonferrous Metals, Except Copper and Aluminum;
    3366 Copper Foundries; 6719 Offices of Holding
    Companies, Not Elsewhere Classified

Inco Limited has been the world's leading producer of nickel since it was founded in 1902. Though it no longer has the monopoly it once possessed, Inco still supplied the majority of the world's nickel with operations in 21 countries. After weathering the commodities recessions of the early and mid-1980s, earnings soared to $753 million in 1989, only to be brought low again in 1992. Yet Inco rallied and continued to dominate the industry, creating new products and applications for its primary product—nickel—while developing a substantial business in cobalt, copper, and other precious metals.

Nickel was first isolated as an element in the middle of the 18th century, but not until the following century did it come into demand as a coin metal. Up to around 1890, coining remained the metal's only use, and most of the world's nickel was mined by Le Nickel, a Rothschild company on the island of New Caledonia. At that time, however, it was determined that steel made from an iron-nickel alloy could be rolled into exceptionally hard plates, called armorplate, for warships, tanks, and other military vehicles, and the resulting surge in demand spurred a worldwide search for nickel deposits.

The world's largest nickel deposit ever discovered was in Ontario's Sudbury Basin; before long, one of the area's big copper mining companies, Canadian Copper, began shipping quantities of nickel to a U.S. refinery in Bayonne, New Jersey, the Orford Copper Company. Orford had devised the most economical process for refining nickel, and its alliance with Canadian Copper proved an unbeatable combination. Orford dominated the U.S. nickel business, supplying much of the metal needed by the growing steel industry, and managed to make inroads into the European market as well.

The U.S. steel industry didn't feel comfortable relying on a single Canadian source for one of its essential materials; so in 1902 Charles Schwab of U.S. Steel and a group of other steelmen used the financial backing of J.P. Morgan to take control of and merge Orford and Canadian Copper. The new company was called International Nickel, nicknamed Inco, and was based in New York. From the first, Inco was able to control a majority of the U.S. nickel market, and had increased its share to 70 percent by 1913. Its large-scale operations in the Sudbury Basin allowed the company to eliminate competition through price wars and sheer staying power. According to *Fortune* magazine in May 1957, Inco had maintained its control of the U.S. market without interruption for nearly 40 years.

As the world's leading nickel producer, Inco enjoyed an enormous increase in business during World War I, when the need for armor- plate drove up steel sales. This good fortune soon changed, when the 1921 world disarmament agreements killed the munitions market and Inco was left with a huge backlog of nickel. Its record 1921 profit of US$2 million slipped to a US$1.2 million loss the following year, and the Sudbury mines were shut down for over six months. The shock of this setback stayed with the company for many years in the form of a conservative management policy and a determination to avoid large inventories. In 1922, Robert Crooks Stanley began a 30-year tenure as president—and later chairman—of Inco, intent upon building new markets in fields other than munitions. Stanley created a vigorous research and development department to find new peacetime uses for nickel. So effective were the Inco engineers that many of the innovations in nickel metallurgy over the next 50 years can be traced to their efforts. In effect, Inco became the research department for the entire nickel industry, sharing its findings with customer and competitor alike. Of course, for many years Inco had few of the latter.

By the late 1920s, Stanley brought Inco sales back up to their wartime peak, much of the peacetime addition coming from the automobile industry. Inco's first major postwar investment was a US$3-million rolling mill in Huntington, West Virginia, designed to produce Monel metal, a widely used copper-nickel alloy. At the same time, Stanley effectively blocked the growth of competition from such newcomers as British America Nickel, which in 1923 made a serious bid for the U.S. market. Inco promptly lowered its price from 34¢ to 25¢ (U.S.) per pound, driving British America to bankruptcy a year later. When no one purchased the fallen company's assets, a little-known firm, Anglo-Canadian Mining & Refining bought them very cheaply. Anglo-Canadian was a dummy corporation owned by Inco, which simply took what it could use from British America's refinery and sold the rest for scrap.

A more serious competitor was handled in a different manner. Mond Nickel Company had been operating in the Sudbury Basin since just after the turn of the century, shipping its nickel to Europe to compete with France's Le Nickel and Inco's European offices. Mond, the creation of Ludwig Mond, the British chemist who founded the great Imperial Chemical Industries (ICI), owned half of the best nickel deposits in Sudbury, in an area known as the Frood. The other owner of these deposits was Inco. In 1928, Inco decided it would wiser to join forces rather than fight over the world's largest nickel mine. Mond and Inco were then merged at the end of that year to form International Nickel Co. of Canada, Ltd., still nicknamed Inco. Mond remained a U.K. subsidiary of Inco, handling both European and Asian customers. By moving its incorporation to a foreign country, Inco was better able to deflect inevitable and periodic attempts by the U.S. Department of Justice to prosecute the company for antitrust violations. The 1929 appearance of a small competitor called Falconbridge Nickel Mines Ltd., another European supplier, was only tolerated to avoid the impression of absolute monopoly.

The Great Depression caused Inco temporary losses for the second time in its history, but the growing number of industrial uses for nickel soon pulled sales back up to a healthy level. By this time, Inco had become a major producer of copper and platinum as well as nickel, thanks to Sudbury Basin's rich supply of minerals. The company was now the sixth largest copper producer in the world and the largest supplier of platinum, a metal whose unusual properties had found many industrial applications; however, it was in nickel that Inco held unchallenged power as the source of 90 percent of the noncommunist world's supply. Inco's metal was needed by all of the world's arms maker and for the production of super-hard steel for a variety of uses, from armorplate to exhaust valves on aircraft engines to gun recoil systems.

In a move that stirred up plenty of controversy, Inco became the nickel supplier to both sides of the approaching World War II, which included signing a long-term contract with Germany's I.G. Farben in the mid-1930s. In antitrust action 10 years later, the Department of Justice charged that Inco's agreement with Farben was part of an effort to form a worldwide nickel cartel, and that in the process it had supplied Germany with a stockpile of nickel critical to its imminent war plans. The antitrust action was settled in 1948 when Inco signed a consent decree, agreeing only that it would sell nickel in the United States at fair prices; its worldwide monopoly, however, was beyond the reach of the U.S. Department of Justice.

World War II taxed Inco's capacity and strained its relationship with the U.S. armed forces. Still mindful of its near collapse after World War I, Inco refused to stockpile the inventory desired by the armed forces, instead committing only to the timely delivery of critical metal. As an insurance policy, the U.S. government financed the creation of Nicaro Nickel Company in 1942, a Cuban venture under the direction of the Freeport Sulphur Company. Although Nicaro managed to produce some nickel, it never really got off the ground and was mothballed soon after the war. Its decline may have been hastened by Inco's price cuts on nickel oxides, Nicaro's specialty. The full extent of Inco's nickel monopoly was further suggested by the fact that, aside from the case of nickel oxide, its nickel price never varied between 1928 and 1946—an indication of complete freedom from the normal pressures of competition. At the war's end, Inco's assets were valued at about US$135 million, sales stood at US$148 million, and the company showed a very healthy net income of about $30 million in U.S. funds.

Inco's hesitation to expand its nickel production helped it to avoid a serious postwar slump, but it also left the company unprepared for what soon followed. In the booming economy of the 1950s, nickel assumed new importance finding applications in stainless steel, home appliances, and its use with chrome for automobiles, jet engines, and atomic power plants. When the Korean War added the usual backlog of orders for armorplate, Inco faced a severe and growing nickel shortage. The U.S. government made the situation more difficult by adding nickel to its list of stockpiled metals critical to national defense, a contract Inco was naturally called upon to fulfill.

Indeed, Inco and the U.S. Department of Commerce together allocated nickel to customers across the country. Yet this nickel shortage had two long-term consequences for Inco: first, it made a rise in prices inevitable, which increased by 60 percent between 1946 and 1950 alone; second, a host of new competitors entered the nickel market, encouraged by the acute shortage, rising prices, and by the U.S. government's willingness to finance alternative suppliers of the important metal. Inco's share of the free-world market, which was estimated at 85 percent as late as 1950, soon began a decline to what would eventually mirror its 1990s level of 34 percent.

Once assured the boom in nickel was permanent, Inco increased production and began to search for new deposits. After several years of exploration, a major find was made in northern Manitoba in 1956, a field it christened "Thompson" after company chairman John F. Thompson, successor to Robert Stanley. Thompson was the most significant new deposit of nickel found since the discovery of Sudbury in the 1880s. After Inco spent about US$175 million building mines, smelters, refineries, a town to house its employees, and a railroad to reach the town, the site added about 30 percent to the company's 1956 sales of US$445 million. Inco remained extremely profitable despite its new competitors and still carried no long-term debt. In the recession of 1958, sales dropped to US$322 million but a strike by the Mill, Mine and Smelter Workers Union kept inventories low and prevented a loss for the year.

After the 1958 recession, sales of nickel took off once again. Inco's research engineers continued to provide a new generation of customers with ingenious uses for nickel, as in the rapidly growing electronics and aerospace industries where the use of stainless steel was just beginning to mushroom. Under the leadership of new chairman Harry S. Wingate, Inco's sales hit US$572 million in 1965, and its net income remained a remarkably high US$136 million. The Thompson field had grown into a thriving town and its deposits proved to be every bit as rich as hoped.

Nickel sales were given yet another boost by the Vietnam War, in which the United States employed a vast array of sophisticated weaponry, the bulk of which required nickel-hardened steel. Responding to the bull market, Inco launched a comprehensive refurbishment and expansion program eventually costing more than US$1 billion. For the first time in its history, Inco borrowed money and chose to continue concentrating on the mining of high-grade, relatively expensive nickel at a time when many competitors had come up with inexpensive, readily available nickel oxides and ferronickels.

The impact of these decisions was felt in 1969-1971, when a devastating strike by 17,000 Sudbury workers was followed by the sharp recession of 1971; nickel sales dropped by 25 percent and Inco's stock fell by 50 percent in a matter of months. The company did not show a loss for the year, but it was thoroughly shaken by the low sales and a mounting debt burden. Wingate retired and his successor, L. Edward Grubb, moved to curtail the expansion program then just coming on line. Grubb cut production back to 80 percent of capacity and reduced labor where possible. To protect Inco against the further erosion of sales by ferronickel competitors, he spent another US$750 million to exploit the company's own ferronickel sources in Guatemala and Indonesia, where nickel was extracted from laterite ore by means of a refining process using petroleum.

In 1974, Inco made its first and only major acquisition, paying US$224 million for ESB Inc., a leading manufacturer of large storage batteries using nickel. Inco believed ESB's sales would help balance cyclical downturns in nickel, and that demand for batteries would increase in a world growing short of oil. Inco's share of the world's nickel sales had slipped below 50 percent by this time. Except in 1974, a boom year for commodities, the nickel market was generally soft for the rest of the decade. More worrisome, the soaring price of oil made Inco's huge investments in laterite nickel practically a dead loss, as the cost of refining the ore with petroleum rendered the product too expensive to sell.

In 1976 International Nickel Co. of Canada, Ltd., officially changed its name to Inco Limited. An additional problem was Inco's US$850-million debt burden, which grew less manageable as interest rates reached a peak in the early 1980s. Additionally, Inco's new battery subsidiary was floundering, and in the severe recession of 1981 Inco found itself in deep trouble. Forced to write off its Guatemalan investment, sales began a steep slide; the company reported a disastrous year-end loss of US$470 million, its first since 1932. In the following three years, Inco's sales fell another US$500 million, as the recession and corporate debt proved an almost fatal combination.

Inco, however, had one asset that remained invulnerable: it still owned the world's richest nickel fields. Under CEO Donald J. Phillips, Inco wrote off its ill-fated battery venture for $245 million, almost halved its work force, closed all excess production facilities, and sat tight, waiting for the severely depressed price of nickel to recover. New techniques allowed the extraction of ore in far bigger chunks than previously possible, and the reduced staff performed the smelting and refining tasks with improved methods. A rebound in the nickel market in 1987 brought the boost Inco needed: an increase in market share to nearly 35 percent and a year-end profit of US$125 million.

When nickel prices reached an all-time high in 1988, Inco's worldwide shipments of 495 million pounds of nickel (its highest level in 14 years) sent profits soaring to US$735 million and a stunning US$753 million in 1989. As a reward for his efforts in raising productivity, Phillips was made chairman and CEO of Inco. His first task was to decide what to do with US$1 billion in retained earnings. Mindful of the poor results of past efforts at diversification, Phillips put some into further production refinements; however, the bulk was used for a $10-per-share special cash dividend as part of a controversial recapitalization and shareholders' rights package. Taking cues from its U.S. neighbors, Inco's "poison pill" plan was the first of its kind in Canada. Spurring heated debate from all sides, Quebec's pension fund management group, Caisse de Depot et Placement du Quebec, filed suit on behalf of its 3.2-million Inco shares to legally overturn shareholders' December 1988 approval of the poison pill.

As the 1990s dawned, environmental issues became an increasingly expensive concern for Inco. The company faced an $80,000 fine for a sulphur trioxide leak from its Copper Cliff refinery in April 1987 and faced repeated requests to regulate the sulphur dioxide released into the atmosphere by its smelting operations in Sudbury. Called "the largest single source of sulphur dioxide pollution on the continent" by *Maclean's* in 1990, Inco launched a series of abatement programs (with a price tag of over $500 million) to substantially lower emissions by 1994. To meet this goal, Inco planned to implement new magnetic separators to extract sulphur from ore and replace natural-gas burning furnaces with oxygen flash furnaces, which used oxygen rather than fossil fuels, eliminating toxic emissions altogether. Additionally, the new processes would significantly lower energy costs and boost efficiency.

In 1991, Michael Sopko, an Inco employee since 1964, was named president while Phillips retained the titles of CEO and chairman. Though annual net sales for 1991 fell to just under US$3 billion, net earnings plunged from 1990's US$441 million to US$83 million. In 1992, Sopko replaced the retiring Phillips as chairman and CEO, and Scott M. Hand assumed the presidency. The changing of the guard, however, had little effect on the continued downward trend of nickel prices, sluggish demand, and increased competition from Russian exports—all of which contributed to a year-end loss of US$18 million from net sales of US$2.56 billion. In response, Inco slashed executive salaries, decreased capital expenditures by $50 million, and closed its Ontario and Manitoba facilities for several weeks to cut production by 40 million pounds. Next Inco sold its 62 percent stake in TVX Gold Inc. for $371 million in 1993 as nickel prices plunged to their lowest since 1987. Finishing 1993 with sales of only US$2.13 billion, the company had managed to post a profit of US$28 million rather than another loss.

Although earnings were not spectacular, they were nonetheless encouraging. The following year, Inco continued to struggle, announcing plans to prune upper management, eliminate 1,000 union jobs, and fund expansion at the company's low-cost Soroako mine in Indonesia—just as 4,900 laborers announced their intention to strike. Narrowly averting the strike, Inco took its employee relations in a different direction, funding more research into automated mining, with which the company had increasing success. The company also increased financing for the research and development of scores of new nickel applications and products. Nickel alloys, foam, foil, and powders, as well as nickel coating on fibers, papers, cloths, and even gold, were providing excellent results.

Just as Inco's worldwide R&D teams developed new uses for nickel, the company secured mining rights to a huge new metals deposit called "Discovery Hill" in Newfoundland in mid-1995. Beating out competitors Falconbridge Ltd. and Noranda Inc., Inco's 30 percent stake (for $700 million) of the Voisey Bay property gave it control of the area's vast copper, cobalt, and nickel deposits, all but assuring its continued domination of the world's nickel supply.

In the second half of the 1990s, Inco seemed ideally prepared to reach its centennial year, 2002, in good shape. The company managed to reduce production costs for its third straight year, to slice debt by $66 million, and to close 1994 with net sales of US$2.48 billion and a profit of US$22 million. On the international front, Inco opened a new facility in Clydach, Wales; increased ownership in Tokyo Nickel Company Ltd.; initiated its first joint venture with China; and not only reached an agreement with Indonesia to extend its contract for the Soroako mine to 2025, but planned for a $500-million mine expansion.

Principal Subsidiaries:

American Copper & Nickel Company Inc.; Compagnie des Mines de Xere (France); Continuous Mining Systems Ltd.; Dardanel Madencilik Sanayai ve Ticaret S.A. (Turkey); Exmibal (Guatemala; 70%); Goro Nickel S.A. (New Caledonia; 85%); IEP Airfoils (U.K.); IEP Doncasters (U.K.); IEP Structures (U.K.); Inco Alloys International, Inc. (U.S.); Inco Alloys Ltd. (U.K.); Inco Brasil Participacoes Ltda. (Brazil); Inco Engineered Products, Inc.; Inco Engineered Products Limited (U.K.); Inco Europe Limited (U.K.); Inco Exploration and Technical Services Inc.; Inco Ltd.; Inco Oceanie S.A. (France); Inco Pacific Ltd.; Inco Specialty Powder Products; Incotherm Ltd.; Inco United States Inc.; Inco Venture Capital Management (U.S.); International Nickel Inc.; P.T. International Nickel Indonesia (58%); International Nickel France, S.A.; International Nickel G.m.b.H.; International Services (U.K.) Ltd.; Jinco Ltd. (China; 65%); John Clark Inc. (U.S.); LaQue Center for Corrosion Technology, Inc. (U.S.); Novamet Specialty Products Corp. (U.S.); International Nickel Oceanie S.A. (France); Inco Gold Inc.; SETTAS S.A.; The International Metals Reclamation Company, Inc. (U.S.); Tokyo Nickel Company Ltd. (51%); Welding Products Company (U.S.); Western Aggregates Inc. (U.S.); Wiggen Steel & Alloys Limited (U.K.).

Further Reading:

Arnott, Sheila, "Inco Shapes Its Labor-Relations Climate," *Northern Miner,* September 5, 1988, p. 6.
Cook, Peter, "More Eye-Popping Facts About Poison Pills," *Globe and Mail,* October 20, 1988, p. B2.
Gilbert, Ray, "Sudbury, Home to One of the World's Premier Mining Companies," *Northern Miner,* October 15, 1990, p. B19.
Heinzl, Mark, "Inco Moves to Take Miners Out of Mining," "Wall *Street Journal,"* July 6, 1994, p. B6.
"Inco Reviews Female Policy After Human Rights Ruling," *Northern Miner,* March 14, 1988, p. 6.
"Inco to Expand Indonesian Operation," *Northern Miner,* November 21, 1994, p. 1.
"Inco to Sell Stake in TVX Gold Unit to Underwriters for $289.4 Million," *Wall Street Journal,* June 29, 1993, p. B1.
"Inco to Spend $26.9 Million on Mine Project," *Northern Miner,* November 16, 1987, p. A1.
Lamont, Lansing, "Inco: A Giant Learns How to Compete," *Fortune,* January 1975.
Lamphier, Gary, "Voisey Secures Inco's Future," *Globe and Mail,* June 9, 1995, p. B1.
McInnes, Craig, "Court Fines Inco $80,000 Over Acid Cloud Incident," *Globe and Mail,* January 10, 1989, p. A1.
Mehr, Martin, "Inco Tries to Clean Up the Air and Its Image," *Marketing,* March 27, 1989, pp. B1, B6.
Melnbardis, Caroline, "Canada's First Poison Pill Is Leaving a Very Bitter Taste . . ." *Financial Times of Canada,* October 24, 1988, pp. 27, 30.
Newman, Peter C., "Canada's Largest Investor Goes to War," *Maclean's,* November 7, 1988, p. 50.
"Report on Corporate Finance: Inco's Move Started Wheels Turning in Canadian Boardrooms," *Globe and Mail,* December 12, 1988, p. B17.
"Retooling Mother Inco," *Northern Miner Magazine,* April 1990, pp. 41-45.
Robinson, Allan, "Inco, Falconbridge Betting Nickel Price Will Keep Shining," *Globe and Mail,* November 21, 1988, p. B1.
———, "Inco Expects Another Good Year After Seeing 5th Record Quarter," *Globe and Mail,* April 20, 1989, p. B11.
———, "Inco Slashes Production," *Globe and Mail,* October 6, 1992, p. B1.
———, "Product R & D Pays Off for Inco," *Globe and Mail,* September 8, 1992, p. B13.
Shortell, Ann, and Melnbardis, Caroline, "Code Name Monticello: Inco Devised One of the Most Potent Poison Pills in North America," *Financial Times of Canada,* December 19, 1988, pp. 1, 14-16.
"The Squeeze on Nickel," *Fortune,* November 1950.
Stackhouse, John, "Inco Bets on Indonesia," *Globe and Mail,* May 19, 1994, p. B1.
Tintor, Nicholas, "Inco Exposure to Gold Increased With New Firm," *Northern Miner,* August 17, 1987, pp. 1-2.
Walmsley, Anne, "An Acid Test," *Maclean's,* September 17, 1990, p. 62.

Zehr, Leonard, and McNish, Jacquie, "Inco Plans $1.05-Billion Dividend in Recapitalization," *Globe and Mail,* October 4, 1988, p. B1.

—Jonathan Martin
—updated by Taryn Benbow-Pfalzgraf

Labatt Brewing Company Ltd.

150 Simcoe Street
London, Ontario N6A 4M3
(519) 667-7500
Fax: (519) 667-7304

Wholly-owned subsidiary of John Labatt Ltd.
Incorporated: 1911 as John Labatt Ltd.
Employees: 5,000
Sales: $1.769 billion
Stock Exchanges: (as LBT) Montreal Toronto
  Vancouver
SICs: 2080, 6719 beverages and brewery.

In its 150-year history, Labatt Brewing Company Ltd. has grown from a local enterprise into Canada's second largest brewing company, with Labatt beverages distributed around the world. As the business expanded, production diversified into new areas, eventually warranting creation of a separate brewing group controlled by the John Labatt Ltd. holding company.

Company founder John Kinder Labatt was born in Ireland in 1803 and, as a young man, moved to London, England, where he met and married Eliza Kell. Together the couple set sail in 1833 for Canada, settling in London, Ontario. Labatt became a farmer and sold prize-winning malting barley to a local innkeeper who had built a small brewery in 1828. Contact with the innkeeper gave Labatt the idea of becoming a brewer himself; in 1847 he formed a partnership with Samuel Eccles, an experienced brewer, and they bought the London Brewery from the innkeeper.

Early annual production capacity of the brewery was 400 barrels. In 1853, Labatt bought his partner's share of the business and increased annual brewing capacity to 4,000 barrels. The newly renamed John Labatt's Brewery had six employees. Despite its remarkable production increase, the young enterprise remained a local operation. The situation changed, however, with the growing presence of the railroads. When the tracks of the Great Western Railway connected London to other cities, Labatt began shipping beer and ale to Montreal, Toronto, and the Maritimes.

John Labatt's third son, John Labatt II, apprenticed as a brewer in Wheeling, West Virginia, while his two older sons, Robertand Ephraim, began their own brewery business. Their departure left the John Labatt Brewery without a brewmaster, as it had been assumed that one of the older brothers would eventually fill the position. As a result, at age 26 John Labatt II became his father's brewmaster. In his new capacity, John II was instrumental in establishing a product with international appeal, India Pale Ale, based on a recipe he had learned in Wheeling. By 1878, the ale had earned high marks and honors at the Canada Exposition in Ottawa, the International Centennial in Philadelphia, the Exposition in Australia, and the International Exposition in France.

In 1866, just two years after John II returned to the brewery, John Labatt died, leaving the company to his wife. Eliza Labatt formed a partnership with her son and renamed the business Labatt & Company. Mother and son operated the brewery together until 1872, when John II bought his mother's interest and became the sole owner. Before the new company leader had much opportunity to establish himself, fire destroyed the brewery. Fortunately, insurance coverage enabled Labatt to build a modern facility at the cost of $20,000. Annual production now reached 30,000 barrels.

In addition to introducing an award-winning ale and expanding production, John II is credited with modernizing the company through the use of refrigeration and distribution networks. Labatt products also reached distant Canadian provinces: by 1900, customers in Manitoba and the Northwest Territories could purchase the brewer's products.

At the turn of the century John II's two sons, Hugh and John III, joined the family business. John III had earned a brewmaster's certificate from the brewing academy in New York after graduating from McGill University. In 1911, John II incorporated his company under the name John Labatt Limited. All but four of the 2,500 shares issued were retained by him. The remainder went to his two sons, a nephew, and his lawyer. Total capitalization amounted to $250,000.

John Labatt II died in 1915 at age 75, and the company presidency went to John III. At that time the various provinces were debating possible Prohibition laws. Unlike the United States, where the liquor industry was regulated by a blanket federal law, in Canada each province created its own standard. While almost all of Canada was legally rendered dry by 1916, several provinces allowed the manufacture of alcoholic beverages for export. By the end of Prohibition only 15 of Ontario's 65 breweries still survived. Labatt was not only one of the survivors, but was also the only such firm to have maintained management continuity throughout the era.

During the 1920s and 1930s, the brewery implemented a number of innovative employee policies. In the 1920s, Labatt workers became some of the first Canadian employees to receive annual vacation pay. In 1932, Labatt set an industry standard by establishing a group insurance plan for its employees, and six years later an annuity plan was created to build pension benefits.

While the nation struggled through the years of the Depression, the Labatt family underwent its own period of misfortune. On August 15, 1934, John Labatt III, already a widely recognized business and community leader, was kidnapped on the way from his summer home in Sarnia to a company board meeting. Later his empty car was discovered with a note instructing John's brother, Hugh, to pay a ransom of $150,000.

For the next several days, the story of the mysterious disappearance appeared in the headlines of major newspapers around the world. The incident was the first kidnap/assault in Canadian history. Detectives concentrated their search around the Detroit, Michigan area as suspicion mounted about the possibility of gangster involvement. During Prohibition, American gangsters had transported alcoholic beverages from Canada into the United States in rowboats down the Detroit River. Authorities believed Labatt had been abducted in a similar fashion. After a few days Labatt was released unharmed. The search for his assailants continued over the next several months until the severely shaken Labatt identified a Canadian bootmaker. Labatt retired from public life for the remainder of his tenure as company president.

After World War II, the company prepared to undertake a major expansion. To raise capital, John Labatt Ltd. became a public company and issued 900,000 shares. Many employees were among the over 2,000 original shareholders. In 1946, the company completed its first acquisition, the Copland Brewing Company in Toronto, which doubled Labatt's brewing capacity. The 1950s saw a number of new beverages added to Labatt's product line. Fiftieth Anniversary Ale, nicknamed "Fifty," commemorated John and Hugh Labatt's years of activity in the company. It later became Canada's most popular ale. Pilsner Lager Beer was Labatt's successful venture in the international market.

In 1951, the company presidency passed from John III to his brother Hugh, formerly vice-president. A year later John died at age 72. The company continued to expand during the decade, most notably with the purchase of Shea's Winnipeg Brewery Ltd., a company dating back to 1873. Labatt also acquired the Lucky Lager Brewing Company of San Francisco, while construction of a $6.5 million brewery in Ville La Salle, Quebec, in 1956, marked the brewer's expansion into other provinces.

When Hugh Labatt died in 1956, W.H.R. Jarvis became the first non-family president of Labatt. The following year he oversaw formation of a Feed Products Department, the company's first entrance into an industry outside brewing. The division manufactured animal feed additives using brewing by-products.

Jarvis died of a heart attack during a board meeting in the early 1960s. John H. Moore assumed the post and supervised the further expansion of Labatt's operations. Acquisition of breweries in Newfoundland and Saskatoon, and later in Halifax and Waterloo, strengthened Labatt's position in the national market. Major structural changes also occurred at Labatt in the next few years. The first came in the mid-1960s when the Milwaukee-based Joseph Schlitz Brewing Company attempted to gain a 40 percent interest in the Canadian brewery. The family trust agreed to sell half its shares and many public shareholders were also willing to sell, but the acquisition was eventually halted by U.S. antitrust laws. An investigation led by U.S. Attorney-General Robert F.

Kennedy alleged that Schlitz wanted to control the California market through a Labatt subsidiary. In 1967, Schlitz was forced to sell its approximately one million shares to a consortium of three Canadian investment groups.

Another major structural change occurred in 1964 when John Labatt Ltd. became a holding company to manage its various company activities; brewing fell under Labatt Breweries of Canada Ltd. The parent company proceeded to make acquisitions in other areas, purchasing its first winery, Parkdale Wines, in 1965. Eight years later, Labatt consolidated its wine holdings under the Chateau-Gai brand name. The Ogilvie Flour Mills Company purchase led Labatt into the dairy and processed food industry, and over the next several years, other food product purchases followed. By 1974, company operations fell into three main divisions: brewing, consumer products, and agricultural products. Fiscal sales for the year reached $2.3 billion (brewery sales accounted for $1.8 million), with profits of $155 million. Brewing operations were later divided into the Canadian and international groups. A major expansion campaign at the London facility in 1965 increased annual capacity to 1.3 million barrels, making it one of the largest breweries in the world. At the same time, Labatt announced plans to form a joint venture with Guinness Overseas Ltd. to produce the famous Irish stout in Canada. At the end of the decade, Moore announced he would leave Labatt to take charge of a company that represented Labatt's largest shareholder. N.E. Hardy, formerly president of Labatt Breweries of Canada Ltd., succeeded Moore.

During the 1970s, Labatt participated in the construction of a brewery in Trinidad, purchased an interest in Zambia Breweries, and a Brazilian brewing company. It also established Labatt Importers Inc. in New York to aggressively develop Labatt's presence in the U.S. market, while acquiring a 45 percent interest in the Toronto Blue Jays, an American League baseball franchise. In 1979, Canadian power players Edward and Peter Bronfman acquired Brascan, Ltd., which held a sizeable stake (nearly 40 percent) in Labatt.

The company continued to grow and diversify in the 1980s, launching the Sports Network (TSN) in 1984, then acquiring rights to Barnes wine and Pennsylvania's Latrobe Brewing Co. (home of the popular Rolling Rock beer) in 1987, which added another million barrels of beer to Labatt's production. Additionally, Labatt even dabbled in biotechnology with experiments and research on the genetic manipulation of yeast, while its parent company purchased half-interest of Supercorp Entertainment, Canada's biggest commercial music production company, and a 45 percent share of BCL Entertainment, one of the world's largest rock-concert merchandisers.

For the fiscal year ending in April 1988, Labatt hit sales of $5.1 billion (with profits of $140.6 million), and was Canada's largest brewing company. With an estimated 41 percent share of the beer market and 12 plants across the country, Labatt's Blue brand continued to dominate its competition as the most popular beer in Canada. Yet in 1989, Molson Breweries managed to capture 52 percent of the market, replacing Labatt as number one, despite several awkward months during Molson's merger with Carling-O'Keefe. To regain the company's former position, Labatt directors looked inward to consolidation and streamlining: the Moretti and Prinz Brau Italian breweries were merged; capital spending for the brewing division increased by $20 million; and the company's senior management underwent reorganization as well.

The 1990s proved increasingly tumultuous for Labatt, beginning with the worst beer sales on record for the summer of 1991 (all brands were down 5.5 percent across the country), and the first of many rumors about the brewery's sale to various conglomerates, most notably Anheuser-Busch (with whom the company had a licensing agreement to brew and sell Budweiser in Canada). In an effort to bolster its brewing and entertainment divisions in 1992, Labatt decided to sell off its $2 billion dairy and food division, representing over half (55 percent) of the company's assets. Labatt also purchased another 45 percent of the Toronto Blue Jays (bringing its ownership to 90 percent of the club). The maneuvering paid off; Labatt's market share grew to a record high of 44 percent (as rival Molson's fell almost three points to 49.5 percent) helped by the launch of Labatt Genuine Draft, and a 14 percent sales increase in the United States.

In 1993, several occurrences put Labatt in the headlines: in February, the Bronfmans unloaded their 37.3 percent share of the company to several investors for $933 million; then the longtime rivalry between Molson and Labatt turned ugly after the introduction of "ice" beer, a process Labatt had been perfecting for years with technology patented in 1982, only to be beat to the market by Molson. Labatt took its ice brewing process seriously; to prove it the company filed suit against Molson and Miller Brewing over what Labatt believed was copyright infringement of its "ice" terminology. The year 1993 also marked Labatt's emergence in Taiwan, where its Blue brand was successfully marketed as "Fong Ye" (maple leaf).

In July of 1994, Labatt paid $720 million for a 22 percent stake in Femsa Cerveza, Mexico's second largest brewer (with 48 percent of the Mexican market), producer of the Dos Equis and Tecate beer brands. Spurred by NAFTA, the partnership increased Labatt's brewing production by 40 percent while allowing Femsa to take advantage of Labatt's more modern production, packaging, and marketing techniques. By the end of fiscal 1994, brewing accounted for nearly 78% percent of the company's total revenue and 89 percent of its $155 million profit. Net sales in the U.S. also rose to $228 million, with Labatt brands increasing their market share by 25 percent over the previous year.

February of 1995 brought a court ruling in favor of Miller Brewing and Anheuser-Busch, who challenged Labatt's exclusivity rights to "ice brewed" and related terms in the United States. Nevertheless, Labatt Ice Beer and Maximum Ice were extremely successful and helped Labatt's market share climb to 44.2 percent, its highest ever. Further, Labatt Ice Beer was a surprisingly big hit in Japan.

At the same time, Labatt was hit hard by the rapid decline in the value of the Mexican peso (the company wrote off a $272-million loss in its Femsa investment) and suffered substantial losses from the 1995 baseball strike. Then rumors began circulating once again of a buyout, this time by the Onex Group in May, with subsequent bids offered by Heineken and Interbrew SA. In the summer of '95, the company was bolstered by the slow recovery of the peso and accepted a $2.7-billion acquisition bid by Interbrew. As the deal was reviewed by Canadian investment officials, Belgium-based Interbrew announced its intention to auction off Labatt's entertainment and sports team holdings. While investors worldwide scrambled for funding, at least Labatt's brewing future seemed secure—the company could once again focus on maintaining the superiority of its ice brewed products, perennial favorite Labatt Blue, and newer products like Wildcat.

Principal Subsidiaries:

Labatt Breweries International; Labatt Breweries of Canada; Labatt's USA; Labatt Breweries of Europe; Labatt Retail UK; Femsa Cerveza CA.

Further Reading:

"Another Beer Blast from NAFTA," *Business Week,* July 18, 1994, p. 46.
Bertin, Oliver, "Labatt Pauses to Reflect on Period of Rapid Expansion," *Globe and Mail,* September 9, 1988, p. B7.
————, "Labatt Looks Abroad for Growth," *Globe and Mail,* September 9, 1990, p. B9.
Bochove, Danielle, "Labatt Heats Up Battle for Ice Beer Name," *Globe and Mail,* August 27, 1993, p. B3.
Bociurkiw, Michael, "Taiwan Develops Taste for Blue," *Globe and Mail,* August 9, 1993, p. B5.
Bourette, Susan, "Labatt Girds for Battle," *Globe and Mail,* May 19, 1995, p. B1.
Daglish, Brenda, "Beer Wars," *Maclean's,* August 15, 1994, pp. 26-27.
Daly, John and Wickens, Barbara, "Billion Dollar Paydays," *Maclean's,* February 22, 1993, p. 22.
David, Gregory E., "Strange Brew: The Remaking of John Labatt, Toronto's Beer and Sports King," *FW,* September 13, 1994, pp. 26-30.
Feschuk, Scott, "John Labatt Spinning Off $2-Billion Dairy Business," *Globe and Mail,* September 11, 1992, p. B1.
————, "Time for Another Southern Marriage?" *Globe and Mail,* January 16, 1993, p. B5.
————, "Sale Lifts Uncertainty Over Labatt," *Globe and Mail,* February 13, 1993, p. B1.
Heinzl, Mark, "Onex Says It May Buy John Labatt; Brewer's Shares Up 12 Percent Since April 1," *Wall Street Journal,* April 14, 1995, p. A4.
"Jury in U.S. Rules Against Brewer Labatt in Trademark Dispute," *Wall Street Journal,* February 13, 1995, p. C19.
Makin, Kirk, "Clash of the Brewing Titans," *Globe and Mail,* May 1, 1993, p. A1.
McMurdy, Dierdre, "Bay Street's Bonanza," *Maclean's,* February 22, 1993, pp. 18-20.
McNish, Jacquie and Strauss, Marina, "Rumours Flying: Talk Concerning a Possible Buyout of John Labatt," *Globe and Mail,* February 22, 1991, p. B1.
Noble, Kimberley, "The Edper Puzzle," *Globe and Mail,* December 9, 1990, p. B1.

————, "Labatt Shuffle Raises Questions," *Globe and Mail,* December 9, 1991, p. B3.

————, "Labatt Will Reduce Size of Board," *Globe and Mail,* September 13, 1991, p. B13.

————, "Sale of Labatt Seen as Capital Idea," *Globe and Mail,* February 13, 1993, p. A1.

Strauss, Marina, "Labatt Fails to Meet Forecast," *Globe and Mail,* July 23, 1990, p. B3.

————, "Labatt puts Down Roots in Mexico," *Globe and Mail,* July 7, 1994, p. B1.

————, "Labatt's Caught in Peso Plunge," *Globe and Mail,* March 10, 1995, p. B1.

————, "Onex Bid $800-Million Short: Taylor," *Globe and Mail,* May 26, 1995, p. B1.

————, "Onex Bids billions for Labatt," *Globe and Mail,* May 19, 1995, p. A1.

————, "Struggle for Labatt Intensifies," *Globe and Mail,* May 20, 1995, p. B1.

————, "Where is Heineken Now?" *Globe and Mail,* June 8, 1995, p. B5.

————, "Where's Labatt Board," *Globe and Mail,* May 25, 1995, p. B1.

Strauss, Marina, and Enchin, Harvey, "Strike is No Ball for Business," *Globe and Mail,* August 22, 1994, p. B1.

Symonds, William C., "Life of the Buyout Party," *Business Week,* June 5, 1995, p. 42.

————, "Can Labatt Shed its Belly but Keep the Beer," *Business Week,* December 14, 1992, p. 70.

—updated by Taryn Benbow-Pfalzgraf

Laidlaw Inc.

3221 N. Service Road
P.O. Box 5028
Burlington, Ontario L7R 3Y8
(905) 336-1800
Fax: (905) 336-3976

Company Type: Public Company
Founded: 1958
Employees: 31,585
Sales: US$2.13 billion in 1994
Stock Exchanges: Montreal Toronto New York
SICs: 4111 Local & Suburban Transit; 4953 Refuse
Systems

Laidlaw Inc. is the largest manager of solid waste in
North America and the leading provider of school bus
transit services. It also provides various related services,
including hazardous waste management and healthcare
transportation, and is active in Europe and Mexico.

Laidlaw was founded and built by Michael DeGroote.
DeGroote emigrated to Canada from Belgium shortly
after World War II, when he was just 15 years old. He
moved to Hagersville, Ontario, purchased an old surplus
army truck, and started his own independent trucking
company. With his lone army truck, DeGroote began
hauling manure from local dairies to tobacco farms in
southwestern Ontario. He persevered despite economic
hard times in the region and the eventual failure of his
hauling endeavor, and in 1958, at the age of 25,
purchased a Hagersville trucking company from a man
named Laidlaw. The enterprise was operating 48 trucks
at the time, serving customers solely in southern Ontario, and its annual revenues were about $400,000. During
the 1960s, workaholic DeGroote built Laidlaw into a
dominant regional trucking company. By the time he
was 35 years old, DeGroote was a wealthy man. His
privately owned company was generating $5.6 million
dollars annually and was still growing.

In 1969 DeGroote took his company public, selling
shares to raise expansion capital. The successful public
offering left Laidlaw rife with cash, which DeGroote
used to initiate a buying spree that would span two
decades and result in one of the most successful
companies in Canada. Indeed, between 1970 and 1985
Laidlaw's stock price rocketed at an annual compounded rate of more than 40 percent. During the same

period, Laidlaw's revenues and profits soared at an
annual compounded rate of 53 percent while the company's debt burden remained relatively low. DeGroote
accomplished the feat by focusing on companies and
industries that were based on his expertise—trucking.
"Whether it was garbage or school kids, that's how
DeGroote built his business," explained analyst Burt
Thompson in the August 1991 *Canadian Business.*
"They might call it waste management and other things
now. But to DeGroote, it was trucking."

DeGroote matched his trucking focus with a buying
strategy that proved remarkably profitable. He issued
stock in Laidlaw when it would bring an extremely high
price, and used the cash to purchase companies that
were undervalued and trading at a very low earnings
multiple. Immediately after going public in 1969, De-
Groote purchased a solid-waste hauling company, giving
him an important entry into what would become a
major growth industry in the 1970s and 1980s. Likewise, Laidlaw entered the passenger services industry in
1973. That move allowed Laidlaw to capitalize on the
increase in the busing of school children that occurred
during the next two decades.

The passenger service and waste hauling industries were
unique in two ways. First, they were much less cyclical
than the trucking business. When the economy flopped,
communities would continue to pay for busing and
waste-hauling services long after the commercial trucking markets had declined. Second, they were dominated
by thousands of local mom-and-pop operations. De-
Groote believed that he could purchase the larger and
more successful of these companies to build networks
that would benefit from economies of scale.

Laidlaw posted big gains during the early 1970s as
DeGroote expanded the company by acquiring numerous busing and waste-hauling concerns. Though most of
his acquisitions flourished, he also experienced some
major failures. Laidlaw's initial foray into the hazardous
waste business, for example, floundered; DeGroote built
up a substantial hazardous waste business in the late
1970s in Hamilton, Ontario, but the effort languished
and DeGroote decided to jettison the operation in the
early 1980s. At about the same time, DeGroote purchased a major trucking outfit, New York-based Boss-
Linco. The operation quickly soured and DeGroote
dumped it, taking $5.9-million write-off in the process.

Laidlaw's slip ups were overshadowed by its surging
busing and waste-management businesses in the 1970s
and early 1980s, when the value of DeGroote's strategy
became clear. During that period, the volatile trucking
industry was hammered by an economic downturn that
crushed many of Laidlaw's trucking company peers.
Meanwhile, cash-strapped school boards were looking
for ways to cut costs. They began privatizing their
busing services to companies like Laidlaw, which were
able to provide better training for drivers and to get
lower insurance rates. Laidlaw seized the opportunity
and advanced its busing division. Similarly, Laidlaw
benefited from trends in the waste industry. Stringent
new environmental regulations concerning the construction of new landfills had the effect of boosting the value
of the many landfills that Laidlaw already owned.
Furthermore, Laidlaw's economies of scale related to

waste hauling were becoming increasingly critical in that industry.

The overall result of the various dynamics impacting Laidlaw during the late 1970s and early 1980s was that DeGroote decided to focus almost solely on the passenger service and waste management industries. To that end, Laidlaw began aggressively expanding its school busing operations in the United States and Canada in 1983. By 1985 Laidlaw had become the largest provider of school busing services in North America with 11,000 vehicles. The company simultaneously began buying up traditional waste haulers and landfills, and branching out into the burgeoning recycling industry. In 1981, Laidlaw began Canada's first "blue box" recycling program in Kitchener, Ontario. Surprised by the high rate of citizen participation, DeGroote decided to expand the program. Eventually, many communities in both the United States and Canada were requiring similar programs.

Laidlaw's growth during the 1970s and early 1980s was primarily the result of acquisitions rather than internal growth. DeGroote bought up dozens of companies that were undervalued or performing poorly, turned them around, and then integrated them into Laidlaw's huge operations. Cost savings resulted from greater buying power related to insurance for school buses, for example, and ownership of both waste hauling services and the landfills to which many of the acquired waste haulers had once paid high dumping fees. The recipe had won praise in the stock market, and investors were expecting similar performance from Laidlaw in the future. To meet those expectations, DeGroote had to step up his acquisition program in the mid-1980s.

Laidlaw conducted its largest-ever acquisition in 1983 and 1984 when DeGroote engineered the buyout of ARA Transportation Inc., a U.S.-based school bus operator active on the East and West coasts. That giant purchase added 4,500 buses to Laidlaw's motor pool and made Laidlaw the single largest bus operator in North America. Laidlaw slashed management at the new operation, decentralized decision making, and reorganized to quickly improve the company's profitability. Laidlaw sustained its buyout rampage in 1985 with the acquisition of 11 bus transportation businesses and 14 solid waste management companies. The buyouts continued through the mid-1980s, punctuated by significant takeover bids like the one for the big U.S.-based Mayflower Corp. By the late 1980s, in fact, DeGroote had purchased about 250 companies.

Laidlaw generated revenue of about $546 million in 1986, about 60 percent of which was attributable to school bus services. By that time, DeGroote had effectively exited the trucking industry and was getting the other 40 percent of sales from his waste management division. Laidlaw netted a healthy $50 million in income in 1986, adding to DeGroote's spiraling net worth, since he still owned more than 50 percent of the company. By the end of 1987, moreover, Laidlaw had grown to include 15,000 buses throughout North America and was fast approaching the $1 billion sales mark. Meanwhile, acquisitions continued. "There is no shortage of companies for us to buy," DeGroote told the *South Florida Business Journal* in 1987. "We get letters

and phone calls every week from people wanting to sell out. The trick is, of course, to be able to select the gems from the duds."

Laidlaw powered into the late 1980s with record sales and profits. Indeed, sales soared well past $1 billion and profits vaulted to about $215 million in both 1988 and 1989. By that time, the still-hard-charging DeGroote decided that his time at Laidlaw was up, and in 1988 he sold his stake in the business to Canadian Pacific Limited for $500 million. Incredibly, DeGroote had delivered compounded annual growth of more than 30 percent since taking the company public in 1969. DeGroote purchased a home in Florida and exited in 1990. He left the company in the hands of protege Donald Jackson, a 46-year-old MBA from the University of Western Ontario. Before taking the helm at Laidlaw in 1990, Jackson had cofounded what became a very large truck leasing company and had served as chief executive at Tricil, a waste management company that he helped to start and then sold to DeGroote for $240 million in 1989.

Immediately after DeGroote's departure, Laidlaw began to stumble. Soon after assuming the chief executive slot, Jackson had to announce a disappointing $33 million write-down of a failed waste-treatment operation in Cleveland. More importantly, the global recession was beginning to take its toll on Laidlaw, despite the company's recession-proof reputation. Higher fuel prices were crimping earnings, and it looked as though Laidlaw's planned expansion into the European waste management market might have to be postponed. Revenue growth slowed in 1991 and profits tumbled. Laidlaw took a total $469 million write-down on a Bermuda-based operation and laid off more than 300 workers as part of a cost-cutting effort. In addition to weak market conditions, some critics pinned the decline on Jackson's management style. Some analysts contended that Jackson was more of a manager than an entrepreneur, and lacked DeGroote's risk-taking acumen.

Although sales increased slowly, Laidlaw's profit margins declined and the company's net income plunged from late 1980s levels. Jackson resigned as chief executive in 1993 and shortly afterward Laidlaw posted an operating loss of $22 million. James Bullock assumed leadership at Laidlaw in October of 1993. Bullock, a board member at Laidlaw since 1991, announced his intent to refocus Laidlaw on its three core businesses: transportation, waste management, and hazardous waste management. Acquisitions continued, however, such as the $225 million buyout of United States Pollution Control Inc. that made Laidlaw the number one hazardous waste services company in North America. Following that purchase, Laidlaw's sales jumped to $2.13 billion in 1994 and the company returned to profitability with a net income of $90 million. Going into 1995, Laidlaw was by far the largest operator of school bus services with a North American fleet of 22,000 buses, and the leading North American manager of solid wastes. It was deriving a hefty 25 percent of its sales from its hazardous waste division, while transportation and solid waste management services accounted for roughly 40 percent and 35 percent of revenues, respectively. During the mid-1990s, Bullock planned to cut costs, streamline existing operations to improve profitability, and continue to acquire companies that complemented Laidlaw's three core divisions.

Principal Subsidiaries:

Laidlaw Passenger Services Group; Laidlaw Waste Services; Laidlaw Waste Systems

Further Reading:

Bott, Robert. "Can Don Jackson Fill DeGroote's Shoes?" *Canadian Business*, August 1991, pp. 22-26.

Damsell, Keith. "Laidlaw to Become No. 1 on Continent," *Financial Post*, November 1, Section 1, p. 3.

Foster, Cecil "Standing in the Shadow," *Financial Post*, March 23, 1991, Section 1, p. 7.

Haggett, Scott. "Bullock's Laidlaw Challenge," *Financial Post*, October 16, 1993, Section 1, p. 3.

Hallman, Mark. "Laidlaw Forecast Optimistic," *Financial Post*, December 4, 1991, Section 1, p. 14.

————. "Laidlaw Seals Mayflower Acquisition for US$175M," *Financial Post*, January 24, 1995, Section 1, p. 40.

Higgins, Will. "Who is Michael DeGroote?" *Indianapolis Business Journal*, June 9, 1986, Section 1, p. 1A.

"Laidlaw Chief to Focus on North America," *Financial Post*, October 19, 1993, Section 1, p. 4.

Lim, Paul J. "There's More to Laidlaw Than Just School Buses: Picketing an International Conglomerate," *Seattle Times*, March 21, 1995, Section D, p. 1.

Livesey, Bruce. "Who Cleans Up?" *Metropolitan Toronto Business Journal*, October 1987, Section 1, p. 49.

Nickell, David. "Ryder Bus Service in High Gear," *South Florida Business Journal*, September 21, 1987, Section 1, p. 1.

Yakabuski, Konrad. "Sagging Laidlaw Returns to Route," *Toronto Star*, October 19, 1993, Section B, p. 3.

—Dave Mote

Loblaw Companies Limited

22 St. Clair Avenue East
Ste. 1500
Toronto, Ontario M4T 2S8
(416) 922-8500
Fax: (416) 922-7791

Public Company
Founded: 1919 as Loblaw Groceterias. *Employees:*
  50,000
Sales: $10 billion
Stock Exchanges: Toronto Montreal Vancouver
SICs: 6719 Holding Companies, nec.

With ownership of 20 percent of Canada's supermarkets in the early 1990s, Loblaw Companies Limited ranked as the country's largest supermarket chain. The company's retail operations encompass conventional supermarkets, superstores or "hypermarkets," and a few wholesale clubs. Loblaw Companies was 70 percent-owned by international conglomerate George Weston Ltd. in 1995.

The supermarket giant was founded in Toronto in 1919 by J. Milton Cork and Theodore Pringle Loblaw as Loblaw Groceterias. Due in part to the supermarketing boom of the late 1940s, the chain grew to include 113 stores in Ontario with $50 million in annual revenues. In 1947, George Weston Ltd.—then under the direction of Garfield Weston, son of the founder and namesake—made its first investment in Loblaw stock. Within less than a decade, Weston had accumulated a majority interest in Loblaw and assumed de facto control. In 1956, Garfield Weston created Loblaw Companies Ltd., a holding company, to consolidate the diverse supermarket chains acquired by his family's company in the postwar era. By the end of the decade, Loblaw had expanded geographically through the acquisition of Saskatoon's O.K. Economy Stores Ltd.; National Grocers Co. Ltd. in central Canada; a controlling interest in Kelly Douglas & Co. in British Columbia; and New Brunswick's Atlantic Wholesalers. The company had even reached southward into the American midwest with the acquisition of a controlling interest in National Tea Co.

But by the mid-1960s, the deadly combination of poor management and tough competition had cost Loblaw leadership of its core Ontario market. Although the number of stores had increased to 1,800 by 1970, the company also racked up $200 million in debt during the late 1960s. Loblaw's management had missed the trend toward suburbanization, and had allowed product selection, staff training, and even the stores themselves to deteriorate. The high cost of unionized labor and expensive urban locations rendered Loblaw unable to compete when it was faced with price wars in the early 1970s. Dominion Stores Ltd. became the new king of the provincial retail food scene; other rivals included Atlantic & Pacific and Steinbergs Ltd. Compared to its price-slashing rivals, Loblaw earned an unenviable—and tough to shake—reputation for high prices.

In 1971 Garfield Weston asked son Galen, who himself had parlayed a single inherited grocery store into Ireland's first supermarket chain in the 1960s, to evaluate the situation at Loblaw. Against the advice of a group of British supermarket consultants, Galen accepted the challenge and moved back to Canada early in 1972, becoming CEO of Loblaw Companies.

Galen Weston called a college friend, Dave Nichol, for advice on how to turn the supermarket chain around. Nichol had roomed with Weston at the University of Western Ontario. Following a post-graduate stint selling industrial ball bearings, Nichol went back to school, earning a law degree from the University of British Columbia and a Master's degree at Harvard. Upon graduation he was recruited by McKinsey & Co., a prestigious management consultancy firm. Nichol, in turn, acquainted Weston with Richard Currie, a colleague at McKinsey and a University of Western Ontario grad with an MBA from Harvard. Weston, Currie and Nichol formed the core of Loblaw's turnaround team. Their strategy had two basic foci: operations and marketing. Weston and Currie concentrated on the operational aspects, and left corporate development to Nichol.

Applying techniques learned at McKinsey, Currie began to repair Loblaw's battered balance sheet. His job, as he perceived it, was to generate a positive cash flow that could be used to overhaul both the physical stores, through remodeling, and the corporate image, through marketing and advertising. Bucking the conventional wisdom of the supermarket industry, Currie disregarded market share to focus on maintaining sales at profitable locations. A total of 1,200 unprofitable stores in Canada and the United States were closed. A reorganization eliminated a dozen corporate bodies through consolidation of all retail, wholesale, finance, and real estate operations. Currie also created centralized purchasing divisions, Intersave Canada and Intersave U.S.A., to buy direct from food manufacturers and therefore eliminate the extra expense of buying goods from outside wholesalers and warehouses. These maneuvers freed up funds for debt reduction, store remodeling, and eventually marketing.

Weedy, crowded parking lots, poor lighting, stained uniforms, outdated and dilapidated display cases were the hallmarks of Loblaw's predominantly urban locations. In the fall of 1972, Galen Weston hired the little-known design firm of Break, Pain & Watt to revamp a downtown Toronto store as a trial. Led by Don Watt, the team revitalized everything from the parking lot to the store logo to the Loblaw product brand. Within a month of the store's grand reopening, weekly sales had quadrupled. Loblaw quickly slated ten more stores for makeovers.

The company also launched an image-changing advertising campaign featuring spokesman William Shatner, well-known for playing Captain James T. Kirk on the popular "Star Trek" television series. Advertising agency Vickers & Benson created a new Loblaw slogan, "More than the price is right—but by gosh the price is right." The new ads helped boost 1974 sales by 10 percent.

Notwithstanding the operational economies, the remodeling, the sloganeering, and an injection of over $165 million from Garfield Weston from 1968 to 1974, Loblaw continued to struggle in the mid-1970s. In fiscal 1976, the company lost $49.8 million on $3.5 billion in revenues. Writing for the *Globe and Mail* a few years later, Paul Taylor characterized Loblaw at that point as "a company without a future." The supermarket chain's deficit became a problem even for the huge, diversified George Weston Ltd., which took the first loss in its history in 1976.

Weston, who in 1974 was named chairman and managing director of George Weston Ltd. while continuing as Loblaw Companies' chairman, tapped Currie to be president of Loblaw Companies Ltd. in 1976. Nichol advanced to the presidency of Loblaw Supermarkets Ltd., which then operated 132 Loblaw stores in Ontario.

Having "cut the fat," Currie worked to bring Loblaw into the black in the late 1970s with a three-pronged plan designed to diversify geographically, achieve parity between wholesaling and retailing, and develop customer loyalty. A combination of acquisitions and organic growth helped the company achieve parity among its Canadian and American divisions by 1980. This regional equilibrium helped shield the company from the effects of localized economic cycles. An aggressive franchising operation helped balance predominantly eastern Canadian retail operations with essentially western Canadian wholesaling. Nichol was assigned the task of generating customer loyalty.

Characterized in Anne Kingston's 1994 book *The Edible Man* as "the consummate marketing man," Nichol became the public face of Loblaw in 1977, when he became the company spokesman. In the style of Frank Perdue of Perdue Farms and Dave Thomas of Wendy's, Nichol's "presidential" testimonials convinced customers that Loblaw really did offer competitive prices. Nichol created a million-dollar in-house advertising department in 1978 and had internalized all Loblaw's advertising by 1979.

Nichol and others in Loblaw's upper echelon soon came to believe that private-label products were the true key to long-term success. For supermarket operators, private-label or house brands offered several advantages over national brands. Manufacturing and distributing its own products allowed the retailer to take bigger profits, while simultaneously offering its customers significantly lower prices. Although many North American supermarketers considered the idea revolutionary, it was by no means original. France's Carrefour chain had already

established itself as the first supermarket with no-name products, Great Britain's J Sainsbury Ltd. made house brands its specialty, and Germany's privately held Aldi Group built one of the world's few intercontinental supermarket chains on the concept. The idea made its way to the U.S. in the late 1970s, but these "generic" products with their unappealing black-on-white packaging were generally perceived as low in quality and sold poorly.

Loblaw already had a private-labeling infrastructure in place with its powerful Intersave procurement and distribution operations, which could negotiate volume discounts on a wide variety of products. Bargaining for (then offering customers) the lowest possible price was the first factor in the private-label equation. Galen Weston budgeted $40 million for a private-label program in 1974. Nichol started work on Loblaw's first generic line, called Exceptional Value, shortly thereafter. The "non-brand" featured large-volume packages of household staples like paper goods, detergent and peanut butter. But customers simply weren't yet prepared to buy in bulk, and the line was quickly pulled.

Undaunted, in 1976 Nichol and designer Watt set out to refine the line under the tongue-in-cheek No Name brand. They lowered the quantities and raised the quality. The products, all staples, were also distinctively packaged. Eschewing the typical, hard-to-read black-on-white label, Don Watt designed a simple but effective label featuring black on yellow, which created an eye-catching display. The 135-store launch in 1978 was accompanied by an aggressive multi-media advertising campaign—starring Nichol—that emphasized the competitive prices and high quality of No Name products. Building on the success of No Name in the late 1970s, Loblaw's created the No Frills chain of stores, which dedicated the vast bulk of their selection to the No Name line.

Together, these operational and merchandising changes helped Loblaw achieve its first annual profit of $43 million on sales of $5.4 billion in 1979. It was just the beginning of a steady string of sales and profit increases. By fiscal 1983, annual revenues exceeded $6 billion, and net income totaled $52.7 million.

But none of Loblaw's top executives were ready to rest on their laurels. In the early 1980s, they began to develop a concept initially known as "No Name gourmet." Nichol believed that the high-flying ethos of the 1980s was conditioning consumers to expect better quality and to willingly pay more for it. These ideas gelled in 1983, when Loblaw tested the first product in what would become the "President's Choice" premium private-label line: President's Blend coffee.

Instead of appealing to the lower end of the market—as traditional house and generic lines had done in the past with their cheap ingredients and bland packaging—the President's Choice line sought to bring "gourmet" or "top shelf" foods to the masses. Nichol sought out unique products, then convinced food manufacturers to "eat" their development costs for the highly profitable privilege of selling to Loblaw. Nichol didn't skimp on packaging, either. His distinctive cursive handwriting combined with full-color product photos distinguished President's Choice from traditional private-label goods and positioned them more on a par with the national brands. The range of products rapidly grew to include specialties ranging from balsamic vinegar to gourmet dog food, and perhaps most celebrated, The Decadent Chocolate Chip Cookie. The President's Choice line became the essence of Loblaw's' differentiation from other supermarketers, and therefore the key to customer loyalty, because, as Dave Nichol told Diane Brady of *Maclean's*, "Anybody who loves this cookie has to shop in my stores." At the same time, an international division of Intersave called International Trade was set up to bypass traditional (and traditionally expensive) food importers. By the end of the decade, this operation made Loblaw the largest offshore importer in the nation, with over $30 million in annual volume.

In 1983, Nichol bought *Insider's Report* from a California grocer for $25,000. This comic book-style flyer was published three to four times annually. It featured recipes and anecdotes plugging President's Choice products, which were introduced chainwide in 1984. Its distribution reached 10 million copies by 1987, and was considered essential to the success of the premium private label.

In 1984, Nichol was placed at the head of Loblaw International Merchants, a new division created to manage the development, production, packaging, and promotion of the premium private-label products. Over the course of the 1980s, this segment of Loblaw Companies' business grew to include several targeted categories of products: Teddy's Choice for children, Nature's Choice and G.R.E.E.N. "environmentally friendly" goods, and Too Good To Be True! for the health-conscious.

The proportion of private-label products sold at Loblaw's stores increased from 6 percent of total sales in 1980 to 32 percent by 1993 and the line expanded to include over 1,500 products. But in spite of the media frenzy and copycatting that surrounded the premium line, it only constituted about one-fourth of Loblaw's annual house-brand sales. Due in part to a late-1980s, early 1990s recession, the lesser-known No Name brand brought in $700 million in gross sales annually compared with $250 million for President's Choice by 1991. That spring, Currie announced that No Name would begin to receive attention more proportionate to its contribution.

The success of the private-label lines contrasted sharply with the poor performance of Loblaw's eastern Canadian superstores and its U.S. locations in the late 1980s. These operations began to pull down overall performance; sales dropped 4 percent, from $8.6 billion in fiscal 1987 to $8.3 billion in fiscal 1988, and net income plunged 45 percent from $73.6 million to $40.8 million. Currie blamed high capital investments in the superstores and price wars in its American markets for the dive.

Frustration with the U.S. market prompted a gradual retreat from the retail portion of the regional supermarket industry. The pull-out culminated in the 1995 sale of Loblaw's 89 remaining National Tea Co. stores in the U.S. to Schnuck Markets Inc., a privately-held St. Louis chain, for an estimated $300 million. During this same period, the company was launching an attack on the U.S. market from a different angle. Loblaw started wholesaling its President's Choice products to non-affiliated supermarket chains, building up a $20 million business by late 1991.

John Thompson, Loblaw Companies' senior vice-president of Finance and Administration, correctly characterized the late 1980s downturn as a "glitch." From 1989 through 1991, the company's net earnings increased steadily to over $105 million. George Weston Ltd. reduced its stake in Loblaw Companies to 71 percent by abstaining from a 1991 public share offering. The five-million-share offering raised $97.4 million and fueled speculation that Loblaw was warming up for a major acquisition.

After more than two decades with Loblaw, corporate icon Dave Nichol resigned in 1994 and eventually became president of Cott Corp., the bottler of President's Choice beverages for Loblaw. Industry observers speculated that internal power struggles, dissatisfaction with his $1 million salary, and even a touch of egomania drove Nichol's decision. Loblaw International Merchants became Loblaw Brands Limited, and Nichol was succeeded by John W. Thompson. Richard Currie continued as president of Loblaw Companies.

After dipping from $105 million in 1991 to $80 million in 1992, Loblaw Companies's profits increased by nearly 59 percent to $127 million in 1994. Sales increased as well, reaching the $10 billion mark that year.

Principal Subsidiaries:

National Grocers; Loblaw International Merchants; Intersave Buying & Merchandising Services; Atlantic Wholesalers Ltd.; Kelly, Douglas & Co., Ltd.; Fortino's Supermarkets, Ltd.; IPCF Properties Inc.; Loblaws Supermarkets Ltd.; National Grocers Co. Ltd.; Zehrmart Inc.; Westfair Foods Ltd.

Further Reading:

Brady, Diane, "The Names Game," *Maclean's*, 3 February 1992, 64-66.
Currie, Richard, "Loblaws: Putting the Super Back in Supermarket," *Business Quarterly*, Summer 1994, 25-32.
Kingston, Anne, *The Edible Man: Dave Nichol, President's Choice and the Making of Popular Taste*, MacFarlane, Walter & Ross: Toronto, 1994.
Strauss, Marina, "Loblaw Offering More Bulk Goods," *Globe and Mail*, 2 May 1991, B16.
———, "Loblaw to Raise $97.4 million," *Globe and Mail*, 16 May 1991, B9.
———, "Marketing: Nichol Has Choice Words for U.S. Viewers," *Globe and Mail*, 12 November 1991, B4.
———, "Super-Store Woes Sink Loblaw Profit," *Globe and Mail*, 23 February 1989, B1.
Taylor, Paul, "Loblaw Achieves Big Leap with New Ideas on Market," *Globe and Mail*, 22 December 1980, B6.

—April Dougal Gasbarre

London Life Insurance Company

255 Dufferin Avenue
London, Ontario N6A 4K1
(519) 432-5281
Fax: (519) 679-3518

*Wholly Owned Subsidiary of London Insurance
    Group Inc.*
Incorporated: 1874 as London Life Insurance
    Company
Employees: 5,719
Sales: $3.73 billion
SICs: 6400 Insurance Agents, Brokers & Service

The largest provider of individual life insurance in Canada, London Life Insurance Company sells a wide variety of insurance and financial services products. Controlling roughly 15 percent of the Canadian life insurance market in 1995, London Life achieved its preeminent position over the course of a century, beginning its rise toward market dominance in 1874 when five businessmen residing in London, Ontario, organized a small life insurance concern. As the decades passed and the Canadian insurance industry matured, London Life emerged as one of the country's leading insurance companies, bolstered by its highly regarded service to Canadian businesses and particularly to Canadian individuals.

London, Ontario, the city from which London Life took its name, began as a small frontier settlement in a region then known as Canada West, the country's western outpost. As befitted the pioneer spirit of the land and its people, the settlement's first building, constructed in 1826, was a tavern, perhaps the only type of business that could be assured a steady flow of customers during the early years on the Canadian frontier. Shortly thereafter, however, the modern trappings of a community emerged. A school, a courthouse, and a jail were established by the village's enterprising innkeeper. All were housed in a two-story log building until 1829, when a brick building outfitted with turrets and battlements was completed; its construction required the recruitment of workers from outlying areas and created the village's first appreciable wave of settlers.

Less than a decade later, London was well on its way toward shedding its status as a village, having grown from a one-tavern settlement into a bustling center of commerce. There were, by the mid-1830s, several taverns competing for the patronage of the village's 1,000 residents, as well as a host of other establishments that were more suggestive of the financial center London was set to become. Several stores, a stagecoach inn, two churches, a bank, two tanneries, grist mills, and a brewery now framed the dirt roads of London, which in 1841, with a population approaching 2,000, was incorporated as a town. Four years later, London's population doubled, then tripled, eclipsing 12,000 people by 1855, when it leaped to the next plateau of community classification and became a city.

A worldwide economic depression, sparked by the end of the Crimean War in 1856, struck a severe blow to London's economy in the years immediately following its incorporation as a city. Already reeling from spiraling inflation, London's citizens were devastated by plunging land prices precipitated by the end of the war. Thousands left the newly designated city; many, it was theorized, to escape debtors' prison. Although the community had experienced its share of disastrous moments in its short history—a fire in 1845, for example, had destroyed three-quarters of the town, reducing 300 stores, homes, and churches to rubble— soaring inflation and plummeting land prices during the late 1850s represented its largest crisis to date. An estimated three-quarters of the city's businesses failed during a two-year span. The city was crippled, and for the next decade—the years immediately preceding the formation of London Life Insurance Company—those who remained in London strove to rebuild their once-prosperous community.

London's economy would recover before London Life first opened its doors, buoyed largely by the discovery of oil west of the city in Enniskillen Township, where the first commercial production of crude oil in North America was drawn from a well dug by hand. The outbreak of civil war in the United States contributed to London's economic rebirth as well, flooding the city with British troops who arrived to assure that hostilities did not spread northward. Roughly 10,000 soldiers were sent to guard the country's border, 2,000 of whom found their way to London, where they boosted the business of those merchants still in operation after the previous decade's economic slide. By the beginning of the 1870s, when Ontario first began exporting oil to Europe, London was once again a thriving hub of commerce. It was also fertile ground for the newest addition to the city's growing ranks of businesses, the London Life Insurance Company, which would dominate Ontario's insurance market for more than the next century.

London Life was formed in 1874, seven years after the Confederation of Canada, emerging at a time when London, after its first half century of existence, had become a hub for the distribution of oil and agricultural products. Approximately 20,000 people resided in the city when London Life commenced operations, but the number of businesses serving and supporting the population suggested that considerably more people dwelled within the city's boundaries. Aside from a host of stores, there were eight banks, three daily newspapers, the head offices of five savings and loan institutions, and, despite the fact that the insurance industry was still in its infancy in Canada, no fewer than 21 insurance companies operating in London. White-collar professionals, the largest segment of London's population to survive the tumultuous 1850s, prospered during the early 1870s, wielding their influence and wealth to boost London's stature as a focal point of business activity in Ontario. Five of these local businessmen were responsible for organizing London Life: two lawyers, Edward Harris and James Magee; a doctor, William Woodruff; a military leader of local fame, Colonel John Walker; and a banker, Joseph Jeffery, who was selected as London Life's first president and whose family would participate actively in the management of London Life for more than the next century. The company was granted a provincial charter on March 24, 1874, and shortly thereafter began selling life, health, and accident insurance to Ontario residents, well before such insurance became a common feature of modern Canadian life.

In Britain and the United States, the concept of insuring one's life had moved into the mainstream at least by the 1880s, but in Canada life insurance was only purchased by the affluent, which severely restricted the market for London Life. During its formative decades, London Life would contribute greatly toward making life insurance a common product by designing policies and payment schedules tailored to the needs and financial limitations of middle- and lower class citizens, but initially the company excluded certain segments of the population. This was also true of other life insurance companies operating at the time, primarily because underwriting life insurance was still an extremely inexact business, not yet built on the foundation of actuarial science.

Accordingly, London Life initially excluded those who put the company at too great a risk, refusing to issue accident policies to travelers bound for the southwestern United States or western Canada. Sailors and railway workers were generally barred from purchasing life insurance, as were hotel and tavern keepers, as their occupations were considered too dangerous. As insurance underwriting became more of a science, the company gradually extended coverage to virtually everyone and steadily built an ample customer base.

London Life sales agents canvassed southwestern Ontario during the company's first decade of existence, traveling by train or horse-drawn carriages to outlying areas in search of new customers. Ten years after the company was formed, London Life received its Dominion Charter and accelerated its growth by focusing on other regions of Canada. By the turn of the century, when London Life had contracts for $6.8 million of insurance, the company had business in Ontario, Manitoba, New Brunswick, and Nova Scotia and was rapidly becoming one of the leading insurers in Canada.

Over the course of the next two decades, London Life's insurance in force increased nearly ten-fold, reaching $60 million by 1918, which positioned the company as one of Canada's largest insurers. The following year a new market for London Life opened up when insurance companies were permitted to write group insurance policies for the first time. An estimated 250 Canadian companies insured their employees during the first year for a total value of $78 million, giving London Life a substantial infusion of new business.

London Life agencies were established in Quebec in 1924, and then the company stretched westward, reaching British Columbia by 1937. Expansion into the Prairie Provinces did not occur until after the Second World War, when group insurance saw another boom. London Life shared in the general economic prosperity that followed the war, growing rapidly during the 1950s as increasing numbers of individuals and businesses insured themselves against accidents, health problems, and death. In the early 1950s, London Life had nearly $2 billion of insurance in force, a total that would rise to nearly $6 billion by the end of the decade.

By the beginning of the 1960s, London Life was writing approximately $650 million worth of new insurance a year, the bulk of which was derived from individual life insurance premiums as opposed to group insurance premiums or sickness and accident insurance premiums. Over the course of the next two decades, the company would continue to depend heavily on individual life insurance business, becoming the preeminent individual life insurer in Canada.

Aside from the company's steady growth during the 1960s, 1970s, and 1980s, the most significant development was a change in ownership precipitated by the financial misfortune incurred by one of the descendants of Joseph Jeffery, London Life's first president. Joseph Jeffery's grandson, Gordon Jeffery, lost millions of dollars when he made an ill-advised investment in an apartment block in downtown London. In order to rescue Gordon Jeffery from financial ruin, Jeffery family members sold some of their controlling shares in London Life, which were then purchased by a company named Brascan. A holding company named Lonvest, owned by Brascan, the Jeffery family, and the Toronto-Dominion Bank, was formed to take control of London Life in 1977. Lonvest controlled London Life for roughly two years until Edgar and Peter Bronfman purchased enough shares of Brascan on the open market to assume control of it, which, in turn, gave the two brothers and their company, Edper Equities Limited, a substantial stake in London Life.

After the fast-paced ownership changes at London Life during the late 1970s, the company went on to record exponential growth during the next decade, particularly during the latter half of the 1980s, when life insurance in force increased from $55.2 billion in 1985 to more than $90 billion by the end of the decade, making the company the largest provider of individual life insurance in Canada. Encouraged by this growth, London Life began, by the decade's conclusion, to expand internationally, seeking to establish a presence in foreign markets through reinsurance business. During the early 1990s, the company began providing specialty insurance products to other insurance companies in the United States and Europe, building a subsidiary reinsurance operation named London Reinsurance Group that by the mid-1990s ranked London Life as one of the 50 largest reinsurers in the world. With no reinsurance operation in 1989, London Life had developed a sizeable new source of revenue that by 1994 had nearly $500 million in capital.

Entering the mid-1990s with more than $100 billion of insurance in force, London Life's management set their sights on the Asian insurance market, hoping to carry their success in the United States and in Europe across the Pacific Ocean. In 1993 London Life entered Taiwan when the company established Shin Fu Life Insurance Company in a joint venture with Central Investment Holding Company, the investment arm of Taiwan's ruling Kuomintang National Party. As the company looked toward the future, the burgeoning Southeast Asian economies represented a strong potential market. The company established a regional center in Malaysia in 1994 in hope of establishing additional insurance ventures in the region. Elsewhere, London Life continued to explore further opportunities in the United States and Europe, supported solidly by its secure market position in the Canadian insurance market, where the company had thrived for more than a century.

Principal Subsidiaries:

London Life Financial Corporation; London Reinsurance Group Inc.; London Life and General Reinsurance Company Limited; London Life and Casualty Reinsurance Corporation; London Life Insurance Co. of Michigan; London Life International Reinsurance Corp. (Barbados); Dubigest Incorporated (67%); Vadis Engineering Ltd. (67%); Toronto College Park Limited (51%); International Care Corporation; Devan Properties (59%).

Further Reading:

"$9.5 Million Tab for London Life," *Financial Post,* February 9, 1963, p. 9.

Aarsteinsen, Barbara, "Insurance Company Defends Policy," *Globe and Mail,* October 5, 1989, p B2.

"Edper: The Good, the Bad and the Ugly," *Globe and Mail,* February 12, 1993, p. B4.

Howlett, Karen, "Reputation Spurs London Life," *Globe and Mail,* April 16, 1993, p. B7.

Jorgensen, Bud, "A Conflicting Look at London Life," *Globe and Mail,* February 23, 1993, p. B12.

Knowles, Robert G., "Retention Is Profit Key for London Life," *National Underwriter Life & Health-Financial Services Edition,* May 21, 1990, p. 3.

"London Life Insurance Co.," *Financial Post,* February 9, 1963, p. 22.

"London Life Insurance Co.," *Financial Post,* March 31, 1962, p. 56.

Noble, Kimberley, "London Life's Dynacare Deal Doubles Retirement Business," *Globe and Mail,* January 13, 1995, p. B6.

Welsh, Lawrence, "London Life Seen Poised to Regain Leading Position," *Globe and Mail,* March 21, 1981, p. B1.

—Jeffrey L. Covell

Maclean Hunter Publishing Limited

Maclean Hunter Building
777 Bay Street
Toronto, Ontario M5W 1A7
(416) 596-5000
Fax: (416) 593-3175

Wholly owned subsidiary of Rogers Communications Inc.
Incorporated: 1891 as J.B. McLean Publishing Company, Ltd.
Employees: 700
Sales: $185 million
SICs: 2700 Printing and Publishing

Until it was acquired by Rogers Communications Inc. in March 1994, at a cost of more than $3 billion, Maclean Hunter Limited was a Canadian communications giant with operations in North America and Europe. In addition to its traditional mainstay, trade publications, the business on which the company was founded, Maclean Hunter held interests in broadcasting, cable television, and various other communication services, generating revenue of $1.74 billion in 1993. Following its purchase of the company—the largest acquisition in Canadian telecommunications history—Rogers retained an interest in most of Maclean Hunter's Canadian cable operations, its publishing assets, its consumer and trade publications, its four radio stations, and the 61.4 percent interest in The Toronto Sun Publishing Company. The periodicals, newspapers and radio broadcasting segments have since been managed by a newly formed corporate umbrella, Rogers MultiMedia Inc. The century-old company name, however, still exists in the form of Maclean Hunter Publishing Limited, a wholly owned subsidiary of Rogers MultiMedia which publishes consumer magazines, business publications and other periodicals, directories and supplements in Canada.

Maclean Hunter began in 1887, when John Bayne Maclean left his post on the Toronto *Mail* to found Grocer Publishing Co. and publish *The Canadian Grocer*, a specialized publication filled with commercial news about the food industry. The first 16-page issue was sent free to grocers all over Canada, who were invited to purchase subscriptions for $2 a year. Within three months, the fledgling publication became profitable and Maclean began to publish weekly. At that time,

he also brought his brother, Hugh, into the business as a partner. Expansion followed in 1888 with the establishment of *Dry Goods Review.*

Success in the grocery area led Maclean to move into other trades, and in 1888, *Hardware & Metal* was established at the invitation of a group of hardware-store owners. By 1890, Maclean was publishing four business journals, and had set up his own typesetting and composition operations. In 1891, the J.B. McLean Publishing Company, Ltd. was incorporated. (Maclean was not always consistent in spelling his own last name.)

By 1893, Hugh Maclean was running the business in Toronto, while his brother J.B. worked in New York City on a short-lived art publication called *Art Weekly.* In the early 1890s, the company began to open advertising sales offices in cities outside Toronto, branching out to Montreal in 1890, and across the Atlantic Ocean to London in 1895. In 1899, John Maclean bought out his brother's one-third share in their company for $50,000.

By 1903, J.B. McLean Publishing Company had grown to employ about 50 people. Two years later, the company was successfully publishing six business papers, including *Bookseller and Stationer, Printer and Publisher*, and *Canadian Machinery & Manufacturing News*, and its founder was anxious to make his mark in a wider field. Using the profits from his commercial journals, he purchased a magazine published by an advertising agency, called *Business: The Business Man's Magazine.* Shortening its name to *The Business Magazine*, Maclean published his first issue in October 1905. The 144-page general-interest publication was made up entirely of condensed articles from other publications. Three months later, the magazine's name was again changed, this time to *Busy Man's Magazine*, with a subtitle that explained its purpose: "The Cream of the World's Magazines Reproduced for Busy People." Maclean edited it personally while also overseeing the company's other publications.

At the start of 1907, the J.B. Maclean Publishing Company introduced another general-interest publication, the *Financial Post.* The weekly was a joint venture between Maclean and Stewart Houston, a well-connected lawyer who wrote and edited the newspaper, which started out with 25,000 copies.

In the first decade of the 20th century, Maclean's publishing enterprise grew quickly. Under the autocratic and frugal leadership of its founder, who became known as "the Colonel" after he was given command of a regiment during the Boer War, in 1899, the company had a high turnover of employees, frustrated by low salaries and the Colonel's constant meddling. In 1911, however, Maclean promoted the man whose name would one day join his in the corporate logo, Horace T. Hunter, to general manager. Hunter raised salaries and brought a decentralized approach to management, improving the company atmosphere and employee productivity. Also in 1911, Maclean changed the title of *Busy Man's Magazine* to *Maclean's.* He continued to act as chief editor for the flagship publication.

Not long after the end of World War I, in August 1919, Maclean's only son died unexpectedly, eliminating the possibility that his company would become a dynasty.

Also that year, Maclean renamed the enterprise the Maclean Publishing Company Limited. Soon afterward, in 1920, Maclean sold 30 percent of the company to Hunter, now a vice-president, for $50,000, and another 10 percent of the stock to his general manager, H. Victor Tyrrell. Other editors and executives were also given the opportunity to buy company stock. At the same time, Maclean undertook a long-overdue company restructuring and bought the one-third of the *Financial Post* that the company did not already control.

In the years following World War I, the Canadian consumer-magazine industry was overwhelmed by an influx of magazines produced in the United States that paid no import duties to enter the country. Nevertheless, throughout the 1920s, Maclean's enterprise continued to grow. In 1922, the company officially branched out from publishing into the related field of commercial printing, an activity that actually had been going on for some time. In 1909, the company had purchased an entire square block of property in Toronto to provide enough space for a printing plant for all its magazines, and over the years, the plant had begun to take on outside work. In 1927, the company first ventured outside Canada with its acquisition of *Inland Printer* and *Rock Products* in the United States, and in the following year it introduced *The Chatelaine*—later simply *Chatelaine*—a women's magazine that soon gained a loyal following. In 1930, the company moved into French-language publishing for Canadians when Maclean purchased *Le Prix Courant*. During this period, Maclean's company felt the impact of the Great Depression. Helped by a government duty on imported magazines, which allowed Canadian publishers to regain some of the market share they had lost to U.S. publishers, Maclean was able to avoid laying off employees by putting workers paid by the hour on shortened schedules, and cutting wages and vacation pay. Maclean Publishing Company's salaried employees suffered two 10-percent cuts in pay. In 1935, the import duties were lifted with a change in Canada's government, and U.S. publications gained predominance once more on newsstands. By 1936, however, Maclean's employees numbered nearly 900, and wages and hours had both increased. By the end of the decade, the company boasted 30 publications.

With the coming of World War II, Maclean coped with wartime rationing and shortages of goods and workers, and a drastic decline in advertising revenue. With the conversion of the economy to a wartime footing, production of consumer goods was drastically curtailed, resulting in a scarcity or disappearance of many goods, and the need for consumer product advertising thus dried up. The company attempted to compensate by encouraging "sustaining" advertising, to maintain the image and familiarity of a brand name, and through the increased use of advertising by the government. The company's business publications became tools in the war effort, monitoring the nationwide war production effort, and publicizing government policies and regulations. Even such publications as *Mayfair*, a society magazine, were transformed, advising women on war charities and economical use of food. In addition, the company produced a free edition of *Maclean's* for distribution to Canadians on active duty overseas, which eventually gained a circulation of 30,000.

In 1945, the company's name was changed to Maclean-Hunter Publishing Company to reflect the contribution of Horace T. Hunter, its president since 1933. Three years later, the company made its most dramatic physical expansion up to that point, when it opened a $3 million printing plant in a Toronto suburb, Willowdale. Throughout the postwar years, the company once again found its consumer publications facing stiff competition for advertising dollars from such U.S. imports as the Canadian editions of *Time* and *Reader's Digest*. By 1948, two-thirds of all magazines purchased in Canada came from other countries.

In 1950 John Maclean died, and Hunter acquired 60 percent control of the company, in which he continued to serve as president for two more years. In 1952, Floyd S. Chalmers, who had been with the company since 1919, became president. Throughout the 1950s, Canadian magazines found themselves challenged by new modes of communication, such as television, as well as by U.S. publications. In 1956, Canadian publishers got some help from their government when it imposed a 20 percent tax on advertising in non-Canadian magazines, but this was repealed the following year under U.S. pressure. By the end of the decade, nonetheless, Maclean-Hunter was publishing 51 different titles.

The 1960s marked a turning point for Maclean-Hunter. What had until then been a staid enterprise, engaged almost exclusively in publishing, became a diversified company, operating in a wide variety of communications fields. In 1960, the company made an unsuccessful attempt to obtain a license for a television station in Toronto, but in the following year it was able to enter the broadcasting industry through its purchase of 50 percent of the radio station CFCO in Chatham, Ontario. The station had been one of the pioneers in Canadian radio, having been founded by a butcher with an interest in radio in 1926. It had used a homemade transmitter until 1948.

Maclean-Hunter also diversified into the event-planning industry. In 1961, the company organized a convention for members of the plastics industry, despite the fact that Canada's main trade association for plastics was headed by a rival trade publisher, who refused to lend the association's support to the show. The show, which became an annual event, was not a great success, nor would it be for many years. Nevertheless, Maclean-Hunter forged ahead in the show-management field, forming Industrial & Trade Shows of Canada, now known as Industrial Trade & Consumer Shows Inc., in 1962.

At this time, the company also expanded its holdings in the media-information services field. Maclean-Hunter had long owned *Canadian Advertising Rates & Data*, a service publication for advertising agencies, and in 1958 it had acquired *British Rate & Data*. Both were doing well, and the company was looking for new areas of growth. The U.S. market was out of the question, dominated as it was by one well-established firm, Standard Rate & Data Service, so Maclean-Hunter moved into continental Europe with the French publication *Tarif Media*. In 1961, it sold 50 percent of this publication to the U.S. company Standard Rate & Data Service, and with this partner formed a European joint venture to launch a West German service, *Media Daten*. Eventually, European operations came to include Austria, Switzerland, and Italy.

The company's Canadian operations, however, were not faring as well. Although the company had continued to expand its French-language offerings, adding its first general-interest publication for the Quebec market in 1960, *Chatelaine-La Revue Moderne*, and following with *Le Magazine Maclean* in 1961, its English-language consumer magazines lost $1.8 million in that same year. This was, as ever, due partly to the domination of the Canadian market by U.S. publications. Despite this, Maclean-Hunter introduced another English-language consumer publication in 1963, targeted at younger women. It was called *Miss Chatelaine*.

A year later, in 1965, the Canadian periodical industry received some government support when the tax deduction for the business expense of advertisements in non-Canadian publications—with the exception of *Time* and *Reader's Digest*—was abolished. This opened up the field somewhat by discouraging the proliferation of U.S.-owned Canadian editions, and driving some of these publications out of business.

Also in 1965, stock in Maclean-Hunter was publicly traded for the first time. Up until this time, the company's shares had been closely held by Maclean's designated successors and a small number of members of senior management, but it became clear that internal mechanisms for distributing stock in the company were no longer adequate, and a sale of 15 percent of the shares was arranged. Of the 15 percent, 40 percent was allotted to meet high employee demand.

The company expanded further into non-publishing fields in the mid-1960s, acquiring Design Craft Ltd., which produced exhibits for trade shows, as a natural complement to its existing interests in that area. It continued to purchase radio stations, adding CHYM, a rural station, in 1964, and CKEY of Toronto, the company's first urban radio property, in 1965. Also in 1965, the broadcasting company's interests were augmented by the acquisition of CFCN radio and television, of Calgary.

Further ventures into the broadcasting field came in 1967 with Maclean-Hunter's entry into the cable television business. The company entered a partnership with Frederick T. Metcalf, who had already built a cable system in Guelph, Ontario, and the result was Maclean Hunter Cable TV. The first market targeted for expansion was Toronto. The company's steady progress in diversification was ratified in 1968 when its name was updated from Maclean-Hunter Publishing Company Limited to Maclean-Hunter Limited.

In the first years of the 1970s, the company ventured into book distribution, purchasing a book wholesaler; into the printing of business forms, with the acquisition of Data Business Forms; and into the paging business, by buying Airtel, which provides personal pagers to relay messages. In 1973, Maclean-Hunter purchased a 50 percent interest in KEG Productions Ltd., which put together television programs on wildlife. The company created "Audubon Wildlife Theater" and "Profiles of Nature," both successful and long-running series.

In the mid-1970s, with further expansion in the Canadian market blocked by the Canadian Radio-Television & Telecommunications Commission, Maclean-Hunter set its sights on cable television in the United States, buying Suburban Cablevision of New Jersey. Unlike Canadian cable systems, which existed to provide clear reception of ordinary network television in remote locations, the New Jersey operations set out to attract customers by offering them access to programs not available on regular television, such as special sporting events. This new concept proved popular, and Suburban Cablevision grew from 10 franchises to 43. In 1975 Hunco Ltd., the Hunter family holding firm, owned a 51 percent controlling interest in Maclean-Hunter. This block of stock was sold to the board of Maclean-Hunter in January 1976, when chairman Donald F. Hunter, facing death from a brain tumor, sold nearly 3.5 million of his family's 4 million shares to a holding company set up to ensure that the company would be safe from unwanted takeover attempts in his absence. The era of family control was over.

Perhaps the most important event of the mid-1970s for Maclean-Hunter took place outside the company: the passage of Bill C-58 in 1976. This amendment to the Income Tax Act removed the exemptions on tax-deductible advertising from *Time* and *Reader's Digest*, and stipulated that three-quarters of a publication's owners must be Canadian and four-fifths of its contents must be original and non-foreign, in order for advertising within it to qualify for a tax exemption. This gave new life to the Canadian magazine industry, in particular *Maclean's*. The flagship publication had long suffered in its head-to-head battle with *Time*, and in addition had fallen into an identity crisis under a series of editors. The magazine, which had lost credibility and had been losing money heavily since the early 1960s, had become a source of embarrassment to all concerned. With the support of Bill C-58, however, *Maclean's* was able to rally in the latter part of the 1970s, and in 1978 stepped up from a biweekly to weekly publication.

By that time, Maclean-Hunter had diversified to such a large extent that income from publishing accounted for only half of all company revenues. Notwithstanding these changes, the company continued to expand its magazine operations in the late 1970s, acquiring four special-interest publications in 1978, including *Ski Canada* and *Racquets Canada*, and founding *New Mother* and its French-language counterpart *Mère Nouvelle* in 1979.

Steady expansion of Maclean-Hunter operations continued into the 1980s, with the purchase of a four-fifths interest in a U.S. form printer, Transkrit Corporation, in 1980; the acquisition of *Progressive Grocer* journal in 1982; the launch of *City & Country Home* in 1982; and the purchase of *Hospital Practice* in 1983. In 1981 Maclean-Hunter Limited dropped the hyphen in its name becoming Maclean Hunter Limited.

In 1982, the company fulfilled a long-standing ambition to include the newspaper business in its ever-widening scope of operations when it purchased a 51 percent share of the *Toronto Sun*, a daily tabloid newspaper. A year later its involvement with the *Sun* led to purchase of the *Houston Post*, in Texas.

Throughout the late 1980s, Maclean Hunter continued to grow in its chosen fields, primarily through acquisitions, as in its purchase of the Yorkville Group in 1985 and Davis & Henderson Ltd. in 1986, both printers. In 1986, it started work on 49 percent-owned Barden Cablevision, which covers all of Detroit, Michigan, and subsequently began construction of a system in the United Kingdom. By 1989, newspaper holdings included *Sun* papers in three Canadian cities outside Toronto, and in 1990 the company purchased Armstrong Communications, a cable system, in Ontario.

In December 1988, Maclean Hunter made the largest acquisition in its history, taking over Selkirk Communications Ltd., a Toronto-based broadcasting and cable company, for an estimated $600 million. It subsequently negotiated deals worth a total of $310 million to sell off large segments of the target company to three other companies, including its rival, Rogers Communications. Although the Canadian Radio-Television and Telecommunications Commission approved the deal the following year, it ordered Maclean Hunter to invest $21.2 million—the size of the financial gain the company stood to make on the purchase and breakup—in a capital fund to be used to strengthen and improve Canadian broadcasting.

As Maclean Hunter entered the new decade, a recessionary economy and a concomitant decline in ad revenues resulted in lower profits. Likewise, the company's stock earnings plummeted to 14 cents per share, a 75 percent drop. According to some analysts, the company's move towards product diversity also contributed to the decline. The cost of the Selkirk acquisition, for instance, while strengthening the company's presence in the broadcasting and cable television markets, offset revenue growths from other segments of the company. As early as February 1994, Maclean Hunter itself became the object of an acquisition. Hoping to create a $3-billion communications conglomerate that would serve a third of Canada's 7.2 million cable subscribers and provide a Canadian analog to U.S. communications giants Time Warner and McGraw Hill, Rogers looked to purchase all of Maclean Hunter's shares, which were valued at $3.2 million. The magnitude of the possible merger and the repercussions in the communications world provoked a variety of responses. Rogers's aggressive chief and founder Ted Rogers expressed the belief held by many that the new conglomerate would help Canada as a whole by securing its place on the information highway and, in the short term, consolidating the country's cable-TV industry and enhancing customer service. Others, however, feared the ramifications such a merger would present for the Canadian populace. Ian Morrison, president of Friends of Canadian Broadcasting, for instance, suggested that the competitive advantage gained by Rogers would hinder the free flow of information and raise prices in the Canadian entertainment industry. "When does a monopoly ever reduce the cost to the consumer?" he told the *Globe and Mail*'s Harvey Enchin and John Partridge.

In an attempt to prevent the hostile takeover, Maclean Hunter chose not to adopt a common strategy known as a "poisoned pill", in which a targeted company sells its assets and loads itself with debt. Rather, after Rogers made an offer of $17 per share, Maclean Hunter chief executive officer Ronald Osborne attempted to obtain more money for shareholders by breaking up the company and selling the individual pieces at a higher rate. But no one could top Rogers's offer. After a month of heated rhetoric between the two companies, Rogers amended his offer, agreeing to pay a special dividend of 50 cents a share, raising the value of the deal by $90-million. On March 9, negotiations were finally completed; nine months later the takeover was approved by the federal broadcast regulator.

After taking full control of the communications giant, Rogers elected to sell Maclean Hunter's U.S. cable-television assets, several radio stations, magazines in the United States and Europe, and printing operations. However, it held on to the company's other broadcasting interests, a 62 percent interest in Toronto Sun Publishing Ltd., and its flagship magazine, *Maclean's*. Maclean Hunter Publishing Ltd., headed by John Tory, now oversees the production of seven consumer magazines, including *L'actualite* and *Chatelaine*, and 35 specialized business periodicals and directories.

Further Reading:

Enchin, Harvey, "It's Official: CRTC Okays HM Takeover," *Globe and Mail*, December 20, 1994, p. B1.
Enchin, Harvey and John Partridge, "Rogers, Maclean Hunter Sign Deal," *Globe and Mail*, March 9, 1994, p. A1.
————, "Rogers Tempers His Takeover Bid," February 25, 1994, p. B1. Gold, Douglas, "Money Managers Like MH Deal," *Globe and Mail*, March 9, 1994, p. B8.
McKenna, Barrie, "Rogers Not Splitting MH Print Empire," *Globe and Mail*, September 16, 1994, p. B4.
Partridge, John, "Media Stocks Hit Hard," *Globe and Mail*, February 23, 1991, p. B1.
————, "Profits Plunge for Newspaper, Media Giants," July 26, 1990, p. B7.
Perry, Robert L., *Maclean Hunter at One Hundred*, Toronto: Maclean Hunter Limited, 1987.

—Elizabeth Rourke
—updated by Jason Gallman

MacMillan
Bloedel Limited

MacMillan Bloedel Limited

925 West Georgia Street
Vancouver, British Columbia V6C 3L2
(604) 661-8000
Fax: (604) 687-5345

Public Company
Incorporated: 1911 as the Powell River Company
  Ltd.
Employees: 12,500
Sales: $3.95 billion *Stock Exchanges:* Toronto
  Montreal Vancouver NASDAQ
SICs: 2620 Paper Mills; 2400 Lumber & Wood
  Products

MacMillan Bloedel Limited is Canada's largest producer
of forest products. Although the majority of its operations are located in Canada, "MacBlo" has facilities in
the United States, the United Kingdom, Japan, Mexico,
and Europe. An early-1990s restructuring changed the
company's organizational structure from a geographic
orientation to a focus on product. As of 1994, the
business was concentrated on three core markets: building materials, packaging, and paper. Within those
categories, the firm manufactures lumber and engineered wood products; pulp, newsprint, and specialty
papers; and containerboard and other packaging materials. Its products are marketed in approximately 40
countries.

MacMillan Bloedel was formed through the 1951 merger of the H.R. MacMillan Export Company with Bloedel, Stewart & Welch. The union created Canada's
biggest lumber products firm. The principals, Wisconsin
native Julius Harold (J.H.) Bloedel and Harvey Regi-
nald (H.R.) MacMillan of Ontario, took different routes
to their shared destiny. Bloedel was more involved in
private lumber production, while Macmillan worked his
way through the civil forestry service.

Bloedel attended the University of Michigan in civil
engineering in the 1880s but left before graduation
because of a lack of money and a desire to start a career.
He worked first for a Wisconsin railway, then in real
estate before moving west, where he became a partner in
the 1890s in two different logging ventures in the state
of Washington.

In 1911, while managing the Larson Lumber Company,
Bloedel heard about an anticipated Canada-U.S. reci-
procity treaty to lift tariffs on lumber and other wood
products and decided to expand his logging operations
into British Columbia to take advantage of the more
favorable business conditions. That same year Bloedel
united with railway contractors Patrick Welch and John
W. Stewart to incorporate Bloedel, Stewart & Welch (B,
S & W) in British Columbia, with Bloedel owning half.
Stewart and Welch remained silent partners who provided critical access to the railway market. Bloedel was
mistaken about the tariffs, which were lifted only on
pulp and newsprint, two products that did not interest
him at the time.

World War I hurt an already ailing lumber industry, and
in 1914 exportation was nearly impossible because of a
shortage of non-military shipping. B, S & W managed to
keep open its logging camps at Myrtle Point during most
of the war — not all firms were so fortunate. When
servicemen returned home in search of work, only two-
thirds of the mills in the province were operating.
Powell River Company ultimately enjoyed a boom
market and rising prices as a result of World War I.

In the meantime, MacMillan pursued a divergent career.
From humble beginnings, he became engrossed in
forestry early in life as a result of mentoring efforts by a
teacher at the Ontario Agricultural College and a 9¢-per-
hour job on its experimental forestry plot. He graduated
from the program in 1906 and became enamored with
British Columbia after scouting timber for a group of
Ontario businessmen in 1907. He moved there soon
afterward, and became the province's first chief forester
after the passage of British Columbia's first Forest Act
in 1912.

During World War I, the Canadian government assigned MacMillan the post of Timber Controller, in
charge of finding world markets for Canadian lumber.
He reported back to the government his dismay that
nearly everywhere he traveled, lumber, including that
from British Columbia, was sold through U.S. firms.
MacMillan's efforts, however, were not in vain; Canadian exports to Allied countries improved dramatically
during the last two years of the war. This government
job, which MacMillan later termed one of the great
opportunities of his life, ended in 1916.

In 1919 MacMillan entered into an agreement with
British lumber importer Montague Meyer to create
British Columbia's first privately owned lumber export
brokerage. MacMillan insisted on an equal partnership,
mortgaging his house to match Meyer's $10,000. The
H.R. MacMillan Export Company was incorporated
that same year. As president, MacMillan ran the firm for
a year before hiring fellow professional forester Whit-
ford Julien VanDusen as manager. By the end of the
1920s Meyer had sold out to MacMillan.

In 1924 B, S & W unintentionally became a manufacturer following the failure of the Shull Lumber & Shingle
Company, which owed B, S & W money. B, S & W,
Shull's main creditor, bought the Shull mill. B, S & W,
however, still focused on logging and buying timber.
Prentice Bloedel, the elder son of J.H. Bloedel, joined
the firm in 1929, a bumper year is sales. A former
teacher, he had worked briefly as a logging laborer. In

1930 Bloedel, Stewart & Welch, like other firms, got caught in the Great Depression, experienced decline, and the following year lost money.

In 1935 B, S & W joined Seaboard Lumber Sales, a subsidiary of the Associated Timber Exporters of British Columbia Limited, (Astexo), a cooperative, and the main competitor of the H.R. MacMillan Export Company. When Astexo, representing about 30 firms, formed Seaboard, it stopped allowing MacMillan to market its British Columbia lumber supplies, forcing MacMillan into a major mill operation and the purchase of timberland. The firm not only survived but expanded, handling logging, sawmilling, plywood and door manufacturing and railway-tie production, as well as shipping and sales. The H.R. MacMillan Export Company was a pioneer in vertical integration, purchasing firms involved in all parts of the lumber trade. During World War II the H.R. MacMillan Export Company's most important acquisitions were timberlands. The firm went public in 1945. In 1948 MacMillan became chairman and VanDusen, vice chairman.

In 1942 J.H. Bloedel became chairman, and Prentice Bloedel supplanted him as president and treasurer of B, S & W, which went public in 1948. B, S & W was a pioneer of post-World War II reforestation efforts, handling 70 percent of all private reforestation and planting two million trees by the late 1940s.

Convinced that smaller firms had no future, Prentice Bloedel approached MacMillan in 1950 about a merger. MacMillan recommended the union to a skeptical VanDusen, arguing it would enable the new firm to find capital to keep the British Columbia forest industry on a competitive footing with its counterparts in the United States and elsewhere. Of the pair, MacMillan had a larger marketing operation, and Bloedel had more timberland. The merger would result in British Columbia's largest lumber and pulp operation.

Not only money was at stake. As Donald MacKay wrote in Empire of Wood, Prentice Bloedel recalled his father's reaction: "It really hurt his pride very much. He was dynastically minded as many people were who were self-made in that generation, and here we were selling out to our arch-enemy." Although he knew his firm would take a back seat to MacMillan as a wholly owned subsidiary, J.H. Bloedel signed the merger documents establishing MacMillan & Bloedel Limited in October 1951 — his last act before retiring. To clear the way for amalgamation, the combined firm paid $2.3 million in taxes to Canada because of $16 million in B, S & W income that had gone undistributed for years.

MacMillan's strong connections with British Columbia's government helped his company garner control of hundreds of thousands of hectares of provincial forest in the postwar era. During the 1950s, the government set up "tree farm licenses," renewable 25-year contracts allowing forest companies to sustainably harvest timber, then pay "royalties" to the province. Most of these contracts went to MacBlo, which accumulated 850,000 productive hectares of "TFL" land. This property constituted the vast majority of MacMillan Bloedel's one million hectares in British Columbia.

In 1956, at age 74, MacMillan resigned as chairman and was succeeded by B.M. Hoffmeister. Tension between them led MacMillan to request his resignation as 1957, a hard year, ended. During that same traumatic year, J.H. Bloedel died at age 93. John Valentine Clyne, a justice of the British Columbia Supreme Court, was named chairman of MacMillan & Bloedel in January 1958. Then 56, Clyne had little experience in business or knowledge of the forest-products industry but had established a reputation in marine law in his native Vancouver. As chairman, he faced challenges: poor timber sales, labor troubles in the pulp and paper area, and U.S. tax and tariff policies.

MacMillan & Bloedel brought its first newsprint machine on line in 1957, bringing the company in direct competition with the Powell River Company Ltd. Founded in 1909 by Dwight Brooks and Michael J. Scanlon, Powell River had grown to become one of Canada's largest newsprint makers and owner of the world's largest newsprint mill. But by the 1950's, outdated machinery and correspondingly high production costs combined with growing competition to erode Powell River's production, sales, and earnings. The firm considered and rejected five merger offers before agreeing to sell 50 percent of its equity to MacMillan & Bloedel in 1958.

Serious talks about a merger began the following year. Powell River Chairman Harold Foley was told that MacMillan & Bloedel would be the main partner of the new firm, with Clyne as chairman. MacMillan, Bloedel and Powell River Limited, the largest forest products company in Canada, was established in January 1960. The union of two different management styles—MacMillan & Bloedel's tight organization and efficiency with Powell River's more relaxed paternalistic management—turned ugly. By 1962, as a result of what was reported to be one of the nastiest corporate fights in Canadian history, most of the senior Powell River executives had resigned or had been "eased out." President (and son of Harold Foley) Milton Joseph (Joe) Foley quit in April 1961 complaining of exclusion from any meaningful participation. His father, who had become vice chairman of the merged firm, followed suit that May.

High taxes, the political climate in British Columbia, and high labor costs were among the reasons behind Clyne's drive to expand MacMillan, Bloedel and Powell River from a regional firm into a global entity. With its emphasis on solid wood products, the company experienced significant growth in pulp and paper manufacturing during the 1960s, becoming an international corporation with production in Europe, the United States, and Asia. MacMillan, however, viewed foreign countries as markets, not production centers. In the company's first successful step into international investment and its initial expansion of manufacturing facilities outside Canada, it bought container plants in Great Britain for $36 million in 1963. The next year a minority interest in the Royal Dutch Paper Company (KNP) was acquired. In 1966 the company name became MacMillan Bloedel Limited (MB or "MacBlo").

Joining with the United Fruit Company, the company built a liner board plant near Pine Hill, Alabama, completed in 1968, later becoming full owner. Later in 1968 MB adopted a policy to move from its traditional operation in wood products, pulp, and paper, and diversify into other businesses. It would look at firms related to the forest products industry but with a lesser priority on those outside the industry.

In 1970 MacMillan and VanDusen resigned from the board. In 1972 Prentice Bloedel, 71 years old, was the final owner-manager to leave the board. He is remembered as building British Columbia's first fully integrated sawmill and pulp unit, designed to obtain maximum use of each piece of timber, and as having developed the hydraulic ring barker, a key step in the processing of logs.

In 1973 Clyne, whose departure, like MacMillan's, was in stages, resigned as chairman. That year sales hit $1 billion. Robert Bonner, president and chief executive officer, replaced Clyne, and Bonner's positions were filled by Denis Timmis. Bonner and Timmis took joint command. A struggle between them, however, led to Bonner's resignation in 1974, and George Currie, executive vice president for finance, became chairman.

One of MacMillan Bloedel's efforts at diversification was the establishment in 1974 of a ventures group to seek small entrepreneurial companies with a potential for growth. The catalyst for an ensuing disaster was the expansion in 1973 of the Canadian Transport Company (CTCO), founded by the H.R. MacMillan Export Company in 1924, to carry its forest products into a general shipping line that competed for cargo with other global carriers. In spring 1974 CTCO was making a significant profit, but March 1975 was the worst shipping market since 1940. CTCO's fleet exceeded its needs. It was to take delivery on yet several more vessels, and it was losing money on many of its other chartered ships. Months later the chartering of ships was ordered stopped, and several CTCO officials were fired. Timmis cut operating and administrative expenses, including executive salaries. For 1975 MacMillan Bloedel suffered an $18.8 million after-tax loss—its first ever—on sales of $1.2 billion. The success of pulp and paper sales prevented a worse loss.

In February 1976 H.R. MacMillan died at his home in British Columbia at age 91. MacMillan was credited with establishing the British Columbia forest products industry.

Timmis had tried to reduce MacMillan Bloedel's dependence on the boom and bust cycles of wood products through diversification, but had made a badly-timed entry into shipping. Timmis and Currie were asked to leave in 1976. Months earlier Timmis had twice offered his resignation, that in each case had not been accepted. In March 1976 J. Ernest Richardson retired from the British Columbia Telephone Company, where he had been chairman and CEO since 1971, to accept the positions of chairman and acting president of MacMillan Bloedel. He had been a director at MB since 1967.

C. Calvert Knudsen, and attorney and specialist in maritime law and a senior vice president at Weyerhaeuser Company in Washington state, became CEO at MacMillan Bloedel in September 1976. His appointment reflected the board's zeal to return the firm to basics—the manufacturing and marketing of forest products. Despite limited success in its bid to become a multinational organization, MacMillan Bloedel was back in the black by October 1976 as market conditions improved. The venture group investments, many of which had lost money, began to be divested. In 1977 the company started a program of replacing and modernizing facilities in British Columbia.

Efforts to rally productivity while cutting costs in existing operations led MacMillan Bloedel to look at acquisitions again. In 1981, in an attempt to acquire Domtar, it became the object of takeover bids itself by Domtar and Canadian Pacific. Following intervention by B.C. premier Bill Bennett, who did not want MacMillan Bloedel to lose its provincial identity, Domtar and MacMillan Bloedel canceled their respective takeover efforts. Canadian Pacific pressed on, but with opposition from MacMillan Bloedel, backed off. MacMillan Bloedel was free for the time being, but the door to takeover had been opened.

In 1979 earnings were very good, in part because of full production and strong markets. MacMillan Bloedel employed 24,500—its largest staff to date. In 1980 Knudsen became both chairman and CEO. Also in 1980 the British Columbia Resources Investment Corporation (BCRIC) hired away MacMillan Bloedel's president, Bruce Howe, to become its president. He was replaced by Raymond V. Smith, senior vice president.

In 1981 MacMillan Bloedel again faced takeover on two fronts. Knudsen opposed a takeover bid from BCRIC but negotiated the transfer of a BCRIC subsidiary to MacMillan Bloedel for company shares. Premier Bennett rejected the plan. Also in 1981 Noranda Mines of Toronto sought to increase its shares of MacMillan Bloedel stock to 49 percent. Moves and countermoves included an offer by Noranda to limit its presence on the MacMillan Bloedel board to less than might normally be expected, which satisfied the government. Noranda hiked its bid and included an all-cash option, which MacMillan Bloedel's board recommended for acceptance, and soon after BCRIC withdrew its bid. When Noranda paid a total of $700 million for 49 percent of MacBlo, five of its executives joined the MacMillan Bloedel board including executive vice president Adam H. Zimmerman, who became vice chairman of MB when Richardson retired. Within a few months, Brascade Resources of Toronto, owned by the Bronfmans of Montreal, acquired 42 percent of Noranda. (Noranda divested its stake in MacBlo in 1993. The $971 million deal was hailed as "the largest equity financing in Canadian history.")

The 1981 recession in the industry, especially lumber, was the worst since the 1930s. MacMillan Bloedel's loss for 1981 was $26.7 million on sales of $2.2 billion. In 1982 it suffered its worst year to that date, losing about $57 million on sales of $1.8 billion. Fighting to survive, the firm downsized by perhaps half during a three-year period starting in 1981. Measures included decreasing capital spending for everything except for safety; reductions in salaries, dividends, and staff; temporary mill closures; and permanent closures or sale of manufacturing plants, subsidiaries, and joint ventures. The company jet was sold as was the firm's 26-story tower in

Vancouver. As many as 40,000 industry workers, nearly 20 percent of whom were MacMillan Bloedel employees, were laid off in British Columbia in late 1981 and in 1982. The decade also saw two industry-wide strikes and one lockout.

Despite Noranda's wish that he stay, Knudsen returned to Washington in 1983, largely for tax reasons, but he remained in the position of vice chairman. He was replaced by Zimmerman, who also retained a title at Noranda. In 1985 MacMillan Bloedel was still talking survival. In 1987 it enjoyed sales of about $3.1 billion, and earnings nearly doubled. With 1988 came improved markets and prices. Sales neared $3.3 billion, and the company earned record profits. Sales rose slightly in 1989, with about 80 percent of the total from international sales; nearly half of the exports went to the United States, lumber accounting for the largest share. A general economic slump in 1990 affected the industry, with declining prices and markets in all product lines, and MacMillan Bloedel plants were operating at less than capacity.

In the early 1990s MacMillan Bloedel's efforts to expand its global presence included a lumber distribution business in Japan, where MacMillan Bloedel Building Materials accounted for more than 25 percent of the total value of lumber that the parent company sold worldwide. Japanese major trading houses do not easily render business to foreign competitors, but MacMillan Bloedel's history of service there began with the Great Kanto Earthquake of 1923, when the firm supplied much-needed lumber.

MacMillan Bloedel's biggest challenge in the 1990s was to meet environmental demands, complying with new pollution standards and land preservation issues. New government regulations regarding pulp and paper operations formulated after dioxins were found in pulp and water effluent caused MacMillan Bloedel to commit $75 million in 1989 to virtually eliminate these unwanted and dangerous by-products from its Harmac and Powell River mills. MacBlo President Smith said in March 1989 that the industry in British Columbia faced up to $1.5 billion in capital investment into the early 1990s to meet new environmental regulations, and potential costs of $3 billion to conform to standards being proposed or being developed.

Environmentalists and native groups dogged MacMillan Bloedel with increasing success beginning in the mid-1980s and won growing public support in the early 1990s. Under pressure from groups like the Western Canada Wilderness Committee, Greenpeace and the California-based Sea Shepherd Conservation Society, Canada's federal and provincial governments rescinded a tree farm license on South Moresby Island that was worth nearly $40 million to MacBlo. It was the largest British Columbian TFL parcel ever taken from a forestry concern— and it was only the beginning. In 1987, the Social Credit administration, under Bill Vander Zalm, reduced the annual allowable cut in the province by 5 percent across the board. In 1988, environmentalists targeted the Carmanah Valley, home of some of North America's oldest and largest trees, for conservation. After initial resistance— which reflected

badly under the light of public opinion—MacBlo agreed to establish a 500 hectare preserve in the area.

The firm has no option but to remain somewhat flexible; nearly half of the forest lands it manages (721,000 hectares of a total 1.6 billion hectares) are under the public domain. In fact, the company only owned 225,000 hectares outright in 1994. Although government expropriations of land have been relatively small—5 percent in 1987 and another 8 percent in 1994—and the company has receive some compensation for the loss of their use, the threat of larger confiscations remained.

MacMillan Bloedel began experimenting with selective logging—as opposed to traditional harvesting methods like clear-cutting and "slash-and-burn"—in 1989. While the process is much more complex and expensive, it is also more palatable to nature-lovers. MacBlo also used million-dollar public relations campaigns to tout its land use planning efforts, which included wildlife and fish surveys as well as long-running replanting programs. A special "Annual Environmental Report" first published in 1993, also publicized the firm's efforts to comply with environmental standards. Nonetheless, public mistrust of MacBlo's stewardship continued to run high in the 1990s. In 1993, the battle moved to the Clayoquot Sound region on the west coast of Vancouver Island. The government, which had formerly protected this region, opened two-thirds of the timberland to harvesting that April. The resulting conflict attracted worldwide attention during the summer of 1993, when 800 protesters were arrested while trying to prevent logging in the region. A government-sponsored evaluation of the area (completed in 1995) determined that Clayoquot could be sustainably harvested, an apparent victory for MacMillan Bloedel. While allowing logging, however, the report also established stringent new controls, limiting the amount of trees taken out and the number of roads into the forest, as well as requiring extraordinary methods of timber removal like helicopters and hot air balloons. The new regulations made Clayoquot one of the most expensive logging operations on the continent. Government sanction also did not exonerate MacBlo from daily protests that continued into 1995.

Stymied by the government, environmentalists took their case to MacMillan Bloedel's customers in Great Britain, Germany and the United States. Under threats of a consumer boycott, the British arm of the Scott Paper Company annulled a US$5 million contract with MacBlo in 1994. In spite of these continued efforts to dissuade Macmillan Bloedel from logging the Clayoquot forest, the company appeared convinced that backing down on this front would only encourage new challenges to its land use policies.

Economically, the early 1990s were distinguished by low demand for pulp and paper, declining prices for MB's largely commodity products, and correspondingly poor financial results. The company lost a record $93.4 million in 1991 and another $48.8 million in 1992. Cost reductions, asset sales, and the beginning of an economic recovery helped lift MB back into the black in 1993. Although 1994's net earnings, at $180.2 million, more than tripled those of the previous year, MB President and CEO Robert Findlay challenged his recently-reorganized company to reach much higher. That year, the firm announced the implementation of "Gap Attack," a strategic plan to raise MB's return on capital employed (before interest and income taxes) to 20 percent, thereby ranking the company among the most profitable in the global forest products industry.

Principal Subsidiaries:

Altair Property and Casualty Corporation; Forest Industries Flying Tankers Limited (57.5%); MacMillan Bloedel Building Limited; MacMillan Bloedel Building Materials Limited; MacMillan Bloedel (Georgia) Limited; Vancouver Marine Engines Ltd.; MacMillan Bloedel of America Inc.; MacMillan Bloedel Financial Inc. (U.S.); MacMillan Bloedel Inc. (U.S.); MacMillan Bloedel Packaging Inc.; MacMillan Bloedel Timberlands Inc. (U.S.); MacMillan Bloedel (Delaware) Inc. (U.S.); MacMillan Bloedel (U.S.A.); MacMillan Bloedel Paper Sales Incorporated; MacMillan Bloedel Energy Inc.; American Cemwood Corporation; Fibres International, Inc. (51%); MacMillan Bloedel Pty. Limited (Australia); Camarin Limited (Barbados); Canadian Transport Company Limited (Barbados); MacMillan Bloedel Finance Limited (Barbados); MacMillan Bloedel FSC Ltd. (Barbados); MacMillan Bloedel Pulp and Paper Sales Limited (Great Britain); MacMillan Bloedel (Asia) Limited (Hong Kong); MacMillan Bloedel (Ireland); MacMillan Bloedel K.K. (Japan); MacMillan Bloedel Guadiana, S.A. de C.V. (Mexico); MacMillan Bloedel (Limburg) N.V. (Netherlands); Canadian Maas River Investment N.V. (Netherlands Antilles); MacMillan Bloedel St. Maarten N.V. (Netherlands Antilles).

Further Reading:

Lush, Patricia, "World Watching as B.C. Releases Clayoquot Report," *Globe and Mail,* May 29, 1995, p. B1.

MacKay, Donald, *Empire of Wood: The MacMillan Bloedel Story,* Vancouver: Douglas & McIntyre, 1982.

Matas, Robert, "Clayoquot: the Sound and the Fury," *Globe and Mail,* May 22, 1993, p. A1.

McMurdy, Deirdre, "Bay Street's Bonanza: the Edper Empire Sells Off Assets to Raise $2 Billion in Cash," *Maclean's,* February 22, 1993, pp. 18-20.

Watt, Keith, "Woodsman, Spare That Tree!," *Globe and Mail,* February 16, 1990, p. 48.

—Gwen M. LaCosse
—updated by April Dougal Gasbarre

MAGNA

Magna International Inc.

36 Apple Creek Boulevard
Markham, Ontario L3R 4Y4
(905) 477-7766
Fax: (905) 475-0776

Public Company
Incorporated: 1961 as Magna Electronics Corporation
  Limited
Employees: 21,000
Sales: $3.56 billion
Stock Exchanges: New York Toronto Montreal
SICs: 6711 Holding Company; 3711 Motor Vehicles
  & Car Bodies

A leading global supplier of automotive systems, assemblies, and components, Magna International Inc. ranks as one of the largest manufacturing concerns in Canada, with 83 operating divisions located throughout North America and Europe. The company recorded rapid growth during the 1970s and particularly during the 1980s, then stumbled during the late 1980s and early 1990s, falling victim to burdensome debt and overzealous management. By the mid-1990s, Magna International had fully recovered and regained its reputation as a powerful force in the automotive parts market. A maker of a wide variety of parts for automobiles, including air bags, seating systems, electro-mechanical devices, and stamped and welded metal assemblies, Magna International recorded $3.56 billion in sales in 1994 and generated $234.4 million in net income.

In 1957, Frank Stronach decided to open his own business and realize an entrepreneurial dream he had held since he was a young tool-and-die apprentice in his native Austria. For the then 25-year-old Stronach, the establishment of his own business, a small tool-and-die company named Multimatic Investments Limited, was a remarkable achievement considering his age and financial standing, but Stronach's inaugural year of business ownership would be overshadowed by his achievements after 1957. In the years ahead, Stronach would become much more than a small business owner of a tool-and-die company; Stronach would become one of the most influential and progressive business leaders in Canada, transforming his stature in the Canadian business world from a fledgling entrepreneur to the revered chairman of a multi-billion dollar automotive parts empire named Magna International Inc.

By the time Stronach was ready to open his own business, he already had been working as a tool-and-die maker for more than a decade. Born in Kleinsemmering, Austria in 1932, Stronach left school at age 14 to train as a tool-and-die-maker, forgoing his education to begin his life's work. Nine years later, in 1954, Stronach left Austria and moved to Canada, arriving with one suitcase and $200. Stronach worked for a year as a tool-and-die maker at Keicher Engineering in Kitchener, Ontario, then moved to Toronto where he worked in the same capacity for Peerless Engineering. It was during these first three years in Canada when Stronach began to develop a management philosophy that proved to be crucial to his future success.

Stronach's fateful lesson came after his employer promised to make him a partner, a promise his employer never kept. Disgruntled, Stronach quit and founded Multimatic Investments Limited, using a $1,000 bank loan to open his own business. As an entrepreneur, Stronach fared well, employing 20 workers in his small shop after two years of operation, including an ambitious foreman who asked to become Stronach's partner. Stronach agreed, but unlike his former employer Stronach fulfilled his promise, reportedly telling his foreman, "Why don't we open up a new factory and give you an ownership in it?" What followed was the genesis of Stronach's unique approach to management, an operating philosophy that ceded considerable power to Multimatic's managers and underpinned Stronach's climb from novice entrepreneur to a position of sweeping influence and substantial wealth. "Fair Enterprise," as Stronach's approach to participatory management was later dubbed, would contribute significantly to Magna International's enviable performance several decades later, but during the late 1950s, when Stronach first was experimenting with his Fair Enterprise management concept, Magna International had yet to be created.

The predecessor company to Magna International was formed in 1961, when six companies banded together to create Magna Electronics Corporation Limited. Magna Electronics represented an amalgamation of Magna Electronics Ltd., Magna Metal Fabricators Ltd., Duncairn Holdings Ltd., Verial Metal Fabricators Ltd., Southern Manufacturing & Equipment Ltd., and Petronics Ltd., the assets of which were purchased through a public offering in January 1962. A maker of precision parts for the electronics, computer, radar, aircraft, and missile industries, Magna Electronics initially conducted its manufacturing operations in five Toronto plants, serving both industrial and defense customers, but quickly grew, acquiring additional businesses and benefitting from a substantial backlog of manufacturing orders.

Bolstered by large contracts with the U.S. and Canadian governments to supply precision parts for military applications, Magna Electronics maneuvered through its first decade of existence, its last without the leadership of Stronach. Stronach, who broadened Multimatic's manufacturing scope by diversifying into the production of stamped automotive components once his tool-and-die business was flourishing, became a controlling shareholder in Magna Electronics when his company merged with Magna Electronics in 1969. For Magna Electronics, the merger was a significant development.

The addition of Multimatic gave Magna Electronics what would later become its core business — the production of automotive parts — and the managerial talents of Stronach, who would transform Magna Electronics into one of the most successful companies of its kind in the world.

Along with the capital assets of Multimatic, Magna Electronics also inherited the decentralized system of corporate governance created by Stronach, which would predicate Magna Electronics' meteoric rise in the years to come and quickly elevate Stronach to the top of the company's leadership ladder. By giving authority and profit incentives to managers, Fair Enterprise imbued Magna Electronics with an entrepreneurial spirit that placed an emphasis on innovation and profitability, particularly after 1971 when all employees and not just management were given a percentage of annual profits and ownership in the company. Stronach was named chairman and chief executive officer two years later, in 1973, when Magna Electronics Corporation Limited became Magna International Inc., marking the formal beginning of the Stronach era at the diversified manufacturing concern.

Once in power, Stronach put his trust in the management structure he had created, delegating much of his authority to his plant managers and employees, all of whom owned a percentage of the company and were entitled to a percentage of the profits generated by the particular factory in which they were employed. The result was a loosely affiliated group of small factories that operated essentially as a corporate fiefdom, a fiefdom superintended by Stronach, who, in turn, relied on his managers to operate the network of manufacturing facilities composing Magna International independently. By operating Magna International in this manner, Stronach eliminated layers of bureaucracy that otherwise would have slowed the company's decision-making process, giving Magna International the agility to respond quickly to changing business conditions. Further buttressing the company's position in relation to its competition was the focus on profitability inherent in the Fair Enterprise concept, which materially rewarded individuals who made prudent decisions and steered the company in the most advantageous direction.

As it had for roughly 15 years, the Fair Enterprise concept of employee equity and profit participation inculcated a spirit to succeed, propelling Magna International's growth as the diversified manufacturer maneuvered through the 1970s. Although enviable annual sales growth was recorded throughout the decade, Magna International's most profitable years arrived during the 1980s, after the company's broad manufacturing scope was narrowed, engendering a more tightly focused manufacturing organization.

The heavy involvement in manufacturing precision parts for the electronics, computer, radar, aircraft, and missile industries that supported Magna Electronics during the 1960s continued to contribute a substantial amount of revenue during Stronach's first decade of leadership, but by the early 1980s this segment of the company's business was divested. In 1981, Magna International sold its aerospace and defense businesses to concentrate more heavily on the automotive sector,

where Stronach's involvement dated back to Multimatic's early years as a manufacturer of stamped automotive parts. Although Magna International retained a 20 percent interest in its defense and aerospace businesses, the company from 1981 on would become chiefly a manufacturer of automotive parts, supplying major North American car manufacturers with automotive components. For Stronach, the decision to carve a greater presence in the automotive market was highly advantageous, sparking a period of unprecedented growth that soon made Magna International one of the largest automotive component suppliers in the world.

Once Magna International's unique managerial system was focused on a single market, the company quickly flourished and secured a commanding position in the automotive parts industry. Expansion-minded managers given the authority and incentive to make Magna International a dominant manufacturer quickly did so, accounting in large part for the company's enormous growth during the 1980s, when annual sales increased 13-fold. By the middle of the decade, with more than 60 manufacturing facilities in the United States and Canada churning out automotive parts, annual sales had eclipsed the $1 billion plateau, up from $300 million in 1983, casting both Stronach and Magna International into the public spotlight.

Encouraged by his success and the praise Fair Enterprise had earned from the North American business press, Stronach began to pursue other interests during the latter half of the decade, entrusting the stewardship of Magna International to the capable managers who had accounted for much of its success. Although he had been working for approximately 40 years by this point, Stronach's sabbatical from Magna International was not spent resting on his laurels; instead he threw himself once again into the role of entrepreneur, launching a variety of business ventures that met with only a modicum of success. He founded a sports clothing company, started a business and lifestyle magazine named *Vista*, opened Rooney's, a Toronto disco, and opened a restaurant named after his daughter Belinda, but his most widely publicized endeavor was his campaign as a Liberal candidate for the 1988 federal election. Running against a little-known Conservative candidate, Stronach was soundly defeated, losing his chance to help implement what he believed was the ideal economic system for Canada. In the years leading up to his bid for a seat in Parliament, Stronach had been known to diagram such an economic model, then autograph it for admirers, but once swept aside by the 1988 Conservative landslide, his political aspirations were dashed and he returned to Magna International the day after his defeat. What he discovered there was more disheartening than the election day results: Magna International, it appeared, was on the brink of failure.

During Stronach's absence, Magna International's management had been overly ambitious, expanding whenever the opportunity to expand presented itself. Operating without the financial and authoritative constraints that held capital spending in check at other companies, Magna International's debt mushroomed, bloated by the same sales and plant managers who had aggressively led the company toward explosive growth earlier in the decade. By the time Stronach returned, the company's debt had reached $1 billion, making as prolific a rise as Magna International's sales volume during the halcyon early and mid-1980s. Stronach's homecoming could not have occurred at a more inauspicious moment. Magna International's situation, however, was about to go from bad to worse.

Magna International's debt threatened to cripple the company to be sure, but the result of over-spending also increased business, fueling a steady rise in sales that lifted the company toward the $2 billion mark. That temporary bubble of hope burst in 1990, when automobile sales plummeted during the onset of a recession. With $1 billion of debt, Magna International was ill-prepared for the situation. For the year, Magna International recorded the first loss in its history, a staggering $224 million, and it appeared, according to the most pessimistic prognostications, that the company was destined for bankruptcy. Stronach, however, was not one of those pessimists.

While the company's financial health deteriorated, anxious bankers began pressuring Magna International's executives to break up the company and sell its assets. Others called for Stronach's ouster, but Stronach moved quickly to restore the company's stalwart position in the automotive parts market. In early 1990, Stronach implemented an austerity program designed to slash debt and to instill greater discipline and more prudent planning among the company's ranks. Nearly half of the company's 120 factories were sold, headquarters staff was trimmed by 50 percent, and 2 of 3 corporate jets were sold, as company-wide cost-cutting measures were effected to reduce Magna International's debt. Additionally, factory managers were stripped of some of their wide-ranging power to authorize new expenditures and instructed instead to clear any major spending with senior executives.

By the following year, in 1991, Magna International amazingly had returned to making a profit, recording $16.5 million in net income after 1990's disastrous $224 million loss. The company's stunning recovery was regarded as one of the largest and fastest corporate turnarounds in Canadian history, a feat one company executive likened to "trying to put a parachute back in the bag during a windstorm." More remarkable was the economic environment in which Magna International's recovery was achieved, as the recession that first precipitated the company's plunge intensified, severely affecting automobile manufacturers and their suppliers. In 1991 alone, the three largest U.S. automobile manufacturers, General Motors, Ford, and Chrysler, collectively racked up $7.6 billion in losses and began closing manufacturing plants, but Magna International continued to record profit gains, generating $98 million in net income in 1992 and $140 million in 1993.

Although its largest customers were hobbled by dropping automobile sales, Magna International's profits and sales volume continued to increase because many of the manufacturing facilities the Detroit automobile makers were closing were their own parts departments. Consequently, Ford, General Motors, and Chrysler increasingly turned to automotive parts makers like Magna International to fill the void created by their scaled-down manufacturing operations. Ironically, the same

expensive and modern manufacturing facilities built during the 1980s that had greatly contributed to Magna International's prodigious debt were now contributing to its recovery, putting the company once again into a commanding position in the automotive parts market.

As Magna International entered the mid-1990s, record profit gains helped erase painful memories of the troubled late 1980s and early 1990s. In 1994, the company collected $234 million in net income on sales of $3.5 billion, both of which were record highs and evidence of robust growth. Encouraged by this success and with debt virtually eliminated, the company was aggressively pursuing a greater presence in Europe as it charted its course for the late 1990s and beyond, confident that expansion overseas would fuel its future growth.

Principal Subsidiaries:

Magna International of America, Inc.; Atoma International Inc.; Cosma International Inc.; Decoma International Inc.; Tesma International Inc.

Further Reading:

Bryant, Adam, "3 Car-Part Makers Worth Watching," *New York Times,* February 10, 1992, p. D4.
Cameron, Stevie, "Magna Chief Is Dreaming of High Office in a Turner Government," *Globe and Mail,* February 18, 1988, p. A2.
"Company Reports," *Financial Post,* January 16, 1965, p. 19.
Dalglish, Brenda, "Defying the Odds," *Maclean's,* October 7, 1991, pp. 52-3.
Daly, John, "Driving in a New Direction," *Maclean's,* December 13, 1993, pp. 40-2.
Doak, Jim, "Don't Get Suckered into Playing It Safe," *Canadian Business,* April 1994, p. 19.
"Electronics," *Financial Post,* February 26, 1968, p. 43.
Enchin, Harvey, "Curbing Expansion," *Globe and Mail,* March 9, 1991, p. B1.
Goold, Douglas, "Magna Prepares for Tough Times," *Globe and Mail,* May 5, 1995, p. B5.
Henry, Jim, "Magna International Grows as Makers Winnow Suppliers," *Automotive News,* January 3, 1994, p. 7.
Johnson, Arthur, "Man of Parts," *Canadian Business,* December 1992, p. 80.
Kidd, Kenneth, "Magna's Next Hurrah," *Globe and Mail,* May 22, 1992, p. P37.
Kindel, Stephen, "Magna International: Northern Phoenix?," *FW,* October 1, 1991, pp. 14-5.
"Magna CEO Quits Job," *Automotive News,* October 24, 1994, p. 2.
"Magna Expects Record Year," *Financial Post,* June 9, 1962, p. 24.
"Magna Jockeys for Europe with New Airbag Partner," *Automotive News,* September 12, 1994, p. 22. Montgomery, Leland, "Magna International," *FW,* April 14, 1992, p. 57.
Pritchard, Timothy, "Magna and No. 2 Man Split," *Globe and Mail,* October 20, 1994, p. B1.
Romain, Ken, "Magna Bites a Big Bullet," *Globe and Mail,* March 17, 1990, p. B1.
Sinek, Jeremy, "Magna Buys Airbag Firm," *Automotive News,* September 27, 1993, p. 2.

————, "New Mantra for Magna: Avoid Debt,"
Automotive News, January 25, 1993, p. 22.
"Small Electronics Firm Gets $540,000 from Public,"
Financial Post, January 6, 1992, p. 4.

—Jeffrey L. Covell

Maple Leaf Foods Inc.

30 St. Clair Avenue West
Toronto, Ontario M4V 3A2
(416) 766-4311
Fax: (416) 926-2018

Public Company
Incorporated: 1927 as Canada Packers Ltd.
Employees: 11,000 *Sales:* $3.2 billion
Stock Exchanges: Toronto Montreal
SICs: 2010 Meat Products; 2015 Poultry
   Slaughtering and Processing; 2030 Preserved Fruits
   and Vegetables; 2051 Bread, Cake, and Related
   Products

Maple Leaf Foods Inc. was formed in 1927 as Canada Packers Ltd., during a period of consolidation among Canadian meat packers. The decade was a hard one for Canadian meat packers, who were increasingly reliant on exports for expansion. Prior to the 1900s, miners and settlers had provided an expanding market, but the domestic market leveled off with the century's beginning. As worldwide demand soared, so did production, creating a volatile industry susceptible to both agricultural and manufacturing cycles.

Meat production had increased to meet the demand during World War I, but in the aftermath Canada was cut off from much of the European market, and in 1921 the United States imposed a tariff on Canadian beef. By the mid-1920s Canada faced new competition for the vast American market from Argentina and Australia. Tariffs and cheaper competition made reliance on the U.S. market difficult for Canadian agricultural producers for many years after.

The Canadian domestic market could not absorb the surplus created by these pitfalls, and the number of meat processing plants dropped from 86 to 76 between 1912 and 1927. For nearly the same period, the number of food producers also decreased, yet employment and value added by the manufacturer grew.

In 1927 the Harris Abattoir Company of Toronto acquired three smaller meat packers. Unlike its competitors, Harris had remained profitable during the 1920s through substantial cuts in personnel. With distribution branches throughout Canada, Harris's earnings easily overshadowed those of the companies it purchased.

Gunns Ltd., a Toronto packer, transferred its stock to Harris in February when it found itself unable to obtain credit. In June Harris purchased the much smaller Canadian Packing Company Ltd., and in August Harris merged with William Davies Ltd., Canada's oldest meat packer. The new holding company was named Canada Packers Ltd., and in its first year it made a profit of more than $1 million.

The four companies remained separate operating units and continued to compete with each other, although by 1929 the Harris Abattoir offices in Toronto had become the central headquarters. However, the companies could not survive the Depression in this manner. Meat prices were high relative to other commodities following the stock market collapse, and drought in the western provinces produced higher unemployment and lower consumer demand for meat. Already merging slowly, heavy losses in 1931 forced the closure of the William Davies Toronto plant and the formation of a single company at the beginning of 1932. By the following year operating expenses had been drastically cut—only five of nine plants remained, the work force had been cut by 40 percent, and total expenses had been reduced by $7 million annually.

During the mid-1930s the company revived. The Ottawa Agreements allowed 280 million pounds of bacon a year to be exported to England, giving Canadian companies entry into a market previously filled by European companies. The agreement increased production at all plants at a crucial point in Canada Packers's development.

Simultaneously, the company's by-product division, which had been selling scraps for fertilizer, began to sell a mixture of scraps as a feed concentrate for animal food, a new venture that proved extremely profitable. Thirty years later the fertilizer business would be sold entirely, but animal feed remained an active and relatively reliable division for the company under the name of Shur-Gain.

In 1936 the company began its first expansion since its formation. It built a meat processing plant in Alberta and acquired a tannery in Ontario. This growth continued as British bacon and American beef imports reduced livestock surpluses. In 1938 Canada Packers opened an additional packing house; renovations of other plants brought capital investment between 1935 and 1938 to more than $2.5 million.

During World War II Canada continued to be a major supplier of meat to England—the amount of bacon shipped overseas more than doubled during the course of the war. Demand increases brought about the first labor shortage in Canada's meat packing history. Canada Packers's work force more than doubled to over 11,000.

Increased postwar demand allowed continued expansion, but improvements in infrastructure and employment for returning soldiers were needed. In response to an anticipated recession, the company stepped up its diversification efforts. The company's work force was nearly as large then as it is now, but overall production constantly expanded in the succeeding decades.

The emphasis on wartime efficiency required the establishment of a research laboratory, leading Canada Packers into synthetic vitamins, gelatin, synthetic detergents, and dairy products by the end of the war. By 1946 the chemical applications of animal by-products being investigated by the research lab would warrant the status of a separate division.

Another wartime development was the creation of union representation. During 1943 and 1944 Canada Packers agreed to representation by the United Packinghouse Workers of America, later the Canadian Food and Allied Workers Union. It was not long before the bargaining unit began to have an impact on earnings, as it would for a number of years to come. In 1947 a nationwide strike involving more than 16,000 meat packing workers occurred. No longer a wartime necessity, food production was once again controlled by the manufacturers. Canada Packers and a competitor negotiated new contracts two months later.

Since World War II, Canada Packers's sales have been greater than its two closest competitors' combined. The anticipated recession never hit the company as population growth and prosperity increased demand for meat and all other food products. The research lab, which had so far worked only on chemical development, began to look for improved production methods. Automated slaughtering operations finally replaced the outdated manual process, and the company kept pace with the industry by applying new technology to the mass production of poultry.

During the decades following the war, Canada Packers made its first significant transition to meet new demand. In the 1950s the per capita consumption of poultry doubled, and it continued to increase during each following decade. Through timely acquisition, investment, and the development of a new feather-cleaning company, the company began to increase its presence in the poultry industry. The company also entered oil production through acquisition in 1951.

Canada Packers's postwar expansion was rapid and prominent. The 1955 purchase of two packers brought the company into a dispute with the Restrictive Trade Practices Commission. However, Canada Packers argued successfully that industry-wide competition had increased and that the purchase would have no restraining effect.

J. S. McLean, president since the company's formation and the man responsible for the company's postwar diversification, retired in 1954 and was succeeded by his son William. Late in the 1950s the company reorganized its many businesses into separate divisions, including feed and fertilizer, consumer products, and canned and frozen vegetables. By 1958 only 55 percent of sales were from meat.

Canada Packers kept capital investment steady throughout the 1960s, continuing expansion and diversification. To meet perennially increasing poultry demand, the company built two plants—in New Brunswick and Quebec—expanded operations in Ontario and Manitoba, and acquired an Alberta plant. In 1963 only 36 percent of its assets were devoted to livestock products.

Although sales had increased more than 50 percent since 1951, the 1960s brought about the most dramatic changes for the food-processing industry to date. As international distribution became more common, production became more specialized. During this period, North American beef came to spend more time in transit than any other meat, reflecting the specialized processes of raising cattle and producing meat. As Canada's largest processor, Canada Packers had much to contribute to this changing environment.

During the 1960s the company created the largest private food-research facility in Canada. Inventories as well as product composition were determined through data processing centers in Toronto, Montreal, Winnipeg, and Edmonton, and new meat packing technology in such areas as packaging and flavoring were implemented in a $10 million Toronto facility.

In addition to these technological advances, Canada Packers expanded internationally during the decade. The company purchased meat packers in England, West Germany, and Australia and set up trading companies in London and Hamburg. Trading operations with the United States also grew, as did its interest in Southeast Asia. By 1969, exports exceeded $145 million, nearly 16.5 percent of company sales.

With the sale of the fertilizer sector, the feed operation became the Shur-Gain division and investment in feed mills intensified. In 1966 the United Packinghouse Workers of America led its first strike since 1947. Although the strike was national, it hit Canada Packers hardest. Another strike in 1969 also affected earnings. Despite inflationary stress and an increasingly competitive climate in the meat packing industry, the company continued to increase capital spending. Between 1970 and 1977 Canada Packers spent $137 million on expanded facilities. It also increased its overseas presence by purchasing two more Australian meat processors. Even though these subsidiaries did poorly for several years, they were expected to fill the growing Asian demand.

During the 1970s Canada Packers became a more diversified food processor and separated the management of its other food production groups from meat packing. The company granted division status to its fruit and vegetable segment in 1970 (York Farms brand), poultry in 1971, and edible oils and dairy in 1975. The chemical division, created in the late 1960s, became more significant with the 1975 establishment of Harris Laboratories, which developed pharmaceuticals for human use. In response to continual growth in demand for drugs related to feedlot production, the division also created MTC Pharmaceuticals for the veterinary-product industry.

Overseas packers and lean margins continued to plague the company, but its diversification kept earnings at acceptable levels. Non-food sales contributed 15 percent of the total; it was the only sector to show significant increases in the early 1970s. Animal feeds did grow steadily, helping to ease the earnings drain caused by meat. Valentine N. Stock became president of Canada Packers in 1978. As the company entered the 1980s, earnings margins were still lower than expected, less than one percent for the third consecutive year. Sales value had increased, but sales volume remained the same. The increases in product value had benefits but also added to higher-cost inventories. With relatively low long-term debt, at $34.7 million, the company planned to grow through acquisitions and to earn higher margins through packaged meats. Because consumers continued to demand convenience, meat processing was the only growth area in the company's core business. Stock also planned to increase non-food and international operations, despite disappointing results overseas.

Canadian food processors experienced a bad year in 1979 due to increased costs for meat and a seven-week labor dispute that closed some facilities. Canada Packers's competitor, McCain Foods Ltd. of New Brunswick, increased its holding in Canada Packers to 10.3 percent, fueling takeover rumors. As a precaution, Canada Packers repurchased 3.5 percent of its shares, but takeover remained unlikely because the McLean family and their associates controlled 34 percent of the company's shares.

As expected, the company looked to international markets by acquiring Delmar Chemicals Ltd., a supplier to the pharmaceutical industry, for $18.2 million. Delmar was coupled with the company's existing pharmaceutical division to increase non-food exports. Nonetheless, the company remained close to its food core and Maple Leaf brand of meats and also accepted a $4 million grant from the Ontario government to construct a canola (rapeseed oil) processing plant.

By 1981 profits had soared 50 percent over their 1979 level, up to a record $30 million. But the cyclical nature of the industry still affected the company as pork operations proved disappointing, carcass prices rose, and a reduction in consumer demand and greater competition among packers continued to erode earnings. Occasional plant closings continued to be the industry norm.

In 1983 the Canadian government began investigations of price fixing involving Canada Packers and four other meat packers. Some of the charges were dropped in 1984, and although the other companies would eventually plead guilty, Canada Packers was completely exonerated and partially reimbursed for legal expenses in 1986.

Profits plunged to their 1979 level in 1983, even though sales continued to grow. Earnings were affected by the cost of plant closings and poor performances in fresh meat operations, and foreign subsidiaries proved disappointing. The packing house division, in fact, suffered the worst loss in its history, but processed meat remained profitable. As a result, the company earmarked $50 million for structural improvements in these profitable areas and cut hundreds of jobs in fresh meat. Although its outlook was better, previous profit levels looked unreachable.

Another strike in 1984 that involved 3,700 workers at most of the company's 12 plants eventually cost Canada Packers $7.5 million. Although it lasted only five weeks, the strike kept the company's Maple Leaf brand from store shelves and strengthened competitors. As the country's largest meat packer, the strike of the United Food Commercial Worker's Union (UFCW) demon-

strated the company's vulnerability to labor disputes. The strike caused a slight earnings decline for 1985.

Non-food products showed a surprising decrease in profits for 1983, proving that the company could not venture far from its traditional core business—one with fiercely competitive margins but with proven cash flow. Although making up less than half of Canada Packers's profits, meat products still accounted for two-third of its sales.

Despite setbacks, however, the mid-1980s were prosperous for the company. Increased cash flow allowed a four-year, $200 million revitalization spending plan. Poultry production was enlarged, reflecting the division's profitability and continued long-term potential.

A reorganization, begun in 1984 and completed by 1985, was the largest and most expensive in the company's history. Unprofitable businesses, including an ice cream plant and five slaughterhouses, were sold, and other meat plants and oil refineries were purchased and upgraded. Earnings for the next four years climbed at record rates from $25 million to more than $38 million. Canada Packers then entered a joint venture with Sea Farm of Norway and began fish farming in New Brunswick. By the late 1980s the company had production facilities on both coasts of Canada and viewed fish farming as one of its most promising growth industries.

Canada Packers circumvented another strike by reducing the scope of nationwide bargaining in 1986, a record year for earnings. By keeping negotiations on a provincial and single-plant level, the company quickly settled with the UFCW. As the meat packer with the most employees, Canada Packers's labor relations had a strong influence on the industry as a whole, making national strikes in the future less likely.

At the beginning of 1987 Valentine Stock died and James Hunter was appointed acting CEO. A. Roger Perretti, former vice-president of finance, became CEO at the beginning of 1989. During Stock's tenure, the company had seen a continued decline in beef demand and completed a ten-year consolidation. It consistently reduced dependence on fresh meat and turned to areas with higher and more reliable margins, like fish farming, processed foods, salad oils, and pharmaceuticals. Under Perretti, the company planned further acquisitions outside the meat industry.

Net income dropped to $12.59 million in 1990 from sales of just over $3 billion. The disappointing results were partially caused by overall market sluggishness. To counter the oncoming economic recession, the company once again responded by reorganizing. Specifically, Canada Packers majority owner, Hillsdown Holdings, consolidated its consumer foods division by closing plants and updating existing equipment. Importantly, Hillsdown officially merged Canada Packers with Maple Leaf Mills to form a new company; Maple Leaf Foods Inc. The company jettisoned non-performing divisions and whipped the organization into shape throughout the early 1990s.

In addition to reorganizing, Maple Leaf also began to focus on its cross-border operations, particularly in the United States. The advent of free trade with the United

States, in fact, had renewed the company's interest in that country, and by 1994 Maple Leaf was generating about eight percent of its sales from its southern neighbor. Likewise, its British, German, and Japanese subsidiaries also showed promise for long-term gains.

Maple Leaf suffered from lean margins during the early 1990s, but continued to show a profit as it had for every one of its more than 60 years in business. In addition, it continued to retain a market share of slightly less than half of all Canadian meat packing—an industry that totaled $8 billion in 1986. Sales during the early 1990s remained sluggish, but the company was able to cut costs through reorganization and boost profits slowly throughout the downturn. In fact, Maple Leaf's sales actually fell to $2.75 billion in 1992 while net income rose to $69.18 million. In 1993, moreover, profits rose to $70.12 million from revenues of $3.03 billion.

Maple Leaf's sales and profits rose again in 1994—to $3.18 billion and $75.73 million, respectively. Shortly after the end of that year, the company became the target of a takeover when Wallace McCain engineered a buyout, taking advantage of Maple Leaf's low debt and strong cash position. McCain had formerly run competitor McCain Foods, a company similar in size to Maple Leaf, before his brother and the board ousted him from his joint-chief-executive post. Meanwhile Maple Leaf Foods looked to the future, continuing to develop new technological applications and entering new food markets.

Principal Subsidiaries:

Clearview Turkey Farms; Corporate Foods Ltd. (68.5%); Buns Master Banker Systems Inc. (52.3%); Northam Food Trading Co.; Cana Foods Inc.; Shur-Gain Agresearch Inc.; Seafood Products Co. Ltd.; Fearmans Inc.; Groupe Shur-Gain Quebec Inc.; P.E.I. Produce Co. Ltd; Archibald Farms Ltd.; Keswick River Investments Ltd.; Sunny Glen Eggs Ltd.; Canada Packers (Japan) Inc. (65%); Canada Packers GmbH (Germany); Belize Mills Ltd.; Canada Packers (U.S.A.) Inc.; Maple Leaf Mills Ltd.; Canada Packers (Hong Kong Ltd.); Liberty Reduction Inc.; Mil'mer S.A. (France, 52%); Marcel Berard Ltee.; National Meats Inc.

Further Reading:

Brent, Paul, "Maple Leaf Foods Looks to U.S.," *Financial Post,* May 19, 1994, Section 1, p. 16.
———, "Maple Leaf Foods Profit Surges," *Financial Post,* March 10, 1995, Section 1, p. 7.
———, "Wallace McCain Makes $1.28 Bid for Rival MLF," *Financial Post,* March 7, 1995, Section 1, p. 1.
Waldie, Paul, "Moving on MLF," *Financial Post,* March 17, 1995, Section 1, p. 6.

—updated by Dave Mote

McCain Foods Limited

Main Street
Florenceville, New Brunswick E0J 1K0
(506) 392-5541
Fax: (506) 392-5332

Private Company Incorporated: 1956 as McCain
  Foods Limited
Employees: 12,500
Sales: $3.2 billion
SICs: 5148 Fresh Fruits & Vegetables; 5143
  Packaged Frozen Foods; 5149 Groceries &
  Related Products Not Elsewhere Classified

With more than 50 food-production facilities spread across four continents, McCain Foods Limited ranks as one of the premier food-processing companies in the world. The company began as a small producer of frozen french fries, then evolved into a diversified conglomerate involved in the production of pizzas, juice, oven meals, cheese, desserts, and vegetables. Roughly 80 percent of McCain Foods business during the mid-1990s was derived outside of Canada, particularly in Europe and Australia, where the company began establishing food production plants early in its history.

In the small town of Florenceville, New Brunswick, Harrison and Wallace McCain became involved in the potato business in the mid-1950s, following in the footsteps of their father. Over the next three decades, the two brothers would build their family-owned business into a multi-billion dollar enterprise, creating an empire that elevated the McCain family name to international prominence and earned its members enormous wealth. Together with the Sobeys, the Southerns, the Irvings, the Bronfmans, and the Lemaires, the McCain family ranked among the most successful and influential families in Canada.

To the residents of Florenceville, the McCain name was a familiar one before Harrison and Wallace started in business together. Their father, Andrew McCain, had owned a company named McCain Produce Ltd. that was involved in exporting potatoes and potato seed, but when he died in 1953 none of his six children took the reins of the family business—at least not immediately. As an inheritance, Andrew McCain left hundreds of acres of choice farmland and an extensive list of potato buyers and growers, which Harrison and Wallace

McCain used to start their own business in 1956, three years after their father's death. Named McCain Foods Limited, the two brothers' company was incorporated in May of that year, and began producing frozen french fries the following year in a small factory in Florenceville.

The newly created McCain Foods produced roughly 1,500 pounds of potato products an hour during its inaugural year of production, employing 30 workers who were able to generate slightly more than $150,000 in sales. It was an encouraging start for the company, but Harrison and Wallace McCain envisioned much more for their company. The two entrepreneurs were intent on dominating the processed potato industry, but instead of taking the conventional path toward growth by expanding into the United States, the McCains looked elsewhere, targeting areas neglected by other North American food processors. It was an astute move, enabling McCain Foods to capitalize on underdeveloped markets rather than butting against stiff and entrenched competition in the United States. The eldest of the two brothers, Harrison, was regarded as McCain Foods' visionary leader, while his brother Wallace was known more for his attention to detail and his ability to oversee the company's daily operation. Their contrasting yet complementary personalities served the company well, with Harrison steering the company in the right direction while Wallace ensured that operations proceeded in an efficient and logical manner. Led by these two men, McCain Foods moved forward after its first year of production, achieving enough success during its fledgling years to finance the company's first overseas expansion by the mid-1960s.

Initially the McCains set their sights on the European market for processed foods, beginning their international expansion in 1965 when they first began selling McCain frozen french fries in England. Three years later the company opened up another front by establishing a sales organization in Australia. Also in 1968 the company formed a subsidiary in the United Kingdom named McCain International Limited. As McCain Foods' first full decade of business drew to a close, its presence in England was strengthened by the construction of a french fry plant in Scarborough in 1969.

McCain Foods also entered the U.S. market for the first time in 1969, but as international expansion continued into the 1970s the company's involvement in the United States would take a back seat to its expansion in Europe and Australia. A french fry plant was acquired in Daylesford, Australia in 1971, then the following year the production capacity of the company's plant in Scarborough was doubled. Next, McCain Foods moved into Holland, purchasing a french fry plant in Werkendam in 1972 and another plant in Lewedorp in 1973. One year after the acquisition of the french fry plant in Lewedorp, McCain Foods diversified for the first time, beginning the production of frozen pizzas in a Florenceville prepared foods plant. The company would diversify again, into juice production in 1980 and cheese production in 1982, but the production of frozen french fries would remain as McCain Foods mainstay business throughout the 1970s, the 1980s and into the 1990s, propelling the company's growth and enabling further penetration into foreign markets.

Such was the case in 1976 when the company acquired a french fry plant in Burgos, Spain. That same year, the company's involvement in frozen pizza production was augmented with the addition of a pizza plant in Grand Falls, New Brunswick—its second in its home province—and another in Daylesford, Australia, the company's first pizza plant established on foreign soil. Two more pizza plants were added to the McCain Foods fold before the decade was through—one in Ballarat, Australia in 1979 and another in Scarborough the same year — while the company's french fry business was solidified with the acquisition of a production facility in Hoofddorp, Holland in 1978 and the construction of another french fry plant in Portage la Prairie, Manitoba.

By the end of the 1970s, annual sales had climbed to $360 million. Although the 1970s had been a decade of robust growth, the company's pace of financial and physical growth would be much greater during the 1980s, when McCain Foods' sales volume would climb from $360 million to more than $2 billion, positioning the company as one of the largest food processors in the world.

During the 1970s, McCain Foods had begun to vertically integrate its operations, purchasing a trucking company called Day & Ross to give the company a fleet of freezer trucks to carry its products across Canada. The acquisition of the trucking fleet marked the beginning of McCain Foods diversification into other business areas. The production of french fries had created a need for freezer trucks, which in turn facilitated the company's entry into the frozen juice market, giving its fleet of trucks a twofold purpose. McCain Foods' diversification into frozen pizza production also engendered the company's diversification into cheese production, enabling it to supply its pizza production plants with McCain cheese. The result was a largely self-sufficient enterprise with a broader scope, the advantages of which were borne out in the enviable growth recorded by McCain Foods' sales volume.

The company entered the juice business with the acquisition of a juice plant in Toronto from Sunny Orange Ltd. in 1980. Two years later the company acquired its first cheese processing operation when it purchased Darigold Products Ltd., a major processor based in Oakville, Ontario. In 1984 another Ontario-based dairy company was purchased, Tavistock Union Cheese and Butter Ltd., then a month later McCain Foods increased its presence in the Ontario dairy industry by acquiring Harrowsmith Cheese Factory Ltd., a medium-sized cheese processor based in Eastern Ontario. With the addition of these three dairy companies, McCain Foods was able to produce 35 million pounds of cheese a year for its frozen pizzas, a production capacity that added roughly $75 million to the company's annual sales volume, bringing the total to $847 million.

Concurrent with its diversification into juice and cheese, McCain Foods continued to increase its presence in the global french fry market during the early 1980s, adding two new plants in 1981 — one in Harnes, France and another in Grantham, England. In 1984 the company diversified again, acquiring a major vegetable processing plant in Smithton, Tasmania, a potato-based

animal food plant in Presque Isle, Maine, and a fish processing plant in Hull, England. In 1985, McCain's sales volume surpassed $1 billion, proving the value of the company's aggressive expansion and methodical diversification.

Since McCain Foods had first entered foreign markets in 1965, the company had opened 27 plants geared for the production of various food products. During a three year span between 1986 and 1989, 16 additional plants were either constructed or acquired, pushing the company's annual sales past the $2 billion mark by the end of the 1980s. Aside from bolstering its already prodigious interests in Australia, Canada, England, and Holland during this three-year span, McCain Foods carved a deeper presence in France and the United States, and entered Belgium for the first time, bringing a 100-percent increase in revenues. Expansion continued during the early 1990s, raising annual sales to $3 billion by 1992. That year, Harrison McCain underwent open-heart surgery, touching off a battle between the two brothers over who would succeed them as McCain Foods' leader. The brothers shared the company's chief executive position, with Harrison serving as chairman and Wallace as president. Each owned 33.4 percent of McCain Foods, with the remainder divided evenly between the families of their two deceased brothers, giving Harrison and Wallace equal say in the affairs of the company. McCain Foods' corporate bylaws, in fact, stipulated as much, placing Harrison and Wallace McCain on equal ground for a bitter struggle over the empire they had built.

As the feud intensified, each brother offered their proposed successor: Wallace opting for his son, Michael McCain, president and chief executive of the company's U.S. operations, McCain USA, and Harrison backing his nephew, Allison McCain, managing director of the company's British operations, McCain Foods (GB) Ltd. Neither brother approved of the other's selection, prompting Wallace to make a $1 billion bid in August 1993 for all the shares he did not own. The offer was rejected by McCain family members, then steps were reportedly taken to usurp Wallace's position at the top of McCain Foods. The rift between the brothers widened as time progressed until Wallace was forced out of the company in October 1994. The seven-member board of the family holding company, McCain Foods Group Inc., voted five to two to strip Wallace of his two titles, president and co-chief executive, ending his tenure at McCain Foods after nearly 40 years at the company's helm.

Bitter about his dismissal, which he described to *The Globe and Mail* as, "a termination without cause based solely on family politics," Wallace McCain left McCain Foods intent on acquiring a new food empire. In March 1995, he made a $1 billion bid for Toronto-based Maple Leaf Foods Inc., a food-processing conglomerate with $3 billion in annual sales and businesses involved in the production of a variety of foods, including french fries. The following month, Wallace McCain became the chairman and largest shareholder of Maple Leaf Foods, the only food-processing company in Canada large enough to rival McCain Foods, pitting the two brothers against each other for dominance in the Canadian food-processing industry.

Against the backdrop of this heated struggle for power, McCain Foods gained a new chief executive, Howard Mann, in March 1995. A British food executive, Mann assumed McCain Foods' chief executive position, with Harrison McCain serving as chairman. With Wallace McCain's Maple Leaf Foods and Harrison McCain's McCain Foods poised for a definitive struggle in the Canadian food-processing industry, the future of McCain Foods promised to include a most intriguing chapter in the company's history.

Principal Subsidiaries:

Bilopage Inc.; McCain Produce Inc.; McCain Refrigerated Foods Inc.; Valley Farms Limited; Thomas Equipment Limited; McCain Fertilizers Limited; Day & Ross Inc.; Day & Ross (Nfld.) Ltd.; Transport de l'Est Ltee.; McCain USA, Inc.; Tater Meal Inc.; McCain Transport Inc.; McCain Citrus Inc.; McCain Ellio's Foods Inc.; McCain Argentina SA; McCain Foods (GB) Limited; PAS (Grantham) Limited; Britfish Limited; Dansco Dairy Products Ltd.; Tolona Pizza Products Ltd.; McCain Foods Pty Ltd. (Australia); Saffries Pty. Ltd. (Australia); McCain Foods Ltd. (New Zealand); McCain Alimentaire SA (France); Beau Marais SA (France); McCain Sunnyland France SA; McCain Foods Holland BV; Keizer BV (Holland); McCain Foods Belgium NV.; McCain GmbH (Germany); McCain Foods Limited (Japan); McCain Espana SA (Spain)

Further Reading:

Burtin, Oliver, "Common Touch, Global Outlook Keys to McCain Foods Growth," *The Globe and Mail,* September 11, 1989, p. B8.
Cox, Kevin, "McCain Empire Poised for Transformation," *The Globe and Mail,* September 12, 1994, p. B1.
Farnsworth, Clyde H., "Canadian Family's Feud," *The New York Times,* October 30, 1994, p. F3.
Gutner, Toddi, "What's Yours Is Mine," *Forbes,* August 2, 1993, p. 68.
Heinzl, John, "Fuel Poured on McCain Fire," *The Globe and Mail,* October 26, 1994, p. B1.
Howlett, Karen, "McCains Spurn $1 Billion Bid," *The Globe and Mail,* August 25, 1993, p. A1.
"McCain and Able," *The Economist,* September 17, 1994, p. 75.
"McCain Court Feud Over as Wallace Drops Appeal," *The Globe and Mail,* May 31, 1995, p. B12.
"McCain Foods Expanding in Japan," *The Globe and Mail,* March 20, 1986, p. B16.
Saunders, John, "N.B. Village Watches in Awe," *The Globe and Mail,* March 9, 1995, p. A1.
———, "Wallace McCain Seeks New Food Empire," *The Globe and Mail,* March 7, 1995, p. A1.
Strauss, Marina, "McCain Purge Over, Official Says," *The Globe and Mail,* March 9, 1995, p. B4.

—Jeffrey L. Covell

Métro-Richelieu Inc.

11011 Maurice-Duplessis Blvd.
Montreal, Quebec H1C 1V6
(514) 643-1055
FAX: (514) 922-7791

Public Company
Founded: 1947 as Magasins La Salle Stores Limitée.
Employees: 6,240 *Sales:* $2.91 billion
Stock Exchanges: Montreal Toronto
SICs: 5141 Groceries, General Line; 5122 Drugs,
   Proprietaries, and Sundries; 6794 Patent Owners
   and Lessors.

With over one-third of Quebec's $12.5 billion food
retailing market, Métro-Richelieu Inc. ranks as the
province's second-largest player. Épiciers Unis Métro-
Richelieu Inc. is Métro-Richelieu's core wholesaling
business, contributing 67 percent of its 1994 revenues.
This subsidiary purchases and distributes produce,
grocery items, meat, frozen foods, and seafood to
affiliated, owned and independent retailers throughout
Quebec. Affiliated stores are operated under the Métro,
Marché Richelieu, and Les 5 Saisons marquees. Following a late-1980s diversification, Métro-Richelieu owned
and operated 25 discount "hypermarkets" under the
Super C banner. These operations contributed 20 percent of revenues in 1994. Institutional food service,
another relatively new business interest, contributed 7
percent to 1994's profits. Pharmaceutical wholesaling
and franchising through the McMahon-Essaim Inc.
subsidiary pitched in the remaining 6 percent of annual
sales. The Montreal-based firm also has a stake in the
Quebec Nordiques hockey club.

Métro-Richelieu retreated from late 1980s forays into
the neighboring province of Ontario and the United
States, limiting its operations to Quebec in the early
1990s. The company emerged from a major shakeout in
the regional food industry as a strong competitor in the
hotly-contested provincial market.

Although Métro-Richelieu has diversified from its historical focus on wholesaling, it retained vestiges of its
cooperative roots. Retailers who operated under the
Métro and Marché Richelieu marquees were required to
invest in Métro-Richelieu Inc. stock. In the early 1990s,
over half of the 480 independent retailers affiliated with
its wholesale business were also shareholders with

privileged voting rights and a significant enough stake in
the company to control its board of directors.

The company was incorporated in 1947 as Magasins la
Salle Stores Limitée. Later known as Métro Food Stores
Ltd., the firm evolved in the late 1970s and early 1980s
into a leading competitor in Quebec's retail food
industry through a series of mergers uniting several
grocery cooperatives. In 1976, the group merged with
Épiceries Richelieu Limitée to form Métro-Richelieu
Inc. The name changed to Métro-Richelieu Group Inc.
in 1979. In 1982, Métro-Richelieu acquired and merged
with United Grocers Inc. to form United Grocers
Métro-Richelieu Group Inc. These amalgamations
created Quebec's third-largest grocery company, a firm
with 75 percent of its volume concentrated in wholesale
distribution for its 660 affiliate-shareholders.

The formation of these cooperatives helped independent
supermarketers retain their autonomy while enabling
them to compete with larger rivals like Loblaw Co. Ltd.
and Provigo Inc. Co-ops pooled warehousing and distribution, thereby eliminating the middleman and cutting
overhead. Shared promotions saved money and increased marketing and advertising clout. Since affiliates
were required to own stock in the cooperative, they were
also entitled to a share of its profits.

The evolution and growth of Métro-Richelieu Inc. (the
name was shortened in 1986) was a manifestation of
declining population growth in the province, the maturation of the region's food distribution market, and the
intensified competition that resulted. By the early
1980s, Métro's merger strategy had earned it a third-
place ranking among Quebec's wholesale food companies. By that time, the wholesaler was racking up over $1
billion in sales and $2.5 million in profits.

In spite of its efforts to build up a strong presence, the
Métro-Richelieu suffered a stunning reversal in 1985,
losing $417,000 on sales of $1.3 billion. Jacques Maltais,
a relative newcomer to Métro with only three years'
experience, advanced to the wholesaler's presidency that
year. Maltais proposed a sweeping "modernization
program" that encompassed Métro's organizational
scheme, its operations, and its growth strategy. The first
part of Maltais's plan entailed the partial dissolution of
the cooperative organizational scheme. The company
went public with the sale of $27.5 million in subordinate
voting stock, but remained under the control of its
grocer-affiliates. Part of this capital infusion went
toward technological upgrades, including the installation of electronic point-of-sale systems, store renovations and expansions and other enhancements.

Following the lead of Quebec grocery industry leader
Provigo, Inc., Métro-Richelieu also undertook a diversification program in the late 1980s. Maltais reasoned
that geographic and product diversification would shelter the food company from economic cycles and supplement its skinny, but typical, one percent profit margins.
According to a December 1986 *Globe and Mail* article,
the new leader's plan enjoyed "a clear mandate from his
controlling shareholders." Over the course of just one
year, 1987, the company bought into restaurant and
sporting goods chains, pharmaceutical wholesaling and
retailing, institutional food service, and its own chain of
retail supermarkets.

Analysts (who enjoyed the 20-20 vision of hindsight) later characterized the diversification program as a miserable failure — four of the seven acquisitions were divested within five years of their purchase, and Métro-Richelieu incurred back-to-back losses in fiscal years 1989 and 1990 totaling over $25 million. The acquisition policy also cost president Maltais his job; he quit early in 1990. Marcel Guertin, who had maintained his position as chairman throughout the crisis, assumed the additional role of interim CEO, while Jacques Obry became president and chief operating operator.

Métro-Richelieu recruited two former executives of its primary competitor, Provigo Inc., and hired them in the fall of 1990. Pierre Lessard had served as Provigo's president for nine years when he resigned in 1985 after being "passed over" when the CEO's position came open. Lessard was characterized as a "cautious, conservative" leader who focused on the basics of the grocery industry — increasing volume and returns. In fact, some industry observers correlated his lack of daring with his lack of progress at Provigo, but by the early 1990s that "flaw" had become a virtue. H. Paul Gobeil formed the other half of the new management team. Gobeil did "double-duty" during the early 1990s, dividing his work week between Métro-Richelieu's vice-chairmanship and his previously-held chairmanship of Royal Trust Co. Called "a firm believer in deficit reduction," Gobeil was put in charge of financial planning. Both aged 48, the partners had worked together at Provigo for almost a decade before going their separate ways in 1985.

Under new direction, the company divested its restaurant and retail sporting goods interests to concentrate on the food and drug businesses. The companies that Métro retained from its ill-fated diversification evolved into vital contributors to the parent company's bottom line. La Ferme Carnaval Inc. had been acquired from Burnac Corp. for $135 million (half cash, half shares) in 1987. Founded in Quebec City in 1982, it had previously been a customer of Métro's warehouse operations. Within just five years, the supermarket chain had captured 20 percent of its hometown retail food market and expanded into Montreal. Although La Ferme Carnaval had been partly to blame for Métro's poor performance, Lessard and Gobeil elected to keep the discount grocery chain. Its positive contributions included the addition of 12 Super Carnaval stores. Carnaval also gave Métro a foothold in the fledgling warehouse/discount sector and vaulted it over struggling rival Steinberg Inc. to become Quebec's second-largest food retailer.

McMahon-Essaim Inc., a wholesale pharmaceutical distributor acquired for $6 million in 1986, also grew under Métro-Richelieu's custody. Over the course of its eight years in the Métro family, the company's sales increased from about $50 million to $186.3 million. An aggressive franchising program for the division's Brunet drugstores helped it evolve into the second largest player in the provincial pharmacy market by the early 1990s.

In 1992, the tough Quebec food market claimed a major victim, number-three chain Steinberg Inc. The three largest remaining competitors (according to rank) — Provigo (which was renamed Univa, Inc. that year), Métro-Richelieu, and Oshawa Group Ltd.'s Hudon et Deaudelin Inc. — divided the spoils of the decade-long battle for the provincial market among them. Métro-Richelieu bought 46 of Steinberg's 102 stores for just over $100 million. The new locations were an instant boon; Métro-Richelieu's profit rose 153 percent in the first quarter of 1993.

From fiscal 1990 to fiscal 1994, in fact, Métro-Richelieu's sales increased 33 percent, from $2.19 billion to $2.91 billion. Net earnings quadrupled during the same period, from a deficit of $9 million to a $37.2 million profit. The company was also able to reduce its long-term debt load by almost 75 percent, from $184.4 million to $46.7 million, thereby freeing up funds for capital investment. Part of the company's success was attributed to an advertising campaign begun in 1991. The ads, which featured the tagline, "Métro, grocers by profession," won numerous accolades from regional, national, and even international industry organizations.

Métro placed increased emphasis on its private label (or house brand) program in the 1990s. Private label products enable retailers to offer their customers a consistently low-priced product, yet retain higher profit margins for themselves. By the early 1990s, Métro-Richelieu's own-label program included over 1,500 products. In 1994, the company launched two new private lines: Éconochoix bargain-priced items and the controversial Norois Premium beer. Retailing at 12 percent less than its next-lowest-priced competitor, Métro's brew was the lowest-priced beer in the province. But Canada's beer establishment was quick to counter this incursion. Molson, Labatt, and the Quebec Brewers' Association filed a lawsuit to stop sales of the beer. Although sales of the brew were halted in 1994, an intermediate ruling allowed Métro to resume sales in 1995 pending a final decision. By mid-year, it was estimated that Norois had captured 2 percent of home consumption sales in the province. The case remained unsettled at mid-1995.

Métro-Richelieu entered 1995 with a bankroll of $32 million intended for renovations, store expansions, and construction of new stores. The company was in a strong competitive position, having increased its market share from 25 percent in 1990 to 32 percent in 1995. It appeared poised to capture the top position in the provincial food market from long-time rival Univa, which remained hobbled by heavy diversification-related debt. By the spring of 1995, Lessard was confident enough to reinstate the company's dividend for the first time since 1990.

Principal Subsidiaries:

Épiciers Unis Métro-Richelieu Inc.; La Ferme Carnaval Inc.; McMahon-Essaim Inc.; Alimentation Dallaire St.-Romuald Inc.

Further Reading:

Clifford, Edward, "Metro-Richelieu Looking Better," *Globe and Mail*, 17 June 1993, B11.
Gibbens, Robert, "Métro-Richelieu Buys Major Food Chain," *Globe and Mail*, 5 May 1987, B1.
_____, "Métro-Richelieu Seeking to Diversify," *Globe and Mail*, 30 December 1986, B6.

Gibbon, Ann, "Lessard Returns," *Globe and Mail*, 1 October 1990, B1.

————, "Métro-Richelieu Posts Profit Rise," *Globe and Mail*, 24 January 1995, B8.

————, "Richelieu Reports Profit," *Globe and Mail*, 29 January 1991, B9.

McKenna, Barrie and Ann Gibbon. "Provigo, Métro-Richelieu, Hudon to Carve up Steinberg," *Globe and Mail*, 23 May 1992, B1.

—April Dougal Gasbarre

Molson Companies Ltd.

1555 Notre Dame Street East
Montreal, Quebec H2L 2R5
(514) 521-1786
Fax: (514) 598-6969

Public Company
Incorporated: December 4, 1930
Employees: 14,700
Sales: $2.97 billion
Stock Exchanges: Toronto Vancouver Montreal
SICs: 5169 Chemicals & Allied Products, nec; 2082
    Malt Beverages.

Established in 1786, Molson Companies Ltd. is perhaps best known for its brewery, which is the oldest in North America. Molson Breweries supplanted long-time leader Labatt Brewing Co. as Canada's leading brewery in 1989, and claimed about half of the country's beer market by the mid-1990s. Molson has nurtured a distinctly Canadian character: its flagship beer brand is "Molson Canadian," its beers are brewed only in Canada, and its advertising aggressively pitches the "I am Canadian" line. Ironically, however, foreigners owned a controlling share of the Molson Companies' historic brewery following the incremental sale of a 60 percent stake in that business in the late 1980s and early 1990s. In the mid-1990s, its partners were Australia's Foster Brewing Group, which owned 40 percent of Molson Breweries, and America's Miller Brewing Co., which held 20 percent.

Under the direction of Marshall "Mickey" Cohen in the early 1990s, the Molson holding company shifted its focus from the low-growth beer industry to a business acquired in the late 1970s—specialty cleaning and sanitizing chemicals. By the mid-1990s, this segment of Molson's operations, the Diversey Corp. subsidiary, had become its largest revenue generator.

The history of Molson brewing began soon after the 18-year-old John Molson emigrated from Lincolnshire, England, during the late eighteenth century. He arrived in Canada in 1782 and became a partner in a small brewing company outside Montreal's city walls on the St. Lawrence River a year later. In 1785 he became the sole proprietor of the brewery, closed it temporarily, and sailed to England to settle his estate and buy brewing equipment. Upon his return in 1786, with a book

entitled *Theoretical Hints on an Improved Practice of Brewing* in hand, the novice started brewing according to his own formula. By the close of the year, Molson had produced 80 hogsheads (4300 gallons) of beer. In 1787 Molson remarked, "My beer has been almost universally well liked beyond my most sanguine expectations." His statement in part reflects the quality of the brew, but it also indicates that Molson had excellent timing; he faced very little competition in the pioneer community.

Before electrical refrigeration became available, Molson was confined to a 20-week operating season because it had to rely on ice from the St. Lawrence River. Nevertheless, production grew throughout the 1800s as the Montreal brewery steadily added more land and equipment. Population growth and increasingly sophisticated bottling and packaging techniques also contributed to Molson's profitability in the early days.

It was not long before Molson became an established entrepreneur in Montreal, providing services in the fledgling community that contributed to its growth into a major Canadian city. Molson first diversified in 1797 with a lumberyard on the brewery property. A decade later he launched the *Accommodation,* Canada's first steamboat, and soon thereafter he formed the St. Lawrence Steamboat Company, also known as the Molson Line. The steam line led to Molson's operation of small-scale financial services between Montreal and Quebec City; eventually the services became Molson's Bank, chartered in 1855. In 1816 John Molson signed a partnership agreement with his three sons, John Jr., William and Thomas, ensuring that the brewery would remain under family control. He was elected the same year to represent Montreal East in the legislature of Lower Canada and opened the Mansion House, a large hotel in Montreal that housed the public library, post office, and Montreal's first theater.

The Molsons established the first industrial-scale distillery in Montreal in 1820. Three years later, the youngest brother, Thomas, left the organization after a severe disagreement with his family. In 1824 he moved to Kingston, Ontario, where he established an independent brewing and distilling operation.

The elder John Molson left the company in 1828, leaving John, Jr., and William as active partners. He served as president of the Bank of Montreal from 1826 to 1830, and in 1832 was nominated to the Legislative Council of Lower Canada. Possibly his most fortuitous venture was his contribution of one quarter of the cost of building Canada's first railway, the Champlain and St. Lawrence. He died in January 1836 at age 72.

Thomas Molson returned to Montreal in 1834 and was readmitted to the family enterprise. Over the next 80 years new partnerships formed among various members of the Molson family, prompting several more reorganizations. The first in the third generation to enter the family business was John H.R. Molson, who joined the partnership in 1848. He became an increasingly important figure in the company as William and John Jr. devoted more of their time to the operation of Molson's Bank.

In 1844 the Molson brewery, now called Thos. & Wm. Molson & Company, introduced beer in bottles which were corked and labeled by hand. Beer production grew faster than bottle production, though, necessitating the company's purchase of a separate barrel factory at Port Hope, Ontario, in 1851. In 1859 Molson started to advertise in Montreal newspapers, while also setting up a retail sales network and introducing pint bottles.

The company became John H.R. Molson & Bros. in 1861 following the establishment of a new partnership with William Markland Molson and John Thomas Molson. In 1866 the Molsons closed their distillery, citing poor sales, and in 1868 they sold their property in Port Hope.

By 1866, the brewery's hundredth year in Molson hands, its production volume had multiplied 175 times but profit cleared on each gallon remained the same—26¢. In the early years of the twentieth century, the company incorporated pasteurization and electric refrigeration into its methods. Additionally, electricity replaced steam power, and mechanized packaging devices sped the bottling process. In 1911 the company became Molson's Brewery Ltd. following its reorganization as a joint-share company. The Molson family would continue to hold a major stake in the company through the mid-1990s. The family's direct interest in banking ended in 1925 when Molson's Bank merged with the Bank of Montreal.

The first half of the twentieth century was a period of rapid growth for Molson. Production at the Montreal brewery rose from 3 million gallons in 1920, to 15 million in 1930, to 25 million in 1949. Molson adopted modern marketing and advertising methods to enhance market penetration, and in 1930 began producing its first promotional items—despite founder John Molson's contention that "An honest brew makes its own friends."

In the mid-1950s Molson management recognized a need to expand operations significantly. By concentrating their resources, other Canadian breweries had finally begun to compete successfully against perennial leader Molson. Molson decided that the appropriate strategy was to have a brewery operating in each province, as distribution from its base in Ontario to other provinces was subject to strict government regulations. With operations in the other provinces, Molson could further build its market throughout Canada. This large-scale expansion began when Molson announced a second brewery would be built on a ten-acre site in Toronto. Modernizations at the Montreal facility had, it was felt, fully maximized output there. The new Toronto installation opened in 1955 and became the home of Molson's first lager, Crown and Anchor. In the next few years Molson acquired three breweries: Sick's Brewery, bought in 1958; Fort Garry Brewery in Winnipeg, 1959; and Newfoundland Brewery, 1962.

The expansion effort resulted in good returns for Molson investors; between 1950 and 1965 earnings more than doubled. Even so, Molson leaders recognized that expansion potential within the mature brewing industry was limited, and further, that growth rates in the industry would always be slow. It was clear that even the most successful brewing operation would soon reach the limits of its profitability. Thus Molson began an accelerated diversification program in the mid-1960s

which heralded in Canada the era of the corporate takeover.

In 1968 Molson made its first major non-brewing acquisition in more than a century. Ontario-based Anthes Imperial Ltd. was a public company specializing in steel materials, office furniture and supplies, construction equipment rentals, and public warehousing. The Anthes executive staff was known to be highly talented in acquisitions and strategic management, two areas in which Molson needed expert help to pursue its goal of diversification. However, because the various Anthes companies required different management and marketing strategies, the acquisition did not benefit Molson as much as its directors had hoped. Soon Molson sold off most of the Anthes component companies. The company had learned that future acquisitions should be of firms that were more compatible with Molson's long-standing strengths in marketing consumer products and service. Molson did retain one important component of Anthes: its president. As Molson's chairman, Donald "Bud" Willmot directed a series of successful acquisitions in the early 1970s. Management felt the ideal candidate must be a Canadian-based firm and must be involved in above-average growth. The do-it-yourself material supplies market seemed to be the ideal candidate: there seemed to be a new trend—consumers doing their own home improvements—and Molson recognized the potential for rapid growth of this market in urban areas, which at that time had few or no lumberyards or similar outlets. Molson began acquiring small hardware, lumber, and home furnishings companies. In 1972 it spent $50 million buying more than 90 percent of the shares of Beaver Lumber, a large Canadian company. During the remainder of the decade Beaver acquired several smaller hardware and lumber operations. Molson's service-center division grew to encompass 162 retail stores, most of them franchises, selling everything from paint to home-building supplies. In the mid-1980s Beaver began importing competitively priced merchandise from Asian countries.

In July 1973 the company's name was changed to Molson Companies Ltd., a reflection of its diversification. The beer-making operations were renamed Molson Breweries of Canada Ltd.

Although Beaver's sales climbed steadily throughout the 1970s, rapidly making it a leader in its industry, profits lagged behind what Molson had anticipated, and initially the company considered the Beaver purchase only a modest success. Struggling at first to integrate the brewing and home improvement divisions, Molson eventually learned that the two industries, and marketing therein, are very different. The beer industry operates in a controlled market; governments regulate sale and manufacture of alcoholic products. The hardware industry, on the other hand, operates in a relatively free market. Furthermore, in brewing, manufacturing efficiency is the key to a profitable enterprise, but the success of a home improvement retail operation hinges on the ability to provide a broad variety of products at competitive prices.

The challenge of integrating two companies operating in such different markets led Molson to a careful reassessment of its diversification criteria; in the future, the company would concentrate on marketing specific product brands. W.J. Gluck, vice-president of corporate development wrote: "We only wanted to go into a business related to our experience—a business in which marketing, not manufacturing, is the important thing." The search for another acquisition began.

In 1978 Molson offered $28 per share of stock in Diversey Corporation, a manufacturer and marketer of institutional chemical cleansers and sanitizers based in Northbrook, Illinois. Contending that their company—which boasted $730 million in annual sales—was worth more, Diversey stockholders contested the sale, but eventually accepted Molson's original $55 million offer. Diversey was Molson's first large acquisition in the United States, though most of its clients and manufacturing plants were in fact located outside the U.S. in Europe, Latin America, and the Pacific basin.

Molson also bought into sports and entertainment during this period, buying a share in the Club de Hockey Canadien Inc. (the Montreal Canadiens) and the Montreal Forum, as well as hosting Molson Hockey Night in Canada and other television shows through its production company, Ohlmeyer Communications.

Molson opened the 1980s with the $25 million purchase of BASF Wyandotte Corporation, an American manufacturer of chemical specialty products related to food services and commercial laundries. The subsequent merger of BASF and Diversey made Molson's chemical products division its second largest earnings contributor. Prior to the merger, Diversey was a weak competitor in the U.S. sanitation supplies market. BASF Wyandotte, however, was a leader in the U.S. kitchen services market. Thus the marriage was a sound move for Diversey, which had found a relatively inexpensive way to increase its share of its market in the United States.

Having concentrated on diversification, Molson found that it had missed the globalization of the brewing industry that had begun in the 1970s. While other major competitors had expanded internationally through acquisition, Molson had not completed a single foreign acquisition. Although the conglomerate remained profitable throughout the 1980s, it became clear to the board of directors—led by eighth-generation heir Eric Molson—that the company would need to make some international connections in order to remain a major, independent participant in the beer market.

In 1988, the board hired Marshall "Mickey" Cohen as president and CEO. A career civil servant who had only entered the private sector in 1985, Cohen was brought into Molson with one objective: to raise the 202-year-old company's sagging returns. His first move was to revive ailing merger talks between Molson and Elders IXL Ltd., Australia's largest publicly traded conglomerate. Elders (subsequently renamed for its beer-making subsidiary, Foster's Brewing Group Ltd.) had recently capped off a five-year amalgamation of global brewing companies with the purchase of Canada's number-three brewery, Carling O'Keefe. The proposed merger of number-two Molson with Carling was called "the biggest and most audacious deal in Canadian brewing history" in a 1989 *Globe and Mail* story, but it required Molson to share control of the resulting company. While it had been difficult for Cohen's predecessors to agree to

relinquish more than two centuries of control, Cohen had no such compunctions.

The resulting union gave Molson access to Foster's 80-country reach, while Foster's bought entree into the lucrative U.S. market, where Molson was the second-largest importer after Heineken NV. The merger also helped lower both participants' production costs: the combined operations were pared from 16 Canadian breweries down to nine, and employment was correspondingly cut by 1,400 workers. As a concession to its larger pre-merger size—Molson's brewery assets were valued at $1 billion, while Carling's only amounted to about $600 million—Cohen also managed to wring $600 million cash for Molson Companies out of the deal.

Some analysts surmised that the CEO would use the funds to further supplement the multinational beer business, but he surprised many with the $284 million acquisition of DuBois Chemicals Inc., the United States' second-largest distributor of cleaning chemicals, in 1991. The addition boosted Diversey's annual sales by 25 percent to $1.2 billion, and augmented operations in the U.S., Japan, and Europe. Unfortunately, the merger proved more troublesome than expected, and a subsequent decline in service alienated customers. While Diversey's sales increased to $1.4 billion in fiscal 1994 (ended March 1994), its profits declined to $72.6 million and the subsidiary's president jumped ship. Cohen took the helm and began to formulate a turn-around plan.

Hoping to boost the Molson brand's less-than-one-percent share of the U.S. beer market, Molson and Foster's each agreed to sell an equal part of its stake in Molson Breweries to Miller Brewing Co., a leader in the American market. Miller's $349 million bought it a 20 percent share of Molson Breweries and effectively shifted control of Canada's leading brewer to foreigners in 1993. Cohen expected the brand to retain its distinctly Canadian character (the beer would continue to be manufactured exclusively in Canada), but hoped that it would benefit from Miller's marketing clout.

Molson's financial results were mediocre at best in the early 1990s. Sales rose from $2.55 billion in fiscal 1990 to $3.09 billion in fiscal 1993, but earnings vacillated from $117.9 million in fiscal 1990 to a net loss of $38.67 million the following year, and rebounding to $164.69 million in fiscal 1993. The company blamed its difficulties on Diversey's money-losing U.S. operations, which faced strong competition from industry leader Ecolab Inc. The following year's sales and earnings slipped to $2.97 billion and $125.67 million, respectively, as Diversey continued to lose money in the U.S. Nevertheless, Cohen remained determined to turn Diversey's operations around. Late in 1994, he announced a decision to divest Molson's retail home improvement businesses to focus on the brewing and chemicals operations. He also planned to invest about $500 million toward increasing Diversey's sales staff and improving its customer service training program from 1994 through 1996.

176   Molson Companies Ltd.

Principal Subsidiaries:

Molson Breweries; Diversey Corporation; Beaver Lumber Company Limited; Sport & Entertainment Group; Club de Hockey Canadien, Inc.; B.B. Bargoon's; Groupe Val Royal.

Further Reading:

Banks, Brian, "Continental Draft: Molson Brews up a Strategy to Export its Canadian Success to the Mighty US," *CA Magazine,* December 1991, pp. 28-31.
Cheers for 200 Years!: Molson Breweries, 1786-1986, Vancouver: Creative House, 1986.
Daly, John, "Miller Time for Molson: The Largest Brewer Gives up Canadian Control," *Maclean's,* January 25, 1993, p. 30.
Denison, Merrill, *The Barley and the Stream: The Molson Story,* McClelland and Stewart, 1955.
Forsyth, Neil, *The Molsons in Canada: The First 200 Years,* Public Archives Canada, 1986.
Joslin, Barry. "Anatomy of a Merger," *The Business Quarterly,* Autumn 1990, p. 25-29.
Molson's, 1961 [175th Anniversary, 1786-1961], Montreal: Molson's, 1961.
Perreault, Michel G. *The Molson Companies Limited: A Corporate Background Report,* Ottawa: Royal Commission on Corporate Concentration, 1976.
Slater, Michael. "Number One at Last," *Globe and Mail,* November 17, 1989, p. 50.

—updated by April Dougal Gasbarre

MOORE®

Moore Corporation Limited

1 First Canadian Place
Toronto, Ontario MSX 1G5
(416) 364-2600
Fax: (416) 364-1667

Public Company
Founded: 1882 as Grip Printing & Publishing
   Company
Incorporated: 1929
Employees: 19,890
Sales: US$2.4 billion
Stock Exchanges: Toronto Montreal New York
SICs: 2721 Periodicals; 2761 Manifold Business
   Forms; 6719 Holding Companies, Nec; 7336
   Commercial Art and Graphic Design

Moore Corporation Limited was built upon the design and manufacture of a simple salesbook using carbon paper inserts. As the world's largest maker of business forms throughout most of its history, Moore has continually redefined the industry. Moore has remained competitive through adaptability and versatility, offering clients a myriad of services to serve their information and communications needs.

Samuel J. Moore immigrated to Canada from his native England as a young boy in 1861. He worked in the printing business throughout his teens; by his early twenties, he was the co-publisher of a Tory newsletter called *The Grip*. When Moore met John Carter, a local sales clerk, who described his idea for a salesbook using a piece of carbon paper to standardize sales slips and provide a record of transactions, Moore seized upon the idea, acquired rights to produce the salesbook, and hired Carter as his first sales representative. With the motto, "Let one writing serve many purposes" and an initial investment of only $2,500, the Paragon Black Leaf Counter Check Book went into production in 1882 at the Grip Printing & Publishing Company. The following year Moore reduced production overhead by 75 percent by purchasing two automatic printing presses; in 1889, he bought the operation that manufactured the presses, Kidder Press Company.

At the same time, Moore had already begun to look beyond the Canadian market. He predicted that the United States—offering a large population and no language barrier—would become his primary market,

and it did. Within two years of the Paragon salesbook's introduction, Grip established a factory in Niagara Falls, New York. Business was so good at the world's first factory devoted exclusively to the manufacture of salesbooks that the owner doubled plant capacity in 1886 and again in 1888. Moore named the U.S. organization Carter & Co. to honor Paragon's inventor.

Europe presented another opportunity for growth, but it took Moore two years of negotiation to enter that market. In 1889 he reached an agreement with the British-based Lamson Store Service Company, securing rights for the salesbook's patents and manufacturing for all of Europe and Australia. Demand for the salesbooks continued to grow so dramatically that the company was left short of boxes for packaging and shipping. Moore's eye for efficiency settled on the night watchman, whom he assigned to produce boxes in his spare time. Soon the company had box orders from shoe stores and other local merchants; in 1909, box-making became a separate business, called the F.N. Burt Company.

Moore also pursued other entrepreneurial notions. A young man brought Moore an idea to make souvenir silver teaspoons that tourists around the world could collect. Moore raised capital and established the Niagara Silver Company, later renamed William A. Rogers Limited. Additionally, in 1902, Moore was a founder of the Metropolitan Bank of Canada and elected its president in 1907. At that time, banks issued their own paper currency, and Samuel Moore's likeness and signature appeared on the bank's $5 bills. When the Metropolitan Bank was absorbed into the Bank of Nova Scotia in 1914, Moore was appointed to the board. Over the years, Moore became president, chairman, and then honorary chairman of the Bank of Nova Scotia.

In 1925 one of several Moore-controlled companies, the Pacific Manifolding Book Company, forged ahead of its competition by developing a single-use, disposable carbon paper. Inspired by a customer who owned a large California poultry business and complained that carbonized paper was too messy, the "Speediset" business form consisted of slips glued together at the ends with a carbon between them, eliminating the need for the customer to touch the carbon paper.

During the 1920s, Moore's network of nine separate companies became the Moore Group. The group was involved in boxing and printing, salesbooks, and other endeavors. Income from the salesbook and related sales counter products still made up 98 percent of the Moore Group's business, but change was on the horizon. Web-fed lithography, a major development in the printing industry in the mid-1920s, brought Moore and other paper-producing businesses into modern times. The web press's high speed allowed mass production and product standardization. As a result, Moore created a machinery division to produce equipment for Moore companies.

On January 1, 1929, the three largest members of the Moore Group formally merged into a public company, Moore Corporation Limited. The companies included under the Canadian corporate umbrella were actually based in the United States: American Sales Book Company; Pacific-Burt Company, Limited (later called Pacific Manifolding Book Company Limited); and Gilman Fanfold Corporation, Ltd. Eventually the remaining six Moore Group members came under the control of Moore Corporation.

In its first year on the Toronto stock exchange, Moore reported a net income of more than $1 million. However, after the market crash of 1929, facing an era of economic depression as well as his own aging, Moore turned his attention toward grooming successors to guide the company's future. This was the year he hired David W. Barr, who eventually became chairman; meanwhile Moore saw potential in Edwin G. Baker, whom he had hired nine years earlier. When Moore made Baker president of the corporation in 1935, he established a tradition of promoting from within rather than seeking executives from outside.

It was also about this time that Moore instituted a separate research subsidiary to oversee research activities for all divisions. Research would play an increasingly vital role at Moore and in the industry in general. As new president Baker secured the threads holding together the loose network of individual companies within the corporation; he also encouraged autonomy of each company's daily operations. In the United States, he divided the organization geographically, giving each region its own executive committee. This helped establish close local ties, and provided a small-scale training ground for future corporate executives. It was to the Moore Corporation that the U.S. government turned in 1936 when it needed a sizable business-form order: the first 40 million Social Security application forms and cards. This government connection proved important to the growth of the company. World War II brought demand for ration booklets, payroll envelopes, and various other forms industry and governments hadn't needed before. This demand hastened Moore's maturation from a salesbook producer to one encompassing all types of business forms. During the war, more than 150 Canadian and U.S. government departments used forms developed by Moore. By 1945, 80 percent of Moore's revenue was generated by business forms other than salesbooks.

The corporation reorganized to reflect the change in 1945, bringing a multitude of companies together under the common name of Moore Business Forms. This division employed half of Moore's total work force. The corporation also realigned its management echelon to prepare for the postwar era. Baker became chairman and W. Norman McLeod, who had joined Moore with Baker in 1920, took over as president, while Samuel Moore kept the title of honorary chairman until his death in 1948. McLeod stepped up a campaign to both specialize the company and to diversify geographically. He increased the number of production plants in the U.S. from 10 to 40, but kept plant size small for greater control as they grew more and more technologically complex.

In 1955, McLeod was appointed chairman and Thomas S. Duncanson became president. Duncanson had joined Moore in 1910, when the F.N. Burt division was added. His most significant contribution as president was to create a central division in the U.S. headquartered in Chicago, dividing the country into eastern, southern, pacific, and central quadrants. Duncanson remained president until 1962, when he was elected chairman and W. Herman Browne was made president.

Browne initiated a policy to broaden Moore's international operations. He cemented the British connection by reaching a formal financial relationship with long-time associate Lamson Industries Limited. Through an exchange of shares, Moore acquired 20 percent of Lamson's equity. Included in the agreement was an exchange of directors and a 10-year pact to share technical information. It was also during Browne's tenure that the U.S. government instituted Medicare, and in 1966, Moore printed more than 25 million Medicare identification cards. The ever-present U.S. tax form, the W-2, also came from Moore.

David W. Barr, whom Samuel Moore had handpicked so many years earlier, was named president in 1968. He professionalized sales representatives' training and followed through on the firm's internationalization, increasing Moore's interest in Lamson Industries to 52 percent in 1973. Packaging took on a bigger role at Moore during this time. The packaging operation in England was assigned to a division called Decoflex Ltd., which also manufactured bags for the clothing industry and currency containers for bankers. At home in 1974, Moore merged its Dominion Paper Box Company Ltd. with Canada's Reid Press Ltd. to establish Reid Dominion Packaging Limited.

Barr became chairman in 1976, when Richard W. Hamilton, who had been with Moore 35 years, moved into the presidency. A year later, Hamilton approved a total acquisition of Lamson. The internationalization plan begun 20 years earlier was now complete: Moore owned Moore Business Forms de Mexico; Moore Business Forms de Puerto Rico; Moore Formularios Limitada, in Brazil; and Moore Business Forms de Centro America, in El Salvador. In addition, ties were established with Formularios y Procedimientos Moore in Venezuela and Toppan Moore Company, Ltd., in Japan.

International expansion wasn't the only concern at Moore during this period: while Moore executives were concentrating on their new foreign operations, they also turned their attention and funding to research: computerization was taking over the industry, and big money awaited companies who could adapt their services to complement the new machines. During the computer era's infancy in the 1960s and 1970s, Moore developed "Speediflo" and "Speediflex" continuous-feed forms and other advances including a carbonless paper; an optical character recognition tester; the "Mooremailer" continuous envelope producer for high-speed addressing systems; and the "Speediread" form with colored highlight lines for easier data reading.

New products meant more divisions and Moore formed a response graphics division in 1974 to develop special products for the U.S. direct mail industry, and acquired the Minneapolis-based International Graphics Corporation in 1977. Despite its pioneering start, Moore had developed a conservative reputation. Thus when the company announced its decision in the late 1970s to enter the small computer systems market, the financial community expressed surprise. Moore executives didn't jump into this extremely competitive field with eyes closed; they had considered the idea for years before acting on it. Yet in the 1970s, it had become clear that although the business-forms industry was still growing, it wasn't booming the way it had been. An annual overall market increase of 15 percent wasn't unusual in the 1960s. By the early 1970s, the industry's yearly growth was down to 9 percent, falling to about 3 to 4 percent in the following decade. Even though Moore held 25 percent of the U.S. business-forms market in the 1970s and continued to gather profits from around the world, the company was accustomed to soaring net figures and the time was ripe for change.

Moore's corporate decision-makers concluded that since 70 percent of business forms were designed for use with a computer, a natural addition to their product line was the computer itself. Hoping to sell computer systems to small companies, Moore set its sights on nearly one million potential buyers, and 40 percent of them had already been customers at one time or another. Now Moore wanted to show each customer how it could tailor software to fit its payroll, inventory, and general accounting needs. As a further commitment to computer sales, Moore also opened retail outlets under the name MicroAge, selling computer supplies designed to service customers after they bought Moore's systems. Yet the microcomputer market proved too much for a newcomer like Moore. After losing about $30 million in the course of a few years, Moore abandoned the retail computer business, selling or closing its 44 MicroAge stores.

Throughout the 1980s, Moore's international operations in Europe, Japan and Brazil continued to fluctuate. As the decade neared its end, however, the company reported the highest returns of its 107-history with a solid $186 million profit on sales of $2.54 billion in 1988. Though 89 percent of Moore's revenue was still derived from business forms, its electronic-based division was slowly evolving and taking shape. By the next year, Moore had diversified with new printing and manufacturing facilities in California, Tennessee and Wisconsin; the acquisition of Sabre Systems and Service Inc., an Ohio-based data processing service for governmental agencies; and a joint venture with Italy's largest business forms maker. They also began construction on a new U.S. headquarters, uniting five operations at one location. Sales figures for 1989 climbed to $2.71 billion, with net earnings breaking the previous year's high by topping $201.7 million.

As the 1990s commenced, Moore's stockholders approved a "poison pill" or shareholders' rights policy, then in anticipation of sluggish sales announced a $55-million provision in the second quarter for worldwide restructuring. Despite a $20-million order from the U.S. Census Bureau to print 100 million census forms, Moore still fell victim to the industry-wide slowdown, reporting sales slightly above 1989 at $2.77 billion and net earnings cut by nearly 40 percent to $121 million.

Although Moore controlled 19 percent of the U.S. and 22 percent of the Canadian market by 1990, it wasn't prepared for how quickly the information superhighway rendered many of its products obsolete. Despite recognizing that computers would one day dominate business, the company's slow response cost it millions and part of an already dwindling customer base as 1991 sales

fell to just under $2.5 billion and net earnings plummeted to $88 million. To offset losses on multi-part sales and business forms, Moore came out with a technologically-advanced plateless printing; automated pressure-seal mailing systems (that could sort, stuff, seal and address envelopes) endorsed by the Xerox Corp.; and peel-off bar code labels that could withstand the heat of laser printers. Then the company persuaded some of its biggest clients to turn over their printing, marketing, and mailing services, allowing Moore to handle most information management and communication services previously handled in-house. Yet new product development wasn't enough and Moore's revenues hovered close to those of the previous year at $2.4 billion, while it reported a loss of $2.3 million, due in part to another restructuring plan costing $77 million. Breaking a 110-year tradition, Moore hired its first president and CEO from outside the company in 1993, naming Reto Braun, formerly second in command at computer giant Unisys, to the post. Goodrich, due to retire in a couple years, remained chairman, and joined Braun in preparing the company for the next century and beyond. After 1993's disappointing figures ($2.3 billion in sales and a record-breaking loss of $77.6 million), Braun instituted another company-wide reorganization beginning with the layoff of 3,000 employees, the closure of several plants and a pretax charge of $210 million.

By mid-1994, things were looking up at Moore: the company paid $20 million for 20 percent of JetForm Corp., a software developer, with a five-year option to purchase an additional 31 percent; then formed a lucrative, double-sided alliance (worth $1.7 billion) with Dallas-based Electronic Data Systems Corporation (EDS). Though EDS and Moore had previously partnered to handle services for tax collecting in Mexico and Britain, the new deal called for Moore to print all of EDS's commercial and operational forms, while in turn EDS would direct all of Moore's information management systems in the U.S. By the end of the year, to free up further funds for expansion, Moore sold most of its 45 percent equity in Toppan Printing Company Ltd., its joint venture with Japan since the 1960s, for US$350 million. Among Moore's new conquests were operations in Hong Kong and Shanghai, and a five-year, $200-million pact with AmeriNet to produce its health services-related forms. Year-end figures reflected Moore's renewed vigor by returning to a profit of $121.4 million on revenues of $2.4 billion.

Continuing its trend in early 1995, Moore's first quarter sales increased by 6 percent and the company introduced several new products, including a check-writing system compatible with Microsoft Windows-based software, and formed an alliance with Indigo N.V. to develop and market a digital color printing process. In April, Goodrich retired after 36 years and Braun was named chairman and CEO in addition to his duties as president. Having tightened its focus and moved firmly into the electronic age, Moore's three divisions (Forms and Print Management, Labels and Labeling Systems, and Customer Communications Services) provided clients with simple, personalized business forms or the complete design and implementation of a global electronic management system.

Principal Subsidiaries:

Command Records Services Ltd.; Formularios Moore de Costa Rica S.A. de C.V. (56%); Formularios Moore de Guatemala, S.A. (56%); Logidec Canada; Moore Asia Pacific Ltd.; Moore Belgium N.V.; Moore Business Forms & Systems Ltd. (New Zealand); Moore Business Forms de Centro America, S.A. de C.V. (El Salvador; 56%); Moore Business Forms de Puerto Rico, S.A.; Moore Business Forms Ltd. (U.K.); Moore Business Systems Australia Limited; Moore de Mexico S.A. de C.V.; Moore Formularios Limitada (Brazil); Moore France S.A.; Moore International B.V. (Netherlands); Moore Nederland B.V. (Netherlands); Moore Paragon (PVT) Ltd. (Zimbabwe); Moore Portuguesa Limitada (Portugal); Sigma Moore S.P.A. (Italy).

Further Reading:

Boyd, Greg, "Managing Moore in a Paperless World," *Canadian Business,* September 1991, pp. 60-3.
Clifford, Edward, "Stock Scene: Moore's Profit Remains Strong," *Globe and Mail,* May 18, 1990, p. B7.
Clinkard, Andrew, "Moore Corp. Gains with U.S. Economy: Should Regain Market Premium," *Investor's Digest,* March 24, 1987, p. 91.
Cuthbert, Wendy, "New Driver to Steer Moore Down Hi-Tech Highway," *The Financial Post,* November 13, 1993, pp. S18-19.
Kinross, Louise, "Going the Extra Mile in Recycling," *The Financial Post,* September 30, 1991, p. 34.
Liepins, Ivar, "Moore Does Better Than Expected," *Investor's Digest,* March 20, 1992, p. 765.
Mahood, Casey, "Moore Breaks Form in Naming New President," *Globe and Mail,* August 10, 1993, p. B1.
————, "Moore, EDS Deal Cements Alliance," *Globe and Mail,* September 27, 1994, p. B1.
————, "Moore Hones Its Asian Strategy," *Globe and Mail,*
————, "Moore to Buy 20% of JetForm," *Globe and Mail,* June 14, 1994, p.B11. December 20, 1994, p. B9.
————, "Moore to Lay Off 3,000, Shut Plants," *Globe and Mail,* January 21, 1994, p.B1.
McMurdy, Deirdre, "Moore Corp. Adopts Poison Pill Plan to Foil Takeover Attempts," *Globe and Mail,* January 19, 1990, p. B9.
Noble, Kimberley, "Forms Maker Moore Looks to New Fields," *Globe and Mail,* April 14, 1989, p. B11.
Pitts, Gordon, "Moore Reorganizing in Europe for '92," *The Financial Post,* July 31, 1989, p. 6.
"Shaking Off the Slump (Moore Corp.)," *Financial Times of Canada,* April 13, 1987, p. 27.
Siklos, Richard, "Moore's Old-School Assault on the '90s," *Financial Times of Canada,* February 27, 1989, pp. 10-11.
Slattery, Patrick, "Moore Corporation: Company Continues on Its Path to Recovery," *Investor's Digest,* June 26, 1992, p. 186.
The Story of Moore, Toronto: Moore Corporation Limited, 1982.
Symonds, William C. "Moore's Recovery Looks Good on Paper," *Business Week,* May 22, 1995, pp. 134, 136.
Willis, Andy, "Gunning for Growth at Moore Corp.," *Financial Times of Canada,* December 16, 1991, p.15.

—Rosanne Ullman
—updated by Taryn Benbow-Pfalzgraf

National Bank of Canada

National Bank Tower 600 de La Gauchetiere West
Montreal, Quebec H3B 4L2
(514) 394-4000
Fax: (514) 394-8434

Public Company
Incorporated: 1859 as Banque Nationale
Employees: 12,227
Assets: $44.77 billion
Stock Exchanges: Montreal Toronto Vancouver
SICs: 6021 National Commercial Banks

The sixth-largest chartered bank in Canada, National Bank of Canada maintains a vast network of branch offices stretching across the globe but primarily serving the Quebec market, where its predecessor companies were founded in the mid-nineteenth century. National was formed in 1979 through the merger of two banks, the Provincial Bank of Canada and Bank Canadian National, in one of the largest bank mergers in Canadian history.

When the National Bank of Canada was formed in 1979, three of Quebec's oldest financial institutions were united after more than a century in the banking business. Two of the three major pillars supporting National Bank of Canada's foundation, Banque Nationale and Banque d'Hochelaga, had merged 55 years earlier to form Banque Canadienne (Bank Canadian National), while the third, Provincial Bank, founded in 1861 as Banque Jacques Cartier, waited until 1979 to join its competitors, finally putting to rest predictions of such a merger after more than six decades of speculation. Upon completion of the 1979 merger, the combined forces of the Provincial Bank and Canadian National immediately created Canada's sixth largest chartered bank with $16.5 billion in assets. The story of how this prodigious banking concern came to be, however, involved considerably more than the signed agreement that created it. The true story of National Bank of Canada's creation took place over 120 years.

Banque Nationale was the first financial institution around which the numerous other banking concerns, both large and small, gathered to eventually create the National Bank of Canada. Like the Banque Jacques Cartier and the Banque d'Hochelaga, the Banque Nationale emerged from fertile ground in 1859, nearly a decade into perhaps the first definitive and pervasive era of prosperity in Canada. Between 1851 and 1861 the number of banks operating in Lower and Upper Canada doubled, increasing from eight to sixteen. Cash deposits bearing interest during this span exponentially increased as well, jumping from $54,858 to $565,326. From this period of burgeoning economic growth, when banks were demonstrating increased stability, greater versatility, and more thorough diversification of risk, Banque Nationale emerged in Quebec City, formed by virtue of an act of Parliament of the Union of Upper and Lower Canada. Over the course of the nineteenth century the bank would slowly expand geographically, extending its presence across the Atlantic by 1907, when it established an office in Paris, but initially Banque Nationale limited its activities to the Quebec City region and in eastern Quebec.

Capital was scarce in the years leading up to Confederation, and it would remain scarce after the formation of the country, particularly in rural areas where farming was the primary economic activity, but also in the region's urban areas, where merchants, craftsmen, and small manufacturing concerns combined to plant the seeds for bustling commercial hubs. Banks were the primary source of capital that farmers, store owners, manufacturers and the like needed to get their businesses established. Banks predicated and fueled the growth of the economies they served, and, accordingly, the Banque Nationale was instrumental to the economic development of the region surrounding Quebec City, helping fledgling rural and urban industries finance the difficult task of establishing commercial enterprise in a new land.

In 1861 the Banque Jacques Cartier was founded in Montreal through the same parliamentary measures that had spawned the Banque Nationale two years earlier. Following a reorganization in 1900, the Banque Jacques Cartier changed its name to the Provincial Bank of Canada, then gradually established a network of branch offices throughout Quebec before spreading into certain regions of Ontario, New Brunswick, and Prince Edward Island.

Six years after the Banque Jacques Cartier commenced operations, the Dominion of Canada was formally brought into existence, engendering a second great wave of expansion and prosperity throughout Ontario and Quebec. From the year of Confederation to 1890, substantial advances were achieved in manufacture, transportation, and general trade, but perhaps the most intense period of growth recorded in the newly created country occurred during the late 1860s and early 1870s. From 1870 to 1875, for instance, railways throughout the country were extended from roughly 2,500 miles to nearly 5,000 miles, quickening the pace and amplifying the magnitude of goods and people transported across Canada. Not coincidentally, the number of banks in the country proliferated as well. Between 1868 and 1874, 28 banks were incorporated in Canada, one of which was the Banque d'Hochelaga, established in Montreal in 1874. Like the Banque Jacques Cartier, the Banque d'Hochelaga would experience its first appreciable growth at the turn of the century after demonstrating only modest growth during its first formative decades.

These three banks would form the nucleus of National Bank of Canada slightly more than a century later, but until then they faced each other as competitors. Following World War I, competition among the Banque Nationale, the Provincial Bank, and the Banque d'Hochelaga intensified, with each recording roughly equal success in serving the same Quebec market, prompting the first public suggestion that the three banks could better promote Quebec's economic development if they banded together. Shortly thereafter, the directors of the Banque Nationale and the Banque d'Hochelaga followed such advice after a particularly harsh economic recession during the early 1920s. In 1924 the Banque Nationale merged with the Banque d'Hochelaga, creating the Banque Canadienne Nationale. The directors of the Provincial Bank declined an invitation to join the merger and continued to independently compete against this newly formed rival.

In terms of growth, the decision to couple the operations of the Banque Nationale and the Banque d'Hochelaga proved more beneficial to Canadian National than the decision by the directors of the Provincial Bank to remain autonomous. As both banks struggled through a decade-long economic depression during the 1930s, World War II, and then flourished during the ensuing post-war economic rebirth, Canadian National emerged as the much larger bank, having developed more rapidly and earned a more prestigious reputation than the Provincial Bank.

By 1970 Canadian National was twice the size of its closest rival, the Provincial Bank, but in the coming decade the Provincial Bank would begin to gain ground on its long-time adversary by adopting a more aggressive program of acquisitions. In 1970 the Provincial Bank acquired the People's Bank, a financial institution with roots stretching back more than a century earlier. Then in 1976, the year the Provincial Bank launched a national expansion program, it acquired Toronto-based Unity Bank of Canada. By 1979, after purchasing Laurentide Financial Corporation Ltd., a Vancouver-based Canadian finance company, the Provincial Bank had narrowed the gap separating it and Canadian National, maintaining $6 billion in assets compared to Canadian National's $9 billion in assets. Later that year, in November 1979, the assets of both were amalgamated, creating a new powerful force in the Canadian banking industry: the National Bank of Canada.

Although Canadian National and the Provincial Bank had expanded nationally and internationally over the course of their existence, particularly during the decade preceding their union, each relied heavily on business generated in Quebec where the two banks had competed against one another for decades. The 1979 merger ended the struggle over native territory, consolidating the two banks' operations in numerous overlapping markets throughout Quebec and enabling the much larger combination to more effectively compete on a national and international scale. Ranking as the sixth-largest chartered bank in Canada after the merger, the newly created National Bank of Canada was poised and equipped to become one of the predominant banks of the 1980s. National entered the 1980s occupying a unique position in Canada's banking industry. The bank was much larger than, the country's numerous smaller banks, but

also was easily outdistanced in terms of assets by Canada's five largest chartered banks: Bank of Nova Scotia, Toronto-Dominion Bank, Canadian Imperial Bank of Commerce, Royal Bank of Canada, and the Bank of Montreal. The gaps separating National from minor and major banks were essentially equal, leaving the newly formed bank occupying the middle ground within the banking industry without any close rivals. With hopes of joining the elite cadre of Canada's "Big Five" banking concerns, National sought to broaden the scope of its operations, using its large and stable retail, or individual, deposit base in Quebec to fuel expansion outside of Quebec and across Canada.

Maintaining slightly less than $17 billion in assets and boasting a branch in nearly every Canadian city with a population of 50,000 or more, National appeared well-equipped for the task at hand, but initially the directors of the bank needed to fully consolidate the operations of the Provincial Bank and Canadian National, particularly in Quebec where the two former competitors had fought for the same markets. In 1980 National closed 79 branches, a majority of which were located in Quebec, then established a national accounts division to bolster its ability to retain large corporate clients. Before the 1979 merger neither bank derived any appreciable revenue from large corporate customers—that lucrative segment of the banking market was largely the domain of the country's larger banks—but after the merger, with greater financial resources at its disposal, National endeavored to retain corporate customers previously lured away by the Big Five. Accordingly, in addition to its national accounts division, National established a staff of corporate specialists and began to offer a range of services tailored to the needs of large corporate customers.

Before National's expansion program and its efforts toward securing corporate clients could record much success, the Canadian banking industry became mired in an economic recession in 1982, saddling it with loan losses largely stemming from rising Third World debt and a crippled Canadian real estate market. National's woes were exacerbated by a large and inefficient branch office network and top-heavy management, two problems resulting from the 1979 merger. The bank's stock plunged from $15.50 per share in 1981 to as low as $4 per share during the 1982 recession, forcing National's management to effect cost-cutting measures in order to halt the retrogressive slide of the bank's financial performance. A wage freeze was instituted and the number of National's branches was whittled from 753 to 610, which produced some positive results, but as the bank returned to profitability its assets slipped in value, dropping from $19.2 billion in January 1982 to $16.9 billion in 1983.

To strengthen its position, National looked toward increasing its presence in the United States in the wake of the recession, adding offices in Dallas and Atlanta in 1984. (Offices had previously been established in 1978 in Chicago and New York City.) The bank's U.S. lending portfolio doubled during the year as a result, jumping from $500 million to $1 billion. On the home front, National looked to increase business at each branch rather than building new branches, continuing, in fact, to reduce the number of branches it operated.

In early 1986, National merged with Montreal-based Mercantile Bank of Canada, which strengthened National's presence in the market for loans to small and medium-sized businesses and gave it an experienced real estate lending division based in Toronto. The deal also added $3.5 billion in assets to National's total, which stood at $26.7 billion after the merger. In 1988, National acquired 73 percent of Quebec's largest independent investment dealer, Levesque Beaubien Inc., then the following year acquired investment dealer Geoffrion Leclerc Inc. and merged it with Levesque Beaubien. Against the backdrop of these two acquisitions, National turned away from expanding nationally and focused its efforts on strengthening its core business in Quebec, hoping to have 100 branches in the province by 1993. The bank opened 11 new branches in 1987, reversing its earlier strategy to halt further branch expansion, then opened 15 additional branches in 1988.

During its first decade as Canada's sixth-largest chartered bank, National had demonstrated torpid profitability as management struggled to divine the proper approach for the bank to take, initially seeking to increase its national presence then turning inward and attempting to build upon its position in Quebec. The 1990s began with more disheartening results when a personal loan made in 1990 to corporate raider Robert Campeau ended up costing the bank $156 million. This loss coupled with the onset of a national economic recession during the early 1990s negatively affected National's bottom line, causing its net income to fall from $186 million in 1991 to $1 million the following year as exposure to a floundering real estate market hobbled the bank's profitability.

Attempting to put its questionable lending practices behind it and to recover from the pernicious affects of the recession, National emerged from the early 1990s ready to intensify its efforts toward becoming the preeminent banking concern in Quebec. In 1993 National acquired three subsidiaries owned by General Trustco of Canada Inc., marking its entry into the trust business. National purchased General Trust of Canada, Sherbrooke Trust, and Gentrust Financial Consultants, a fund management company, which, after the two trust companies were combined, gave National the second-largest trust company in Quebec, $3.6 billion in assets, and 33 branch offices. As the directors of the bank charted their course for the mid-1990s and beyond, profitability had once again been restored after the

discouraging early 1990s. From the $1 million recorded in net income in 1992, National recorded resolute growth, generating $175 million in net income in 1993 and $217 million in 1994, sparking hope that National would continue to demonstrate such success into the future.

Principal Subsidiaries:

Natcan Trust Company; General Trust Company; National Bank Export Finance Co. Inc.; NBC Export Development Corporation Inc.; Levesque, Beaubien and Company Inc. (67%); National Bank Securities Inc.; NBC holdings USA, Inc.; National bank of Canada (International) Limited (Bahamas); Natcan Finance (Asia) Ltd. (Hong Kong); National Bank of Canada (Asia) Ltd. (Singapore); Mercantile Canada Finance B.V. (Netherlands); Natcan Insurance Company Limited (Barbados)

Further Reading:

Breckenridge, Roeliff Morton. *The History of Banking in Canada.* Washington: Government Printing Office, 1910.

Chisholm, Patricia, "Keepers of the Vaults," *Macleans,* July 30, 1990, p. 30.

Fleming, James, "The Players," *The Globe and Mail,* January 18, 1991, p. P17.

Gordon, Sheldon, "Banking on U.S. Customers," *Canadian Banker,* January-February 1994, p. 24.

Hartley, Tom, "Canadian Eyes Operation in Buffalo," *Business First of Buffalo,* May 20, 1991, p. 2.

Ingram, Mathew, "Bank Profits to Top $4 Billion," *The Globe and Mail,* November 21, 1994, p. B1.

Gibbons, Robert, "Absorbing Mercantile Key Task at National," *The Globe and Mail,* April 7, 1986, p. B7.

Johnson, Arthur, "Small Risks and Lots of 'Em," *Canadian Business,* May 1994, p. 33.

Kerr, Wendie, "National Becoming More National," *The Globe and Mail,* February 23, 1981, p. B37.

McKenna, Baebie, "National Bank Acquires Trust," *The Globe and Mail,* July 23, 1993, p. B7.

Phillips, Dana, "Montreal Bank Gets Fed S&L Charter," *South Florida Business Journal,* December 23, 1994, p. 1A.

Racine, Pierre, "Accidental Banker," *Canadian Banker,* July-August 1993, p. 20.

—Jeffrey L. Covell

Noranda Inc.

BCE Place
181 Bay Street
Toronto, Ontario M5J 2T3
(416) 982-7111
Fax: (416) 982-7423

Public Company
Incorporated: 1922 as Noranda Mines Ltd.
Employees: 31,000
Sales: $6.76 billion
Stock Exchanges: Toronto
SICs: 1031 Lead and Zinc Ores; 1310 Crude
  Petroleum and Natural Gas; 2610 Pulp Mills;
  2421 Sawmills and Planing Mills; 3330
  Nonferrous Metals.

Noranda Inc. is one of the largest companies in Canada
and one of the largest mining companies in the world.
The firm has three industry segments with activities
throughout the world: mining and minerals (70 percent
of 1994 revenues); pulp, paper, and lumber products (27
percent); and oil and gas (3 percent). In 1995 the
company was 41.4-percent-owned by Brascan Ltd.

The history of Noranda begins with the story of a
prospector named Edmund Horne, and a hunch. During
the early 1920s, at a time when northern Canada was
unchartered the area was mostly wilderness and prospectors preferred to stay on the familiar grounds of
Ontario, Horne was drawn to the Rouyn district in
northeastern Quebec. He visited Rouyn repeatedly,
because he believed it "didn't seem sensible that all the
good geology should quit at the Ontario border!" Horne
could reach Rouyn only by way of a chain of lakes and
rivers.

His enthusiasm was contagious, and soon a group of
twelve men had raised $225 to finance further explora-
tions. The effort paid off when word of Horne's first
strike made it to S. C. Thomson and H. W. Chadbourne,
two United States mining engineers with a syndicate of
investors interested in exploring Canadian mines. In
February of 1922 the syndicate bought an option on
Horne's mining claims in Ontario and Quebec and
exercised it. Noranda Mines Ltd. was incorporated in
1922 to acquire the U.S. syndicate's mining claims.

The next task was to make the area more accessible to
miners. Roads were cut through the forests, and travel
often required skis and sleds. Some equipment arrived
by barge and ski-equipped plane, both of which could
travel the lakes and rivers with relative ease. The mine
began producing gold, copper ore, sulfur, and iron, and
Noranda convinced the Canadian government to lay
roads, railways, and power lines. Eventually, Noranda
Mines Ltd. constructed a mill and a smelter, and a city
began to take shape in what was once untamed wilderness.

Not satisfied with this initial success, Noranda Mines
began to acquire other holdings. In 1927 it bought 80
percent of the stock in Waite-Ackerman-Montgomery
Mines, which changed its name six years later to Waite
Amulet Mines Ltd. Also that year Noranda acquired a
majority interest in Aldermac Mines Ltd., of Rouyn.

Because it believed strongly that Canadian ore should be
processed in Canadian plants, Noranda Mines eventually acquired or built several processing companies.
Canadian Copper Refiners, Ltd., a company in which
Noranda Mines held majority interest, was constructed
in eastern Canada in 1929 as a joint effort of Noranda
Mines, London's British Metal Corporation, and Nichols Copper Company of New York City. The following
year, Noranda Mines purchased a rod and wire mill just
east of the copper refinery and bought a substantial
interest in Canada Wire & Cable Company, Ltd., of
Leaside, Ontario.

In the early 1930s Noranda Power Company, Ltd., a
new subsidiary, was formed. In 1934 this company took
over the parent firm's power rights and leases on the
Victoria River, only to transfer the rights to the government's National Electricity Syndicate under a new
agreement four years later.

The 1930s set the stage for a decades-long tradition of
growth through acquisitions, as Noranda made its climb
to the ranks of Canada's largest companies. In 1935 the
firm bought a substantial interest in Pamour Porcupine
Mines, Ltd., located in the Porcupine district of Ontario. A few years later, it also acquired a 63.75 percent
interest in Compania Minera La India for its gold mines
in Nicaragua. In 1939 Noranda bought the controlling
interest in Aunor Gold Mines, Ltd., which was formed
earlier that year to take over additional Porcupine
property. The late 1930s also saw the creation of
Noranda Exploration Company, Ltd., a subsidiary
formed in 1938 to undertake exploration work in
Quebec.

By 1936 output of metals in the province of Quebec
totaled well over $30.6 million, thanks to the develop-
ment sparked by Noranda Mines. From 1926 to 1936
Noranda stimulated the nation's economy by pouring
into it approximately $71 million in supplies, transpor-
tation, salaries, and taxes. By the end of World War II,
the area's mineral production had climbed to $150
million annually.

Perhaps due to the events of World War II, however, the
1940s and even the 1950s saw less corporate activity
than earlier decades. Still, the company made two major
acquisitions, including Castle Tretheway Mines Ltd.'s
Omega Gold Mines, which Noranda Mines bought

jointly with Anglo-Huronian Ltd. in 1944. Four years later, Noranda Mines and a subsidiary, Waite Amulet Mines, bought more than 500,000 shares of Mining Corporation of Canada Ltd. In 1956 Noranda acquired a sizable interest in Bouzan Mines Ltd.

By the early 1960s the company began a flurry of activity, beginning with the acquisition of Western Copper Mills Ltd., located near Vancouver, in 1963. The new acquisition joined with Noranda Copper & Brass Ltd., a Noranda Mines subsidiary, to form Noranda Copper Mills Ltd. Also that year, the company acquired the remaining shares of Mining Corporation of Canada, which continued the firm's exploration efforts. In addition, Anglo-Huronian, Bouzan Mines, Kerr-Addison Gold Mines, and Prospectors Airways—all Noranda affiliates—merged to form Kerr-Addison Mines Ltd.

In December of 1964 Noranda Mines made its most important acquisition when it merged with Geco Mines Ltd. The new company retained the name Noranda Mines Ltd. Based in Manitouwadge, in northwestern Ontario, Geco was a major producer of copper, silver, and zinc. The following year, Canada Wire & Cable, in which Noranda Mines had an interest since 1964, became a wholly owned subsidiary. In 1966 the firm also bought 80 percent of Norcast Manufacturing Ltd., which then purchased shares in Wolverine Die Cast Group. Also that year, Noranda Mines formed Noranda Manufacturing, Ltd., a holding company for its various manufacturing subsidiaries. Noranda Mines also acquired a controlling interest in Pacific Coast Company in 1967.

By 1968 Noranda Mines had become a widely held mining company with most of its activities centered around Quebec. Employees numbered 5,000. It was also in 1968 that 37-year-old Alfred Powis became president of Noranda Mines. Formerly a financial analyst in Montreal with Sun Life Assurance Company of Canada, Powis joined Noranda Mines in 1955 as an assistant to the firm's treasurer. Under Powis's leadership, the company began its evolution from a regionally based mining firm to an industry leader with subsidiaries involved in energy and forestry, in addition to mining.

It seems that Powis's aggressive tactics, including a chain of takeovers, were key contributors to the company's success. Powis's success did not come overnight, however. The company first had to weather the impact of several large investments made in the late 1960s.

In the early 1970s the mining industry, as a whole, was depressed. Consequently, Noranda Mines had limited earnings from 1966 to 1972, increasing in that period by only 21 percent. In addition, gross capital employed rose from $500 million in 1967 to $1.5 billion in 1973. The rate of return on that capital dropped from 16 percent in 1966 to only 9 percent in 1972. Powis worked through the cyclical, industry-wide recession, and finally, in 1973, investments began to pay off; Noranda's sales climbed 75 percent to $121 million, a company record.

Additional investments made in the early 1970s included Tara Exploration and Development Ltd., which owned lead and zinc properties in Ireland, and Belledune Fertilizer Ltd., acquired from Albright & Wilson Ltd. in 1972. The year 1974 saw even more acquisitions, including a 55 percent stake in Fraser Companies Ltd. and Alberta Sulphate Ltd., and 38.5 percent of Frialco, a Cayman Island firm with controlling interest in Friguia, a bauxite mining company in the Republic of Guinea. In addition, Noranda Sales Corporation of Canada Ltd., a subsidiary, bought in the spring of 1971 a 50 percent interest in Rudolf Wolff & Company, a British trading firm dealing with metals and other commodities.

The mining industry, known for caution, watched Powis march on this unusual acquisition path, then witnessed Noranda sales climb from $60 million in 1972 to $155 million two years later. It was during this era that a *Canadian Business* contributor referred to Powis as "the Houdini of the Canadian mining industry."

What goes up, however, often comes down, and in 1976, earnings dropped to $47 million. Demand for the two biggest contributors to the company's sales, copper and zinc, began to lag. The automobile industry was replacing zinc die castings with plastics. Copper, too, was being supplanted by various substitutes, from aluminum for power lines to glass fibers for communication cables.

In addition, many of the firm's earlier investments had been financed with short-term loans, which seemed like a good idea when business was booming. Although Powis acknowledged that money was tight at Noranda Mines in 1977, he defended his decision to load up on short-term debt, telling *Canadian Business:* "We put restraints on at the end of 1974 when we could see that things were getting grim. Those clamps have stayed on." Powis also indicated he was prepared for the tight zinc market.

To help wait out the cyclical downturn in the mining industry, the company diversified, concentrating on other business segments, such as manufacturing and forestry. As Powis stated in the July 22, 1974, issue of *Iron Age,* the future of Noranda would be "where our nose takes us. . . . We originally got into manufacturing so we could have a home for our products." In addition, the company invested millions of dollars in efforts to convert some old saw mills into profitable lumber plants. That marked its entry into the forestry industry.

In 1981 Powis lost a long-running, highly publicized battle with Brascan, Ltd., a Toronto holding company owned by Edward and Peter Bronfman. Brascan became Noranda Mine's largest stockholder, and Powis, who became accountable to the Bronfmans, stayed on as chief executive officer. Brascan added $500 million to Noranda Mines's bankroll, and set the company back on its acquisition path.

In 1981 Noranda Mines first picked up Maclaren Power and Paper Company, a newsprint, pulp, and woodproducts enterprise located in Buckingham, Quebec. The following year it bought 49.8 percent of MacMillan Bloedel, Canada's largest paper company. The minority shareholding was sufficient to give Noranda Mines control of the company. While the acquisitions were intended to decrease the company's concentration on the lagging copper market, the expansion of the early 1980s initially resulted in decreased profits: in 1980 the firm had record earnings of $408 million, while in 1983 it lost $117 million due to interest payments on the

186   Noranda Inc.

acquisitions and expansion loans, which totaled $169 million in 1983.

Powis and Adam Zimmerman, president of Noranda Mines, shared an optimism that began to pay off in the mid-1980s. Sales of zinc, fine paper, and other products began to recover, and, just as Noranda Mines finished a $300 million addition to its aluminum smelter, demand for the element skyrocketed. Diversification was paying off, and to reflect its expanded activities, the company changed its name from Noranda Mines Ltd. to Noranda Inc. in 1984.

In 1986, after a $253,900 loss caused by strikes and other labor problems in 1985, the firm's net income stood at $43,300, and total revenue was $3.55 billion. In 1987, as various labor strikes were resolved, company officials predicted the firm would see its highest earnings since 1980. Also in 1987, the company was restructured, dividing its various business segments into four subsidiaries: Noranda Energy, Noranda Forest, Noranda Minerals, and Noranda Manufacturing.

In October of 1989, after a heated battle between Powis and former protege William James who had left Noranda and become chairman of Falconbridge, Ltd., a rival mining company Noranda bought 50 percent of Falconbridge. Ownership of the multibillion dollar company is shared by Trelleborg A.B., a Sweden-based conglomerate. The move not only gave Noranda half of Falconbridge, but also ownership of Kidd Creek, a Timmins, Ontario, copper and zinc mine that Noranda had long coveted.

Although most of Noranda's assets are located in North America, Noranda markets its products globally. The firm's goal is to be a premier diversified natural resources company. Under the leadership of President David Kerr, the company remains committed to a sensitive environmental policy, a pledge necessary for any business to be well received in the 21st century. But the company's professions of environmental responsibility and the public's perception of its efforts often diverge. Noranda's Forest division has been a frequent target of criticism. While environmental groups decry clear-cutting, Noranda Forest officials cite reseeding programs that plant twice as many seedlings as are cut. Although the company has been unable to meet environmentalists' demands in some areas, Noranda Forest has been compelled to meet consumer demands for recycled paper.

Noranda Forest Recycled Papers was established in 1989 and operates at a mill with a 50-year history of recycled paper production. The mill was the first to receive the Canadian Standards Association's Environmental Choice designation for its inclusion of more than 50 percent recycled paper and five percent postconsumer fiber in its fine paper. The operation has been very successful, and Noranda has raised the postconsumer content of its recycled paper to ten percent in line with 1991 federal guidelines.

Noranda made halting progress in its handling of labor relations in the 1990s. When officials at a subsidiary, Brenda Mines Ltd. in British Columbia, realized that the mine's ore vein would be exhausted within three years, the company took steps to ensure a more stable transition for its workers. With the cooperation of the Canadian government's Department of Employment and Immigration, the provincial Ministry of Advanced Education Training and Technology, representatives of management, and hourly and salaried employees, a job placement center was created to help employees recognize and prepare for new job prospects. The program earned an award from the Canadian Mental Health Association for "excellence in addressing the personal issues" related to the closure.

The Brenda Mines scenario, however, did not necessarily characterize labor relations in the late 1980s and early 1990s. A 94-day strike at the Noranda Aluminum smelter in New Madrid, Missouri, capped a 20-year adversarial relationship at that Noranda division. And a ten-month strike that started in July of 1990 at Brunswick Mining and Smelting's huge zinc/lead mine near Bathurst, New Brunswick, threatened to shut down that division. Noranda executives admitted that management-labor relations were never lower, but agreements in 1991 at both subsidiaries focused on more open communications at all levels.

The lingering recession of the early 1990s hit Noranda hard in 1991, when it posted a $133 million loss for the year. Although the mining and metals and oil and gas groups posted net gains, a $75 million loss in the forest division cut into those profits. The balance of the losses was blamed on overproduction and the high level of the Canadian dollar relative to the U.S. dollar. The poor financial performance inspired management throughout the conglomerate to focus on cash conservation, cost containment, and asset sales. To that end, the Canada Wire and Cable division was sold to Alcatel Cable for more than $400 million in 1991. Following that sale were several dispositions that reduced Noranda's owned assets but buoyed its profit potential.

Noranda's profits were spotty during the early 1990s as the company scrambled to regroup. As it sold off poorly performing or noncomplementary assets, the company's assets plunged to about $7.34 billion in 1993. Meanwhile, sales dropped from $9.43 billion in 1990 to $5.26 billion in 1993. During that period, Noranda lost more than $500 million, much of which was due to restructuring. Reorganization paid off in 1994, however, when Noranda posted a net income of $303 million—its best year since 1989.

Noranda's long-time executive stepped down from his post early in 1995 after he had a heart attack. The 64-year-old Alf Powis had worked for the company for 40 years, serving as chief executive beginning in 1968 and also as chairman beginning in 1977—he eventually relinquished his chief executive duties. "I'd like to be remembered for the fact that I'm leaving Noranda in terrific shape," Powis said in the March 1, 1995, *Financial Post*. During his tenure, Powis had helped to grow the company into a diversified natural resource company with operations throughout much the world.

Principal Subsidiaries:

Noranda Mining and Exploration Inc.; Noranda Forest Inc. (74 percent); Canadian Hunter Exploration Ltd.;

Noranda Aluminum, Inc.; Wire Rope Industries Ltd. (90 percent).

Further Reading:

Antoniak, Jane, "Profile: Green Giant," *CA Magazine,* March 1991.
Beizer, James, "Metal Mining Troubles Loom Large in Canada," *Iron Age,* July 22, 1974.
Daly, John, "The Final Victory: Falconbridge May Prove to Be Too Expensive," *Maclean's,* October 9, 1989.
Francis, Diane, "Alfred Powis as Corporate Superman," *Maclean's,* November 27, 1989.
Haliechuk, Rick, "Noranda Forest Rewards President for Turnaround," *Toronto Star,* March 17, 1995, Section B, p. 3.
———, "Powis to Retire After 27 Years at Noranda Helm," *Toronto Star,* March 1, 1995, Section B, p. 7.
Kennedy, Peter, "Powis Bowing Out as Noranda Chairman," *Financial Post,* March 1, 1995, Section 1, p. 12.
Roberts, Leslie, *Noranda,* Toronto: Clarke-Irwin, 1956.
Young, Jim, "Noranda Meets New Fine Paper Postconsumer Waste Standards," *Pulp & Paper,* March, 1991.
Zuehlke, Mark, "The Right Way to Handle a Closure," *Canadian Business,* August 1991.

—Kim M. Magon
—updated by Dave Mote

NORTEL

Northern Telecom Limited

3 Robert Speck Parkway
Mississauga, Ontario L4Z 3C8
(905) 566-3000
Fax: (905) 803-4660

Partially Owned Subsidiary of BCE Inc. (52 percent)
Incorporated: 1914 as Northern Electric Company
    Limited
Employees: 57,054
Sales: US$10.79 billion
Stock Exchanges: New York Toronto Montreal
    Vancouver London Tokyo
SICs: 3600 Electronic & Other Electrical Equipment;
    3661 Telephone & Telegraph Apparatus; 3670
    Electronic Components and Accessories; 3610
    Electric Distribution Equipment; 3620 Electrical
    Industrial Apparatus

From its base in Canada, Northern Telecom Limited
has grown steadily during its long history to become a
leading global supplier of telecommunications systems.
In the United States, for example, Northern Telecom
was in the early 1990s the second-largest manufacturer
of telecommunications equipment after American Telephone and Telegraph (AT&T). Northern Telecom sells
its products in more than 80 countries and operates 42
manufacturing plants in the United States, Canada,
France, Australia, Thailand, Malaysia, the Republic of
Ireland, and the People's Republic of China. Its products include telephones, networks, wire and cable,
telecommunications and transmissions systems, fiber-
optic cable and equipment, and other equipment for
both public and private communications networks.

To reach such a position, Northern Telecom implemented bold and aggressive economic strategies throughout
its history. During four years alone, from 1981 to 1985,
the telecommunications giant's net profit margin
jumped by 30 percent, and its sales doubled. In 1985
sales were US$4.3 billion.

Northern Telecom's origins can be traced back to 1880,
four years after Alexander Graham Bell invented the
telephone in 1876. In that year Bell Telephone Company of Canada (Bell Canada) was founded. To develop
adequate telephone equipment for the fledgling company, Bell established its mechanical department on July
24, 1882, in Montreal, Canada, with a staff of 3 that

soon expanded to 11. Success came early to the company, and five years later the mechanical department
moved to a larger facility to accommodate a staff that
had increased to 54.

The growth led to Bell Canada taking out a charter in
1895 for a separate company to take over the mechanical department's work. On December 7 of that year,
Northern Electric & Manufacturing Company Limited
was incorporated under the dominion charter. With
C.F. Sise as president, the company called its first
general meeting of stockholders on March 24, 1896. By
1902 Northern Electric employed 250 people and occupied a 48,000-square-foot plant, which it leased from
Bell Canada. That plant had expanded to 241,000
square feet in 1912, the year Northern Electric and Bell
Canada worked out a deal whereby Northern would
become the storekeeper and purchasing agent for Bell.

In 1895 C.F. Sise had bought a small plant from
Alexander Barrie that was involved in manufacturing
rubber-coated wire for the fast-growing electrical industry. In turn, Sise offered the company to Bell Canada for
what it had cost him. Bell Canada accepted the offer,
and on December 19, 1899, the Wire & Cable Company,
as the enterprise became known, was granted a province
of Quebec charter. Sise was appointed president and
Barrie superintendent. A big success, the Wire & Cable
Company replaced its provincial charter with a dominion charter in 1911 and changed its name to Imperial
Wire & Cable Company.

By then both Northern Electric and Imperial Wire &
Cable were playing vital roles as Canada's major suppliers of telephone equipment. In many operational areas,
however, their needs and interests overlapped. The
management of both companies realized that to increase
efficiency and to reduce overhead, the two enterprises
should amalgamate. On July 5, 1914, they consolidated
under the laws of Canada into Northern Electric Company Limited. While the general sales division continued to be located in Montreal, the company established
supply and repair divisions for western Canada in 1929
and for the Maritime region in 1944. Despite the Great
Depression, which forced Northern to cut back production, the company still managed to grow. It established
the electronics division in 1931 and expanded its base of
operations by purchasing a majority interest in Amalgamated Electric Company Ltd. in 1932 and, in 1935, by
launching Dominion Sound Equipment Ltd., a wholly
owned subsidiary that supplied Canada with electric
sound equipment, acoustic and sound proofing supplies,
radio and broadcasting sound equipment, and other
lines of electrical equipment.

When the Depression ended, Northern became involved
in Canada's World War II effort, converting 95 percent
of its operation to war production. By 1944 most of the
company's 9,325 employees were engaged in this activity. Soon after the war's end in 1945, Northern immediately began a flurry of construction to meet the expanding communications needs of Canada's growing communities. As a measure of its continuing growth, Northern's
work force expanded to 12,775 by 1948.

The company was gradually losing its independence. By
1956 the U.S. company Western Electric, the manufacturing arm of AT&T, owned 40 percent of Northern

Electric, an economic situation that forced Northern to operate much like a "branch plant." During this period, the company had a small research and development staff, and its sales efforts were confined to Canada. As its main function was to manufacture Western Electric products for Bell Canada, Northern Electric's product line generally lagged behind Western Electric's by two to three years. Northern Electric ceased operating like a branch plant in 1956 when Western Electric signed a consent decree with the U.S. Department of Justice in which it agreed to relinquish its interest in Northern Electric. Bell Canada acquired most of Western Electric's interest in Northern Electric in 1957 and the remainder in 1964. With no product line of its own, and with management knowing that it must start one to remain competitive, Northern Electric stepped up its research and development efforts, establishing Northern Electric Laboratories—with a staff of 30 to 40 people—in 1958. In 1965 the company made a commitment to develop a switching device known as SP-1, stored program switch system, which it believed would meet the needs of the Canadian market and spur economic growth. From 12 researchers in 1965, the product development team working on SP-1 grew to more than 100 by the end of the decade. The commitment paid off when Northern put its product on the market. By 1975 not only had every major telephone company in Canada bought the switch, but 25 percent of all sales were being made in the United States.

Northern Electric's research and development division had become a conglomerate itself, mushrooming to more than 2,000 employees, and eventually incorporating as a separate entity. On January 1, 1971, Northern Electric's subsidiary, Bell-Northern Research Ltd. (BNR) was formed. In the early 1990s, BNR operated research and development facilities in ten cities: four in Canada, five in the United States, and one in the United Kingdom. In 1973 Bell Canada sold a portion of Northern Electric's shares to the public, while retaining a majority holding. During the 1970s the company established many new subsidiaries, such as Northern Telecom (International) B.V. in Amsterdam, and Northern Telecom (Asia) Limited in Singapore and Hong Kong, both established in 1974. These subsidiaries reflected its increasingly strong presence in the international marketplace. In 1976 the company's name was changed to Northern Telecom Limited (Northern) to reflect the great advances it had made in manufacturing modern telecommunications equipment.

The same year Northern introduced the first fully digital switch. Although AT&T did not immediately authorize its affiliates to buy the switches, independent U.S. telephone companies quickly did, and by 1978 Northern sales had jumped by 130 percent from the previous year. The demand for the company's digital switches received a big boost in 1981 when AT&T approved the purchase of the switches for its affiliates. In 1984 the U.S. government broke up AT&T, and sales of Northern's digital switches skyrocketed, and volume increased by 1,200 percent over that of 1976.

Northern had ignored conventional business wisdom and taken chances to get where it had arrived. As one company official said, "When we started to work on the digital central office switches in the 1970s, we were advised to follow AT&T and continue making old analog switches since digital switches would be too expensive." Fortunately for Northern, it did not, and the introduction and marketing of the switch proved to be a major milestone in its history. By 1990 one research firm estimated that the company held close to one-third of the U.S. market for the digital switches.

Northern's fortunes, however, began to change by the mid-1980s. While AT&T was making a comeback with its own switch, Northern made a technological blunder. It began selling new software to provide its phone company subscribers with advanced service capabilities based on new technology. Poor marketing, bugs in the software, and the fact that the processor in Northern's switch could not keep up with all the new tasks the expanded software had to do alienated many company customers. One disgruntled business executive told *Business Week* in 1987, "Their software and capacity problems are still driving us wild. We're giving our orders to AT&T."

Northern launched a public relations campaign to reassure its customers that it had solved the software problems. It also announced the availability of Supercore, a new processor that cost $50 million to develop. "[Supercore] will double the capacity of our switches and eventually increase it to whatever we want," maintained Northern President David G. Vice.

Many in the telecommunications market remained skeptical, however, and rival telecommunications companies like Japan's NEC, Sweden's Ericsson, and Germany's Siemens began to make a move for Northern's markets. Despite the setbacks, Northern had become one of the giants in the telecommunications industry. Consolidated revenues for 1989 were US$5.41 billion, up from US$4.44 billion in 1986.

Northern repositioned in 1988 because of concerns that the intense global competition combined with the money it had invested in product and market development had affected its financial performance. Under the newly elected chairman, chief executive officer, and president, Paul G. Stern, who took over in March 1989, Northern embarked on a program to restructure the corporation.

Stern's association with Northern began in April of 1988 when the company elected him to its board of directors and to membership on the executive committee. He brought to the job a strong background in advanced-technology company management and a reputation for making tough cost-cutting decisions at large corporations. He had previously served as an executive for Burroughs, Unisys, IBM, and Rockwell. Within nine months after Stern assumed the helm, Northern had reshuffled management, cutting 2,500 jobs; closed 4 of its 41 plants, selling one-fifth of the plants to employees; and changed its bonus system, tying employee incentives in each business unit to company performance.

The dramatic changes caused a stir in Canada. Northern's plans to move its research and development operations from Toronto to Texas and California made Canadians wonder if the company would move its headquarters as well. As of 1991, however, it was still a Canada-based company.

Northern, however, quickly saw positive results from the tough measures it took. In 1989 company expenses fell 18.5 percent from the year before, while profits jumped 18 percent on a 13 percent increase in sales. The company was making a push to garner a bigger share of the market outside the United States, not only by increasing sales of its switches, but by marketing a line of fiber-optic transmission systems and a network design concept called Fibre World. "Invariably, [customers] buy a product because a supplier has an uniqueness," Stern said. "When you're first, the perception lingers." Introduced in February 1989, the concept and its systems are based on a set of international standards established in 1988 called synchronous optical network, or Sonet, which, Northern officials said, would assure compatibility among equipment from different manufacturers, thus permitting the establishment of extensive networks and improving the speed and volume of information that telecommunications systems could carry.

To maintain its position in the highly competitive world of communications technology, Northern continued to invest heavily in research and development. Northern was spending more on research and development than any other company in Canada, and through its subsidiary, Bell-Northern Research Ltd., it had become the biggest employer of telecommunications research professionals in the country; it hired each year between one-quarter and one-third of all available electrical engineering doctoral graduates of Canadian schools. In total, Northern was employing more than 6,100 research and development staff. "For us, there is no question that the major opportunity before the telecommunications industry today is to develop innovative solutions that can link different manufacturers' equipment in public, private and hybrid networks," said Greg Sakes, president of Bell-Northern Research Ltd.

Northern's pioneering work in telecommunications during the 1980s was illustrated by the development of the international services digital network (ISDN), the company's control switching system. Two years after using the technology to make the first ISDN telephone call in North America in November 1986, Northern introduced the technology commercially throughout the continent.

By 1990 Northern was the world's sixth-largest telecommunications company, but corporate management publicly stated that it was preparing for an even more ambitious goal—to become the world's leading supplier of telecommunications equipment by the year 2000. Soon after, it took a major step in that direction when it purchased STC PLC, a large British telecommunications company in January 1991 for about US$2.6 billion. The acquisition put Northern in third place behind Alcatel NW of Belgium and the United States-based AT&T. Northern had already owned 27 percent of STC PLC when it made the deal. The purchase increased Northern's total debt to $4.3 billion, 50 percent of its equity, compared to 29 percent before the buyout. Northern said, however, that it planned to help relieve the debt using the $1.6 billion from the sale of STC's computer's division, ICL Ltd., to Fujitsu Ltd. of Japan.

In February 1991 Northern and Motorola, the world's largest supplier of cellular transmission gear, formed a cellular equipment alliance. Observers saw the alliance as the first step in a joint venture to market and develop equipment in the United States and overseas. In preparation for its international push, Northern also announced at the same time that it had undertaken a significant reorganization of its operations. Among other changes, the marketing, sales, and service activities of Northern were divided into four geographical areas: the United States; Canada, including activities in Mexico, the Caribbean, and Central and South America; Europe, including Africa and the Middle East; and Asia and the Pacific Rim. The effort represented management's intent to push Northern Telecom's sales past the $30 billion mark by the year 2000.

Northern Telecom experienced only tepid gains during the early 1990s. Sales hovered around the US$8 billion mark between 1991 and 1993. Profits also remained steady with the exception of 1993. In that year, in fact, Northern took a staggering US$940 million restructuring charge. That deduction resulted in a total loss of US$848 million for the year, which was much greater than many analysts had projected. Although the restructuring costs were immense, the investment was intended to set the stage for long-term growth. Northern's reorganization during that period took two main courses: 1) a reemphasis on the company's core profitable businesses, and; 2) and a shift toward new, high-growth businesses.

To those ends, Northern jettisoned several subsidiaries during the early 1990s, including STC Submarine Systems PLC of the United Kingdom, U.S.-based Northern Telecom Finance Corp., and several manufacturing facilities throughout North America. The proceeds from the sale of STC Submarine and Northern Telecom (U.S.) alone brought $1.5 billion into the organization's coffers. Besides dumping noncore businesses, Northern also consolidated remaining operations and implemented various cost-cutting efforts. It eliminated more than 2,000 workers in 1993 and 1994, for example, and shifted 3,000 employees to new business segments that it had targeted for growth. The effects of the reorganization were already apparent by 1994. Profit margins increased, sales surged to nearly US$8.9 billion, and net income recovered to a healthy $404 million in that year.

By 1995 Northern Telecom was generating about 32 percent of its sales overseas—up from just 13 percent in 1990. Besides diversifying globally, Northern was successfully moving toward its goal of achieving a leadership position in the global electronic information, communication, and networking industries. That intent was evidenced by the company's $1.16 billion—13 percent of revenues—1994 investment in research and development. It was also indicated by the adoption of a new corporate logo that identified the company as NORTEL, which was designed to reflect the company's global presence.

Principal Subsidiaries:

Bell Northern Research.

Further Reading:

Anderson, Mark, "Leaner, Refocused Northern Ringing up Solid Profits," *Financial Post,* October 26, 1994, Section 1, p. 5.

Brehl, Robert, "Northern Telecom Leaps on News of Recent Deals," *Toronto Star,* March 16, 1995, Section B, p. 2.

Crawford, Anne, "Purchase of NovAtel Pays Off for Northern," *Calgary Herald,* January 24, 1995, Section C, p. 2.

Mukherjee, Sougata, "In Focus: Northern Telecom—Switching On," *Triangle Business Journal,* December 2, 1994, Section 1, p. 7.

"Nortel Says Global Recognition Behind Name Change," *Ottawa Citizen,* March 28, 1995, Section C, p. 1.

Wickens, Barbara, "Becoming a Global Giant," *Maclean's,* January 14, 1991.

—Ron Chepesiuk
—updated by Dave Mote

North American Life™

North American Life Assurance Company

5650 Yonge Street
North York, Ontario M2M 4G4
(416) 229-4515
Fax: (416) 229-6594

Wholly Owned Subsidiary of The North American Group, Inc.
Incorporated: 1881 as North American Mutual Insurance Company *Employees:* 1,840
Sales: $1.95 billion
SICs: 6400 Insurance Agents, Brokers & Service

One of the largest and oldest insurance companies in Canada, North American Life Assurance Company offers a wide range of financial products and services, including registered retirement savings plans, annuities, registered retirement income funds, disability income plans, deferred profit sharing plans, and mutual funds. With offices spread throughout Canada and the United States, North American Life has been a pioneering force in the Canadian insurance industry.

By the 1880s, the concept of insuring one's life had moved into the mainstream in the United States and Britain, but in Canada it had not. Those life insurance companies that did exist in Canada at the time catered almost exclusively to the affluent residing in large urban centers; for the rest of the country, life insurance was an eccentric luxury afforded to only the wealthy. On January 4, 1881, some of the most powerful figures in Canada gathered in the Temple Chambers in Toronto to organize the North American Mutual Life Insurance Company, which, they hoped, would provide all Canadians with the opportunity to obtain life insurance.

In attendance were Oliver Mowat, the premier of Ontario; Alexander Morris, the former lieutenant-governor of Manitoba; Senator G. W. Allan, one of the fathers of the Confederation; and George Brown, editor of the *Toronto Globe.* A former prime minister of Canada, Alexander Mackenzie, was named the company's first president, and soon thereafter North American Mutual Life began selling life insurance.

Despite the prestige of North American Mutual's board of directors, the fledgling enterprise started modestly, operating with one room, two desks, several chairs, a stove, and a work force of two: William McCabe, managing director, who promoted the company during its formative first decades, and Leopold Goldman, North American Mutual's secretary. After six months, however, business was brisk enough to warrant the hiring of an additional employee—a 13-year-old English boy named Thomas Bradshaw, who tended to North American Mutual's stove and other sundry chores for $5 a month. He went on to become a leading Canadian financier.

With McCabe, Goldman, and Bradshaw running the day-to-day operation of the company, North American Mutual recorded $56,948 in life insurance premiums after its first year of business, an encouraging start for company that sought to revolutionize the Canadian life insurance industry. North American Mutual, which would undergo a name change to North American Life Assurance Company by 1883, was a for-profit enterprise, but underpinning the company's corporate philosophy was a belief that life insurance should be available to everyone, not just the well-to-do. Accordingly, for as little as five cents a week, Mackenzie's company offered "industrial" workers' insurance—which provided protection against death and medical check-ups—as well as policies created to address the special needs of wealthier customers, such as a policy that included investment features in addition to the conventional protection against death. North American Life attempted to embrace the entire country's population, which, as Mackenzie theorized, would move life insurance into the Canadian mainstream, give it mass-market appeal, and fuel the company's growth.

After ten years, North American Life had more than $10 million worth of insurance in force and annual revenues had climbed to more than $350,000; nevertheless, the directors of the company were disappointed. Despite their efforts to cultivate a clientele of lower-income individuals, the affluent continued to hold an overwhelming majority of the life insurance in force. The company rededicated its efforts during the 1890s toward building a more balanced clientele, sending salespeople to sparsely populated rural areas and as far away as the Yukon in an attempt to spread North American Life's unique corporate perspective throughout the country.

By 1900 there were 35 companies selling life insurance in Canada, 18 of which were Canadian. North American Life headed the pack, ranking as the dominant life insurance company in the country with 17,402 policies valued at more than $25.5 million. Growth continued to bolster the company's market position and finances as the new century progressed, despite a Royal Commission investigation of corruption in the insurance industry during the century's first decade, when North American Life's business increased 75 percent and its assets tripled under the intense scrutiny of a government inquiry.

North American Life emerged from the investigations unscathed and continued to grow during the 1910s. In 1919, the year insurance companies were first permitted to write group insurance policies, 250 Canadian companies insured their employees for $78 million, giving North American Life a substantial infusion of new business.

In 1925 Leopold Goldman, North American Life's first secretary, retired as the company's president and was replaced by W. B. Taylor, nephew of William McCabe, the company's first managing director. Taylor, as executor of the McCabe estate, held a sizeable block of North American Life's shares—enough to wield control over the company—which raised concern over the future direction of the company once Taylor retired. If Taylor's shares were sold once he left the company, as they presumably would be, control of North American Life could fall into potentially hostile or at least unfamiliar hands, something those within the company wished to avoid. The solution to the problem was found in Thomas Bradshaw, the former teenage apprentice to Goldman and McCabe who had joined North American Life in 1881 and remained there until 1897. After his departure at the age of 29, Bradshaw went on to establish a distinguished career for himself as a businessman and an investment banker. He also served for a time as the treasurer and finance commissioner for the City of Toronto, earning praise for stabilizing the city's finances and restoring its credit. Bradshaw approached Taylor about acquiring his shares, and Taylor agreed. Taylor retired as president in 1928, and Bradshaw took his place, making what could otherwise have been a problematic transition of power a natural segue between long-time North American Life employees.

For the troubled times ahead, North American Life could not have had a more qualified leader. Bradshaw became president of the company one year before a precipitous stock market plunge sent the Canadian economy into a tailspin. To protect North American Life from potential takeovers, Bradshaw acquired another large block of shares, making him the company's major shareholder, then in 1931 mutualized North American Life, giving its ownership to North American Life policyholders. With the ownership issue resolved and the possibility of a hostile takeover eliminated, Bradshaw employed his considerable financial acumen to steward the company through the tough economic times, recording enviable success given the financial climate of the 1930s. Business increased every year during the Depression except one—1933—further bolstering North American Life's market position for the more profitable years to come.

Assets swelled from $65 million to $96 million during World War II, and group insurance enjoyed a sharp increase in popularity following the conclusion of hostilities, giving North American Life a total of nearly $500 million of insurance in force. In the coming years, the company continued to grow while becoming increasingly efficient. From 1946 to 1955 the company's sales force was trimmed from 875 to almost half that figure, while insurance in force nearly tripled to more than $1 billion. The value of the average policy sold leaped from $3,018 to $7,510, and the average annual production of insurance sold by each North American Life salesperson made a remarkable jump from $68,000 to $368,000.

Expansion beyond Canada's borders had begun earlier in the century, when Ed Sears, an enterprising salesman who traveled to the Yukon, finally settled in Seattle, Washington, and established an office there, and when North American Life agents began selling insurance throughout the Caribbean during the 1920s. Geographic expansion began in earnest following World War II, particularly in the United States. By the mid-1950s, North American Life had offices in Chicago, Philadelphia, and Southfield, Michigan. With more than $2 billion of insurance in force by the end of the 1950s, North American Life was well prepared for further expansion. The company established a network of additional sales offices in the United States during the next two decades and diversified as well, once changes in insurance legislation were enacted during the 1960s that permitted insurance companies to invest more heavily in real estate. From the mid-1960s to the end of the 1970s, North American Life's mortgage and property holdings increased from roughly $200 million to nearly $650 million, which buttressed the company's mainstay insurance business. By the end of the 1970s North American Life offices operated in Atlanta, Baltimore, Connecticut, Washington D.C., Fort Lauderdale, Minneapolis-St. Paul, Pittsburgh, and Cleveland, in addition to the four original U.S. sales offices the company had established by the mid-1950s.

Entering the 1980s the company acquired two life insurance companies that substantially increased its stature. In 1982 North American Life acquired The Monarch Life Assurance Company of Winnipeg for $68 million, which increased the company's assets and life insurance in force roughly 25 percent, while nearly doubling its sales force in Canada. That same year, North American Life acquired Capital Bankers Life Insurance Company of Milwaukee, Wisconsin. The following year it recorded its largest profits ever, collecting $16 million, or more than double its pre-acquisition total.

After these two pivotal acquisitions, North American Life spent the remainder of the decade acquiring additional properties, including Calvin Bullock Ltd., Elliott & Page Ltd., and a 50 percent stake in Garyrock Shared Venture Ltd. As competition within the life insurance industry intensified, however, the company began to look for relief from outside the life insurance industry, which was experiencing intense competition from banks, trust companies, credit unions, and securities firms. Instrumental to its diversification was the Edgecombe Group, Inc., a wholly owned subsidiary of North American Life. Edgecombe, which offered financing, sales, property management, and real estate development services, provided North American Life with its best opportunity to diversify beyond the strictly regulated life insurance industry, and as the company headed toward the 1990s, it looked toward the expansion of Edgecombe's business to provide a needed boost to business.

In 1992 North American Life acquired First City Trust, which was renamed North American Trust after the purchase. While the acquisition was expected to strengthen North American Life's involvement in the real estate market, the value of commercial real estate plummeted shortly afterward, and by 1994 the company was resold.

Thereafter North American Life focused on strengthening its activities in its core markets, where it looked to increase the profitability of its products and services. In 1994 North American Life completed the acquisition of

Sun Alliance and London Assurance Company, the Canadian life insurance subsidiary of Sun Alliance Group P.L.C., based in the United Kingdom. A stock life and health insurer licensed in all provinces and territories in Canada, Sun Alliance and London Assurance sold insurance products similar to those sold by North American Life, which, according to company officials, would enable North American Life to increase productivity by administering a greater number of policies and reduce its unit costs. As the company planned for the remainder of the 1990s and the coming of its third century of business, its focused approach buoyed hopes that North American Life's future would be as successful as its past.

Principal Subsidiaries:

Elliot & Page Limited; NAL Resources Management Limited; North American Security Life Insurance Company; Seamark Asset Management Ltd.

Further Reading:

Findlay, Gordon S., "Monarch Merger Steps Are Ahead of Schedule," *Best's Review—Life-Health Insurance Edition,* July 1984, pp. 82-83.

Koco, Linda, "North American Life Group Term Adds 'Free' Living Benefits," *National Underwriter Life & Health-Financial Services Edition,* January 20, 1992, pp. 17-18.

Lee, Betty, "Life Insurance: Risky Business," *Canadian Business,* June 1984, pp. 92-93.

North American Life Assurance Company, *North American Life Centennial—100 Years of Assuring Bright Financial Futures,* North York: North American Life Assurance Company, 1981, 24 p.

—Jeffrey L. Covell

NOVA Corporation

801 Seventh Avenue Southwest
Calgary, Alberta T2P 3P7
(403) 290-6000
Fax: (403) 290-6379

Public Company
Incorporated: 1954 as The Alberta Gas Trunk Line
    Company Ltd.
Employees: 6,600
Sales: $3.27 billion
Stock Exchanges: Toronto Montreal Alberta New
    York London Geneva Zürich Basel
SICs: 4922 Natural Gas Transmission

NOVA Corporation is the primary natural gas pipeline
company in Canada, transporting over three-fourths of
the natural gas sold domestically. The firm's 12,600
miles of pipe delivered 4.1 trillion cubic feet of natural
gas to Canada and the United States in 1994. NOVA is
also a major participant in the North American petrochemicals industry, producing several types of polymers.
Under the guidance of Robert Blair throughout the
1970s and 1980s, NOVA grew to become the country's
premier Canadian-owned gas and petrochemical multinational. But poorly-timed acquisitions in the mid- and
late-1980s combined with poor market conditions hobbled NOVA's performance in the early 1990s. With the
benefit of new management, two major restructurings,
and improved chemical prices, NOVA was able to
achieve record earnings in 1994. After the ill-fated
diversification of the 1980s, NOVA appeared committed to its two core groups— natural gas services, which
contribute approximately 71 percent of annual revenues, and petrochemicals, which furnish the remainder.
These two primary interests were represented by the
company's Nova Gas Transmission Ltd. and Novacor
Chemicals Ltd. subsidiaries.

NOVA's origins can be traced to 1954, when it was
incorporated as The Alberta Gas Trunk Line Company
Ltd. (AGTL) by the premier of Alberta, Ernest Man-
ning. Although AGTL was not government-owned, the
provincial legislature retained the right to appoint four
of the company's directors until 1994. Initially AGTL
was involved in gas gathering within the province. By
the mid-1960s, several Canadian gas companies were
vying for the National Energy Board's permission to
compete in the gas export market. In 1967 the United

States approved a pipeline that would stretch from the
north central U.S. to eastern Canada, with the potential
of bringing billions of dollars in revenue to the gas
industry in Alberta.

In an effort to assert itself in this growing marketplace,
AGTL announced in 1970 its plans to build a $1.5
billion Alaskan pipeline. This was the brainstorm of
Sidney Robert Blair, who came on board as executive
vice president of AGTL in 1970 and was appointed
president and chief executive officer later that year. A
Trinidad-born Canadian nationalist, Blair would serve
as the outspoken "Boss-a-NOVA" for over twenty years,
expanding the provincial utility into a diversified multinational.

Blair's lofty plans for AGTL included a pipeline that
stretched from Prudhoe Bay, Alaska, to Alberta, cover-
ing AGTL's existing transmission system, and then on
to the rest of Canada and the United States, ultimately
drawing from and including the gas fields in the mostly
untapped Canadian Northwest Territories. In an effort
to make this dream a reality, AGTL joined forces with
other interested parties to form a study group to
research the feasibility of the plan. Economic restrictions, protests by environmental groups, and logistical
concerns slowed down the plan's momentum, however,
and by the time the pipeline's proposed completion date
drew near in 1974, AGTL had withdrawn from the
consortium that had grown to 26 companies. Instead,
perhaps in reaction to the rerouting of the pipeline solely
through the United States, AGTL proposed to develop
its own all-Canadian pipeline stemming largely from the
Northwest Territories. Ultimately, this project, the
Alaska Natural Gas Transportation System, received
approval from the Canadian and U.S. governments. As
of the mid-1990s, it had not been built, but was expected
to be constructed when demand for Alaskan gas increased in the lower 48 states.

Arthur Johnson of *The Globe and Mail* has called the
1970s "Blair's golden decade." AGTL grew rapidly
through organic growth and acquisition, and profits
multiplied just as fast. The company first formed and
incorporated several subsidiaries related to the gas and
oil industry. AGTL formed Alberta Gas Chemicals Ltd.;
Algas Resources Ltd. (later renamed Noval Enterprises);
Algas Engineering Services Ltd. (later renamed Novacorp Engineering Services Ltd.); and Novacorp International Consulting Inc. The company also acquired a
controlling interest in Pan-Alberta Gas Ltd., which
AGTL had used previously to supply gas to companies
outside of Alberta. In 1974 AGTL incorporated The
Alberta Gas Ethylene Company Ltd. and Algas Mineral
Enterprises Ltd. (later renamed Novalta Resources
Ltd.). The latter was formed to carry out gas exploration
and development. Later that year, AGTL formed Foothills Pipe Lines Ltd., a joint venture with Westcoast
Transmission Company Ltd. to continue its work on the
Arctic pipeline project. By the end of 1974, AGTL's net
income was $17.8 million, almost three times more than
its earnings a decade earlier.

In 1975 AGTL began to explore possibilities for produc-
ing ethylene, a derivative of natural gas used in plastics.
At this time, Dow Chemical Company of Canada and
Dome Petroleum Ltd. were also exploring petrochemi-

cal possibilities in Alberta, and Dow had plans to build such a plant. After resistance both from industry officials, about the need for two plants, and from the Alberta government, which had already given AGTL the go-ahead, the three companies decided to merge their plans. AGTL would build the plant near Red Deer, Alberta, supply Dow with the ethylene the plant produced, and allow Dome to build the pipeline that would transport the surplus chemicals to eastern Canada and the United States.

AGTL continued to acquire companies in 1975 and 1976, including Grove Valve and Regulator Company through its U.S. subsidiary, A.G. Industries International Inc., and WAGI International S.p.A., now Grove Italia S.p.A. In 1977 Q & M Pipe Lines Ltd., which formed a joint venture with Trans-Canada Pipe Lines Limited, was incorporated. The pipeline joint venture, Trans Quebec & Maritimes Pipeline Inc., was created to build a pipeline connecting Montreal to Nova Scotia. AGTL's net income in 1977 had grown to nearly US$58 million, and Blair was ready for his biggest move to date — a 35 percent share purchase in Husky Oil Ltd.

Husky Oil was a prominent oil and gas producer and marketer in Canada. Blair had watched Husky as a possible acquisition, but when another Canadian oil company, Petro-Canada, placed its bid, AGTL was forced to act. In the meantime, Husky called on U.S.-based Occidental Petroleum to counter the Petro-Canada bid. While officials of Occidental and Petro-Canada fought over the legalities of the takeover, AGTL, in what is known as a "creeping takeover," was buying shares in Husky openly, confounding both the Toronto Stock Exchange and the Ontario Securities Commission, which held that AGTL should have made its acquisition intentions public. AGTL had made its purchases in the New York market, however, outside of these bodies' jurisdiction. The Husky coup was a much-discussed incident in the industry, and once again, it was speculated that nationalism provided extra incentive for Blair, who wanted to rescue Husky from Occidental. By the following year, AGTL had purchased 69 percent of the Husky stock.

In 1980 AGTL changed its name to NOVA, an Alberta Corporation, an appellation that better reflected both the company's diversified activities and its distinctively Canadian character. NOVA continued to assert itself in the marketplace, acquiring Western Star Trucks, Inc., a truck manufacturer, and forming a joint venture with the Alberta government for NovAtel Communications, a cellular telephone company. It also dissolved some joint ventures it had owned with Shell Canada Ltd. and built a polyethylene plant in Joffre, Alberta, in addition to the new plant it was planning to build with Dome Petroleum Ltd. at Empress, Alberta, for liquefied natural gas extraction. With its increased interests in petrochemicals, NOVA formed Novacor Chemicals Ltd. in 1981 to manage and operate the plants.

These changes, however, could not deter such problems as a declining petrochemical industry and subsidiaries that were losing money. By 1982 a recession, coupled with severe price restrictions and higher taxes from Canada's national energy program, threatened the profitability of NOVA's Husky Oil and Alberta Gas Chemi-

cals. By the end of 1983, stockholders saw stock prices that had peaked at $14.38 two years earlier plummet to $6. The year 1984 was better for the company. Husky was able to sell off some of its assets, earning NOVA a US$505 million profit, and NOVA put its valve companies up for sale. Net income for that year quintupled 1983 income at $203.4 million.

The year 1985 brought the deregulation of crude oil pricing, as well as a positive shift in taxes and other charges. Blair became chairman of NOVA, in addition to his titles as president and CEO.

At this time, the company was also dealing with a scandal surrounding Husky Oil and its US$5 million lawsuit against John A. Grambling Jr. for breach of contract. Grambling had conspired with another businessman, Robert H. Libman, to borrow US$100 million illegally from several banks to buy Husky's Denver, Colorado-based refining and marketing unit. Eventually, the complex network of loans began to unravel, and both businessmen were caught. Grambling was indicted on 32 counts of bank fraud and Libman was indicted on two counts of conspiracy, among other charges. The year 1985 had been a difficult one in the oil industry overall, with a fall in crude oil prices and a large decrease in net income. Blair and other NOVA officers took a 15 percent pay cut, and the company reported its first annual loss, of $82.4 million.

Blair had to do some quick restructuring to rescue the company; in 1986, after much discussion, NOVA took Husky private, retaining a 43 percent share and transferring 43 percent to a Hong Kong investment group led by billionaire Li Ka-shing, for $855 million. The Canadian Imperial Bank of Commerce also retained some shares. The company name changed to NOVA Corporation of Alberta, and shareholders' rights were reorganized so that class B shareholders, primarily gas companies, would no longer be allowed to elect members of NOVA's board. Class A shareholders received full voting rights through the conversion of their shares into ordinary common shares. Blair also replaced NOVA's president, Robert Pierce, with James Butler, chairman of Novacor Chemicals Ltd., NOVA's petrochemicals subsidiary, and consolidated Novacor into NOVA.

In 1988 Blair launched a corporate takeover that became one of Canada's largest and most acrimonious. The eight-month battle ended only when NOVA agreed to pay Polysar Energy & Chemical Corporation of Toronto, a multinational petrochemicals company, its asking price of nearly $1.92 billion. Blair ultimately felt the battle was worth it because it allowed NOVA to expand its role in the global marketplace and achieve prominence as one of two of the largest ethylene producers in North America. At the same time, Husky bought Polysar's subsidiary, Canterra Energy Ltd., for $400 million. Later that year, Husky was given permission through government financial backing to upgrade its Lloydminster plant, and NOVA was guaranteed by the government a sustained supply of ethane, a necessary material for the production of ethylene, so that it could move ahead with plans to expand its petrochemicals output. The Canadian government, eager to build domestic resources, was very supportive of the growth of

NOVA Corporation. By the end of 1988, NOVA reported record profits of $402 million.

The following year, import tariffs between Canada and the United States were eliminated, and the National Energy Board, which previously had placed certain controls on the export of natural gas, loosened its restrictions. In addition, Canada gained access to U.S. oil from the north slope of Alaska. Such changes encouraged an increase in natural gas trade between the two countries. Buoyed by his Polysar success and these positive regulatory developments, Blair forecast that 1989's profits would exceed $540 million.

Other market conditions conspired to undercut NOVA, however, and it soon became apparent that Blair had "bought high," at the peak of an economic cycle that quickly reversed course. Plastics and petrochemicals prices plunged rapidly in 1989. High debt service on NOVA's $4.2 billion debt exacerbated the situation, paring 1989 earnings to $186 million. In the absence of lasting price increases, NOVA was forced to sell assets in order to stay in business. Perhaps the most painful aspect of the divestments was the fact that many of the new owners were foreigners. In 1990, NOVA sold Grove Italia for approximately $114 million to an Italian bank subsidiary. The biggest divestment came mid-year, when NOVA sold its Polysar rubber operations—the "crown jewel" of the 1988 acquisition—to Bayer AG of Germany for $1.48 billion. Novalta Resources, Western Star Trucks, and Trans Quebec & Maritimes Pipelines were all sold that year as well. The company also unloaded NovAtel Communications Ltd., which had lost more than $540 million over the course of its scant decade in business, to Alberta Government Telephones, its Crown-owned partner. NOVA's remaining operations were restructured internally into autonomous divisions of petrochemicals, plastics, and rubber.

NOVA's net income in 1990 was $185 million, considerably lower than projected, due to volatile prices in the petrochemicals and plastics industries and the continuing debt caused by the acquisition of Polysar. In addition, both Canada and the United States continued to suffer a recession in 1991. The company's stock dropped from a 1988 high of $14.75 to $7 in 1990.

Early in 1991, Blair revealed a plan to split NOVA into two separate entities—a pipeline concern and a petrochemical concern. But as pricing of commodity chemicals and plastics continued to slide, it became clear that the spin-off was simply not marketable. Long criticized for "running a one-man show," Robert Blair announced in July that he would be resigning as soon as a successor was found. He retired just two months later, and was succeeded as president and chief executive officer by J. E. "Ted" Newall.

Formerly chairman and chief executive officer of DuPont Canada Inc., Newall was recognized as "a senior statesman of Canadian business" in a 1991 Globe and Mail essay. Even Blair praised the outsider as "an absolutely top Canadian executive." Newall moved quickly to rehabilitate NOVA, commissioning a comprehensive corporate review and initiating an immediate management decentralization. Although the sale of the Husky Oil stake brought in $325 million that same year, NOVA suffered an overall loss of $937 million, due partly to restructuring costs. But sales and earnings increased in 1992 and 1993, as Nova concentrated on trimming general and administrative costs by $10 million annually.

With the results of the corporate review in hand, Newall set out on a second restructuring in 1994. He personally took the lead in this effort, eschewing a conventional salary and instead accepting 68,000 shares of NOVA stock in 1994 and 1995. The CEO hoped that reforming NOVA's natural gas services as a wholly-owned subsidiary would allow the organization—known as NOVA Gas Transmission Ltd.—to raise its own equity and pursue overseas expansion. At the same time, NOVA's petrochemicals business was boosted through the purchase of a 24 percent stake in Vancouver-based Methanex Corporation, the world's largest methanol producer. Increased overseas investments were also expected to pay off during the late 1990s. Newall's plan appeared to be working; in 1994, NOVA achieved record net income of $575 million on revenues of $3.72 billion.

Principal Subsidiaries:

NOVA Gas Transmission Ltd.; Pan-Alberta Gas Ltd.; Foothills Pipe Lines Ltd. (50%, U.S.); Novagas Clearinghouse (50.01%); Novacorp International Inc.; Novacor Chemicals Ltd.

Further Reading:

Carlisle, Tamsin, "Blair Driven to Rekindle NOVA: Vindicating Corporate 'Child' a Personal Quest," *Financial Post,* March 22, 1990.
Enchin, Harvey, "Nova Plans Major Decentralization," *Globe and Mail,* December 3, 1991, p. B1.
Johnson, Arthur, "Shrinking Horizons," *Globe and Mail,* September 21, 1990, p. 104.
Motherwell, Cathryn, "NOVA Shareholders Back Restructuring," *Globe and Mail,* May 7, 1994, p. B20.
Newman, Peter C., "Thinking Man's Energy Baron: Boss-a-Nova Bob Blair," *Maclean's,* February 26, 1990, p. 36.
Phillips, Ed, *Guts and Guile: True Tales From the Backrooms of the Pipeline Industry,* Vancouver, British Columbia: Douglas & McIntyre, 1990.
Wickens, Barbara, "Postponing NOVA's Dream," *Maclean's,* June 4, 1990, pp. 52-53.

—Susan Telingator
—updated by April Dougal Gasbarre

Ontario Hydro

700 University Ave.
Toronto, Ontario M5G 1X6
(416) 592-3345
Fax: (416) 971-3691

State-Owned Company
Incorporated: 1974
Employees: 20,500
Sales: $8.36 billion
SICs: 4911 Electric Services

Ontario Hydro is a government-owned electric utility corporation, regulated by the Ontario Energy Board, that is run as a business. Employing 28,000 full-time workers, and with assets of over $43 billion, it is one of the largest utility companies in North America. The company produces electricity and provides electrical service to the people of Ontario.

While Ontario Hydro produces most of its electricity today from nuclear and fossil-fueled generators, until the 1950s most of Ontario's electricity was derived from water or "hydro" power. Though Ontario is blessed with an abundance of water, much of it does not provide the pressure necessary to generate power because the province's terrain is relatively level and the water does not "fall." Thus electricity was initially provided to larger cities by small, privately owned thermal-electric plants run by fossil fuels.

However, the powerful Niagara Falls is located in Ontario, in an area that was populated by the majority of the province's citizens in the late nineteenth century. In 1895 the first major generating station was built, harnessing the power of the Niagara Falls, which was for many years the province's most vital source of electricity. Still, only local areas were able to take advantage of the power provided by a number of private companies given water-power leases on the falls.

At the turn of the century, a group of prominent citizens began to advocate public ownership of the hydroelectric industry. Foremost among the proponents was Adam Beck, the mayor of London. A vociferous, energetic supporter of public ownership of electric power, he threw the entire weight of his office and his powerful connections behind lobbying the Ontario legislature in favor of the idea, arguing that the thinly populated province would benefit from having a one-company monopoly rather than rival private competitors. Before approval could be given, however, legal battles had to be fought with the United States to regain control of parcels of the Canadian Niagara Falls that had been purchased by American companies. In addition, the public had to be won over to the idea of a government monopoly of electric power.

Finally in 1906 the Ontario legislature passed a statute creating the Hydro Electric Power Commission of Ontario, headed by Sir Adam Beck, as he later became. The commission was given a mandate to provide all citizens with electricity at the lowest possible cost. This "socialist" measure, although viewed with alarm in the United States and Great Britain, achieved its desired results.

Initially Hydro purchased electric power from private entrepreneurs for distribution to those municipalities that had contracts with the commission. However, the utility gradually began to purchase and, much later, to build its own hydroelectric generators, in addition to transmission systems.

The First World War enormously expanded the need for electricity. The demand for electric power in Ontario tripled during the war and continued at the higher rate even after the war's end. In 1914 Hydro purchased its first generating station, and later the same year construction was completed on the first generating station to be built by the commission. Thus began an aggressive purchasing and building campaign, necessary to meet the increased demand, due in part to the soaring popularity of such electric appliances as irons, vacuum cleaners, and washing machines.

By 1922 Hydro was the largest, most powerful utility in the world, with a demand for electricity of 496,000 kilowatts, up from 4,000 kilowatts just 12 years before. To help meet the growing demand, in 1922 Hydro completed construction of its first major power station, Queenston-Chippawa, later renamed the Sir Adam Beck-Niagara Generating Station No. 1. It had taken two thousand men to build, and was the largest power generator in the world.

In the 1930s the commission took over administration of a series of small northern systems—later to be known as the Northern Ontario Properties—that primarily provided service to the paper and mining industries in that region. Three systems, serving the southern, more populated, area of Ontario, were consolidated into the Southern Ontario System in 1944. These two systems were eventually combined into one in 1962, although two others, divided at Sault Ste. Marie into the East System and West System, remained separate. In 1970 all of them were finally merged into one province-wide integrated system, with enough capacity to supply electricity to the United States at a handsome profit.

The years after World War II saw a huge expansion of utility companies, including the Hydro Electric Power Commission of Ontario. Immediately after the war, Hydro began construction of eight additional hydroelectric stations. In the late 1950s—with demand for electricity still unsatisfied—the commission decided to harness the St. Lawrence River, Ontario's last major undeveloped hydraulic site. The St. Lawrence project was undertaken jointly with the State of New York, and, when completed, added an extra one million kilowatts to the Hydro system, which, at the time, included 65 hydro stations and two fossil-fueled plants.

With the completion of the St. Lawrence project in 1958, Ontario had only minor waterways available for hydroelectric development. While thermal-electric plants are efficient generators during peak usage periods, these did not provide a viable alternative to meeting the spiraling demand for electricity, due to the expense of importing the fossil fuels necessary to run the plants. Nuclear power seemed to be the answer, and Ontario was richly endowed with the uranium that was used in the nuclear reactors. As early as 1951 Hydro had begun to experiment with nuclear power for commercial use, completing its first experimental nuclear power plant in 1962, followed in 1967 by a much larger one. While nuclear power is clean and efficient, it is also costly. Hydro engineers began experimenting successfully with increasing the size of nuclear power generators, developing the CANDU, or Canada Denterium-Uranium, that all nuclear power stations in Canada now use. CANDU reactors were successfully installed in the Pickering A generating station, Canada's first major nuclear power facility, completed in 1971. Diminishing natural resources, soaring costs, growing environmental consciousness, and the rise of aboriginal movements in Canada signaled that it was time for the Hydro Electric Power Commission to evaluate its direction for the future. An Ontario legislative task force was established in 1971 to examine these changes and to determine how Hydro could best meet them. The result was a major reorganization that enabled the company to better respond to the social and economic complexities of the late twentieth century. Hydro ceased being a commission and became incorporated as a Crown Corporation in 1974, adopting the name Ontario Hydro. While still a government monopoly, the company became financially independent and was expected to turn a profit. The new Hydro was managed by a 17-member board of directors, 16 of which, including the chair, were appointed by the provincial lieutenant-governor, while the president was appointed by the board itself. Although the newly reorganized company began to focus on social and environmental issues in addition to producing electricity, Ontario Hydro's mandate remained as it was in 1906, although expanded: not only electricity, but also electrical services including inspection and repair of electrical wiring and equipment, would be provided to Ontario citizens.

Throughout the 1970s and 1980s Ontario Hydro faced the public's growing concern about the world's shortage of fossil fuels and mounting damage to the environment. In an effort to deal with these problems, as well as keep costs down and moderate demand, conservation became an important company initiative. By late 1991 Ontario Hydro had invested nearly $179 million in energy conservation, which produced a reduction in demand, in that year, of 250 megawatts and resulted in a savings to customers of $28 million. This commitment to a responsible environmental policy intensified in 1992 with the appointment of Maurice Strong, Canada's best-known environmentalist, as chairman. Other measures undertaken to aid the environment included company-wide recycling and the installation of scrubbers in many of the hydroelectric plants.

Although Ontario Hydro continued to show a modest profit, it found it necessary to reduce its work force and restructure its operations in response to the recession of the early 1990s. Throughout the early 1990s Ontario Hydro executives worked to streamline the organization. The company was praised, however, for its humane downsizing, in which employees whose jobs were targeted for elimination were given the option of assessing their abilities and determining how and where they could best fit into other areas of the company. Those employees who left the company received generous severance packages. Salary freezes were approved for senior management for the foreseeable future. To further offset increased costs and the effects of the recession, the Ontario Energy Board gave its approval for a sizable rate hike of 11.8%.

Ontario Hydro continued to generate profits and increase its exports during the early 1990s. It signed 76 new contracts to provide its services abroad in 1991, for example, and managed to boost revenues ten percent to about $7.14 billion. Sales grew similarly in 1992 and net income increased to a healthy $312 million. Throughout the period, Ontario Hydro managers worked to cut costs and improve efficiency. In 1993 Ontario Hydro appointed Allan Kupcis CEO. Strong continued as Chairman.

Under Kupcis's direction Ontario Hydro continued to cut costs, reduce the size of its work force, and reposition itself for future gains. Restructuring efforts showed up on the bottom line in 1994 when the company recorded net income of $855 million. Although its debt was still more than $34 billion going into 1995, the company's liabilities had been significantly reduced since the late 1980s. Furthermore, Ontario Hydro had reduced its work force to less than 21,000 from more than 32,000 just a few years earlier. Although Ontario Hydro's competitive stance was improved over the early 1990s, it long term success was contingent on some factors outside its control—including the possibility of deregulation, or "open access," in the Ontario electricity supply market.

Further Reading:

"Canadians Replace Layoffs with Voluntary Rightsizing," *Personnel,* May 1991.
"Marc Eliesen: Ontario Hydro's New Chairman Says the Public's Interests Are Best Served by Ensuring That It Remains a Crown Corporation," *Financial Times of Canada,* October 14, 1991.
Nelles, H. V., *The Politics of Development: Forests, Mines and Hydroelectric Power in Ontario, 1849-1941,* Toronto: Macmillan Publishing Co., 1974.
"Ontario Hydro Privatization Urged," *Petroleum Economist,* May 1991.
"Ontario Hydro Profit $587 Million for 1994," *Toronto Star,* March 14, 1995, p. D7.
"Ontario Hydro Says Savings Will Allow It to Defer New Plants," *Wall Street Journal,* January 17, 1992.
"Utility Chooses Nuclear Power," *Christian Science Monitor,* January 16, 1990.
Van Alphen, Tony, "Hydro's Failed Overhaul," *Toronto Star,* October 24, 1994, Section B, p. 1.

Weber, Terry, "Ontario Hydro Confirms New CEO," *Financial Post,* January 28, 1995, Section 1, p. 11.
————, "Ontario Hydro Trims 1,025 Jobs in Buyout Program," *Financial Post,* March 23, 1995, Section 1, p. 12.

—Sina Dubovoj
—updated by Dave Mote

The Oshawa Group Limited

302 The East Mall, Suite 200
Etobicoke, Ontario M9B 6B8
(416) 236-1971
Fax: (416) 236-2071

Public Company
Incorporated: 1957 as Oshawa Wholesale Ltd.
Employees: 19,000 *Sales:* $6 billion
Stock Exchanges: Toronto Montreal
SICs: 5120 Drugs, Proprietaries & Sundries; 5140
  Groceries & Related Products; 5400 Food Stores;
  5912 Drug Stores & Proprietary Stores; 8742
  Management Consulting Services

The Oshawa Group is one of Canada's largest suppliers of food, operating in both the wholesale and retail sectors. In 1995 the company was franchising 645 IGA food stores and about 800 stores under the Knechtel, Food Town, and Bonichoix banners. It also owned 111 supermarkets in Ontario and Nova Scotia under various banners, owned 143 pharmacies in Ontario and Manitoba, and operated the country's largest food service company, SERCA Foodservice Inc.

The Oshawa Group has experienced steady growth since it was established in 1957. It registered record sales and earnings for the 12 consecutive years preceding 1989—a remarkable feat considering the generally cyclical nature of its primary industry—and the company was well positioned to continue its progress going into the mid-1990s.

The company was originally incorporated in Ontario on June 18, 1957 as Oshawa Wholesale Ltd., and operated as a distributor to grocery stores during its first few years. But as the company grew in the early 1960s, it quickly began to diversify. In 1963 Oshawa purchased a controlling interest in the Dominion Mushroom Company, a large mushroom growing and packing concern. Earnings surpassed $1 million in 1963, and Oshawa soon invested heavily in supermarkets. In September of 1964, the company acquired full control of the Independent Grocers Alliance (IGA) Distribution Company. Two months later it purchased the eight units of Bassins Food Chain located in Toronto and Ajax, Ontario, and transformed them into IGA stores. Throughout the rest of the decade the company built a formidable chain of supermarkets through acquisition.

Oshawa diversified into general merchandise retailing in January of 1966 when it purchased a 75 percent interest and took over management of the six-store Rite-Way Department Store chain, which operated throughout Ontario. A year later the company acquired the rest of Rite-Way's shares and purchased Allied Towers Merchants Ltd., another department store chain, combining the operations of the two under one management group.

Oshawa continued its diversification into other businesses and new geographical areas in the late 1960s. In July of 1968, the company purchased Kent Drugs Ltd. The acquisition added about $7 million to Oshawa's annual sales, and Oshawa President Ray D. Wolfe announced the company's plans to put Kent Drug store units in new Towers Department stores. Also in 1968 Oshawa purchased Rockower of Canada Ltd., a firm which operated the men's and boys' departments in 26 of Oshawa's Towers stores. Oshawa's food distribution unit was greatly expanded late in the year by the purchase of Shop & Save Ltd., an IGA supplier in Quebec. The company branched into the Maritimes when it acquired Bolands Ltd., which as supplier to 45 IGA stores in that region had accounted for about $27 million in sales the previous year. By the end of its shopping spree Oshawa was the supplier to 325 IGA stores in five provinces and had become well diversified in the general merchandise and drug store markets.

In the 1970s Oshawa became more involved in real estate dealings. In mid-1970 the company purchased an interest in Baxter Estates, a real estate partnership which owned an apartment building in Winnipeg and a shopping center in Calgary. (The company sold its interest in Baxter three years later for a nearly 100 percent profit).

In November of 1971, three months after it changed its name to The Oshawa Group Ltd. to reflect its diversity, the company purchased the rest of Marchland Holdings Ltd., a real estate developer it already half-owned. At the time of the acquisition Marchland owned four Towers-Food City shopping centers and a commercial complex in Sudbury, Ontario that included a shopping mall, hotel, office center, theater, and parking garage. Oshawa also purchased the remaining third of the modular home developer Systems Construction Ltd. of Ontario.

In early 1972, Oshawa moved into Western Canada by acquiring Codville Distributers Ltd. Oshawa's bid was accepted over the competing bid of Westfair Foods Ltd., a subsidiary of George Weston Ltd., because Oshawa's offer was more attractive to Codville's minority stockholders.

In October of 1973, Harvey S. Wolfe succeeded his brother Raphael Wolfe as president of Oshawa; Raphael became chairman and CEO. In 1976 Oshawa bought out its partners in the Decairie Square shopping mall in Montreal. In December of 1977, Norman S. Lipson, former president of Oshawa's Tower Department Stores unit, pleaded guilty to four counts of fraud which involved kickbacks of $411,000. Lipson had resigned from his position in late 1976. He was sentenced to two years' imprisonment and fined $30,000.

In the late 1970s the Wolfes began to slim Oshawa's operations a bit. The company shed its 50 percent interest in the Consumers Distributing Company, Ltd. in 1978. Consumers Distributing sold brand-name general merchandise at reduced prices in large, no-frills showrooms; Oshawa had entered into a joint venture with the limited-service retailer, providing capital for the chain's expansion eight years before. Oshawa also sold its 90 percent interest in Coinamatic Laundry Equipment in late 1978.

The early 1980s saw Oshawa emphasize its core businesses—food wholesaling and retailing. In 1983 group sales surpassed $2 billion. In 1985 the company strengthened its presence in the Atlantic provinces when it acquired nine supermarkets and a distribution center in Nova Scotia from Dominion Stores Ltd. and bought 22 Canada Safeway supermarkets in the Toronto-Hamilton area. In 1986, as group sales passed the $3 billion mark, Oshawa divested its Dominion Mushroom farm due to both erratic earnings and the unit's need for a major capital reinvestment, and sold its Decairie real estate in Montreal and its Sudbury shopping center.

In the late 1980s Oshawa took bold steps to improve its food retailing business. Oshawa's corporate-owned Food City stores took on a new "streetscape" look. The store layout was intended to resemble an old-fashioned sidewalk merchant atmosphere, and at the same time appeal to young urban professionals as well as retirees. Oshawa targeted upscale consumers wherever possible with specialized services and fancy merchandising. For example, in 1987 the company's Thornhill, Ontario Food City superstore added a kosher deli, bakery, and meat department to appeal to the community's large Jewish population. By specializing wherever possible, Oshawa commanded beefier margins on premium products and services. In 1988 Oshawa tripled its drug store chain by acquiring the 109 retail units of Boots Drug Stores for $45 million. The stores were renamed Pharma-Plus Drugmarts and joined the 34 Kent Drugs and 12 Metro Drugs units in operation. The addition helped Oshawa's sales top $4 billion in 1989. That acquisition was the first in a string of buyouts during the early 1990s that were part of Oshawa's aggressive growth strategy. Sales had already climbed from $2.7 billion in 1985 (fiscal 1986, year ended January 25) to $4.38 billion by 1990.

During the early 1990s, though Oshawa's revenues surged to a record $5.7 billion by 1993. Earnings declined during the period as a result of weak markets, but still hovered between a healthy $35 million to $60 million. Greatest sales growth during the early 1990s occurred in Oshawa's food service and wholesale/retail food sales divisions, while contributions from the companies drug and real estate divisions remained flat.

In 1994 Oshawa reorganized its core food distribution business into three regional operation segments and grouped all of its foodservice holdings into a single division. The move reflected the company's overall effort to reduce costs associated with purchasing and marketing, partly through the integration of advanced electronic information systems. Oshawa continued its legacy of profitability in 1994 when it earned $53 million from record sales of more than $6 billion. By the end of that year the company was operating about 1,500 stores, about 110 of which it owned.

The Oshawa Group's aggressive growth efforts combined with its conservative financial strategy—Oshawa's long-term debt was less than $125 million in 1994—suggested a bright future for the company. Going into 1995, the company continued to concentrate on what it called the mainstream of the market, rather than change store formats to superstores or specialty stores. Although the trend in Europe and the United States was toward increased size and cross-merchandising between food and nonfood retail stores, Oshawa had downplayed that trend in its regions. Instead it was focusing on retail presentation in its department stores and drug stores and broader product lines in its existing supermarkets.

Principal Subsidiaries:

IGA; Knechtel; Food Town; Bonichoix; Food City; Dutch Boy; Price Chopper; SERCA Foodservice Inc.; Pharma Plus.

Further Reading:

Brent, Paul, "Oshawa Group Ahead 15 Percent," *Financial Post,* November 19, 1994, Section 1, p. 5.

—updated by Dave Mote

O & Y Properties Inc.

2 First Canadian Place
Toronto, Ontario M5X 1B5
(416) 862-6100
Fax: (416) 862-5349

Private Company
Incorporated: 1969
Employees: Not available
Sales: $300 million (estimated)
SICs: 6500 Real Estate

During the 1980s and early 1990s, Olympia and York Developments Limited was one of the most respected merchant real-estate companies in the world. With an estimated US$31 billion in assets, a staggering collection of the world's finest office towers, and a fair number of Canada's leading industrial corporations, the company maintained a reputation for honesty and a passion for privacy unusual in the world of big-time real estate. But in May 1992, the privately held creation of three brothers named Reichmann, its resources drained from a tumbling real estate market and mishandled building projects, filed for bankruptcy protection, with a long-term debt of $18.6 billion. Unable to engineer a successful debt restructuring plan, the Reichmanns were forced to dismantle their empire, retaining control only of a modest Toronto-based property management company named O & Y Properties Inc. Since gaining complete control of the fledgling company in July 1993, however, the Reichmann family has acquired management contracts for about 12 million square feet of office and mixed-use buildings, mostly in Toronto, Calgary and Ottawa, and has slowly begun to rebuild its empire.

Albert, Paul, and Ralph +Reichmann were born in pre-World War II Vienna, to a family headed by Samuel Reichmann. Originally from Hungary and of Jewish heritage, Samuel Reichmann led his family on a series of traumatic escapes from Nazi persecution, eventually settling in the free port of Tangier, Morocco. There Reichmann built a reputation for wizardry in banking while preparing his children for a life in business. Albert Reichmann, eldest of the three brothers, joined his father's business; Paul Reichmann went on to Talmudic colleges in England, and in 1957 joined Ralph Reichmann and began another family exodus, to Canada, starting a tile import business in a Toronto suburb. An ancient Greek culture enthusiast, Ralph named this

venture Olympia Floor & Tile Co. Within a few years Paul and Ralph were joined by the rest of the Reichmann family.

Later the prospering tile company needed a new warehouse, and the Reichmanns built it themselves for about half of the contractor's bid. They decided to pursue opportunities in suburban real estate, beginning with building more warehouses. The strong economy of the early 1960s provided ample room for expansion in Toronto industrial real estate, and the Reichmann family soon became known as a leading local builder of high-quality industrial space. The Reichmanns early learned the importance of streamlined construction practices, developing a knack for money-saving innovations that would later prove to be worth many millions of dollars. Their real-estate business was organized in several companies. One of them was called York Developments, and in 1969 the three brothers consolidated their various concerns under the name of Olympia & York Developments Ltd.

The Reichmanns already had established a number of operating principles from which they would never deviate. They were scrupulously honest in their negotiating, earning a reputation as people whose handshake was as good as a contract. They built solid structures on time and under budget, maintained excellent relations with tenants, and came up with ingenious financing packages designed to keep ownership of all properties within the family. The brothers paid close attention to the desires of municipal and state government officials, whose cooperation became increasingly important as the size of their projects grew. The Reichmanns also remained devoutly Orthodox, stopping all work by sundown every Friday and on Jewish holidays throughout the year.

In 1965 the brothers demonstrated the last ingredient in their formula for success—a willingness to gamble. When U.S. real estate mogul William Zeckendorf fell on hard times, the Reichmanns seized a chance to buy from him 500 acres of land just outside Toronto for $18 million. After selling off a few parcels to reduce debt, the brothers began a series of highly successful office buildings on the site. The Reichmanns were able to build the complex office structures with their usual efficiency, advancing from projects on the Zeckendorf purchase to bigger and more profitable ventures in Ottawa, Calgary, and downtown Toronto.

The brothers were as yet little known when they acquired a valuable piece of property in the heart of Toronto in 1973 and announced plans to construct the tallest building in Canada, a 72-story office tower called First Canadian Place. The proposal was considered too grand for Toronto's market in some quarters—its 3.5 million square feet represented a 10 percent increase in the city's available office space—but the Reichmann brothers went to work with their customary ingenuity. They devised a new method of construction in which all activity took place within the building; a complicated network of elevators and turntables moved supplies and men to where they were needed. The Reichmanns estimated that the technique saved up to 2.5 hours of labor per worker every day, a saving that became of critical importance when the building was slow to lease.

Despite the leasing problems, the Reichmanns refused to cut their rents and eventually managed to raise them 350 percent during the four years it took to fill the building. First Canadian Place permanently changed the Toronto high-rise market and became the flagship of O & Y's real estate empire.

Having amassed a net worth estimated at US$1 billion by the time First Canadian was finished in 1976, the Reichmanns began to look farther afield for their next project. In New York City, the National Kinney Corporation was trying to sell a block of eight Manhattan office buildings known as the Uris portfolio. At the time, the city was flirting with bankruptcy and its real estate market was severely depressed. It was not clear whether New York would retain its position as the world's most important business center or slide into a decline. The Reichmanns concluded that, unless New York's recession was permanent, the Uris land alone was worth more than the US$320 million asking price, and in 1977 they used the equity built up in First Canadian Place to finance the deal. Within a few years the glut of Manhattan office space had become a shortage as the local economy roared back, and the Reichmanns were able to triple rents while still keeping their eight new buildings nearly full. The Uris acquisition proved to be a tremendous coup for the Reichmanns, their investment of US$320 million growing in five years to an estimated value of US$3 billion, and providing an equity base sufficient to launch O & Y on to bigger developments.

O & Y moved on to the World Financial Center at Manhattan's extreme southern tip. This Battery Park site, adjacent to the World Trade Center, had been entangled in political and financial difficulties since its creation out of landfill. Olympia joined 11 other bidders in a 1980 competition to gain approval for construction, and eventually emerged as the winner. World Financial Center was a gigantic project: six buildings with two-thirds as much space as the towering World Trade Center next door, 250,000 square feet of shops and restaurants, and four acres of well-designed public spaces. The project, in which the Reichmanns poured US$300 million of their own money, also provided for the construction of low-cost public housing in the area. The Reichmanns were able to do all of this with money borrowed below prime rate against their Uris properties, and by implementing the same highly efficient construction methods as they had used at First Canadian Place. At the same time, they were erecting US$750 million of office towers in other U.S. cities, all during a period of severe recession. To land the prestigious tenants the World Financial project needed to assure its success, the Reichmanns took the unusual step of buying the buildings housing the tenants' previous offices in exchange for long-term lease commitments. In this way both American Express Company and City Investing Company agreed to take large blocks of space.

The Reichmanns also had begun buying stock in major industrial corporations. In 1981 the brothers paid $618 million, most of it, again, borrowed against the Uris properties, for about 90 percent of the stock in Abitibi-Price, the world's largest manufacturer of newsprint paper. They soon added large pieces of MacMillan Bloedel Ltd., another forest-products company; Hiram Walker Resources Ltd., the liquor giant; and also bought into a number of other important Canadian real estate developers. In 1983 the brothers joined forces with Canada's Bronfman family, taking a 13 percent interest in the Bronfman's Trilon Financial Corporation, a fast-growing diversified marketer of financial services. During the next few years the Reichmanns increased their holdings in Hiram Walker to 49 percent, but in 1986 they lost a bidding war for control of the company and traded their stake for US$360 million in cash and a 10 percent share of its new owner, Allied-Lyons plc of the United Kingdom. More successful was a 1985 bid for Chevron Corporation's 60 percent interest in Gulf Canada Ltd., one of the country's leading oil producers; O & Y's US$2.1 billion offer was accepted, and the brothers subsequently increased their stake to nearly 75 percent. Finally, in 1987, they took part in a restructuring of Santa Fe Southern Pacific Corporation, buying 19.6 percent of the enormous railway, oil, and real estate concern.

With all that, the brothers remained primarily real estate developers, and in 1987 they took charge of a yet vaster project in the United Kingdom. London's Docklands, just east of the bustling city center, had been a severely depressed area for years due to England's declining shipping business and the closure of most of the city's docks. The local government had launched a project designed to transform a part of the Docklands, called the Isle of Dogs, into a new center of white-collar business. The development foundered until the Reichmanns took over in 1987. In their boldest venture yet, the brothers financed construction of what amounted to a small city that was expected to provide 12 million square feet of offices in 24 buildings, one of them to be the tallest in the United Kingdom. The project, called Canary Wharf, was an enormous undertaking—the largest real estate development in Europe—and aimed at a permanent restructuring of London's downtown office market, much as First Canadian Place had done in Toronto. The project's future depended on construction of a new subway route and the upgrading of available rail service, as well as the success in attracting London's prestigious clients with the promise of low rents and modern working space.

A phenomenal boom in the British economy, aided by deregulation and the emergence of information age technology, suggested to the Reichmanns that a modern office tower in London would help turn the city into the financial capital of a resurgent, post-Cold War Europe. But the reunification of Germany and the resurgence of its economy threatened London's status in the financial community: many foreign banks that had entered the city during the late 1980s returned home after suffering heavy losses. And while tenants had once been desperate to get into any development, by the early 1990s vacancy rates were as high as 20 percent. "We had anticipated the change in the market," Paul Reichmann stated in the *Globe and Mail,* "but not the depth of the change." With just half the complex rented by late 1991, and interest payments believed to have been as high as $20 million a month, O & Y's losses continued to climb to upwards of $3 billion. The losses suffered in the Canary Wharf project, however, were symptoms of an even larger financial crisis. The famous Reichmann mystique that had led creditors to lend the company billions of dollars, reportedly without scrutinizing its balance sheets, proved disastrous. The recession of the early 1990s, an ensuing decline in the Toronto and New York real estate markets, and a collapsing stock market that brought about a $1.25-billion loss to the Reichmanns' extensive portfolio, left the company unprepared to meet its financial obligations. The news of the company's financial crisis only served to exacerbate its problems: as more and more information was released and the number of O & Y's multi-million-dollar creditors multiplied, it became more apparent that the company would have no choice but to seek bankruptcy protection.

After several failed restructuring attempts and a refusal of the Canadian government to bail out the real estate giant, O & Y finally filed for protection in Canada under the Companies Creditors Arrangement Act. According to a *Globe and Mail* report by Brian Milner and Margaret Philip, when asked whether this signified the end of the company, Steve Miller, a chief advisor to the company, responded, "Absolutely not. Olympia & York is continuing in business. If I can make an analogy for you, it's as though you're walking down the street, you notice it's raining, you open your umbrella and keep going."

Despite such optimism and numerous negotiations with the company's nearly 100 banks, O & Y failed to keep its empire in tact. In February 1993, a Toronto judge signed a court order approving the dismantling of the company. Their multi-billion-dollar operation reduced to a modest real-estate management firm, O & Y Properties, the Reichmanns had come full circle. It would not take long, however, for the family to start its comeback. Just a few days after the decision, Paul Reichmann, behind the financial strength of a New York financier, launched an international real estate firm. Meanwhile, Philip Reichmann, Albert's son, and Frank Hauer, Paul's son-in-law, took over control of the O & Y remnant.

In May 1995, O & Y Properties showed further signs of a comeback, acquiring a 50 percent interest in Paseo Gestion Immobiliere Inc., a property manger based in Montreal, and announcing plans to create a new, joint venture management company, O & Y Services Immobilieres Inc. Having established a strong base in Toronto, the company looked to expand its business in Montreal, a city that has one of the highest concentra-

tions of high-quality office buildings in the country. While the O & Y portfolio of the mid-1990s paled in comparison to its properties of the previous decade, the company had slowly begun to rebuild its reputation. As Donald Fitzpatrick, an executive vice-president of CB Commercial Real Estate Group Canada Inc. of Toronto and a satisfied O & Y customer, told the *Globe and Mail*'s Leonard Zehr, "I give Philip a lot of credit for regaining the credibility that the family lost." Whether or not the banks that lost hundreds of millions of dollars on the Reichmanns would renew their faith in the company, however, remained to be seen.

Further Reading:

Foster, Peter, *Towers of Debt: The Rise and Fall of the Reichmanns,* Key Porter, 1993.
Greenspon, Edward, and Enchin, Harvey, "O & Y's Myth Meets its Match," *Globe and Mail,* May 16, 1992, p. A1.
Howlett, Karen, "Reichmanns Retain Hold on Remnant of Their Empire," *Globe and Mail,* July 27, 1993, p. B3.
Mason, Todd, and Weiner, Elizabeth, "Inside the Reichmann Empire," *Business Week,* January 29, 1990.
McNish, Jacquie, "How Banks Flubbed O & Y," *Globe and Mail,* December 4, 1992, p. A1.
_____, "One Year after the Fall: The Lessons of Olympia and York," *Globe and Mail,* March 22, 1993, p. B1.
_____, "Peace Pact Frees O & Y Unit to Restructure," *Globe and Mail,* June 24, 1993, p. B1.
Milner, Brian, and Bourette, Susan, "O & Y Seeking Cash Infusion," *Globe and Mail,* January 18, 1995, p. B1.
Milner, Brian, and Philip, Margaret, "O & Y Puts on Brave Face to Mask Predicament," *Globe and Mail,* May 16, 1992, p. B1.
Stewart, Walter, *Too Big to Fail: The Story Behind the Headlines,* McClelland & Stewart, 1994.
Philip, Margaret, "Old O & Y Hands Land on Feet," *Globe and Mail,* March 22, 1993, p. B2.
Tully, Shawn, "The Bashful Billionaires of Olympia & York," *Fortune,* June 14, 1982.
Zehr, Leonard, "O & Y Properties Flexes Its Muscles," *Globe and Mail,* May 29, 1995, p. B1.

—Jonathan Martin
—updated by Jason Gallman

PanCanadian Petroleum Limited

PanCanadian Plaza
150 Ninth Avenue SW
Calgary, Alberta T2P 3H9
(403) 290-2000
Fax: (403) 290-2950

Public Company
Incorporated: 1958 as Canadian Pacific Oil and Gas
  Limited
Employees: 1483
Revenues: $1.48 billion
Stock Exchanges: Montreal Toronto Alberta
SICs: 1311 Crude Petroleum & Natural Gas; 1321
  Natural Gas Liquids; 2911 Petroleum Refining;
  4920 Gas Production & Distribution; 5169
  Chemicals & Allied Products Nec; 5172 Petroleum
  Products Nec.

With production of over 130,000 barrels of oil and 574 million cubic feet of natural gas each day, PanCanadian Petroleum Limited ranks among Canada's largest producers of oil and natural gas. Following a stunning turnaround in the early 1990s, the company initiated the most ambitious capital investment program in the Canadian oil industry, plowing over $850 million into new exploration and development—including over 1100 new wells—in 1994 alone. At that time, PanCanadian's four most important revenue streams were oil, which contributed 42 percent of annual sales; natural gas, at 27 percent; fuel marketing, at 11 percent; and syncrude (synthetic crude), at 10 percent.

In 1995, over four-fifths of PanCanadian's shares were held by Canadian Pacific Enterprises Limited, a subsidiary of Canadian Pacific Ltd., Canada's biggest non-government enterprise, with interests in steel, mining, hotels, agricultural chemicals, financial services, and pulp and paper, as well as its once-core railroad. PanCanadian Petroleum has been one of Canadian Pacific's most profitable diversifications.

The Canadian Pacific Railway Company (CP) was founded in 1881 to build a transcontinental railroad across Canada. In order to promote the project and thereby encourage western settlement, the Canadian government ceded 25 million acres of Crown-owned land in Manitoba, Alberta and Saskatchewan to the railway company. PanCanadian Petroleum was a logical

extension of the Canadian Pacific's activities, its origins dating back to 1883, two years before Canadian Pacific's transcontinental railroad was completed. That December, a crew working near Medicine Hat, Alberta, was drilling for water when (to their disappointment) they instead found natural gas. On that site, the company built Alberta's first producing gas well which fueled street and residential lighting through the 1930s.

Ironically, however, the resources that would form the basis of one of Canadian Pacific's most profitable subsidiaries were virtually ignored for nearly seven decades. CP didn't begin to take advantage of the vast potential of its land and mineral rights until after World War II, when several trends converged to compel the company's diversification. Competition from automobiles in the passenger sector and trucking in the freight sector cut into the railroads' traffic base. Federal regulations, however, required the trains to maintain certain lines even if they were unprofitable. In the face of these hurdles, the company needed large amounts of cash to build, maintain, and upgrade its operations to remain competitive. Burgeoning gasoline demand and major discoveries of oil in western Canada revealed one way to parlay the company's real estate holdings into ready cash.

Under the leadership of Norris Crump, CP became one of the first North American railway companies to see the writing on the wall and begin diversifying. Crump had first started with the railroad in 1920 and moved up through the ranks to become president in 1955. He created Canadian Pacific Oil and Gas Limited to undertake exploration of the railway's properties in 1958.

Crump created Canadian Pacific Investments to serve as the parent company's vehicle for diversification in 1962. A public share offering in 1967 helped raise investment funds, but CP retained a controlling interest. A reorganization shifted the petroleum operations to CP Investments (which was later renamed Canadian Pacific Enterprises Ltd.), where they remained throughout the ensuing three decades.

In 1963, CP Oil and Gas started to accumulate shares in Central-Del Rio Oils Limited, a small producer that first incorporated in 1947 as Central Leduc Oils Limited. The two companies' stakes in each other increased over the course of the 1960s until 1971, when they were merged as PanCanadian Petroleum Limited.

By virtue of a transfer from its ultimate parent, PanCanadian instantly became Canada's largest owner of freehold oil land, most of it in Alberta's "oil patch." The company's outright ownership of nearly 11 million acres of previously public land has long been recognized as its most valuable asset and most important competitive advantage. (After more than three decades of exploration and development, the company still boasted 6.8 million acres of undeveloped land.) The majority of PanCan's rivals leased exploration and production rights on Crown lands, and were given a maximum of five years to look for and retrieve any resources found therein, paying the government an additional 30 percent royalty in such a case. PanCanadian also paid royalties, but its writeoffs for exploration expenses could reduce that bill by over one-fourth. It also enjoyed an unlimited amount of time to explore and drill on its lands, which undoubtedly contributed to its status as one of the most inquisitive of Canada's oil companies.

Pan Canadian's competitive advantage could have contributed to a freewheeling corporate strategy, but instead caution became a company hallmark. PanCan built up its reserves during the 1970s, often discovering more oil and gas than it sold. By the latter years of the decade, the company's revenues neared $500 million and net profits topped $155 million.

The firm's heritage of conservatism was embodied in Bartlett B. Rombough, who advanced to PanCanadian's presidency in 1980. The circumstances at the time of his rise to leadership may have contributed to his prudence: a global petroleum glut exacerbated recession-induced problems in the early 1980s. But while many competitors suffered losses and piled up debt, PanCanadian breezed through the first half of the decade with relative ease. Profits slid 16 percent from 1980 to 1981, then joined revenues in a persistent climb. In 1984, annual sales surpassed the $1 billion mark and profits increased to $300 million, up 29 percent from 1980's $232 million. But market conditions and bad luck caught up with PanCanadian in the late 1980s. Plummeting oil and natural gas prices slashed PanCanadian's profits in more ways than one. In 1986, the company was compelled to "write down" the value of its foreign natural gas properties to the tune of $94.8 million. The streak of bad luck continued when the company rushed to buy land in northwest Alberta in the hopes of making a big natural gas find, as had competitor Shell Canada Ltd. By the time PanCan gave up on that project in 1988, its annual revenues had declined to $674 million and profits had shrunk to $124.5 million.

In 1990, PanCanadian's board brought in David P. O'Brien to replace Rombough as president and chairman. O'Brien had held top positions with industry leaders Petro-Canada Inc. and Noverco Inc. The 49-year-old made no bones about his plans to shed PanCan's reputation for stodginess. His three-pronged plan focused on increasing profitability through sale of non-core businesses, reduction of operating expenses, and increases in production.

By 1993, the company had divested its U.S. gas and oil assets, sold the Langevin Resources subsidiary, and liquidated a heating oil distributor. O'Brien set out to improve the performance of the remaining operations. But in spite of (or perhaps because of) the many time-, money-, and labor-saving ideas implemented, O'Brien was unable to avoid a 14 percent staff reduction in 1992. The new president "moved [PanCan] up the risk curve" with increased investment in exploration and development. Capital expenditures more than doubled, from around $300 million in 1989 to $854 million in 1994. O'Brien leveraged the increased budget by forming strategic alliances with other firms in the oil industry.

Whereas virtually all of the company's capital budget had previously been invested in North American projects, O'Brien began to look overseas for new opportunities. His desire for geographic diversity was driven in part by declining reserves and the correspondingly high cost of Canadian exploration. In 1992, PanCan formed an international division to coordinate these

projects. The vast majority of PanCan's foreign business consisted of joint ventures, which helped to spread the operations' political and economic risk. The core of the international division was a strategic alliance in Russia known as Samotlor PanCanadian Fracmaster Services. This unwieldy name incorporated the names of the partners: Russia's Samotlorneft owned 50 percent of the project, while PanCanadian and Canadian Fracmaster each held 25 percent.

By 1993, PanCan had also formed operations in Asia, Australia, and Africa. The company's Australian project enlisted the cooperation of Amoplex Ltd. (which owned 65 percent) and Bridge Oil Ltd. (which controlled 10 percent). PanCanadian owned 60 percent of a partnership with Canadian Occidental Petroleum Ltd. to explore a site in Indonesia. PanCanadian's 15 percent interest in a joint venture with Fina Exploration Libya BV took the company to Africa's Sirte Basin, where 12 wells were planned.

O'Brien's multi-faceted revitalization program kept PanCanadian from following its rivals into the red in the early 1990s. From 1990 to 1994, production (in oil and gas equivalents) increased from 78,500 barrels per day to 130,000 barrels per day. After dropping to $852.7 million in 1991, revenues increased 73.6 percent to $1.48 billion by 1994. Due in part to a $100 million write-down of assets, net income dropped to $47.5 million in 1991, then grew sixfold to $287.3 million in 1994. The turnaround won O'Brien accolades and set the stage for a major advancement in his career.

At the end of 1994, PanCan lost its energetic leader to Canadian Pacific after CP president James Hankison abruptly resigned and O'Brien was called up to take his place. O'Brien continued as chairman of PanCanadian's board, and was succeed as president and CEO by 20-year PanCanadian veteran David Tuer early in 1995. Tuer's resume also included a stint as Alberta's Assistant Deputy Minister of Energy from 1985 to 1988, after which he returned to PanCanadian.

By this time, market imperatives again called for a change in strategy. Burdened by 36 percent export taxes and a disintegrating infrastructure, the company's Russian venture was only marginally profitable. In 1994, PanCanadian indicated that it would be limiting its overseas activities and refocusing capital expenditures on its domestic interests.

One indigenous project in particular garnered much attention and spurred rampant speculation. In 1995, PanCanadian formed a 50-50 joint venture with Dallas's privately and closely held Hunt Oil to survey on- and off-shore plots in areas of Newfoundland that had not been explored since the early 1970s. The region had for the most part been abandoned due to a dearth of commercially viable finds. But armed with new technology that allowed for ever-deeper drilling and a strong hunch, Hunt and PanCanadian pursued secretive exploration. They reasoned that since the region's geological formations closely matched those of Oklahoma's Arkoma Basin and Texas's Midland Basin, it could contain similarly large reserves of oil. By the fall of 1994, they had invested millions and drilled a "wildcat well" on Newfoundland's west coast. Whereas previous crews had only drilled to depths of about 700 meters, Hunt-

PanCanadian drilled more than six times deeper, to 4,600 meters. This activity titillated locals, analysts, and competitors alike. Residents hoped that a major oil strike would relieve high levels of unemployment. Market speculation drove up PanCanadian's stock by over 35 percent in the spring of 1995. And rivals hoping to cash in on Hunt-PanCanadian's legwork began snatching up petroleum leases in the region. But in spite of the clamor for information, the partners remained firm in their desire to keep their findings under wraps until mid-1996. The most PanCan President Tuer would reveal was that he and his partners were "encouraged by [their] progress to date."

PanCanadian also took some tentative steps into refining and transportation in the early 1990s. A 1993 joint venture with Amoco Canada Ltd. planned to build at least one $30 million natural gas processing plant near Medicine Hat, Alberta. The facility was projected to have the capacity to process 800 million cubic feet of fuel per day. A deal with Alberta Natural Gas Co. Ltd. transferred that company's natural gas liquids and crude oil brokerage business in Canada, as well as a stake in a Michigan storage facility, to PanCan in 1994. PanCanadian executives hoped that these new capabilities, which amounted to 11 percent of 1994's revenues, would enable the company to retain increased profits.

Principal Subsidiaries:

Langevin Holdings (Barbados) Limited; Langevin Insurance (Barbados) Limited; PanCanadian Energy Inc.; PanCanadian Exploration and Production B.V.; Pan-Canadian Gas Products Ltd.; PanCanadian Kerrobert Pipeline Ltd.; PanCanadian Petroleum (Australia) Limited; PanCanadian Petroleum (Libya) Limited; PanCanadian Petroleum (North Caspian) Limited; PanCanadian Petroleum (U.K.) Limited; PanCanadian Petroleum Company; PanCanadian Petroleum Holdings B.V.; PanCanadian Petroleum Holdings Limited; PanCanadian Petroleum International Limited; PanCanadian Petroleum Netherlands B.V.; PanCanadian Petroleum Offshore (Cyprus) Limited; PanCanadian Ventures Inc.; PCP (KLP) Cogeneration Ltd.; PCP Fuel Management Ltd.; 2891174 Canada Ltd.; 592284 Alberta Ltd.; Maxim Petroleum Marketing Partnership; PanCanadian Resources; Siding Resources; Kinetic Resources (LPG) (75%); Kinetic Resources (U.S.A.) (75%).

Further Reading:

Donville, Christopher, "CEO Has Big Plans for PanCanadian," *Globe and Mail,* November 19, 1990, p. B10.
Foster, Cecil, "Energy Accord Held Beneficial to Pancanadian Pete," *Globe and Mail,* June 10, 1985, p. B12.
Goldenberg, Susan, *Canadian Pacific: A Portrait of Power,* Methuen Publications: Toronto, 1983.
Hunter, Nicholas, "PanCanadian A Top Investment Based on Land Riches," *Globe and Mail,* October 21, 1985, p. B6.
Jang, Brent, "Hunt Followed Hunch in Newfoundland," *Globe and Mail,* May 3, 1995, p. B8.
Motherwell, Cathryn, "The Change Page: Pumping Up the Oil Patch," *Globe and Mail,* August 25, 1992, p. B20.
————, "Canadian Oil Firms Hang Tough in Russia," *Globe and Mail,* November 8, 1994, p. B21.
————, "CP's New Boss Set For 'Enormous Challenges,'" *Globe and Mail,* December 15, 1994, p. B1.
————, "Report on Energy: Far Fields Beckon Energy Firms," *Globe and Mail,* December 15, 1993, p. B21.

—April Dougal Gasbarre

Petro-Canada

150 Sixth Avenue S.W.
P.O. Box 2844
Calgary, Alberta T2P 3E3
(403) 296-8000
Fax: (403) 296-3030

Public Company
Incorporated: 1975 as Petro-Canada
Employees: 6,353
Revenues: $4.73 billion
Stock Exchanges: Toronto Vancouver Alberta
  Montreal
SICs: 1311 Crude Petroleum and Natural Gas; 2911
  Petroleum Refining; 5172 Petroleum Products,
  nec.

Known by some as "the oil company Canadians love to hate," Petro-Canada ranked among the country's top three integrated petroleum companies in the mid-1990s. The firm's most distinguishing aspect has been its operation as a Crown corporation substantially owned by the government of Canada. As such, the government owned any property held by Petro-Canada, which is commonly known as Petrocan. Common shares in the company were held in the name of the Minister of Energy, Mines, and Resources. Almost since its founding, proposals had been made to sell Petro-Canada's common shares to the public. After 16 years under this ownership structure, the company's equity was transferred to the Minister of Privatization, who made an initial public offering of 15 percent of its equity in July 1991. Subsequent offerings reduced the government's holdings to about 70 percent of total equity by Fall 1994. This privatization and an early 1990s recession were followed by the deposition of Petrocan "czar" Wilbert Hopper as well as a much needed rationalization.

Petro-Canada's interests fall into two categories. Petro-Canada Resources explores, produces, and markets crude oils, natural gas and its liquids, sulfur, and bitumens. Petro-Canada Products refines, markets, and distributes various petroleum products and by-products, and offers other related goods and services. In the mid-1990s, it was the largest Canadian-owned petroleum firm. The giant corporation has built an energy network that sells more than 17 percent of the country's gasoline, placing it second among fuel retailers in 1994. Petro-

Canada's 2,200 gas stations sell an average of 2.5 million liters each year.

Created by an act of parliament in 1975, Petro-Canada was a product of the oil crisis that shook the world in 1973 and 1974, driving oil prices up and creating havoc with the energy supply. When OPEC substantially increased oil prices, Canada became aware of the vulnerability of its foreign oil supplies. The energy crisis focused the country's attention on the extent to which foreign countries dominated domestic oil production. Coincidental with the OPEC price increases, a sharp downward revision of Canada's oil reserves created substantial fears about whether supplies of domestic crude oil would be adequate for future needs. Petro-Canada was originally established as an effort to provide more Canadian control over the domestic oil industry, to ensure that the nation would receive its fair share of remote and difficult-to-reach energy resources, and to provide the federal government with a listening post on the country's oil industry.

Maurice Strong, who earlier had helped establish Dome Petroleum, served as Petro-Canada's first chairman. It was Wilbert Hopper, more than any other individual, however, who made Petro-Canada a success story. Ottawa-born Hopper, with degrees in geology and business administration, started in the oil business as a geologist for Imperial Oil Ltd. in the 1950s. In the early 1960s, he was senior economist for the Canadian National Energy Board, before joining the Cambridge, Massachusetts-based international consulting firm of Arthur D. Little. With a solid reputation in the oil industry, Hopper caught the attention of Canadian Prime Minister Pierre Elliott Trudeau, who sought Hopper's advice in forming a state-owned oil company. Thus began Petro-Canada. Hopper started his association with the company as a vice president in 1976. Six months later, he was named president and chief executive officer. In 1979 he became chairman as well as CEO.

The initial holdings of Petro-Canada included properties previously owned by the government of Canada, that were conveyed to the company after its formation: a 12 percent interest in Syncrude oil-sands mining project in northern Alberta; a 45 percent interest in Panarctic Oils, and a stake in the Polar Gas project, which was set up to operate a gas pipeline from the Arctic. With access to large amounts of money, Petro-Canada bought several Canadian-based oil companies that significantly increased its land holdings and oil and gas reserves, and quickly made it a giant in the oil industry.

The company's first purchase, Atlantic Richfield Canada, was made in 1976 for $342 million. Assets acquired from Atlantic Richfield included both producing and undeveloped oil and gas properties in western Canada, natural gas-processing facilities, undeveloped oil and gas properties in the Arctic, and an additional interest in oil-sands leases. The cash flow from the producing assets funded exploration and development of new sources. Two years later, in 1978, Petro-Canada borrowed US$1.25 billion from Canadian banks to finance the purchase of Pacific Petroleum, which tripled the company's oil production and quintupled its gas production. Pacific Petroleum's assets added also coal leases in western Canada, oil properties outside of Canada, and distribution and sales facilities—among them being 400 retail outlets. Among Petro-Canada's mandates set forth by the federal government was that of special emphasis on exploration in remote frontier regions. In 1977 the company made its first discoveries of oil and natural gas pools in the Brazeau River area, southwest of Edmonton, and in the late 1970s, it participated in several oil discoveries in the Utikuma Lake area, northwest of Edmonton. Since 1979 Petro-Canada conducted an international exploration program that has included activities in Colombia, Ecuador, Indonesia, Papua New Guinea, and offshore China.

Petro-Canada's development has been controversial from the beginning. Members of the country's private oil industry have charged that the state-owned corporation has received preferential treatment and has a significant political and financial advantage over its private-sector competitors. Petro-Canada's easy access to government funding, which enabled it to expand through acquisition of competitors into one of the industry's top three players within barely a decade, was particularly irksome to the Canadian oil establishment. The counter-argument was that Petro-Canada has been required to undertake high-risk projects in the public interest, such as investment in frontier exploration, that can only be done with the infusion of government funds.

After briefly losing power in the late 1970s, the Liberal government forged ahead with its agenda, introducing federal legislation under the National Energy Program (NEP) that gave Petro-Canada 25 percent rights on all federal land, including potentially rich frontier acreage. Those rights have been described by the Canadian Petroleum Association as retroactive confiscation of assets. The NEP also gave Petro-Canada more power over the nation's energy resources, including acquiescence to the company's continuing takeover of competitors.

One of Petro-Canada's few unquestionable successes was its major role in increasing domestic ownership of integrated oil companies from 26 percent of industry revenues in 1980 to 48.2 percent in 1985. The 1981 acquisition of Petrofina Canada, Inc. for US$348 million represented not only the nationalization of a Belgian-owned oil company, but also the expansion of Petro-Canada's activities from long-term frontier exploration and development projects—its original mandate—into refining and marketing. Petrofina's over 1,100 service stations throughout Canada more than tripled the acquiring company's previous retail operations. Two years later, Petro-Canada bought BP Canada for $425 million, adding another 1,640 service stations and 108 terminals and bulk plants.

Canada's private oil sector strongly protested these two major purchases, arguing that publicly funded competition in the oil industry had become a destructive practice. Hostility to the company was displayed in the press, and some oil men began to refer to Petro-Canada's 52-story red-granite clad headquarters in downtown Calgary as "Red Square." The private sector also fumed over a federal government decision in mid-1982 awarding acreage in a Sable Island area off Nova Scotia to a group headed by Petro-Canada, protesting that Petro-

Canada had not had to compete with other companies for the rights. Relations between the state-owned oil company and the private sector reached an all-time low in 1985 when Hopper announced at a public conference that his company was withdrawing membership from the Independent Petroleum Association of Canada.

By the mid-1980s Petro-Canada was an established major player on the Canadian oil industry scene, the existence and mandate of which was supported by a clear majority of Canadians. With the purchase of the Petrofina and BP interests, Petro-Canada became Canada's fifth-largest company, with nearly 6,000 employees. It was the country's third-largest gasoline marketer and the only nationwide station chain. The company continued with successful oil discoveries during the 1980s, principally in Saskatchewan, including the Cactus Lake field in 1980, the Salt Lake field in 1984, and the Hoosier South field in 1987.

The Progressive Conservative Party swept into power in December 1984, determined to reduce the national government's role in business. "Reform is urgently needed," Prime Minister Brian Mulroney declared. "Crown corporations have become a state within a state," as reported in Business Week of September 24, 1984. Petro-Canada, the new government mandated, must be regarded less as an instrument of national policy and more as a commercial operation. By the mid-1980s Petro-Canada seemed to be moving in this new direction, a change signaled by Chairman Hopper in the company's 1984 annual report. He wrote: "The corporation has now been given a new mandate by its shareholder [the Canadian government]—to operate in a commercial, private sector fashion with emphasis on profitability and the need to maximize return on the government of Canada's investment."

Soon after taking office, the Conservatives replaced Petro-Canada board members appointed by the previous Liberal government and canceled about US$250 million in additional funding for 1985 that had been Liberal-approved. The government also told the company it had to finance its operation from revenues or market financing.

In 1985 Petro-Canada made a deal that appeared to reflect its new mandate and to mark a turning point in the history of the company. Petro-Canada purchased Gulf Canada Limited's refining, distribution, and marketing assets in Ontario, western Canada, the Yukon Territory, and the Northwest Territories for $896 million by using its own internally generated funds and short-term debt—not taxpayers' money. Among the assets acquired were a lubricants plant, an asphalt plant, and 1,800 additional retail outlets. The acquisition increased the size of Petro-Canada, giving the company at that time about US$10 billion in assets and making it an even bigger force on the Canadian petroleum scene.

For the next three years, the federal government talked of privatization but allowed Petro-Canada to consolidate and rationalize its operations. In 1988, for example, Petro-Canada significantly increased its expenditures in natural gas development, reflecting the company's increased focus on the natural gas business, and also entered into a preliminary agreement providing for the potential development of an oil-sands mining project, the OSLO project, at Kearl Lake, Alberta, and for the Hibernia oil field off Newfoundland's east coast.

By 1988 the private oil sector's hostility seemed to have dissipated. Peter Foster, a long-standing critic of Petro-Canada and the petroleum industry in general, speculated that private-sector oilmen had been mollified by the Crown corporation's investments in their high-risk joint exploration ventures. Hopper was elected president of the Canadian Petroleum Association and public support ran relatively high: one poll showed a 45 percent public approval of the company, with 35 percent of the public indifferent or ambivalent, and only 20 percent opposed outright to the company's existence. In order to maintain its improving public image, Petro-Canada sponsored an 18,000 kilometer cross-country relay of the Olympic torch dubbed "Share the Flame." The 80-day promotion drew 7,000 torch bearers and cost Petro-Canada $5.5 million to stage. It was just one of many patriotic campaigns carried out during the late 1980s.

The future looked rosy indeed for the oil giant when it reported 1987 to be its most profitable year ever. But when put in perspective, those "record earnings" weren't much to crow about. Over the course of the 1980s, the company earned total profits of $38 million. Its return on shareholders equity lagged comparable competitors by a wide margin. Whereas Imperial Oil Ltd. earned an average return on equity of 10.8 percent and Shell made 9.46 percent from 1980 to 1989, Petro-Canada made a paltry 1.43 percent. CEO Hopper acknowledged this in a 1991 interview with *Maclean's,* noting that "compared with our competition, we are well aware of our lower performance." A high rate of debt service on the company's $1 billion in long-term financing, in fact, led to a shift in the company's economic strategy from aggressively investing in remote areas toward enhancing the company's financial health and operating capability.

In 1989 Petro-Canada began a $50 million internal reorganization that led to a staff reduction of over 1,000 positions. After several years of equivocation, the Progressive Conservative government appeared to be ready to move firmly toward privatizing the state oil company. Energy Minister Marcel Masse said the move would be carried out through a general sale to the public. Petro-Canada's continuing cash problems led the company to announce in December 1989 that it was looking for an infusion of money to help it develop the country's energy resources. In January 1990 Hopper gave testimony before a government panel studying Petro-Canada's future. He served notice that the oil company would not be able to carry out its commitment to costly frontier development without private capital.

A new era began for Petro-Canada in February 1990, when the Honorable Michael Wilson, Canada's Minister of Finance, indicated that Canada would begin the privatization of Petro-Canada. According to the announcement, in 1991 the government would offer to the public about 15 percent of the shares of the government-owned company, but individual ownership would be limited to 10 percent and foreign ownership to a cumulative 25 percent of the publicly held shares. Wilbert Hopper welcomed the government's announcement. The generated equity capital, Hopper said, would

help Petro-Canada participate in developing several oil projects, including the Hibernia oil field.

In April 1990 the Canadian government went one step further, announcing that Petro-Canada would eventually be sold in its entirety to the public. After much talk and speculation, the Canadian government had decided to get out of this segment of the energy business.

After years of debate over whether or not Petro-Canada should be privatized, the decision to do so sparked new questions. Paramount among them was a dispute over who should receive the proceeds of the sale—the company or the government. Although the federal government, which was carrying a high debt of its own and had pumped billions into the enterprise over the years, certainly had a claim to the income, officials turned the funds over to CEO Hopper with nary a peep. It would be used, he said, to finance continuing exploration of the frontier areas at Hibernia and Terra Nova. Petro-Canada expected its commitments there to cost $3 billion between 1990 and 1996.

On February 1, 1991, the government-owned shares of Petro-Canada were transferred to the Minister of State for Privatization and Regulatory Affairs; and Petro-Canada was authorized to issue and sell its own shares. The company made its initial public offering on July 3, 1991, selling 19.5 percent, or 42 million, of its shares on Canadian stock exchanges for $13 each. The sale gave the federal government's remaining stake a market value of about half of its previously estimated worth and thereby effectively raised the nation's debt. To make matters worse, the initial public offering was poorly-timed. Uncertainties related to the Persian Gulf War, as well as Petro-Canada's continuing poor performance combined to reduce its stock price to around $9, where it stood through the end of 1992.

In 1991, CEO Hopper stepped up downsizing efforts that had already eliminated 1,000 employees from the corporate roster. By Fall 1992, he had cut total debt by about $1 billion to $1.25 billion, slashed the employee roster from a high of 10,000 in 1985 to 8,200, and divested assets worth nearly $850 million, including about 1,200 of the company's ubiquitous service stations. Although the company lost $603 million in 1991, the changes began to reflect on the bottom line in 1992, when Petrocan recorded a $5 million profit.

Ironically, the announcement of this return to profitability (albeit meager) brought with it the ouster of Wilbert Hopper, the only leader Petro-Canada had ever known. Long criticized as a mere "civil servant" and "fat cat" who enjoyed taxpayer-funded perks like an executive chef and jet, Hopper was nonetheless considered a "Teflon" man, able to deflect blame for his company's long-running problems. That reputation came to an end in January 1993, when he was removed without comment by Petro-Canada's board of directors. James Stanford, who had served as president of the company since April 1990 and was a 15-year veteran of the company, succeeded Hopper as CEO.

Stanford continued the rationalization program, reducing employment to 6,200 and maintaining a debt-to-equity ratio of around 28 percent (considered "reasonable" by petroleum industry standards) through the end of 1994. After declining throughout the early 1990s, revenues increased from $4.6 billion in 1993 to $4.73 billion in 1994. More importantly, the company achieved record earnings of $262 million that year, nearly seven times its total take for the entire decade of the 1980s.

In Petro-Canada's 1994 annual report, Stanford complained that the government's controlling interest in the company was a significant factor in the undervaluing of its shares. The stock had fallen to a low of $7.25 early in 1993 and only rebounded to about $11.50 by the end of 1994. Around that time, the government committed itself to divesting its remaining 173 million shares "when market conditions permit."

Petro-Canada's downsizing, an anticipated increase in oil prices as the country cycled out of the early 1990s recession, and a long-anticipated payout from the expensive Hibernia project were expected to make the company a legitimate competitor in the nation's petroleum industry.

Further Reading:

Bliss, Michael, *Northern Enterprise : Five Centuries of Canadian Business,* Toronto: McClelland and Stewart, 1987.

Donville, Christopher, "Good Timing," *Globe and Mail,* May 18, 1991, p. B1.

Fleming, James, "Petro-Canada Gets the Lead Out," *Globe and Mail,* January 28, 1994, p. 44.

Foster, Peter, *The Blue-Eyed Sheiks : The Canadian Oil Establishment,* Don Mills, Ont.: Collins, 1979.

————, *Self Serve : How Petro-Canada Pumped Canadians Dry,* Toronto: MacFarlane Walter & Ross, 1992.

————, "Hopper's Folly," *Globe and Mail,* July 19, 1991, p. 18.

McMurdy, Deirdre, "A Matter of Privacy," *Maclean's,* March 4, 1991, pp. 42-44.

Motherwell, Cathryn, "Petrocan Battles For Respect," *Globe and Mail,* 13 October 1992, p. B9.

"Petro-Canada: How it Grew and Where it Likely is Going," *Oil & Gas Journal,* December 9, 1985.

Phillips, Ed, *Guts and Guile: True Tales From the Backrooms of the Pipeline Industry,* Douglas & McIntyre, 1990.

—Ron Chepesiuk
—updated by April Dougal Gasbarre

Placer Dome Inc.

P.O. Box 49330
No. 1600-1055 Dunsmuir St.
Vancouver, British Columbia V7X 1P1
(604) 682-7082
Fax: (604) 684-7261

Public Company
Incorporated: 1987
Employees: 7,000
Sales: $899 million
Stock Exchanges: Montreal New York Toronto
SICs: 1000 Metal Mining; 1021 Copper Ores; 1041
Gold Ores; 1044 Silver Ores; 1081 Metal Mining
Services

Pacer Dome Inc. is a leading global mining company
whose primary emphasis is gold, followed by silver,
copper, and molybdenum. The company was formed in
1987 by the merger of Placer Develop Limited and
Dome Mines Limited, both of which were gold mining
companies formed in the early 1900s. Both companies
grew steadily during the mid-1900s before they joined
forces to become the second largest gold producer in the
world. Going into 1995 Placer Dome was operating 16
mines, 13 of which were gold mines, in Australia,
Canada, Chile, Papua New Guinea, the Philippines, and
the United States. It was also planning to open new
mines.

Placer Dome's chief predecessor is Dome Mines Limited, a gold mining company founded in 1910. Dome
Mines was distinguished for its discovery of the first
large Canadian gold mine. The year was 1909 and the
place was the backwood's of northern Ontario. For
years, prospectors had suspected that the region contained commercially viable gold deposits but had been
unable to prove it. Many geologists had simply given up
on the region. When the railroad was extended northward in the early 1900s, though, a prospecting revival
occurred. Among the many teams searching for gold in
the area was one lead by Jack Wilson. Wilson, his friend
Harry Preston, and the rest of the team reached Porcupine Lake in May of 1909. They set up camp on
Graveyard Point and began scouring the area for gold.

As legend has it, one day when they were out prospecting, one of the men slipped and fell on a rock outcrop
and dislodged a chunk of moss—gold appeared. The
men stripped back the moss to reveal a dome-shaped
structure studded with gold. In a less entertaining
version of the story, the party discovered a dome-like
mass of quartz. In any case, after several days of
trenching and cleaning part of the formation, Wilson
discovered a "spectacular piece of gold in a thin seam of
schist." Drilling and blasting then revealed a stunning
display described by a visitor (as recorded in company
annals): "The gold was in blobs, like candle dripping,
and in sponge-like masses, some of them as large as a
cup, lying under the moss in a dome-shaped outcrop of
quartz. 'The Big Dome,' they called it."

Wilson found a Chicago investor, W. S. "Pop" Edwards
to help him secure his claim to the find. Dome Mines
Company Limited was incorporated on March 23, 1910,
for the purpose of extracting gold from the "Big Dome."
Edwards got the hefty financial backing needed to build
a mine from the wealthy Monell Syndicate, a family
empire that included the lucrative International Nickel.
Construction of the mine was difficult because of the
lack of good roads in the area. Heavy equipment could
be hauled only during the winter and by horse-drawn
sled, and workers lived in a crude tent city. Nevertheless, by the end of 1910 the mine was in operation and
producing a trickle of gold and silver ore. Early in 1911
a branch off of the railroad was added that reached the
Dome mine, and a town was built to house workers for
the Dome and other emerging mining and exploration
operations.

Dome Mines suffered a major setback in the summer of
1911. A fire, driven by hurricane-like winds, rapidly
swept across the mine and the burgeoning town. 73
people were confirmed dead, although the count may
have been much higher—many of them drowned while
seeking protection from the fire in the nearby lake. All
surface buildings and equipment were destroyed, bringing total property damage to over $500,000 for Dome
Mines alone. The only benefit of the unfortunate tragedy
was that the fire burned off scrub in one area and
unveiled a vein that contained almost solid patches of
free gold. The exposed vein became known as "The
Golden Sidewalk." That find proved to be a major boon
for Dome, and helped to fund the rapid reconstruction
of the mine and the town. By 1913 the company was in
full operation and generating half million dollars in
profit annually.

World War I crimped Dome's work force, which was
comprised largely of young, able-bodied men. The mine
was even forced to shut down late in 1917 and did not
reopen until 1919. The company used its depleted work
force during that period to improve and expand the
mine. By 1920 Dome was again up-and-running, and
was as financially sound as it had ever been. Dome
continued to prosper throughout the 1920s until 1929,
when a second fire destroyed the operation. Fortunately
for Dome, the fire coincided with the stock market crash
that kicked off the Great Depression. Dome quickly
rebuilt and by 1930 was enjoying fat profits as a result of
rocketing gold prices. Healthy gains proceeded through
the 1930s as Dome opened new mines and increased
production.

Dome's labor force was depleted again when World War
II erupted. Dome never had to close its mines, though.

Furthermore, the War gave Dome a reason to begin branching out into new minerals like tungsten and molybdenum, which were needed for the war effort. After the war, Dome invested in another mining operation—the Campbell Red Lake Mines—that quickly surpassed output by Dome's original claim and became the largest gold mine in Canada. Unfortunately, global government intervention effectively capped gold prices and quashed Dome's profits. Government subsidies were created to keep producers like Dome from going under. The net result, however, was that the gold mining industry had changed and had become less volatile.

During the 1950s and 1960s Dome focused on exploration for gold and other metals. Several major discoveries boosted the company's reserve base and pushed Dome's sales and profits up. In 1968 Dome poured its ten thousandth gold bar for a total of $280 million worth of gold produced since the company started mining in 1910. During the late 1960s and early 1970s, moreover, governments, particularly in Britain and later the United States, began deregulating gold prices. The result was that Dome prospered during the early 1970s as gold prices rose and it dumped gold into the newly freed markets. Gold prices fluctuated throughout the 1970s and early 1980s. After faltering in the mid-1970s, for example, they surged in 1977. Importantly, gold prices rocketed skyward during the early 1980s to all-time highs. Prices eventually tumbled, but Dome continued to pay dividends. Going into the mid-1980s, in fact, Dome was expanding its production capacity to more than 3,000 tons of ore daily.

As Dome Mining evolved during the 1900s, the other half of the Placer Dome story was being written by a company called Placer Development Limited. Placer Development was created in 1926 by Arthur Banks, a New Zealand-born mining engineer who managed a British silver mining company, and Addison Freeman, one of Australia's most successful entrepreneurs. Freeman and Banks met in Vancouver in 1926 through their mining interests and quickly found that they had a lot in common. In a handshake deal, Freeman agreed to back Banks in a new mining venture—The W. A. Freeman Company, which was soon incorporated as Placer Development Company Limited. The enterprise was founded with $200,000 and a broad goal to "buy, sell, manufacture, and deal in minerals, plants, timber, machinery, implements, conveniences, and other things."

Placer Development burned through much of its money during its first two years in several failed attempts to find gold in the United States and Canada. Placer's situation was bleak. In a final attempt to strike gold, Banks took his prospecting team to New Guinea to search for gold that he had heard may exist below the Bulolo River. Initial drilling indicated that the deposits were much richer than even Banks had suspected they might be. Placer's working capital was immediately boosted to $500,000 and Bank's began making plans to extract the rich ore. Because the location was so remote, Banks realized that he would have to bring equipment in by air to build the mine and get the ore. He purchased three old German trimotor planes and built a landing strip near the banks of the Bulolo. For ten years he flew equipment and workers into his makeshift town. By the

end of the 1930s, he had brought in eight large dredges, a hydro-electric power plant, a machine shop, and living and recreational facilities for more than 1,000 workers. The feat earned him the American Mining and Metallurgical Society's gold medal in 1938 for pioneering air transportation in mining.

Placer's Bulolo mines bore much more gold than even Bank's geologists had expected. Placer's board of directors dumped the excess cash into a number of new ventures, including oil interests, exploration operations, and other gold mining companies. Among the company's most successful efforts was Pato Consolidated, a gold mining operation in the equatorial region of Columbia, the effort depended on air transport to develop facilities in the blazing hot, insect-infested, malaria-ridden jungle. But Pato was just one of hundreds of properties that Placer acquired or investigated throughout North America and South America during the 1930s and 1940s. The company remained dependent on Bulolo and Pato, though, and almost went bankrupt when the Bulolo mines were knocked out of commission for several years during and after World War II.

After the war, Placer's directors stepped up their efforts to diversify, investing in oil, tungsten mining, and lead and zinc production. Importantly, Placer acquired the Emerald underground tungsten mine in southern British Columbia. Placer eventually employed a work force of more than 1,000 at that and a nearby mine, and the operations became major producers for the company. In fact, the success in Canada came at a good time. Both the Colombian and New Guinea mines had passed their prime in the early 1950s, and they were expected to contribute much less to Placer's bottom line in the future. With the boost from the Canadian mines, Placer was able to post a record profit of $11 billion in 1955. Thus, in 1957 the company began moving its headquarters from San Francisco to Vancouver.

During the 1960s Placer became involved with the well-known Mattagami zinc-copper mine in Quebec. The giant project was financed by Placer and several other major mining companies. Through that project, Placer became engaged in other major projects, including the successful Craigmont copper mine. Placer followed that venture with the development of the world's largest molybdenum open pit mine in British Columbia, which began production in 1965. By that time, the Bulolo and Colombian gold mining operations had effectively been shuttered. To make up for the slowdown of several of its operations, Placer stepped up exploration and development efforts in the late 1960s and 1970s. New ventures included zinc and lead mining in Portugal, cattle-ranching in New Guinea and Australia, and coal mining in Nevada. Most vital to its gains during the period, though, were giant new copper mines that Placer developed in British Columbia and the Philippines. By the late 1970s the company was generating record sales and boasting a diversified portfolio of mining and related ventures throughout much of the world.

Placer's long-time leader, J. D. Simpson, retired in 1975. The aggressive and astute Tasmanian businessman had relentlessly built Placer into a leading global mining concern by the time of his departure. Although he left Placer during a peak in the mining industry, the company reorganized during the late 1970s. It jettisoned many of its poorly performing operations, and reentered the gold mining industry in the early 1980s with open pit mines in the United States and Australia. By the mid-1980s, Placer was operating seven mines in four countries. It was at that time that executives from Placer and Dome began discussing the possibility of joining forces.

The decision to merge Placer and Dome into a single giant mining company made sense. Each company complemented the other; Placer was an international operator with skills in open-pit mining and hefty interests in non-precious metals, while Dome brought a dominant North American presence and experience in gold mining to the table. Both companies boasted healthy balance sheets with little long-term debt. Furthermore, several tax advantages were possible. For example, Placer's development expenses could be written off against Dome's Canadian income. Thus, in 1987 the two companies officially merged to form Placer Dome Inc., a company with 19 mines and 4,500 employees. Placer Dome's annual gold production—gold was by far its largest product—was nearly 900,000 ounces annually, making the company one of the largest gold producers in the world. Importantly, Placer Dome was sitting on a war chest of about $760 million that it could use to acquire or develop new mines.

Rather than expand during the late 1980s, Placer focused on restructuring operations, cutting costs, and improving the productivity of its mines. Its efforts were largely successful, although many shareholders were eager for the company to begin taking some risks and growing. Placer did begin working to boost output, as evidenced by the rise in the number of ounces produced from 952,000 in 1987 and 964,000 in 1988, to nearly 1.2 million ounces in 1989. And during the early 1990s Placer Dome's gold output surged to nearly two million ounces annually by 1992. At the same time, however, its total base of gold reserves dwindled by about 15 percent between 1988 and 1991. To steer Placer on a new course, the board hired John Wilson, a mining industry veteran.

Under Wilson's direction, Placer intensified its efforts to move from a bureaucratic organization to a more decentralized, entrepreneurial concern. To that end, Placer was broken up into for major operating units: Placer Dome Canada, Placer Dome U.S., Placer Dome Latin American, and Placer Pacific. Wilson announced his intent to see Placer boost gold production to 2.5 million ounces by the year 2,000 while at the same time

increasing its reserve base through exploration and development. Although Placer's gold output dropped slightly during 1993 and 1994 as a result of market conditions, its gold reserves did surge to nearly 20 million ounces. Meanwhile, total revenues dropped from $1 billion in 1992 to about $900 million in 1994, reflecting static market prices for gold. However, increased productivity allowed Placer to keep its net income steady at approximately $107 million annually during the period.

Going into 1994, Placer Dome was operating 16 mines, 13 of which were gold mines, in Australia, Canada, Chile, Papua, New Guinea, the Philippines, and the United States. And it was planning to open two new mines in mid-1995 in Australia and Chile. Placer's stated long-term goals were to increase gold production, intensify exploration and development efforts throughout the world, and become a global low-cost leader in the gold mining industry. Placer's improving productivity and strong cash position, combined with rising minerals prices in mid-1995, suggest a healthy future for the gold-mining pioneer.

Principal Subsidiaries:

Placer Dome Canada Limited; Placer Pacific Limited; Placer Dome U.S. Inc.; Placer Dome Latin America Limited; Placer Dome Exploration Inc.

Further Reading:

Adams, R. A., *Placer—An Historical Outline,* reprint of 1976 essay, Vancouver: Placer Dome, Inc., reprinted in 1995.
The Big Dome—Over 75 Years of Gold Mining in Canada, Toronto: Cybergraphics Company Inc., 1983.
Crespo, Mariana, "All That Glitters," *Financial World,* September 13, 1994, p. 58.
Danielson, Vivian, "Latin America Special—Placer Dome Eyes Acquisitions," *Northern Miner,* March 27, 1995, Section B, p. 1.
The Glitter of Gold From the Beginning, Vancouver: Placer Dome Inc., 1995.
Ross, Alexander, "Is Bigger Better for Placer Dome?," *Canadian Business,* January 1990, pp. 38-43.
Schriener, John, "Placer Dome Aims to Be No. 1 in Gold," *Financial Post,* April 23, 1994, Section 1, p. 16.

—Dave Mote

Power Corporation of Canada

751 Victoria Sq., 44th Fl.
Montreal, Quebec H2Y 2J3
(514) 286-7400 Fax: (514) 286-7424

Public Company
Incorporated: 1925
Employees: 9,800
Revenues: $6.9 billion
Exchanges: Montreal Toronto Vancouver
SICs: 6719 Holding Companies, nec; 6282
   Investment Advice; 6099 Functions Related to
   Deposit Banks; 2711 Newspapers; 4833 Television
   Broadcasting Stations; 4832 Radio Broadcasting
   Stations.

Power Corporation of Canada is a holding company whose interests are focused primarily in the financial services and communications sectors. Although it has been characterized as a conglomerate, it is better described as an investment vehicle. In 1995, the firm held controlling interests in leading financial service and media companies. Financial services were grouped under Power Financial Corporation (68.7 percent owned by Power Corporation), which in turn held controlling interests in Great-West Lifeco Inc., Investors Group Inc., and Pargesa Holding S.A. Great-West Lifeco was itself the holding company for 99.5 percent of The Great-West Life Insurance Company, one of North America's largest life insurance providers. With eleven mutual funds under its administration, Investors Group Inc. ranked as Canada's leading sponsor and distributor of mutual funds. Owned through an intricate series of intermediate holding companies, the Pargesa group stood as one of Europe's top investment companies.

Power Corporation's media interests were divided among the wholly-owned Gesca Ltée and Power Broadcasting Inc. subsidiaries. Gesca controlled four daily newspapers—including the nation's largest French-language paper, La Presse—eight weeklies, and several retail book outlets. Power Broadcasting held stakes in television and radio stations in Ontario and Quebec.

With over $30 billion in assets under its control, Power Corporation bears the indelible stamp of Paul Desmarais, who led the firm from the late 1960s into the mid-1990s and personally owned over 60 percent of its voting rights. Frequently referred to as one of Canada's wealthiest and most powerful men, the reserved French-Canadian billionaire readied his two sons, Paul Jr. and André, to succeed him in the mid-1990s.

Paul Desmarais was born in the northern Ontario mining town of Sudbury in 1927. He had planned to follow his father into the field of law, but changed course in 1951 after failing a legal history course at the University of Toronto's Osgoode Hall school of law. Fortunately, Desmarais had a "fallback position:" a small, ailing trolley company that had been in his mother's family. The company had done well transporting miners from Sudbury to the outlying mines, but began to lose money when faced with competition from busing companies and personal automobiles in the post World War II era. To make matters worse, the enterprise was compelled to operate certain unprofitable routes deemed necessary for the public good. By 1950, the transition to motor transport had put the family firm $300,000 in debt. When Paul Desmarais asked to try his hand at the troubled family business the following year, his parents agreed to sell him the company for $1 on the condition that he assume its liabilities. Desmarais was able to turn the company around within five years. That's when he started to focus on growth.

He expanded the bus system throughout his home province, then won a contract to provide municipal service to Quebec City. At the time, it was considered quite a feat for someone from outside Quebec to win a public contract in the province. But as the years went by, this episode would become just a small example of Desmarais's diplomatic acumen.

The young entrepreneur didn't limit himself to transportation. When his cash flow permitted, the budding magnate began to dabble in other interests through investment. In 1968, he traded a company he controlled, Trans-Canada Corporation Fund, for a dominant equity position in Power Corporation, an industrial and financial holding company. Incorporated in 1925, the firm had invested in domestic electric utilities (hence its name) for about three decades before beginning a diversification program in the 1960s. More than one analyst characterized the company as a poorly coordinated "hodgepodge" of investments. By the time the 41-year-old Desmarais took over, Power Corporation's most vital holdings included Canada's second-largest pulp and paper concern, Consolidated-Bathurst Inc.; Canada Steamship Lines; and Laurentide Financial Corp. Ltd., a national consumer finance company. Desmarais reorganized the firm, refocusing on acquiring controlling stakes, rather than short-term portfolio investments. Under Desmarais's leadership, Power Corporation's earnings multiplied from under $4 million in 1967 to $98.4 million by 1979.

That decade's phenomenal growth was not without setbacks, however. In 1970, Desmarais made a mercifully brief, but significant, investment in Robert Campeau's namesake real estate company. He exchanged Power Corp.'s broad real estate holdings for a controlling interest in the ill-fated Campeau Corp. But the two leaders' management styles proved too contrary: Desmarais was known for his caution, and Campeau's speculative nature was equally infamous. Within just two years, the two parted ways.

The Franco-Ontarian businessman also found himself positioned between two powerful interest groups: radical Quebec separatists who denounced him for "collaborating" with the Anglo establishment, and the Anglo-dominated business community that resisted penetration by outsiders. Although the violent threats of the Quebecois never materialized, English-speaking businessmen were said to have thwarted Desmarais's $150 million bid to gain control of the Argus Corp. in 1975. After striving three years to acquire voting shares, he sold the 26 percent stake he had accumulated to Ravelston Corp. for $80.5 million.

In 1980, Power took a deceptively small 2.5 percent stake in Compagnie Financiére de Paris et des Pays-Bas (Paribas), an international investment holding company that has been referred to as "France's most powerful banking group." The investment got interesting in 1981, when François Mitterand's Socialist administration took power and took steps to nationalize Paribas. In an effort to protect his investment, Desmarais conspired with the bank's chief executive and other interested parties to coordinate a complicated movement of stock between Europe's financial capitals of Paris, Geneva and Brussels. By the time their machinations were complete, they had shifted controlling interests in two of Paribas's most profitable affiliates, Paribas Suisse and Copeba (Belgium) to Paribas's Swiss affiliate, Pargesa Holding S.A. Not coincidentally, Power Corporation held 10 percent of Pargesa, whose capital quintupled to $186 million practically overnight. Ironically, this ingenious scheme left Power Corporation with an irate minority investor: by the end of 1982, the French government owned Paribas, giving it control of Paribas's 20 percent stake in Power. Power Corporation sold its stake in Paribas for $19.5 million in 1982, and Paribas (which was de-nationalized in the late 1980s) transferred its stake in Power to a Pargesa affiliate.

In 1981, Desmarais moved to fulfill a long-term ambition; acquiring control of the country's biggest company, Canadian Pacific Ltd. (CP). According to a 1986 *Maclean's* article, at 24 Desmarais had written a treatise "on how an individual could take control of CP." Although he succeeded in becoming CP's second-largest individual shareholder, Desmarais was unable to parlay the 5.8 percent share of the widely-held company into an influential position. In 1985 he sold out his stake for $218 million.

The proceeds of this and other asset sales (including $178 million from the 1981 divestment of Power's transportation interests) helped reduce long-term debt that had ballooned to over $300 million by the end of 1984. In 1983 these liabilities cost Power Corporation $27 million in interest payments. The debt was pared to nil by the end of 1985.

In light of the deregulation of the financial services industry in the early 1980s, Desmarais consolidated his financial holdings as Power Financial Corporation in 1984. The reorganization clustered Investors Group, Great-West Life Assurance Co., and Montreal Trustco Inc. with the 25 percent share of Pargesa Holding S.A. This reconfiguration allowed cross-selling and packaging of products from each of the separate businesses. For example, a Great-West agent could offer customers the opportunity to invest in one of Investors Group's mutual funds, and vice-versa. This sales strategy would concentrate more investment dollars in Power's coffers. Great-West also diversified into property and casualty insurance during this period. Power Corporation owned 80 percent of the newly formed group, while the Caisse de Depot et Placement du Quebec (an influential public pension fund) purchased 15 percent of the remaining shares. The Royal Bank of Canada and the Bank of Nova Scotia each took 2.5 percent of Power Financial.

Fueled by the increasing profitability of its financial operations, Power Corporation's earnings continued their upward climb in the early 1980s, nearly doubling to about $200 million in 1985. An estimated $120 million of that year's net income came from the company's financial group.

Unlike his financial holdings, Desmarais's publishing properties (then limited to Gesca Ltée) had virtually no profit growth in the early 1980s. In 1985, the investor attempted to boost those operations with the $97.8 million acquisition of 41 percent of the highly profitable Télé-Métropole, Inc. Télé-Métropole controlled Canada's largest francophone television station, Montreal's CFTM or "Canal Dix," as it was better known. When the Canadian Radio-television and Telecommunications Commission (CRTC) nixed the controversial Canal Dix deal, Power targeted some lower-profile television and radio stations. In 1987 the company acquired Katenac Holding Ltd. and Prades Inc. for a total of $35.8 million. The companies were consolidated and reorganized as Power Broadcasting Inc.

Over the years, Desmarais had developed a particular investing style, favoring "friendly" deals over hostile acquisitions. His acquisition standards required a 15 percent return on investment, a significant percentage of a company's outstanding shares, and a seat on the board of directors. Desmarais's preference for cash trades and aversion to debt contrasted strongly with the 1980s predilection for leveraging. That discretion became something of a point of contention in the early 1990s, in fact, when Desmarais was criticized by some analysts for sitting tight on a multi-billion dollar "nest egg."

After being thwarted in a late 1980s attempt to form the world's largest paper company through the merger of Power Corp.'s Consolidated-Bathurst with Domtar Inc., Desmarais sold Power Corp.'s 40 percent stake in Consolidated-Bathurst to Chicago-based Stone Container Corp. The value of the pulp and paper company's shares had multiplied 60 times, from $5 to $300 each (adjusted for stock splits) over the course of their twenty years under Desmarais's control. That same year, he divested Power Corporation's share of Montreal Trustco Inc. (a Power Financial holding) to BCE Inc. (formerly Bell Canada). The timing of the two transactions could not have been better, bringing in $1.8 billion in cash just before a recession and positioning Power Corp. to take advantage of the downturn.

Having built up a $2.5 billion "war chest" in all, Desmarais turned over control of Power Financial to eldest son Paul Jr. and leadership of Power Broadcasting to son André and began to focus more closely on the international arena. In 1988, he parlayed years of political contacts to create an international advisory board whose membership roster included Seagram Company Ltd. Chairman Charles R. Bronfman; West Germany's Helmut Schmidt; Dwayne O. Andreas of Archer-Daniels-Midland; and former Canadian Prime Minister Pierre Trudeau, among other influential business and political leaders. Desmarais's international strategy reached out in two directions: Europe and Asia.

Desmarais's Continental designs focused on Pargesa, through which he befriended Belgian banker and international advisory board member Albert Frere. By 1990, Power Corporation had accumulated a 25 percent stake (worth $500 million) in Pargesa, which had performed well until 1989, when its profits plummeted from $180.03 million to $4.07 million. Together with Frere, Desmarais engineered a 1990 mutiny at Pargesa Holdings that got Desmarais elected chairman of the $2 billion Swiss holding company and earned both men seats on the de-nationalized Banque Paribas's board of directors. Like Power Corporation, Pargesa was poised for growth, with a $1 billion cash hoard to invest in companies devalued by the economic downturn of the early 1990s.

Desmarais had shrewdly laid the foundations for his Asian assault in the 1970s and build on them over the ensuing quarter-century. His methodical strategy included business trips, creation of a bi-lateral trade council, a joint venture with the Chinese government in a British Columbian pulp mill. When he created Power's international advisory committee in 1988, he invited Rong Yiren, chairman of China's foreign investment office, to join its membership. As the Chinese government became more amiable to foreign investment in the early 1990s, Power Corporation stood poised to partake in the country's economic growth. Together with two of Canada's largest hydroelectric companies, Ontario Hydro and Hydro Quebec, Power Corporation formed Asia Power Group Inc., a $100 million joint venture that sought to meet China's growing power generation needs. Other investments in the region included a $60 million real estate development, a gold mining cooperative with American Barrick Resources Corp. (later renamed Barrick Gold Corporation), and a highway project. Power augmented its media holdings with two high-profile, yet relatively small, investments in 1993. That March, the company announced its purchase of a 16.8 percent stake in Southam Inc., a leading, but struggling, firm with interests in publishing and broadcasting. Founded in 1877, Southam was called "Canada's premier newspaper chain" in a March 1993 *Globe and Mail* article. Power Corporation's $180 million cash infusion helped substantially reduce Southam's debt, and it was hoped that the resulting lower interest payments would bring it into the black after two consecutive annual losses. Then

in May, Power took a 1 percent stake in Time Warner Inc. at a cost of US$100 million.

Although Desmarais loosened Power Corporation's purse strings somewhat to make his European, Asian and media investments, the potential for ever-greater exploits remained. At the end of 1994, the company still had over $900 million in cash and marketable assets on hand. Power's assets had increased steadily from $23.86 billion in 1990 to $31.5 million in 1994, but net earnings did not follow that trend. In fact, profits declined from a 1989 peak of $221 million to a 1991 nadir of $136 million, then gradually recovered to $186 million in 1994.

While Paul Desmarais continued to exert control over Power Corporation as chairman and CEO, the 67-year-old had clearly positioned his two sons to succeed him by that time. Paul Jr. advanced to vice-chairman of the parent company in 1991, the same year that André became its president and chief operating officer.

Principal Subsidiaries:

Power Financial Corporation (68.7%); Investors Group inc. (67.4%); Power Financial Europe B.V.; Power Communications Inc.; Power Broadcasting Inc.; Gesca Ltée.

Further Reading:

Came, Barry, "Paul Desmarais," *Maclean's,* 27 December 1993, 38.
Enchin, Harvey, "Power Adds to Stake in Southam," *Globe and Mail,* 20 March 1993, B1.
Gibbon, Ann, "Power Strategy," *Globe and Mail,* 8 August 1991, B1.
Greber, Dave, *Paul Desmarais, Un Homme et Son Empire,* Montreal: Editions de l'Homme, 1987.
Grenspon, Edward, "After Months of Murky Machinations, Paul Desmarais and a Belgian Tycoon Have Taken Control of a Swiss Holding Company," *Globe and Mail,* 18 September 1990, B1.
Koselka, Rita, "Cash-Rich and On the Prowl," *Forbes,* 16 April 1990, 56.
McDonald, Marci, "Warfare in the Corridors of Power," *Maclean's,* 7 December 1981, 22.
McMurdy, Deirdre, "Power Play," *Maclean's,* 5 April 1993, 36-38.
"Power Plays China Hand," *Globe and Mail,* 4 March 1994, B1.
Wallace, Bruce, "The Power Establishment," *Maclean's,* 24 February 1986, 46-47. Walmsley, Ann, "Stalking a Media Empire," *Maclean's,* 15 July 1985, 24.

—April Dougal Gasbarre

PROVIGO

Provigo Inc.

1611 Cremazie Blvd. East
Montreal, Quebec H2M 2R9
(514) 383-3000
Fax: (514) 383-3088

Public Company
Incorporated: 1961 as Couvrette & Provost Limited
Employees: 14,300
Sales: $6.18 billion
Stock Exchanges: Montreal Toronto
SICs: 5141 Groceries, general line; 5411 Grocery
   stores; 5541 Gasoline service stations

Provigo Inc. is the food industry leader in Quebec and one of the largest food retailers and distributors in Canada. The company operates through three subsidiaries: Provigo Distribution Inc. in Quebec, under the store names Provigo Supermarkets, Maxi, and Héritage; LOEB Inc. in Ontario and western and northwestern Quebec, under the store names LOEB, Marché Plus, and Votre Epicier; and C Corp Inc., a network of convenience stores in Quebec, Ontario, and Alberta, under the names Provi-Soir, Winks, Top Value, Red Rooster, and Pinto. Provigo's wholesale activities are carried out through its Distribution Group, a single entity consisting of a network of 42 cash and carries, Presto and Linc; 900 retailers affiliated with the L'Intermarche, Axep, Jovi and Proprio banners; and 1,500 food service restaurants, hotels, cafeterias and institutions served through the Dellixo unit. Provigo employs 14,300 people directly and an additional 30,000 indirectly through affiliated and franchised retailers.

Provigo was founded in Montreal when Bernard and Jacques Couvrette and Roland, Ernest, and René Provost decided to link their family businesses. The new wholesale grocer was incorporated in 1961 as Couvrette & Provost Ltd., dealing mainly in dry goods, tobacco, candy, and toiletries.

Couvrette & Provost's first president, Bernard Couvrette, established a precedent for aggressive acquisition, and over the next eight years the company integrated ten food wholesalers in an effort to diversify its food lines with dairy products, meats, vegetables, and health and beauty aids.

As a wholesaler and distributor, the company depended on independent grocers for its business. At the beginning of the 1960s, a supermarket chain boom consumed much of the smaller grocers' market share, but by 1964, in Quebec at least, these independents had won back most of what had been lost and held 70 percent of the market. Couvrette & Provost was supplying about 800 grocery stores, 300 of them affiliated with the company under various names. The small grocers' success was largely due to their growth in rural Quebec areas, but in some provinces the chains still dominated.

Couvrette & Provost was also diversifying into new areas of the food-service industry. Its subsidiary, Provost & Provost, served restaurants, hotels, schools, and other institutions, and another subsidiary, Les Epiceries Presto Limitée, operated eight cash-and-carry stores. Couvrette & Provost also organized Primes Régal Incorporated, a trading stamp system for retailers to offer their customers. The stamps were redeemable for prizes the shopper could choose from an illustrated catalogue, and the promotion was successful in bringing some of the supermarket glitz to smaller groceries.

In 1965, the company acquired Magasins Régal Stores, a cooperative of several Quebec food retailers that worked through pooled purchases to allow the group to run its own warehouse to keep prices lower. Also that year, Conrad Lajoie Limitée, a small distributor, was acquired as a subsidiary. The company also underwent a five-for-one stock split in 1965, feeling that its $30 to $35 unit price was too high for ordinary investors and that the company would benefit from more shareholders and shares outstanding to increase its leverage on the stock market.

During the mid-1960s, profits continued to increase by as much as 29 percent a year, and in 1967, Couvrette & Provost made a change in capital structure. Previously, the company had used the two-class structure of A and B shares that was common for newly incorporated Quebec companies. Only the B shares, which were held by the Couvrette and Provost families, had voting rights. Under the new plan, both classes of shares were converted into no-par-value common shares.

In August, 1967 Bernard Couvrette became chairman of the board and René Provost was named president. During the next two years, the company became a leader in the Quebec market. It acquired P. D'Aoust Limited, a family-owned wholesale grocery business, and then merged with Lamontagne Limited and Denault Limited through an exchange of shares. This was the first merger of its kind in the province, and it expanded the company into new territories: Saguenay, Quebec City, Sherbrooke, and the Eastern Townships. One of the main results of the merger was an overall reduction of operating costs through the integration of management, distribution, advertising, and purchasing, which helped sales to increase at a rapid rate over the next 20 years. *The Financial Post* called the firm's progress in nine years "most impressive," saying, "management appears to be very aggressive and forward looking and has shown sound judgment in the recent mergers."

In 1969, Antoine Turmel became CEO, while René Provost remained president and general manager. In

September of the next year, Couvrette & Provost changed its name to Provigo Inc.

As rural citizens of Quebec began to move to the cities in larger numbers in the early 1970s, their lifestyle changes included patronizing independent grocers less and chain supermarkets more. The chains used modern merchandising techniques and muscular ad campaigns to attract more consumers to their strategically placed sites in shopping centers and suburbs. Because of the volume of their sales and the strength of their purchasing power, the supermarkets could afford to offer lower prices, and soon had launched price wars.

In food distribution, often called the "penny business," profit margins are tiny and must be compensated for with a large sales volume. To counteract the supermarket price war, wholesalers began to band together and distributors forged closer links with their independent grocers by affiliating retailers and franchising convenience stores. In 1970, Provigo merged with ProviFruit Inc., and over the next five years, Provigo concentrated on developing its retail sector by establishing a network of 50 supermarkets and 800 affiliated or franchised stores. The company had opened its first warehouse market in 1969; by 1972, it had a dozen warehouse operations. Because of this wise planning during the price wars, Provigo was the only publicly owned food distributor in Canada whose earnings did not decline at all but, in fact, increased.

In 1974, Provigo implemented a new approach to retailing and developed a chain of franchised convenience stores under the name Provi-Soir. In 1975, Provigo purchased Jato, a company operating nine supermarkets. In November 1976, the company moved into the meat sector and created its own subsidiary, Provi-Viande.

Provigo made an audacious move in 1977 when it acquired M. Loeb Limited, a company with larger sales and territories than its own, more than doubling Provigo's size. The company's sales rose from $500 million to $2 billion in the next two years. The acquisition was not only shrewd but well timed, since price competition in food retailing lessened during 1977 and sales growth was outrunning inflation. Along with M. Loeb, Provigo acquired Loeb's subsidiaries in Washington, D.C. and northern California, thus gaining a foothold in the United States. Provigo also acquired National Drug Limited, a pharmaceutical distributor.

Provigo's dominance in the food industry so far was mainly due to its wholesale activities, which still earned about 75 percent of the company's sales. In Quebec, the market for independent grocers was growing again as more women were working, families were smaller, and fewer people were shopping in large supermarkets.

Provigo decided to expand its retail operations, extending its Jovi, Provibec, and Provigo stores into all areas of Quebec City. In November 1980, it bought all the shares of Abbatoir St.-Valerien Inc., which operated a large slaughterhouse. In January 1981, the company acquired Sports Experts Inc. In February, Provigo bought 87 of Dominion Stores' Quebec operations and distributing facilities. Pierre Lessard, who had become president and general manager in 1976, told *The Wall Street Journal* that "getting a larger presence in Montreal was the key to the transaction."

From the beginning, the Dominion stores had trouble. The managers responsible for integrating the new stores did not always agree with the managers of other Provigo supermarkets, and because of their differences, the stores had to be transformed one by one, taking six months longer than expected. As operational losses grew, the acquisition put several other projects on the shelf and cost the company a great deal of money and work. By 1984, Richard Constantineau, who had managed the Dominion stores, had resigned, several of the Dominion stores were sold to affiliates, and about 30 were closed. Others continued to do business until 1986, when the last were closed.

Provigo was involved in another price war in 1983, this time as a retailer. It began when Provigo's competitor, Steinberg Inc., started giving its customers coupons worth 5 percent of their total purchase, redeemable at the next purchase, a plan that won over shoppers immediately. Two days later, Provigo retaliated by offering a 6 percent discount on most products, which could be applied immediately to the purchase, as well as accepting discount coupons issued by Steinberg. When asked what it would take to end the price war, Turmel told the *Globe and Mail*, "I think it will be over when our competitor sees our results. They'll see we can withstand it better than they can. . . . We don't like it, but we can stand it." Provigo's colorful advertisements drew more customers during the war, and attracted wide press coverage.

In October, the company suffered another crisis when 45 of its Montreal-based Provigo stores were shut down by a strike, following a one-week strike at Steinberg. About 2,200 workers asked for increased job security and wages. After four weeks, Provigo offered a contract that matched Steinberg's contract with its workers, and the Provigo labor force accepted.

In 1984, Provigo extended its reach in the fast-food area by becoming a majority owner of Restaurants Les Pres Limitée, which operated four restaurants and was set to open eight more. Provigo also planned to focus on the convenience-store industry, which was blossoming in Quebec. In addition, the company began installing automatic banking machines in its major stores. In July, company stores also announced price cuts on many items with a campaign called Permaprix. Between 1980 and 1985, Provigo more than doubled its profits.

In April, 1985, Antoine Turmel retired, and the president of the Montreal stock exchange, Pierre Lortie, resigned that post to take control of Provigo as CEO. Later in the year, Pierre Lessard, who many had believed would take Turmel's place, stepped down from his position as president.

That year was also full of new ventures. Capitalizing on the many young couples who were buying and repairing old houses, Provigo went into the home-renovation business in February, becoming partners with a building supply firm, Val Royal LaSalle, to open a large home-renovation center in Montreal. That month the company also joined with Collegiate-Arlington Sports Inc. in Toronto, merging its Sports Experts division to form a new national business called Sports Experts Inc. In August, Provigo purchased a majority stake in Consumers Distributing Company, a catalogue showroom firm in Ontario. The company broadened its presence in eastern Quebec by purchasing Alphonse Allard Inc. and Approvisionnement Atlantique, both food wholesalers.

In an effort to increase profits as well as geographical growth, Provigo divided its businesses into five groups: food distribution (still comprising about two-thirds of its business), pharmaceuticals, convenience stores, non-food distribution, and Provigo U.S.A. Lortie believed this restructuring would enhance Provigo's national presence and help block competition from other firms. Provigo's U.S. subsidiaries had merged under the new restructuring, and sales increased to account for about 14 percent of the annual total. In 1986, Provigo acquired Pharmacom Systems Limited, a supplier of computer systems to pharmacies. The Sports Experts subsidiary opened five stores, the National Drug subsidiary opened a new distribution center, and several new food-distribution centers and cash-and-carry warehouses were also opened. Provigo undertook a joint venture with McKesson Corporation in San Francisco to distribute health supplies and equipment in Canada. In the supermarket division, the company expanded its fresh-foods and specialty departments.

By 1987, the pharmaceuticals operation was Provigo's fastest-growing business, and in February, the company consolidated its $1 billion operation into one company called Medis Health and Pharmaceuticals Services Inc. The move was viewed by many as a guard against Steinberg, Provigo's fiercest competitor; analysts had predicted that Steinberg would enter the drug distribution market soon. Provigo also planned to spend $18 million building drug distribution warehouses in Montreal and Toronto. In November, the company bought the remaining shares of Consumers Distributing Company.

In 1988, Unigesco Inc., a holding company, and Empire Company, a supermarket concern, raised their joint stake in Provigo stock from about 41 percent to 51 percent, and the president of Unigesco, Bertin Nadeau, who had been a director at Provigo since 1985, gained control of the company as the head of this 51 percent consortium.

Steinberg had been seeking bids for its supermarkets due to a quarrel in the Steinberg family, and in April, 1988 Provigo and Metro-Richelieu Inc., another food wholesaler, made a joint bid for its Quebec stores, planning to convert them into their own. Provigo and Metro-Richelieu were very competitive, and the joint bid insured that a bidding war would not occur between them. In the end however, with a new labor agreement, Steinberg opted not to sell its supermarkets after all.

In June, 1988, Provigo began to act on its plans for expansion in the United States, purchasing the Petrini's upscale supermarket chain in San Francisco, ten Alpha Beta stores, and five Lucky Supermarkets throughout northern California. The company also made plans to establish itself in Europe and Japan by organizing Provigo International to increase exports.

Provigo's traditional core business has been in wholesaling. Instead of focusing on vertical expansion into food manufacturing like many similar companies, it chose to test its retail and distribution skills in businesses other than groceries. In order to reflect this broadening focus, the company changed its name to Univain May 1992. The diversification strategy begun in the mid-1980s proved largely unsuccessful and was described by the *Globe and Mail*'s Ann Gibbon as "a disastrous journey into non-grocery areas." According to her report, operating losses from Sports Experts, Consumers Distributing, and Medis combined with the charges the company sustained in selling them in the early 1990s, and foregone profit from strong assets, such as the Alberta supermarket chain Horne Pitfield, are said to have cost the company as much as $1 billion between 1985 and 1995.

The decentralized management style and diversification that defined the company in the late 1980s and early 1990s came to an end when Pierre Michaud and Pierre Mignault entered the company in 1993, taking over as chairman and chief executive, respectively. In addition to restoring the company name Provigo, the new management team instituted a new organizational structure, implementing a more centralized decision making process at corporate headquarters in an attempt to reduce administrative overhead. That same year the company disposed of its unprofitable subsidiary, Sports Experts Inc., underscoring its renewed emphasis on its core business of food retail and distribution.

In January 1995, Provigo took another major step towards fully implementing its restructuring plan by closing the sale of its California subsidiary, Provigo Corporation, which had been unprofitable since 1990 despite several attempts to turn the subsidiary around. The company also continued to cut its losses from other non-performing operations, while introducing other cost cutting measures, which included closing sixteen unprofitable stores, consolidating warehouse functions through the closing of two distribution centers, and eliminating 500 support positions. In 1994, for the first time in several years, all of Provigo's subsidiaries operated in the black.

By streamlining operations and focusing on the business of selling groceries in Canadian stores, the company has attempted to make room for a three-year $250 million investment plan that was instituted in 1994, focused on the technological upgrading of existing stores and distribution facilities, the construction of state-of-the-art new stores, and the further development of its smaller independence and convenience store group. Once the program is fully implemented, the company expects to generate annual sales growth of 10 percent. Whether or not Provigo will be able to achieve this goal will depend largely on its continued ability to cut costs and on the strength of the Canadian economy.

Principal Subsidiaries:

LOEB Inc.; Provigo Distribution Inc.; C Corp. Inc.

Further Reading:

Given, Ann, "Can Provigo Turn Things Around?" *Globe and Mail*, February 3, 1995, p. B1.

Goold, Douglas, "The Long Road Back for Provigo," *Globe and Mail*, November 8, 1994, p. B13.

McKenna, Barrie, "Provigo Plans to Shed U.S. Subsidiary," *Globe and Mail*, April 9, 1991, p. B13.

———, "Univa Plucks New Chief from Rival," *Globe and Mail*, September 3, 1993, p. B3.

Melnbardis, Robert, "Provigo's Dubious Steinberg Purchase," *Financial Times of Canada*, June 1, 1992, pp. 19-20.

Provigo Inc. Annual Reports, 1992-1995, Montreal, Quebec.

Provost, René and Maurice Chartrand, *Provigo: The Story Behind 20 Years of Entrepreneurial Success,* Prentice Hall, 1989.

—updated by Jason Gallman

QUEBECOR GROUP INC.

Quebecor Inc.

612 Rue St. Jacques
Montréal, Quebec H3C 4M8
(514) 877-9777
Fax: (514) 877-9757

Public Company
Incorporated: 1965
Employees: 25,307
Sales: $3.08 billion
Stock Exchanges: Montréal New York Toronto
SICs: 2711 Newspapers: Publishing or Publishing &
Printing; 2731 Books: Publishing or Publishing &
Printing; 2752 Commercial Printing, Lithographic;
2754 Commercial Printing, Gravure; 2759
Commercial Printing Not Elsewhere Classified

Quebecor Inc. is a vertically integrated company specializing in publishing and distribution, printing, and forest products. The publishing and distribution arm, Quebecor Group Inc., produces daily and weekly newspapers, as well as magazines, books, and print advertisements. It is Quebec's largest publishing firm and largest magazine and newspaper distributor. Quebecor Group also distributes books, musical recordings, and photographic equipment. The company's printing division, Quebecor Printing Inc., is the largest diversified commercial printing concern in Canada and the second largest in the United States and North America. Quebecor Printing also has holdings in France and Mexico. Subsidiaries of Quebecor Printing make advertising insets and circulars, catalogues, telephone directories, magazines, books, checks, money, and passports. Quebecor Printing customers include Bloomingdale's, L.L. Bean, Radio Shack, Sears, and the magazines *People, Sports Illustrated, Time,* and *TV Guide.* Donohue Inc., Quebecor's forestry products subsidiary, manages forest tracts, operates mills, and produces newsprint, pulp, and lumber.

Pierre Péladeau, Quebecor's founder, president, and chief executive officer, bought his first newspaper in 1950 when he was 25 years old. His father had been successful in business, but lost his fortune by the time of his death when his son was only ten. His mother managed to send Péladeau to an exclusive school and he continued his education at elite universities. At an early age, Péladeau decided he would control his own financial destiny. "I always created my own jobs," Péladeau

told *Forbes.* A graduate of McGill University with a degree in law and of the University of Montreal with a master's degree in philosophy, Péladeau borrowed $1,500 from his mother to buy the ailing weekly *Le Journal dé Rosemont,* and worked hard to make the paper a success. In 1953 Péladeau bought his first printing press. More dailies and printing presses followed, until Péladeau had built the beginnings of his empire.

A 1964 strike at Quebec's leading French language daily, *La Presse,* gave Péladeau a big opportunity. In *La Presse*'s absence, Péladeau launched his own daily, *Le Journal de Montréal.* The tabloid, which featured graphic pictures of crime scenes, heavy sports coverage, pin-up girl photos, and no editorials, met with immediate success. *La Presse*'s return to the stands seven months later slowed but did not halt that success. In fact, circulation rose during the following years until *Le Journal* became Quebec and North America's leading French language daily in the late 1970s, a status it maintained into the 1990s.

After an entrepreneurial beginning and incorporation in 1965, Quebecor Inc. pursued a decade long course of acquisition and expansion that aimed to consolidate the company's leading position in the fields of publishing and printing in Canada and the United States. Since 1965, over 100 subsidiaries have been added to the Quebecor empire. The location and business activity of Quebecor's subsidiary purchases indicates the success of the company's stated strategic objective: "[To] Broaden its reach across North America and overseas; to acquire additional product market share and diversity; to target and acquire underperforming assets that are geographically well situated and improve their performance; and to achieve a size that maximizes the benefits of economies of scale."

In 1967, Péladeau founded *Le Journal de Quebec,* and later added an entertainment magazine and *Winnipeg Sun* to his newspaper holdings. Labor lawyer Brian Mulroney, eventually to become Canada's prime minister, worked out *Le Journal*'s first labor agreement. Péladeau's generous dealings with labor cemented his positive reputation with the public. In 1972, Péladeau offered shares in Quebecor.

In 1977, Péladeau gambled in the U.S. newspaper market by launching the *Philadelphia Journal.* But this venture turned out to be one of Péladeau's few misjudgments of the market and the competition. He thought the extensive sports coverage and tabloid format used in *Le Journal* would be a big hit in Philadelphia. Yet the paper's competition simply increased its sports coverage and cut advertising rates to squeeze Péladeau out of the market. Five years later, at a loss of US$14 million, the paper closed its doors.

In the next several years, Péladeau undertook a more aggressive campaign to establish a presence in the U.S. market and to take the number one position in Canada. He saw that technology and economies of scale were becoming increasingly important to success in the printing and publishing industries due to changes in technology and a more competitive world economy. His strong customer orientation and grasp of client needs, both in business-to-business and consumer markets, were great assets in the strategic expansion of Quebecor. Quebecor invested in emerging technologies, allowing retailers and advertisers to regionalize product offerings and prices. Bar code technology allowed the creation of large databases from which computers could determine demographic buying patterns, making it possible to tailor publications to specific regions, neighborhoods, or even individuals. These technologies required specialized capabilities such as special binding techniques to allow customized compilation of pages destined for different markets.

Péladeau and British publishing magnate Robert Maxwell teamed up in 1987 to form Mircor Inc., a joint subsidiary created to purchase—for $320 million—a 54 percent stake in Donohue Inc., a leading forest products company in Quebec. Quebecor took a 51 percent share of the newly-formed Mircor. The Donohue acquisition gave Quebecor its status as one of the most vertically integrated communications companies in the world, for it allowed the company to do everything from cutting the tree to distributing the printed product. Donohue supplied paper for Quebecor's journals and magazines and for direct mail advertising for its retail clients.

In 1988, Quebecor bought almost all of the printing assets of BCE Inc., the owner of Bell Canada, for $161 million and a 21 percent share of Quebecor capital stock. The acquisition expanded Quebecor's printing capabilities and brought in lucrative contracts for printing telephone directories, currency, and passports. This acquisition made Quebecor first in printing in Canada and gave the company significant economies of scale, positioning it well for success in the increasingly competitive and technology-driven industry.

In 1990, Quebecor bought Maxwell Communication Corp.'s 14 U.S. printing operations, forming the basis of Quebecor Printing. The US$510 million deal included a non-competition agreement and the purchase by Maxwell of a 25.8 percent interest in Quebecor Printing for US$100 million. According to Michael Crawford in *Canadian Business,* the purchase gave Quebecor access to a C$744 million customer list and rotogravure presses tailored to U.S. advertisers and catalogue companies. Only a year later, Robert Maxwell's death revealed his holdings to be in a financial mess. Quebecor bought back its shares from Maxwell for US$94.8 million dollars, US$5.2 million less than Maxwell had paid for it, giving Quebecor 100 percent ownership of Quebecor Printing.

Quebecor was not immune from the recession in the early 1990s. Plummeting newsprint prices in 1991 created heavy losses at Donohue, substantially eating into Quebecor's revenues. Advertising was down as well, putting pressure on the publishing and printing segments. In anticipation of the North American Free Trade Agreement, Quebecor established a foothold in Mexico by buying Mexican printer Graficas Monte Alban S.A. The move was another step forward in Quebecor's determination to become a truly North American company and gave Quebecor a presence in all three North American countries. Graficas prints books for Mexican and South American publishers. With about 200 employees and annual sales of US$4.5 million, Graficas was not a large acquisition. Neverthe-

less, it provided a starting point from which to learn the Mexican market and expand holdings in the fast growing market of 80 million people.

Quebecor expanded further in 1992 as it made large investments in its printing facilities and took Quebecor Printing Inc. public with an initial public offering that left the parent company with a 67.57 percent share of its printing subsidiary. Proceeds from the offering were used to reduce bank debt. In the same year, Quebecor won two lucrative five year contracts to print and bind Canadian telephone directories. The value of the contracts over five years was estimated at a combined total of $505 million.

In 1992 and 1993, Quebecor Printing acquired Arcata Graphics, San Jose, and three major Arcata Corporation printing plants, bringing in clients such as *Reader's Digest, Parade,* and *TV Guide.* The acquisition of these plants substantially expanded Quebecor's market share and capacity in producing catalogues, magazines, and books. Advanced web offset publication, special binding, ink jet printing, and shorter run production capabilities were some of the technologies enhanced by the purchase. In 1994, Quebecor completed its buyout of Arcata when it exercised its option to buy the company's outstanding shares. The final acquisition added five book manufacturing plants and a distribution facility to Quebecor, making the company the second largest book fabricator in the United States.

The strategic importance of Quebecor's expansion of its printing operations and move into the United States market was apparent from financial figures. By the end of 1993, U.S. sales represented more than 73 percent of Quebecor Printing's revenues and 64 percent of Quebecor Inc.'s revenues.

Quebecor's launch of *Le Magazine Provigo* with Provigo supermarkets in early 1993 was another example of Quebecor management's insight into consumer trends and changing markets. Four years before the magazine was introduced, Quebecor had approached the supermarket chain with the idea of differentiating itself from competitors by producing a monthly magazine on nutrition and health, with bits about local sports and entertainment celebrities. Quebecor hoped the magazine would join its information and distribution networks with Provigo's large target market to produce an effective advertising vehicle. Though Provigo wasn't ready to make the investment at the time, increased competition increased and narrowing profit margins in the retail grocery business eventually compelled Provigo to embrace the more upscale image offered by the magazine.

Quebecor Printing continued its international expansion with purchases and contracts in France, India, and Lebanon. Quebecor chose France because it is strategically situated to serve the European market, the world's second largest market for printed products after the United States. In 1993, Quebecor acquired 70 percent of the shares of commercial printer Groupe Fécomme for about US$12 million. The concern was renamed Imprimeries Fécomme-Quebecor S.A. The operation included three printing plants that made magazine covers, advertising inserts and circulars, and direct mail. Quebecor signed a letter of intent a few months after the Fécomme purchase to buy 49 percent of the shares of

Groupe Jean Didier, the largest printer in France, for US$27.6 million. The deal was completed in early 1995. The company produced magazines, catalogues, and inserts. With the two acquisitions, Quebecor established a significant foothold in Europe.

A partnership was formed in 1993 with Tej Bandhu Group in India to construct a printing plant, called Tej Quebecor Printing Ltd., for printing the majority of telephone directories in India. With a population of 850 million, the establishment of a subsidiary in India provided great potential for future expansion. In 1994, Quebecor was awarded a contract to produce bank notes for the central bank of Lebanon. The job specifies at least 29 million large denomination pound notes. The new issue is the first time Lebanon has printed its currency outside of England since its independence in 1943.

On the domestic front, 1994 saw the loss of one of Quebecor's major contracts, the printing of the U.S. edition of *Reader's Digest*, the largest paid monthly circulation magazine in the United States. Quebecor lost the US$20 million-a-year, ten-year contract to its major U.S.-based competitor, R. R. Donnelley & Sons Co. Donnelley was the largest commercial printer in North America and the world, with three times the revenues of Quebecor Printing. The contract was apparently awarded to Donnelley because of the company's technological capabilities in targeting advertising to specific subscriber groups. Another factor in the loss of the contract may have been the refusal of some unionized workers at Quebecor Printing of Buffalo Inc., where the magazine was printed, to accept a ten year no-strike/no-lockout amendment to the contract. Quebecor planned to make up the lost volume with growth in book printing.

While Quebecor appeared to be well positioned strategically and financially to meet the changing demands of its industries going into the twenty-first century, several management and business issues will have to be handled carefully to ensure future success. The ever-increasing competition and costly technological changes in Quebecor's main business sector will continue to present strategic challenges. The other main issue facing the company was the succession of founder Pierre Péladeau, whose flamboyant entrepreneurial style was an integral part of the company's development. Péladeau, 70 years old in 1995, planned to relinquish his position as president and CEO and take the slot of chairman of the board of directors "soon," though he had not specified what soon means. Two sons, Pierre Karl and Érik, held executive positions in the company and were considered likely candidates for the top slot.

Principal Subsidiaries:

Donohue Inc. (63.6 percent); Quebecor Printing Inc. (75.4 percent); Imprimeries Fécomme-Quebecor SA (70 percent; France); Quebecor Printing Corp. (USA); Tej Quebecor Printing Ltd. (40 percent; India).

Further Reading:

Bomberger, Paul, "Donnelley Planning Big Expansion Here," *Intelligencer Journal,* September 15, 1994, p. A1.
"Business Brief—Quebecor Inc.: Mexican Printer Is Acquired by a Unit of the Company," *Wall Street Journal,* January 7, 1992, p. 2.
Coles, Alex, "Quebecor Inc.—Sanford Evans Communications Ltd. Restructures Its Direct List Brokerage Services," *Business Wire,* February 22, 1993.
Crawford, Michael, "Prey for the Paper Tiger," *Canadian Business,* November 1993, p. 22.
Dougherty, Kevin, "The Powerful World of the Péladeaus," *Financial Post,* March 21, 1992, p. 2S16.
Dunn, Brian, "Provigo and Quebecor Launch Magazine for Grocery Shoppers," *Montreal Gazette,* March 1, 1993, p. C15.
Gray, Alan, "Quebecor Makes Paper, Prints on It and Distributes the Published Product," *Montreal Gazette,* March 22, 1993, p. F8.
McIntosh, Andrew, "Pierre Péladeau to Quit Quebecor—Next Year," *Monteal Gazette,* April 29, 1994, p. 1.
Palmeri, Christopher, "Nietzsche's Out God's In," *Forbes,* December 10, 1990, pp. 40-41.
"Quebecor Earnings Fell 89 Percent in Quarter, Revenue Declined 9 Percent," *Wall Street Journal,* February 13, 1992.
"Quebecor Finalizes Arcata Deal," *Graphic Arts Monthly,* August 1994, p. 21.
"Quebecor Printing Gets Contract," *Wall Street Journal,* September 29, 1992, p. B8.
"Quebecor Printing Gets 5-Year Contract to Print Directories," *Wall Street Journal,* July 6, 1992, p. 27.
"Quebecor Unit Acquires Plant," *Wall Street Journal,* January 23, 1992, p. 4.
"Quebecor Unit Sets Initial Public Offering of 14 Million Shares," *Wall Street Journal,* April 13, 1992, p. C11.
"Reader's Digest Selects Donnelley as Printer for Its U.S. Edition," *Wall Street Journal,* September 14, 1994, p. A4.
Rojo, Oscar, "Canadian High-Tech Firms Heading Overseas," *Toronto Star,* April 4, 1994, p. F3.

—Katherine Smethurst

Rio Algom Limited

Rio Algom Ltd.

120 Algom Ltd.
Toronto, Ontario M5H 1W5
(416) 367-4000
Fax: (416) 365-6870

Public Company
Founded: 1960 as Rio Algom Mines Ltd.
Employees: 2,575
Sales: $1.21 billion
Stock Exchanges: Montreal Toronto American
SICs: 1021 Copper Ores; 1031 Lead and Zinc Ores;
   1081 Metal Mining Services; 1094 Uranium-
   Radium-Vanadium Ores; 1221 Bituminous Coal
   and Lignite Surface Mining

Rio Algom Ltd. is a leading Canadian mining company with operations throughout the world. Since its inception in 1960, the organization has grown steadily by emphasizing underground uranium mining. It has also diversified into open-pit copper, zinc, and metallurgical coal, among other mining interests, and has developed extensive operations related to metals processing and distribution services. After nearly 30 years of growth, Rio Algom experienced declining sales and profits as a result of weak markets and slumping demand for uranium. Going into the mid-1990s, the company was benefiting by shifting its focus from uranium to other minerals, particularly copper.

The Rio Algom story began shortly after World War II, at the beginning of the cold war. The atomic age had arrived and demand for materials to make nuclear weapons was growing. Prospectors had long suspected that radioactive materials existed in Ontario north of Lake Superior and Lake Huron. Exploration began in earnest after the war. A few isolated finds during the late 1940s and early 1950s failed to expose significant uranium reserves, but they did generate a sort of uranium fever. By the early 1950s the woods were full of wishful amateur prospectors, tramping through the underbrush with their Geiger counters and headphones looking for the valuable radioactive bomb-making materials.

Among the greenhorn prospectors was Aime Breton, a hotel owner and manager who began looking for uranium in his spare time. In the late 1940s Breton stumbled upon what he suspected was a promising find on rough terrain about 75 miles east of Sault St. Marie in the Algoma woods. Breton's partner and full-time prospector Karl Gunterman confirmed Breton's suspicions, although he was unsure of the size of the find. They had a more experienced and educated mineral expert, Franc Joubin, take a look at the discovery, but preliminary tests indicated that the find was not substantial. A few years later, though, Joubin came across an article in a technical journal that suggested his testing methods might have missed something. To find out if the site was valuable, however, he would have to do expensive drilling.

Joubin approached a friend of his named Joseph Hirshhorn. Hirshhorn was a New York entrepreneur who had dabbled in uranium investments in Canada. To Joubin's surprise, Hirshhorn immediately agreed to front $30,000. Drilling began in 1953. Of 53 cores drilled on the site, 50 suggested that the site may have valuable uranium reserves. They named the find Pronto because they wanted to move on it quickly. The deposit, Joubin determined, was contained in a giant rock formation that stretched for 90 miles like a giant Z through rugged, uninhabited bush. Hirshhorn scrambled to protect the find and secure rights to the land. By law, he and his partners had just 30 days after staking their claim to get rights to the land. They hired 75 men who worked for 30 days securing property rights in the Algoma woods. Hirshhorn eventually filed claims on 1,400 separate properties on 56,000 acres. The find was valued at about $2 billion, or roughly two-thirds of the value of all the uranium in the Algoma area.

News of the giant Pronto discovery spread fast and a wave of prospectors flooded the region. Within a few months, 8,000 more claims had been filed in the area, including some that would soon become as well-known as Pronto. The first Pronto mine opened late in 1955. It had a daily production capacity of 1,500 tons of ore. Other mines were gradually added to tap into the long formation, for which long roads and accommodations for workers and their families had to be built. All of the claims under the Hirshhorn umbrella were separated and given to different operating companies for the sake of efficiency. A company called Preston East Dome—its workers had helped secure the land rights to the find—and a new company called Algom Uranium Mines were allotted about half of the claims. Pronto Uranium Mines Limited, the only company bearing the name of the original venture, was created to control about 140 claims. Other companies included those bearing the names Nordic, Lake Elliot, and Quirke.

The leading buyer of Canada's uranium in the 1950s was the United States. During that decade, demand for Canada's uranium was strong because the United States was still working to develop its own reserves. By the mid-1950s, however, the United States had started to create its own supply and the long-term future of the Canadian uranium industry was uncertain. It was about that time that Hirshhorn sold out. Rio Tinto Limited, a giant British corporation, began acquiring most of his interests in 1955. All of the interests were eventually grouped under a parent company called Rio Tinto Mining Company of Canada Limited. Joubin stayed on with Rio Tinto as a consulting geologist.

By 1959 Rio Tinto was supplying about 40 percent of Canada's uranium oxide. Unfortunately, the United States announced in 1959 that beginning in 1963 it would purchase no more uranium from Canada. Contracts were renegotiated to stretch until 1966, but the industry still deteriorated. Most mines closed during the early 1960s. Rio Tinto reacted to the 1959 decision by consolidating its floundering operations in 1960 into one company; Rio Algom Mines Limited. Many of the uranium companies in Canada simply dissolved. Rio Algom, however, survived by diversifying into copper and molybdenum mining, and into steel production. Under the agile management of Bob Winters, all of Rio Algom's debt was paid off by 1961 and Rio even found itself in relatively sound health by 1966, when its U.S. uranium sales ended. Besides diversifying into other businesses, Winter managed to find new uranium buyers in Great Britain, Japan, and Canada. In fact, it had secured long-term contracts in Britain and Canada to supply about 14,000 tons of uranium oxide between 1970 and 1983.

Despite the serious downturn in the Canadian uranium industry during the 1960s, Rio Algom remained focused on those operations. Sales and profits were sporadic during the early 1960s while Winters and his associates scurried to reposition the organization to compete without its major uranium customer. By 1963, though, sales began picking up as a result of acquisitions, diversification, and new uranium customers. In 1962, for example, Rio purchased the steel business of Atlas Steels Ltd. Rio's sales more than doubled in 1963, and net income (before extraordinary items) surged about 20 percent to more than $10 billion. From that point on, Rio achieved steady revenue gains almost every year throughout the 1960s, 1970s, and 1980s. It achieved those gains partly because of its status as the leading Canadian producer of reactor-grade uranium-oxide, but also through its success in other mining industries and in metals processing and distribution.

As Rio's uranium business recovered during the 1970s and even into the 1980s, management continued to pursue new interests related to various types of metal and precious-metal mining and metals services. Its metals services including warehousing, processing, and distribution of metals for other mining companies and for manufacturing companies that utilized Rio's output. Rio even began extending its operations outside its borders with acquisitions in the United States, and later in South America, Australia, and New Zealand. Sales shot up about $183 million by 1970, and $15 million was netted as income. By 1980, moreover, Rio was generating about $850 million in revenues annually and capturing a record $75 million in profits. Furthermore, despite acquisitions and expansion, Rio managed to keep its total debt load at relatively low $100 million.

Expired contracts combined with volatility in key markets caused Rio to stumble in the early 1980s. As sales and profits slipped, management began looking for new opportunities. In April of 1984 Rio purchased Vincent Brans and Aluminum Co. Inc. of the United States for about $60 million in cash. Vincent (renamed Vincent Metals Division) operated ten metal service centers in the midwestern and southeastern United States. That acquisition reflected Rio's intent to become more active

in metals processing. To that end, in 1986 Rio invested in Al Tech Specialty Steel Corp.—also in 1986, Rio bought an American potash mining company with mining operations in Canada. By the mid-1980s, Rio's metal processing operations were accounting for a major portion of its revenues, although mining operations continued to supply the majority of profits. Largely as a result of its acquisition drive, but also because of rebounding markets, Rio's sales rocketed more than two-fold during the mid-1980s to nearly $2 billion by 1988. Meanwhile, profits climbed to a record $114 billion.

Rio's mid-1980s gain was short-lived. In fact, an economic downturn beginning in the late 1980s, made worse by serious structural problems that developed in Rio's key uranium markets, pummeled the company. Revenues plunged about 50 percent between 1988 and 1993, in fact, and profits dwindled. To make matters worse, Rio was abandoned by its major shareholder in June of 1992 when British conglomerate RTZ Corp. sold its 51 percent stake. The company continued to post profits, as it had for more than 30 consecutive years, but its long-term outlook was suddenly clouded by a general lack of corporate direction. Disappointed with the company's strategy, Rio's board decided to bring in a new chief executive. Ray Ballmer stepped aside in 1991 and was replaced by Rio insider Colin Macaulay.

The 59-year-old Macaulay had received degrees in both Canada and the United States before beginning a career with various subsidiaries of RTZ Corp. He started out in 1958 with one of the mining companies that was merged to form Rio Algom. He later worked for other RTZ subsidiaries in Canada and Africa before returning to Rio in 1988 to be groomed for the chief executive post. Under his leadership beginning in June of 1991, Rio intensified its efforts to develop a new corporate identity and long-term strategy. Macaulay initially planned to jettison the remainder of Rio's steel distribution operations and focus on mining. He also wanted to tap Rio's giant reserve of capital to acquire new companies that would complement existing operations. To that end, Rio did acquire or become a partner in various mining related ventures in the early 1990s that bolstered mining revenues. But it remained active in steel, aluminum, and other metals processing and distribution businesses.

Rio suffered major setbacks in its uranium division, as evidenced by a production decline from more than eight billion pounds in the early 1980s to less than two billion by the early 1990s. Two of its uranium mines were shuttered in the early 1990s and a third was scheduled for closure in 1996. To make up for the loss, Macaulay shifted gears and targeted the copper market. In fact, the overall strategy that emerged during the early 1990s was to focus on mining operations, particularly copper mining. Meanwhile, Rio restructured and consolidated its metals processing and distribution businesses in North America and Australia, significantly improving their competitiveness and providing a much needed boost to Rio's bottom line when minerals prices slumped in 1993. Macaulay's long-term strategy was to position Rio as a low-cost leader in the base-metals mining industry, and to achieve long-term growth through a conservative asset-building approach.

Rio drew fire for its lackluster performance during the early 1990s, mostly from critics that believed its management lacked aggressiveness and was afraid to take risks. But the company was actually in good condition and was suffering largely from circumstances outside of its control, such as weak minerals prices. Importantly, the company's conservative approach toward debt and diversification had left it with plenty of cash to survive even major market fluctuations, and it was well positioned for future growth. The value of its long-term growth strategy was validated by recovering markets in 1994. Helped mostly by rising copper prices, Rio Algom's revenues jumped 27 percent in 1994 to $1.21 billion, while net income vaulted to a recent high of more than $75 million. 1994 became Rio's 35th consecutive year of profitability.

Going into 1995, Rio was operating copper mines in Chile and British Columbia, a uranium mine and coal mine in British Columbia, a zinc mine in the Canadian arctic, extensive metals distribution businesses in North America and New Zealand, and both processing and manufacturing businesses in Australia. In addition, Rio was managing and developing mineral exploration projects in North and South America. Mining was accounting for about 31 percent of revenues and 68 percent of profits, while metals distribution made up 69 percent and 32 percent, respectively. Low debt and rising minerals prices suggested short-term growth and long-term stability.

Principal Subsidiaries:

Atlas Steels Ltd. (60.9 percent; Australia); Compania Minera Cerro Colorado Limitada (Chile); Compania Minera Riochilex S.A. (Chile); Rio Algom Exploration Inc.; Rio Algom Mining Corp. (U.S.A.).

Further Reading:

Cambell, Tom, "Al Tech Looks for Capital Projects From New Owner," *Business First-Buffalo,* March 27, 1989, Section 1, p. 13.

Carrington, John, *Risk Taking in Canadian Mining,* Toronto: Pitt Publishing Company Ltd., 1979.

Fowlie, Laura, "Rio Algom Has Lower Profit, Gloomy Outlook," *Financial Post,* April 25, 1991, Section 1, p. 15.

Fung, Victor, "New CEO Seeks to 'Purify' Rio," *Financial Post,* May 31, 1991, Section 1, p. 39.

———, "Rio Algom Proceeds with Chile Mine," *Financial Post,* January 28, 1992, Section 1, p. 16.

Historical Reports: Rio Algom Limited, The Financial Post Datagroup, July 5, 1995.

Joubin, Franc R., *Not For Gold Alone,* Toronto: Deljay Publications, 1986.

Kennedy, Peter, "Rio Algom Counts on Move to Copper," *Financial Post,* January 16, 1993, Section 1, p. 10.

Kryhul, Angela, "Steel, Metals, Mining Spur Rio Algom Earnings," *American Metal Market,* March 8, 1988, p. 3.

Munford, Christopher, "Rio Algom Casts Eye to Mining: Looks to Sell Metals Distribution Business," *American Metal Market,* March 1, 1991, p. 1.

"Rio, Exxon Team Up in Wisconsin," *Northern Miner,* September 20, 1993, Section 1, p. 1.

—Dave Mote

Rogers Communications Inc.

Scotia Plaza, Suite 6400
40 King Street West, Box 1007
Toronto M5H 3Y2
(416) 864-2375
Fax: (416) 864-2375

Public Company
Incorporated: 1920 as Famous Players Canadian
   Corporation
Employees: 6,540
Sales: $2.25 billion
Stock Exchanges: Toronto Montreal Alberta
   Vancouver
SICs: 4812 Radiotelephone; 4813 Telephone
   Communications except Radiotelephone; 4832
   Radio Broadcasting Stations; 4833 Television
   Broadcasting Stations

The largest communications company in Canada, Rogers Communications functions as the holding company for four main operating companies: Rogers Cantel Mobile Communications Inc., Rogers Cablesystems Limited, Rogers Multi-Media Inc., and Unitel Communications Holdings Inc., a 29.5 percent-owned subsidiary. Cantel is Canada's largest wireless telephone company and the only company licensed to provide cellular and paging services nationwide. Cantel serves nearly 800,000 subscribers and owns a national network capable of providing service to 24 million people, or 85 percent of the Canadian population. Rogers Cablesystems is Canada's largest cable company, serving nearly 2.6 million subscribers, or 33 percent of nation's cable subscribers. Rogers Multi-Media, created after the 1994 acquisition of Maclean Hunter Limited, owns radio and television broadcasting properties, Canadian business and consumer periodicals, and a 62 percent interest in Toronto Sun Publishing Corporation. Unitel, jointly owned by Rogers Communications, Canadian Pacific Limited, and AT&T, provides public switch and private line voice and data service through a national digital network.

On three notable occasions, Edward S. Rogers, Jr., challenged conventional wisdom while orchestrating the development of his company, refusing in each instance to heed the advice of those purporting to know better. Each instance proved to be instrumental to the growth of Rogers Communications and greatly contributed to

Rogers' personal success, helping him earn the epithet most sought after by entrepreneurs: self-made billionaire. First, Rogers decided to enter the FM radio broadcasting business, which raised the eyebrows of disbelieving critics who declared that FM radio would never be popular. Next he made the decision to enter the cable television business, while onlookers proclaimed that consumers would never pay for television. Then, in the mid-1980s, Rogers set his sights on the nascent cellular telephone business, but the board of directors of Rogers Communications rejected his proposal. Rogers reacted characteristically: he went ahead anyway, using his own money to help launch the venture. By the mid-1990s, despite all the pessimistic predictions, Rogers Communications was one of the largest communications companies in the world.

Rogers inherited some of his pioneering and entrepreneurial spirit from his father, Edward S. Rogers, Sr., who, in 1921, was the first Canadian to transmit a radio signal across the Atlantic. At the time only 21 years old, Rogers went on to become much more than a historical footnote by inventing the radio amplifying tube, a device that revolutionized the radio industry by eliminating the need for cumbersome, leak-prone acid batteries, enabling consumers to operate their radios on alternating current. Rogers's invention led him to found CFRB (Canada's First Rogers Batteryless), which became the most popular radio station in the country, and Rogers Majestic Corporation, a manufacturing concern devoted to producing his invention. Rogers moved on to break ground in another direction in 1931 when he was granted the first license in Canada to broadcast experimental television, but eight years later, when Edward S. Rogers, Jr., was five years old, the elder Rogers died of overwork and a bleeding ulcer, leaving no one in charge to supervise his various business interests. The Rogers estate floundered and the popular CFRB station was lost.

The younger Rogers, who preferred to be called Ted, was affected deeply by the death of his father. He followed his father's footsteps in his first big business deal, purchasing radio station CHFI-FM in 1960 while studying for a law degree at Osgoode Hall Law School. Rogers used a life insurance policy as collateral to take out a $63,000 loan and paid $85,000 for the station, an intrepid move considering that only five percent of the Toronto market possessed FM receivers at the time. Undaunted by critics who dismissed the FM concept, Rogers plunged into the FM radio broadcasting business, establishing Rogers Radio Broadcasting Limited as the owner of CHFI. To help promote the station, Rogers, then 26 years old, approached Westinghouse Canada and convinced the company to manufacture inexpensive ($39.95) FM radios, which he then sold or gave away to listeners. Two years later, a year after earning his law degree, Rogers purchased CFTR-AM, then went on to win other radio licenses, initially using money from his parents' estate and later soliciting financial assistance from the Bank of Montreal and Toronto business leaders. By the mid-1960s, Rogers was ready to steer the Canadian communications industry in a new direction. While his father had shown himself to be an ingenious engineer, the younger Rogers was carving his niche in the communications industry as a marketer, transforming existing but little-used technology into widely sought-after services. His entry into FM radio broadcasting had proved to be an insightful move, the first of his successful efforts to broaden the appeal of existing communications technology, but when he was awarded Canada's first cable franchise in 1965 his abilities produced success of a much higher magnitude. Competing against industry stalwarts such as Gulf & Western and CBS for the first rights to broadcast cable, Rogers emerged victorious, registering one of the several key licensing coups that would carry him to the top of the communications industry.

After slightly more than a decade in the cable business, Rogers had established a formidable presence, constructing a cable network that had few rivals. In 1978 he made an aggressive move to bolster his company's position further when he acquired Canada's second-largest cable company, Canadian Cablesystems Limited, in an unfriendly takeover. At the same time, Rogers began collecting cable franchises in the United States. The following year he took his company public as the largest cable operator in Canada. Another leading cable company, Premier Communications Limited, was added to Rogers's stable of cable properties in two transactions—85.1 percent in 1979 and 14.5 percent in 1980—extending the company's coverage to British Columbia, where Premier served three urban centers. In 1981 Rogers targeted UA-Columbia Cablevision Inc. as his next acquisition, offering his family's five radio stations, owned by a private company named Rogers Telecommunications Ltd., and his extensive cable television interests for a loan to secure UA-Columbia's 450,000 cable subscribers. Rogers bid $152 million for 51 percent of UA-Columbia, teaming up with United Artists Theater Circuit Inc. to beat out competing bids offered by Knight-Ridder Newspapers and Dow Jones. When the deal was concluded in November, Rogers's cable properties served 1.75 million subscribers, making the company the largest cable operator in North America.

Rogers's frenetic growth slowed during the early 1980s after the acquisition of UA-Columbia, as an economic recession inflated interest rates to 20 percent between 1982 and 1983. Saddled with $750 million in debt it had assumed to finance its growth, Rogers Communications staggered through the early and mid-1980s, divesting assets and abandoning plans to expand into Europe. "We sold off everything we could, just to keep afloat," Rogers reflected later to *Forbes*. "It was like flying a plane and you're just tossing stuff out of the plane just trying to keep above the trees." The company paid its price for two decades of aggressive expansion, losing more than $100 million between 1982 and 1987, but the losses, although severe, were of secondary importance to Rogers. More important was securing commanding control over emerging communications technologies, even if that goal was achieved through lackluster financial performance.

Prompted by recent developments in cellular telephone technology, Rogers began exploring the possibility of entering the business in 1982. In February of the following year he approached the company's board of directors, who, considering the financial condition of the struggling company at the time, rejected his proposal to obtain a cellular telephone license. Rogers persevered,

looking elsewhere for financial support. Assistance was obtained from the Belzerg family of Vancouver-based First City Financial Corporation and Philippe de Gaspee Beaubien of Montreal-based Telemedia Inc. Rogers then invested $2 million of his own money to launch the venture, which was incorporated in May 1984 as Rogers Cantel Mobile Communications, Inc. Over the next four years, after investing an additional $5 million, Rogers bought out his partners to become the sole owner of Cantel, giving his company a third leg to stand on.

The future of the communications industry, as Rogers and others perceived it, entailed all communications services being transmitted via a single wire into businesses and individual residences, preferably by one company with broad communications capabilities. As a result, Rogers sought to become a communications conglomerate capable of bundling telephone, television, and paging and wireless services in one monthly bill to consumers throughout Canada.

One important branch of the communications field was missing from this growing empire, however: Rogers Communications did not maintain a stake in providing telephone service. Rogers attempted to fill this void in 1985 by making a bid for CNCP Telecommunications Limited, a subsidiary of Canadian Pacific Limited, but the attempt was rejected. Four years later Rogers tried again, but first he made an uncharacteristic move by selling his U.S. cable properties to Houston Industries, Inc., in February 1989 for $1.58 billion. Instead of using the money to support an aggressive expansion program, he ploughed the money back into Rogers Communications, with $525 million earmarked for refurbishing the company's cable operations and another $600 million dedicated to strengthening Cantel, which by this point had captured more than 50 percent of the Canadian mobile telephone market.

One month after Rogers Communications sold its U.S. cable properties, Rogers made another bid for CNCP Telecommunications to end what he referred to in an interview with the *Globe and Mail* as "Soviet-style communications monopolism." This time around Rogers was successful, acquiring a 40 percent stake in the company from Canadian Pacific Limited and spawning a new business arm for Rogers Communications, which was later named Unitel Communications Inc. In June 1992, Unitel received permission from the Canadian Radio-Television and Telecommunications Commission to compete against the telephone companies in the public long-distance market, making the company one of the largest of the long-distance companies in the country, trailing only Bell Canada.

Unitel, however, proved to be a drain on Rogers Communications' profits, losing a total of $600 million between 1992 and 1995. Rogers Communications had experienced its fair share of losses, sacrificing annual earnings for market share and for financing entry into new business areas, leading Rogers to casually note in a 1994 *Macleans* interview, "All this company has to do to make money is stop growing." Nevertheless, more than $500 million in losses racked up between 1990 and 1994 were cause for concern, and by 1995 Rogers was beginning to pin some of the blame on Unitel, confiding to Rogers Communications shareholders that year, "Our policy is to be in long-distance, but not necessarily in Unitel." Earlier, the company's interest in Unitel had been dropped to 32 percent after AT&T signed on as a partner in January 1993 when it purchased a 20 percent stake and as Rogers Communications mapped its plan for the mid-1990s it appeared Unitel would have perhaps a more distant relationship with Rogers Communications.

Despite mounting losses, Rogers Communications concluded a pivotal deal in 1994 when it acquired Maclean Hunter Limited for an enormous $2.5 billion. Financed largely by bank loans, the acquisition of Maclean Hunter, a cable and publishing conglomerate, gave Rogers Communications a 62 percent stake in Toronto Sun Publishing Corporation, which owned the *Toronto Sun,* the *Financial Post,* tabloids in Edmonton, Calgary, and Ottawa, and nearly 200 other publications, including *Macleans, Chatelaine,* and *Canadian Business.* These properties were organized into a new operating company for Rogers Communications named Rogers Multi-Media Inc., formed in late 1994.

Maclean Hunter's numerous cable properties which ranked the company as Canada's fourth-largest cable operator. With 700,000 cable subscribers in Canada (compared to Rogers Communications' 1.9 million), Maclean Hunter also owned U.S. cable systems in Florida, New Jersey, and the Detroit area that served more than 500,000 subscribers, as well as numerous other non-cable properties, including 21 radio stations, a CTV affiliate in Calgary, a home security division, a business forms company, and a trade show management group.

The acquisition of Maclean Hunter represented an enormous undertaking, strengthening Rogers Communications' own 14 Canadian cable systems, 16 radio stations, and one television station, as well as other diverse business interests, including a chain of video rental stores the company had acquired in 1988 and a stake in Canadian Home Shopping Network Limited. As the company prepared for its future after the acquisition, it planned to sell Maclean Hunter's U.S. cable properties to reduce the company's long-term debt, which had swelled to more than $2 billion, and contemplated conducting its long-distance telephone business through Cantel rather than through its troubled 29.5 percent-owned Unitel Communications.

Principal Subsidiaries:

Rogers Multi-Media Inc.; Rogers Broadcasting Ltd.; Rogers Cable T.V. Ltd.; Rogers Cablesystems Ltd.; Rogers Canada Inc.; Rogers Cantel Mobile Communications Inc.; Rogers Cantel Mobile Inc.; Rogers Ottawa Ltd./Lte.; Rogers Telecom Ltd.; Unitel Communications Holdings Inc. (32%); Unitel Communications Inc.

Further Reading:

Dalglish, Brenda, "Up in the Air: Long-Distance Competition Squeezes New Phone Companies," *Maclean's,* May 8, 1995, p. 50.

"Famous Players Canadian Corp.," *Financial Post,* June 5, 1965, p. 35.

Fisher, Ross, "Ted's Team," *Canadian Business,* August 1989, p. 28.

Garneau, George, "Maclean Hunter Agrees to Be Bought by Rogers," *Editor & Publisher,* March 19, 1994, p. 50.

Hawkins, Chuck, "A Cable Mogul with a Live-Wire Idea," *Business Week,* July 4, 1988, p. 39.

Jackson, Basil, "Building Hustle Ahead as Movies Try Comeback," *Financial Post,* September 12, 1962, p. 36.

Marion, Larry, "The Legacy," *Forbes,* July 6, 1981, p. 81.

Mason, Todd, "Houston Industries Splurges on Cable TV," *Business Week,* September 12, 1988, p. 40.

Meeks, Fleming, "This Will Be a Very Political Issue," *Forbes,* February 19, 1990, p. 80.

Munk, Nina, "Ted Rogers' New Apartment," *Forbes,* April 24, 1995, p. 42.

Newman, Peter C., "The Ties that Bind," *Maclean's,* February 21, 1994, p. 34.

Osterland, Andrew W., "Cable's Other Ted," *Financial World,* October 25, 1994, p. 36.

Partridge, John, "Rogers Gives His Rival More Reasons to Worry, '" *Globe and Mail,* April 3, 1989, p. B1.

Stoffman, Daniel, "Great Connections," *Globe and Mail,* August 18, 1989, p. P37.

—Jeffrey L. Covell

ROYAL BANK

The Royal Bank of Canada

1 Place Ville Marie
Post Office Box 6001
Montreal, Quebec H3C 3A9
(514) 874-2110
Fax: (514) 874-7197

Public Company
Incorporated: 1869 as the Merchants Bank of
   Halifax
Employees: 41,215
Total Assets: $173.73 billion *Stock Exchanges:*
   Toronto Montreal London Tokyo
SICs: 6021 National Commercial Banks

The Royal Bank of Canada is Canada's largest financial institution and ranked among the 50 largest banks in the world going into 1995. The bank maintained more than 1,500 branches and 4,000 banking machines, and offered a full range of banking services in the United States, Europe, Asia, Latin America, and the Caribbean.

Founded in 1864 by a group of eight businessmen in Halifax, Nova Scotia, the Merchants Bank, as it was then called, began with $200,000 in capital to support local commerce. The bank's establishment coincided with a sharp increase in the area's commercial activity, a result of the American Civil War—Halifax was a thriving center for blockade runners crossing the U.S. border. The bank made a successful start under these conditions, and was incorporated five years later as the Merchants Bank of Halifax. Thomas C. Kinnear, one of the original founders, was its first president.

From these early beginnings, the bank expanded conservatively, opening branches in several more Maritime towns until a business depression in the latter 1870s slowed the expansion. In 1882 Merchants opened its first branch outside Canada, in Hamilton, Bermuda—before it had even expanded as far as Ontario domestically. Although this branch closed in 1889, the bank remained committed to international operations, opening several branches in Latin America before it was well established in western Canada.

By 1896, Merchants Bank's assets totaled $10 million. The gold rush in the early 1890s in southern British Columbia, along with the completion of the new Canadian Pacific Railway in 1885, provided the impetus for the bank's western expansion. In 1899 two more branches were established in New York and Havana. The bank took a conservative approach in developing its Cuban business and made only a handful of initial loans. But as confidence in Cuba's future grew, particularly with the formation of the Republic in 1902 and the continuing growth of the sugar industry, the bank gradually expanded, opening several branches around the country. This business upswing came to a temporary halt when the sugar market suffered its first collapse, in 1920.

The dawn of a new century heralded a period of growth and prosperity in Canada, especially in the area between Winnipeg and the Rocky Mountains. The bank, renamed the Royal Bank of Canada in 1901, grew too, opening more branches and acquiring several smaller institutions. With this growth, the bank decided in 1907 to relocate from Halifax to Montreal, where the general manager was based. The move reflected Montreal's growing importance as a financial center and the relative decline of maritime commerce.

By the following year, the Royal Bank of Canada had 109 branches and $50 million in assets. This strong base provided the foundation for the acquisition, in 1910, of the 54-year-old Union Bank of Halifax. Subsequent acquisitions of the Traders Bank of Canada and the Bank of British Honduras in 1912 more than doubled the number of operating branches and doubled its asset base by the end of the next year.

At the start of World War I, the Canadian real estate market had collapsed and very little capital was flowing into the country from abroad. In this uncertain atmosphere, the bank could not even promise staff who had enlisted reinstatement upon their return. Soon, however, business expanded sharply as wartime industry geared up, and the bank was forced to break with tradition and hire women.

Although the war put pressure on the Royal's day-to-day operations, the bank continued to grow, buying the Quebec Bank in 1917, the Northern Crown Bank in 1918, and two other banks in British Guiana and Nassau. By the end of the war, the Royal was the second largest bank in Canada, with 540 branches, assets of more than $422 million, and a new foreign trade department to handle its growing international presence.

The Royal Bank weathered the period of economic collapse that followed the end of World War I and, by 1925, had resumed its quest for expansion with the purchase of the Bank of Central and South America and the Union Bank of Canada. The Union Bank was the Royal Bank's largest takeover yet, and strengthened its presence in the three Prairie provinces. Royal's solid structure and leading position in the banking industry helped it survive the stock market crash relatively well, but it was not totally unscathed. Asset and profit levels fell, branches were closed, staff were laid off, and expenditures and the salaries of remaining employees were cut. Yet, while banks in the United States were closing in record numbers, not one Canadian chartered bank failed during this time.

By 1939, total assets were more than $1 billion and the bank was ready to take advantage of the opportunities World War II offered. In cooperation with other banking institutions, the Royal actively participated in war measures, and it was instrumental in operating a ration coupon system for food and gasoline. But basically the war meant increased government expenditures for the war effort. The bank's domestic business flourished, though internationally its European branches were constrained under German occupation.

After World War II, the Royal helped develop Canada's oil, gas, and resource exploration industries by providing banking services in remote locations. It opened an oil and gas department in Calgary in 1951, and also established banking services in cities along the British Columbian route connecting a massive project undertaken by the Aluminum Company of Canada. The bank continued its international expansion with the establishment of the Royal Bank of Canada Trust Company in New York in 1951 as well.

When Fidel Castro came to power in Cuba in 1959, the Cuban banking system was nationalized. The Royal Bank of Canada and the Bank of Nova Scotia were, alone among banks, permitted to operate independently, but the losses they incurred, as nationalized businesses transferred their banking to the nationalized system, were too heavy, and the Royal Bank sold its Cuban assets to the Banco Nacional de Cuba in December of 1960.

In 1962, almost 100 years after its founding, The Royal Bank of Canada adopted a new emblem to replace its original coat of arms. The emblem's design incorporated a lion, a crown, and a globe to symbolize the bank's position as a leading force in international banking. That same year, the bank's offices moved into a new, 42-story skyscraper—the construction of which helped set in motion a large-scale urban development plan that turned midtown Montreal into a vital commercial district. At the same time, the bank sharpened its focus on consumer-oriented financial services by entering the market with a product called TermPlan, a package of credit and insurance benefits. Six years later, in partnership with three other banks, the bank introduced Chargex, a credit card that allowed holders to make purchases within a specified credit limit and obtain cash advances through any of four participating institutions.

The 1967 revision of the Bank Act sparked vigorous competition among Canada's chartered banks, which had long operated under a morass of special restrictions. In removing or casing these constraints, the new law permitted banks to vie for loans, deposits, and conventional mortgages on an equal basis with other lending and borrowing institutions. By 1967 the Royal Bank had written more than half of the residential mortgage loans provided by all of the chartered banks combined.

In the early 1970s, the Royal Bank joined forces with five other banks to form Orion, a London-based merchant banking organization designed to enter the financial services market. Although Canadian law prohibited banks from entering this market domestically, Orion competed successfully in placing international bond issues and securities. Orion became a wholly owned subsidiary of the Royal Bank in 1981, enabling the bank to diversify its operations up to the limits imposed by Canada's banking laws and position itself for the possibility of international banking deregulation.

In 1979 Rowland Frazee, who had been with the bank for 40 years, was appointed chief executive officer. He replaced W. Earle McLaughlin, who became chairman after an eighteen-year reign as CEO. By this time the Royal Bank was the fourth largest bank in North America, with assets of $53 billion. Although one-third of that total was attributed to its international activities, the bank had lost its early advantage in many foreign markets to other institutions. One of Frazee's first orders of business was to strengthen the bank's influence in the United States. He poured new capital into the Royal Bank and Trust Company, in New York, and increased its staff. A second Frazee priority was the development of a Global Energy Group, based in Calgary, to provide technical consultation as well as capital for energy-related projects on an international basis. To manage its newly aggressive stance, the bank reorganized into four groups, two responsible for Canadian retail and commercial business, and two to handle corporate banking and international operations.

In 1986, Allan Taylor became chairman of the Royal Bank. Taylor's rise from junior clerk at the age of 16 to chairman 37 years later has become a company legend. His appointment as chairman replaced the bank's traditional conservatism with a more entrepreneurial approach to the Royal's modern banking challenges. One of the first problems Taylor faced was the relaxation of rules governing the ownership of brokerage firms by banks. The Royal began negotiations with Wood Gundy, a leading Canadian brokerage firm, in the spring of 1987, some months before the law actually changed. That deal fell through, but the Royal went on to acquire Dominion Securities, the largest investment house in Canada, just after the stock market crash in October that year. Although it was one of the last of Canada's big banks to enter the brokerage market, by waiting, the Royal got the best deal of all because it saved a significant amount over pre-crash prices. Taylor was also credited with helping to reduce Royal's net exposure to Third World debt from 200% of shareholder equity to 75% going into the early 1990s.

During the early 1990s Royal executives continued to work to cut costs, reduce problem loans, and expand into new businesses. Largely as a result of restructuring, but also because of economic factors such as fluctuating interest rates and sporadic securities markets, Royal's revenues and income bobbled. Sales declined from about $14.63 billion in 1990 to just $11.68 billion in 1993 as net income plunged to a deficit of $16 million in 1992. By the mid-1990s, though, the banks efforts began to pay off. Revenue rose to $13.43 billion in 1994 and net income vaulted to a record $1.1 billion—that made Royal the first Canadian bank to clear the $1 billion profit hurdle. Ongoing efficiency initiatives in that year, the bank's 125th anniversary, were evidenced by a work force reduction of 4,000.

Having improved the bank's health during his short stint as chairman and chief executive, Taylor stepped down in January of 1995. He was succeeded by John Cleghorne, an industry veteran and long-time ally of

Taylor's. Cleghorne planned to continue cutting costs, including the elimination of 1,000 jobs in 1995, and to consolidate existing operations. His top priority, though, was revenue growth and market diversification. For example, Royal was eyeing a foray into the insurance market in 1995 following related government deregulation of the banking industry that took effect in that year. The bank's long-term prospects were positive going into the mid-1990s, especially given Royal's improved financial condition and sheer size.

Principal Subsidiaries:

Royal Bank Holding Inc.; Royal Bank Mortgage Corporation; Royal Trust Corporation of Canada; RBC Finance B.V.; Royal Trust Corp. of Canada; Atlantis Holdings Limited; RBC Holdings (USA) Inc.; Royal Bank of Canada Reinsurance (Cayman) Limited.

Further Reading:

Blackwell, Richard. "Royal Bank Profit Beats the Street," *Financial Post*, March 2, 1995, Section 1, p. 4.

Blackwell, Richard. "Royal Stalls Dividend Hike Despite Record Earnings," *Financial Post*, January 27, 1995, Section 1, p. 5.

Haliechuk, Rick. "Bank Shareholders Cheer Retiring Taylor Royal's Future Bright, He Says," *Toronto Star*, January 27, 1995, Section B., p. 1.

Ince, Clifford, *The Royal Bank of Canada: A Chronology: 1864-1969,* Montreal: The Royal Bank of Canada, 1969.

—updated by Dave Mote

Saskatchewan Wheat Pool

2625 Victoria Avenue
Regina, Saskatchewan S4T 7T9
Canada
(306) 569-4411
Fax: (306) 569-4708

Cooperative Company
Incorporated: 1923 as Saskatchewan Co-operative
  Wheat Producers Limited
Employees: 3,202
Sales: $2.08 billion
SICs: 0100 Agricultural Production—Crops; 2090
  Miscellaneous Food & Kindred Products; 2875
  Fertilizers—Mixing Only

The largest of three agricultural cooperatives that handle the bulk of the grain grown in Canada, Saskatchewan Wheat Pool was formed in 1923 at roughly the same time the country's two other agricultural pools, Manitoba Pool Elevators and Alberta Wheat Pool. Initially, Saskatchewan Wheat Pool handled and marketed the wheat grown by its member farmers, enabling them to sidestep a host of intermediaries that took much of their profit. As the cooperative evolved over the decades, its scope broadened to embrace a wide variety of agricultural and non-agricultural interests including oilseed processing, publishing, doughnut franchises, flour milling, insurance, and barley malt production.

In theory, Saskatchewan would seem to be a farmer's paradise. Grain fields spread across fertile ground in every direction, ending with the horizon, blanketing the countryside with an agricultural abundance seen in few regions of the world. Its vast southern prairies feed the country's citizens, produce wheat and other grains for global export, and underpin the province's economy, making the Saskatchewan farmer an integral contributor to not only Canada's agricultural output but to the world's as well. During the mid-1990s, Saskatchewan ranked, as it had for decades, as the greatest wheat-growing region in North America, providing half of Canada's wheat and containing two-fifths of the country's farmland—more than any other province.

Despite the region's bountiful agricultural yields and its outward appearance as a haven for farmers, the southern prairies of Saskatchewan for years were the site of a bitter struggle between farmers and, among others, grain elevator companies, a struggle the area's farmer were losing. Operating independently, Saskatchewan farmers were at the mercy of grain elevator agents who in many instances colluded against the farmers, determining the quality of the wheat delivered, the price paid for it, and, in the process, the fate of the farmers themselves. Saskatchewan Wheat Pool, organized in 1923 and 1924, enabled tens of thousands of farmers working the wheat fields to band together and wrest control of their livelihoods away from those with contrary interests.

By the time Saskatchewan Wheat Pool was formed, the battle to improve the farmers' position had raged for nearly three decades, with numerous cooperatives and government agencies searching for an equitable solution to what was widely perceived as an unjust system of marketing wheat that awarded the bulk of the profits to speculators. Between 1899 and 1915 no fewer than 14 royal commissions were formed to investigate the grain-handling business. An early cooperative that attempted to quell the farmers' growing bitterness was the Territorial Grain Growers' Association, formed in 1901. Five years later, the Grain Growers' Grain Company was formed, then in 1911 the Saskatchewan Co-operative Elevator Company. A three-member board of grain commissioners was established by the 1912 Canada Grain Act to tighten grain-trade regulation and grain inspection, but every attempt, whether initiated by government authorities or labor organizers, fell short of expectations and the pursuit of a solution continued on.

The outbreak of the First World War offered, if not a respite, then an easing of tensions in the Saskatchewan agricultural community, primarily because the price of wheat soared during the war. Once the war ended and the price of wheat plunged precipitously, farmers and labor organizers redoubled their efforts to combat the grain elevator companies. Speculators, who purchased wheat futures from the grain exchange, were prospering from farmers' harvests, as were grain elevator agents, railway owners, and a host of other intermediaries, but not the farmers themselves.

Those campaigning for the establishment of the Saskatchewan Wheat Pool sought to change the system by creating an organization that had a democratic structure and paid members patronage dividends, two of the chief characteristics that separated Saskatchewan Wheat Pool from earlier efforts. After considerable debate and province-wide campaigning, the cooperative pool, known informally as Saskatchewan Wheat Pool, was incorporated on August 25, 1923, as Saskatchewan Co-operative Wheat Producers Limited.

Although Saskatchewan Wheat Pool was a legal entity, the cooperative needed to secure contracts for at least 50 percent of the province's total wheat acreage before it could officially begin operating, with a deadline of September 12th stipulated in the farmers' contracts. Realizing several day before the deadline that the cooperative would fall short of its goal, the provisional directors of Saskatchewan Wheat Pool asked those who had signed contracts to waive the deadline condition, and the cooperative rallied forward, planning to become operational once the 50 percent target was reached, regardless of when that occurred.

Through the winter and spring months of 1924 it seemed that day would never arrive. Many farmers had opted not to sign the waiver, and as a result the cooperative had slightly more than three million acres of wheat under contract by March 15th, or four percent less than it had six months earlier. Nevertheless, on June 16, 1924, Saskatchewan Wheat Pool reached the 50 percent plateau. With 45,725 farmers and more than 6.4 million acres of farmland behind it, Saskatchewan Wheat Pool set itself to the task of giving farmers the economic power they lacked and eliminating the speculative system of grain marketing that had spawned rich corporate empires but left little for the farmer. To accomplish this goal, the cooperative had little beyond the the expectations of thousands of farmers. Although technically operational, the wheat pool was in no position to handle the grain that soon would be arriving. In fact, Saskatchewan Wheat Pool was so ill-prepared for the massive job at hand that during the cooperative's first board meeting two directors were dispatched to purchase 20 chairs so the board members could plot their first moves while seated. More important than chairs, however, was the desperate need to acquire facilities to handle the grain set to arrive. The first such facility, an old warehouse located in Scobey, Montana, was purchased in September 1924 for $2,280, but the wood structure represented only a partial and temporary solution to the cooperative's considerably larger needs. Consequently, the cooperative's directors ordered the construction of Saskatchewan Wheat Pool's own grain-handling facilities, which led to the incorporation in February 1925 of a subsidiary, Saskatchewan Pool Elevators Limited, to supervise the construction.

Construction of Saskatchewan Wheat Pool's first grain elevator was completed in July 1925. By October of that year, 85 additional grain elevators were added: 51 were constructed by Saskatchewan Pool Elevators Limited, and the others were purchased. Less than a year later, in August 1926, Saskatchewan Wheat Pool augmented its grain-handling facilities considerably when it purchased Saskatchewan Co-operative Elevator Company for slightly more than $11 million, an acquisition that gave the cooperative 451 grain elevators. By the end of 1928, Saskatchewan Wheat Pool owned 727 grain-handling facilities. By the end of 1929, it owned nearly 1,000, a substantial total amassed just in time for the collapse of the stock market and the subsequent decade-long depression.

The economic collapse precipitated by the stock market crash delivered a staggering blow to Saskatchewan's economy and, not surprisingly, to the province's wheat farmers. The price of wheat plunged from $37.85 per tonne in 1929 to $17.27 per tonne by 1930. In addition, the 1930s were disastrous years for farming, as weather and natural calamities conspired to drastically reduce grain volumes throughout the southern prairies. The farmers endured grasshoppers, drought, and hail, and in mid-May 1934 an estimated 300 million tons of topsoil was sent skyward by a dust storm. In 1937, perhaps the worst year for crops, wheat crops averaged 2.8 bushels an acre, far below the 16.5 bushels wheat farmers had averaged for years. After recording such promising growth during the 1920s, the cooperative was left nearly bankrupt.

Saskatchewan Wheat Pool did not fully recover until the end of World War II. The cooperative changed its name from Saskatchewan Co-operative Wheat Producers Limited to the shortened and more general Saskatchewan Co-operative Producers Limited, although informally it continued to be known as Saskatchewan Wheat Pool, which was adopted as the organization's official title in 1953.

The cooperative launched a diversification and expansion campaign in 1944 that added a new flour mill, a crushing-processing plant for vegetable oil, and a large printer operation during the next five years. The cooperative also opened livestock sales yards in Swift Current, Yorkton, and North Butterfield, expanding its involvement in agribusiness.

The transition was difficult for Saskatchewan Wheat Pool, as the cooperative struggled to quickly gain the needed expertise in new industries. The new businesses lost money for years, causing concern to members and observers, but diversification ultimately gave Saskatchewan Wheat Pool's members a more solid economic foundation.

The cooperative established a farm supplies department in 1963 and bolstered its grain handling operations, most notably in 1972 when Saskatchewan Wheat Pool, Manitoba Pool Elevators, and Alberta Wheat Pool jointly acquired Federal Grain Company, the largest Canadian grain company outside the cooperative movement. The cooperative also formed, through a joint venture with Manitoba Pool Elevators in 1975, CSP Foods Limited, which processed and marketed oilseeds and oilseed products.

By the 1980s, Saskatchewan's agricultural community had undergone a significant transformation. Fewer, yet considerably larger, farms populated the province's southern prairies, while farmers, after decades of concentrating almost exclusively on the production of wheat, turned increasingly to raising livestock and poultry to avoid the risks of relying on a one-crop industry.

During the late 1980s, when the agricultural community in Saskatchewan was hobbled by the worst slump in farm prices since the 1930s, the cooperative continued to make strategically important diversification moves, such as its 1987 purchase of a share of Northco Foods, which owned the Robin's Donuts chain.

By the mid-1990s, the directors of Saskatchewan Wheat Pool were mapping the cooperative's plans for the 21st century, intent on remaining a guiding force on Saskatchewan's southern prairies. Plagued by repeated financial losses from its non-wheat-related business ventures and the cyclical nature of agricultural business, the cooperative faced a difficult future to be sure, but the organization's proven ability to adapt to turbulent change buoyed hopes for whatever the future held.

Principal Subsidiaries:

AgPro Grain Inc.; AgPro Grain Inc. (United States); AgPro Grain Holdings Inc. (United States); CSP Capital Corporation (66.66%); SM Prairie Management Ltd. (66.66%); CF Edible Oils Inc. (33.33%);

CanAmera Foods (33%); 605056 Saskatchewan Ltd.; 605058 Saskatchewan Ltd.; DF Foods Mfg. Inc. (50%); Dawn Foods Mfg. Inc. (49.5%); Burnt Lake Livestock Mart Ltd.; InfraReady Products Ltd.; SWP Venture Capital Corporation (91.9%); Bioregional Food & Science Corp. (20.8%); Canadian Pool Agencies Limited (33.33%); MAALSA Investments Ltd. (40%); Northco Foods Limited (35%); Pacific Elevators Limited (30%); Pool Insurance Company (50%); Pound-Maker Agventures Ltd. (22%); Prairie Malt Limited (42.4%); PrintWest Communications Ltd. (56.2%); Saskatoon Livestock Sales Ltd. (25%); Western Co-operative Fertilizers Limited (33.33%); Western Pool Terminals Ltd. (30%); XCAN Grain Pool Ltd. (33.33%).

Further Reading:

Bertin, Oliver, "Co-ops Keep Corporate Philosophy Alive," *Globe and Mail,* December 29, 1988, p. B1.

Cox, Bob, "Prairie Spaceships May Create Ghost Towns," *Canadian Press,* August 22, 1988, p. B4.

Donville, Christopher, "Pool Diversification Helps Profits," *Globe and Mail,* April 30, 1990, p. B3.

Enchin, Harvey, "Farm Background Helps Head of Saskatchewan Corporate Giant," *Globe and Mail,* April 30, 1990, p. B3.

Fairbairn, Garry Lawrence, *From Prairie Roots: The Remarkable Story of Saskatchewan Wheat Pool,* Saskatoon: Western Producer Prairies Books, 1984, 318 p.

Motherwell, Cathryn, "Inside Saskatchewan," *Globe and Mail,* July 14, 1994, p. B3.

Pitka, Pat, *Saskatchewan Business,* July/August 1991, p. 5.

—Jeffrey L. Covell

The Seagram Company, Ltd.

1430 Peel Street
Montreal, Quebec H3A 1S9
(514) 849-5271
Fax: (514) 987-5214

Public Company
Incorporated: March 2, 1928 as Distillers
  Corporation
Employees: 15,800
Sales: $7.99 billion
Stock Exchanges: New York London Toronto
  Montreal
SICs: 2082 Malt Beverages; 2084 Wines, Brandy,
  and Brandy Spirits; 2085 Distilled and Blended
  Liquors; 2086 Bottled and Canned Soft Drinks;
  5182 Wine and Distilled Beverages

In 1889 the Bronfman family fled Czarist anti-Semitic pogroms in Bessarabia to make their home in Canada. A wealthy family, they were accompanied by their rabbi and two servants. In the century since, the Bronfmans (whose name, ironically, means "liquor man" in Yiddish) experienced a brief period of poverty but then went on to build the world's largest distilling business. Going into the mid-1990s, The Seagram Company Ltd. and its subsidiaries was selling its full line of beverages in more than 150 countries throughout the world. Many labels owned by the family make no reference to their Seagram connection, and many apparently independent producers are nothing more than Seagram subsidiaries.

Soon after the family's arrival in Canada, patriarch Yechiel Bronfman learned that tobacco farming, which had made him a wealthy man in his homeland, was incompatible with the cold Canadian climate. The Bronfmans found themselves without a livelihood, and Yechiel was forced to leave his family to work as a laborer clearing the right-of-way for a line of the Canadian Northern Railway. He bought a shed for $12 for his family and after a short time moved to a better job in a sawmill. Yechiel Bronfman and his sons then started selling firewood, making a fairly good living, and began a trade in frozen whitefish to earn a winter income. Eventually they turned to trading horses, a venture through which they became involved in the hotel and bar business. On reaching adulthood, two of Yechiel Bronfman's sons, Harry and Sam, took charge of the family's business interests. Harry Bronfman owned his first hotel in 1903 when he was 17 years old.

When Prohibition came to Canada in 1916, the Bronfmans decided to leave the hotel business and enter the whiskey trade. Canada had implemented Prohibition only to appease foes of drinking; in reality, alcohol consumption remained high in Canada. The Bronfmans took advantage of the imprecise Canadian Prohibition laws to maximize their bootlegging profits. Sam Bronfman bought the Bonaventure Liquor Store Company, conveniently located near the downtown railway in Montreal, in 1916. People traveling to the "dry" west could stock up on liquor before boarding the train. Business was brisk until March 1918, when a law was passed that prohibited the manufacture or importation of alcohol containing more than 2.5 percent spirits.

The prohibition excluded alcohol intended for medicinal purposes, so Harry Bronfman promptly went into the drug business. He bought a Dewar's whiskey sales contract from the Hudson Bay Company and began selling straight liquor through drugstores and to processors who made "medicinal" mixtures. One such concoction was known as a Dandy Bracer—Liver and Kidney Cure; it contained sugar, molasses, bluestone, 36 percent alcohol, and tobacco

When the Volstead Act instituted Prohibition in the United States in 1919, the Bronfmans imported 300,000 gallons of alcohol from the United States, enough to make 800,000 gallons of whiskey. They reduced 65-overproof white alcohol to the required bottling strength by mixing it with water, some real whiskey and a bit of burnt sugar to provide color. A shot of sulfuric acid brought on a quick simulated aging process. The Bronfmans' mixing equipment could fill and label 1,000 bottles an hour. All the whiskey came out of the same vats, but it was bottled under several different labels to raise the liquor's value. Materials cost of the whiskey mixture was no more than $5.25 per gallon. Bottled, the whiskey sold for the equivalent of $25 a gallon.

In 1924 the Bronfmans opened their first distillery in La Salle, across the St. Lawrence River from Montreal. In the same year they incorporated under the name Distillers Corporation Limited.

Two years later the family sold a 50 percent interest to Distillers Company, an amalgamation of British distillers that controlled more than half the world's scotch market and from which the Bronfmans had been importing scotch in bulk. In exchange for a half share in Distillers Corp., the British Enterprise gave the Bronfmans Canadian distribution rights for its brands, which included Haig, Black & White, Dewar's, and Vat 69.

At about the same time the Seagram family's distilling business became a public company. The enterprise had begun in 1883 when Joseph Emm Seagram became sole proprietor of a distillery in Waterloo, Ontario where he had worked since the 1860s. Seagram later turned to politics (he was a Conservative Member of Parliament from 1896 to 1908) and also devoted much of his time to horse racing. His company was a leading Canadian rye producer with two popular brands, Seagram's '83 and V.O., which was introduced in 1909. (Joseph

Seagram's racing colors, black and gold, still appear on the labels of V.O. bottles.)

In 1928, two years after Seagram went public, the Bronfmans' Distillers Corp. acquired all stock in the distillery and itself became a public company. The merged company took the name Distillers Corp-Seagram Limited. W.H. Ross was president and Sam Bronfman was vice president. In its first year the company netted $2.2 million in profits, most of it from the Bronfman's busy bootlegging work. In 1929 Sam Bronfman prepared a $4.2 share offering to finance expansion in the highly successful export business. By 1930, however, company profits were declining, and the share offering had to be postponed.

By that time the border between Canada and the United States was extremely dangerous for illegal alcohol transport, so most trading was done by sea. The Bronfmans had established warehouses on the coast and subsidiaries called Atlantic Import and Atlas Shipping. Schooners shipped the contraband goods into the United States in the dead of night. Prohibition ended in the United States in 1933. The next year a lawyer Richard Bedford Bennett was chosen to head the federal Conservative Party and immediately launched an investigation into the liquor smuggling industry. The Bronfmans were arrested, and a year later they were tried. The judge threw the case out of court.

In 1928 Sam Bronfman had anticipated the end of Prohibition and begun to stockpile and age whiskey. Now the company owned the largest private stock of properly mellowed whiskey. This lucrative position enabled it in 1933 to acquire 20 percent of Schenley, whose product line included the well-known Golden Wedding brand of rye whiskey. When Sam Bronfman informed the Distillers Company board in Scotland of the move and requested an increase in whiskey prices, he was told at an acrimonious board meeting that Distillers would not agree to either proposal. In response, the Bronfman brothers raised $4 million and bought out the Distillers Company's holding in Distillers Corporation-Seagrams Limited. W.H. Ross resigned after the split, and Sam Bronfman became president. The company then purchased the Rossville Union Distillery in Lawrenceburg, Indiana, and set up Joseph E. Seagram and Sons Inc. to operate the U.S. venture. Schenley's board of directors suggested an equal partnership in the operation, but when Sam Bronfman found out that Golden Wedding was not aged before it was sold, he immediately rejected the plan. Soon afterward, Seagram and Schenley parted company. Schenley held the top position in the whiskey market until 1937, lost it to Seagram until 1944, regained it until 1947, then lost it to Seagram for good.

Blending and aging became Seagram's hallmark. Sam Bronfman wanted to quash the somewhat dubious image of whiskey drinking that had developed in the bootlegging era and replace it with a more respectable and refined one. In promoting his products he would use one of three descriptions of the blending process: a formal outline of the details of the process; a short definition ("Distilling is a science; blending is an art"); and an informal explanation ("Look, when a man goes into a store for a bottle of Coca-Cola, he expects it to be the same today as it will be tomorrow. . . . The great products don't change. Well, our product's not going to change either."). Seagram still has "blending libraries" at its offices in New York, Montreal, and Paisley, near Glasgow, where samples of the company's different types of straight whiskeys are continually catalogued and tested.

The company purchased Maryland Distillers, Inc and its Calvert affiliate in Relay, Maryland in 1934 and imported its own aged Canadian stock to blend with its new U.S. distillates. The resulting product came out under the Five Crown and Seven Crown labels. A few years later the company built a new distillery in Louisville, Kentucky. By 1938 Distillers-Seagram had approximately 60 million gallons of whiskey aging in its three U.S. plants.

The Bronfman brothers revolutionized liquor marketing by selling their products to distributors already bottled. Other distillers sold liquor to local rectifiers in barrel consignments, thereby losing control over the final product. The Bronfmans' method allowed Seagram to maintain the kind of quality control that builds brand loyalty. The practice is now industry standard. By the end of 1936, Seagram sales were up to $60 million in the United States, with another $10 million in Canada. By 1948 total sales exceeded $438 million, and the company posted an after tax profit of $53.7 million.

Sam Bronfman had always been impressed with British aristocracy. When George VI and Queen Elizabeth visited Canada in 1939, Bronfman blended 600 samples of whiskey before creating the prestigious Crown Royal brand in their honor. He also purchased the Chivas distillery in Aberdeen, Scotland because its operators owned a grocery store that served the royal family when they were in Scotland. Chivas Regal is now the best-selling deluxe scotch whiskey in the world.

In the 1940s Seagram expanded from the whiskey business into the larger liquor industry. Its entry into the wine markets began with a 1942 partnership with German vintners Fromm & Sichel to purchase the Paul Masson vineyards in California. (Seagram sold its 96 percent interest in Paul Masson in the mid-1980s). Eight years later the company bought a majority interest in Fromm & Sichel. During World War II Seagram imported rum from Puerto Rico and Jamaica and acquired several West Indies distilleries which would later introduce the Captain Morgan, Myers's, Woods, and Trelawny labels. Seagram also purchased Mumm's Champagne, Perrior-Jouet Champagne, Barton & Guestier, and Augier Frères.

Sam Bronfman took the company in a dramatically new direction in 1950 when he invested in the Alberta oil company Royalite. He later sold his interest in Gulf and purchased the Frankfort Oil Company. In 1963 Seagram acquired the Texas Pacific Coal and Oil Company for $276 million.

In 1957 Edgar Bronfman, Sam Bronfman's son, became the company's president. He resurrected Calvert Reserve by remarketing it as Calvert Extra and promoting it with a personal tour. He also expanded Seagram's brands of rum, scotch, and bottled cocktails (manhattans, daiquiris, whiskey sours, and martinis), and began to import wine on a large scale. By the end of 1965, the company was operating in 119 countries and had surpassed $1 billion in sales.

Between 1961 and 1971, sales of blended whiskey by all makers dropped from 60 percent to 20 percent of the total hard liquor market, but Seven Crown, V.O., Chivas, and Crown Royal continued to capture an increasing share of their shrinking markets and Seagram revenues and profits maintained their growth. In 1975, a year after the company name was changed to The Seagram Company, Ltd., Seagram's earnings slipped 9 percent to $74 million. Seven Crown sales dropped by 600,000 cases, and V.O. was down 300,000 cases. Edgar Bronfman decided to reorganize the company's board of directors and management. A new executive committee was formed with another Bronfman brother, Charles, at its head. In 1977 Seagram recorded a net income of $84 million on sales of $2.2 billion.

In the late 1960s Edgar Bronfman decided to get involved in the film industry. He bought $40 million of MGM stock and in 1969 replaced Robert O'Brien as the studio's chairman. MGM lost $25 million in the next year, and Bronfman resigned from the studio. Seagram lost about $10 million in the short-lived venture. He found some success in the entertainment industry later when his Sagittarius Productions Inc. staged several Broadway successes.

The fabulously wealthy Bronfman family received extensive media attention in the 1970s. Details of Edgar's private life, exposed in divorce proceedings, were eagerly reported in the tabloids; and in 1975, the family had to contend with the alleged kidnapping of Edgar's 23-year-old son, Samuel II. The incident and subsequent trial became headline news in many countries. Mel Patrick Lynch, the defendant (a fireman from Brooklyn, New York) was acquitted of kidnapping charges but convicted of extortion. Throughout the trial, Lynch maintained that Sam II was his lover and that the kidnapping was a hoax cooked up by Bronfman in order to lay his hands on some of the family cash. Sam II was reunited with his father; both of them hotly denied Lynch's version of events.

In 1980 Seagram sold Texas Pacific to the Sun Company for $3 billion, but when Edgar wanted to reinvest the money in St. Joe Minerals, he was turned down even though he offered $45 a share for stock that had been selling at $28 a share. Conoco also rejected Seagram's advances. Du Pont, Seagram's third choice, accepted a bid on 19 percent of the company's stock. Seagram remained the single largest shareholder in Du Pont going into the 1990s.

Seagram continued to diversify in the 1980s. In 1981, for example, the company formed Westmount Enterprises to finance its beverage ventures and market its new gourmet frozen dinners. Seagram also manufactured and marketed premium mixers jointly with the Coca-Cola Bottling Company of New York. In addition, the company has purchased 11.6 percent of Biotechnica International and had ventured increasingly into the wine industry through its Seagram's Vinters division.

In 1985 Seagram underwent a thorough reorganization of its companies, brands, and personnel. It also launched a new advertising campaign aimed at upgrading the image of liquor consumption. Those efforts, combined with ongoing diversification into new businesses, allowed Seagram to prosper during much of the late 1980s and early 1990s. By 1990, in fact, Seagram was generating global sales of $6.63 billion and netting income of about $850 million. It sustained that income level throughout the early 1990s, with the exception of 1993 when the company was took a write-off of expenses related to restructuring.

In 1994 control of The Seagram Company again changed hands. This time the reins were handed to 39-year-old Edgar Bronfman, Jr., Edgar's son and the grandson of founder Sam Bronfman. When he took the helm, Edgar Jr. promised a new cost-cutting initiative. "We'll examine everything we do in the next two or three years, eliminating overlap and designing new products," the junior Bronfman stated in the June 2, 1994, *Financial Post*. "It means sweeping changes, but lower costs and higher shareholder value." He also laid plans to continue increasing Seagram's global reach, particularly in Asia. In fact, he envisioned Asia becoming a more important market for the company than either Europe or North America.

Edgar Jr. was also eager to break into new business. Interestingly, he began pursuing interests in the entertainment industry. In 1994, in fact, Seagram purchased a 15 percent stake in Time-Warner for about $2 billion. Then in April 1995, Bronfman acquired 80 percent of entertainment giant MCA Inc. for US$5.7 billion. Said Bronfman at the time, "We believe that the entertainment sector has unusually high future growth and profit potential." The interest in that particular industry was partly attributable to Edgar Jr.'s experience as a Hollywood producer and song writer. But it also mimicked efforts by his father in the 1960s to buy into the Hollywood scene. His father's effort ultimately failed, causing some analysts to predict a similar fate for the younger Bronfman.

In any case, Seagram remained a power player in the global alcoholic beverages industry and was placing relatively little at risk with its sideline forays into the entertainment industry, or any other businesses. Indeed, by 1994 Seagram was capturing revenues of $8 billion, about 75 percent of which came from wine and spirits operations. It was shipping its products to more than 150 different countries. Besides Seagram, The Bronfmans owned assets including shopping malls, office complexes, and resorts and were among the wealthiest families in the world.

Principal Subsidiaries:

Centenary Distillers, Ltd.; Seagram International BV; Joseph E. Seagram & Sons, Inc.; Distillers Products Sales Corp.; General Beverage Co.

Further Reading:

Ferrabee, James, "Serene Family Succession in Sharp Contrast to Brutal Media Baptism of Seagram's CEO," *Gazette*, June 2, 1994, Section C, p. 8.
Gibbens, Robert, "New Chief Promises Big Changes," *Financial Post*, June 2, 1994, Section 1, p. 1.

Heinrich, Jeff, "Hollywood Hunger; Seagram Appears Posed to Take a Shot at Entertainment Giant MCA," *Gazette*, April 6, 1995, Section D, p. 1.

McIntosh, Andrew, "Seagram Pours Out $736-Million Profit," *Gazette*, March 16, 1993, Section C, p. 6.

Newman, Peter C., *King of the Castle: The Making of a Dynasty: Seagrams and the Bronfman Empire,* New York: Atheneum, 1979.

Schatz, Robin, "Seagram Chief has Stars in His Eyes," *New York Newsday*, April 8, 1995, Section A, p. 13.

—updated by Dave Mote

Southam Inc.

1450 Don Mills Road
Don Mills, Ontario M3B 2X7
(416) 445-6641
Fax: (416) 442-2077

Public Company
Incorporated: 1871 as Southam Ltd.
Employees: 10,764
Sales: $1.20 billion
Stock Exchanges: Toronto Montreal
SICs: 2711 Newspapers; 2721 Periodicals

Southam Inc. is a Canadian communications conglomerate engaged primarily in the newspaper publishing business. With an average daily circulation of 1.5 million, it is the largest publisher of daily newspapers in Canada. Its two divisions, Metro Newspapers and City and Community Newspapers, publish 17 daily newspapers, including the *Montreal Gazette* and the *Windsor Star*, and 33 weekly newspapers across Canada. Southam also manages trade and consumer shows, publishes business-to-business magazines, and provides electronic news services.

Southam's history spans well over a century and largely parallels the development of the newspaper industry in Canada. William Southam, a self-made man, left school in 1855 at age 12 and got his first job delivering papers for the *London Free Press*. In 1871 Southam, then 33 years old, bought a failing newspaper in Hamilton, with partner William Carey. He paid $4,000 for his part in the venture. Southam was off to a small start but already had his eye on the *Spectator*, a much larger venture.

During this time, newspapers survived largely on government patronage. The *Spectator* and *Journal of Commerce* had prospered due to favorable government advertising contracts secured from the Conservative administration, which lasted until 1873. But by 1877 the rival Liberals ruled and advertising and printing contracts slumped. Southam and Carey were betting on a Conservative victory in the upcoming elections, which would assure better fortunes for the *Spectator*. To this end, after becoming half-owner of the publication, Southam made sure the newspaper backed the Conservative Party in the election. The gamble paid off: on September 17, 1878, the *Spectator*'s presses ran late announcing the Conservative return to power.

In 1881 Southam and Carey branched out by purchasing a printing firm in Toronto, the Mail Job Printing Co. They printed railroad timetables and folders and eventually theater programs, posters, and even shredded paper flakes for parades. The *Spectator* also expanded by beginning a book printing business. Then, in 1896, after the Liberal government regained power, the owners of the *Ottawa Citizen*, another Conservative paper, feared a slump in government advertising and printing contracts. They turned to Southam as a buyer and a second newspaper was added to the company's stable. Wilson Southam, the eldest son in the family, was pegged to run the *Citizen*. He was soon joined by Harry, the fourth eldest son of William Southam. The Southam family's control over the company then expanded further. In 1889, Southam's second son, Frederick Neal, was sent to Montreal to open a printing shop to serve the railway industry headquartered there. For a mere $1,500, Neal was able to buy two ticket presses and a cutting machine and hire seven staff members.

In 1904 the company was reorganized and renamed Southam Ltd. Its portfolio included ownership of the *Citizen*, half of the *Spectator*, printing plants, and investments in steel making and other manufacturing concerns. Five years later, the Mail Job Printing Co. in Toronto was renamed Southam Press Ltd., and operations were moved to Duncan and Adelaide Streets in Toronto.

Seeking expansion by penetrating new markets, Southam acquired other newspapers. In 1908 Southam bought a controlling interest in the *Calgary Herald*, the *Mining and Ranch Advocate*, and the *General Advertiser*. Four years later, the *Edmonton Journal* became the property of Southam Ltd.

In the early part of the century, brothers Wilson and Harry Southam became involved in a controversey with the Canadian government for encouraging critical coverage by *Citizen* reporters. The elder Southams hoped matters might repair themselves when the Conservative government of Robert Borden returned to power in 1911. But the Borden regime became so critical of *Citizen* coverage of its affairs that it threatened to open a rival newspaper in Ottawa. Matters grew to a head in 1912 when founder William Southam canceled his own home subscription to the *Citizen* over its editorial trespasses. The company began a policy that grants newspaper editors independence from Southam's owners and, because of the company's size, from local pressures. The newspaper chain would have, in theory, no Southam-mandated editorial policy. Instead, each paper would develop an independent editorial line.

Despite these troubles, in 1920, Southam purchased the *Winnipeg Tribune* and was well on its way to becoming among Canada's largest newspaper and communications chains. Two years later, the company—now known as William Southam and Sons—pushed even further westward with the purchase of a controlling interest in the *Vancouver Province*. Soon, the rival Vancouver daily, the *Sun*, ran into financial trouble under owner Robert Cromie. He knew who to turn to for help, and Frederick Neal Southam offered a lifeboat, offering to assume a third of the *Sun*'s mortgage.

Frederick Neal Southam would serve as president of William Southam and Sons from 1928 to 1945. He replaced his brother Wilson, who had served from 1918 out of Ottawa. After the First World War, company founder William Southam began gradually ceding control to his five sons.

In the 1920s, Southam newspapers branched out into the emerging radio broadcast market. The first was the *Vancouver Province*, which broadcast on station CDED to crystal radio listeners beginning on March 13, 1922. Both the *Edmonton Journal* and the *Calgary Herald* went to the airwaves six weeks later, taking a 60 percent stake each in stations CJCA and CFAC, respectively. In 1924 the *Hamilton Spectator* traded advertising space in its newspaper for the right to operate its own radio station.

Three years later, Southam went through a thorough restructuring, changing its name to the Southam Publishing Company Ltd. The reason for this move was to gather all outstanding shares Southam held, many reflecting minority stakes in regional newspapers and broadcasting concerns, and exchange them for shares and securities of the new company. The company also established offices in Montreal and Toronto in order to be able to sell advertising space throughout the newspaper chain. In addition, Southam sent reporters to bureaus in Ottawa, Washington, and London. Through this network, reporters could file stories for use in any of the Southam newspapers. This was the beginning of Southam News Services.

In 1945 union staff at the *Winnipeg Tribune* went on strike. Southam's head office refused to intervene, declaring the dispute a local matter. But the International Typographical Union, in solidarity with the striking Winnipeg staff, brought Southam papers in Hamilton, Ottawa, Edmonton, and Vancouver out on strike. The Vancouver strike turned bloody when printers attempted to cross the picket line and were beaten back. Trucks attempting to move newspapers from the printing plant were overturned and burned.

Earlier, in 1938, the company's name had been changed yet again to the Southam Company. Shares in the company were first issued to the public on the Toronto Stock Exchange in 1945. Three years later, Southam purchased all outstanding shares belonging to the *News of Medicine Hat* in Alberta for $125,000. In 1955 the company took full control of that newspaper. By the 1960s the company was branching out into other industries. In 1960 St. Clair Balfour, then president of Southam, concluded a deal to buy Hugh C. MacLean Publications Ltd., which led to the formation of Southam-MacLean Publications Ltd., a business and professional trade magazine venture. Under Southam's stewardship, it began conducting trade shows, seminars, and market research and expanded its range of trade publications. Southam-MacLean also formed Videosurgery, which tapes medical operations and sells them to doctors and medical schools in North America for training and instruction.

In the next four years, Southam purchased up to 20 business publications of varying sizes, including 14 journals bought as part of Age Publishing Co. Ltd. of Toronto for $792,000. By far the largest of these acquisitions was Southam-Maclean Publications' purchase of the *Financial Times of Canada* from the E.C. Ertl estate in 1961. By 1965, Southam moved its head office from Montreal to Toronto, nearer Bay Street and that city's banking and financial core. Also in 1965, Southam formed Southstar Publishers Ltd., a joint venture with Toronto Star Ltd., to publish the *Canadian*, a weekly glossy magazine that would eventually appear weekly in many Southam newspapers.

A year later, the company scooped up the *North Bay Nugget* after that employee-owned newspaper was put on the market. At the same time, Don Cromie, who had taken control of the *Vancouver Sun*, encountered financial problems of his own and turned once again to Southam for help. A handshake aboard a boat in the Vancouver harbor between Cromie and St. Clair Balfour, then managing director of Southam, solved matters. The Southam-owned *Providence* would print a morning edition and the *Sun* would retain the afternoon slot. Both newspapers would be sold to a third company, Pacific Press Ltd., to be jointly owned by Southam and Sun Publishing.

Meanwhile, across the country in Weston, Ontario, Southam bought Murray Printing & Gravure for $700,000, a move that increased Southam's printing capacity by 50 percent. The Murray plant was modernized and Southam's Toronto printing capacity was relocated to the new site. In 1969 Southam expanded yet again by purchasing the *Windsor Star* and the *Brantford Expositor*. By the end of 1971 Southam had also purchased the *Owen Sound Sun-Times* for $950,000 and the *Prince George Citizen* for $2 million.

In November 1973 the *Ottawa Citizen* moved to a modern, purpose-built plant. Here it would become the first newspaper in Canada to use video terminals for editing newspaper articles, as opposed to running a red pen over type-written copy.

In 1975 Gordon Fisher took over from Balfour as president of Southam. That same year the company purchased the *Daily Star* in Sault Ste. Marie, Ontario. In 1976 the *Hamilton Spectator* moved into a new $23 million plant, complete with a newsroom the size of a football field. Two years later, the name of the company was changed to its current name, Southam Inc. The company also made a strategic purchase to go into bookselling, buying Coles Book Stores Ltd. at $23 a share. Coles would subsequently become Canada's largest book seller, with over 250 outlets in 124 cities and towns, including 58 U.S. outlets.

Meanwhile, Southam strengthened its hold on both the major eastern and western newspaper markets. In early 1980, Southam bought a one-third interest in the *Montreal Gazette* from F.P. Publications for $13 million. This move gave it full control of Montreal's leading English-language newspaper. That same year, Southam strengthened its hold on the Vancouver newspaper market when it bought outright control of Pacific Press Ltd. for $42.25 million. A year later, the *Kamploops News*, in British Columbia, was added to the company's newspaper stable.

The early 1980s recession hurt advertising revenues at Southam's newspaper operation, with western Canada hit the hardest. With the western newspaper sector struggling, the focus was on Southam's non-newspaper assets to perform and make up for lost advertising revenue. One competitive measure was to expand into the U.S. market; in October 1983, Southam acquired Dittler Brothers, of Atlanta, Georgia, for $67.6 million. Southam was branching out from its core newspaper operation with gathering pace. In fact, in 1984, revenue from Southam's newspaper operations and other business segments balanced out for the first time. Such progress was welcome because labor lock-outs in Vancouver and Montreal the previous year had cost Southam $6.5 million in earnings.

In 1985 Gordon Fisher, Southam's president, died suddenly after an unexpected illness, leaving no clear successor. That opened the way for rumored takeover bids for the company and a slumping share price. The slide in stock value was eventually halted by a share exchange worth $225 million between Southam and rival Torstar Corporation. Torstar gained a 23 percent stake in Southam but signed an agreement barring it from purchasing a controlling interest in its rival for at least ten years. For Southam, the Torstar arrangement enabled the Southam family to retain control of the company while holding only 23 percent of outstanding shares.

In 1986 Southam consolidated its newspaper assets by forming the Southam Newspaper Group, led by Paddy Sherman. The company also established four other separate business segments: Southam Printing Ltd, Coles Book Stores Ltd., Southam Communications Ltd., and Southam Inc., which included a 30 percent investment in Torstar.

Sales and acquisitions highlighted much of Southam's business activity in 1987. Further expansion continued as Southam expanded into the Quebec French-speaking market by publishing *Le Matin*, an up-scale tabloid daily. In total, Southam spent $77 million in 1987 on new newspaper acquisitions throughout Canada. Southam also sold its 49 percent interest in Sun Publishing Company to majority shareholder L. D. Whitehead; and Coles Book Stores sold its 48 U.S. outlets to Waldenbooks Inc. of Stamford, Connecticut.

In 1988 the company resolved a bitter, six-month-long strike at the *Montreal Gazette*. Despite this, sales for the year increased by 13.5 percent to $1.45 billion. In August of that year, Coles Book Stores launched its first Active Minds store, aimed at younger readers, in Calgary. A second store soon opened in Toronto.

Heading into the 1990s, a slowing Canadian economy was cited as evidence of a need for caution ahead for Southam's business plans. Hugh G. Hallward, now chairman of the company, said in the 1989 annual report: "Looking ahead to 1990, we see slower economic growth for Canada as a whole than in 1989, but better in the West than in the East." Hallward was essentially drawing the lines of the forthcoming recession, which hit Eastern Canada, and especially Ontario, harder than elsewhere. In late 1990 Southam sold the money-losing *Financial Times of Canada*, based in Toronto, to rival Thomson Press, for an undisclosed sum. Troubles continued into 1991. Southam saw its advertising sales drop five percent compared with a year earlier. A

number of acquisitions boosted total company sales, which jumped nine percent to $1.8 billion in fiscal 1990. But profits were down sharply to $2.7 million in 1990, compared to $90.5 million in 1989.

Further complicating Southam's troubles, the government brought an anti-trust case against the company. Southam was ordered to sell three community newspapers it had bought in 1990, all based in and around Vancouver. The government argued that Southam had monopolized the Vancouver market through its ownership of Pacific Press Limited. Divesting itself of the three newspapers, it was argued, would create room for potential competitors in the Vancouver market.

In October 1991, the 114-year tradition in which a member of the Southam family controlled the business empire ended. William Ardell, previously head of the Coles Book Stores chain and Southam Business Communications, was named to succeed John Fisher as CEO. Ardell was seen as the turnaround specialist Southam needed to restructure itself during the early 1990s recession. The downside was that Ardell had no experience running newspapers, Southam's principal business.

Uncertainty regarding the future of the company fed rumors in financial circles about impending takeover. One persistent rumor was that Torstar, with its one-third ownership of Southam, was displeased with its slumping profit line and was again entertaining takeover designs. But in 1992 Conrad Black, head of newspaper and magazine publisher Hollinger Inc., bought Torstar's 22.6 percent stake in Southam for $259 million, bringing Hollinger's vast international experience in the newspaper business to the company.

Meanwhile, Ardell moved quickly to develop a strategy that would enable the company to survive in an increasingly competitive environment. The new plan consisted of two basic components: a reduction in size and a renewed emphasis on its core newspaper business. While implementing a workforce reduction program that would eventually cut about 1,200 jobs from its newspaper division by 1995, the company helped to reduce its debt by divesting its graphics and audio visual assets. To that end, the company sold its Canadian Web Group printing operations to G.T.C. Transcontinental Group Ltd. for just under $105 million, its 35 percent interest in Telemedia Publishing Inc. for $18 million, and its entire stake in Torstar. In an effort to restore profitability to its newspapers, Southam divided the newspaper group into two divisions—Metro Newspapers, and City and Community Newspapers—with Jim Armitage and Ray Elliot appointed presidents of the respective groups.

By the end of 1992, Southam had reduced its debt by 56 percent, laying the groundwork for a return to profitability the following year. While continuing to lower costs through workforce reduction, the company looked to increase revenue and lessen its dependency on advertising. Toward that end, in late 1993 the company launched a national advertising campaign called ADitus, which standardized the advertising rates and services for customers across the country. That same year, Southam attempted to increase efficiency and reduce costs by amalgamating some of its editorial services and production facilities at daily newspapers. Although one of the company's strengths has been in the editorial independence of its individual papers, the rapid evolution of information sharing technology promised to broaden the amount of information made available to readers, while reducing editorial costs at individual papers. In addition, by entering into a joint-venture with Knight Ridder's Dialog services, Southam positioned itself for the future development of the information highway, helping to create the largest commercial electronic news information service in Canada.

Southam's strategy of greater efficiency and cost control continued to pay off in 1994: the company more than doubled its net income to $44 million behind a strategy aimed at improving the content, quality, and marketing of information. In an effort to coordinate editorial objectives for all its newspapers and facilitate the process of information sharing, the company created a new Vice President, Editorial position. Likewise, the company introduced a common organizational structure throughout all its newspapers, making the transfer of skills and ideas across various papers easier. Finally, the company made the decision to sell its book retailing subsidiary, Coles Book Stores Limited, to SmithBooks. The deal was completed in April 1995 for an estimated $35 million.

Southam's long-term future will depend largely on its continued ability to improve the efficiency of its core business while also keeping pace with the rapid technological advances of the Information Age. Having survived more than a century of depressions and recessions, Southam, as its progress in the 1990s would indicate, expects to retain its position as one of Canada's more competitive communications conglomerates.

Principal Subsidiaries:

Southam Newspaper Group; Southam Magazine and Information Group; Southam Show Group

Further Reading:

"A Century of Southam," Gazette Canadian Printing Ltd., 1977.
Charles Bruce, *News and the Southams,* Toronto: MacMillan of Canada, 1968.
Dunnett, Peter, *The World Newspaper Industry,* London: Croom Helm, 1988.
Enchin, Harvey, "Financiers Running Show at Southam," *Globe and Mail,* May 31, 1993, p. B1.
Goold, Douglas, "Conrad Black's Quest for Southam," *Globe and Mail,* October 21, 1993, p. B1.
Mahood, Casey, "Southam Getting Back to Newspaper Basics," *Globe and Mail,* February 10, 1995, p. B1.
"No Tears for Southam-Torstar Split," *Globe and Mail,* July 24, 1992.
"The Southam History Series: How It All Began," *The Torch: A Magazine About Southam Inc.,* Summer 1989.
Wells, Jennifer, "Get-tough CEO Bill Ardell Inherited a Culture of Complacency," *Globe and Mail,* July 24, 1992, P17.

—Etan Vlessing
—updated by Jason Gallman

stelco

Stelco Inc.

Post Office Box 2030
Stelco Tower
Hamilton, Ontario L8N 3T1
(416) 528-2511
Fax: (416) 577-4449

Public Company
Incorporated: 1910 as Steel Company of Canada
  Ltd. *Employees:* 11,768
Sales: $2.79 billion
Stock Exchanges: Toronto Montreal Vancouver
SICs: 3312 Blast Furnaces and Steel Mills.

Canada's top steelmaker, Stelco Inc., produces nearly 5,000 tons of steel each year at two primary plants located at Hamilton harbor on Lake Ontario and another site on nearby Lake Erie. In addition there are fabricating units responsible for production of pipes and tubes, wire and wire products, and fasteners and forgings. Stelco survived the North American steel shakeout of the late 1980s and early 1990s through large-scale cutbacks and painful but essential capital investments.

Stelco prides itself on being a Canadian company. A predecessor firm was Canada's first fully-integrated iron and steel manufacturer. But like many segments of the Canadian economy, Stelco's origin reflected both British and U.S. influences. The firm was formed through a series of turn-of-the-century mergers combining the Ontario Rolling Mills, which was run by a group of Americans; the Hamilton Blast Furnace Company, a Canadian-run company; and the Montreal Rolling Mills, which had British investors. These predecessor companies traced their histories back to the mid-nineteenth century.

During the 1850s the Montreal merchant house of Moreland and Watson imported British iron to meet investment needs in the burgeoning Canadian economy. Moreland and Watson established the Montreal Rolling Mills (MRM) in the 1860s to reroll wrought iron and scrap imported from Britain into nails and other hardware. Charles Watson served as the mill's first managing director. In 1873, he appointed William McMaster as secretary; McMaster then succeeded Watson in 1888.

The 1880s were a decade of transition for Montreal Rolling Mills. This was an era of increasing protection-ism by both Canadian and U.S. governments following the devastating trade depression of the 1870s. Tariff increases helped to preserve a role for British metal in the Canadian market, but the advantage was gradually passing to U.S. suppliers whose raw material and transportation costs were falling rapidly. These trends increasingly handicapped the MRM, whose trade relied on the reworking of metal from Great Britain.

Montreal Rolling Mill also faced competition from the Ontario Rolling Mills (ORM), which was established at Hamilton in 1879 by a group of Ohio businessmen. These U.S. tradesmen and investors were representative of many who migrated north to create industrial enterprises in early Ontario. The ORM used an abandoned mill to reroll scrap iron rails and rework metal for use by local machine shops and hardware manufacturers.

The ORM and other Hamilton-area secondary metal firms created a growing local demand for primary metal. Favorable tariff and transportation changes made it profitable by the early 1890s to establish a blast furnace on Hamilton harbor using U.S. ore and coal. Local foundry owners and the Hamilton municipal council were instrumental in launching the Hamilton Blast Furnace Company (HBFC) in 1894, after U.S. investors withdrew from what seemed a risky prospect. Alexander Wood, a hardware merchant and later a Liberal senator, was the largest HBFC shareholder. By 1899 HBFC had proven its value to the ORM leadership, who agreed to merge the two firms. The resulting company, the Hamilton Steel and Iron Company (HSIC), quickly erected steel furnaces using its capitalization in excess of $1 million. The company's vice-president and general manager was Robert Hobson, son-in-law to Wood and later president of the Canadian Manufacturers Association.

The HSIC was Canada's first fully integrated iron and steel company. It flourished during the massive wave of investment that swept over the Canadian economy between 1900 and 1910. In the later year William McMaster offered to bring the Montreal Rolling Mills into a larger organization that would provide a secure supply of primary metal. The successful Maritime financier, Max Aitken, later Lord Beaverbrook, promptly brokered yet another merger of the HSIC with the MRM and several smaller secondary metal companies, resulting in the Steel Company of Canada, or Stelco as it was soon unofficially labeled.

Stelco's first president was Charles Secord Wilcox, who had arrived in Hamilton by horseback in 1880 to join other family members in the ORM. Wilcox was president of Stelco from 1910 to 1916 and chairman of the board from 1916 to 1938. He instituted a policy of plowing back as much profit as possible into the company. The firm's location in southern Ontario, which minimized transportation costs on material assembly and product delivery, was the most attractive possible in the fragmented Canadian market. Government tariffs and cash subsidies also augmented company profits and permitted the financing of new investment from retained earnings.

During World War I Stelco produced large quantities of shell steel, but the production of munitions did not prevent the company from establishing a sheet mill to widen its potential product base, and ore and coal mines to facilitate raw material supply. Stelco's diversified product base and concentration on light steel products served it well during the Great Depression of the 1930s, as its share of the Canadian steel market rose from 17 percent in 1918 to 45 percent in 1932.

Two presidents served Stelco during this era. Robert Hobson, along with Wilcox from the Hamilton side of the company, presided from 1916 to 1926. Ross McMaster, son of the MRM's William McMaster, had stayed to manage the Montreal works after its sale in 1910; he became president from 1926 to 1945.

The outbreak of World War II inaugurated a new era for Stelco as it did for the Canadian economy. Stelco expanded its finishing capacity with the erection of plate and hot strip mills in 1941 and cold and tin mills in 1948. The growth of the finishing mills resulted in the use of more primary metal. In 1951 Stelco expanded its primary production facilities by building a 226-foot blast furnace and new open hearth steel furnaces sufficient to increase Canadian ingot capacity by 20 percent.

Hugh Hilton, president from 1945 to 1957 and board chairman from 1957 to 1966, oversaw a period of postwar expansion. The last of the steelmaking engineers to head the company, Hilton's best-known technical innovation had been a 1928 fuel-saving improvement for the system of distributing waste gas from the furnaces to other applications in the plant. Hilton was followed by Vincent Scully, an accountant who had come to Stelco as comptroller in 1951. Scully was president from 1957 to 1967 and chairman of the board from 1966 to 1971.

The continued use of open hearth furnaces until the 1980s reflected the slow introduction of basic oxygen furnaces first available during the 1950s. Stelco demonstrated considerable prowess in the development of secondary production technology. In 1959 David McLean, superintendent of Stelco's shapes division, organized a team to improve the cooling and coiling of steel rods in a high speed mill. By 1961 the solution was found in an adaptation of a U.S. patent leading to the Stelmor process for high quality and low cost rod cooling and coiling. During the 1970s the manager of product design services, Bill Smith, pioneered a coilbox technique used for intermill transfer of hot bars; this technique remained proprietary technology.

The 1970s comprised the Gordon era of Stelco, named after Peter Gordon, who served as president from 1970 to 1976 and chairman of the board from 1976 to 1985. Gordon guided the company through a major expansion, as the number of Stelco employees mushroomed from 12,500 to 25,000 during the 1970s. Gordon's lasting contribution was the establishment of a new plant on Lake Erie.

Strong market growth before the 1973 oil shock and subsequent economic slowdown led Stelco in 1974 to begin construction at a new location, the Lake Erie works (LEW). This plant began production during 1980. Annual capacity was 1.7 million tons of semi-finished steel. The LEW has large production runs of continuous cast low carbon steel that is cold-rolled into auto sheet and steel used in pipes.

The older and larger Hilton works on Hamilton harbor had an annual capacity of 2.8 million tons. This plant produced diverse and sometimes specialized high- and low-carbon steel in strip, bar, and rod forms. The average production run at Hilton was smaller than at LEW. Between 1985 and 1987 financing and technology from the Japanese firm Mitsui assisted in a major upgrading of the Hilton facilities that included the introduction of basic oxygen technology and continuous casting. The Quebec and Alberta plants had small production runs from mini-mills of a capacity less than one million tons, each from electric arc steel furnaces.

Stelco's four primary plants were part of an integrated production process spanning from the mine to a wide array of finished steel, including nails, sheet metal for appliances and vehicles, long-distance gas pipes, springs for vehicles, structural members for bridging and building, steel fencing and a variety of hardware. During the 1980s the final destination of output was the construction industry, automobile assembly, shipbuilding, as well as railways, agricultural and other machinery parts, and packaging. Stelco undertook secondary processing at Hilton and in more than a dozen subsidiary plants scattered from Montreal to Niagara and in Alberta.

The 1980s proved a difficult decade. Stelco lost its position as Canada's largest steelmaker to hometown rival Dofasco. Employment declined from a high of over 26,000 in 1981 to 16,100 by 1990. Competition from inexpensive South American and Asian imports compelled heavy investments in new technology. Between 1978 and 1988, Stelco spent more than $2 billion in an effort to increase productivity and enhance competitiveness. At the same time, demand for steel declined as a result of slow economic growth from 1973 to 1984, and the substitution of other materials for steel for a variety of products. Stelco's debt rose to $935 million and the company recorded a devastating string of losses in the 1980s. But at least the firm survived; many U.S. steelmakers didn't, and several Canadian companies moved south. And in spite of its ongoing difficulties, Stelco's stock held its own, declining from the low 30s early in the decade to $26 in 1989.

Another difficult circumstance for Stelco was the need to reduce its impact on the air and water around its plants. Perhaps most notorious was the company's contribution to high pollution levels in Hamilton Harbor, called "one of the dirtiest water bodies in North America" in a 1991 Globe and Mail article. Poisonous coal-tar derivatives and ammonia discharged by Stelco's main plant deprived the harbor floor of oxygen and hence killed fish. Increasing public concern to minimize environmental damage prompted Stelco to invest in a variety of devices to control pollution. By 1985 the Hilton works alone had 49 facilities to clean waste water and 54 facilities to clean the air. From 1970 to 1990, the company invested an average of $17 million per year on environmental equipment. In 1991 there were some signs of improvement in Hamilton-area air and water, although Stelco's sulfur dioxide emissions remained a concern. In contrast to and perhaps because of the pollution problems at Hilton, the Lake Erie works had been built under careful government scrutiny to minimize environmental concerns. Difficult relations with organized labor were a perennial problem at Stelco. The

Hilton workers are represented by Local 1005 of the United Steelworkers of America, which historically had been one of the most militant of Canadian locals. Violence marred an 85-day strike in 1946 that is often seen as a turning point in the modern history of Canadian industrial relations. Another, 86-day, strike in 1958, a violent wildcat strike in 1966, a legal strike in 1969, a 125-day strike in 1981, and a 97-day strike in 1990 continued the record of debilitating labor-management relations.

More significant than resulting wage adjustments was the damage to both workers and investors of a persistently and seriously discordant industrial relations atmosphere. An individual worker needed a very long time to recoup the loss of three months pay. On the other side Stelco had been disadvantaged by disruption of supply continuity and other costs of bitter collective bargaining.

In 1991 there were signs that the challenge of competition from east Asia would force labor and management to collaborate in forging a new survival strategy. The union had agreed to set aside traditional job categories in a steel coating mill within the Hilton works. The new mill was a joint venture with Mitsubishi Canada Ltd. to improve the rust-resistance of sheet metal. Hand-picked Hamilton have visited Japan to acquire technical knowledge and improve their understanding of the Japanese culture of company-worker cooperation.

The new coating mill was one aspect of Stelco's campaign to win contracts from Japanese-owned auto assembly plants located in southern Ontario. This response to change in secondary markets reflects the same careful attention to customer needs embodied in nineteenth-century mergers with the Montreal Rolling Mills and Ontario Rolling Mills. Stelco policy has returned the company to its historically successful strategy of careful integration between primary production and the secondary industry.

But in spite of the admirable efforts of both management and labor, the 1990s proved even more difficult for Stelco than the 1980s had been. A recession, global over capacity in the steel industry, intense competition, low demand, and high labor and production costs combined to keep profitability out of reach. Stelco lost half a billion dollars from 1990 to 1993. Its stock, which had held fairly steady throughout the difficult 1980s, plummeted from $26 in 1989 to less than $1 in 1992. As rumors of bankruptcy swirled and the company's debt rating was lowered to "junk bond" level, one shareholder dumped 1.5 million shares of stock at $1 each that November.

Frederick H. Telmer, a career Stelco employee in marketing, succeeded John Allan as chairman of the board and chief executive officer in 1991. One of his first moves was to eliminate the dividend, which didn't help the steelmaker's stock price, but freed up operating funds. Asset sales also helped keep the company afloat. Telmer cut staffing by one-fourth, from 16,000 in 1989 to 12,000 in 1993, and decentralized the remaining pool of managers. One of his key objectives was to reduce costs to their 1989 level — the last year the company

had earned a profit. The Hilton, Lake Erie and McMaster plants all exceeded that goal by 1993.

That year, Stelco (along with other Canadian steel manufacturers) was taken to task for unfair trade practices, as determined by the U.S. Commerce Department. The company was found guilty of dumping—selling below market price or below cost—specific, limited categories of steel products. As a punishment, the U.S. agency imposed import duties as high as 68.7 percent on the commodities, making it virtually impossible for Stelco to market the products there.

The penalties were not debilitating, however, and Telmer's cost-cutting combined with the expensive technological upgrades of the 1980s helped bring Stelco slowly but steadily out of the red. As sales increased from $2 billion in 1991 to $2.5 billion in 1993, net losses shrunk from $136 million to $36 million. In 1994, the steelmaker recorded its first profit since 1989, a net of $115 million on sales of $2.8 billion. Telmer remained cautiously optimistic about Stelco's future, citing the ratification of North American Free Trade Agreement (NAFTA) as a positive influence and the uncertainty of the automobile market (on which Stelco was dependent for about one-third of its sales) as an unreliable influence.

Principal Subsidiaries:

Stelco-McMaster Lté; AltaSteel Ltd.; Stelwire Ltd.; Frost Wire Products Ltd.; Stelco Fasteners Ltd.; Stelfil Lté; Stelpipe Ltd.; Welland Pipe Ltd.; CHT Steel Company Inc.; Stelco USA, Inc.; Chisholm Mine; Z-Line Company (58 percent); Baycoat (50 percent); MOLY-COP Canada, Alta. & B.C. (50 percent); Fers et Métaux Recyclés Lté, Que. (50 percent); Torcad Limited (50 percent).

Further Reading:

Chisholm, Patricia, "Showdown at Stelco: The Steel Industry Girds for a Bitter Strike," *Maclean's,* August 13, 1990, pp. 40, 42.
Feschuk, Scott, "Stelco Awash in Gloom," *Globe and Mail,* November 5, 1992, p. B1.
Inwood, Kris, "The Iron and Steel Industry," in *Progress without Planning: The Economic History of Ontario from Confederation to the Second World War,* Toronto: University of Toronto Press, 1987.
Kilbourn, Williams, *The Elements Combined: A History of the Steel Company of Canada,* Toronto: Clarke Irwin, 1960.
McMurdy, Deirdre, "Stelco Slims Its Structure to Cut Costs and Boost Productivity," *Maclean's,* January 10, 1994, pp. 18-20.
Mittelstaedt, Martin, "Cleanliness Is Next to Profitability," *Globe and Mail,* June 26, 1991, p. B1.
Saunders, John, and Alan Freeman, "Steel Firms Dodge U.S. Trade Bullet," *Globe and Mail,* July 28, 1993, p. B1.
Stinson, Marian, "Stelco Cutting 800 Jobs at Plant in Hamilton," *Globe and Mail,* September 24, 1992, p. B1.

—Kris E. Inwood
—updated by April Dougal Gasbarre

Stone-Consolidated Corporation

Stone-Consolidated Corporation

800 Rene-Levesque Boulevard West
Montreal, Quebec HB3 1Y9
(514) 875-2160
Fax: (514) 394-2223

Company Type: Subsidiary of Stone Container
   Corporation (Chicago)
Founded: 1931
Employees: 4,087
Sales: $1.09 billion in 1994
Stock Exchanges: Toronto Montreal
SICs: 2620 Paper Mills

Stone-Consolidated Corporation is one of the world's largest manufacturers of newsprint, uncoated groundwood papers, and lumber. Headquartered and with most of its operations in southern Quebec, Stone-Consolidated also operates divisions in the United States and the United Kingdom. The enterprise was named Consolidated-Bathurst until 1989 when it became a wholly-owned subsidiary of Chicago-based Stone Container Corporation. Stone-Consolidated posted net losses throughout the early 1990s, although its performance was improving going into the mid-1990s.

Consolidated-Bathurst (the predecessor to Stone-Consolidated) was formed in 1931 by the merger of the five major pulp and paper mills that were operating in southern Quebec at the time: Laurentide; Belgo; Wyagamack; St. Maurice Paper; and Port Alfred Pulp & Paper. Between 1925 and 1931 those companies gradually joined forces in an effort to survive an ugly industry downturn caused by plunging paper prices and excess production capacity. The history of each of those mills is a story in itself, and reflects the pioneer attitude and perseverance that built Quebec's pulp and paper industry during the late 1800s and early 1900s.

Evidencing the historical importance and intrigue of Quebec's early timber industry was Laurentide, the oldest of the five companies that eventually merged to form Consolidated-Bathurst. Laurentide was inspired by John Forman, a Montreal trader of Scottish origin. Forman visited the timber-rich region of Ste-Flore in Quebec in 1881. Lumbering in that region had been going on since 1852, when the Lower Canadian government designated vast areas of timberland to merchant George Baptist in an area south of Ste-Flore. From

Baptist's timberlands, settlers had moved upstream to Ste-Flore, not far from a major waterfall. When Forman visited the area in 1881, he realized that the natural resources of the St. Flore area could be put to use to create a pulp mill—the waterfall would provide hydro power to mill the high-quality timber. Thus, in 1882 he formed the Canada Pulp Co. Ltd.

Forman's initial effort went bankrupt before the mill was even completed. Undeterred, Forman spent the next four summers buying up more land around the waterfalls and looking for investors to fund his venture. In 1887, Forman and four partners formed the Laurentide Pulp Co. Ltd. One of the partners, Albrecht Pagenstecher, had previously patented the once-renowned Voelter groundwood process, and had also invented a revolutionary papermachine. The group's technical expertise and fat financial backing of nearly $500,000 allowed the company to enjoy heady gains throughout the late 1880s and early 1990s, despite periods of temporary economic turmoil. Indeed, by the late 1920s Laurentide was generating revenues of nearly $3 million annually, employing thousands of workers, and was a leader in the North American pulp, paper, and newsprint industry.

Although Laruentide and other Quebec paper companies enjoyed fat sales increases during the newsprint boom of the early 1920s, the industry deteriorated rapidly after paper prices plunged. Financially strapped mill companies banned together rather than close their doors. The stock market crash in 1929 intensified the regional downturn and the Quebec timber and pulp industry spiraled into a severe depression. By late 1931 the companies had merged to form Consolidated Paper Corporation Ltd., which was based in Port Alfred in Southern Quebec. Most of the mills closed during the Depression. In fact, only Laurentide and one other mill managed to keep operating throughout the period, though they were often running only a few days each week.

Frustrated bondholders brought in LaMonte J. Belnap to save their investments in Consolidated. Belnap was large, imposing, and authoritative. After taking the helm at the newly formed Consolidated, he launched an aggressive campaign to eliminate the company's debt and put Consolidated in a position where it would never again need to borrow money. To that end, he would go to almost any length to cut costs. At one point, for example, he ordered employees to type their memos single-spaced on both sides of the page to save paper. And he supplied workers only with a low grade, inexpensive paper. Known as tough and demanding by his peers, Belmont was recognized by his juniors for taking a sincere interest in their careers. Under his disciplined leadership, Consolidated managed to completely eliminate its debt by 1955.

Although Consolidated survived and even managed to pare its debt under Belnap's leadership, the company skated on the brink of bankruptcy for several years after it was incorporated. For example, immediately before Consolidated was officially incorporated in 1931, the company learned that a huge contract to supply newsprint to the U.S.-based Hearst media empire was at jeopardy—Hearst did eventually purchase some of his newsprint from Consolidated, but he never paid for much of what was shipped to his companies and Consolidated carried more than $2 million in bad debts from that account alone into the 1940s. The overall situation was so bad during the early 1930s that the company set up a depot to distribute basic foodstuffs to its employees still living in the area. To make matters worse, a devastating 1932 fire that burned for ten days destroyed 90 percent of Consolidated's reserve of pulpwood.

Consolidated staggered through the 1930s with lackluster improvements in its finances. Nevertheless, the company continued to progress with its eye on the future. Belnap even managed to set up a research and development department that introduced a number of breakthrough innovations. For example, Consolidated is credited with developing a process known as "centrifugal pump cleaning" using a device initially dubbed the "Vortrap." The company also invented a special splicing film made with vinyl acetate that could be used to splice breaks in rolls of newsprint. Interestingly, Consolidated's research team, searching anywhere for profits, even devised a doomed scheme to market a deer horn derivative to China, where the substance was considered an aphrodisiac.

When World War II started up, the Canadian government assigned production quotas to all operating paper mills. Belnap opened all of Consolidated's closed plants just long enough for them to receive their quota allocation. He then reassigned production to the company's most efficient mills. That strategy helped Consolidated to square away its finances during the War. In 1946, after the War's end, Consolidated was even able to pay a dividend to investors—the first dividend in the company's history. Consolidated was also able to restore and modernize its outdated and mothballed mills. Besides bringing its facilities up to speed, the company began using revolutionary new chainsaws, which were invented in the 1940s in Sweden. By the early 1950s Consolidated's productivity and production capacity had soared. Steady increases in newsprint prices, moreover, allowed the company to achieve healthy growth.

Having restored Consolidated's balance sheet, the 68-year-old Belnap considered retiring. When his wife died in 1947, though, he changed his mind. Belnap would remain as chief executive of Consolidated until his 82nd birthday in 1962. Under his leadership, Consolidated would eliminate its debt entirely, invest in new facilities and equipment at a rate of about $4 million annually, and boost sales and profits to record figures. Although Consolidated's progress may have seemed impressive to some observers, critics derided Belnap's management style. Indeed, they believed that Belnap's frugal, Depression-influenced thinking was outmoded and severely hindered Consolidated's growth potential. Thus, several members of Consolidated's executive ranks were relieved when Belnap finally stepped aside and handed the reigns to George Hobart.

Hobart quickly began to invest some of the huge cash reserves that Consolidated had accumulated under Belnap's direction. He replaced several of the company's aging machines, many of which had been installed in the 1920s, with state-of-the-art equipment that vastly in-

creased the company's capabilities and productivity. More importantly, Hobart wanted to build a completely new mill. He decided to buy the milling operations of the Gillies company, which included 2,000 square miles of woodlands, and to build a new mill. Not long after Consolidated began construction on the new mill, though, Hobart lost his position as CEO. Indeed, after waiting in the wings for more than 20 years for Belnap to retire, Hobart was replaced as chief executive following the 1966 merger of Consolidated Paper Corporation and Bathurst Paper Limited. The resulting organization was called Consolidated-Bathurst, and was headed by former Bathurst head Spike Irwin.

Consolidated's decision to team up with Bathurst was prompted by several factors. Bathurst, founded in 1907, was itself a long-time leader in the Canadian timber, groundwood, and newsprint industry. During and following World War II, Bathurst converted from newsprint to the primary production of packaging products. And in the 1950s Bathurst expanded by purchasing six packaging companies. During the early and mid-1960s Bathurst cemented its leadership position in the packaging industry with the construction of several new facilities and state-of-the-art mills. Bathurst's largest shareholder was Power Corporation, and in 1965 Power became the leading shareholder of Consolidated as well when it managed to accrue about 16 percent ownership in the company. Power Corp. believed that Consolidated, with its strength in the newsprint industry, and Bathurst, with its packaging supremacy, complemented each other.

Hobart resisted Power Corp.'s initial proposal to combine the two companies. He eventually relented, however, and the two companies were officially merged on October 1, 1967. Irwin became chief executive of the new company and Hobart's role was relegated to that of chairman. The new company was now one of Canada's largest integrated pulp, paper, and packing manufacturers. While its operations were technically under the same roof, however, the two companies remained philosophically divided. Many of Consolidated's employees felt that their company had been coerced into a merger that primarily benefited Bathurst. Furthermore, Consolidated's corporate culture was technical, centralized, and frugal, while Bathurst tended to be decentralized and marketing oriented. Throughout the late 1960s Irwin struggled to integrate the two segments into a cohesive, streamlined whole.

Irwin's failure to successfully join Consolidated and Bathurst came to a head in 1970, when the organization suffered a disappointing $10.7 million loss. By that time, Consolidated-Bathurst's stock price had plummeted from $44 at the time of the merger to $5.25. With their prize asset teetering on the edge of disaster, Power Corp. stepped in, investing more money in Consolidated-Bathurst in 1970. It also moved Irwin to Chairman and installed Power Corp. executive Bill Turner, a Harvard MBA, as chief executive. Turner quickly jettisoned some of the company's non-vital assets and returned the enterprise to profitability in 1972, following an ugly 1991 loss of $18.8 million.

By the mid-1970s, Consolidated-Bathurst was back on track. During the late 1970s and early 1980s it invested heavily in new equipment and production facilities and began increasing its overseas activities, adding operations in the United Kingdom to complement existing divisions in Germany. Going into the 1980s, Consolidated-Bathurst was among the 30 largest publicly traded manufacturing companies in Canada, was running a pulp and fiber mill in England, and had packaging operations in Germany. The company also maintained significant interests in Canadian oil and gas production and exploration industries. By 1981, Consolidated-Bathurst was generating $1.5 billion in annual sales and looking forward to sustained growth.

Despite expectations, Consolidated-Bathurst's fortunes began to turn in the early 1980s. Indeed, demand growth for newsprint stalled and companies like Consolidated-Bathurst were stung by industry-wide overcapacity. Demand recovered during the mid-1980s and even outstripped supply in North America for a short time. Some product segments, such as uncoated groundwood paper used for advertising and graphics, realized steady gains throughout the decade. Consolidated's overall business realized less encouraging gains, however, largely as a result of general malaise in newsprint markets. The company restructured during the early and mid-1980s and jettisoned some underperforming operations. By the late 1980s, the company was enjoying moderate profitability.

Consolidated-Bathurst was purchased from Power Corp. in 1989 by Stone Container Corporation of the United States. Stone Container viewed the $2.6 billion buyout as a means of diversifying into Canada and the newsprint industry and strengthening its position in the global pulp and paper industry. Stone renamed its new subsidiary Stone-Consolidated. Unfortunately for Stone, a nasty recession pummeled the industry in the late 1980s and early 1990s. As demand plummeted, Stone-Consolidated's sales and profits crumbled. The company lost money in 1990, 1991, and 1992. Finally, Chairman and Chief Executive Roger Stone decided to take action. In 1993, in an effort to raise cash, he spun off the newsprint and groundwood paper divisions of the subsidiary as Stone-Consolidated Corp. The linerboard and packaging division of the original Consolidated-Bathurst was retained as part of Stone Container Corp.'s operations.

The new Stone-Consolidated Corp. was spun off in 1993—Stone Container remained the new company's chief shareholder. With a chunk of its operations severed, Stone-Consolidated's aggregate sales for 1993 were about $927 million. That figure reflected the start of a recovery in newsprint markets. Indeed, the newsprint and groundwood operations of Stone-Consolidated generated sales of only $840 million in 1992 and showed a staggering loss of $110 million. The loss declined in 1993 to about $69 million. In 1994, moreover, Stone-Consolidated generated sales of about $1.09 billion and managed to reduce its loss to just $7.8 million. James Doughan, chief executive of Stone-Consolidated in 1995, expected the division to post a profit in 1995 as a result of surging newsprint prices and improving margins.

Principal Subsidiaries:

Bridgewater Paper Company Limited; Stone-Consolidated Paper Sales Corporation.

Further Reading:

Gibbens, Robert. "Despite Regrets, Stone has Faith in Consolidated," *Financial Post*, June 9, 1994, Section 1, p. 5.
Leger, Kathryn. "Stone Defends Newsprint Costs," *Financial Post*, May 24, 1995, Section 1, p. 9.
MacKay, Donald. *Anticosti*, Montreal: McGraw-Hill Ryerson Limited, 1979.
Schabas, Bill. "Consolidated-Bathurst: From Many Into One, 50 Years of Progress," *Pulp & Paper Canada*, November 1981.

—Dave Mote

Sun Life Assurance Company of Canada

Sun Life Centre
150 King Street West
Toronto, Ontario M5H 1J9
(416) 979-9966
Fax: (416) 595-0345

Public Company
Incorporated: April 14, 1871 as Sun Mutual Life
   Insurance Company of Montreal *Employees:*
   14,788
Revenues: $8.27 billion
SICs: 6311 Life Insurance; 6371
   Pension/Health/Welfare Funds; 6282 Investment
   Advice; 6733 Trusts, nec; 6321 Accident and
   Health Insurance.

The Sun Life Assurance Company of Canada is the country's foremost life insurer, with over $300 billion in life insurance in force, a surplus of over $4 billion, and more than $107 billion in total assets under management. The company celebrated its 125th anniversary in 1996. Notwithstanding its name, the firm had operations in the United States, Great Britain, Ireland, the Philippines, and Hong Kong, as well as its native Canada.

The Sun, as it is commonly known, was founded in 1871 by Mathew Hamilton Gault, a native of Ireland who immigrated to Canada with his parents and siblings in 1842. After his father's death, Gault dabbled less than successfully in banking, farming, and whatever else he thought would enable him to sustain his six brothers and sisters to maturity. Then in 1851, Gault found his career course, becoming an agent for two leading life insurers: British America Assurance Company of Toronto and the Mutual Life Insurance Company of New York. By 1865, this assiduous worker was also employed as a manager of the Royal Canadian Bank.

After many years of watching Mutual Life and British America grow in Canada's veritable insurance void, Gault convinced George Stephen and several other leading Montreal businessmen to invest in a new *Canadian* insurance company. Although their company was not the country's first indigenous life insurer, The Sun Mutual Life Insurance Company of Montreal would one day become its largest.

Thomas Workman was its first president and Gault was installed in the post of managing director. The first year's premiums totaled $14,000, and insurance in force quickly rose to $404,000. Sun Life's first years of steady growth fostered a false sense of security in its board and director. With the insurance business running seemingly effortlessly, Gault accepted the presidency of the Exchange Bank of Canada — in addition to his responsibilities at the Sun — in 1872. When an international depression began to impact the fledgling Canadian life insurance industry in 1873, Gault soon realized that he had bitten off more than he could chew.

In 1874, Sun's board hired Robertson Macaulay to oversee the firm's day-to-day operations as secretary. Macaulay discovered an operation replete with discouraged, indifferent, and even embezzling agents. He also soon realized that Sun's investments in the Exchange Bank and the Montreal Loan and Mortgage Company had been devalued by over one-third over the course of The Sun's short history. When it came to light that both the sales and investment sides of Sun's business had been impaired on his watch, Gault resigned in 1879. Macaulay advanced to managing director and gave the firm a name that matched his wider aspirations for it: The Sun Life Assurance Company of Canada. Macaulay soon showed an innovative bent as well, establishing operations in the West Indies and offering the world's first unconditional life insurance policy — all in his first year as managing director. He was elected president in 1889. By the turn of the twentieth century, The Sun had total assets of about $11 million and nearly $50 million of insurance in force.

Macaulay's son Thomas Bassett Macaulay had come on board in 1877 at the age of 17. After advancing to the post of secretary in 1889, the young executive, known as T.B., spearheaded the firm's international expansion. Faced with slow population growth at home, the company pursued business in Asia, Africa, Central and South America, Europe, and the United States. Boosted by 15 percent annual increases, Sun Life surpassed its elder rival, Canada Life, to become the country's largest life insurer in 1908.

Acquisition of competing companies also helped increase Sun's stature. In 1910 the company added Royal-Victoria Life Insurance Company of Canada's $4.6 million in business. Home Life Association of Canada was acquired in 1913, bring an additional $5.1 million in business. Two acquisitions in 1915 — the Federal Life Insurance Company of Canada and The Security Life Insurance Company of Canada — added a total of $29.3 million in business. The first decade and a half of the century had seen Sun's insurance in force multiply nearly five times, to $257 million. During that same period, the surplus grew to $7.5 million and total assets expanded to $74 million.

The younger Macaulay succeeded his father as managing director and president in 1915. Like his father — and unlike the typical life insurer — T.B. was an innovator and a risk-taker. In 1919, for example, he made Sun Life Canada's first life insurance company to offer a group life policy. Using funds earned on the high-flying stock market of the 1920s, he acquired several less fortunate life insurers in China and the United States. Sun's own stock price multiplied from $560 in 1927 to $4,100 in October 1929.

But T.B.'s venturesomeness caught up with The Sun after the collapse of the U.S. stock market began to reverberate throughout the global economy as the Great Depression. His investment of more than half of the firm's assets in common stocks proved devastating: the actual value of Sun's surplus shrunk from $60 million in 1929 to $30 million in 1930, $16 million in 1931, and bottomed out at less than $6 million in 1932. At its nadir, the technically bankrupt company was kept afloat by special insurance valuation regulations sanctioned by the federal government.

This crisis utterly transformed Sun Life's corporate culture, ushering in a multi-decade period of conservatism that ensured stability, but paid for that safety with correspondingly low earnings. Arthur Barton Wood, who was characterized in Mark Witten's 1982 *Saturday Night* essay on the company's history as "an able though colourless actuary," succeeded T.B. upon his resignation in 1934. Whereas the Macaulay era had been conspicuous for its innovations — new products, geographic expansion, and high-risk/high-return investments — the post-Macaulay era was characterized by rigid conservatism. Witten's 1982 evaluation noted that for most of the twentieth century, product development was based more on actuarial and investment standards than on consumer demands and needs, and that technical and financial expertise, rather than managerial competence, were the favored qualities for ascension through the management ranks.

The Sun's withdrawal from its far-flung international operations was one manifestation of its reticence. Faced with the challenges of nationalism, war, over-regulation, inflation, and nationalization, the insurer pulled out of country after country. For example, The Sun had grown to become China's largest foreign life insurer by 1948. But the post-World War II political climate combined with 4,000 percent inflation to chase Sun from the country. In 1945, the geographic distribution of insurance in force stood at: 32.7 percent in Canada, 41.5 percent in the United States, 12.1 percent in the United Kingdom, 9 percent in Asia, and 4.5 percent in Central and South America. By 1957, the concentration had shifted: 51 percent of business was in Canada, 34 percent in the United States, 13 percent in the Commonwealth countries, and 2 percent from other regions. From a high of 50 countries in the 1930s, its business was limited to seven nations by the 1970s. Like other insurers across the continent, The Sun strove to regain its pre-Depression stature in the 1930s and early 1940s. The company reduced its investment in common stocks to 33 percent of assets, and by 1936 had built its surplus back up to $18 million. The Sun appeared to have made a full recovery by 1945, when insurance in force reached $3.5 billion (a mere $465 million more than in 1931) and assets increased to $1.3 billion. Rising standards of living kept the company's policy holders alive and paying premiums longer, as well as protecting ever-larger amounts of property. Per capita life insurance increased 30 percent from 1945 to 1950 alone. This growth trend continued in the prosperous 1950s; Sun's insurance in force more than doubled from 1947 to 1957, to $7.5 billion.

An unofficial twenty-year hiring freeze made for an orderly pattern of succession at The Sun. Wood served as president until 1950 and chairman until his death at the age of 82 in 1952. George Bourke served as Sun's president from 1950 until 1962. Alistair Campbell became president in 1962. The popularity of group life insurance policies and pension plans helped make the 1960s The Sun's most prosperous decade since the 1920s. This period also saw the dawn of a new era of efficiency with the launch of the Univac II electronic data processing system. By 1967, insurance in force totaled $15.5 billion and assets amounted to $3.2 billion.

Campbell advanced to chairman in 1970 and was succeeded as president by Tony Hicks. Hicks, who was characterized as being cast in the mold of T.B. Macaulay, launched an important restructuring that included the creation of a marketing division under George Clarke. Hicks' aggressive ideas and manner clashed with Sun's entrenched, conservative corporate culture. The board of directors waited until 1972, the year after Sun's big centenary celebration, to oust Hicks.

This uncharacteristically abrupt change in leadership was a harbinger of a tough decade for The Sun. High inflation devalued life insurance policies as investment vehicles. As clients shifted their funds from low-interest insurance policies to higher-return vehicles, insurance companies were forced to lower premiums and raise dividends, thereby squeezing profit margins. The increasing popularity of term life insurance, where policyholders only pay for the coverage and do not chip in additional funds as savings (which the insurance company invests to make its own money), was just one sign of the times. Under the presidency of Thomas Maunsell Galt from 1972 to 1978, The Sun had resumed its conservative tendencies. The company was slow to react to the imperatives of an inflationary economy, and as a result it lost ground to innovative competitors like Great-West Life Assurance Company. While still strong, growth lagged the rate of inflation in the early 1970s: assets only increased from $3.9 billion in 1971 to $4.2 billion in 1974.

One of Galt's last actions as president of Sun Life was also one of the most dramatic in the company's history. In 1976, Quebec elected its first Parti Qubecois government. The new officials promptly enacted legislation (Bill 101) making French the official language of the province. On 6 January 1978, Galt made the stunning announcement that, "because Quebec had, by law, become largely French, the company could no longer envisage recruiting or retaining people sufficiently competent in English to continue its head office operations in the province." After over a century in Montreal, Sun Life moved its headquarters to Toronto. The reaction in Quebec was predictable: sales of new insurance policies dropped, and about one-fourth of The Sun's provincial sales force resigned.

George Clarke became president of Sun that same year. Clarke was the company's first leader to come up through the sales side of the organization, as opposed to the actuarial side. His background in marketing helped drive a fundamental shift at the insurance company. Within months of his ascension, the new leader brought in an outside consultant to evaluate a reorganization of the company.

The convergence of several trends in the early 1980s transformed the life insurance industry and imparted a sense of urgency to Sun's internal soul searching. Inflation continued to make standard whole-life policies (Sun's traditional strong suit) less attractive as investments. Deregulation of financial services opened the market to competition from innovative newcomers like banks, trust companies, and even the government. At the same time, both individual and institutional investors began to favor high risk-high return investments over safe and steady vehicles like life insurance.

Although these market imperatives required Sun to overcome decades of inertia, it had one thing going for it: a huge financial surplus of almost $1.4 billion more in assets than liabilities. The company's 20 percent surplus ratio (the proportion of surplus assets) nearly doubled the industry average. These excess funds, which had served as Sun's security blanket, gave the company the ability to engage in some cutthroat competitive strategies. For his part, George Clarke wanted to start leveraging the surplus to Sun's advantage.

In 1984 Galt was succeeded by John Brindle, although he remained chairman. Over the course of Brindle's four-year tenure, Sun's net income more than doubled, from $118.2 million to $248 million, on a 40 percent increase in annual revenues. The increased profitability was attributed to expanded operations in the United States and Hong Kong, as well as increased productivity due to staff reductions.

The installation of John McNeil as chairman and CEO and John Gardner as president in the late 1980s inaugurated a team that would lead Sun into the mid-1990s. McNeil had first joined Sun in 1956, but left the company ten years later to take positions in a mutual fund and at the Bank of Montreal, returning to The Sun in 1978. The new leaders launched an acquisition program that broadened Sun's product offerings. In 1989, the company purchased Coronet Trust Co., a mortgage company, from Crownx Inc. and renamed it Sun Life Trust. The new business anticipated competition from banks, which were expected to receive legislative approval to enter the life insurance industry.

Within just a couple of years, Sun Life Trust had grown to rank among Canada's top ten trust companies. In 1990 the parent augmented those activities with the acquisitions of Counsel Trust Co. and Pacific Savings and Mortgage Corp., two regional mortgagors. But in the early 1990s, a glut of loan delinquencies and a number of commercial and residential mortgage defaults led to a string of losses for the subsidiary.

High rates of domestic taxation drove Sun to re-emphasize international growth in the late 1980s and early 1990s. For example, federal taxes alone increased 62 percent to from 1990 to 1991, while the company's assets only increased 12 percent and its revenues increased less than 14 percent. The $111 Sun paid in federal, provincial and local taxes in 1991 surpassed its dividend payout of $98 million to policyholders.

In 1991, The Sun acquired Massachusetts Financial Services Company, the United States' third-largest mutual fund management company. The acquisition enabled Sun to offer its insurance clients higher-yielding products, while retaining their investment dollars. When the opportunity to nearly double its British operations arose in 1994, the company did not hesitate. The $440 million (£200 million) acquisition of the bankrupt Confederation Life Assurance Company's British business boosted Sun's operations there to one-third of total assets. The company also targeted its old stomping ground, Asia, especially focusing on Taiwan, Singapore, Thailand and Malaysia. (It already had operations in the Philippines and Hong Kong.)

Sun Life's revenues nearly doubled, from $5.7 billion in 1989 to $10 billion in 1994, but its net income did not follow suit. Profits rose from $239 million in 1989 to $267.8 million in 1991, then declined to $151 million by 1993. The decrease was attributed in part to Sun Life Trust, which had not made a profit since 1989 and was not expected to return to the black until 1996. A dramatic increase in the profitability of The Sun's Canadian operations, however, helped increase 1994's profits to $304.5 million.

Principal Subsidiaries:

Spectrum Bullock Financial Services Inc.; Calvin Bullock, Ltd.; Sun Life Trust Company; Sun Life of Canada Investment Management Limited; Sun Life Assurance Company of Canada (U.S.); Sun Life Insurance and Annuity Company of New York (U.S.); Massachusetts Casualty Insurance Company (U.S.); Massachusetts Financial Services Company (U.S.); New London Trust F.S.B.; Sun Life Assurance Company of Canada (U.K.) Limited; Confederation Life Insurance Co. (U.K.); Sun Life of Canada Unit Managers Limited (U.K.); Sun Banking Corporation Limited (U.K.).

Further Reading:

Reier, Sharon, "Return of the Globalist," *Financial World*, 4 September 1990, 77.
Schull, Joseph, *The Century of The Sun: The First Hundred Years of Sun Life Assurance Company of Canada.* Toronto: Macmillan of Canada, 1971.
Slocum, Dennis, "Sun Life Fed Up With Taxes," *Globe and Mail*, 6 May 1992, B11.
Witten, Mark, "Sun Life at The Crossroads," *Saturday Night,* March 1982, 15-22, 24+.

—April Dougal Gasbarre

TELEGLOBE

Teleglobe Inc.

1000 de La Gauchetière Street West
Montreal, Quebec H3B 4X5
(514) 868-8124
Fax: (514) 868-7275

Public Company
Founded: 1949 as Canadian Overseas
   Telecommunications Corporation
Employees: 1899
Operating Revenues: $643 million
Stock Exchanges: Montreal Toronto Vancouver
SICs: 4813 Telephone Communications Not Radio;
   1623 Water, Sewer, and Utility Lines; 7372
   Prepackaged Software

With over $2 billion worth of facilities, Teleglobe Inc. ranks among the world's ten largest telecommunications concerns in terms of minutes of outbound traffic. In the early 1990s, the company's primary business was the provision of overseas communication services between Canada and the rest of the world (except for the United States, which was served by domestic companies) through its chief subsidiary, Teleglobe Canada, Inc. The company's network of transoceanic cables and satellites connects Canadians with over 240 countries and territories around the world. Other services include undersea cable installation, telecommunications consulting, and mobile communication. Under the direction of Chairman and CEO Charles Sirois after a 1992 "boardroom coup," the former Crown company aimed to become one of the world's three largest telecom companies by the end of the twentieth century.

The impetus behind the creation of Teleglobe came with the 1948 ratification of the Commonwealth Telegraph Agreement, a treaty among the members of the British Commonwealth. Among other things, this contract stipulated that overseas telecommunication services be publicly owned. In accordance, Teleglobe was founded in 1949 as Canadian Overseas Telecommunications Corporation (COTC) to acquire the overseas communications businesses of Cable and Wireless Ltd. and Canadian Marconi Ltd.

In order to reassure domestic phone companies that this government-supported newcomer would not infringe on their established territories, the enabling legislation prohibited the COTC from providing Canada-U.S.

service. At the time, that segment of the telecommunications market accounted for fully 85 percent of the country's international traffic; the COTC was limited to the remaining 15 percent stake. COTC had one competitor at the outset, but when this single rival went out of business a few years later, the Crown corporation was left with a defacto monopoly in its assigned territory. The company enjoyed steady, if modest, profitability throughout its first few years in business, during which it concentrated almost exclusively on the provision of international telegraph services.

Then, in 1956, the company participated in the installation of the world's first transatlantic coaxial cable, which linked Newfoundland and Scotland. The project signaled COTC's shift from telegraph to telephone services and ushered in a period of growth and profitability uncommon among Canada's Crown corporations. Profits skyrocketed from under $500,000 in 1958 to $2.4 million in 1964, as the company and its Commonwealth counterparts created and operated an expanding network of undersea telephone cables. This profitability—and the capacity to finance its own growth without dipping into the public coffers—enabled the COTC to maintain a high level of autonomy from the federal government. The company's activities included a leading role in INTELSAT, the International Telecommunications Satellite Organization.

Like many Canadian businesses, the COTC was dominated by Anglos from its inception until the 1970s, when government pressure brought an influx of French Canadian managers and the introduction of bilingualism. This shift was outwardly represented by a 1975 name change, when the company became Teleglobe Canada Inc.

Rapid increases in international telephone traffic during the 1970s fueled continuing growth. From 1975 to 1985, Teleglobe's retained earnings increased by 400 percent and its annual return on equity averaged 17 percent, but its employment level only increased marginally. The combination of these three factors led inexorably to increased profitability. The federal treasury took notice of Teleglobe's fantastic performance and ordered the company to pay its first dividend, of $3.8 million, in 1980. The dividend became a regular feature of Teleglobe's annual report.

It was also around this time that the first rumblings of privatization began to sound. The 1984 inauguration of the Mulroney government brought a push to divest many Crown corporations and use the proceeds to pay down the national debt. Several sources noted that Teleglobe was considered "the jewel in the Crown."

Government officials had hoped to complete Teleglobe's privatization by 1985, but the process was held up by debate over whether any telecommunications carriers would be allowed to enter the bidding. A compromise plan that prohibited foreign telecommunications companies from buying shares and limited domestic telecoms to a minority stake finally reopened the bidding in November of 1986. Other terms of the sale restricted foreign ownership to 20 percent of shares and mandated that Teleglobe would continue to have a monopoly on international telecommunications for a set transitional period. This last provision made Teleglobe's "initial public offering" even more marketable.

Bids came in from some of the country's most important firms, including Canadian Telecom Carriers International Inc., Spar Aerospace Ltd., Inter-City Gas Corp., Power Corporation of Canada, and First City Financial. But the winning bidder came as a complete surprise to nearly all observers. It was made by Memotec Data Inc., a firm one-sixth the size of Teleglobe.

The ten-year-old company was first created to produce and sell several types of communication processors that link computer networks. Within just two years of its 1977 establishment, Memotec was acquired by International Syscoms Ltd. Under the direction of Syscoms' president Eric Baker from 1979 to 1984, Memotec expanded internationally, launching operations in the United States, South America, and Asia.

Baker left Syscoms and Memotec in 1984 to create Altamira Capital Corp., a venture capital firm that enjoyed the support of several important individual and institutional investors. Then, barely a year later, Baker and his supporters accumulated a controlling interest in Memotec from Innocan Investments Inc., Syscoms' parent. Baker was "re-installed" as Memotec's chairman in 1985. William McKenzie, who had been hand picked by Baker to lead Memotec in 1983, continued as president and chief executive officer.

The company grew quickly in the years leading up to its acquisition of Teleglobe. Sales multiplied from $8 million in 1984 to $57 million in 1986, largely on the basis of the acquisition of Real Time Datapro Ltd., an insurance services company, in 1985 and the purchase of data communications products maker Infinet the following year.

Memotec won the bidding war by offering the government $488.3 million in cash, repayment of $143 million Teleglobe owed the treasury, and about $16 million from Teleglobe's 1985 profits. Other terms of the sale included: the provision of an employee share purchase option, honoring all existing labor agreements, promising no layoffs, and reducing overseas telephone and telex rates by 13.5 percent and 10 percent respectively in 1988.

Shortly after the sale was announced on February 11, 1987, provincial and federal agencies suspended trading of Memotec shares to investigate purported insider trading. The Quebec Securities Commission subsequently charged seven individuals (including Peter Blaikie, former president of the Progressive Conservative Party) with insider trading. It seems that on February 5—the day that the federal government decided to accept Memotec's bid—over 23,000 shares in Memotec were traded on the Montreal Stock Exchange at a 20 percent premium to their price from the day before. Memotec's activity on the Toronto Exchange was only 3,725 shares that day. After more than a year of investigation and courtroom testimony, the unusual—and profitable—activity was chalked up to "coincidence."

Although it entailed the assumption of $225 million in short-term debt, the acquisition of Teleglobe catapulted

Memotec to the vanguard of Canada's telecommunications industry. Within months of the purchase, Bell Canada Enterprises (BCE), the country's largest telephone concern, gave it a vote of confidence with the purchase of one-third of Memotec's shares. (This was later reduced to 22 percent.)

Memotec, which adopted its famous subsidiary's name in 1991, expanded through acquisition as well as organic growth in the latter years of the 1980s. A flurry of activity in 1988 included purchase of a controlling stake in Polycom Systems Inc., the outright acquisition of Datagram Inc., and the purchase of a minority position in Infotron Systems Corp. Teleglobe International Inc. was formed that same year to pursue global opportunities for growth. While leading telecoms fought over the world's largest markets, Teleglobe International targeted such small and mid-sized countries as Ukraine, Poland, and the Republic of Moldova, that they had overlooked. Teleglobe International formed a joint venture to create mobile communications networks for ships and aircraft with IDB Communications Group, Inc., a satellite transmission company, in 1990. Teleglobe Marine Inc., was also created in 1988 to provide installation and maintenance of undersea telecom cables. Teleglobe expanded its insurance services business with the 1989 acquisitions of Equifax Insurance Systems and ISI Systems Inc.

While Teleglobe's activities resulted in a 21 percent increase in operating revenues, from $276 million in 1987 to $333 million in 1990, the company's profits plummeted from $48 million to $8 million. After a slight rebound in 1991 to $26 million, the company resumed its losing ways with a $51 million loss in 1992.

These disappointing results prompted an investor revolt led by Charles Sirois. Sirois' career had been launched in high style when, shortly after securing his master's degree in finance in 1979, the 24-year-old's father and uncle gave him $1.5 million in start up money to invest as he wished. Over the next 15 years, Sirois built that nest egg into National Telesystem Ltd., a multi-million-dollar holding company that managed over 100 Canadian telecoms.

Sirois had personally invested $83.3 million to buy a 20 percent stake in Teleglobe from former top shareholder Bell Canada Enterprises. (Perhaps not coincidentally, Sirois had served as the director of BCE's Mobile Communications division.) He joined forces with the Caisse de Depot et Placement du Quebec, an influential provincial pension fund that owned another 16 percent of Teleglobe; the Ontario Municipal Employees Retirement Fund, which held 9 percent; and fellow telecom magnate Ted Rogers, who owned 4 percent. In 1992, the co-conspirators forced Chairman Eric Baker and CEO William McKenzie off Teleglobe's board of directors.

After being installed as CEO, Sirois set out to move Teleglobe into the upper echelon of the global telecommunications industry. To achieve that goal, the relatively small company would have to surpass such multi-billion-dollar competitors as U.S. Sprint Communications Co. And although attaining the number three spot by the turn of the century has been characterized as an "unlikely objective" by Peter C. Newman of *Maclean's*, the analyst acceded that more time may be all Sirois needs to consummate his objective.

Sirois targeted his objective with a $900 million, five-year capital expansion plan funded in part by the 1993 spin-off of Memotec's original communications products business. Many of its major projects are multi-company ventures that hearken back to the days of INTELSAT. One of the biggest was CANTAT 3, an alliance of 37 international telecoms. Late in 1994, this consortium completed the first leg of this multi-level project, a $385 million, high-capacity, fibre-optic system, that linked Canada with England, Denmark, Germany, and Ireland, and extended into Eastern Europe. The next phase of the project, dubbed CANUS 1, planned to link the United States to the CANTAT 3 network.

In 1994, Teleglobe signed an agreement with TRW to form Odyssey Worldwide Services, a consumer mobile phone system that proposed to use 12 medium altitude satellites to create a global communications system. The project, which was expected to cost $2.5 billion, was joined by Spar Aerospace, Harris Corp., and Hitachi Ltd. early in 1995.

Also in 1995, Teleglobe became the first telecom company to launch low-earth orbiting satellites (LEOS) as part of its ORBCOMM joint venture with Orbital Sciences Corp. The partners planned to launch a total of 36 LEOS to complete a global wireless data and voice communications system by 1997. Teleglobe expected transport, trucking and energy companies to use the system, which offered access to databases, messaging services and other advanced functions throughout the world.

In his quest for greatness, Sirois has boldly eschewed the two-edged sword of Teleglobe's monopoly status (which was extended for a second five-year period in 1992 and prevented the company from competing in the United States). In 1994, he told Peter C. Newman of *Maclean's:* "I don't believe Teleglobe's future resides in perpetuating its [Canadian] monopoly. We have to become a North American, not just a Canadian or overseas player. We need to grab enough market share in the United States to go head to head with AT&T. At the moment, with 100 percent of the Canadian traffic, we have only seven percent of North America's overseas communications. I want 20 percent. We also intend to become an active partner in a global mobility concept that will link nearly everybody anywhere on earth through satellites." Sirois' anticipation of a deregulated market led to the 1994 formation of an alliance with Formento Radio Beep (of Mexico) and IXC Communications and Westel (both of the U.S.) to supply local and long-distance services in Mexico.

The CEO's visionary leadership also brought about a breathtaking financial turnaround at Teleglobe. From its 1992 deficit, the company's net results boomeranged to back-to-back record profits of $71.9 million in 1993 and 90.9 million in 1994. Operating revenues continued their climb, rising nearly 47 percent from $438.1 million in 1992 to $643 million in 1994.

Principal Subsidiaries:

Teleglobe Canada Inc.; Teleglobe International (U.S.) Inc.; Teleglobe Mobility; Teleglobe Cable Systems; Teleglobe Marine Inc.; Teleglobe International Inc.; Teleglobe CANTAT-3 Inc. (Barbados); Teleglobe Insurance Systems; ISI Systems, Inc. (United States); Teleglobe Limited (England).

Further Reading:

Burke, Dan, "A Personal Nightmare," *Maclean's*, February 1, 1988, p. 32.
"A Buyer for Teleglobe," *Maclean's*, February 23, 1987, p. 38.
Fennell, Tom, "Memotec's Tangled Roots," *Maclean's*, March 23, 1987, p. 42.
Moeller, Michael, "LEOS Technology Lifts Off the Launching Pad," *PC Week*, April 17, 1995, p. 31.
Newman, Peter C., "An Electronic Highway Ready for Traffic," *Maclean's*, April 11, 1994, p. 43.
Schultz, Richard, *Teleglobe Canada: Selling the Jewel in the Crowns*, Montreal, Centre for the Study of Regulated Industries, McGill University, 1988.

—April Dougal Gasbarre

TELUS

Telus Corporation

10020 100th St., 31st Fl.
Edmonton, Alberta T5J ON5
(403)498-7320
Fax: (403)498-7322

Public Company
Incorporated: 1990
Employees: 9,300
Sales: $1.36 billion
Stock Exchanges: Alberta Montreal Toronto
SICs: 6719 Holding Companies

Telus Corporation was created in 1990 to serve as a holding company for the privatized assets of Alberta's government-owned telephone utility. In 1995 Telus was managing $3.2 billion in assets and generating annual revenues of $1.36 billion. Through its subsidiaries, Telus provides voice, data, video telecommunications, and other communications services to Alberta's population of nearly three million people. The young company was experiencing a rapid transition from a public bureaucracy to a contender in the free market in the mid-1990s.

Telus Corporation was created on October 4, 1990, following several years of effort by both public and government entities to privatize the public telephone system in Alberta. In the largest share offering in Canadian history, more than 130,000 Albertans purchased 74.7 million common shares of Telus. A sale of remaining government shares on the Alberta, Montreal, and Toronto stock exchanges about one year later made Telus a 100-percent publicly traded company. The overall privatization scheme garnered $1.8 billion and spread ownership of the company to 55,000 Albertans.

Several subsidiaries were organized under the Telus holding company umbrella. The largest of those underlings was Alberta Government Telephones (AGT), which was formerly Alberta's telephone utility. AGT's history reaches back to the early 1900s when Canada was installing its nationwide telephone network. Because of the advanced technology and massive infrastructure required to develop regional telephone systems, government-backed companies were usually established to generate funding, build, and then manage the equipment and services. The first of those utilities in Canada was the Bell Telephone Company of Canada

(Bell Canada), which was established in 1880 to bring telephone service into Montreal, Ottawa, Quebec, and other of Canada's eastern cities.

Within a year of its inception, Bell Canada was supplying telephone service to 14 major cities, employing about 150 workers, and servicing more than 2,000 telephones. Furthermore, the company had set up agencies in a number of other towns to secure subscribers and develop new exchanges. In fact, Bell Canada's long-term goal was to extend service throughout Canada. The company obtained rights to provide service throughout much of the country and began investing in the construction of equipment and facilities in several provinces. Soon, telephone infrastructure was being built as far west as Alberta and was even being extended to very small towns.

It eventually became apparent that Canada's vast geography would preclude a single company from efficiently developing and managing a system for the entire country. Among other operations, therefore, Canada Bell sold its telephone operations in Prince Edward Island, Nova Scotia, and New Brunswick in the late 1880s. Many citizens in the Prairie Provinces, including Alberta, were dissatisfied with Bell Canada by the early 1900s. That was partly because Bell Canada had been successful mostly in bringing service only to urban areas (voice clarity was possible only over distances of less than 20 miles). To get phone service from the city to rural residents, public telephones were commonly installed at the ends of the Bell Canada lines. Thus, many Alberta customers wanted to transfer ownership of the telephone system to the province government, which they felt would be able to provide a more cohesive system that focused on their needs.

In 1906 Alberta's first legislative sssembly approved the province's entry into the field of telephone service. Two years later the province purchased all of Bell Canada's plants and equipment along with the privileges and rights to provide service throughout Alberta. The entire telephone system was placed under the control of the Alberta government, although several small farmer-owned services remained intact. To help balance the will of bureaucrats with the needs of the citizens, the province placed the telephone system under the regulation of the Alberta Public Utilities Board in 1915. Then, in 1927, the system was placed under the control of an autonomous Ministry, with the general manager elevated to the rank of deputy minister. The service remained in that form until 1958, when Alberta Government Telephones Commission was established to end direct government control of the phone system. Thus, AGT became what is known as an agency of the crown.

Under various forms of government control, AGT picked up where Bell Canada left off and expanded service throughout Alberta during the early and mid-1900s—the exception was Edmonton, Alberta, which continued to be handled by the independent Edmonton Telephone into the 1990s. Telephone technology advanced rapidly during the period. Importantly, the vacuum tube repeater was introduced in 1915. That mechanism, which could theoretically transmit a voice an infinite distance, allowed AGT to become part of a transcontinental telephone network that gave an entirely new meaning to "long distance" telephone communication. Of similar import was an improvement over early telephone systems that required batteries to be installed at the subscriber's premises. "Central energy switchboards" eliminated that inconvenience. Another major breakthrough was the phantom circuit, whereby two pairs of wires with special equipment at each end could transmit a third conversation—the third "phantom" line even offered higher quality transmission than the other two lines.

By the 1950s telephone technology had improved to the point where the service was viewed as a necessity by many people. To expand and improve service, AGT initiated a $93 million, 10-year effort in 1964 to bury rural telephone cables and bring four-party, dividedringing service to virtually every farm in Alberta. Meanwhile, AGT continued to buy up the old farmerowned phone systems to secure its monopoly on the Alberta phone system (still with the exception of Edmonton Telephone). In 1976, in fact, AGT purchased the last of the farmer-owned systems. Two years later the number of telephones serviced by AGT reached one million. In 1983 AGT Limited was incorporated to act as the owner of AGT and to separate nonregulated operations. During the 1980s AGT also branched out into communications services other than basic, traditional, regulated telephone service.

The government supported, regulated, monopolistic environment that characterized Alberta's (and much of Canada's) telephone system served the country well for roughly a century. Governments often mandated that all customers requesting service receive a phone line, regardless of their location, and multi-million-dollar projects were forced into action through political mandate. The result was that everybody got quality telephone service and equipment, and usually at reasonable rates. By the 1980s, though, many people were beginning to question the validity of the system. Much of the costly infrastructure was already in place, so the role of the bureaucracy had diminished. And many people felt that the system was antiquated and was hindering innovation and growth. A number of new technologies, such as wireless telecommunications, were poised to take off, and many insiders believed that add-on telephone services were not being developed quickly enough.

In fact, AGT was widely believed to have become a cumbersome, inefficient bureaucracy. The utility had long been as much a political tool as it was a member of the business community. For example, politicians often appointed people to executive posts in the company as a political reward rather than because they were the best person to handle the job. AGT did introduce new services. In 1982, for example, AGT commenced operation of Canada's first cellular telephone system using 400 megahertz bandwidth. Three years later AGT began offering conventional 800 megahertz cellular service, and also launched Individual Line Service for all Albertans. Despite those initiatives, however, many customers and government insiders believed that change was due. Throughout the 1980s public pressure to privatize AGT's long-distance services mounted.

In 1990 the Alberta legislature passed the Alberta Government Telephones Reorganization Act. That Act was designed to reorganize the Alberta Government Telephones Commission and to place all of the shares of AGT under a holding company to be named Telus Corporation. The idea was to privatize the phone system and allow the free market to exert greater influence on the long-distance telecommunications sector. The effort had a big impact on AGT, which began a turbulent transformation from a government-regulated monopoly to a relatively unprotected combatant in the increasingly competitive world of telecommunications. Indeed, during the next few years the company was forced to slash its long-distance rates by 40 percent and to eliminate fully 25 percent of its staff. The huge work force cutbacks, which seemed to confirm critic's claims that the organization was bloated and inefficient, did little for employee morale.

Besides reducing long-distance rates and cutting payrolls, AGT attempted to diversify its service offerings to compensate for profit stagnation in its traditional businesses. The company had already started AGT Directory in 1988, which was a Talking Yellow Pages service offered to customers in Calgary. AGT Directory also offered *Yellow Pages* books. Telus started another subsidiary after privatization called AGT Mobility, which became the first North American company to offer digital cellular service. Within two years the division was serving 15,200 paging subscribers and about 100,000 cellular telephone customers. Also in 1992, Telus launched ISM Alberta, a joint venture, to provide state-of-the-art computer systems and technical expertise on a contract basis to business and government customers.

At about the same time that it joined ISM, Telus became involved in Stentor, an alliance owned by nine Canadian telecommunications companies. The consortium company offered better long-distance services, as well as commercial satellite service between Canada and 240 countries and territories around the globe. In 1993 Telus entered the cable television/telephony business in the United Kingdom through a partnership with CUC broadcasting. Dubbed Telecential, the pioneer venture combined telephone and cable television services and managed to accrue about 150,000 customers by the end of 1993. AGT Mobility became profitable for the first time that year, adding to Telus' overall net income for the year of about $180 million. Indeed, despite turbulence in its core AGT subsidiary, Telus managed to keep sales and net income steady around $1.2 billion and $180 million, respectively, during the early 1990s.

Regardless of its rapid diversification and stable earnings, Telus' board of directors decided that the company was due for a management shakeup in 1993. Shortly before Telus was formed, in fact, the last political appointee to head AGT was named. Neil Webber took the helm as chairman in 1989. Webber had worked in government for several decades before being tapped as chairman by political ally and premier Don Getty. He was considered a member of the old guard, so his retirement was greeted with enthusiasm by many investors. Still, under Webber's command Telus managed to post major gains. The number of AGT employees per 1,000 telephone access lines, for example, plummeted from about 9.3 in 1991 to just 5.8 by late 1993. At the same time, the number of access lines increased by more than 100,000.

George K. Petty took over as chairman and chief executive of Telus late in 1994. A telecommunications veteran, Petty had worked for telecom giant AT&T from 1969 to 1994 and had most recently served as vice-president of global business services. Before AT&T he had been a U.S. Navy communications officer after graduating from New Mexico State University with a degree in electrical engineering. At Telus, he quickly announced his intent to slash costs, diversify services, and focus on customer satisfaction. He also welcomed increased efforts by the CRTC to increase competition within the industry. "From my experience, deregulation immediately increases the ability to communicate," Petty said in the January 13, 1995, *Calgary Herald*.

Importantly, in 1995 Telus finalized the acquisition of the operations of Edmonton Telephones Corporation (Ed Tel) for $465 million. Ed Tel was incorporated in 1893 as Edmonton District Telephone Company and owned by the city of Edmonton from 1904 to 1995. Throughout the century it survived as the only telephone company in Alberta outside of AGT's control. By 1994 Ed Tel was supporting about 400,000 access lines in the Edmonton area, or about one-third the number of lines operated by AGT. Ed Tel also had about 36,000 cellular subscribers. The merger brought 2,000 new employees to Telus, which had managed to cut its AGT payroll from 10,200 workers to just 6,300 by 1994. Telus management believed that it could integrate Ed Tel into its operations to achieve economies of scale. Telus also hoped to cut costs and improve efficiency at the new subsidiary.

By 1994 Telus was operating, or partnering in, six subsidiaries. Most of its sales and profits were derived from AGT Limited. Telus' subsidiaries, though, were expected to contribute much more to the holding company's bottom line in the future. Indeed, most of Telus' companies were achieving steady sales and earn-

ings gains going into the mid-1990s and were building market share in growing niches of the fast-paced communications industry. The holding company's sales increased to $1.36 billion in 1994 while net income jumped a healthy 18 percent to $212 million. Ed Tel was expected to add about $325 million to Telus' revenue base for the 1995 year. Despite ongoing upheaval in Canadian telecommunications industries, strength in its core markets and its growing diversification made Telus a weighty contender in the newly deregulated telecommunications sector.

Principal Subsidiaries:

AGT Limited; ED TEL; AGT Mobility; AGT Directory; Telecential; ISM; Canadian Mobility Products

Further Reading:

Campbell, Donald. "Webber Boasts AGT's Now in Fighting Form," *Calgary Herald*, December 22, 1993, Section D, p. 3.
Cattaneo, Claudia. "Telus Profit Climbs 17 Percent," *Calgary Herald*, February 9, 1995, Section C, p. 2.
Crawford, Anne. "Quantum Change; AGT, for Years Operated As a Government-Run Monopoly, is Trying to Adapt to Face Stiff Corporate Competition," *Calgary Herald*, June 26, 1993, Section F, p. 1.
————. "Taking Care of No. 1: New Telus Boss Puts Customers First as the Company Faces Stiff Competition," *Calgary Herald*, January 13, 1995, Section E, p. 6.
Geddes, Ashley. "Edmonton Tel Takeover Approved," *Financial Post*, March 1, 1995, Section 1, p. 6.
Powell, Johanna. "Brighter Future Seen for Telus," *Financial Post*, May 30, 1991, Section 1, p. 13.
Urlocker, Mike and Daren Schuettler. "1,500 Worker to Lose Jobs at Telus," *Financial Post*, September 25, 1992, Section 1, p. 5.
Urlocker, Mike. "Telus Reports Modest 1990 Gain," *Financial Post*, March 9, 1991, Section 1, p. 21.

—Dave Mote

Toronto-Dominion Bank

Post Office Box 1
King Street West and Bay Street
Toronto, Ontario M5K 1A2
(416) 982-8222
Fax: (416) 982-6335

Public Company
Incorporated: 1955
Employees: 22,853
Total Assets: $99.8 billion
Stock Exchanges: Toronto Winnipeg Montreal Tokyo
Vancouver London Alberta
SICs: 6011 Federal Reserve Banks; 6021 National
Commercial Banks

The Toronto-Dominion Bank's hyphenated name suggests its origins: the amalgamation of the Bank of Toronto and of the Dominion Bank. The Bank of Toronto missed celebrating its centennial by six weeks when the new bank's charter was signed on February 1, 1955. Going into 1995 the Toronto-Dominion Bank was Canada's fifth-largest bank in terms of assets, and among the most profitable Canadian banks. It maintained nearly 1,000 branches in Canada and had offices in the United States, Tokyo, London, Hong Kong, Taipei, and Singapore.

Founded by flour producers who wanted their own banking facilities, the Bank of Toronto was originally chartered on March 18, 1855. The Millers' Association of Canada West, as Ontario was then known, coordinated its preliminary affairs, and on July 8, 1856, the bank opened its doors to the public.

From its initial service to wheat farmers, millers, and merchants, the Bank of Toronto quickly expanded to the lumber industry and to other agricultural interests, mirroring the expansion of business activities on Canada's frontier as pioneers pushed west. In addition to this expansion, railroad booms both in England and in the United States increased the demand for flour and timber. Unfortunately, both booms collapsed at the same time, sharply curtailing the Canadian economy and with it, the westward growth of railroads and towns. Entire communities that had borrowed heavily to finance the building of rail service to their areas went bankrupt.

Although geographically in the middle of this national crisis, the Bank of Toronto was not as imperiled as many other businesses that had invested in the promise of the railroads because it had been established too late to provide much of the financing to the industry. Nor was it directly affected by the radical swings in real estate prices, dependent on the coming of the railroad, because its first officers did not believe in investing in an asset which fluctuated in value. While the business of the bank did contract, wheat was still grown, milled, and shipped.

The Canadian economy rebounded when markets in the United States reopened after the American Civil War in 1865. Fledgling businesses in leather, tanning, and liquor distillation sprang up, but the harvest still formed the backbone of business for native Ontario banks. A good year brought prosperity and a bad one meant hardship.

The Bank of Toronto was not without competition. The Bank of Montreal, older and larger, attempted to have the new bank's status limited to that of a community bank with no authority to establish branches. This debate was settled by Lord Durham's Report of 1850, which established branch banking as the national structure for the industry and guaranteed that successful banks could compete within their provinces and beyond, giving all institutions the opportunity to establish national identities.

The volume of business in Ontario in general and in Toronto specifically encouraged a group of professional men to seek a charter and to found the Dominion Bank, which opened for business on February 1, 1871. The Toronto-Dominion Bank was foreshadowed from the start: stock subscriptions for the Dominion Bank were deposited in the Bank of Toronto. Although originally incorporated to facilitate and promote agricultural and commercial growth, the Dominion Bank stressed the commercial end of banking, investing heavily in railway and construction ventures as well as in the needle trade in Ontario and Montreal.

Over the next several decades, through a series of booms and busts, Canada's economy grew and new industries were established: dairying, textiles, pulpwood, mining, and petroleum. Both the Bank of Toronto and the Dominion Bank responded to the opening of the prairies with a pioneering spirit. Many a new office shared the counter of a town's one general store, while a one-man staff slept with deposits beneath his mattress and a revolver under his pillow.

The outbreak of World War I brought great demand for Canada's natural resources. Within a year the country had erased its trade deficit and become a creditor nation. A few brief years of prosperity followed Germany's surrender in 1918, but the depression and panic preceding World War II appeared at the Dominion Bank on October 23, 1923. Sometime that Friday morning a foreign customer presented a check that was uncashable due to insufficient funds in the account. The teller attempted to overcome the customer's lack of fluency by raising his voice. "No money in the bank," he said. Those five words began a run that lasted until Tuesday afternoon, when rational voices finally overruled rumors.

Hastily established branches were another symptom of the shaky ground on which growth was built. For example, when three banks, one of them the Bank of Toronto, decided simultaneously to open an office at Cold Lake, Manitoba, the Bank of Toronto's officer rushed to be the first—with the help of Western Canada Airways. Although undocumented, he claimed it was the first bank in the world to open with the help of aviation.

The impact of the 1929 stock market crash in New York was compounded in Canada by the beginning of a seven-year drought. Foreign trade decreased, inventories accumulated, and factories closed. Both banks compensated by closing unprofitable branches, writing off bad debts, and reducing assets. Public criticism abounded. Partly as a response to the outcry but also as an attempt to coordinate the industry, the Bank of Canada was founded in 1934 to issue currency, set interest rates, and formulate national monetary policy. During World War II, the Foreign Exchange Control Board had issued regulations for all foreign transactions. Both banks worked under these restrictions and cooperated with the Bank of Canada to raise $12.5 billion from Canadian citizens to finance the war effort. In another major contribution, 707 employees of the Dominion Bank and more than 500 of the Bank of Toronto, approximately half of each staff, served with the Canadian forces while their jobs were held for them.

By 1954, both the Bank of Toronto and the Dominion Bank occupied a special position among the nine major banks in Canada. Each had achieved national prominence through its own efforts rather than through merger or acquisition. Each bank, however, realized that to retain its position, it needed to improve its capital base. Only a merger would support the size of industrial loans, which had grown from thousands to millions of dollars. The Minister of Finance approved the merger on November 1, 1954 and it was enacted on the following February 1, the first amalgamation of chartered banks since 1908 and only the third in the nation's history.

On opening day, the Toronto-Dominion Bank operated 450 branches, including offices in New York and London. It controlled assets of $1.1 billion and a loan portfolio of $479 million. During its first 15 years the new bank devoted a great deal of effort to establishing a unified image. In 1967, it moved into the 56-story Toronto-Dominion Bank Tower of the Toronto-Dominion Centre. During the 1970s, the Bank began to expand internationally—within three years it opened branches in such diverse locations as Bangkok, Frankfurt, and Beirut. During the mid-1970s, Toronto-Dominion issued the $65 million offering for the Toronto Eaton Centre, a 15-acre urban redevelopment project in downtown Toronto.

Toronto-Dominion prospered during the late 1970s and 1980s under the leadership of Richard Murray Thomson, who became chairman at the institution in 1976. By the late 1980s the bank was consistently outperforming its rivals both in return on assets and in stock performance, and was one of only two non-regional banks in North America to enjoy an AAA credit rating. Thomson was independent enough during the 1980s to refuse the government's request to provide free services to retail depositors, and to have led the opposition against the bailout of two regional banks in Alberta. On the other hand, he willingly stopped the flow of money to Canadian firms for the purchase of foreign oil companies because it was causing a run on the already weak dollar in 1981. During the 1980s, in fact, Thomson and Toronto-Dominion were credited with two major successes: reducing problems related to third world debt and helping to finance the largest merger in Canadian history.

Indeed, developing countries offered a financial frontier for large banks during the 1960s and 1970s. By 1987, though, Brazil's debt alone totaled $90.4 billion. Of that amount, Brazil owed $7.1 billion to Canadian creditors, including $836 million to Toronto-Dominion. In February 1987, Brazil suspended payment on the entire debt. After months of negotiation, a settlement was reached in which several Canadian banks, including Toronto-Dominion, agreed to assist Brazil with a $2 billion interest payment to the United States by loaning the country an additional $6 billion. This action protected the U.S. banks from classifying Brazil's loans of $37 billion as uncollectible and preempted a banking crisis in that country. Internally, Toronto-Dominion reclassified most of its Brazilian loans as non-accruing in the second quarter of 1987. Thomson reduced the risk from all Third World debt further by selling off $411 million in loans for 66 cents on the dollar.

The other major liability resolved under Thomson's guidance involved a merger between Dome Petroleum and Conoco, Inc. Problems began in 1981 when Dome purchased Conoco, Inc. for US$1.7 billion. As oil prices fell, Dome attempted to restructure its debt, but only succeeded in prolonging the inevitable. By early 1987, Dome was entertaining buyout discussions with several different companies. Amoco Canada Petroleum emerged as the early leader among the bidders and signed an agreement with Dome in April. It took eight months and an additional $400 million for Dome's creditors to approve the largest buyout in Canadian history. The final $5.5 billion offer provided 95.4 cents on the dollar to each secured creditor.

Toronto-Dominion continued to prosper in the late 1980s and to expand into new businesses and regions. Some analysts criticized the bank's performance during that period, implying that it was failing to take advantage of real estate industry gains. Fortunately, though, Toronto-Dominion stayed the conservative course. The real estate market crashed, bringing many banks along with it. Toronto-Dominion suffered during the downturn, which lingered throughout the early 1990s. But it continued to post profits, increase its asset base, and enter new service businesses. After bottoming out in 1992 at about $6.14 billion, the bank's sales jump to about $7 billion in 1994 as net income recovered to about $640 million. Meanwhile, Toronto-Dominion's asset base swelled past $100 billion early in 1995 from just $67 billion in 1990.

Toronto-Dominion's gains following the banking industry downturn of the early 1990s reflected its healthy future prospects. Besides building its traditional banking operations, the organization was aggressively chasing new markets in an effort to keep pace with changing technology and to compete against new competitors in the financial services arena. To that end, Toronto-Dominion was among the first Canadian banks to offer mutual funds. By 1995 the bank was offering nearly 50 different funds. Toronto-Dominion was also boosting its investments in electronic and home banking services, trust administration, retail brokerage, credit card services. Importantly, Toronto-Dominion was permitted by the federal government to enter the property and casualty insurance business beginning in 1995. In the first month following the announcement the bank received 40,000 inquiries and 1,000 new customers. Meanwhile, Thomson was searching for a successor to fill his shoes after his planned 1998 retirement.

Principal Subsidiaries:

TD Mortgage Corporation; Toronto Dominion Securities Inc.; TD Pacific Mortgage Corporation; Toronto Dominion Limited (Singapore); TD Ireland; Toronto Dominion N.V. (Barbados); Toronto Dominion Holdings, Inc. (United States); Toronto Dominion Investments B.V. (The Netherlands); Toronto Dominion Australia Limited (Australia).

Further Reading:

Blackwell, Richard, "TD Bank Licensed to Sell Home and Auto Insurance," *Financial Post,* February 8, 1995, Section 1, p. 3.

Blackwell, Richard, "TD, National Profits Higher," *Financial Post,* February 24, 1995, Section 1, p. 5.

Haliechuk, Rick, "TD Bank, National Bank Post Solid Profit Gains," *Toronto Star,* February 24, 1995, Section B, p. 4.

McFarland, Janet, "Baillie to Become TD President," *Financial Post,* September 23, 1994, Section 1, p. 7.

McQueen, Rod, "Thomson Insists on Hand-Picking His Heir," *Financial Post,* September 24, 1994, Section 1, p. 4.

Schull, Joseph, *100 Years of Banking in Canada: A History of the Toronto-Dominion Bank,* Toronto: Copp Clark, 1958.

—updated by Dave Mote

TransAlta Utilities Corporation

110 12th Ave. SW
Box 1900
Calgary, Alberta T2P 2M1
(403) 267-7110
Fax: (403) 267-4902

Public Company
Incorporated: 1947 as Calgary Power Ltd.
Employees: 2,506
Sales: $1.26 billion
Stock Exchanges: Toronto Montreal Alberta
SICs: 4911 Electronic Services

TransAlta Utilities Corporation is the largest investor-owned electric utility in Canada. TransAlta supplies electricity directly and indirectly to about 1.7-million Albertans. Its principal subsidiary, TransAlta Resources Corporation, handles the company's non-utility investments, which include oil, computer hardware and software, and technological research.

The forerunner of TransAlta Utilities, Calgary Power Company, was founded by banker W. Max Aitken in 1903. Aitken, who later became Lord Beaverbrook, reorganized a number of utilities as a subsidiary of his Royal Securities Company. He was joined in this venture by his friend and mentor R. B. Bennett, who served as Canadian Prime Minister from 1930 until 1935. Some business leaders felt that Aitken and Bennett were an unlikely team, since Bennett was known as an upstanding young man, while Aitken had earned a reputation as something of a renegade. Nonetheless, the pair joined several other prominent Canadian businessmen on Calgary Power's initial board of directors. Among these board members were: A. E. Cross, one of the founders of the Calgary Exhibition and Stampede; Herbert S. Holt, a Montrealer who was later knighted; and C. B. Smith, president of Calgary Power's forerunner, Calgary Power and Transmission Company Limited. Aitken soon became Calgary Power's first president.

Beginning as early as 1887, there were numerous small, privately owned firms that supplied towns across the province of Alberta with electricity. However, service was often inconsistent limited to a select number of businesses and provided only for a few evening hours. In an attempt to meet people's energy needs more fully, Bennett negotiated a contract to supply the city of Calgary with electricity. Calgary Power's first major project became the construction of the province's first large-scale hydroelectric plant, located at the Horseshoe Falls. The Horseshoe Falls Plant's opening on May 21, 1911, allowed Calgary Power to meet the needs of the city. According to the *Morning Albertan,* Calgary mayor J. W. Mitchell was aroused from a Sunday nap to flip the switch which officially opened the plant and connected the city with its first large-scale source of electricity. By 1913, Calgary Power had constructed the Kananaskis Falls Plant as an additional source of power.

In 1911, Calgary Power supplied 3,000 horsepower of electricity to the city at a cost of $30 per horsepower. By way of comparison, Calgary required 1.3 million horsepower in 1986 at a cost of $170 per horsepower. There were 44,000 people who called Calgary home in 1911, and the emerging need for mass transportation was met by the booming streetcar industry. Streetcars accounted for a significant share of the city's electric usage.

Aitken, the company's founder, left Calgary Power and sold Royal Securities in 1919, after he moved to England to pursue other business interests. The buyer was financial wizard Izaak Walton Killam, who started his business career as an innovative 15-year-old paperboy. Killam soon acquired the franchises from the five daily newspapers that supplied his hometown of Yarmouth, Nova Scotia, and hired other paperboys to deliver for him. Killam remained owner and chairman of the board of Calgary Power until his death in 1955. During Killam's tenure, Calgary Power developed a close professional relationship with another company he owned, Montreal Engineering Company, which eventually became one of the largest engineering firms in Canada. The two companies participated in a mutually beneficial system of exchanging management personnel for many years, which led to increased opportunities in both firms.

The 1920s became a decade of expansion for Calgary Power. In 1927, the same year that Charles Lindbergh flew solo across the Atlantic Ocean, the team of Geoffrey Gaherty and Harry Thompson travelled the province in a Model T, signing city electric franchise agreements for Calgary Power. Gaherty was an engineer and visionary who provided the technical expertise. Thompson was a businessman with an ability to deal well with people. The pair signed franchises with fifteen towns and villages, including Claresholm, Nobleford, Stavely, Taber, and Vulcan. Gaherty eventually earned a spot on the company's board of directors.

In 1928, Calgary Power bought out its chief competitor, the Calgary Water Power Company, for the price of $600,000. Calgary Water Power had supplied electricity to a section of downtown Calgary. In the same year, Calgary Power opened its Ghost River Hydro Plant and continued its power-line expansion that would eventually provide electricity to rural areas. The 1920s also brought Calgary Power its first female employee, Margaret Collett. She was originally hired to emboss customer addresses during the company's first attempt to send out bills by machine. Collett stayed with the company until 1963, when she retired from her last-held position as an arrears clerk.

The stock market crash of 1929 brought Calgary Power's period of rapid growth to an end. The 1930s saw poverty and unemployment rise across Canada. Bread lines formed, and relief camps became necessities. The prairie provinces were hit particularly hard by the Great Depression. Wheat sold for as low as 25 cents per bushel and steers sold for just three cents a pound. Calgary Power, however, managed to maintain its entire staff throughout the Depression. In order to avoid losing their jobs, employees volunteered to take a 10 percent pay cut. As a result, there were no layoffs or staff reductions made. Calgary Power actually hired in a handful of engineers straight out of college in 1935. The company did so anticipating future need, despite the fact that few other companies in Canada were hiring at this time. The immediate need, however, was in areas besides engineering, so Calgary Power set its new employees to work at a variety of menial tasks like srubbing floors and digging holes for power poles.

If fighting the Depression wasn't enough, fire nearly brought Calgary Power to its knees in 1936. A brush fire blazed just west of the city of Calgary and wiped out three of the company's main power lines. Calgary Power was limited to its Victoria Park Steam Plant and a power line from Lethbridge as its only supply sources until the fire was contained and the downed lines could be replaced.

The most positive aspect of the 1930s for Calgary Power was the anticipation of the coming acceptance of electric appliances. The company put together its "Modern All-Electric Kitchen" as a travelling exhibit to showcase such innovations as a range, refrigerator, mix-master, dishwasher, and coffee maker. The exhibit provided an abundance of publicity for the company, including winning the Mercantile Section of the Calgary Stampede in 1937.

When Canada entered World War II in 1939, public utilities alerted their employees to the possibility of sabotage. Prisoner of war camps were set up near Calgary to house German and Italian soldiers. The Canadian army issued Calgary Power employees handguns and rifles to defend themselves and the utility against escaped prisoners, though the need never arose. Since many employees were sent overseas in the armed forces, the company experienced a temporary manpower shortage during the war years. Demand for electric services also increased at this time, particularly with the development of large refrigeration plants to store food.

What the company did find itself fighting in 1940 was another fire. All of Calgary Power's employees were awakened and called into action on a September night when the Horseshoe Falls Plant caught fire. The blaze was eventually controlled and the plant was only temporarily out of service.

In 1947, two years after the war ended, Calgary Power moved its head office from Montreal, then the nation's largest city and prime business center to Calgary, reorganized, and incorporated as Calgary Power Ltd. At that time, Calgary Power supplied the province of Alberta with 99 percent of its hydroelectric power. Also in 1947, Calgary Power built its Barrier Hydro Plant and used it to test the use of a newly developed remote-control operation system. The automation efforts

worked well enough that Calgary Power soon converted all of its plants to the Barrier Plant system. A control center that could operate the company's entire system was built in Seebe in 1951. The company continued its string of innovations by testing "mobile radio" communications in its line patrol trucks.

Although electricity had begun to spread to rural areas in the 1940s, only 5 percent of farmers in the province had electricity of any kind. The majority of farmers were hesitant to adapt until it became obvious that electric service could increase farm production as well as provide modern conveniences. The main problem for utilities in supplying farms was a financial one: at the time, it was estimated that it would cost $200 million or twice the provincial debt to expand service and supply all of the farms with electricity. This dilemma led to an unprecedented cooperative effort between Calgary Power, farmers, and the provincial government. Calgary Power established a subsidiary, Farm Electric Services, as the company's rural branch. Farm Electric Services kept separate records and made an extra effort to keep costs low. Farmers joined together to form Rural Electrification Cooperative Associations. With funds provided by farmers themselves, supplemented with government loans at a small rate of interest, these co-ops eventually brought electricity to Alberta farms and new customers to Calgary Power through its Farm Electric Services.

By 1949, Calgary Power's service area reached from the United States border to as far north as 60 miles past Edmonton. The extensive service area brought the need for a substation near Edmonton to supplement Calgary Power's control center in Seebe. The substation was fully operational in 1954. Also in 1954, Calgary Power began construction on the Bearspaw Plant near Calgary. It was the first of three major projects Pocaterra and Interlakes hydroelectric plants were the others that were undertaken in the mid-1950s. By 1955, Calgary Power boasted 540 employees, and its subsidiary, Farm Electric Services, employed 166 workers. There were more than 25,000 farms receiving power through Calgary Power by this time. This was also the year that longtime owner Killam died, prompting the company to offer stock first to employees and then to the general public.

The Alberta economy had received a tremendous boost in February of 1947 when oil was discovered in Leduc. By the end of the year, there were 30 wells producing 3,500 barrels of oil per day. Calgary Power supplied much of the needed electricity for pipeline pumping installations, oil refineries, and natural gas processing plants. The entire province benefitted from the oil industry boom. By 1956, Alberta's population had grown enough to support four television stations and five daily newspapers. There were 250,000 cars registered that year in the province, up almost 100,000 from 10 years earlier.

Calgary Power continued to expand through the 1950s and 1960s, developing its first underground distribution lines and building dams on the Brazeau and North Saskatchewan rivers. The reservoir built on the North Saskatchewan project, Lake Abraham, became the largest man-made lake in the province. Also at this time, Calgary Power began exploring thermal energy generation, since few sites remained that were suitable for hydro power development. The company built its first thermal generating plant in 1956 near Wabamun Lake, west of Edmonton and near large coal reserves.

The recession of the 1970s slowed the growth of Calgary Power. Food prices in Alberta had increased by 96 percent from 1961 to 1972. Housing costs were up 70 percent. In 1972, Calgary Power held a hearing to increase its rates for the first time in the company's history; until then, all rate changes had been decreases. Despite the dire economic situation, the company still managed to finance a new thermal energy station, the Sundance Generating Plant. Construction began in 1967, and the final unit was completed in 1980. Following the increased environmental concerns that surfaced in the 1970s, Calgary Power instituted a new electrostatic method to catch the byproduct fly ash produced at the two thermal generating plants.

Following an unsuccessful 1980 takeover attempt by a fellow Alberta company, ATCO Ltd., Calgary Power changed its name to TransAlta Utilities Corporation in 1981. With a service area that had outgrown Calgary decades earlier, the company's new name reflected its province-wide operation. By 1985, TransAlta provided 81 percent of the province's electricity needs. Along with its name change, the company formed a wholly owned subsidiary, TransAlta Resources, to handle its non-utility investments. TransAlta Utilities also used technology to improve efficiency and productivity in the 1980s. New systems implemented ranged from office computers to automated facility planners to hand-held meter readers. In 1985, the plant remote-control center at Seebe was retired, and a new System Control Centre in Calgary took its place.

With the new decade, TransAlta has attempted to strengthen its position as Alberta's leading supplier of electricity, while expanding its operations through geographical diversification both in Canada and on an international scale. The firm looked southward for expansion in 1991, entering into a contract to supply power to the Bonneville Power Administration in the northwest United States. The contract was expected to generate $25 million in net revenues for TransAlta over a four-year period. The company also began exploring exports to British Columbia as part of its ongoing effort to expand its operations.

The early 1990s saw TransAlta continue to extend its core business of power generation outside the Canadian borders. In December 1993, the company joined Duke Energy Corporation of the United States and Chilgener S.A. of Chile in purchasing a 59 percent interest in Piedra del Aguila, a hydroelectric facility in Southwest Argentina on the Limay River. The 1,400 megawatt facility, which was completed on schedule and on budget in 1994, has supplied approximately 10 percent of the country's electricity needs. The company has also signed a number of other joint-venture agreements to develop potential projects in New Zealand, Chile, and China. The early stages of these projects, which represent a mix of generation including coal, natural gas, and biomass, were initiated in 1995.

While expanding geographically, TransAlta has also explored new methods of generation to expand its non-regulated business and position itself for long-term growth. In 1990, the company began actively pursuing the process of cogeneration, which uses natural gas to generate steam, which in turn is used to generate electricity. Two years later, construction was completed on two cogeneration plants in Ontario. Expected to be one of the chief sources of power for the 1990s, cogeneration produces both electricity and useful thermal energy (steam, hot water, and chilled water) from a single fuel source, making it a more environmentally safe method of energy production.

TransAlta's commitment to the environment has also been demonstrated in its efforts to help customers be more energy efficient. Through Power Smart programs, such as the Old Fridge Round Up, where customers were encouraged to dispose of their inefficient refrigerators and freezers, the company has helped customers to save money and reduce their impact on the environment as well. In 1994, the company launched the Enviro-Partner$ program, a state-of-the-art community-based program designed to help commercial, institutional, and residential customers make more efficient energy decisions. Among the many features of the program include auditing municipal facilities for energy efficiency improvements and coordinating financing, contractors and other professionals to ensure that the work is properly completed.

Having remained Alberta's leading supplier of electricity through the Depression, World War II, and various recessions, TransAlta has attempted to position itself favorably for what promises to be an increasingly competitive market. With the anticipated passage of the Electric Utilities Act and the Electric Energy Marketing (EEMA) Repeal Act, introduced into the Alberta Legislature in May of 1995, a new regulatory framework that allows for greater competition among generators and offers incentives for greater efficiency will be established. The lowest-cost major producer of electric energy in the province, TransAlta has viewed deregulation as leading to opportunities for growth. And with such innovative projects as a $70 million Edmonton plant designed to recycle municipal wastes and several international partnerships on the drawing board, the company is expected to strengthen its reputation as one of Canada's leading utilities.

Principal Subsidiaries:

TransAlta Utilities Corporation; TransAlta Energy Corporation.

Further Reading:

Clifford, Edward, "TransAlta Looks Outside for Growth," *Globe and Mail,* July 16, 1992, p. B9.
Cox, Kevin, "TransAlta Set to Raise Power Sales to U.S.," *Globe and Mail,* May 13, 1988, p. B6.
Jang, Brent, "Utilities Want City Out of Power," *Globe and Mail,* May 30, 1995, p. B4.
McMurdy, Deirdre, "TransAlta Getting into Cogeneration Deals," *Globe and Mail,* May 12, 1990, p. B17.
Motherwell, Cathryn, "Calgary: Rising Cost of Power Is Splitting Province," *Globe and Mail,* August 7, 1991, p. A6.

TransAlta Corporation News Releases, TransAlta Corporation, 1994-1995.

—Bruce MacLeod
—updated by Jason Gallman

TransCanada PipeLines

TransCanada PipeLines Limited

111 Fifth Avenue Southwest
Calgary, Alberta T2P 3Y6
(403) 267-6100
Fax: (403) 267-8993

Public Company
Incorporated: 1951
Employees: 1,800
Sales: $5.2 billion
Stock Exchanges: Toronto Montreal Vancouver
   Alberta Winnipeg New York
SICs: 4924 Natural Gas Distribution; 4922 Natural
   Gas Transmission

Canada's largest pipeline company, TransCanada Pipe-Lines Limited (TCPL) also ranks as a major North American natural gas transportation and marketing corporation. While the firm is headquartered in Calgary, its executives are based in Toronto. The core of Trans-Canada PipeLines is its mainline gas transmission system—more than 13,000 kilometers of pipeline—which runs from the Alberta-Saskatchewan border to the Quebec-Vermont border. A wholly owned subsidiary, Western Gas Marketing Limited, is the leading Canadian gas marketer and has the largest supply pool in North America. Beginning in 1989, the company undertook a major expansion of its mainline system to meet the increased demands of markets in eastern Canada and the northeastern United States. The early 1990s also witnessed TCPL's first expansion beyond North America, through participation in a major Colombian petroleum project.

In the early 1990s, the company also held investments in electric power generation projects, including full ownership of the 36-megawatt Nipigon Power Plant, which used waste heat from TransCanada's adjacent compressor station. Another subsidiary, Cancarb Limited, was the leading international manufacturer of high-quality thermal carbon black.

The company overcame engineering and financial hurdles in its early years. Building a gas pipeline across Canada was a project equal in scale to the building of the cross-country railway and was one of the most contentious chapters in Canada's economic and political history.

Although a trans-Canadian natural gas pipeline had been proposed as early as 1931, its actual establishment was linked to political, social, and economic events that took place in an atmosphere peculiar to 1950s Canada. For one, the country's population was booming, especially in the cities. The population of metropolitan Montreal alone grew from 1.83 million in 1956 to 2.57 million in 1966. The 1950s also witnessed the greatest economic boom in Canada's history, and the energy shortage was real. At no period of history was this more apparent than during the World War II era, when Canadians learned that they could not depend on energy from the United States, as the United States put its own energy needs first. The young generation of the 1950s was self-consciously Canadian and deeply suspicious of its neighbor to the south. Although economic prosperity increased, so did American ownership of most of Canada's wealth: approximately 70 percent of Canada's oil industry, 56 percent of its manufacturing industry, and 52 percent of Canadian mines were owned by U.S. businesses, and these percentages would grow. Growing national sentiment called for railways and a trans-Canadian pipeline to be built completely within Canada, regardless of cost.

Economic boom times, the looming energy shortage, and the election of a new government in 1957—which brought renowned nationalist Prime Minister John Diefenbaker to the helm—all set the stage for the adoption of a plan to harvest Alberta's rich deposits of natural gas. At the same time, the St. Lawrence Seaway, which would enable Canadian agricultural and industrial products to be shipped worldwide, was under construction.

As it turned out, it took an almost epic struggle to build the trans-Canadian pipeline. L. D. M. Baxter, a Canadian financier, was the first to advocate a trans-Canadian pipeline to bring Alberta natural gas to eastern Canada, although even he had doubts about the plan's feasibility. The obstacle, as he saw it, was the Laurentian Shield of northern Ontario, a vast rocky area that is the chief geological barrier separating eastern from western Canada. Canadians were not alone, however, in perceiving the value of a pipeline. On the U.S. side, the prospect of natural gas from Canada also tempted some businessmen to invest in such a venture. Clint Murchison, a Texan and head of Canadian Delhi Oil Company, believed the pipeline could be run through the Laurentian Shield. By 1954 both Canadian and U.S. interests had agreed on the usefulness of a pipeline through Canada that also would export gas to the United States. The difficulty, however, was in reaching agreement on the financing of the scheme. Since it was to be an all-Canadian route, the U.S. participants—who had formed a company called TransCanada PipeLines—insisted that financing should be split evenly, while the Canadian interest group, Western Pipe Lines Limited, opposed this 50-50 proposal because the United States had far greater financial resources at its disposal than did Canada. The Canadian group wanted the United States to take on 90 percent of the cost. In the end the Canadian investors agreed to the 50-50 split and sought to persuade their government to finance the pipeline. The person sponsoring the pipeline bill in Parliament was Minister of Transport C. D. Howe. An engineer by training, he would come to view the pipeline as the crowning achievement of his career.

TransCanada PipeLines was incorporated in 1951 to undertake the pipeline project. The first president of the new company was Nathan Eldon Tanner, who remained at the helm until the pipeline was completed. While other members of the board of directors had greater influence and experience, Tanner was a mediator. The major problem to be negotiated in 1955 was convincing the government of the financial viability of the company. After prolonged negotiations, the Royal Bank of Canada loaned TCPL $25.5 million, and a Montreal financier successfully negotiated large loans from the Canada Bank of Commerce as well as from the Royal Bank, thus enabling the company to win crucial government backing. The pipeline bill reached the floor of Parliament in 1956, and engendered months of rancorous debate and fears of a tighter U.S. hold, despite the strenuous effort of Transport Minister Howe to convince doubters of the wholly Canadian nature of the enterprise. By then, Canadian interests lobbying against the pipeline bill regarded it as a sellout to U.S. interests. Opponents felt that the pipeline would only provide the United States with cheap Canadian gas. Even in the United States opposition was beginning to mount. In the coal industry in particular fears were voiced that Canadian natural gas would displace coal and lead to layoffs, while only Canadians would benefit. Howe was not a smooth negotiator, but his expertise and influence ultimately combined to steer the bill successfully through Parliament. The pipeline was finally approved in June 1956.

Building commenced on a monumental scale in 1957. By December 1, the Toronto-to-Montreal segment had been completed. The entire project was finished in October 1958, as originally scheduled. More than 2,200 miles long, it was the longest pipeline in the world, and was expanded almost continuously.

In 1958 Tanner resigned as chief executive officer and president; his replacement was James Kerr. Kerr was new to the pipeline business. He had worked for Canadian Westinghouse since 1937, becoming a divisional vice president of Westinghouse in 1956. Like others on the board of directors of TCPL, Kerr was a Canadian nationalist who accepted the offer to become head of TCPL out of a sense of patriotism. At this time, TCPL's deficit was the company's biggest problem, one which it would not overcome until 1961.

In the 1960s the company entered the computer age, developing a highly sophisticated computer system that could measure and control the flow of gas precisely; the first such system devised for pipelines. The company diversified into the chemical industry during this decade, establishing the first of numerous gas-extraction plants in Empress, Alberta. In 1967 TCPL was permitted to extend its pipeline along the Great Lakes in the United States, an extension that was completed that same year. One year later, TCPL celebrated the tenth anniversary of its pipeline operations. Between 1958 and 1968, operating revenue had multiplied nearly sevenfold, from $30 million to $200 million. Net income had risen from a deficit of $8.5 million to a surplus of $17.5 million, while the proportion of Canadian shareholders had grown to 94 percent.

By the 1970s TCPL already was a world leader in pipeline technology. Vast subterranean natural gas pockets lay untouched in northern and western Canada, and exploiting this natural wealth was the goal of the company in the 1970s. The publicly-traded company was owned by Dome Petroleum Ltd. from 1979 to 1983, when Canada's largest and most profitable conglomerate, Bell Canada Enterprises Inc., purchased a 44 percent interest in TCPL. The new shareholder gave TCPL the extra financial support it needed to focus on geographic expansion, rather than diversification, as annual growth in Canadian demand for natural gas slowed to about 2 percent in the late 1980s. Beginning in late 1985, deregulation of the Canadian natural gas industry led to price competition. By 1988, prices for TransCanada's gas—which had previously been locked in with long-term contracts—ran about 80 percent higher than many competitors' prices. At the same time, growing demand in the U.S. that was unmet by American energy companies helped draw TransCanada into that market.

In 1990, TCPL proposed the biggest pipeline construction project in Canadian history: a $2.4 billion expansion of its system. The expansion called for erection of about 1,600 kilometers of pipeline, a 15 percent increase in TransCanada's total system capacity. Unlike the vast majority of its previous growth, about 75 percent of the gas transported by this pipeline was designated for the Iroquois Gas Transmission System (of which TCPL would own a 29 percent interest), and eventual use in American residences and businesses in coastal New England.

Not surprisingly, the primary stumbling block to this international expansion was the question of who would pay for it. TCPL's Canadian customers (especially industrial gas users) resisted footing the bill, saying that the U.S. customers who would benefit from the "megaproject" should pick up the accompanying "megacheck." But in spite of this opposition, TCPL won approval from the U.S. Federal Energy Regulatory Commission (FERC) to deliver western Canadian gas to the northeastern United States. Other FERC and Canadian National Energy Board rulings gave TCPL permission to expand its Great Lakes gas transmission system and mainline systems respectively, which allowed Canadian natural gas to be carried through TCPL's mainline system to Iroquois, Ontario, across the St. Lawrence River to the U.S. states of New York, Connecticut, and New Jersey.

The company also obtained a contract to sell to the California market and received a license to export natural gas to Michigan in 1990. These authorizations not only gave TransCanada one of the world's largest pipeline construction projects and entree into the competitive U.S. natural gas market, but also helped siphon off a glut of gas in Alberta and thereby boost gas prices deflated by post-deregulation competition. In April of 1992, TCPL sought approval of another construction project, a $500 million expansion of domestic services in Saskatchewan, Manitoba and Ontario.

The company appeared to have been unaffected by the recession of the early 1990s, with President and Chief Executive Officer Gerald Maier expecting an annual earnings growth rate of from ten percent to 15 percent in the 1990s. Like most established utilities, TCPL was accustomed to making slow but steady increases in profits. Net income in 1990 rose a surprising 14.9 percent from 1989, while the company pursued stream-lining, divesting itself of unprofitable businesses, such as its interests in Les Mines Selbaie and the Montreal Pipeline Ltd. in Quebec province. Then, in the first half of 1992, the company's overall profit jumped 30 percent, making TransCanada one of Canada's "10 most popular stocks." The company took advantage of its popularity with new stock and debentures issues. In the Spring of 1993, BCE divested the last of its TCPL holdings, "selling high."

In the fall of 1994, TCPL bought into its first major venture outside North America with an investment in a US$2.5 billion Colombian pipeline project. TCPL was a primary participant in the undertaking, sharing about 40 percent of the investment and responsibility with fellow Canadian company IPL Energy Inc. Other partners included British Petroleum Co. PLC; Total S.A. of France; Triton Energy Corp. of Dallas, Texas; and Ecopetrol, a state-owned Colombian oil company. The project proposed to develop one of the world's largest oil discoveries, the Cusiana oil field. It was estimated that the area contained 1.5 billion barrels of oil. Slated for completion in 1997, this US$2.3 billion venture was considered TransCanada's shot at "international credibility." At that same time, TransCanada was an investor and participant in a US$4 billion pipeline linking the United Arab Emirates and Pakistan as well as a US$200 million project in Tanzania.

Gerald Maier, who advanced to chairman and was succeeded as CEO by George Watson in 1994, hoped that these international efforts would serve as a launch-pad to accelerated earnings growth and elevation into the ranks of "world-class" pipeline companies.

Principal Subsidiaries:

Western Gas Marketing Limited; Iroquois Pipeline Operating Company (U.S.A.); Alberta Natural Gas Company Ltd; Northridge; Cancarb Limited; Great Lakes Gas Transmission Limited Partnership (U.S.A.); Trans Québec & Maritimes Pipeline Inc.

Further Reading:

Fagan, Drew, and Christopher Donville, "TCPL Wins Regulatory Battle," *Globe and Mail,* November 7, 1990, p. B1.
————, "$2.4 Billion TCPL Project Approved," *Globe and Mail,* May 10, 1991, p. B1.
Kilbourn, William, *Pipeline: TransCanada and the Great Debate, A History of Business and Politics,* Toronto: Clarke, Irwin & Co. Ltd., 1970.
Motherwell, Cathryn, "IPL, TransCanada Seal $2.5 Billion Deal," *Globe and Mail,* September 23, 1994, p. B6.
Newman, Peter C., "Tending Canada's Only Megaproject," *Maclean's,* March 2, 1992, p. 32.
Sheppard, Robert, "Report on Energy: Suppliers See Profit in Hunger of the U.S.," *Globe and Mail,* March 20, 1989, p. B27.
Walmsley, Ann, "Always a Bridesmaid," *Maclean's,* May 4, 1987, p. 42.

—Sina Dubovoj
—updated by April Dougal Gasbarre

Trilon Financial Corporation

BCE Place
181 Bay Street Suite 4420
P.O. Box 771
Toronto, Ontario M5J 2T3
(416) 363-0061
Fax: (416) 365-9642

Incorporated: 1982
Employees: 23,500
Revenues: $5.03 billion
Stock Exchanges: Toronto Montreal Vancouver
SICs: 6311 Life Insurance; 6282 Investment Advice;
   6531 Real Estate Agents and Managers; 6029
   Commercial Banks, nec.; 6021 National
   Commercial Banks; 6211 Security Brokers and
   Dealers; 6150 Business Credit Institutions.

Trilon Financial Corporation is a diversified Canadian financial services company that offers insurance, investment banking, real estate brokerage, and commercial financing through several operating subsidiaries. Trilon is substantially and indirectly owned by Edper Equities, the Toronto-based holding company of Seagram Company heirs Peter and Edward Bronfman. Edper Equities has been characterized as a complex "pyramid" of holding companies whose structure is legal in Canada, but not in the United States or Great Britain. In the mid-1990s, Trilon's chain of ownership could be traced to principal shareholder Trilon Holdings Inc., which owned 48 percent of Trilon Financial's equity in 1994. Trilon Holdings, in turn, was a subsidiary of Brascan Limited, which owned 75 percent of its equity. Brascan, a natural resource recovery and power production company founded in 1899 by Brazilian and Canadian entrepreneurs, was acquired by Edper Equities in 1979.

At the time of its acquisition by the Edper group, Brascan had completed the sale of its primary Brazilian subsidiary, Light-Servicos de Eletricidade S.A., to the Brazilian government for US$380 million. Under the direction of Edper's chief strategist, Trevor Eyton, Brascan made plans to use the proceeds of that sale to finance expansion in its three principal areas of strength: consumer goods, natural resources, and financial services. With limited debt and a substantial cash reserve, Brascan planned to create Canada's largest diversified financial services corporation. The 1982 creation of Trilon was a cornerstone of Eyton's strategy.

Trilon was in the vanguard of the Canadian trend toward one-stop financial service companies. The movement began in the United States, when several large financial companies such as Merrill Lynch and Prudential Insurance Company sought to offer a full range of financial services. Restrictive legislation had prohibited diversification in Canada until the 1980s, when deregulation permitted companies to enter new markets.

The economic climate was ripe for the formation of diversified financial companies. The Canadian life insurance industry had endured several years of poor performance in the 1970s and early 1980s. Inflation had devalued traditional insurance products like whole life policies and deregulation brought increased competition from products offered by banks, trust companies, and governments, all of which had begun to offer similar products to compete for Canadians' savings.

Trilon was created in 1982 to take advantage of the new imperatives of the financial services market. As a foundation for its operations, Trilon acquired significant stakes in the London Life Insurance Company and the Royal Trust Company, both companies in which Brascan held substantial minority positions. London Life had originally been founded in 1874 and had grown to become Canada's fourth-largest life insurer, boasting over one million policyholders and 11,000 corporate customers. A 1993 *Globe and Mail* article called London Life "the crown jewel of Edper's insurance operations." With $26 billion in fiduciary assets, 83-year-old Royal Trust (later renamed Gentra Inc.), was the country's largest trust company.

Under Canadian legislation, insurance companies were prohibited from directly owning trust companies. However, insurance and trust activities could be coordinated under the direction of a holding company. Soon after its November 1992 formation under federal charter, Trilon increased its holdings in London Life to 80 percent and then in February 1983 to 98 percent. Shortly thereafter, Trilon made a $102 million share offering, the proceeds of which were used to acquire a 42 percent controlling interest in Royal Trust in July 1983.

Trilon's management hoped that, by offering a full range of financial services to London Life's and Royal Trust's massive customer base, it would be able to capture more of each family's or business's investment dollar. The company's strategy was to link trust, insurance, and brokerage operations to take advantage of broadened investment powers which would not be available to each independently. This would enable Trilon to capture and retain a larger portion of its client's investment dollar. Though critics said the formation of Trilon and similar companies presented opportunities for conflict of interest, Trilon argued that the arrangement would bring greater convenience, to the overall benefit of both stockholders and clients.

Trilon's management came primarily from within the ranks of Brascan, Edper, and the network of companies they had acquired. Allan Lambert, the former chairman of Toronto-Dominion Bank, was appointed chairman, and Melvin Hawkrigg, the former senior vice-president of Brascan, was named president and CEO.

Trilon grew rapidly through a series of acquisitions backed by Brascan's substantial capital base. The company's strategy was to acquire existing companies with the necessary expertise in their respective fields. Within just six months of its formation, Trilon earned a ranking among Canada's tens largest financial institutions. Trilon's resources were so extensive that it was able to devise a marketing plan to target all of Canada's six million families.

To coordinate and manage the diversification of its operations, Trilon formed intermediate companies corresponding to its respective services. Lonvest Corporation was formed to manage insurance operations. In its insurance operations, Lonvest reorganized and acquired in an attempt to broaden the range of its services. At the time of its acquisition, London Life, Lonvest's primary component, was trying to regain its place as one of the top five companies in the Canadian life insurance industry. It began revamping traditional whole life policies and introduced new insurance and annuity products, including "savings and accumulation" plans similar to plans being sold by banks and trust companies as well as auto, and homeowner policies. In 1985 Lonvest acquired all of the outstanding shares of Fireman's Fund of Canada for $143 million. Fireman's Fund, subsequently renamed Wellington Insurance Co., had been operating as a general insurer in Canada since 1840. In September, 1986, Lonvest acquired a 59 percent interest in The Holden Group for $57 million. The Holden Group was a U.S.-based specialty insurer that provides individual and group benefit plans for educational institutions and public employees. In 1987 the company acquired a 60 percent interest in The Optimum Financial Services Limited, a manager of automobile and property insurance for members of professional and alumni associations in Quebec, Ontario, and Alberta. The following year, Optimum acquired both Reed Stenhouse Personnel Insurance Ltd. and Security National Insurance Company for $15 million.

Trilon created Royal Trustco Ltd. to manage Royal Trust's operations. Under Trilon's direction, the subsidiary began to shed its long-held reputation as a conservative financial institution, taking bold measures to compete with Canada's banks. In 1984 Royal Trust expanded into real estate operations through the acquisition of A.E. LePage, merging Canada's largest real estate brokerage with its second largest provider of mortgages. Though the banks with which Royal Trust competed had access to greater resources, Royal Trust's smaller size gave its flexibility and the ability to process transactions more rapidly. Recognizing this advantage, the company streamlined operations even further through greater use of computer technology and the elimination of as many as seven layers of management between the chairman and customers. In 1987 Royal Trust introduced several innovative products in the guaranteed investment certificate markets (GICs), including guaranteed market index investments, stock price adjusted rate certificates, and diversified guaranteed investment certificates. These allowed investors to protect their principal while taking advantage of rises in the stock market.

Trilon also formed a corporate financial services division to manage its own investments and to provide brokerage services. In 1986, this division became Trilon Bancorp Inc., an independent subsidiary. Like Trustco and Lonvest, Trilon Bancorp also expanded actively and widely. In March, 1985, it formed a leasing division by acquiring a controlling interest in CVL Inc., Canada's largest fleet leasing company, for $1.5 million. The following year it changed the name from CVL to Triathlon Leasing Inc. Through the acquisition of City National Leasing in 1986 and Kompro Computer Leasing in 1987, Triathlon also began to lease equipment and computers. Triathlon is Canada's largest leasing operation, with more than 40,000 vehicles under management. In 1986 Trilon Bancorp acquired an 11 percent interest in the Great Lakes Bankgroup, a banking and hydroelectric energy production company in the Brascan group, and also acquired Eurobrokers Investment Corporation, a wholesale money broker. Trilon Bancorp expanded into real estate in 1987 by purchasing Trustco's 51 percent interest in Royal LePage. That year it also formed Trilon Capital Markets and Trivest Insurance Network to conduct merchant banking activities for small- and medium-sized businesses. Trivest Insurance Network was a risk management company which at its formation planned to spend nearly $100 million to acquire minority equity positions in general insurance brokers.

In addition to establishing itself as an important player in the domestic financial industry, Trilon made significant, trend-setting international moves. In 1986 Royal Trustco acquired Dow Financial Services Corporation, Dow Chemical's financial services subsidiary, for $239 million. Following this purchase, Royal Trust established R.T. Securities and Royal International in Amsterdam and opened an office in Tokyo to promote trade between Japan and Canada. This international expansion continued through the remainder of the decade, when Trilon opened offices in Geneva, Hong Kong, Luxembourg, Austria, and Singapore. In 1987, Trilon Bancorp also entered into a joint venture with Taiwanese investors, obtaining a $6 million, 49 percent common equity interest in China Canada Investment and Development Company.

Expansion into the United States focused on the thrift industry, which was rife with "bargain" remnants of the savings and loan debacle. Royal Trust acquired Pacific First Financial Corp., a Seattle, Washington savings and loan company, in 1989, then snatched up parts of Oregon's American Savings and Loan and Williamsburg Federal Savings and Loan the following year.

George Myhal, formerly of Hees International Bancorp Inc., was elected to Trilon Financial's board of directors in 1992 and president in 1993. One of Myhal's first tasks as head of Trilon was the sale of the majority of Royal Trustco's operations in the wake of losses totaling over $900 million in 1990 and 1992. While Trilon retained its 47 percent interest in the firm—renamed Gentra, Inc.—it sold the affiliate's choicest assets to the Royal Bank of Canada. Left with a portfolio of hard-to-collect loans, Gentra continued to suffer losses into the mid-1990s. Difficult conditions in the real estate market contributed to successive losses at Trilon's Royal LePage affiliate as well during this period.

Following the lead of ultimate parent Edper Equities—which liquidated over $3 billion in holdings in 1993 and 1994—Trilon sold Triathlon Leasing Inc. to General Electric Capital Canada for $225 million. The 1994 transaction permitted Trilon to concentrate more fully on its core interests, provided funds for debt reduction, and helped it achieve its first net profit since 1991.

Principal Subsidiaries:

London Insurance Group Inc.; London Life Insurance Company; The Holden Group Inc. (U.S.); Meloche Monnex Inc.; Trilon Securities Corporation; Trilon International Inc. (Barbados); Royal LePage Limited; Trilon Bancorp Inc.

Further Reading:

Collard, Edgar Andrew, *A Very Human Story: A Brief History of the Royal Trust Company, Its First 75 Years,* Montreal: Royal Trust Co., 1975.
Howlett, Karen, "Trilon Upbeat Over Trust Stake," *Globe and Mail,* 22 June 1993, B13.
Newman, Peter C., "Canada's Growing Economic Outreach," *Maclean's,* 23 January 1989, 42.
Noble, Kimberley, "Trilon Determined to Stand Pat," *Globe and Mail,* 20 March 1993, B8.
Olive, David, "And Now for Something Completely Different," *Canadian Business,* April 1984, 107.

—April Dougal Gasbarre

Westcoast Energy Inc.

Suite 3400, Park Place
666 Burrard Street
Vancouver, British Columbia V6C 3M8
(514) 861-9481
Fax: (514) 861-7053

Company Type: Public Company
Founded: 1957 as Westcoast Transmission
Employees: 6,000
Sales: $3.71 billion in 1994
Stock Exchanges: Montreal, Toronto, Vancouver,
  New York, Pacific
SICs: 1300 Oil & Gas Extraction; 1311 Crude
  Petroleum & Natural Gas; 1321 Natural Gas
  Liquids; 4911 Electric Services; 4922 Natural Gas
  Transmission; 4923 Gas Transmission &
  Distribution; 4924 Natural Gas Distribution

Westcoast Energy Inc. is a regulated monopoly that provides power generation and natural gas distribution, storage, and processing services throughout Canada and the United States. The company is one of the largest processors of natural gas in the world and, with more than $7 billion in assets in 1995, is among the biggest companies in Canada. Westcoast stumbled during the late 1970s. Following a turnaround in the early 1980s, the company achieved explosive sales and profit growth and continued to post healthy gains going in the mid-1990s.

Westcoast was incorporated in 1949 under a Special Act of Parliament. It began operations in 1957 when it opened the first natural gas transmission pipeline in British Columbia. That pipeline was developed under the direction of chief executive and swashbuckling oil-and-gas pioneer Frank McMahon, one of the McMahon brothers credited with building British Columbia's gas industry. McMahon and his associates labored during the 1950s to develop a transmission system that, among other benefits, would deliver gas throughout the west coast and carry surplus gas from British Columbia and Alberta to the United States. After opening its first pipeline in 1957, Westcoast began trying to expand its system with the ultimate goal of building a pipeline that would bring in gas from the Arctic.

The Canadian gas industry during the 1950s and 1960s was still relatively young and entrepreneurial. Compa-

nies competing to locate, tap, and deliver oil and gas were often engaged in ventures punctuated by numerous political, financial, and competitive risks. Among the industry-renowned pioneers was Westcoast's McMahon. McMahon, a wildcatter, drilled for several years in search of oil and gas. After pouring millions of dollars into mostly dry holes, he scored big, boosting his reputation in the energy industry with major gas finds in northern British Columbia and Alberta. McMahon pursued his goals of bringing oil and gas to the west coast and the United States, and from the Arctic, through Westcoast Transmission. His drive to carry his oil and gas to the United States reflected his desire to circumvent domestic regulations that suppressed profit opportunities—Westcoast Transmission was a government-regulated monopoly at the time, and its oil and gas profits were indirectly controlled by federal regulators.

Despite its successes, including rising sales throughout the 1960s, Westcoast was still struggling several years after it opened its first pipeline. It took ten years for the company to pay its first dividend, for example, and the price of the company's stock had fallen from its early days when its future seemed so promising. Part of the problem was that the company's supply and purchase contracts were generating measly margins that barely covered operating costs. Furthermore, McMahon had sold much of the gas he had discovered to pay for more wildcatting, which had been only semi-productive. By the late 1960s Westcoast was headed for bankruptcy. To alleviate problems, management restructured the company. Among other moves, executives spun off Westcoast's oil and gas production division in an effort to intensify the organization's exploration efforts. The spun-off division, Westcoast Petroleum Ltd., went public to obtain financing and Westcoast Transmission became a minority shareholder in the operation. Besides spinning off the exploration operations, McMahon initiated a management shakeup.

The renegotiation of certain supply and purchase contracts buoyed Westcoast temporarily, but new problems arose. Importantly, although Westcoast's relationships with its U.S. buyers improved, relationships with its major Canadian customers deteriorated for a number of business and political reasons—rifts with those buyers would haunt Westcoast into the 1980s. Also hurting Westcoast was a major setback in 1973. A summer flood at two major gas fields on which Westcoast was heavily dependent virtually destroyed their gas-producing capacity. Almost overnight Westcoast lost about 30 percent of its total gas supply. Westcoast tried to ration the gas to all of its customers, but its Canadian buyers, in a move that further stressed relations with Westcoast, succeeded in getting the provincial government to order Westcoast not to curtail their supply. Thus, Westcoast was forced to make its higher profit U.S. buyers bear the burden of its reduced supply. U.S. buyers, stung by massively reduced gas supplies supposedly guaranteed by contract, were irate. One official in the state of Washington even suggested that the U.S. Marines be brought in to open Westcoast's gas valves. The curtailment lasted six years.

Westcoast scored a major victory in 1977 that largely overshadowed many of its setbacks during the late 1960s and early 1970s. In that year, Westcoast's proposal for a gas pipeline connecting the Alaska and the Arctic region with southern Canada and the United States was approved. The award was the result of a four-year competition in which Westcoast and its associates were the underdogs. The giant project was a major coup for Westcoast and represented the achievement of the company's founder's dream. Importantly, the "Foothills" pipeline project suggested a brighter future for Westcoast Transmission because it would give the company access to both the arctic region and to the east of Canada and the United States. Westcoast would participate in the construction of the giant pipeline and would be part owner of a major section traversing Alberta and Saskatchewan.

Shortly before the project was awarded, 58-year-old Ed Phillips was named president and chief executive at Westcoast. Phillips had joined Westcoast in 1968 at the request of McMahon. Previously, he had worked as president of Trane Company of Canada Ltd., but had been involved in the energy industry beforehand. During the management shakeup of the late 1960s and early 1970s, McMahon was one of the few top managers that kept his job. Indeed, heavy-handed Kelly Gibson was hired to restructure Westcoast and succeeded in getting many of the company's executives to leave. Phillips stayed and was even able to climb the ladder to the top post by 1976, although Gibson stayed on as chairman and continued to have the ultimate say for a few years in what went on at the company.

During the late 1970s Westcoast continued to provide its primary service of transporting large amounts of gas from central British Columbia to bigger markets in the lower mainland and in the United States. It also labored to make its contribution to the arctic pipeline project, and even tried to diversify into other related businesses. Unfortunately, Westcoast's efforts under Phillips leadership were often squelched by forces outside of its control, and the company stagnated. Indeed, because it was effectively a type of regulated utility, Westcoast's future was increasingly being determined by expanding provincial and federal regulatory agencies staffed by armies of intrusive bureaucrats in Victoria and Ottawa.

For example, at one point Phillips accused Victoria of vindictively thwarting its effort to win a bid to build the Vancouver Island Pipeline. Among other projects that became snared in political traps was a $750-million fertilizer complex that Westcoast had proposed, a $2-billion project to export liquefied natural gas by tanker, and a methanol plant. By the early 1980s Westcoast was faced with a growing list of enemies, both bureaucrats and customers, that were dampening its drive to grow and diversify. Phillips began looking for a way out of the dilemma. "We felt we had to add to our roster of promotable executives a person with skill sets none of us possessed," Phillips recalled in the August 1990 *BC Business*. "We needed someone who had experience in public service and understood the process and the minds of politicians."

Enter Mike Phelps, a 34-year-old attorney working for the Ottawa energy ministry. Phelps had served in the ministry during the creation of one of the most controversial energy policies—the National Energy Program (NEP)—ever imposed by the federal government. The bill effectively diverted vast amounts of money from energy-producing western provinces, particularly Alberta, to the federal government. Phelps first met Phillips when Phelps was sent out as part of a task force to explain the NEP to energy industry participants and others. Although Phillips was adamantly opposed to the NEP, he was impressed by Phelps demeanor and presentation, partly because he felt that Phelps looked out of place in the stifling bureaucratic environment. He soon lured Phelps away to Westcoast, and Phelps progressed rapidly within the company.

Phillips retired in 1982. His successor, John Anderson, died soon thereafter of cancer. The company's senior vice-president stepped in as temporary CEO, delaying his own retirement until a permanent chief executive could be located. In 1983 the Westcoast board put the 40-year-old Phelps at the helm. Although Phelps was considered young for the job, it was not the first time that he had been in that position. In fact, shortly after joining the federal government in 1976 Phelps had been selected to serve as executive assistant to the energy minister, an extremely challenging and high-profile job. It was in that post that he began to learn many of the political nuances that would help him in his career at Westcoast.

When Phelps took control of Westcoast the company was facing a generally lackluster future. Its existing businesses were sound, but they were government regulated and offered little opportunity for growth. Following a 1994 study that he headed, Phelps announced a new corporate strategy designed to boost Westcoast's revenues from the non-utility sector to 50 percent. To that end, Phelps and his associates aggressively pursued a diversification program during the 1980s that lead to a number of acquisitions in the oil and gas industry. Bolstering their diversification efforts, moreover, were a number of positive political and economic developments. In the mid-1980s, for example, Canada began deregulating and privatizing its energy industries. Gas prices fell and Westcoast's sales slumped between 1986 and 1989. But there were some victories. Canadian gas exports to California and the Pacific Northwest, for example, shot up about 50 percent in 1987 alone. Furthermore, Westcoast continued to post healthy profits.

By the end of the 1980s Westcoast was becoming a large, diversified player in the increasingly profitable and deregulated gas and oil business. It was producing 15,600 barrels of oil and 60 million cubic feet of natural gas daily, in fact, making it one of the top 20 oil and gas-producing companies in Canada. Those output figures reflected a surge in Westcoast's output in 1990 that resulted from Phelp's ongoing acquisition efforts. Importantly, the company acquired Inter-City Gas Corp.'s gas utility division in 1989 for $462 million, giving it access to 440,000 new customers in Manitoba, Ontario, Alberta, and British Columbia. That acquisition doubled Westcoast's number of employees and increased its asset base by 50 percent. Shortly after that purchase, Westcoast began construction on the Vancouver Island pipeline—the project that had been a political hot potato in the early 1980s. Early in 1990, Westcoast purchased an interest in Kanger Oil, a major operator in the British sector of the North Sea that gave Westcoast a potential entry into the international oil business. Westcoast's stock price climbed.

Westcoast's impressive gains during the late 1980s were dwarfed by ongoing expansion in the early 1990s Indeed, Westcoast executives intensified their acquisition drive and began pursuing multiple avenues of growth. The company even changed its name to Westcoast Energy to reflect is diversity. Besides building new pipelines and purchasing competitors, the company vastly increased its drilling activity to keep up with its competitors. Sales climbed from $700 million in 1989 to $1.46 billion in 1992, and then to a $3.63 billion in 1993. Meanwhile, operating income more than doubled. Westcoast retained its unique status as a regulated monopoly, despite its diversification, by including processing and gathering costs in its transmission tolls. Some observers and potential competitors claimed that Westcoast was benefiting from an unfair advantage and that the company had defied deregulation efforts. Defenders of the company pointed to its healthy profit growth and efficiency as evidence of the success of its strategy and status.

Westcoast's sales rose to $3.7 billion in 1994 as net income surged to a record $173 million and total assets swelled to $7.4 billion. Going into 1995, the company was operating more than 3,000 miles of pipeline and five processing plants with a processing capacity of 1.9 billion cubic feet of gas per day. The company also owned interests in power facilities in Canada and was building a power plant in southern Ontario. Furthermore, Westcoast was engaged in a number of new ventures both at home and abroad, including cogeneration plants as far away as China.

Principal Subsidiaries:

Centra Gas Alberta Inc.; Centra Gas British Columbia Inc.; Centra Gas Manitoba Inc.; Centra Gas Ontario Inc.; Pacific Northern Gas Ltd.; Union Gas Limited; Westcoast Gas Services Inc.; Westcoast Power Inc.

Further Reading:

Baines, David, and Daphne Bramham, "Little Guys Challenge Westcoast Plan," *Vancouver Sun,* February 25, 1995, Section F, p. 1.
Doyle, Richard J., *Guts & Guile,* Vancouver: Douglas & McIntyre, 1990.
Ludwick, Laurie, "Westcoast Set for Pipeline Expansion," *Financial Post,* September 8, 1994, Section 1, p. 3.
Lyon, Jim, "Gassed Up: Remember Westcoast—Yawn—Transmission?," *BC Business,* August 1990, Section 1, p. 12.
McIntyre, Hugh, "Imaginative Proposals," *BC Business,* February 1988, Section 1, p. 23.
Morton, Peter, "Westcoast Energy Takes First Step Overseas," *The Oil Daily,* December 7, 1994, p. 2.
Nutt, Rod, "Energy Conglomerate Romps to Humongous $136 Million Profit," *Vancouver Sun,* July 30, 1994, Section C, p. 6.

—Dave Mote

INDEX TO COMPANIES AND PERSONS _____

Listings in this index are arranged in alphabetical order. Company names beginning with a letter or proper name such as George Weston Limited will be found under the first letter of the company name. The definite article "The" is ignored for alphabetical purposes. Company names appearing in bold type have full essays. Company and personal names in light type indicate references within an essay to that company or person.

INDEX TO INDUSTRIES

Index to Industries

NOTES ON CONTRIBUTORS

BADARACCO, Claire. Professor and author of annotated edition of *The Cuba Journal of Sophia Peabody Hawthorne*, 1984, and *R.R. Donnelley's "Four American Books Campaign" at The Lakeside Press 1926-1930*, 1990.

BELSITO, Elaine. Free-lance writer and editor. Assistant managing editor, *Archives of Physical Medicine and Rehabilitation*, 1988-90.

BENBOW-PFALZGRAF, Taryn. Free-lance editor, writer, and consultant in the Chicago area.

BROWN, Susan Windisch. Free-lance writer and editor.

CHEPESIUK, Ron. Free-lance writer and professor. Author of *Chester County: A Pictorial History*, 1985.

COLLINS, C.L. Free-lance writer and researcher.

COVELL, Jeffrey L. Free-lance writer and corporate history contractor.

DUBOVOJ, Sina. History contractor and free-lance writer; adjunct professor of history, Montgomery College, Rockville, Maryland.

FARQUHAR-BOYLE, Allyson S. Analyst, Mercy Health Services, Department of Strategic Planning and Analysis. Author of "Strategic Planning as a Process," *Court Management and Public Administration*.

GALLMAN, Jason. Free-lance writer and graduate student in English at Purdue University.

GASBARRE, April Dougal. Archivist and free-lance writer specializing in business and social history in Cleveland, Ohio.

GROSSMAN, William R. Free-lance writer. Author of *The Dating Maze*, 1989.

KEELEY, Carol I. Free-lance writer and researcher; columnist for *Neon*; researcher for *Ford Times* and *Discovery*. Contributor to *Oxford Poetry*, 1987, and *Voices International*, 1989.

MAGON, Kim M. Consultant KGM Communications; free-lance editor, *World Facts and Maps*. Associate Editor, Technical Reporting Corp., Chicago, 1985-88.

MARTIN, Jonathan. Free-lance writer.

MOTE, Dave. President of information retrieval company Performance Database.

ROURKE, Elizabeth. Free-lance writer.

SAHAFI, Maya. Free-lance writer. Developmental editor, Arab Bank Limited, 1988.

SMETHURST, Katherine. Free-lance writer.

TELINGATOR, Susan. Free-lance writer. Author of *The Chicago Arts Guide*.

TUCKER, Thomas M. Free-lance writer.

VERNYI, Bruce. Reporter, *Plastic News*. Former reporter *Toledo Blade* and *American Metal Market*; free-lance contributor to *Business Week, Wall Street Journal, National Real Estate Investor,* and *American Banker*.

VERZHBINSKY, Moya. Free-lance writer; graduate student in business administration, University of California, Berkeley.

VLESSING, Etan. Free-lance writer and editor. Former editor of *Insight;* news editor, *Financial Weekly*.